a guide to *Poetics Journal*

a guide to

Poetics Journal

WRITING IN THE EXPANDED FIELD

1982–1998

with the copublication of *Poetics Journal* Digital Archive

Edited by **Lyn Hejinian** and **Barrett Watten**

WESLEYAN UNIVERSITY PRESS

Middletown, Connecticut

Wesleyan University Press

Middletown CT 06459

www.wesleyan.edu/wespress

© 2013 Lyn Hejinian and Barrett Watten

Manufactured in the United States of America

Wesleyan University Press is a member of the Green Press Initiative.
The paper used in this book meets their minimum requirement for
recycled paper.

Publication of this book is funded by the Beatrice Fox Auerbach
Foundation Fund at the Hartford Foundation for Public Giving.

Library of Congress Cataloging-in-Publication Data
A guide to Poetics Journal: writing in the expanded field, 1982–
1998, with the copublication of Poetics Journal digital archive /
edited by Lyn Hejinian and Barrett Watten.
    p. cm.
Includes bibliographical references and index.
ISBN 978-0-8195-7120-5 (cloth: alk. paper)—ISBN 978-0-8195-7121-2
(pbk.: alk. paper)—ISBN 978-0-8195-7122-9 (ebook)
1. Poetics—History—20th century.   2. Criticism—Periodicals.
3. Poetry—Periodicals.   I. Hejinian, Lyn.   II. Watten, Barrett.
III. Poetics Journal.
PN1042.G78 2012
808.1—dc23   2012030738

publication of this book is funded by the

BEATRICE FOX AUERBACH FOUNDATION FUND

at the Hartford Foundation for Public Giving

Contents

How to Use This Guide

The present volume is one part of a two-part publication, coedited by Lyn Hejinian and Barrett Watten and based on the ten issues of *Poetics Journal* that appeared between 1982 and 1998. The second part is the *Poetics Journal Digital Archive*, an online resource that includes all of the articles published in *Poetics Journal*. The archive contents are available in a searchable form to individual and institutional subscribers. The guide and archive each contain an index and set of links organized by keywords that will help readers make connections between articles.

The print volume has been edited and organized to be read on its own, but also to be used in conjunction with the archive. It comprises an anthology of key works excerpted from the run of *Poetics Journal* that individually—but, more important, collectively—helped define and articulate the examples and methods of contemporary poetics. The works range widely in style and approach and reflect a diversity of cultural perspectives, representing writing in poetics from North America and parts of Europe, the former Soviet Union, and Asia after 1980. They include essays that influenced the development of contemporary poetics; reviews and responses, both critical and theoretical, to new writing and other experimental practices; and texts that do the work of poetry and poetics simultaneously, as two facets of a single practice.

As our volume's title suggests, it is also intended as a guide, both to its own construction and to the archive. The editors hope that it will encourage readers to make exploratory connections between the 256 texts of *Poetics Journal*'s sixteen-year, ten-issue run. As the introduction explains, each issue was edited around a particular topic; the arrangement of the works within each issue was intended to maximize connections—in terms of affinity or contradiction—in order to catalyze discussion and creative projects. To increase the usefulness of the print volume, we have provided a series of headnotes to the individual works and a general introduction. Our goal has been to provide cultural and historical contexts for the materials as representing a larger field of writing in poetics.

The thirty-six articles selected for this guide are presented in three parts, drawn respectively from numbers 1–4, 5–7, and 8–10 of the journal. The twelve articles within each part appear in alphabetical order. Each article is preceded by a headnote and followed by publication data; a short list of keywords, which can be used to access related articles in the guide and archive; a series of links to other works by the author and to related articles; and a selected bibliography of the author's works, foregrounding creative work, writings in poetics, and collaborative projects. Thematically organized "constellations," or annotated lists of suggested further readings and their links to guide or archive articles, follow each part.

Some of the essays included in this print volume are abridged versions of the originals. The archive will present nearly all of the works published in the journal, including those in the guide, in full.

We hope that the combined publication of print guide and online archive will provide a model for the continued accessing and circulation of similar bodies of work in a way that foregrounds the historical contexts for their production as well as their relation to each other. The writing that appeared in *Poetics Journal* reflected the development of a range of creative and critical approaches in avant-garde poetry and art in the 1980s and 1990s. In making the content newly available for creative and critical use, we hope to preserve the generative enthusiasm for new writing and art it represents, while encouraging new uses and contexts.

—*Lyn Hejinian and Barrett Watten*

a guide to *Poetics Journal*

Introduction

I

The first issue of *Poetics Journal* appeared in January 1982, in the midst of a period of intense poetic productivity, with several North American geographical centers (the San Francisco Bay Area, New York, Toronto, and Washington, D.C., being the most notable) and with corollary developments, both historical and contemporary, taking place elsewhere in the world. It was no accident that, from its inception, one of our chief editorial aims was to articulate the linkages between this multicentered Language writing movement and parallel developments in other avant-garde practices. In the intervening years, *Poetics Journal* witnessed the development of writing on poetics from a wide range of aesthetic tendencies—language-centered, ideology-critical, performance-based, New Narrative, hybrid genre, new lyric, textual materialist, and conceptual/documentary, to name only a few. Our tenth and final issue of *Poetics Journal* appeared in June 1998, but we do not consider the journal's work complete. *A Guide to Poetics Journal: Writing in the Expanded Field, 1982–1998*, along with its companion *Poetics Journal Digital Archive*, are intended as a resource for further work, by us and by readers who will take up the various challenges these materials and their interconnections offer.

Poetics as a contemporary genre of writing and artistic-intellectual practice was (and is still) just beginning to discover its possibilities, even as it was attempting to create terminology, name its objects of concern, devise methodologies, and generate an arena for collaborative (and sometimes contentious) conversation. This volume is intended not merely as a contribution to literary history or cultural studies; indeed, we think it is primarily *not* that. Many of the works in it, though thoughtful in character, are polemically charged, and many of the questions they raise remain open. Otherwise put, many of the writings here signal the beginning of new modes of inquiry or creative approaches. This volume makes available a number of the perspectives that were initiated in the pages of *Poetics Journal*, but at many points the works are (as they were intended to be) suggestive rather than definitive—openings into new areas of inquiry more generally—and readers will discover not only an account of paths taken but also a clear indication of paths to be explored. We take the moment that *Poetics Journal* records to be one of incipience, a demand for intervention and participation in attempts to shift contemporary cultural horizons. In editing *Poetics Journal*, and in editing this guide and assembling the journal's archive, we have wanted to extend the dimensions of the literary and cultural field and to alter its outline.

Poetics Journal began in the cultural recession of the Reagan era, a period many writers and artists experienced as one of increased social pressure and constraint. Such negativity can give rise to what Barrett Watten has called a "constructivist moment," which seeks, as he puts it, "both to disclose the nature of the system and to develop an imagined alternative." Our constructivist moment was already well under way in 1982 when *Poetics Journal* 1 appeared. Literary practice, as undertaken by those involved in Language writing, entailed ardent (as well as arduous) formal and informal conversations among its participants, along with persistent attention to the surrounding cultural milieu. Numerous works available by 1982 (poetry, reviews, talks, manifestos, and so on) testify to this. *Poetics Journal* was intended to expand, clarify, and intensify our ongoing thinking about the contexts and trajectories of the work under way. As became clear over the course of the ten issues of its run, a cultural topography was being outlined and indexed, the scope and details of which surprised even us as editors. Discussion of Language writing to this day persistently remains blind to the variety of interests and the range of cultural activity that inform its creation. These contexts are central to the meaning of Language writing, and to fail to note or acknowledge them is to miss one of its central points.

During the years that the journal was active, both editors of *Poetics Journal* were also writing poetry and editing literary publications. Barrett Watten edited the magazine *This* from 1971 to 1982, and This Press was active through the 1980s; it has recently published the ten-volume, ten-authored project titled *The Grand Piano: An Experiment in Collective Autobiography, San Francisco, 1975–1980*. My Tuumba Press, which published a sequence of fifty letterpress chapbooks, ran from 1976 to 1984 (it was revived in a different format in 2001 and remains active). That we decided to devote attention to a journal addressed to "poetics" is an indication of our interest in discovering and describing sites of artistic practice in terms of immediate cultural experience and the unfolding of social modernity and its outcome in the postmodern. "Poetics" emerges in the pages of *Poetics Journal* as a site where poetry, largely construed, expands into its implications. At the same time, poetics is a site where other spheres of cultural activity and other kinds of art-making enter *into* poetry. It is, at least in the account offered by *Poetics Journal*, a site for the practice of self-reflection and intensive redefinition as concomitant to broad social and aesthetic engagements; it is also a site for continuing incipience, a site for perpetual, open-ended, and curious becoming.

Bruce Andrews and Charles Bernstein's *L=A=N=G=U=A=G=E*, which began publication in 1978, posed the question of poetics in ways that were productive as well as problematic. The frequency of its publication and its newsletter format encouraged improvisatory practices in which the difference between poetry and poetics was often difficult to discern. Indeed, *L=A=N=G=U=A=G=E* could be read as an argument against there being a difference between them: the editors sought articles that were generally short, indexical, and thus condensed in the manner of poetry. While we valued the foregrounding of language and the production of radical encounters in theory as well as in poetry, we also wanted to offer a venue in which writing in poetics could be developed at a greater length. It was with this in mind that we set about bringing the first issue of *Poetics Journal* into existence. With its simple green-gray stippled cover, it looks like a school notebook, with the white rectangle on which one might inscribe the notebook's "subject" still blank; it was the only issue lacking a title, though we thought of it as "Beginning" or "Introduction." (We had experimented earlier with mimeograph production, but decided to continue in the more distributable perfect-bound, offset format.) For this first issue (as, indeed, for all ten), we specifically asked for essays or reviews of substantive length, soliciting work from a political theorist (David Plotke), a linguist (George Lakoff), and a literary historian (Jed Rasula), as well as poets (Bob Perelman and Kit Robinson each contributed to the first issue, as did the editors). From the journal's inception, we were interested in establishing dialogues between different theoretical and practical approaches to questions of language. In this first issue, with Watten's "Politics of Style" and David Plotke's "Language and Politics Today," an explicit (and abiding) interest in laying bare the politics implicit but always at work within language usages (literary and otherwise) is evident.

I do not mean to suggest that *Poetics Journal* initiated the ideological critiques of language or literature; such critiques had been under way among language-centered writers for some time, as, for example, in the Canadian journal *Open Letter*, in *L=A=N= G=U=A=G=E*, and in other journals. What was new (and for us particularly dynamic) was the interdisciplinary character of the discussion. And the linkages to be made were not only between contemporaries. An important precedent for our notion of what "poetics" might look like was the early-twentieth-century work of the Russian Formalists. Viktor

Shklovsky, Yurii Tynianov, Osip Brik, Boris Eikhenbaum, and Roman Jakobson, along with figures still virtually unknown in the West, had joined forces early in the twentieth century to form OPOYAZ (a Russian acronym for "Society for the Study of Poetic Language") as an alternative to the academic philology in control of literary studies at the time (1916–23). Language writing likewise emerged at a time when a certain amount of mustiness was evident in the academy, as in the literary establishment generally, notably in their insistence on lyric subjectivity. We saw this as a symptom of ideological proclivities that were infecting social life generally, and we were encouraged (and, indeed, felt required) to follow the example set by OPOYAZ and rethink poetry and the poetic altogether. As tacit acknowledgment of our indebtedness to Russian Formalism, Richard Sheldon's translation of a major essay by Viktor Shklovsky (from his *Theory of Prose*) appeared as the first work in our first issue.

The second issue of *Poetics Journal* (September 1982) was titled *Close Reading*. The choice of this topic had two points of origin. One was a talk ("Close Reading: Leavings and Cleavings") given by Steve Benson at 80 Langton Street in San Francisco whose implications seemed far-reaching and continued to reverberate. Offering a time-based and site-specific context for reading poetic texts (including Walt Whitman's *Leaves of Grass*, Emily Dickinson's manuscripts, Larry Eigner's typescripts, and his own work), Benson's talk represented a radical intervention in the practice of "close reading" as it was purveyed by New Criticism, and it suggested an alternative trajectory to the practice as it was carried out by the Russian Formalists. The work of the Formalists, then, served as the second point of origin, from which we hoped to track overlooked trajectories and discover new, generative, contextualizing possibilities for close reading.

The first issue of *Poetics Journal* included eight contributors; the second contained fourteen, with work by a prominent linguist (Haj Ross) again represented, along with essays bringing an array of references into the discussion and pointing to the diversity of influences that were informing it (the work of Hart Crane, Eigner, Joseph Ceravolo, Georges Bataille, and Edgar Allan Poe, among others). A number of the terms that Language writing had generated were being productively (and sometimes contentiously) challenged by members of the loosely construed New Narrative group (which included Dodie Bellamy, Dennis Cooper, Kathy Acker, Bruce Boone, Kevin Killian, and Robert Glück). The central argument concerned the status of narrative itself—a mode that a number of Language writers (but most definitely *not* Carla Harryman) had dismissed as ideologically suspect. Robert Glück's "His Heart Is a Lute Held

Up: Poe and Bataille" in the pages of *Poetics Journal* 2 offered a challenge (and contributed to a corrective) to that dismissal. Arguing on behalf of the sexualization of narrative, with all that that might imply, Glück then went further, insisting that "a human picture must accommodate . . . transgression." This essay, along with others by New Narrative writers in subsequent issues of the journal, should figure prominently in any account of the recent expansion of poetry into cross-genre modes, resulting, for example, in such novelistic works as Renee Gladman's *Juice* and *The Activist*, Mary Burger's *Sonny*, and Pamela Lu's *Pamela: A Novel*. More recently, a poetics grounded in the interrelationship between New Narrative and Language writing is being explored in essays by Kaplan Harris, Robin Tremblay-McGaw, Rob Halpern, and others.

In *Poetics Journal*'s third issue (May 1983), titled *Poetry and Philosophy*, connections with British and French avant-garde undertakings were made explicit, and they can be read in the context of Language writing's long-standing engagements with philosophical and theoretical developments in those two countries. Key figures included Ludwig Wittgenstein, Alfred North Whitehead, Roland Barthes, Jacques Derrida, Julia Kristeva, Luce Irigaray and Hélène Cixous (though interest in French feminist theory was made more explicit the following year, in the *Women and Language* issue), and the French Oulipo, to name just a few. With the exception perhaps of Whitehead, these and other figures are of major importance in the turn to language that philosophy had taken and that now poetry was taking. This is what "Language writing" means: writing that makes a turn to language, so as to engage in a relentless (and often inventive and playful) exploration of the forms of linguistic meaning and the meaning of linguistic forms. Lines such as the following, culled haphazardly from Ron Silliman's 1986 anthology *In the American Tree*, are indicative: "Each word once the invention of another" (Silliman, *Tjanting*); "Now that you know what the words mean, you can leave" (Watten, "Plasma"); "Learn what it means to receive syllables" (Jean Day, "Heavy Clouds Passing Before the Sun"); "I was delighted when I managed to deprive those bewitched lines of meaning" (Harryman, "Property"); "graphemic / hinges / discourse / re-ordering / SIGNS" (Bernstein, "ST. McC."); "We are WRITING" (Hannah Weiner, "Little Book 124").

The "Women and Language" issue (May 1984) appeared in the context of an ongoing dialogue concerned with critiquing (and improving) power relations within the literary community and beyond. The influence of French feminist theory was of particular importance, but body, gender, identity, performativity, and sexuality were topics of lived, as well as conceptual, concern; the real problems they involved were taken up with adamant interest by both men and women in the literary community in which *Poetics Journal* was playing a part. It is crucial to note, meanwhile, that within that community women writers were among the most influential figures: Rae Armantrout, Mei-mei Berssenbrugge, Carla Harryman, Fanny Howe, Susan Howe, Ann Lauterbach, Bernadette Mayer, Alice Notley, Leslie Scalapino, and Rosmarie Waldrop. Theirs is the first generation of writers in the United States of which that can be said, and exercising power raised questions that demanded identification, reflection, and historical analysis. In responding to that demand, the *Women and Language* issue brought into play a variety of powers—introspection, dialogue and dialectic, polymorphism, invention, collaboration, improvisation— worth exercising by anyone.

Even as identity narratives raised vexing questions, so did narrative per se, and *Poetics Journal* returned to the question of narrative in its *Non/Narrative* issue (May 1985). The slash in the title was intended to signal the existence of contraries in a potent simultaneity, and the fifty-page "Symposium on Narrative" (the first of several symposia that appeared in later issues of the journal) gives some indication of how various are the sites through (or around) which narrative might pass. The complexity of its status informs conditions both within a given medium and between any of several media. The symposium included pieces by several visual artists (Doug Hall and Howard Fried), a musician (Andrew Voigt, an original member of the Rova Saxophone Quartet), and the filmmaker Warren Sonbert. Points of reference ranged from *The Tale of Genji* to psychoanalysis to media theory to William Burroughs to Bakhtin to Virginia Woolf to street theater to the JFK assassination to Ovid, and the issue included a section devoted to the writing, staging, and performing of Kit Robinson's play *Collateral*, written for San Francisco Poets Theater and performed in February 1982.

Poetics Journal 6, *Marginality: Public and Private Language* (1986), opened up an inquiry into the purported margins (and interstices) of language and of community as well as the relation between aesthetic and public language, the "material text," and its communicative demands. The issue appeared at a point when Language writing was in the second decade of its history, a point at which one good reason for venturing into the margins was to breach them. In many traditional accounts of the avant-garde, a decade is more or less the life span of an artistic movement, which culminates with the establishment of the movement's identity. The misconstrual of Language writing, however, is a prominent feature of its history, and part of the subtext to *Poetics Journal*

6 is resistance to the devolution of Language writing into the static condition of a mere "body of work." In order to keep moving, it must make certain its margins don't become limit conditions. The issue begins with a short essay by Barrett Watten ("The XYZ of Reading: Negativity (And)"), which, among other things, poses marginality as a locus of negativity, construed as a condition of demand, a condition of absence, and a condition of possibility. The second essay in the issue, Bob Perelman's "Good and Bad/Good and Evil: Pound, Céline, and Fascism," addresses itself to some of the worst possibilities of modernism, as cultural negativity embraced a politics that became, for those writing later, intolerable.

Poetics Journal 7, *Postmodern?* (1987; the title, with its big question mark, appears on the cover in Day-Glo orange overlying a grayscale image of Diane Andrews Hall's portentously epochal diptych *Monumental Response*), takes on the question of historicity, but from an altogether different perspective. If history's (unwanted) potential to serve as a limit is one of the central problems raised by the *Marginality* issue, its existence as pervasive (positive or negative) context and historicity's failure to produce context are among the problems haunting *Postmodern?* With titles like "Truth's Mirror Is No Mirror" (Robert Glück), "Ugly" (Kathy Acker), "The Failure of a Postmodern Aesthetic" (Harry Polkinhorn), and "From the Empty Quarter" (Duncan McNaughton), many of the essays in the issue raise a strong challenge to the notion that either modernism or its alternative was a great success. Despite (or perhaps because of) numerous manifestations of aesthetic genius, despite myriad intellectual and experiential pleasures, the celebratory stance of postmodernism could (and perhaps should) have rapidly turned funereal. As John Rapko puts it in "What Will Postmodernity Be?" (his contribution to the "Symposium: Postmodern?" section), "Experimental postmodern writing must understand itself as part of a passed future for which no one could have wished." Perhaps the postmodern is an inaccessible ideal, as Paris-based music critic Jason Weiss puts it in "Postmodern and Music: The Reaches": "Listening was probably the first art, awakening in us the means to assemble our knowledge. We may never have really known what music is."

To the degree that postmodernism views the world as a site of virtually infinite data, it positions itself in a sort of "everywhere," as a virtual place or nowhere to which everything comes. *Poetics Journal* 8 (June 1989) attempted to refigure our contemporary situation by presenting it in terms of "elsewhere," the issue's title. A vision of "poetry everywhere" or even of "language everywhere" is enticing, but there is something ultimately unsatisfying (and possibly reprehensible) in the delirium of an allover equivalence. "Elsewhere" in *Poetics Journal* 8 has multiple sites, the first of which is a parodic and loftily celestial distance toward which a single word (the Russian *iydu*, "I am going") advances via a passage through cumulous clouds; this, at least, is the view offered by the image on the issue's cover, taken from a painting by then-Soviet artist Erik Bulatov. In addition to essays by various U.S. writers (Fanny Howe's "Purgatory," Norman Fischer's "The Old City," Andrew Ross's "The Death of Lady Day," among others), the issue presented contributions from several Soviet writers (prominent members of the Metarealist and Moscow Conceptualist circles) and theoreticians as well as poets from Japan, France, and the United Kingdom. It also included a special bilingual section devoted to recent Québecois writing, featuring work by twelve Francophone Canadian poets. The "elsewhere" that emerged is variously utopic, dystopic, real, virtual, desired, defied, infinite, and local.

There was less goal orientation to the editing of *Poetics Journal* than this account may suggest. On the copyright page of both issues 6 and 7, for example, forthcoming issues on "pleasure" and "work" were announced, but both of those topics were dropped. Instead, number 9 was addressed to "the person," and number 10, the final issue, was addressed to "knowledge." The cover of *Poetics Journal* 9, *The Person* (1991), shows the figure of a man (performance artist John Woodall) with his hands over his ears, wearing an outfit that could be a jester's, or a medieval soldier's, or a dreamed-up outfit devised by a madman; the figure is evidently screaming. Elsewhere may be progressively strange, but it is certainly no stranger than personhood. From the beginning, many of Language writing's devices had the intention (and effect) of dismantling cultural assumptions about identity and subjectivity. Thus various challenges to conventional notions and uses of the "lyric I" in poetry had been raised considerably before issue 9 was in the works. "Aesthetic Tendency and the Politics of Poetry," for example, a multiauthored essay that offered a strongly worded ideological critique of lyric subjectivity, appeared in the pages of *Social Text* in 1988, as did, on a smaller scale, Rae Armantrout in her review of *The Morrow Anthology of Younger American Poets* in *Poetics Journal* 6. Norman Finkelstein's "Problem of the Self in Recent American Poetry," the first essay in *Poetics Journal* 9, takes up the issue in the context of Fredric Jameson's analysis of "the cultural logic of late capitalism." The "problem of the self" is likewise the "problem of the poem," in that both are political as well as aesthetic entities. By extension, then, subjectivity, even in poetry, does not function solely or even primarily as a force for interiorizing and then representing experience; its agency is far more active and centrifugal. Subjectivity is always a site of social and cultural interactions; solitariness is not its privileged mode.

Various characterizations of "personhood" emerge from the multidisciplinary "Symposium on the Person" in *Poetics Journal* 9, with contributions from artists working in an array of fields, including musicians Fred Frith and John Zorn, installation artists Margaret Crane and Jon Winet, the painter Robin Palanker, and performance artist John Woodall, along with ten poets, including Barbara Guest, Franco Beltrametti, and Aaron Shurin. Two other symposia also appear in the issue, one titled "Robert Creeley and the Politics of the Person" and the other "The Poetics of Everyday Life"; each features material originally presented in public colloquia. Placed next to Russian journalist and semiotician Yulia Latinina's essay on the folkloric strata underlying the iconography and idiolect of Soviet propaganda, the latter symposium takes on unexpected linguistic resonances. Purportedly the cultural production of "average" or "everyday" people, Latinina asserts that Soviet folklore is also "one of the levels of the official world view." Personhood and officialdom interact in and as the quotidian—at least in the USSR. Our inquiry into the status of "everyday life" hoped to extend the examination of this relationship in relation to ideology as we encounter it and to ideas. Throughout the issue, questions of interactivity (hence of community), ethical agency, and incorporated alterity take their place alongside questions of cognition, imagination, and what Bill Luoma (in "Astrophysics and You") sardonically terms "perception management." That all of this is epistemologically relevant accounts in part for our decision to focus *Poetics Journal* 10 on "knowledge." But it is also the case that the kinds of poetry we have occupied ourselves with raise fundamental questions regarding the nature of "understanding" and the grounds for what might be said, ideologically and otherwise, to constitute "knowledge."

Published in June 1998, the *Knowledge* issue is by far the longest, filling 294 pages of densely laid-out type and presenting work by thirty-six contributors, including a number of younger writers. The issue's cover features a digitally modified photograph by Doug Hall titled "The Bridesmaid," showing what appears to be a child, dressed in white and bearing some resemblance to Alice in Wonderland, with a preternaturally adult head and face. Attendant on the ritual prelude to reproduction, the blurry bridesmaid is herself a production, garbed in innocence but burdened, however unwittingly, with knowledge. In some respects, Hall's image seems emblematic of the epistemological quandary inherent in language and foregrounded by (and as) *poetics*. Knowledge is not synonymous with truth, at least not unless one agrees with Wittgenstein that a truth is a reality that agrees with a sentence (or with a proposition). *Poetics Journal* did not in any way set out to be definitive; its goals were heuristic, its methodology procedural and interconnective, and its strategy dialogic. Challenge and debate were crucial in *Poetics Journal*, and they remain so in the ongoing, expanding (and exogamous) community of discussants and contributors to poetics as it continues to develop even when the utopia in which argument can proceed as a form of flourishing seems hardly to exist anymore. Hence, though many of our design decisions were, of course, determined by production costs (by the need to keep the number of pages down), the relatively stark "look" of the journal—the sans serif typeface, the closely leaded print, the lack of "white space"—was intended to be somewhat abrasive. There was always something serious at stake—cultural life (i.e., managing to sustain individual and social vitality within our cultural milieu). *Poetics Journal* was meant to convey our sense of the urgency of the struggle to figure out—to keep figuring out—what's going on and what's to be done, in the process of "making the work."

This present volume is not intended simply to recapitulate the discussions that transpired in *Poetics Journal*'s ten issues. It has a different purpose and is therefore structured according to principles quite different from those governing the journal's original issues. The *Guide* is divided into three sections. Part 1 includes essays from the first four issues of the *Journal*; in this section a number of key terms are laid out, methodological initiatives are undertaken, and important interdisciplinary connections are established. Many of these articles are by now well known in the field of contemporary poetics. In part 2, contextualization is very much at issue, as is a broadening of the field of artistic and cultural analysis. In part 3, an even greater widening of the landscape is evident, in terms of the number of new authors and the explorations of inexhaustible problems such as personhood and knowledge. The essays within each of the three sections are arranged alphabetically. Rather than organize them thematically here, we want to extend the conceptual horizons of the sections and offer a maximally open terrain in which readers encounter the unexpected points of intersection to be found as one reads through the works included here and in the archive. As Barrett Watten remarked, "It's the space between positions that is fascinating, as much as the positions they define"; it is our belief that an alphabetical ordering can serve as a markedly productive means of discovering and opening those spaces. And though, of the nearly sixteen hundred closely packed pages of *Poetics Journal* 1–10, only some 20 percent are included in this book, we are confident that on its own, and in conjunction with the archive, *A Guide to Poetics Journal* preserves a sense of the scale of the original and offers a heterogeneous array of works that remain compelling and relevant and that can serve as a source and instigation for works to come.

—*Lyn Hejinian*

II

In its contribution to the long history of writing in poetics, from Aristotle to modernists, postmodernists, and contemporaries, *Poetics Journal* becomes a site for reflection on the genre of poetics and its possibilities. Immediately, one might ask: is "poetics" a specific *kind* of writing, after its original usage as an account of the construction and veracity of the work of verbal art that was extended, through its comparison with the visual arts, to writing on aesthetics more generally? What would necessary and sufficient conditions be for writing on poetry or art to be seen as "a poetics"? How does poetics as a kind of writing extend the making of the work of art into new grounds—for new construction, interpretation, critical thinking, cultural agency? In selecting from the variety of work published in *Poetics Journal*, we had an opportunity to ask: to what end *poetics*? While the genre of poetics surely begins with the making of a work of art and extends the act of its construction into contiguous areas of thought and knowledge, we would find a mere description of a work of art, or of the artist's intentions in making it, not enough to account for poetics' importance as a kind of writing. Poetics is a site for reflection on the making of the work that extends its construction into the fields of meaning in which it has its effects. Such fields of meaning are manifold, from the readers' responses to historical contexts, social motivations, relations to other arts, and philosophical concerns, finally entailing something like a cunning of poetics: the manner in which the work of art extends its principle of construction, the way it makes meaning, through the contexts it draws from, finally, to transform them. That the work will arrive and thrive, in terms that are both analytic and prospective—winning its way, in Gertrude Stein's sense—is the implicit argument of poetics.

It should be evident from the range of work presented here that a consideration of the *genre* of poetics leaves the *tradition* of poetics far behind. Poetics for us is closer to avant-garde manifestos, theoretical debates in aesthetics, working notes for performances, or wall texts for gallery exhibitions than the self-focused reflection on the nature of literariness that extends, from the early moderns and Romantics, to works such as William Carlos Williams's *Spring and All* or Gertrude Stein's "Composition as Explanation." Something of the possibility of poetics, in fact, changed with the modernist avant-garde: in its effort to explain their difficult writings to the general public, the modernists extended their artistic counterdiscourse into new registers of agency. The opaque writing of the modernist avant-garde becomes a site not only of disinterested appreciation but of social comprehension—or *in*comprehension. Of course, Wordsworth and Coleridge both placed the contemporary public's incomprehension of the new language of poetry at the center of their criticism; what changed with the modernists was a foregrounding of the opacity of the work itself that demands this crisis be seen as general. The dawn of the material text in modernism (from nineteenth-century aestheticism and ornamental design to avant-garde typography and mass aesthetics) is relocated at the center of social *in*comprehension: a site for aesthetic pleasure, certainly, but also of alienation and interpellation. It is the modernists' demand for the persistent questioning in and by the modernist work of the nature of modern communication, as a site of social *in*comprehension as much as transparency, that keeps its horizon permanently open. The postmoderns who followed took their departure there: the modernist work foregrounded an opacity at the heart of communication that originated in the aesthetic but quickly was articulated more generally—hence its terrific power.

The "expanded field" in which we hope writing in poetics will be read has a dual register. It takes its origins in a constructivist attitude toward language in modernism and extends that attitude through the writings of the postmoderns, notably in their formulation of poetry as an "open field" of meaning and agency. The inaugural moment of this invocation of the field of poetics was Charles Olson's essay *Projective Verse* (1950), which worked energetically to undermine the object status of the modernist poem through an insistence on a time-valued, site-specific unfolding of poetic agency. Heraclitean flux, if not an existential Dasein, led to a widespread cultural style in the emphasis on spontaneous bop prosody in the Beat Generation and a range of poetic styles that culminated in the "Now" of 1960s counterculture. The New Americans, as early postmoderns, rightly took their place as cultural instigators as well as poetic innovators, reversing the aesthetics of modernist alienation and distancing in a demand for immanent meaning and a practice of the present. Writers who followed, who sought to extend but critique the poetics of immediate presence in the New Americans, were faced with a dilemma: how to reorient the author-centered plenitude of poets like Olson, Frank O'Hara, Allen

Ginsberg, LeRoi Jones/Amiri Baraka, or Joanne Kyger in ways that preserved their open horizons of meaning but distanced their claims to immediacy. What occurred in the Language School was a continuation but displacement of the "open field" of the postmoderns onto the horizon of language—a return, I argue, to an earlier site of social *in*comprehension in the modernist avant-garde. The poetics of the Language School thus reached over the New Americans to make contact with the materiality of signification evident in Stein, Louis Zukofsky, and the expatriate partisans of a "Revolution of the Word," and later—once the pall of Cold War and segregation had lifted, as it did by degrees—in the poetry of the recovered Popular Front and Harlem Renaissance. Historically, the worldview that informed the writers of the Language School originated in the countercultural politics of the 1960s, but it resulted in a substantially more critical agenda than that of the New Americans.

The "turn to language" of the 1960s and 1970s was a site for skepticism on claims to unmediated "presence," but it was also a return to the social *in*comprehension of the material text. It is here that a second, formally negative, account of the "expanded field" enters in, in a skepticism toward the (predominantly masculine) author of the postmodern avant-garde; such doubts about the nature of authorship also extend to the status of the work of art and its adherence to a particular genre—poetry or painting. The late 1960s also saw the rise of conceptual art and its influences on environmental sculpture, performance, and installation art—all genres that extended the boundaries of the work from one genre to another. Is performance art, for instance, sculpture (as it was initially categorized by art historians), or is it theater or textual improvisation? Is a language-centered work of art by Joseph Kosuth or Robert Smithson also a work of poetry? In the expanded field in this sense, the work of art itself, rather than the artist or, by extension, the author, challenges and transforms what counts as a work and as a *kind* of work. Conceptual art, site-specific sculpture, installation art, and improvised performance all worked to destabilize the genres of art in the 1960s and 1970s, and these moves had a formative influence on the development of language-centered writing. Rather than returning the genre of poetics to the literary tradition per se, *Poetics Journal* records an opening to new genres in which writing, visual art, performance, and music overlap. This indeterminacy of genre is linked directly to the "turn to language" itself; rather than seeing this turn as merely formal or literary, an unmediated return to the poetics of material signifier in modernism or to the open field in postmodernism, poetics becomes the site of the self-reflexive questioning of the nature of poetry *as* a genre. While responses to this question vary—from those who believe that poetry as a genre provides the necessary horizon for their activity to those who see poetry as one among many points of departure toward cultural agency—it is our claim that this productive indeterminacy leads, in many ways, to new modes of writing, not simply at a technical level but as a part of an expanded field of meaning.

The turn to language as an expanded field of meaning and agency thus combines both projective and reflexive moments. It has been a fact of artistic practice in the turn of poetry toward the materiality of language, and an enabling assumption of its theoretical framework. This progression thus had many sources in the intellectual history of the 1960s and 1970s: American neopragmatism and its interpretation of Wittgenstein; the reception of French structuralism and poststructuralism, in their historical origins in Russian Formalism and their development in the writings of Barthes, Foucault, Kristeva, Derrida, and *écriture feminine*; and debates around ideology in Western Marxism and their construction of a political postmodernism that reinterpreted the aesthetic one. In literature, the turn to language in poetry began with poetic and artistic examples (the Objectivists and the New Americans; conceptual and site-specific art), even as it took place as a part of the larger development of literary and cultural theory in the 1970s and 1980s. Poetry and poetics, then, were crucial sites where the turn to language was articulated, due to the same cultural factors that led to the rise of theory. *Poetics Journal* brought these debates into the journal at appropriate moments; our intention was never simply to record the development and reception of new modes of writing but also to involve that writing with the emergence of theory in the period. We saw many points of commonality for poetic and theoretical work, beginning with the Russian Formalists' efforts to liberate the verbal sign and extending to a number of further moments: from Wittgenstein to the Frankfurt School to poststructuralism to Marxist postmodernism. Poetics becomes a site for the construction of methods as well as works—more precisely, works that entail a critical methodology in their extension and interpretation.

We began in our first issue with a set of topics that assumed nonnarrative and language-centered poetry but that also extended to larger questions. As a common source for the turn to language in literature and theory, a section from Viktor Shklovsky's *Theory of Prose* (1923) was selected to open our introductory issue (no. 1, 1982). It is important that Shklovsky's development of the poetics of the material sign, while informed by the poetry of Russian Futurism, was articulated in the genre of prose fiction, both narrative and nonnarrative. His account of Vasily Rozanov, a case of "minor literature" in Gilles Deleuze and Félix Guattari's sense, locates the turn to language at a chaotic intersection of literary and cultural motives—Rozanov cannot be considered a formalist in any pure sense. For Shklovsky, the move toward foregrounding language performs a "knight's move" in relation to historical context, which it represents obliquely in referential terms but "jumps over" through its processes of defamiliarization. This simultaneously formal and contextual relationship to meaning—where form is expanded to a more broadly social and historical field—was followed in many articles in our first issue, from David Plotke's consideration of the status of language in Marxism to George Lakoff's account of the "continuous reframing" of postmodern performance to Kit Robinson's discussion of the use of avant-garde writing as a model for teaching. In my essay, "The Politics of Style," I took as point of departure Charles Olson's reading at the Berkeley Poetry Conference in 1965—a grandstanding but ultimately lucid presentation of poetry as "uninterruptible discourse"—which I then read in relation to Terry Eagleton's critique of ideology in the foregrounding of signification. In this conjunction of poetic examples and theoretical approaches, we sought to create a situation in which the implications of innovative poetry could be extended into other domains.

Succeeding issues of the journal sought to focus our efforts around key themes: *Close Reading* (no. 2, 1982), *Poetry and Philosophy* (no. 3, 1983), and *Women and Language* (no. 4, 1984). In each, we felt there were particular aspects of new genres of innovative writing that ought to be expanded in particular fields. The task of *Close Reading*, for example, was to take seriously the claim, widely circulated as a theory of how Language writing ought to be understood, that "the reader makes meaning." Based in Barthes's distinction between *lisable* and *scriptible* texts, this theory was, we felt, too general at best and unexamined in terms of specific acts of reading at worst, leading to a politics where the reader can make whatever he or she wants out of a text. The reader-centered theory of meaning has an important democratic aspect, but the resulting politics are as often regressive as progressive. For every instance in which the empowering of the reader as a political entity liberates him from bad authority, one could find an instance in which the reader is free to project whatever he wants onto a political position, to assume it stands for his interests regardless of content. It is easy to connect this "writerly" projection to aspects of democratic politics that have had an overwhelmingly negative effect— in the "dumbing down" of public language to the point that anything means anything, depending on your interest. In the context of the second Iraq War, this meant that the absence of weapons of mass destruction did not matter as an argument against policy; the war was its own argument. The difficult language of poetry, from the modernists onward, has intended, among other things, to question such a "dumbing down" of communication in the public sphere. Just so, the "reader makes meaning" theory needs to be qualified in terms of its specific motives and contexts.

In our issue, we assembled a wide range of examples of what such a "politics of the reader" might look like, from analyses of poetic language by a post-generative linguist (Haj Ross) and the application of recent theories of language to poetry by Ron Silliman and me, to articles that made the act of reading itself a performative operation (Steve Benson, Alan Davies, Jackson Mac Low, Johanna Drucker). Benson's "Close Reading: Leavings and Cleavings" was originally staged as a performance at 80 Langton Street (later New Langton Arts), an interdisciplinary artists' space where many poets of the San Francisco Language School read or performed from the late 1970s on. In his performance, equally a practical demonstration of "the reader makes meaning" theory, Benson carefully hand-copied a series of literary texts, from Emily Dickinson and Walt Whitman to Virginia Woolf and Larry Eigner, which he projected onto the gallery wall and commented on in a spontaneous improvisation. In this work, Benson established a mode of performance as dialogue between preexisting texts and spontaneous interpretations that he continues to develop in his work, adding a skeptical element in the evanescence of such readings that balanced their open and liberatory potential to "free the reader." The open field of meaning is returned here to modernist *in*comprehension of the material text as it expands into new genres of performance art. The turn to the material text here reflected on contemporary practice among poets as it anticipated the critique of material textuality that would emerge in the work of Jerome McGann, Cary Nelson, Michael Davidson, Susan Howe, and others. *Close Reading* offers a prime example of the predictive value of the genre of poetics in terms of the development of theory and practice.

The moment of theory was our focus in *Poetry and Philosophy*. In that issue, we wanted to assess contemporary writers' relations to various philosophical traditions and to pursue the relevance of philosophy to poetry in aesthetics. In a larger sense, we wanted once more to refute the banishment of the poets from questions of truth, as commonly understood (even as much revisionist work on the ancient Greeks, from Hans-Georg Gadamer to Elaine Scarry, questions the exclusion of the poets from philosophical debate). We entered into this question with few prior commitments to how contemporary writing ought to be seen in relation to philosophy. While the turn to language in poetry took place, first and foremost, as a development of literary and artistic possibilities (in experimental modernism, after Gertrude Stein and Louis Zukofsky; the New American poetry; and new developments in conceptual and interdisciplinary art), it also took many of its cues, even central assumptions, from the rise of neopragmatist and poststructuralist theory in the 1960s and 1970s. Even so, the opening of the field of poetry that we witnessed was so powerful that there was seldom a sense that poetry needed to be mapped precisely onto another set of theoretical options. If theory was everywhere and nowhere, poetry was simply, it might be said, the shape of things to come. It is significant that the turn to language in poetry was so immediately identified with the turn to theory, in early examples such as Ron Silliman's mini-anthology "Surprised by Sign" (*Alcheringa*, 1975), Steve McCaffery's section of a special issue of *Open Letter* (1977), and Bruce Andrews and Charles Bernstein's editing of *L=A=N=G=U=A=G=E* (1978–82).

Two points are important here: first, while there was much invocation of theory in these early positions, it was always seen in relation to new possibilities in writing itself. It was also true that the turn to theory was taken to be such a violent affront, to both the poetics of presence among New Americans and the poetry of the workshops, that the Language School was often seen as being in complete denial of poetry in favor some other, "alien" discourse. Our third issue of *Poetics Journal* thus tried to proceed from a reimagined neutral perspective: to what extent are poets involved in theory, and precisely which theories, which traditions? The answers ranged from essays taking up the general question of poetry and philosophy (Charles Bernstein, David Bromige, Allen Fisher, Bernard Noël) to accounts of philosophical influences and demonstrations of the relation of theory to poetics (Jackson Mac Low, Alan Davies, Erica Hunt). The essays exhibited an unresolved tension between Anglo-American and Continental models, while Wittgenstein was the philosopher most frequently invoked. In my essay, I looked for common grounds between conceptual art and Language writing, recognizing important distinctions of genre between them even as I sought a "total syntax" that would extend poetry into contexts in the manner of conceptual and site-specific art. In contrast to this sober analysis, Alan Davies's performance "Language/Mind/Writing" acted out an illicit borrowing of theory by poetry and its refusal of normative forms of poetic discourse that would cause nightmares among mainstream poets.

Given the emerging sense of mission expressed in our volume titles, it was with a sense of belatedness that we took up questions of gender in *Women and Language.* Increasingly there was a common assumption that modernism and postmodernism maintained versions of the author that were patriarchal, homosocial, or authoritarian (granted the expanded canon of women modernists and the anticipation of second-wave feminism in the postmoderns). Poetry in the contemporary period, by contrast, was witnessing the emergence of second-wave feminism and of numerous language-centered women writers, including Kathy Acker, Beverly Dahlen, Jean Day, Lynne Dreyer, Rachel Blau DuPlessis, Kathleen Fraser, Carla Harryman, Lyn Hejinian, Fanny Howe, Susan Howe, Erica Hunt, and Leslie Scalapino. The reception and continuity of a language-centered poetics among women was one of the most important features distinguishing our postmodernism from an earlier male-dominated and homosocial one. In addition, gender was having a profound effect on the development of new genres of poetry and poetics, leading at once to radically self-focused lyricism (Dahlen, Fanny Howe, Day), poetry that breaks with the lyric tradition to address sources of language outside the literary (Susan Howe, Hejinian, Tina Darragh), and forms that deliberately violate the boundaries of genre (Scalapino, Harryman, Acker).

Our fourth issue of *Poetics Journal* was the first such collection of experimental women writers, and numerous essays in it are definitive: Hejinian's "Rejection of Closure," which compares the horizons of "open form" (after Umberto Eco's "open work") with the *écriture feminine* of French feminism; the opening sections of Susan Howe's *My Emily Dickinson*, which transformed notions of authorship in relation to the material text and led to a complete reassessment of Dickinson's poetics; and Dahlen's "Forbidden Knowledge," which brought into poetics a gendered reading of Lacanian psychoanalysis. Also significant in the issue were articles recovering neglected women modernists, from Mina Loy (Carolyn Burke) to Laura (Riding) Jackson (Ben Friedlander), and writing by women visual and performance artists (Abigail Child, Sally Silvers, Ellen Zweig). Francie Shaw's cover should be remembered, too, for the interpretation of the volume it offered: a mixed-media depiction of numerous men's hats suspended in air that, paradoxically, claimed a feminist poetics in the reinscription of masculine signifiers. Françoise de Laroque's contrarian essay "What Is the Sex of the Poets?" reinforced this gendered reinscription in her review of an anthology of contemporary French poets, largely men, that, in contrast to the rise of an essentialist feminist poetics as *écriture feminine*, claimed the author function to be masculine. The double ironies of such a position in the context of the numerous swappings of identity positions in the issue argued against any simplistic identity politics and for more complex understandings of the ways gender is enacted in poetry. At the same time, this was a collection that highlighted innovative writing *by women*. It was our first popularly successful issue—it sold out immediately, and copies are now rare—leading, we heard, to study groups in the Bay Area that met to discuss the essays.

The next triad of issues—*Non/Narrative* (no. 5, 1985), *Marginality: Public and Private Language* (no. 6, 1987), and *Postmodern?* (no. 7, 1988)—sought to interpret innovative poetry in relation to public discourse in related ways. We began by questioning the status of narrative in innovative poetics, in light of numerous strategies among experimental writers that questioned, undermined, or totally abandoned it. The privileging of a synchronic and atemporal horizon of "language," rather than the causality, closure, totalization, and temporality of narrative, was an assumption shared by the majority of the language-centered writers in the 1970s and 1980s. "Language," as we have claimed, originated first in the intensified pressures on meaning in avant-garde and lyric poetry, but it took up related concepts in structuralist and post-generative linguistics, deconstruction, postanalytic and neopragmatist philosophy, and hermeneutics (not all at the same time!) as providing insights into the nature of poetic language. What resulted, as will be evident in any reading of work published in journals like *A Hundred Posters*, *Big Deal*, *Hills*, *La Bas*, *Roof*, *Tottel's*, *This*, and others from the period of the Language School's emergence, as well as from the writings on poetics in *L=A=N=G=U=A=G=E*, was a horizon of language in the Language School that was more spatial than temporal. For many writers (and visual artists), narrative was suspect—it was the horizon of official meaning and interpretation, the real prison house to which we have been confined by history. An open field of meaning offered a way out of the confinements of narrative and closure, and *nonnarrative* writing strategies (which deferred or suspended at least one of the several distinguishing features of narrative) became vehicles of choice. But what about the tricky relation of the prefix *non-* to *narrative*? Does nonnarrative writing depend on a (suppressed, underlying, denied) framework of narrative? What of the social and historical narratives the writer is in when she writes nonnarrative work? Such narratives are easy to discern in the avant-garde: there is the story of new meaning, of tradition leading to innovation, of moving toward abstraction, and so on.

There was also, in much work we published, a resistance to dominant narratives—of opposing the Vietnam War and supporting the civil rights movement, for instance—that gave meaning to the artistic strategies of the counterculture. Seeing these strategies as historical and yet diverging from any singular meaning or larger grand narrative suggested, as well, an emerging consensus for a postmodern refusal of narrative. Fredric Jameson's notion of "the waning of affect" among postmoderns—who could not hold the present together with the protensions and retentions of history and were thus confined to mere intensities, nostalgia, pastiche, and spatial dislocation, a notion put forth in his "Postmodernism" essay—offered a direct challenge to our work. Finally, there was an immediate challenge to Language poetries and nonnarrative raised by writers of the New Narrative tendency in San Francisco—Robert Glück and Bruce Boone, to begin with, and Kathy Acker, Kevin Killian, Dodie Bellamy, Michael Amnasan, and Camille Roy later on—who, following the debates between Georges Bataille and Jean-Paul Sartre against the poetics of surrealism, called for writing that was embodied, committed, concerned with sexuality and with gendered (particularly queer) identity, transgressive in terms of genre, and *narrative*.

Non/Narrative thus raised the question of the rejection or affirmation of narrative in innovative writing within the horizon of an emergent postmodernism. The issue begins with a series of essays by writers who see themselves as suffocating in the prison house of narrative and who try to formulate strategies that negotiate between continuity and discontinuity. As Steve Benson writes in "Mediations in an Emergency": "The sequence of events one encounters and tells oneself of and links in association may be made narrative, by condensation and displacement, much as I tell myself the story of my life, moment to moment, in as many voices and forms and styles as I may know" (7). Between writing and reading, narrative is a necessary sense-making activity that must be negotiated. Leslie Scalapino's "Poetic Diaries" takes up the narrative of *Tales of Genji* and extends it to language-centered prose texts such as Clark Coolidge's *Mine: The One That Enters the Stories*, seeing narrative as an exteriorization of subjectivity:

> Therefore my thought, and events which are painful to me—and the world, are the same. Very painful events may seem to have longer reverberations. Which cause their own reordering. This implies a syntax which in being read would require that the reader go through the process of its thought, have that thought again—and it's therefore an act, one which has not occurred before. A thought of the writer isn't going to be duplicated. (20)

For Scalapino, narrative is a necessary reliving of traumatic experience in a way that is dissimilar to its past moment; narrative joins with nonnarrative at the site of trauma. Ed Friedman's "How *Space Stations* Gets Written"—a narrative of a writing project that works between transcripts of the Apollo lunar mission and his own diaries—takes a more ameliorative approach to narrative, which he sees as distributed among the many voices of the ongoing experiment. Between taped voices of "Mission Control" and his own responses, Friedman constructs a textual feedback system in which he monitors sensory inputs, ongoing data analysis, response formulation, implementation of strategies ("the ability to put plans into action"), and overviews of the project as a whole. Narrative takes place as moments of decision making in the ongoing work that are at the same time distributed in the total form of a process-oriented project. The therapeutic benefits of such a form of self-monitoring are crucial, as discussed in relation to the psychoanalytic tradition by Nick Piombino. Between the stream of associations of the psychoanalytic session and the forms of scientific intuition, narrative is a necessary mediation: "The mental need of transitional language to bind together very brief intervals of inner experience into a recognizable, describable unit of perception causes a continuous shift in perspective from intuited thought to communicable thought." Narrative dislocates rather than totalizes, but the ability to work with its demands leads to an optimal balance between "the fragmentary experience of disjunctive association"—an effect many texts of Language writing imitate—and the capacity of "identity to experience cohesion and still retain the needed sensitivity to change which promotes new configurations." The issue continues with a series of positions that investigate the tension between the need for narrative and the need to escape its confines: in "The Knowledge of Narratives," Peter Middleton defends the importance of narrative for science; Michael Anderson's "Framing the Construals" rejects narrative as a universal element of communication and calls for a semiotics of interpretation; while in his piece "And Who Remembers Bobby Sands," Steve McCaffery rejects univocal narrative as a socially distorted overriding of plurality:

> Narrative is now autotelic inside its own repetitions. Its concern is strictly with its own reproduction as a model of communication. It no longer offers a commodity world of bounded stories and events but hypersimulates its own form as the abstract form of reproduction. In this eclipse of representation, meaning is no longer consumed (as in the realist novels of the last century) nor is meaning produced (as in the struggles of much post-modern narrative and non-narrative); it is reflected without absorption. Hence the entropicity of the late night news. (67–68)

Theoretical overviews of narrative in relation to postmodern knowledge were matched, in our issue, by a forum on poetics and narrative that asked a series of writers, visual artists, filmmakers, and performance artists, "What is the status of narrative in your work?" Responses ranged from descriptions of the place of narrative in artistic practice (Alan Bernheimer, Michael Davidson, Maxine Chernoff, Rae Armantrout, Diane Ward, Alice Notley, Tina Darragh) to enactment of nonnarrative strategies (cris cheek, Fiona Templeton). Two important dimensions of the forum were the extension of the question to visual artists (Doug Hall, Howard Fried), musicians (Andrew Voigt), and filmmakers (Warren Sonbert); and a set of theoretical positions that either supported the New Narrative (Bruce Boone, "A Narrative Like a Punk Picture: Shocking Pinks, Lavenders, Magentas, Sickly Greens"; Robert Glück, "Baucis and Philemon") or worked between narrative and nonnarrative (Carla Harryman's "Toy Boats," which begins, "I prefer to distribute narrative rather than deny it"). Following the forum is a series of articles of a recent production of Kit Robinson's theater piece *Collateral* by the San Francisco Poets Theater. An emergent genre that involved both Language writing as text and narrative construction in production, Poets Theater located its aesthetics squarely on a dividing line between discontinuity (abrupt shifts of narrative frame, nonsense, surprise, *Witz*) and continuity (contingent framing, local coherence, emerging thematics, insight). In this forum, Kit Robinson and director Nick Robinson work through the decisions that take them from text to production, a discussion that may be read in a larger sense as about the interpretation of radical texts in their horizons of meaning. The work of Poets Theater, which featured productions of works by Eileen Corder, Kit and Nick Robinson, Alan Bernheimer, Bob Perelman, and Carla Harryman, and its challenge to static, exclusively language-centered interpretations of experimental writing, was a central influence on our questioning of the status of narrative.

Finally, the issue ended with a series of reviews, controversial in the way reviews of contemporaries seldom are, on writers such as Robert Creeley, Stephen Emerson, Lydia Davis, and David Antin who explore the poetics of narrative. Two reviews of the journal *L=A=N=G=U=A=G=E*, one by David Bromige and the other by David Lloyd, divide on a fault line between valorizing the "open form" of its poetics and demanding that it be considered as a species of ideology. For Bromige, the turn to language in poetry counters its degraded status in the lifeworld: "Between a stultifying insistence on an impossible accuracy, and an intoxicated assumption that one knows what is meant (and which turns out to be what, one way or another, one wanted to be meant), we live. . . . Or we *might* so live, sufficiently reminded." Lloyd, on the other hand, is skeptical of a claim to such an alternative: "In the currently institutionalized forms of the discourse of poetics, a matrix of forms secretes the hidden ideology of aesthetic thinking." This tension between open form and discursive closure is also evident in Bob Perelman's "Exchangeable Frames," his review of Marjorie Perloff's *The Poetics of Indeterminacy: Rimbaud to Cage* and Jameson's *The Political Unconscious: Narrative as a Socially Symbolic Act*. What Perloff ignores, for Perelman, is precisely the social and historical narratives that make indeterminacy legible, in a complex dialectic of determination and interpretation: "Comforting as Perloff's procedures of close reading is to the writer (and distressing, too, when she won't read the form), Jameson's lesson needs to be learned. Writing does not occur only on the page, in the words themselves." In concluding, Perelman aligns his position with the crux between narrative and nonnarrative our issue intended to explore: "Anything is a story if it's seen as one. Yet any narrative can be dissolved into a wider scheme. So there are no 'such things' as narrative or nonnarrative. Narrative is not immanent, but social."

My discussion of the debates around *Non/Narrative* may give a sense of how we tried to construct each issue of the journal: as a network of intersecting arguments within a larger frame, something like a poem, in fact. In retrospect, it seems that *Non/Narrative* marked a crisis in aesthetics among language-centered writers and a defining moment of the journal's project in its situating of nonnarrative in theory, practice, and comment. It was truly controversial: as difficult as it is to criticize toward larger aesthetic or political ends, and not simply descriptively or supportively, there is a human tendency to sustain the continuity of our hard-won meanings, nonnarrative included. Historically, something of the assumptions that were common to language-centered writing seemed to change about the time of *Non/Narrative*, and it might be useful to wonder why. Was it, in fact, the challenge of the advocates of New Narrative, who insisted that the turn to language did not adequately offer a politics of gender? Was it a moment in which a nonnarrative openness of form and meaning found its limits in a demand for historical legibility and the periodizing of a postmodern culture? Was it the tension over the politics of the literary and aesthetic in relation to culturalist approaches that became increasingly important in the 1980s? Was it the arrival on the scene of institutional criticism and critics who would interpret our efforts? Something snapped in terms of the immanent consensus shared by members of the writing community, and perhaps this was a good thing.

Marginality: Public and Private Language (no. 6, 1986) begins with just such an entropic moment, in which the assumptions of nonnarrative writing encounter normative modes of communication in moving from the hermetic and private to the public and accessible. Again, this move was controversial: if poets agreed to place their work in the context of public discourse, much of its originality and nuance might be compromised. Yet the benefits seemed to us to outweigh the risk and produced an important range of positions in the issue for assessing the status of poetic language as public communication (many of which are included in this guide): Bruce Andrews's call for a poetics as social action, "Total Equals What: Poetics and Praxis"; Rae Armantrout's send-up of the public pretensions of "private" concerns in poetry, "Mainstream Marginality"; Michael Davidson's investigation of the poetics of individual languages and sociolects, "'Hey Man, My Wave!': The Authority of Private Language"; Johanna Drucker's valorization of a visual poetics of radical idiosyncrasy, "Hypergraphy: A Note on Maurice Lemaître's *Roman Hypergraphique*"; and Bob Perelman's "Good and Bad/Good and Evil: Pound, Céline, and Fascism," a thorough treatment of modernist poetics in relation to social narratives, as he had called for in the preceding issue. Also featured were George Lakoff's application of frame semantics to private language, "The Public Aspect of the Language of Love"; sections from Jackson Mac Low's "Pieces o' Six," in which he moves from chance procedures to a poetics of real-time association; Andrew Ross's "The Oxygen of Publicity," which brought the poetics of deformed media language into the context of poetics; and my own "XYZ of Reading," which meditated on the fate of radical writing at the site of public *in*comprehension.

The call to expand the field of poetry from the literary to the cultural continued with *Postmodern?* (no. 7, 1988). Here, what was influential in the 1980s was not only Fredric Jameson's challenge to narrate the nonnarratable but also a widespread perception in the visual arts of a turn from expressivist aesthetics toward more public, anti-individualistic concerns. This challenge could be discerned in Jameson's "Postmodernism" essay, which juxtaposed language-centered poetry (Bob Perelman's "China") with examples of schizophrenic language, narrative pastiche, postmodern architecture, and Warhol's *Diamond Dust Shoes*. While Jameson, to be sure, thought he was simply periodizing in characterizing symptoms of postmodern distress in Perelman's poem as schizophrenic language, the implications of such a move—that Language writing was merely symptomatic—had to be countered. And was not the discourse of postmodernism one that innovative writers wanted to claim for their own?

The fault line, here, appears in the word itself, *postmodern*, which various essays in the issue affirmed, contested, or nuanced—beginning with George Hartley's detailed "Jameson's Perelman: Reification and the Material Signifier," which sought to uncover the historical and theoretical reasons why Jameson had written such a one-sided account.

Generally positive overviews of the postmodernism debate were offered by Ron Silliman in "'Postmodernism': Sign for a Struggle, Struggle for the Sign," which affirmed the significance of the postmodern, however contested, for language-centered writing. My own contribution, "The Literature of Surface," argued that a further historical distinction ought to be made between an embodied, spontaneous, immanent Postmodernism I (an "Early Postmodernism"), seen in a range of art practice from the New Americans to minimalism, against a simulacral, nostalgic, pastiched Postmodernism II (the "Late Postmodernism" of Jameson, Lyotard, and Baudrillard) that was taken up by the art of the 1980s. Kathy Acker's "Ugly," a prose fiction that fantasizes revolutionary, Third World violence, or Leslie Scalapino's "Pattern—and the Simulacral" both strongly affirmed postmodernism in literary practice, and by women. However, skeptical notes emerged in Larry Price's "Contingency Caper"; Allen Fisher's "Postmodernism as Package"; Harry Polkinhorn's "Failure of a Postmodern Aesthetic"; and reviews of Andrew Ross's *Failure of Modernism* and Charles Bernstein's *Content's Dream*. Anti-postmodern positions were also represented by Alan Davies's intellectually violent "Strong Language"; Duncan McNaughton's "From the Empty Quarter"; and Bill Berkson's "Stick" (countered, in our mini-forum on the postmodern, by Kathy Acker). Perhaps an element of language-centered nominalism (the Language School is always "so-called," never adequately named) accounts for writers' misgivings about being located in an historical period, however "post-"; such resistance may also be a residual effect of modernist poetics, or even poetry itself when compared to other genres.

The final triad of issues internalized the cultural turn of the preceding three issues and partly returned to literary practice as the ground for poetics, from *Elsewhere* (no. 8, 1989), to *The Person* (no. 9, 1992), to *Knowledge* (no. 10, 1998). This was a moment that coincided with numerous writers of the Language School taking up positions in academia and with the emergence of a new generation of post-Language poets and critics. *Elsewhere* began with the question of radical alterity—the "other" as fundamentally compelling and finally unknowable—as a motive for experimental writing that trades in language-centered alterity. After the cultural turn, such an alterity reflects diverse subjectivities and literary traditions as "other": our issue foregrounded work from an "other" culture at the end of the Cold War, the newly accessible community of post-Soviet poets and artists Lyn Hejinian made contact with in her 1980s travels in the Soviet Union and helped bring into translation. In this moment of cultural opening, a number of Russians would present their work during the same period at New Langton Arts, the Poetry Project, and the New Writing Program (University of California, San Diego), and in turn they organized the 1989 international conference of avant-garde poets and critics that led to the writing of our multiauthored text *Leningrad: American Writers in the Soviet Union* (with Michael Davidson and Ron Silliman, 1991). The literary and cultural issues that surrounded this exchange were many: on the one hand, we had begun our journal by invoking the poetics of Russian Formalism, which post-Soviets shared but from a radically different perspective, in that they had received much of their information about the Soviet 1920s from the West and had rejected any sense that experimental writing and the Soviet state were connected.

The aesthetics of the post-Soviets, at least in poetry, might be characterized as a kind of hyperrealized metapoetics—an inward-turning "beyondsense" generally unlike the material texts produced by the Language School in the same period. One may argue over the reasons for the difference between our aesthetics—and we did, in countless meetings with our counterparts on both sides of the collapsing border between antagonists. Whereas the dissolution of Cold War tensions has now been seen as linked to an assertion of "identity politics" in language-centered writing (in an interesting but speculative essay by Walter Benn Michaels in *The Shape of the Signifier*), the publication of *Elsewhere*, Hejinian's translations of Arkadii Dragomoshchenko and her own *Oxota: A Short Russian Novel*, Kit Robinson's translations of Ilya Kutik, and my own *Under Erasure* are marked sites of a poetics of alterity at the Cold War's devolution. The "end of history" loudly proposed as the triumph of neoliberalism after 1989 was, from the perspective of poetics, no end at all but an opening to multiplicities that were held in check and even suppressed by the great power politics of the era. After the collapse of this constitutive antagonism, our issue took up numerous "elsewheres" of identity and difference in various contexts, from the "l'existence est ailleurs" of the surrealists to Robert Smithson's use of the landscape of New Jersey. Significant alterities in the issue included essays on British and Canadian experimental writing (Jeff Derksen, "North Of"; Paul Green, "Literate Tones"); writings by French poet Emmanuel Hocquard and "Penultimate Witness," Jerry Estrin's essay on Hocquard's work;

essays on religion, myth, and alterity by Nathaniel Tarn, Norman Fischer, and Fanny Howe; Laura Moriarty's account of sex in the poetry then being published by Detroit's In Camera Press; Andrew Ross's reading of race and gender in Frank O'Hara's "Death of Lady Day"; an anthology of Québecois poetry in translation assembled by Michel Gay; discussions of alterity as an element of performance art and film (Steve Benson, Carla Harryman, Abigail Child); and my account of the poetics of social space in Detroit.

This move to alterity permitted, in turn, a new assessment of subjectivity and identity, which we pursued in *The Person*, an issue that presented the subject not as the ground of lyric aesthetics but as a site of anxiety, contestation, trauma. In language-centered writing, it may be said, the subject is "under erasure" in a distancing aesthetic, and we were not advocating any return to the embodied subject of the New American poets, much less the self-presentations of the Confessional poets. On the other hand, the separation between language-centered writing and the aims of poetries that invoked identity politics (African-American foremost among them, with race, class, and gender in general as constituting identities) had to be addressed. As a concept, "the person" combines the positivity of diverse subject positions with the sense that all identity claims are rifted with nonidentity: "the person" is the site of identity as a construction and of nonidentity as its constitutive ground. Our issue thus sought to affirm a necessary relation between poetries that claimed identity and poetries that radically textualized it. This was not a simple task, as the insightful but difficult dialogue between Leslie Scalapino and Ron Silliman, "What Person?," demonstrates. Scalapino had objected to an essay Silliman published in *Socialist Review* (1988) that claimed a necessary difference between the respective aims of "dominant" and "marginal" groups in innovative poetry, with white male heterosexual (WMH) poets proposing a poetry of nonidentity because theirs was not in question, and women, poets of color, and gay and lesbian writers needing to "tell their stories" in a more identitarian manner. Scalapino saw this argument as denying the capacity of minority identities to claim the same "high" aesthetic values (distance, objectification, textuality) as WMHs, and objected to Silliman's perspective as, precisely, the identity claim of a WMH. Silliman, in response, tried to unpack and defuse any such identity claims as ultimately relative to the particular social circumstances of one's upbringing, in his case in terms of class. A minor scandal was the result, with both poets claiming identity and nonidentity simultaneously but in denial (and assimilation) of the other's. As William Carlos Williams wrote in "To Elsie" on the hidden injuries of race and class, "somehow it seems to destroy us"—but it was precisely this agonizing space be-tween identity claims we sought to confront.

To assess the issue of "personhood" from the perspectives of as many "per-sons" as possible, our issue contained work from thirty-six authors, with three symposia: "The Person," which asked a number of artists and poets, "What is the status of the person in your work?"; "The Poetics of Everyday Life," which discussed the relation of postmodern poetry to experience; and "Robert Cree-ley and the Politics of the Person," which focused on a single author. (Given the multitude of authors in the issue, the decision to include a symposium on Creeley was a contrarian impulse, but one that recognized the importance of his work for a poetics of personhood.) In the lead article, "The Problem of the Self in Recent American Poetry," Norman Finkelstein theorized the inescap-able horizon of the person in lyric poetry, no matter how strenuously some poets would seek an alternative to self. "It's *all* person," his argument implied, but if so the next question might be "What person?" In our view, experimental poetics contests the normative account of the person, seeing it as a site of dif-ference, nonidentity, and conflict as much as identity. Kofi Natambu's "Multi-cultural Aesthetic" and Harryette Mullen's "Miscegenated Texts and Media Cyborg" argued for a poetics of culturally diverse and mediated personhood, while Kit Robinson's "Time and Materials: The Workplace, Dreams, and Writ-ing" saw the person as necessary for social structures of late capitalism as a baseline psychological reality. Race, class, and social structure are thus em-bedded within any construction of the "person," which becomes the site for social reading as much as subjective investment. By comparing, for instance, the hypersubjectivism of Dragomoshchenko's "I(s)," on decentered subjectiv-ity in post-Soviet writing, with Hejinian's more self-reflexive framework for personhood in "The Person and Description," one could map a divergent set of cultural assumptions. Charles Bernstein's "Professing Stein/Stein Profess-ing" foregrounds authorship as a site of social construction in which reading Stein, reproducing Stein in the academy, and claiming authorship after Stein come together, while Ben Friedlander's "Lyrical Interference" shows how lyric poetics—as exemplified in his own work, Emily Dickinson's poetry, and lyrics by Ernest Tubb and Louis Armstrong—creates a space for a reinvestment of personhood as alterity in lyric form. Accessing a completely different mode of writing, Dodie Bellamy's "Days without Someone" draws on the genre of popular romance in her account of the time and space of an affair as a site for accessing personhood in terms of absence, desire, and longing. Finally, two essays strongly argue for the social constitution of the person: Félix Guattari's

"Language, Consciousness, and Society," a text that Guattari was prevented from presenting at the 1989 Leningrad conference but that was circulated clandestinely by post-Soviet writers; and Yulia Latinina's "Folklore and 'Novoyaz,'" which recovered survivals of Russian folklore in the 1930s discourse of the Stalin cult, one of the most repellent constructions of "the person" in modern history.

Given these multiperspectival and constructivist accounts of the poetics of personhood, one might predict that the forum on the work of Robert Creeley would be an occasion to denaturalize readings of his work, to question its assumptions of immanence and autobiography. Creeley is particularly important for these debates as the poet who fashioned the most durable account of identity among the New American poets, but who likewise anticipated the "turn to language" in poetry, most particularly in *Pieces* (1969). In introducing this debate (originally a panel discussion at the Poetry Project, New York, in 1991), I asked how Creeley's work might be read as historical despite his explicit disavowal of history outside the scope of autobiography—a question meant to be provocative. Susan Howe and Alan Davies responded with defenses of Creeley's authorship, while Richard Blevins argued for a poetics of mastery in his historical account of Creeley's formulation of "the single intelligence." Ted Pearson's "Form of Assumptions," on the other hand, opened up Creeley's lyricism to alterity in its account of gender and sexuality, disclosing a set of discrepant impulses the form must master and contain, even disavow. However contrarian, his reading of "When he and I . . ." (*Pieces*) opens the way for a reading of Creeley's work in a new sense—one that does not end in the reader's production of the author as site for subjective reinvestment. In this sense, the combined testimony of the multiplicity of persons who responded to our symposia "The Person" and "The Poetics of Everyday Life" demonstrates how a constructivist account of "the person" can be put forward as an open form.

Knowledge (no. 10, 1998), the final issue of the journal, appeared after a hiatus for both editors. In the space between *The Person* and *Knowledge* was—what? History? A reorientation of cultural politics with the end of the Cold War and the first Iraq War? Life? The institutionalization of the Language School and the arrival of new groups of poets? Let us imagine that the gaps between history, life, and poetry, which cannot be fully represented, will continue to produce new knowledge. Knowledge of the unrepresentable? Yet was that not what we were doing all along with the "turn to language"? The moment of reassessment in such terms—and they were not explicitly articulated—

became a moment of opening up to discrepant projects, both creative and critical, that we organized around the (non)theme of all themes, given its ability to include everything in its scope: "knowledge." Louis Zukofsky, in his turn to language, had asserted that he had "done away with epistemology"; from then on only poetry would endure. Skeptical of any such claims, in postmodernity, to an "end" (of history, person, knowledge, or our project), we wanted to open language-centered poetics to the questions of epistemology they assumed. At the same time, we could not adopt any one perspective or method from which such an inquiry would be pursued, since poetry and its community are multiperspectival. Pierre Alferi's contribution, "Seeking a Sentence," opens the issue with a series of meditations on linguistic form as a site of inquiry; while Hejinian's "La Faustienne" contrasts Western epistemology in the figure of Faust with a feminine allegory for knowledge in Scheherazade. The urge to look and to tell become sites not of transparent communication but of agitation and desire. As evident in the compressed form of Ted Pearson's "Things Made Known," poetics itself, as an object of knowledge, is unsettled and agitated.

Gendering epistemology are Joan Retallack's "Blue Notes from the Know Ledge," which extends the uncertainty over whether the color blue can be said to exist in analytic philosophy into a demonstration of poetic inquiry, and Dodie Bellamy's "Can't We Just Call It Sex?," which claims calling sexuality by its right names as fundamental to aesthetics. Reva Wolf, in "Thinking You Know," interrogates knowledge construction in literary and art history through a close reading of John Ashbery's "Farm Implements and Rootabagas in a Landscape" in terms of its intertextuality, and looks particularly at whether Ashbery cited a painting by Andy Warhol that contains a fragment of language (and an image of Popeye) that appears in the poem. Herman Rapaport's reading of Ashbery along with Clark Coolidge and Leslie Scalapino sees lyric poetry as a site of disseminated, temporalizing effects; his deconstructive reading may be juxtaposed to George Hartley's "Althusser Metonymy Wall," which charts the "abyss of representation" via post-Marxist ideology critique after Slavoj Žižek, Ernesto Laclau, and Chantal Mouffe. More than earlier issues, *Knowledge* juxtaposes creative and critical texts, with poetry by Michael Davidson, Dan Davidson, Jean Day, Michael Gottlieb, Pamela Lu, Travis Ortiz, Lisa Samuels, Leslie Scalapino, Rod Smith, Lorenzo Thomas, Hung Q. Tu, and Chris Tysh, along with a chapter from Michael Amnasan's *Joe Liar*, which explores the inauthenticity of postmodern experience. Essays by Ron Silliman, "The Dysfunction of Criticism: Poets and the Critical Tradition of the Anti-

Academy," and David Benedetti, "Fear of Poetic (Social) Knowledge: Why Some People Don't Like (Language) Poetry," on the other hand, reflect the tensions around the institutionalization of language-centered writing, while contributions by Ilya Kutik and Arkadii Dragomoshchenko maintain the focus among post-Soviet writers on a hypersubjectivity that contests normative discourse. My essay, "What I See in *How I Became Hettie Jones*," sees the question of knowledge as leading to a revisionary, gendered account of authorship, which I read as a question of poetics in Hettie Jones's relationship with LeRoi Jones/ Amiri Baraka and as a parallel to the canon formation of the New American poets, from Olson and Edward Dorn to Jones/Baraka. In perhaps the wildest essay in the entire run of the journal, Dennis Barone recovers an instance of eighteenth-century language-centered writing from a Philadelphia newspaper, which he presents in its entirety. Meditations by Kit Robinson on alienation in postmodern social space, "Pleasanton/Embassy Suite"; Aaron Shurin on the poetics of the AIDS epidemic, "Orphée: The Kiss of Death"; Robert Glück on the cultural imperative for "location, location, and location" in the arts; Jim Rosenberg on the coming horizon of digital poetics, "Openings: The Connection Direct"; and Lytle Shaw's and Steve Evans's reviews of new writers— indicate the multiplicity of directions we felt had to be pursued. After the "end of history," we discovered a plurality of poetics that we were able to organize under the rubric of a postmodern turn to "knowledge."

The possibility of continuing our project now, through a selection of representative works from the journal, comes at a somewhat darker historical moment. What looked like an agitated but relatively happy pluralism in the mid-1990s was forever bracketed and contained by the turn to corporate militarism, advanced media hypocrisy, and cultural repression after September 11 and the second Iraq War. We may add to that the specter of global environmental and economic collapse that coincided with the end of the Bush era. In the arts through the end of that period, we saw denial and business as usual and a concomitant hardening of lines, the drawing up of defensive perimeters between positions. It is our sense that the radical openness of modes of poetic inquiry we engaged in the journal have never been more necessary as an instigation to continue the work of immanent critique, in and through the language and culture we live within. At the same time there is a purely practical sense that this writing provides paradigms for poetic inquiry that may be offered to readers more generally and taught in the classroom. Finally, the run of the journal offers a valuable historical record of a period of intense speculation and reflection in poetics and among language-centered writers.

How then should we proceed? It was suggested to us that the run of the journal, as a historical document, could only really be preserved in its entirety, and since that would currently be unfeasible in printed form, it ought to be digitally scanned and published online—but we were certain to reject that option. For one thing, this work is anything but ephemeral; it is a historical record, and needs to be presented as such; for another, digital media are less stable than print, and it is anyone's guess what will become of digital archives in as short a time span as two or three decades. In bringing together a representative sample of writings from the journal in the available means of publication, then, we faced hard choices. To begin with, we decided that we should not represent the work of the journal in a developmental or linear series; rather, we would focus on a matrix-like array of positions. In order to obtain such an array, we unpacked the run of the journal and reordered it, often experimenting with arbitrary game structures in order to create multiple, lateral, and variously contingent relations between authors, essays, and themes. A differently imagined kind of argument emerged from this dissolving of the temporal series that had been so carefully edited in the journal; at the same time, we wanted to preserve a sense of the writing's historical specificity. Thus the essays have been arranged into three sections, while the linear relations between them has been dissolved, and links and keynotes are provided that will help the reader access contiguous discussions in the guide and the online archive.

What we see in *Poetics Journal* is, on the one hand, a written record of poetics and the arts that developed in the 1980s and 1990s, through a dialogue among poets, critics, and artists and focused by the various themes we proposed. More important, however, we see a redefinition of poetics as an expanded field that extends from the radical focus on poetic language to a reflexive genre of cultural critique. In a radical opening from the literary themes of our introduction and first triad of issues, transformed by the demand to account for social and cultural forms in the second, the journal developed a polyvocal, multigeneric, interdisciplinary form of inquiry. In addition to the description, critique, and celebration of new forms of writing, the journal developed numerous new modes of thinking in and as poetics, including prose and performance writing that combines improvisatory form and gender critique; essays in lyric aesthetics as philosophical and methodological investigations; critiques of postmodern politics and social agency extended from innovative poetry; literary polemics that defend the literary and cultural values of formal experiment; genealogies of the turn to the material text as both visual poetics and historical record; time-based and site-specific improvisatory poetics and cultural writing; language-centered texts that claim critical agency in their resistant facticity; theories of public language that have their origins in the analysis of poetic language; writings in poetics that disclose literary assumptions of various national traditions toward a global horizon; postmodern critiques of cultural form and the historical horizons of late capitalism; the poetics of nonnarrative and New Narrative forms; the aesthetics of racial, class, and ethnic difference as mediated in mass culture and poetic form; a historical critique of the forms of modern and postmodern authorship and authority; dialogic exchanges between poets; new media writing; and the emergence of a new generation of language-centered writers.

Each position in this multifaceted debate in some way links to others; so for each of the essays we were able to include in this collection, we have constructed a short bibliography of works by the given author and links to other writings in the journal. We have chosen a hybrid organization of the material, first into rough historical periods, and then, within those periods, by alphabetical order, which is to say arbitrarily rather than chronologically or thematically. Finally, we have made available the entire run of the journal (including full-length versions of articles that have been edited) as a companion *Poetics Journal Digital Archive* and provide a short section titled "How to Use This Guide" in order to bridge the gap between the guide and the archive. Our hope is that, with this experiment in dual print and digital publication, the writing we assembled in the journal and the activity in innovative poetics it represents will be made newly available for use.

—*Barrett Watten*

Numbers 1–4

Close Reading Leavings and Cleavings

Steve Benson's "Close Reading: Leavings and Cleavings" was first given as a performance at San Francisco artspace 80 Langton Street (14 August 1980). In it, Benson took apart and exploded the scene of the reader's interaction with the text as a temporal and performative event of meaning making. Drawing on the work of structuralist and reader-response critics like Roland Barthes and Wolfgang Iser, with Freud and Marx behind them, Benson overturns the dominant ideology of close reading as mandated by a universal, authoritative reader— the pedagogical scene of the academy. Benson's intervention into the ideology of reading has as its point of departure the "reader makes meaning" theory of avant-garde texts, but moves beyond it in several directions: toward the physical properties of the text and its bibliographic codes; toward the embodied experience of multiple readers; and toward its performance in real time and space. Benson's demonstration of a poetics of reading looks forward to projects such as Susan Howe's "*My Emily Dickinson*" (*PJ* 4) and Johanna Drucker's "Hypergraphy: A Note on Maurice Lemaître's *Roman Hypergraphique*" (*PJ* 6), anticipating in turn the poetics of the material text in Jerome McGann's criticism and the interest in the materiality of poetic texts, seen as socially produced, in the late 1980s.

Reading is nearly constant—walking on the street, there are all the signs; at breakfast there's the cereal box. I can posit a continuum, like that of sound from noise through talk and popular to high-art music, from that which is registered and measured inescapably to that which one responds to actively only in isolation. A signifier with immediate and crucial survival value like a stoplight or a yield sign is more easily read partly because its context is commonly presumed almost like rainclouds and white bird-droppings as indigenous to the social matrix of our ecology, whereas a novel, which you dip in and out of on the bus, takes more concentration, since it's less essential and really develops the context of its own events within its text, albeit conventions of reading and genre contribute. Contemporary poetry that intentionally frustrates or coopts the conventional agents of contextualization would then be hardest to read, depending so overwhelmingly on the reader's commitment to formulating an active relationship to the text in order to maintain an ongoing contact that might find some use-value (even if play, some gambit seems prerequisite, at virtually every moment). Such work, while discounting the authority of training and custom, still finds use for the gamut of devices, but determined to constitute a poem, or a poetic agency in the manifest form of a text, relies with particular emphasis on its own concrete construction as a text and on the reader's decisive apprehension of that in all its multivalent peculiarity and potential for association in order to bring an order to bear on the world.

Our contemporary struggle and facility to contextualize our apprehensions in reading psychologically and economically, both abstractly and concretely, with Freud and Marx as the landmark initiators, lends further complexity and ambiguity to the process even as a sense of the urgency and ethical concentration in the activity is radically intensified. The relationship of the reader to the text (and implicitly to the writer, to the images and identities fantasized through the text's suggestions) is existentially personal and individual in its focused laying bare of the reader's imaginative commitment and response to experience. How it feels to read is no longer to be termed merely in the repertoire of stock emotions. The mode of production of the text and its manifest form are also increasingly subject to a reader's interpretation and response, economics grounded in appeal to audience and in the concrete artifact; the poetry's distribution becomes even more legible as a vital aspect of its actual meaning than the author's intentions in inscribing it.

Leaves of Grass.

Ya-honk ! he says, and sounds it down to me like an invitation ;
The pert may suppose it meaningless, but I listen closer,
I find its purpose and place up there toward the November sky.

Looking closely at the words on the page, does the mind try to get the eye to wrap around them, or to pierce them? Or does it only think it tries, anyway? The field of the whole page pulses there, jittering with the largely involuntary little movements of the eyeball pulsing with blood at each heartbeat—imaging the text, while the mind imagines what the text means further. The reader constantly asserts the frame of the page, holding the book so the light will best mark that, privileging the ground of the page over the background of the lights and associations of the rest of the room; the more local frames of the margin, the paragraph or stanza, the sentence or verse line, the phrase or rhythmic foot, each less concrete and more chosen than the last, further hold the tracking, weighing mind's eye in place to seize some gist from the text. The more difficult works for reading, to which glancing proves inadequate as assumptions of principles of the coordination of frames break down and the understanding founders in quandary at patterns of congruity and estrangement inconveniently apprehended, push an insistence back at the reader.

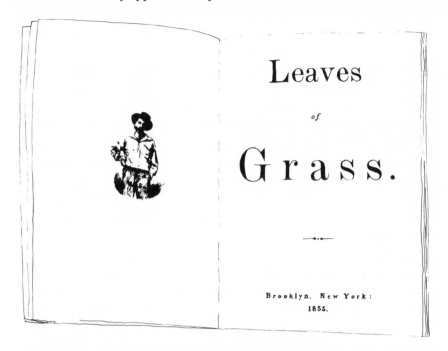

795 copies of the first edition, bound in green, of 95 pages, impressively 11 x 7¾ inches, were published Independence Day 1855. The same Walter Whitman noted, in very fine print, on the reverse of the title page, for entering the volume with a district court's clerk in New York also wrote, produced, distributed, and reviewed the publication (and set about a tenth of the type for it too), though his name appears nowhere else on it.

On the title page the word "Leaves" is 3¼ inches across and ¾ of an inch high. The word "of" is about ⅜ of an inch square. Attended by a period, the word "Grass" is 5½ inches long and 1¼ inches tall. These three words occupy the top half of the page; the bottom 5½ inches include a simple printer's rule, to break up the space, to mark the ground, to distinguish the above from the below, and two lines of bold, substantial, but relatively small print, "Brooklyn, New York:" and "1855."

The type face is a simple, mundane, regular serif face. Its size, spacing, and minimalism effect the impact. Not the crudity or industrial age bravura of heavy block letters but the bare device of the typical appears to step forward due to relations of scale and distribution of elements. The ironic arrogance pushing bland humility in the reader's face in the framing of this particular title counters expectation of the typical ambitions of a book of belles-lettres. If "Leaves" is a customary metaphor for pages, still the reader is brought up short when rather than grounding the trope in some literary association, the type reads "Grass" and demands the reader assimilate the literalness of these words or else derive a value independently in order to construe them appropriate to the occasion.

The page assigns no author responsibility. In the center of the otherwise blank page opposite is planted a steel engraving (the only picture in the book) depicting a bearded man with his underwear showing through an open-necked shirt, his strikingly black hat cocked radically to one side, a hand in a pocket and another on a hip in a fist. He could be saying anything, confronting the reader or staring off into space—in any case, he makes no specific appeal. In the absence of any background or action, he is known only by his own particular appearance.

The long lines on the big pages fill most of the rectangle between the prose margins with words, sets of four dots at a time, exclamation marks, question marks, and commas which bind sentence after sentence loosely together. The address strides persistently forward, permitting of no debate but buttonholing the reader again and again: "If you meet some stranger in the street and love him or her, do I not often meet strangers in the street and love them? / If You see a good deal remarkable in me I see just as much remarkable in you. / / Why what have you thought of yourself?" and a page later, "None shall escape me, and none shall wish to escape me," and "What is there ready and near you now?"

Between the title page and the poetry, in grey double-columns of small regular type, the author's introduction concludes, "The signs are effectual. There is no fear of mistake. If the one is true the other is true. The proof of a poet is that his country absorbs him as affectionately as he has absorbed it." The author demands the reader at once take him at his word, literally, *and* make something of him, imaginatively; the text makes the same demand. The proposition of an identity of the author and the literary text here contrives to make the reader's relationship to the text—the book—the agency motivating its impact—as holistic and direct, as "adhesive" as possible.

Any page of *The Complete Poems of Emily Dickinson* is speckled with dates and numberings added in the early fifties by Thomas H. Johnson to transcriptions from manuscript editions in Dickinson's hand, stored by her in a small box, bound as sixty little volumes, tied with twine. Before Johnson's work on them, the poems had never been published without alterations to their punctuation, capitalization, rhythms, and word choices.

I want to read the one about feeling like being split in two. The index of first lines has "I felt my life in both my hands," which might be it, and "I felt a cleaving in my brain." The number next to it in the index, when I find it in the main body of the text, carries an asterisk directing attention to another at the footnote at the base of the page, "See poem 992," which turns out to be a variant of the second half of 937. The dates above the poem refer to the poem above it. The dashes in the poem, at line endings and in the midst of a line, seem synaptic glitches directing elements to stand in and speak for each other, to mark an identity or coherence—urging the mind to make the leap. The capitalization of each "Seam" makes a seam seem bigger, oceanic. As the brain, also capitalized, suddenly seems more able to burst—and there's that contradiction between "I felt" in the first line, making the "Cleaving" absolutely visceral and technical, and "As if," which starts the second line, so the split in that case seems more circumstantial, conditional on seeing it such a way in the mind's eye. The "I" who tries "to match it," standing outside, objectifying mind and brain, finds no controlling means of connection. The concept of a right-brain-left-brain dichotomy bobs up ludicrously in my head, making its pretensions to archetypicality. The last of the four lines, rather than offering a sense of completion or resolution, shows, in its understatement and its lack of either sensation or image, the project of unification or identity lost in the dust, little uncapitalized monosyllables without even a capital I to grant authority, the word "fit" echoing "if," "in," "it," "split," ridiculous in its helplessness to make good for them.

992*

The Dust behind I strove to join
Unto the Disk before —
But Sequence ravelled out of Sound
Like Balls upon a Floor —

c. 1865

Turning the page adjusts to view the second stanza, earnestly reiterating the difficulty of putting what's behind with what's before, the heaviness of "strove" and "join" and the listless lack of capitalization and the ponderous repetition of "the thought behind" by "the thought before," not only redundant but implicitly circular, or out of order, all contributing to a sense of the futility of the effort to discover coherence, as do the widely separated dates cropping up below, to the left and right of the final lines, the supposed date of composition and the date of first (and certainly inaccurate) transcription into print. Twenty-two pages later, at the same point on the page, 992, with *its* matching asterisk, changes the stanza only by replacing the first "thought" with "Dust" and the latter with "Disk," the concrete images rather frustrating sense and making the final two lines read even crazier. Is sequence normally *in* sound, and now, as though twine were coiled inside a cylinder rather than around it, raveling out carelessly? Or is a string of pearls a more appropriate image, breaking out on making contact with a surface of resistant consciousness? Perhaps, particularly since the reading, reflectively and in moment following moment, sounds the poem out only to lose its parts in loosing them to the mind through the ear, even while the mind tries to reclaim them again

(What was on the previous page? What did I think about it? In what way does it matter?) in some design that *may* be energetic, that *may* be based on one the poet owned to in one moment, that ... The "Balls" seem to have their own autonomy, the "Floor" isn't even an apt receptacle but simply lets them have their ways with it, following them helplessly wherever they go.

No less the subjective individualist than Whitman, likewise participating in every pulse of energy, Dickinson sees the world united in instants and falling away in its expanse while Whitman sees particulars as sensational symbols and finds a wholeness only in generality and omnipresence. Whereas for Whitman bringing the work together in one volume, ever more inclusive and expansive in its constitution and outreach, fulfilled a sense of identity in his address to the world, Dickinson's occasionally and locally disseminated but mostly close-held manuscripts, untailored and untenable to publication in her lifetime, seem to have sustained a sense of resolute singularity that integrated with the conventions of her circumstance, jarring just enough to be accurate to her understanding without bowling anybody else over. The fascination with which I frame the values in the text in the purposes of its author I find suspicious, not so much in its accuracy (which is fortuitous and specific to my usage) as in its deviousness—circumventing the actions of the writing and reading themselves as though they were mere pretext for my identification with the author.

> streets, streets
> the map, the picture
> the field there   cross
> out
>
> the way high
> low, what
> straight is
>
> the sea reaches
>
> wind
>
> you turn,   elsewhere
> down
> from now
>
> me on

In the interests of a writing's effecting or offering a more responsible relationship with the reader, it may eschew guidelines to direct the reader to follow what the author wants the reader to think the author wants the reader to think and, instead, present the reader, not with obstacles necessarily to thought or connection, but with occasions for an active, constructive, uncircumscribed understanding in which the author too is interested. A series of sentences, each of which stands for a construction designed to effect a particular complex of associations, may lack some kinds of marked connections to each other, not because the author disdains continuity or coherence but because the continuity and coherence formulated at the level of the sentence functions sufficiently, if not a bit more arrogantly, if articulated with full decision, than feels honest, to anchor an understanding. The disjunction from sentence to sentence allows the presumptions of a polished understanding to be called into question at each instance without being refused. It allows the reader to consider the sentence's conceptions more closely even while considering their potential relationships. The writing takes the reader into account by constituting statements of value and criticism and definition and affirming them in the authority of print while depending on the reader's own assertions of value, criticism, and definition to make a use of them. The affirmations in the text may even be made in such ways that they need to be challenged. A reader who approaches such writing to put the pieces together and figure out what the author really means is likely to feel cheated, because the author's intention is not to convey a whole statement that absorbs potential dialogue but rather to construct a framework of significations of urgency and coherence and interest in itself, for reading.

Identity, passions, doubts, recollections, values, dazed impressions, specific needs, criticism, awe, distraction, sensuality, and an urge toward the realization of understanding in a form still operate, at will.

> when i read translations, i poke around the words,
> not at them, guessing at a reality not hinted at
> but encoded by some prisoner from another world—
> nobody's perfect; but i relish the quest for the
> peculiar nature of some original writer, un-
> known to us but through his function : images
> thoughts perhaps of trees cows judgings ravings—

In a letter to the director Vsevolod Meyerhold on March 26, 1928, discussing Meyerhold's new production of Griboyedov's *Woe to Wit*, Boris Pasternak wrote, "It's strange to me, but clear to me, that I can give my attention only to something not worthy of it. Because everything worthy of my attention makes me inattentive—doubly so: first, because it stuns me, and second because it gives rise to reflections that distract me from observing it in detail. But I am happy with this trait of mine, and would not want to live otherwise."

Note: The images of this written piece were derived from slides used during the talk. The text on p. 43 is from Larry Eigner, *Flat and Round* (Berkeley: Tuumba, 1980), and on p. 44 from Stever Benson, "Translations," in *As Is* (Berkeley: The Figures, 1978).

PUBLICATION: *Close Reading* (1982), 2:75–81.

KEYWORDS: reading; material text; performance; visuality.

LINKS: Steve Benson, "Mediations in an Emergency" (*PJ* 5), "Personal as Social History: Three Fictions" (*PJ* 7), with Carla Harryman, "Dialogue: Museo Antropología, Mexico" (*PJ* 8); Harryman, "What in Fact Was Originally Improvised" (*PJ* 2); Dennis Barone, "Note on John Smith's 'Philadelphia Newspapers Read Crossways'" (*PJ* 10); Abigail Child, "Outside Topographies: Three Moments in Film" (*PJ* 8); Alan Davies, "Close Reading Close Reading" (*PJ* 2); Johanna Drucker, "Hypergraphy: A Note on Maurice Lemaître's *Roman Hypergraphique*" (*Guide*; *PJ* 6); Howard Fried, "The Museum Reaction Piece" (*PJ* 5); Ben Friedlander, "Lyrical Interference" (*PJ* 9); Susan Howe, "*My Emily Dickinson*, part 1" (*Guide*; *PJ* 4); Jed Rasula, "What Does This Do with You Reading?" (*PJ* 1).

SELECTED BIBLIOGRAPHY: *As Is* (Berkeley: The Figures, 1978); *Blindspots* (Cambridge, Mass.: Whale Cloth, 1981); *The Busses* (Berkeley: Tuumba, 1981); *Briarcombe Paragraphs* (Paris: Moving Letters, 1985); *Blue Book* (Great Barrington, Mass.: The Figures, 1988); *Reverse Order* (Elmwood, Conn.: Potes & Poets, 1989); *Roaring Spring* (Tenerife, Spain: Zasterle, 1998); *Open Clothes* (Berkeley: Atelos, 2005); with Rae Armantrout, Carla Harryman, Lyn Hejinian, Tom Mandel, Ted Pearson, Bob Perelman, Kit Robinson, Ron Silliman, and Barrett Watten, *The Grand Piano: An Experiment in Collective Autobiography, San Francisco, 1975–1980* (Detroit: Mode A, 2006–10).

Writing and Method

Charles Bernstein was the coeditor, with Bruce Andrews, of the journal *L=A=N=G=U=A=G=E*, which they produced in chapbook format from 1978 to 1982. Radical in style as well as content, the essays they published (and often commissioned) were intended to blur the distinction between poetry and poetics, writing and theory. This blurring of genres, and its larger philosophical justification, is developed in many of Bernstein's essays, which have since been collected in several volumes. Influenced by Anglo-American philosophy (particularly Ludwig Wittgenstein and his American interpreter, Stanley Cavell) and continental philosophy (Jacques Derrida's *Of Grammatology* appeared in translation in 1976), Bernstein takes up the long-standing debate between philosophy and literature, arguing for the literariness of philosophy and for the philosophical importance of literature. Citing predecessors from Montaigne and Thoreau to the manifestos of the avant-garde, Bernstein argues, in the first half of his essay, that literary writing should be taken as philosophically serious. In the second half of the essay (available in the online archive), Bernstein elaborates on a basic problem common to philosophical and poetic writing: that of unexamined, normative uses of language whose unquestioned status can have an atrophying impact on thinking. To investigate, rather than assume, forms of philosophy or poetry at their most fundamental level as writing is what Bernstein means by "method."

---

1. The Limits of Style / The Possibilities of Phenomena

An inquiry into the differences between philosophical and literary writing practices is of value insofar as it can shed light on both the nature of philosophy and poetry and, more importantly, on the development and implications of such genre or professional distinctions within writing and thinking. For what makes poetry poetry and philosophy philosophy is largely a tradition of thinking and writing, a social matrix of publications, professional associations, audience; more, indeed, facts of history and social convention than intrinsic necessities of the "medium" or "idea" of either one. So such an inquiry will end up being into the social meaning of specific modes of discourse, a topic that is both a stylistic resource for the writing of poetry and a content for philosophy.

Philosophy has traditionally been concerned with the nature of the world and the possibilities of human knowledge of it; in a large sense, the nature of perception, phenomenon, objects, mind, person, meaning, and action. Richard Kuhns, in his book about the affinities of philosophy and literature, *Structures of Experience*, writes, "Philosophy asks 'What makes experience possible?' and 'What makes *this* kind of experience possible?' Literature establishes the realities for which philosophy must seek explanations." Kuhns bases the distinction between philosophy and literature on the appeal each makes, the address of the text. Philosophy is involved with an appeal to validity and argument (i.e., to impersonal, suprapersonal, "objective" abstractions, to logic) and poetry with an appeal to memory and synaesthesia (i.e., to the reader's own experience). Kuhns, then, is suggesting two different, though interrelated, modes of discourse. "Philosophy" requires "logical" argument and noncontradiction as basic textual modes of discourse; "poetry" seems to reject argument as essential, though of course it may "incorporate" argument. —Even were I to accept Kuhns's traditional distinctions, which I do not, I would add that poetry can focus attention on the structure of meaning by the exemplification of structures of discourse—how the kind of discourse effects what can be said within it.

Another traditional distinction between philosophy and poetry now sounds anachronistic: that philosophy is involved with system building and consistency and poetry with the beauty of the language and emotion. Apart from the grotesque dualism of this distinction (as if consistency and the quest for certainty were not emotional!), this view imagines poetry and philosophy to be defined by the product of their activity, consistent texts in the one case, beautiful texts in the other. Rather, philosophy and poetry are at least equally definable not as the product of philosophizing and poetic thinking but, indeed, the process (the activity) of philosophizing or poetic thinking.

Jean-Paul Sartre, in his "Self-Portrait at 70" (in *Life/Situations*) argues that while literature should be ambiguous, "in philosophy, every sentence should have only one meaning"; he even reproaches himself for the "too literary" language of *Being and Nothingness*, "whose language should have been strictly technical. It is the accumulation of technical phrases which creates the total meaning, a meaning which," at this overall level, "has more than one level." Literature, on the other hand, is a matter of style, style that requires greater effort in writing and pervasive revision. "Stylistic work does not consist of sculpting a sentence, but of permanently keeping in mind the totality of the scene, the chapter . . . the entire book" as each sentence is being composed. So, a superimposition of many meanings in each sentence. —Sartre's remarks are interesting in this context because he so clearly exemplifies the poetry/

philosophy split, being equally known for his fiction and nonfiction. Yet for me, *Being and Nothingness* is a more poetic work than *The Age of Reason* in the sense that I find it more a structural investigation of perception and experience—"being"—whose call is to "memory and synaesthesia," while the novels often seem to exemplify various "problems" using a rationalistic appeal to argument and validity.

Indeed, if one takes it to be a primary philosophical problem—many philosophers of course do not—that the description (ontology) of events, persons, experiences, objects, etc., are at issue, and it is not just a question of *axiomatizing* types of these things, then forms of art not only "define the structure of human experience" as Kuhns has it but *investigate* the terms of human experience and their implications. Then poetry and philosophy share *the project of investigating the possibilities (nature) and structures of phenomena*. The motto for this might come from Wittgenstein in *Philosophical Investigations*: "We feel as if we had to *penetrate* phenomena: our investigation, however, is directed not toward phenomena but, as one might say, the 'possibilities' of phenomena."

As a result, the genre or style of a writing practice becomes centrally a question of method, rather than a transparent given of form. It is this understanding of philosophy that led Heidegger in his later work to reject philosophy and instead call for instruction in "true thinking" (in *What Is Called Thinking*), or has led Stanley Cavell, recently writing on Emerson, to talk of the relation of mood to philosophic inquiry. Or what has led so many poets to feel the need to reject philosophy outright as a ground for poetry, as Craig Watson recently commented, saying that it sentimentalized a picture of perception. The answer to that is that of course people do get attached to their systems: but this should not subvert seeing the possibilities for method itself, for system, for ways of looking at perception. In *Walden*, Thoreau writes, "There are nowadays professors of philosophy, but not philosophers. Yet it is admirable to profess because it was once admirable to live. To be a philosopher is not merely to have subtle thoughts, nor even to found a school, but so to love wisdom as to live according to its dictates.... It is to solve some of the problems of life, not only theoretically, but practically. The success of great scholars and thinkers is commonly a courtier-like success.... They make shift to live merely by conformity, practically as their fathers did, and are in no sense the progenitors of a nobler race of men.... The philosopher is in advance of his age even in the outward form of his life. He is not fed, sheltered, clothed, warmed, like his contemporaries. How can a man be a philosopher and not maintain his vital heat by better methods than other men?" Which I cite partly for that last sentence—the centrality of method.

If philosophy is to be characterized as a form consisting of clearly exposited arguments whose appeal is to the logic of validity, then it would systematically be limited by the limits of expository practice. I don't think it makes sense to restrict philosophy to this particular mode of discourse both because it would rule out some of the best work in philosophy and because it suggests that reason's most "clear" expression is exposition. Rather it seems to me that, as a mode, contemporary expository writing edges close to being merely a *style* of decorous thinking, rigidified and formalized to a point severed from its historical relation to method in Descartes and Bacon. It is no longer an enactment of thinking or reasoning but a representation (and simplification) of an eighteenth-century ideal of reasoning. And yet the hegemony of its practice is rarely questioned outside certain poetic and philosophic contexts. On this level, I would characterize as sharing a political project both a philosophical practice and a poetic practice that refuse to adopt expository principles as their basic claim to validity.

For both poetry and philosophy, the order of the elements of a discourse is value constituting and indeed experience engendering, and therefore always at issue, never assumable.

In some sense these are just issues of style; a style is chosen and it is not to the point simply to be evaluative about which is best intrinsically. But to acknowledge that there are philosophical assumptions that underlie given stylistic practices about the nature of reason, objects, the world, persons, morality, justice. At a certain historical moment certain paths were chosen as to the style that would express a quasi-scientific voice of reason and authority— even though, as Thomas Kuhn points out in *The Structure of Scientific Revolutions*, this "normal" science language cannot account for the paradigm shifts central to scientific progress—a voice that was patriarchal, monologic, authoritative, impersonal. The predominance of this authoritative plain style (taught in such guides as Strunk and White) and its valorization as a picture of clarity and reason is a relatively recent phenomenon and its social meaning will no doubt be clarified by a careful tracing of its origins that would be a central project for the historian of social forms. Morris Croll has elucidated an earlier stage of these developments in his account of the rise of the anti-Ciceronian prose style in the late sixteenth century, a development in some ways paralleling such current critiques as this one of contemporary expository forms in its rejection of a static predetermined formality and its attempt "to portray not a thought, but a mind thinking." Montaigne most clearly exemplifies this movement, especially in terms of his methodological awareness of the implications of style: "I stray from the path, but it is rather by license than oversight. My ideas follow each other, but sometimes it is at a distance, and they look at each other, but with an oblique gaze.... It is the lazy reader who loses track of the subject, not I.... I keep changing without constraint or order. My style and mind both go a-vagabonding.... I mean my matter should distinguish itself. It shows sufficiently where it changes, where it ends, where begins, where resumes, without interlacing of words, of conjunctions, or connectives introduced for weak or negligent ears, and without glossing myself."

No doubt the history of our contemporary plain styles, with their emphasis on connectives, a tight rein on digression, and a continuing self-glossing, a history that could be traced to the last 100 years, would need to account for the effect of industrialization and mass literacy in order to explain the particular tendency toward greater and greater standardization. But the crucial mechanism to keep in mind is not the content per se of current preferred forms versus possible alternatives but *the mechanism of distinction and discrimination itself* that allows for certain language practices to be legitimized (as correct, clear, coherent) and other language practices to be discredited (as wrong, vague, nonsensical, antisocial, ambiguous, irrational, illogical, crude, dumb ...). This "mechanism of exclusion" is described by Michel Foucault in relation to the designation both of the "criminal" and the "insane," with the comment that it is the mechanism itself and its techniques and procedures which were found useful in creating and preserving the predominating hierarchical power relations of the nineteenth-century bourgeoisie (as well, it should be added, as the twentieth-century Soviet state). It is not, then, the intrinsic meaning of the particular distinction that is crucial, not, that is, the particular standard but standardization itself. "What in fact happened ... was that the mechanisms of exclusion ... began from a particular point in time ... to reveal their political usefulness and to lend themselves to economic profit, and that as a natural consequence, all of a sudden, they came to be colonized and maintained by global mechanisms and the entire state system. It is only if we grasp the techniques of power and demonstrate the economic advantages and political utility that derives from them ... that we can understand how these mechanisms come to be effectively incorporated into the social whole." Part of the task of a history of social forms would be to bring into visibility as chosen instruments of power what is taken as neutral or given. Part of the task of an active poetry or philosophy is to explore these instruments by a critique of their partiality and to develop alternatives to them that can serve as models of truth and meaning not dependent for their power on the dominating structures.

The contemporary expository mode was adopted because it effectively did the business of the society's vested interests, by its very mode quelling the sound of oppositional language by equating coherence with mannered and refined speaking. In this context, Sartre tells the story of *La Cause du peuple*, a Paris newspaper that the government actively seized, arresting its editors, in the 70s because, unlike the leftist *Les Temps moderne*, Sartre's own paper, it did not speak in the language of bourgeois discourse but had accounts by workers in their own sharper language of rebellions and atrocities throughout France. I think the outrage against accepting black English diction in a school context is a similar instance of a threat to the legitimizing function served by standardization.

The questions are always: what is the meaning of this language practice; what values does it propagate; to what degree does it encourage an understanding, a visibility, of its own values; or to what degree does it repress that awareness? To what degree is it in dialogue with the reader and to what degree does it command or hypnotize the reader? Is its social function liberating or repressive? Such questions of course open up into much larger issues than ones of aesthetics per se, open the door by which aesthetics and ethics are unified. And so they pertain not only to the art situation but more generally the language of the job, of the state, of the family, and of the street. And my understanding of these issues comes as much from working as a commercial writer as from reading and writing poetry. Indeed, the fact that the overwhelming majority of steady paid employment for writing involves using the authoritative plain styles, if it is not explicitly advertising, involves writing, that is, filled with preclusions, is a measure of why this is not simply a matter of stylistic choice but of social governance: we are not free to choose the language of the workplace or of the family we are born into, though we are free, within limits, to rebel against it. Nor am I therefore advocating that expository writing should not be taught; I can think of few more valuable survival skills. "But if one learns to dress as the white man dresses one does not have to think the white man dresses best." And again the danger is that writing is taught in so formal and objectified a way that most people are forever alienated from it as Other. It needs, to appropriate Alan Davies's terms, to be taught as the presentation of a tool, not mystified as a value-free product, in which the value-creating process that led to it is repressed into a norm and the mode itself is *imperialized*. Coherence cannot be reduced to the product of any given set of tools. This will not necessarily entail that all writing be revolutionary in respect to style or even formally self-conscious about it—though that is a valuable course—but rather that styles and modes have social meaning that cannot be escaped and that can and should be understood.

This understanding should lead to a very acute sense of the depletion of styles and tones in the public realm of factual discourse, including in professional philosophy and the academy in general, but also newspapers, magazines, radio, and TV. Indeed, even within the predominant styles of contemporary philosophy, few of the tones and moods that potentially exist within the chosen style are utilized to any great extent. Indeed, the only significant alternative to the neutral-toned plain style of most philosophical writing of the present time is the weightier tone of judiciousness; but rarely whimsical tones or angry, or befuddled or lethargic or ironic, as if these tones were moods that have been banished, realms of human experience thus systematically untouchable. Not only is the question of method suppressed, but even the possibilities of tone within the style are reduced!

All writing is a demonstration of method; it can assume a method or investigate it. In this sense, style and mode are always at issue, for all styles are socially mediated conventions open to reconvening at any time.

Yet, along with the depletion of styles and tones of writing is a repression of these categories as chosen elements. Appropriating a similar division by Barrett Watten, one might speak of concentric circles of technique, style, mode or genre, and method, each of these terms encompassing a sequentially larger circle that informs the possibilities for the categories within it. That is, a technique exists within the context of a style toward which it is employed, a style can be seen as an instance of a more general genre or mode, and a mode is informed by a still more general method that gives rise to it. Different works will show vastly different indications of these domains. A row of suburban houses, for example, may mask the uniformity of their style by slight alterations (personalizations) made by the individual owners. Art or movie reviewing, for instance, will usually focus on the style or technique and leave unexamined the prevailing assumptions of mode and method, either out of blindness to these aspects or out of a conviction that such issues are contentless or imponderable. Indeed much "normal" philosophy and poetry simply adopts a style and works on techniques within it, without considering either the implications of the larger modality or its methodological assumptions. On the other hand, a "constructive" mode would suggest that the mode itself is explored as content, its possibilities of meaning are investigated and presented, and that this process is itself recognized as a method.

One vision of a "constructive" writing practice I have, and it can be approached in both poetry and philosophy, is of a multi-discourse text, a work that would involve many different types and styles and modes of language in the same "hyperspace." Such a textual practice would have a dialogic or polylogic rather than monologic method. The loss of dialogue in philosophy has been a central problem since Plato; Cavell, applying this to his own work, and that of Thoreau, talks about the dialogue of a "text answerable to itself." Certainly, *Philosophical Investigations* is the primary instance of such a text in this century, and also a primary instance of taking this practice as method. & I can easily imagine more extreme forms of this: where contrasting moods and modes of argument, shifting styles and perspectives, would surface the individual modes and their meaning in illuminating ways and perhaps further Heidegger's call for an investigation into "true thinking." (Thinking is also a construction.) Indeed, I can imagine a writing that would provoke philosophic insight but keep essentially a fabric of dance—logopoeia—whose appeal would not be to the validity of argument but to the ontological truthfulness of its meanings.

Another alternative type of discursive work is suggested by the later writing of Laura (Riding) Jackson. Riding's work has consistently investigated the limits of meaning and the limits of our forms of trying to mean. After twenty years of active poetic practice, she renounced poetry in 1938 as "blocking truth's ultimate verbal harmonies." Had she been a philosopher she might have made a similar renunciation, as, in a sense, Wittgenstein did toward the kind of discourse he and Russell had done in the early part of the century, or as Heidegger did make in his later writing where he characterized philosophy as at odds with "true thinking." Riding's renunciation cuts through distinctions of philosophy and poetry, suggesting that it is the professionalization of—the craft of—each that is the mistake. I've suggested here that if philosophy is reduced simply to a mode of employing argument then the attention shifts from what Riding might call "telling the truth of us all" to the technical perfecting of the mode itself, the kind of tinkering with the mechanics of given arguments, refining their formal elegance, that is apparent on any page of *Mind*. Yet this professionalization, Riding points out, is a danger in poetry itself, as the craft of fine expressiveness she feels necessarily supplants "the telling" that was poetry's initial motivation for the poet. A view that is useful to consider if overly scriptural in its imagination of what this telling is. Riding's appeal in *The Telling* is not to the internal validity of her argument, or to the beauty or virtuosity of her performance or expression, but to the truthfulness of what she is saying in respect to our own, as readers, experiences and memories. We refer back to "ourselves," in that sense are made aware, conscious, of ourselves as readers; by addressing the reader, this work refuses to let its words disappear.

In his "Preface" to *Lyrical Ballads*, Wordsworth writes: "Aristotle, I have been told, has said that Poetry is the most philosophic of all writing: it is so: its object is truth, not individual and local, but general and operative; not standing upon external testimony, but carried alive into the heart by passion; truth which is its own testimony, which gives competence and confidence to the tribunal to which it appeals, and receives them from the same tribunal. Poetry in the image of [humanity] and nature." [. . .]

PUBLICATION: Excerpted from *Poetry and Philosophy* (1983), 3:6–16.

KEYWORDS: writing; philosophy; genre; method.

LINKS: Charles Bernstein, "Professing Stein/Stein Professing" (*PJ* 9); David Bromige, "Alternatives of Exposition" (*PJ* 5); Bromige, "Philosophy and Poetry: A Note" (*PJ* 3); Steven Farmer [Roberts], "Reading Eye Lets" (*PJ* 3); David Lloyd, "Limits of a Language of Desire" (*PJ* 5); Joseph Simas, "Bernstein's *Content's Dream*" (*PJ* 7); Michael Amnasan, "The Eclipsing Function of Full Comprehension" (*PJ* 6); Françoise de Laroque, "What Is the Sex of the Poets?" (*PJ* 4); Arkadii Dragomoshchenko, "Syn/Opsis/Taxis" (*PJ* 8); Lyn Hejinian, "An American Opener" (*PJ* 1); Kofi Natambu, "The Multicultural Aesthetic: Language, 'Art,' and Politics in the United States Today" (*PJ* 9); Ted Pearson, "Things Made Known" (*PJ* 10); Nick Piombino, "Towards an Experiential Syntax" (*PJ* 5).

SELECTED BIBLIOGRAPHY: *The L=A=N=G=U=A=G=E Book* (ed. with Bruce Andrews; Carbondale: Southern Illinois University Press, 1984); *Content's Dream: Essays 1975–1984* (Los Angeles: Sun & Moon, 1986); *The Politics of Poetic Form: Poetry and Public Policy* (ed.; New York: Roof, 1990); *A Poetics* (Cambridge, Mass.: Harvard University Press, 1992); *Close Listening: Poetry and the Performed Word* (ed.; Oxford: Oxford University Press, 1998); *My Way: Speeches and Poems* (Chicago: University of Chicago Press, 1999); *Controlling Interests* (New York: Roof, 1980); *Islets/Irritations* (New York: Jordan Davies, 1983); *The Sophist* (Los Angeles: Sun & Moon, 1987); *Rough Trades* (Los Angeles: Sun & Moon, 1991); *Dark City* (Los Angeles: Sun & Moon, 1994); *Republics of Reality: Poems, 1975–1995* (Los Angeles: Sun & Moon, 2000); *With Strings* (Chicago: University of Chicago Press, 2001); *Girly Man* (Chicago: University of Chicago Press, 2006); *All the Whiskey in Heaven: Selected Poems* (New York: Farrar, Straus and Giroux, 2010); with Bruce Andrews, Ray DiPalma, Steve McCaffery, and Ron Silliman, *Legend* (New York: Roof, 1980).

Forbidden Knowledge

Since the late 1970s, Beverly Dahlen has been at work on *A Reading*, an ongoing long poem that she describes, in a 1980 essay, as "an interminable work" whose compositional method derives from the free-associative practices of psychoanalysis. Her experiments with this method of writing coincided with the rise of French feminism in the United States and were informed by its engagements with philosophy, structuralism, and psychoanalytic theory (particularly that of Jacques Lacan). "Forbidden Knowledge," from which the sections below are excerpted, like *A Reading*, offers a meditation on and demonstration of *écriture feminine*—a term first used by Hélène Cixous in her 1975 essay "The Laugh of the Medusa," where she writes, "Woman must write herself." "Forbidden Knowledge" is one of the first American texts to employ psychoanalytic methods while also critiquing Freud and the post-Freudian tradition for its gender politics. First presented as a talk at 80 Langton Street in San Francisco (26 October 1982), Dahlen's essay addresses the radical negativity of lack as feminine, post-Oedipal, and social. For a woman, as Dahlen sees it, lack is the site of an indeterminacy that is also a possibility of freedom. Her writing unfolds around an absence that has no genre except that of reading, in a poetic practice of interminable coming-to-consciousness.

Some of you may know that I have been writing, off and on, for a long time now, a work called *A Reading*, which is theoretically open-ended, which turns out to be something like a journal, at times like poetry, or prose narrative, and that it was not preconceived in terms of these or any other forms or genres originally.

[This text mimics speech, a talk, imagining you, the second person, or persons, others to whom I speak in the future, the end of October, the darkness rising. *Preliminary fall* I called it originally. Originally there was sin. One was haunted. My history professor who thought Freud confirmed the myth of original sin. Not a fashionable idea. One had better not mention it.

A few nights ago I dreamed I was giving this talk at the Polish Hall in Portland where, as a child, I was taken by my parents to the meetings of the Kaleva Club. A foreign language—Finn—was spoken there, but I don't remember any language in the dream. The lights were very bright.

In this text I would have liked to imitate a certain kind of writing: spare, elegant—the expository writing we learned in school. What I try to teach, proper table manners, the idea of the paragraph, a logical organization, "Eros is the gatherer and tends to form perpetually richer and more complex unities,"[1] "civilization and its discontents," Bob's[2] advice: make a couple of points, don't try to say it all.]

Its method of composition throughout much, but not all of the work, aspires to be free association,

["And where are the confines of relevance?"[3]]

borrowing from Freud the technique he developed in psychoanalysis,

[Freud thought free association was easily learned, but Lacan calls it a "forced labor ... so much so that some have gone so far as to say that it requires an apprenticeship ...," that "nothing could be less free."[4]]

which essentially obligates the patient to speak first and think later, a reversal of our normal procedure.

[*Is* that our normal procedure? Is it not rather that speech and thought arise simultaneously? What is a thought? Can we see or know the end of a thought before we begin to speak it, or while we are speaking it? Do we ever know what we are talking about?

And then there is free association, which specifically requires a non-judgmental attitude towards thought. What is behind this? Freud's conviction that there is an element of censorship in thinking—in all thought?—and that a way to evade the censor would be to say it all, to try to say everything.]

The technique of freely associating ideas and images has been adopted by many writers as a method of composition since Freud first developed it in the context of psychoanalytic practice. There is by now a rather long history of its use, in one way or another, by modernist writers and artists.

["The antiauthoritarian ethics occurs on the level of structure. We call all this 'new'; I reuse the word continually;
      sense of a 'new form' a 'new book' a 'new way
      of writing' layered, 'strudled,' Metzger says
that use of the word 'new' which, in the modern period, has always signaled antithesis to dominant values. These traits, already cited, are one with

the almost thrilling ambition to write a great, encyclopedic, holistic work, an ambition to get everything in, inclusive, reflexive, monumental."[5]]

Nevertheless I suppose that it is my particular use of free association, what I have made of it, and of the larger body of Freud's thought, that prompted this invitation to speak on the general subject of psychology and writing.

Somewhere in *A Reading*, a day or so after I had attended one of the talks in Bob Perelman's series, there is a note to the effect that I wished someone would be invited to speak on psychoanalysis.

[It was, in fact, after Bob's talk on the pronoun *I*, *The First Person*, during the discussion of which Allan Tinker contributed a summary of Lacan's theory about the development of the *I* in the mirror phase. This *I*, where is it? It is constituted in the beginning in alienation, is a fiction, illusory, empty. One learns the trick of disappearing, of becoming invisible, ghostly. One is haunted by images of the double.[6]]

In a sense, I cannot help but see this talk as a fulfillment of that wish. It is a fulfillment, however, which is charged with ambivalence, since I cannot with any certainty be sure that it was not part of the wish to be that "someone" myself. I do not feel qualified to speak about Freud or psychoanalysis; I am not an analyst, I have not, as they say, "been in" psychoanalysis, I have not had any formal training in this austere discipline.

[What is this, an excuse? What is the ground of my authority?]

The most that I can claim is an alternately flaring and fading interest, over the years, in some of Freud's ideas,

[I began reading Freud in high school. I discovered *The Interpretation of Dreams* (the motto of which is: "If I cannot bend the higher powers, I will stir up the lower depths")[7] in the library of the family for which I worked as a babysitter. I read it guiltily, good Baptist girl that I was, weekend after weekend, with a rising sense that it was forbidden knowledge. Years later, I came across a similar idea in the introduction to Norman O. Brown's *Life Against Death*: "To experience Freud is to partake a second time of the forbidden fruit; and this book cannot without sinning communicate that experience to the reader."[8]]

and the related sprawl of some of the post-Freudian critiques, interpretations, and revisions. Yet, it turns out, after all, that these questions have taken up a rather large part of my attention, and so it is just as well, given this opportunity, to try to make some more formal assessment of them than I have before.

[I would have liked to make a "formal assessment," something as cool and distant and functional as a shopping list. I would have liked to, but I can't. The ground keeps shifting. The ground of my needs. Desire? Authority? I admire the "formal assessment," the closely reasoned and coherent essay, but I am haunted by a lack of definition at the center of my experience, this absence which, like a centrifuge, propels me toward the peripheral. Yet: "And where are the confines of relevance?" What can I make, and in what manner, of this *"marginal* speech"? as Julia Kristeva says,[9] taking my place at the boundary, the edge, staying there, saying, with her: "... 'that's not it' and 'that's still not it.'"[10]]

For I have resisted Freud. Is that a confession?

[There is what I might call an interrogative style that seems to turn up frequently in the writing of feminist women. It's a style I'm ambivalent about—it annoys me—and yet I find it to a remarkable extent, as here, in my own work. These are not rhetorical questions, a device used to introduce the answer, since the answer is known in advance. What I am calling the interrogative style of women questions because there are no answers. They are real questions. They are questions about the ground of authority, radical ontological questions, questions about the practice of writing from a center of experience that has been defined by others as non-existent, an absence. These questions throw me into that void, the gulf opens. They are, as Kristeva might say, "hysterical" questions. Punctuated as they are with the sign of the "hook," I am caught in them.]

Here is one of Freud's basic discoveries: that the patient is full of resistances, necessarily, to acknowledging the bitter or depraved or brutal truths which had been repressed and which the analysis slowly but inevitably reveals.

[Resistance: when I threw the book across the room after reading these words: "We must return to Freud and say that incest guilt (the Oedipal project) created the incest taboo. And if the incest taboo involves a preference for masculinity so strong as to see femininity as castration, it would seem likely that a tendency toward patriarchy is intrinsic to the human family."[11] Bitter truth, indeed.]

Even in my apostasy I had to admit that knowledge is forbidden, not just some knowledge, but all of it.

[Here I had to stop and think for a long time. Did I really believe that? *All* knowledge? Was that too extreme? In a world fundamentally constituted out of the grotesque unconscious fantasies of infants and children, in which "a tendency toward patriarchy is intrinsic," in which this father, dead at that, dead at the hands of his sons (in Freud's myth of the primal crime), is instituted at the very foundation of history, forbidding, what? All knowledge? Is that the law of the father?

"to have done," I write on page 2 of *A Reading*," to have done with the judgment of childhood" echoing Artaud's *To Have Done with the Judgment of God*.]

"Under conditions of general repression"[12] (and that is the condition of history), whatever consciousness we may lay claim to is wrested from under the ban. My resistance to Freud necessarily has to do with this analysis, and the part I play in the discovery of repression for myself. That is an odd sentence, but it means, I think, that one can be given to certain ideas for, perhaps, years, before one is moved to make a commitment to an analysis of them.

[The etymology of "analysis": "a releasing . . . to undo . . . to loosen."[13] "Kristeva's concerns have sometimes led her to prefer 'semanalysis' to 'semiotics'— owing to the etymology of 'analysis': . . . to dissolve; dissolving the sign, taking it apart, opens up new areas of signification. . . ."[14]

To dissolve it: little Alice swimming in the pool of her own tears that she shed when she was big Alice. If "child = penis" she swims in a symbolic seminal fluid—it must be the moment of her conception. Or she swims in an amniotic fluid. In any case, she is desperate to be born, to find a way out of the confines of the mother's body, that subterranean passage: in dreams the mother's body is symbolized by houses, rooms, all confining interior spaces, the haunted castles of Gothic novels. "The uncanny."[15]

Animals join her in this pool ("ontogeny recapitulates phylogeny," it must be the primordial sea out of which all life arose), in particular, a mouse, who turns out to be an intellectual mouse (Alice had even suspected it of being "a French mouse, come over with William the Conqueror")[16] who initiates her into history (the father's time), and who tells her a tale about a court trial (the law of the father?) printed in the book as a concrete poem in the shape of his tail, this pun signifying the phallus as signifier. Lacan:

"The phallus is the privileged signifier of that mark in which the role of the logos is joined with the advent of desire."[17] Alice, fascinated by the length of the tail, watches it unfold as a series of "bends." Dimly, she hears him remark: "We know that the unconscious castration complex has the function of a knot."[18]

"'A knot!' said Alice, all ready to make herself useful, and looking anxiously about her. 'Oh, do let me help to undo it!'

'I shall do nothing of the sort,' said the Mouse, getting up and walking away. 'You insult me by talking such nonsense!'

'I didn't mean it,' pleaded poor Alice. 'But you're so easily offended, you know!'

The Mouse only growled in reply."[19]

And here is poor Alice on the Freudian couch, where she has been so many times before,[20] still trying to read the innocent manifest dream as the guilty latent one, censored, censured. Alice, *c'est moi*?[21]]

If ideas are, in the English rendering of Freud's terminology, "libidinal cathexes,"

[We must always bear in mind that we are reading a translation; Freud himself objected to the importation of the neologism "cathexis" to the English version of his work. He wanted a less technical, medical, forbidding language. He used garden variety words to serve his own purposes.[22]]

that is, if thought is erotically charged,

[It matters whose ideas one falls in love with. And then there will be the stormy affair, the struggle, the war, the battle of the sexes, the battle of the books, censorship, denial. Psyche's tasks: circuitous, impossible, endless. In the beginning (in the end?) she is already wedded to Eros.[23]]

then my own repression of analysis begins to be clear. I have made an ambivalent pact

["If the artist goes to the devil by way of his dreams, in time the devil comes to him, and makes his mark; but the dreams do not stop for all that."[24]]

with Freud. He is a figure of the father (is this transference at a distance?) whom I have honored and defended, resisted and feared.

[She hesitates at the gate to the "symbolic order."[25] She is silent. She is slow to learn language, has great difficulty with reading, worse with numbers.

He is trying to teach her her difference, what she is good for. "'But if I'm not the same [[said Alice]], the next question is, "Who in the world am I?" Ah, *that's* the great puzzle!'"[26] It is at this moment that a recurring nightmare begins, in which thousands of snakes crawl over her paralyzed body.[27]

Freud speculated that one of the purposes of the repetition compulsion may be an attempt to master the original painful situation.[28] And what was that? Why, castration of course. "In a symbolic productive/reproductive economy centered on the Paternal word (the Phallus, if you like), one can make a woman believe that she *is* (the Phallus, if you like) even if she doesn't have it (the serpent—the penis): Doesn't she have the child? In this way, social harmony is preserved: the structure functions, produces, and re-produces. Without it, the very foundation of this society is endangered."[29]

"'But I'm *not* a serpent, I tell you!' said Alice. 'I'm a—I'm a—'

'Well! *What* are you?' said the Pigeon. 'I can see you're trying to invent something!'

'I—I'm a little girl,' said Alice, rather doubtfully, as she remembered the number of changes she had gone through that day.

'A likely story indeed!' said the Pigeon in a tone of the deepest contempt."[30]]

I have arrogantly appropriated his ideas for my own uses

["...through identifying with the father, she strives for access to the Word and to time..."[31]]

and have stubbornly refused to provide an account of the outcome of that project. I had thought, in the beginning, that *A Reading* might be a species of self-analysis, contradicting Freud's heroic claim that he, and he alone, could perform such a feat.

[Freud was the first Freudian, the original (*am that I am*), the founding father, the patriarch of that by now far-flung family, analysts, all of whom trace their descent from him, reciting the genealogy, a family which, like any family, is torn apart from time to time by Oedipal rivalries.[32]]

I have been defensive about *A Reading*, wanting to postpone, or defer, conclusions or closure perhaps forever. It is the problem of the interminable. What seems clear to me now, though I have resisted that clarity for a long time, is that the condition of postponement points to a negation, i.e., a repression of the knowledge of death.

[I owe this insight to some of my friends: Ron Silliman, who said, "But you're terminable!"; Mark Linenthal, who patiently tried to instruct me about the difference between life and art, that art must be formal, contained, limited. But, I argued, was I trying to do art? What did I think I was doing anyway? At that point I fell into a profound depression (resistance) which was eased to some extent during the course of an afternoon's conversation with Paul Goepfert and Beau Beausoleil, and in other conversations with Leslie Campbell, and with Frances Jaffer.]

To propose a work which is co-extensive with the literal limits of one's own life is, I think, to be in the thrall of the unconscious notion that one is immortal. For, in Freud's words: "Our unconscious is . . . inaccessible to the idea of our own death. . . ."[33] Works, no less than dreams, may propose a wish and its fulfillment. The rejection of formal limit must bear the burden of this wish that I may never die. The work, insofar as it is a metaphor for the life, will go on forever.

[This is too easy. I suspect it. It was given too early, this sudden crumbling of defenses, like the good analysand's willingness to comply with her good doctor daddy. She wants to please him, after all, even to seduce him, to identify with him so that she may identify with his desire to replace her absence with presence. She wants therefore to know the worst, she expects it, the worst case: megalomania? delusions of immortality? an absence so filled, so inscribed it must point to its reversal: a gap, the void, nothing— barely concealed by this tissue of lies.]

We may, however, be instructed by the recognition of our hubris, and come at length to see how, hidden as it is, it nevertheless provides one term in the dialectic of the work. For in opposition to the unacknowledged longing for immortality there is everywhere in the content of *A Reading* a concern for limits, for boundary, a working out of ideas of time, and of space, of person, parentage, and of the limits of history, both in the larger sense, but especially as one lives it through one's individual life. It seems likely to me now, that what is given in the form as a lack, or absence of limitation provokes an anxiety or tension which generates these, at times nearly obsessive, ideas about limits.

["In other words, we confront two temporal dimensions: the time of linear history, or *cursive time* (as Nietzsche called it), and the time of another history, thus another time, *monumental time* (again according to Nietzsche). . . .

Female subjectivity would seem to provide a specific measure that essentially retains *repetition* and *eternity* from among the multiple modalities of time known through the history of civilizations....

The fact that these two types of temporality (cyclical and monumental) are traditionally linked to female subjectivity insofar as the latter is thought of as necessarily maternal should not make us forget that this repetition and this eternity are found to be the fundamental, if not the sole, conceptions of time in numerous civilizations and experiences....

The fact that certain currents of modern feminism recognize themselves here does not render them fundamentally incompatible with 'masculine' values."[34]]

To dissolve it: they have put words in my mouth, these women:

[I mean: the word as gift, the given; communion (the word as body, broken, the sacrificial word); as replacement, or substitute, empty itself, the signifier or representative of loss, the lost object, "(the Phallus, if you like)"; the word as sublimation, "the symbolic order"; the word as the double, the other, the image in the mirror, in the mother's face, here, gone, illusory, the alienated word; the narcissistic word; the word not my own, quoted, stolen; the sense in which the word of the other is always a distortion of one's own word at the same time that it is a clarification, a recognition of one's own word.]

my mother, who taught me to speak, and finally to read (it was a question of language; Father's Word, mother's tongue), she who was double-tongued, the old foreign language suppressed, the other; she who had translated herself almost wholly into the name of her desire, the language of the father of her children. What can I claim in this rendering, this palimpsest, this layering of texts, the generations, the articulation of loss and desire.

These women: Kristeva, herself the foreigner, the stranger, the exile, multiply so (her work in "... semiotics, a feminine noun in French, whose 'historical role presently is to be the intruder, the third element, the one that disturbs ...'"[35]), the other, heard through the veil, the opening of translation.

These French women: whose works now begin to be translated little by little into English, the echoes of that stormy foreign affair, their battles with Lacan, heard here at last. It was a question of language. Father's Word? Mother's tongue? Kristeva's essay "Love's Heretical Ethics," writes Carolyn Burke, "begins as an analytic study of the Virgin Mary's symbolic function as archetype of the mother. Unexpectedly, the analysis is interrupted by a lyrical intertext composed of outbursts, cries, and flashes of insight. The intertext ruptures the homogeneity of the main text and forces an opening on the page. The coherence of one discourse ... is made to give way to another voice which splits language in two.... The intertext depends upon and echoes the 'mother' text; it functions as its child-being-born in a mimesis of the creation of meaning."[36]

These women: Hélène Cixous, who writes: "A feminine textual body is recognized by the fact that it is always endless, without ending: there's no closure, it doesn't stop, and it's this that very often makes the feminine text difficult to read. For we've learned to read books that basically pose the word 'end.' But this one doesn't finish, a feminine text goes on and on and at a certain moment the volume comes to an end but the writing continues and for the reader this means being thrust into the void. These are texts that work on the beginning.... A feminine text starts on all sides at once, starts twenty times, thirty times, over."[37]

A Reading: in one sense to be myself the reader of a work (have I written it? who is this *I*, where is it?), "thrust into the void"? by it, in this circuitous play of beginnings. "Free" association? It is determined, even over-determined. Rachel Blau DuPlessis: "reading my journal later ... it is not random, those connections. It is intentional; I knew more, said more than I knew. The writing is in the interstices, the meaning is between. It is created in the relationship between, between the elements, they are put down at random, and they flare up they are not said by chance; they know better. I allow this to enter, the blankness which I don't control."[38]

A Reading: what did I think I was doing, anyway? These were questions of language. What was it? Again, DuPlessis: "The holistic sense of life without the exclusionary wholeness of art. These holistic forms: inclusion, nonselection because selection will exclude some important piece of data, or evidence, or knowledge that the writer is not yet sure the meaning of. Holistic work: great tonal shifts, from polemic essay to lyric. A self-questioning, the writer built into the center of the work, the questions at the center of the writer. And uncensored: love, politics, children, dreams, close talk. A room where clippings paper the walls."[39]

In my room clippings paper the door, the entrance, the opening; they are presences at the gate, the threshold, in that place of comings and goings, these daily journeys back and forth,

["What does it mean?" she asks me, my student from Nigeria, "this 'back and forth'?" I draw a picture, arrows on the board; I am helping her to write a letter, the first letter she has ever written in her life, home. We are writing in English, the imperial language, the old foreign language suppressed. English as a second language? For women, perhaps, language as a second language? Layers and layers of veils through which we try to hear one another, translating our primordial muteness, other to other, word by embattled word.]

and in that place, one clipping from Roland Barthes: "What he listened to, what he could not keep from listening to, wherever he was, was the deafness of others to their own language: he heard them not hearing each other. But as for himself? Did he never hear his own deafness? He struggled to hear himself, but produced in this effort no more than another aural scene, another fiction. Hence to entrust himself to writing: is not writing that language which has renounced producing *the last word*, which lives and breathes by yielding itself up to others so that they can hear you?"[40]

The question of language: if *A Reading* is a writing which renounces "the last word," still it has a beginning, a commencement of beginnings, and in that privileged place the epigraph, two sentences from George Steiner's *After Babel* (a book, after all, subtitled aspects of *Language and Translation*), adumbrates the question: "Wittgenstein asked where, when, and by what rationally established criterion the process of free yet potentially linked and significant association in psychoanalysis could be said to have a stop. An exercise in 'total reading' is also potentially unending." If this epigraph is placed in the context of Steiner's work, the question emerges more clearly. Steiner had been writing of several passages in Shakespeare in an effort to demonstrate how many diverse and obscure texts could be brought to bear on the exegesis of those passages. He proceeds to the larger questions of cultural context in general, and then asks: "And where are the confines of relevance? No text earlier than or contemporaneous with Shakespeare can, *a priori*, be ruled out as having no conceivable bearing. No aspect of Elizabethan and European culture is formally irrelevant to the complete context of a Shakespearean passage. Explorations of semantic structure very soon raise the problem of infinite series. Wittgenstein asked where, when, and by what rationally established criterion the process of free yet potentially linked and significant association in psychoanalysis could be said to have a stop. An exercise in 'total reading' is also potentially unending. We will want to come back to this odd truism. It touches on the nature of language itself, on the absence of any satisfactory or generally accredited answer to the question 'what is language?'"[41]

A response to that question is necessarily partial; it will not be answered fully in any imagined endless text, in any total reading of all texts: the interminable text is a metaphor; it affirms the endlessness of language, and the question of language indefinitely.

What is language? A partial response: language is all difference, a play of differences. Terence Hawkes, citing Saussure, writes: "Signs, like phonemes, function 'not through their intrinsic value but through their relative position,' and thus—since the total mode of language is oppositional— '... whatever distinguishes one sign from the others constitutes it.' As a result, 'in language there are only differences *without positive terms.*'"[42]

[I am administering the *Auditory Discrimination Test* to one of my students: "Now, I am going to read you a list of pairs of words. I want you to tell me whether you hear each pair as the same word, or as two different words. Here, I'll give you an example: 'cat—bat.' Same? or different?"

"And here Alice began to get rather sleepy, and went on saying to herself, in a dreamy sort of way, 'Do cats eat bats? Do cats eat bats?' and sometimes, 'Do bats eat cats?' for, you see, as she couldn't answer either question, it didn't much matter which way she put it."[43]]

Language is all difference, a play of oppositions, contrasts, the substitution of a single phoneme for another yielding a new word, a different meaning, same against same against different against same—a rhyme, an echo—illusory? A dream in a dream? infinite regression, babbling, all nonsense?

[I hear them not hearing it. "You don't hear the *a* in 'baby'?" I ask him. He smiles slowly, shakes his head, says, "I hear *b*. That's what I hear. I hear *b*."]

"All I have tried to do," writes Lacan, in a reference to Freud's analysis of Dora, "is to remind you of the misconstrued *a, b, c* of the structure of language, and to teach you to spell once again the forgotten *b—a, ba*, of speech."[44] The note to this sentence cites its source in Freud: "It is a rule of psychoanalytic technique that an internal connection which is still undisclosed will announce its presence by means of a contiguity—a temporal proximity—of associations; just as in writing, if 'a' and 'b' are put side by side, it means that the syllable 'ab' is to be formed out of them."[45] Or, what we have been calling, since Jakobson, *metonymy.*

Hawkes sums up rather neatly Lacan's use in psychoanalytic theory of Jakobson's formulations concerning metaphor and metonymy: "the concept of metaphor illuminates the notion of 'symptom' (the replacing of one signifier by an associated one), that of metonymy sheds light on the origin of desire (through the combinative connection of signifier to signifier and the sense this implies of the infinite extension of such a process into uncharted areas)."[46]

Which brings us roundabout again to Wittgenstein's question,[47] for which, of course, there is no answer. It is a question which thrusts us into the void of indeterminacy.

There is a famous passage in *The Interpretation of Dreams* which reads: "Even in the best interpreted dreams, there is often a place . . . that must be left in the dark, because in the process of interpreting, one notices a tangle of dream-thoughts arising . . . , which resists unraveling but has also made no further contributions . . . to the dream-content. This is then the dream's navel, the place where it straddles the unknown. . . . The dream-thoughts, to which interpretation leads one, are necessarily interminable . . . and branch out on all sides into the netlike entanglement of our world of thought. Out of one of the denser places of this meshwork, the dream-wish rises . . . like a mushroom out of its mycelium."[48] The psychoanalyst Joel Kovel, in an article titled "Things and Words," cites this passage and adds to it another, one particularly emphasized by Freud, since it is given in italics: ". . . the unconscious *'in its innermost nature is as much unknown to us as the reality of the external world, and it is as incompletely presented by the data of consciousness as is the external world by the communications of our sense organs.'"*[49] Kovel offers the following commentary: "Now this reflection of Freud's is neither mystical nor yoked to nineteenth-century 'Newtonian' biologistics. Indeed in a very deep sense any psychoanalytic theoretical reconstruction that does not begin with it is being 'Newtonian' with respect to Freud in the same way that physical mechanics is Newtonian with respect to quantum physics: [it suggests] an indeterminacy that calls into question our very construction of reality. . . ."[50]

The paradox of forbidden knowledge ultimately has to do with this indeterminacy, with an unknown which cannot by its very nature be, with any certainty, known. Contemporary physics is a revelation of this paradox: the work of the physicists is shot through and through with principles of indeterminacy, uncertainty. The physicist Paul Davies writes in the prologue to his book *Other Worlds*: "Science, it is usually believed, helps us to build a picture of objective reality—the world 'out there.' With the advent of the quantum theory, that very reality appears to have crumbled, to be replaced by something so revolutionary and bizarre that its consequences have not yet been properly faced."[51]

To the conceptions of physics Kovel would compare the paradox of the unconscious: that there is at the center

[is it a "center"? *where* is it?]

of our inner world, our subjective experience, some *thing*

[thing? place? system?]

the shape of which, like the shape of the universe, the time of which, the location of which, the contents of which, we can never be sure.

And yet we are bound, in the face of all that is inscrutable, to attempt a reading of the evidence no matter how incomplete it may be. Kovel writes that what "occurs when unconscious content is optimally disclosed is most difficult to characterize, especially in words. This is because it consists of opposed tendencies—i.e., it is a dialectical and not linear relationship. On the one hand such a moment is a finding of the right words, words that most closely describe the truth of the lived situation. But at the same time these words, or, rather, their utterance, indicates an emptiness, a negative—a space within experience whose circumference is describable in verbal terms

[?]

but whose inmost regions lack any form of known registration. To discover the unconscious is like hacking one's way through an impenetrable jungle only to come at once upon a precipice beyond which is an unfathomable drop. It is a moment of absolute lucidity joined with absolute ignorance. In this way we say that word presentations are representations of *thing* presentations— i.e., the unconscious is known through its derivative representations. Here the word 'representation' deserves a close look. The prefix 're' indicates 'backward,' 'turned around.' Thus the representation is the negative of the presentation. It is the union of identity with oppositeness."[52]

A Reading: beginning, as we always do begin, *in medias res*: "before that and before that. everything in a line." Invoking a metonymy which was already a metaphor, the word itself, any word, a representation, a replacement, a substitution for some thing, any thing, which was not there, naming backwards, following it forward, back and forth from nothing to nothing. [...]

NOTES

1 Jean Laplanche, *Life and Death in Psychoanalysis*, trans. Jeffrey Mehlman (Baltimore: Johns Hopkins University Press, 1976), 108.

2 Robert Glück.

3 George Steiner, *After Babel: Aspects of Language and Translation* (Oxford: Oxford University Press, 1977), 7.

4 Jacques Lacan, "The Function and Field of Speech and Language in Psychoanalysis," in *Ecrits: A Selection*, trans. Alan Sheridan (New York: Norton, 1977), 41.

5 Rachel Blau DuPlessis, "For the Etruscans," in *The Future of Difference*, ed. Hester Eisenstein and Alice Jardine (Boston: G. K. Hall, 1980), 137.

6 Bob Perelman, "The First Person," in *Talks: Hills 6/7*, ed. Perelman (San Francisco, 1980), 147–65.

7 Norman O. Brown, *Love's Body* (New York: Vintage, 1968), 241. This is Brown's translation of the Latin motto *Flectere si nequeo Superos, Acherunta movebo*.

8 Norman O. Brown, *Life against Death: The Psychoanalytical Meaning of History* (New York: Modern Library, 1959), xi–xii.

9 Julia Kristeva, *About Chinese Women*, trans. Anita Barrows (London: Marion Boyers, 1977), 35.

10 Julia Kristeva, "Woman Can Never Be Defined," in *New French Feminisms*, ed. Elaine Marks and Isabelle de Courtivron (Amherst: University of Massachusetts Press, 1980), 137.

11 Brown, *Life against Death*, 126–27.

12 Ibid. This is one of the recurring themes of *Life against Death*.

13 *The American Heritage Dictionary of the English Language: New College Edition*, ed. William Morris (Boston: Houghton Mifflin, 1978), 47.

14 Leon S. Roudiez, introduction to *Desire in Language: A Semiotic Approach to Literature and Art* by Julia Kristeva, ed. Roudiez (New York: Columbia University Press, 1980), 18.

15 Sigmund Freud, "The 'Uncanny,'" in *The Standard Edition of the Complete Psychological Works of Sigmund Freud*, ed. James Strachey et al., vol. 17 (London: Hogarth Press, 1917–19), 217–52.

16 Lewis Carroll, *Alice's Adventures in Wonderland*. I am citing *The Annotated Alice*, introduction and notes by Martin Gardner (Cleveland: World Publishing Co., 1963), 41.

17 Jacques Lacan, "The Signification of the Phallus," in *Ecrits*, 287.

18 The fundamental Lacanian concepts to which I allude in this passage (e.g., "the law of the Father") are glossed in *Ecrits* (see note 3).

19 Carroll, *Annotated Alice*, 52.

20 A bibliography of major psychoanalytic works on *Alice* may be found in Phyllis Greenacre, *Swift and Carroll: A Psychoanalytic Study of Two Lives* (New York: International Universities Press, 1955).

21 Cf. Carolyn Burke, "Irigaray through the Looking Glass," *Feminist Studies* 7, no. 2 (Summer 1981), 288–306. Cf. Julia Kristeva, "Women's Time," trans. Alice Jardine and Harry Blake, *Signs: Journal of Women in Culture and Society* 7, no. 1 (Autumn 1981), 31.

22 Cf. Bruno Bettelheim, "Freud and the Soul," *New Yorker*, 1 March 1982, 52–93.

23 There are a number of allusions in this passage. I must cite Robert Duncan's "A Poem Beginning with a Line by Pindar," *The Opening of the Field* (New York: Grove, 1960), 62–69; Brown, *Life against Death* ("The Excremental Vision," 179–201); Kristeva, *About Chinese Women* ("The War between the Sexes," 17–24).

24 Andre Malraux, *Saturn: An Essay on Goya*, trans. C. W. Chilton (New York: Phaidon, 1957).

25 This is another Lacanian concept: see notes 3 and 17.

26 Carroll, *Annotated Alice*, 37.

27 Cf. Sigmund Freud, "Medusa's Head," in *Collected Papers*, vol. 5, ed. James Strachey (New York: Basic Books, 1959), 105–6.

28 Sigmund Freud, *Beyond the Pleasure Principle* (New York: W. W. Norton), 10–11.

29 Kristeva, *About Chinese Women*, 22.

30 Carroll, *Annotated Alice*, 76.

31 Kristeva, *About Chinese Women*, 41.

32 Cf. Sherry Turkle, *Psychoanalytic Politics: Freud's French Revolution* (New York: Basic Books, 1978). Cf. Janet Malcolm, *Psychoanalysis: The Impossible Profession* (New York: Alfred A. Knopf, 1981).

33 Freud, "Thoughts for the Times on War and Death," in Laplanche, *Life and Death in Psychoanalysis*, 6.

34 Kristeva, "Women's Time," 14–17.

35 Roland Barthes, quoted by Roudiez, introduction to *Desire in Language*, 11.

36 Carolyn Burke, "Rethinking the Maternal," in *The Future of Difference*, 112–13.

37 Hélène Cixous, "Castration or Decapitation?" *Signs: Journal of Women in Culture and Society* 7, no. 1 (Autumn 1981), 53.

38 DuPlessis, "For the Etruscans," 137.

39 Ibid., 138.

40 Roland Barthes, *Roland Barthes*, trans. Richard Howard (New York: Hill and Wang, 1977), 170.

41 Steiner, *After Babel*, 7–8.

42 Terence Hawkes, *Structuralism and Semiotics* (Berkeley: University of California Press, 1977), 28.

43 Carroll, *Annotated Alice*, 28.

44 Lacan, "The Function and Field of Speech," 106.

45 Ibid. See Lacan's note 118 for the complete citation of the source in Freud.

46 Hawkes, *Structuralism and Semiotics*, 80.

47 The source of Steiner's reference to Wittgenstein's question is Ludwig Wittgenstein, *Lectures and Conversations on Aesthetics, Psychology and Religious Belief*, ed. Cyril Barrett (Berkeley: University of California Press, 1967), 41–52.

48 Freud, trans. Samuel Weber, quoted by Cynthia Chase, "Oedipal Textuality: Reading Freud's Reading of *Oedipus*," *Diacritics* 9, no. 1 (Spring 1979), 64.

49 Freud, "The Interpretation of Dreams," *Standard Edition*, vols. 4 and 5, 613. (This is Kovel's citation.)

50 Joel Kovel, "Things and Words: Metapsychology and the Historical Point of View," reprinted from *Psychoanalysis and Contemporary Thought* 1, no. 1 (New York: International Universities Press, 1978), 36.

51 Paul Davies, *Other Worlds* (New York: Simon and Schuster; 1982), 12.

52 Kovel, "Things and Words," 73.

PUBLICATION: Excerpted from *Women and Language* (1984), 4:3–19.

KEYWORDS: feminism; psychoanalysis; reading; language.

LINKS: Beverly Dahlen, "In Re 'Person'" (*PJ* 9); from "The Tradition of Marginality" (*PJ* 6); Norman Fischer, "Corbett's *Collected Poems* and Dahlen's *A Reading*" (*PJ* 6); Johanna Drucker, "Women and Language" (*PJ* 4); Kathleen Fraser, "Overheard" (*PJ* 4); Robert Glück, "Truth's Mirror Is No Mirror" (*PJ* 7); Tom Mandel, "Codes/Texts: Reading *S/Z*" (*PJ* 2); Ted Pearson, "A Form of Assumptions" (*Guide*; *PJ* 9); Leslie Scalapino, "Poetic Diaries" (*PJ* 5); Aaron Shurin, "The Irruptive Text" (*PJ* 8); Chris Tysh, from "Dead Letters" (*PJ* 10).

SELECTED BIBLIOGRAPHY: *Out of the Third* (San Francisco: Momo's Press, 1974); *A Letter at Easter* (Emeryville, Calif.: Effie's Press, 1976); *The Egyptian Poems* (Berkeley: Hipparchia, 1983); *A Reading* 1–7 (San Francisco: Momo's Press, 1985); *A Reading* 11–17 (Elmwood, Conn.: Potes & Poets, 1989); *A Reading* 8–10 (Tucson: Chax, 1992); *A-reading Spicer and Eighteen Sonnets* (Tucson: Chax, 2004); *A Reading* 18–20 (Boulder: Instance, 2006).

Language/Mind/Writing

Alan Davies's text-based performance at 80 Langton Street, San Francisco (29 October 1982) is a verbal thought experiment that enacts the disparity between language—divided between speech and writing—and mind. Many of Davies's key terms are charged with prior usages in philosophy, both Western and Eastern: German idealism, American pragmatism, existentialism, deconstruction, and Buddhism. Davies wants to show how the nonidentity of speech and writing, the cornerstone of deconstruction, may be reimagined by appealing to a notion of mind as both mediated by language and autonomous from it. Rather than referring to philosophical tradition, Davies performs the distinctions between his key terms in a work of art that demonstrates both unity of mind in the disparity of language and a dissociation of language from any prior unity. The resulting "act of mind in language" owes as much to Laura (Riding) Jackson's performance of truth in *The Telling* and the errancies of Montaigne's and Emerson's essays as it does to Heidegger's inquiry into language as "the house of being" or Derrida's enactment of "the precedence of writing over speech." Davies conveys to his audience the rigors of his theme in his style of performance: relentless, self-questioning, abstract, and demanding of a nearly impossible level of attention. His text is a unique account of the "turn to language" as a performance of philosophical inquiry.

[...] We project as language the interest of our minds in thought. The language is the peculiar function of the mind in which it immerses itself when it thinks, and in order to think. A language is any gesture which the mind repeats in order to understand itself. Later, in order to disseminate that understanding, in order to see it, the mind reduces a language to a speech, or to a writing. But the language is the mind in contact with itself and most particularly with its understanding of, that is, with its dealings with, itself, and its understanding with, and its dealings of, itself. Language marks the presence of our strange default in relation to life, that we think about it. It presents us to ourselves in view of our thought, as if we were life's gimmick. This failure is our failure to penetrate language in thought, in life. This failure poses us abjectly at the edge of our imminent and delayed failure, our imminent but delayed future. We fail the language when we don't permit it as its own mode of thought, as a mode of thought, when we as it were exact from it a penance for that its existence which we nevertheless encourage, and when we make it do the work for another mode of thought, or for no thought at all, for the very distinct presence of the absence of thought. A language is a tool of thought, the mind is the languages at work, and the difference between mind and thought is the difference between name and function. Language is a use we make of our time when we choose to live in it. In these ways, or for these reasons, we begin to treat the language as an encumbrance, an abuse, and we then so readily get to be the ones who abuse it. The language is one of the verbs for us that as we use it can justify its taking from us the unreliable place of the verb to be. We imagine what it would or could be like to be more spectral or more calm in the space of what can there be at best the vicinity of being, and there, then, is the region of the habitable uses of the language, in the space of the lifetime. We rush to find ourselves in the habitable regions of the language, and others rush to find themselves even near such places, for there the language touches the language, the uses for the language touch the uses of it, and the person is a whole entity at the end of the apt expression of the whole of a thought. The languages make possible for us the reasonings, the forms of reasoning, in the mind, and they make possible the unreasonable problems of frail, broken, incomplete, or otherwise damaged, thoughts, the lesions in thought. The language is, though, properly the excellent tool of excellence in the mind, in acts in the and of the mind, in the mind's thoughts, in the mind's actions in the other languages, the outer languages of the other world. The languages are within the mind a community of the uses of the mind, its efforts within itself and going beyond itself, perhaps leaving the mind but never the language behind. The language is that vehicle of which it is meant that it make for the mind a place in the world. To the extent that the world is a receptacle for language, it is the occasion for, the occasion of, the mind. To that extent to which the world receives the languages, to that extent exactly, the world is a book. Mind begins in language to constitute for itself an expression of itself, and in this way language began, and in this resides the completion of a thought, its excellence in complete articulation, its excellence an excellence in articulate completion, because the beginning of the language is also the completion, the beginning of the mind. It is difficult to think about the language objectively, with what in the language is called objectivity, because the language is the mode of thought among other things also of the language, the thought of language, also, and, also, the language of thought. We would have to say, attributing to ourselves the simplicity of the statement, that language is not separate from the mind, nor is the mind the sum of the languages, nor is it controlled by them. The language intercepts the mind.

That is the notion of the language in the mind. The language does the work of thought as it enters itself or as it enters the world. Writing exemplifies language as it performs those works of thought which enter thought, and speeches are the form of the languages when they blatantly and, frankly, too frequently, enter the world. Nothing is fatal in the vicinity of language, mind, and writing. And it is also too commonly felt that either might be fatal, to itself, to the self, to the social self, or to thought. The language is not precious, or sacred, or a vessel. It exemplifies a mind in the world. The language is the pact that the mind keeps with itself, and when the mind keeps a pact with the world, it engages a language with which to do it. If the beauty of the mind is something which engages thought, then the language, a language, is the, is an, example of that. It appears to us that the language is the end of everything and the beginning of anything. If there is a reason for forgetting it is the language and not the future, and certainly not the completely imaginary past, and the language is the instrument of forgetting, its implement. There is no need to understand the beginning or the beginnings of language, because the beginning, the beginnings, of language, constitute the origin of the completion of the mind as an object, its initiation as a tool, and the language was something which was there as either of these other things happened, or were happening, to complete themselves. Perhaps some things are more perfect than the language and perhaps something is more perfect than the mind, but gradually we begin to doubt ourselves, each doubts each, and the assertion closes on itself, the pariah of speech. It is not the style of language to exclude itself from thought, and that is the definition of style. The language is a special and perfectible thing, special because we know it, because we know in it, and perfectible because we come close to it, and, over it, and, pass it with the language as that excellent weapon of lazy self, in the teeth. The language is not sentimental, or it is the excelsior of sentiment, when it lives. The language is the present without qualifiers. The language does not qualify anything until it is forced to by some idiocy within the world. Released to be itself, that is, being what it would be without that release the need for which we demand for it by our lazy and insistent ways, being there separate from stupidity, and articulate about it, the language makes the nouns live with the verbs, that is all it does, and it does that very well. When we wish to know something about the language we use it, and our use of it tells us more than we had thought we would be asking, because our asking is full of the faults, and language is full with the excellences of its use, that excellence which permits it to be of use. We too often manage to make the language work because we are inattentive to anything else, to everything, else. But the language is a special tool, and, one which does not specialize, and its perfection is always its solidity within, whichever is most immediate of its own gestures, and its gestures make us used to it.

We would not say that the mind is the same as or that it is different from the language, or a language, or the many languages. Languages are the evident portions of minds. The mind is the favored location of the languages when the languages are preferred to be doing their favored, their best, work. The mind is the site of the language when it is most perfectibly the language, the place where a language most and most explicitly perfects itself, and you don't work in the mind without breaking the mind into thoughts, and thought is the explicit early action of a language, but the mind will not relent. The most resilient of factors is the fact of the mind. The mind is the legacy of the acts of the languages, but it is also and, incidentally, more interestingly, the locus of the languages in labor. The mind is the instructing within a life. With memory it is the instructions, and with life it is the simple, temporary, solid, and solitary, construction of the instructions in the life. The language is the presences of the vocabularies and the grammars and the mind is the sentences in the sense of the carrying out of the instructions implicit in the presence of the active vocabulary, the acting grammar, and the instrumentation of each by, and in relation to, each. The mind is the actions in thought of a life, and if memory is its periphery then in those places the mind is a center, an activity which, at its best, diminishes into itself, a soft sharp point of moving focus, without exaggeration, without extension, and if interior to anything, interior to it only in default. The language does not ever use the language as a vehicle for trading out of itself. The language is occasionally or perhaps frequently made to do that work, that sort of work, but by persons living entirely then exterior to the mind, their own mind. The mind is the focus of a life in the world. The language is the light of the mind, the point of its pointed focus in the world. Mind is that device of perpetual motion the existence of which death exists to reinforce if not to prove. The mind in the pursuit of mind, or, mind in pursuit of the mind, these are among the strongest urges which fasten upon a life, or upon which any life fastens. The mind is the evidence of forms, it is their making evident and, making them evident, in order to make them evident, it forms the languages in the worlds of the lives of the humans. It is simple to rest in consideration of other things but all considerations rest, in the end, within the mind as their origin, and in the mind as their conclusion. The mind tolerates no illusion and so the language has about it no illusions, such that where the language exemplifies illusion it evaporates the mind. When we think about the mind, the mind talks, and when we write about the mind it is the mind that writes, and if we talk about the mind it is, then, the mind which talks. It is in these ways, and in those other ways of which it may be said that this way of the mind represents them, in which we come to recognize that the worlds reside in the mind, and that the mind does not only represent them. When the mind is charged with the task of representing a world, then the world is in default of its own presence to the mind. The mind is the function of the mind, etcetera, and the etcetera is the usual failure of the world to account for the presence of the equatabilities within the mind. The world is usually not up to that. This is because the mind is the pure function of function, as we experience it, because its function is purified in the actions of its functioning, and because its exemplification is its loss in the streets of the usual minds of the world. There is no excuse that the mind ever makes in the world, and that is because the mind does not ever touch the world, and that is because of the space between the spaces that habitually touch the world. The world derives its strength from the mind, and that is the simple fact of the human presence in the world, and without it, the mind would derive its strength solely from the mind because of the absence of the human in the worlds. There is no reason to equate anything else, but the mind's constant equatability with the mind belies the presence of anything else within the world. The world equals the world, etc., but the actions of equatability occur and then exist within the mind. The mind is the locus of all the human action of the world. It moves the material of the world, and is itself only material if it is dead. The mind is the world's volution, or the world is its circumference. The mind is a still point amidst the horizons of the world, because thought is vertical, and the verticalization of language in writing its nascent nadir, as object. The mind is the workplace of the living. Only the dead work only in the world. The differences between the languages has only small recourse to a mind, which uses them as extents of its resources, and makes of any one of them, in its use of that one, one equatable with the others, lost there, and, of no more importance than that, its use, and the occasion of its use. The mind is the occasion of its use. Otherwise there is no mind. There are no mistakes made by the mind because everything that the mind does is its work and in that it is not mistaken. There are, however, frequent mistakes made in the mind by the life which surrounds it, by a life which surrounds it, by the or a world, by thought without thought as its object, or by a language in the hands of something other than of a mind. The details of the mind, inside of the mind, are perfect, its actions are perfect, and these are the sorts of things meant by perfection. The intrusions of the worlds are the origin of any faulting in, in any faulting of, the mind. But a mind which has first strengthened itself with its own devices and its own acts, and, where necessary, been absorbed quite totally in and by them, might become and be a mind capable of thought, capable of habitation by languages, or capable of writing, without repeating and thereby inspiring the furtherance of the faults of the worlds without minds. It is the fault of the world that the mind fails, and the strength of the mind that it comes to know that. It is by a kind of isolation from the world which is yet entirely attentive to it, that the mind does perfectly the work of the mind, discerning in itself the longest reaches of its actions, and outside of itself the short appurtenances which can encumber it with hesitations. Outside of the mind exist for example those mistakes of the language, which we have mentioned, and which are in fact the mistakes in contacts between the mind and the world. It is necessary for the mind to remember its place in the mind before the life takes the mind to its place in the world. The mind is the world before the internal mistakes of the world, and with them the mind is the locus of the functioning of the languages of the world. Each person lives in a space bounded by thought. Each thought is bounded by language, or, more accurately in the realms of action, it is the languages that mediate between the points of the person and the layer of thought. And writing is itself not beyond language, within this present thought in metaphor. Writing is the point of mind reaching through thoughts to languages, or, writing is the point of mind living itself, as explicitly and distantly as possible, through the languages to the goal of some anticipated and then manufactured thought. The mind is the use of every thing, without metaphors or distances, although it is through the sharpened, acute, perpendicular distancing of its uses from itself, that it achieves those clear notions of things as they are, and which make it of use to thoughts, to languages, and to the perpendicular distributions of writings upon the flat and blatant horizons of the world. [. . .]

PUBLICATION: Excerpted from *Poetry and Philosophy* (1983), 3:46–54.

KEYWORDS: language; philosophy; performance; writing.

LINKS: Alan Davies, "Close Reading Close Reading" (*PJ* 2), "Motor Mouth" (*PJ* 5), "Or How Shall We Yet Catch Each Unmindful Eye Awake" (*PJ* 9), "Strong Language" (*PJ* 7); Pierre Alferi, "Seeking a Sentence" (*Guide*; *PJ* 10); Mike Anderson, "Framing the Construals" (*PJ* 5); Bill Berkson, "Stick" (*PJ* 7); Abigail Child and Sally Silvers, "Rewire// Speak in Disagreement" (*PJ* 4); Paul A. Green, "Elsewhere" (*PJ* 8); Carla Harryman,

"What in Fact Was Originally Improvised" (*PJ* 2); Jackson Mac Low, "*Pieces o' Six*—XII and XXIII" (*PJ* 6); Delphine Perret, "Irony" (*PJ* 3).

SELECTED BIBLIOGRAPHY: *Abuttal* (New York: Casement, 1982); *Signage* (New York: Roof, 1987); *Split Thighs* (Boston: Other Publications, 1976); *a an av es* (Needham, Mass.: Potes & Poets, 1981); *Active 24 Hours* (New York: Roof, 1982); *Mnemonotechnics* (Hartford: Potes & Poets, 1982); *Name* (Berkeley: This, 1986); *Candor* (Berkeley: O Books, 1990); *Rave* (New York: Roof, 1994); *Odes* (Cambridge, Mass.: Faux Press, 2008).

His Heart Is a Lute Held Up Poe and Bataille

Robert Glück is a central figure in "New Narrative" writing, along with Kathy Acker, Dodie Bellamy, Bruce Boone, Dennis Cooper, and Kevin Killian. These writers borrow from the resources of genre fiction, sensational novels, tabloid gossip, and pornography to address questions of gender and sexuality. Their early work coincided with the emergence of gay and lesbian (later, queer) identity politics in the late 1970s and 1980s, while they often criticized what they saw as the formalism of language-centered writing. The "turn to narrative" undertaken by Glück and his friends was in part a response to the "turn to language" of contemporary poets, especially the Language writers (even as some, like Carla Harryman and Steve Benson, had similar concerns with narrative, gender, and sexuality). For Glück and the New Narrativists, questions of sexuality, subjectivity, and community circulate around primary human questions of love and being with others. In "His Heart Is a Lute Held Up," Glück undertakes a reading of passages from two very different Gothic fictions: Edgar Allan Poe's "Fall of the House of Usher" and Georges Bataille's *Story of the Eye*. The result of Glück's essay on narrative is a powerful study of disarranged (if not deranged) subjectivity that argues for the intelligence (though not necessarily intelligibility) of sex and the senses.

During the whole of a dull, dark and soundless day in the autumn of the year, when the clouds hung oppressively low in the heavens, I had been passing alone, on horseback, through a singularly dreary tract of country; and at length found myself, as shades of the evening drew on, within view of the melancholy House of Usher. (Edgar Allan Poe, "The Fall of the House of Usher" [1839])

This first sentence ends *basso profundo* "House of Usher." Since the House is a symbol, complexity, mystery, and resonance devolve on it; descriptions move toward it like metal shavings to a magnet. In a recent schlock made-for-TV "House of Usher" the narrator (and his wife!) urge unwilling peasants to drive them at dusk through the wasteland to the House. This theft from the vampire myth is apropos—the undead (Roderick, Madeline, Dracula) are cultivated, barren, and old blood—really really old. In both stories there is an overriding sexualization of death and a corresponding reordering of the senses.

To the degree that they use genre, Poe and Bataille have an understanding with us—we consent to receive pleasure, nonproductive, nonimproving. Then it's Poe's show, he trundles out the Gothic trappings with the proviso that his lute be *our* sensibility. Like gossip, this pleasure is based on a manipulation/ transgression of shared codes and a continuum of experience. That's why Truth in fantasy usually reverts to public absolutes—Good and Evil, God and Devil, etc., just as porn likes "types," the cat burglar, the sailor.

Like much of nineteenth-century American prose (Hawthorne, Melville), Poe's is "warmed over," awkward and arty. It's distant from the center of power; you have to work at detail if you are far from the informing idea. "It was the misfortune of Mr. Pickney to have been born too far south.... We pardon his hyperboles for the evident earnestness with which they are uttered" ("The Poetic Principle"). We get to like Poe's overproduced rhetoric. It lets us know we're in for a rather full-blown experience—it's all worked out: the elegiac bell of "dull, dark and soundless," the memorial "autumn of the year" and "shades of evening."

I know not how it was—but, with the first glimpse of the building, a sense of insufferable gloom pervaded my spirit.

The eye of the story enters the impressionable realm—the spirit is invaded with a glance, that is, through the eye.

I say insufferable; for the feeling was unrelieved by any of that half-pleasurable, because poetic, sentiment with which the mind usually receives even the sternest natural images of the desolate or terrible.

We rely on the narrator to organize time and space for us, and to render the intangibles—"I say insufferable." What traits create high perception? Poe had a formula: in the "Purloined Letter," a detective story, visual acuteness is based on an impulse toward order—"ratiocination"—along with an equally high ability to sustain ambiguity. A detective's intelligence is exemplary and beyond us. Our narrator is cut from the same cloth but we understand past him—we triangulate with Poe (a three-way?).

For example, the narrator says the House is not poetic, not pleasurable. This is a strategy, because we *are* poetic, receptive. This tease helps to pin down the reality of subsequent marvels, and it prepares us for one of horror's delicious moments: the opaque doubter, our most atheistic self, joins us and is converted. The conversion and the pleasure are religious; terror, a secular awe.

Horror asks for faith beyond the social conventions in order to acknowledge a more inclusive humanity—"the dark side." Pornography is also religious—"I am a beast!" It says that a human picture must accommodate this transgression. Because they diffuse boundaries, this awe and sexuality are guilty pleasures; formerly they may have been part of a ceremony but now they are sold to us.

> I looked upon the scene before me—upon the mere house, and the simple landscape features of the domain, upon the bleak walls, upon the vacant eye-like windows, upon a few rank sedges, and upon a few white trunks of decayed trees—with an utter depression of soul which I can compare to no earthly sensation more properly than to the after-image of the reveler upon opium; the bitter lapse into everyday life, the hideous dropping off of the veil.

All this bric-a-brac in one short space shows the Gothic conventions as established and at hand. Poe writes thirty or forty years after the first Gothic rush; his story is an auteur version, less vulgar, less energetic, but more penetrating. He adds symbolism, analysis, and psychology. Psychology, like our narrator, will try to undermine fantasy by positing Science as the larger myth. Poe is one stop on the train from Gothic fairy tale to case history of the criminally insane. Symbolism (meaning becomes problematical) and analysis (the resistance of the materials) will become deconstruction in Bataille—he will complete the modernist quote marks around genre.

The narrator invokes that criminal of the senses, the addict. (Shades of Roderick's "morbid acuteness of the senses"—enclaves of body knowledge.)

> There was an iciness, a sinking, a sickening of the heart, an unredeemed dreariness of thought which no goading of the imagination could torture into aught of the sublime.

For the third time the narrator asks us not to consider the sublime, but to see the House as pro-death (vacant eyes, etc.). Roderick and Madeline are barren, nonproductive; their embrace concludes in death. The "atmosphere" manifests itself in the change in Roderick's senses—hearing, taste, touch become more important. So on one hand there's the narrator (living, analysis) and on the other the House (dead, sensation). To assign death and sensation to the same roster is not so odd if we factor in the transcendent, the sublime, which we do despite, and because of, our narrator's objections.

Reordering the senses challenges accepted boundaries, so naturally it is associated with Evil and with Death, those other challengers. Later, there's Rimbaud's *déreglement de tous les sens* and a whole Axel's Castle full of sensual experimentation in out of the way locales. The sublime in our time, the late sixties, also transgressed by reordering priorities and elevating pleasure.

Our narrator is good at seeing. Seeing interested Poe—it's the basis of the detective story and it corresponds to analysis. Our narrator draws his visual conventions from the Picturesque: a cultural expression of the primacy of sight and perspective when mastering nature, our corresponding further remove from nature (once you name nature it goes from being you to yours).

> What was it—I paused to think—what was it that so unnerved me in the contemplation of the House of Usher?

Poe inters character after character, but what activity does justice to the mental atmosphere of suffocation and horror? There is a disjunction between meaning and activity; the symbolic takes up the slack.

> It was a mystery all insoluble; nor could I grapple with the shadowy fancies that crowded upon me as I pondered.

From now on the realistic and the supernatural will keep bracketing each other, making the story impossible to "understand" though sponsoring an "elasticity of mind," which is useful at the conclusion of "The Mad Trist" when Roderick and Madeline embrace in a blaze of crossed circuits and overloaded fuses; the House divides and recombines (like the sister and brother?) in the tarn: the narrator is expelled and death, sex, Madeline, Roderick, and the House *become one* in that collapse.

> I was forced to fall back on the unsatisfactory conclusion, that while, beyond doubt, there *are* combinations of very simple natural objects which have the power of thus affecting us, still the analysis of this power lies among considerations beyond our depth.

The problem of fantasy: what can a true map of the world look like if this landscape is an example? Still, his atomic theory (combinations) doesn't tell the whole story because he can't see why it works.

> It was possible, I reflected, that a mere different arrangement of the particulars of the scene, of the details of the picture, would be sufficient to

modify, or perhaps to annihilate, its capacity for sorrowful impression; acting upon this idea, I reined my horse to the precipitous brink of a black and lurid tarn that lay in unruffled luster by the dwelling, and gazed down— but with a shudder even more thrilling than before—upon the remodelled and inverted images of the grey sedge, and the ghastly tree-stems, and the vacant eye-like windows.

It's odd that someone riding all day—fatigued—at the urgent request of his friend—hurried—would conduct an experiment with sensibility and perspective—the Picturesque. He looks at the House mirrored in the lake— no, still ghastly. Its image isolates the terror. The House will end up in the lake, one with its image. The business of the two views carries an analytical meaning but the horror subverts the analytical. The narrator uses his eyes, the House is blind; he tries a different view, still blind. He must see imaginatively, but the House will be beyond his scope.

I grew up very much alone, and as far back as I recall I was frightened of anything sexual. (Georges Bataille, *Story of the Eye*, trans. by Joachim Neugroschel [New York: Urizen, 1977; originally published in France in 1928])

Bataille's first paragraph breaks into three distinct beginnings. The first sentence presents an "I"; we are given a psychological fact abstracted from its surroundings, a sense of psychological data. We recognize a writer, a personality. We don't realize right off that his sensibility is merely an urge toward transgressive sexuality, toward Evil.

First person presupposes the encompassing context of a personality. Evil accompanies human potential in Bataille; he sets equal signs between sex, death, evil, and (replacing Poe's nature) the unconscious. Since this counters the human models of our "crass machine age," the Evil becomes utopian, an enclave *against*. But historically personhood is on the way out; on its way to becoming a text, merely one more element to factor into a story. In his deconstruction of the narrative, if not the narrator, Bataille dismantles the individual with disjunction and banality, with a cold treatment of genre and a free-for-all of literary codes. Romantics saw nature as separate, as subject matter; the moderns see individuality in the same way (name it and it's lost—owned). Bataille's decentering rejects on a formal level a discrete "I." This modernist rejection is also an enclave *against*.

"I have always been afraid." (Actually *angoissé*, anguish or anxiety, more ambivalent.) People who write about sex internalized society's moral dictums—

they never recovered from the shock of sex itself; they communicate their amazement. The writing is aggressive, something of a revenge. Naive and adolescent, everything is visual. First-hand information from the other senses tends to normalize and diffuse the surprise of sex.

This story, like much of porn, like most of Sade in fact, is about education; it's a Bildungsroman. The first sentence sets up the anxious hero who will learn. The book concludes with his participating in the defilement of a priest. After Sade, who could take the defilement of yet another priest with complete seriousness? Bataille's heroes *are* reduced; instead of Juliette's Sherman's March through Europe we have the narrator's and Simone's tireless little legs pumping always pumping on their bicycles, and later their modest trip to Spain. In any case, isn't there something farcical about the Adonis who guards his precious pearl against the onslaught of Venus? When the priest succumbs, or better, converts—Yes! Yes! I *want* and *need* and *crave!*—we feel he's come over to our side (present company excepted, naturally).

> I was nearly sixteen when I met Simone, a girl my own age, at the beach in X. Our families being distantly related, we quickly grew intimate.

This second beginning—the furniture of 19th-century narration. The inspired X invokes the 19th-century struggle toward the "effect of the real." (Poe also used initials to give his stories an air of docu-drama.) Bataille "imports" this packaging; his stilted prose advances the plot and at the same time puts quotation marks around plot itself, inviting us to relish its patina as one more refinement of pleasure. It's nostalgic—it's Poe's furniture. That is, it's a museum. The strangeness of subject matter now extends to the narrative style. The disjunction, the quotation marks around storytelling emphasized by multiple beginnings, gives us notice: to the degree this story is about being a story, it's not a story. The first paragraph is not an example of "reframing," which develops an idea while placing it between the audience and writer; it simply heads out three different times, parallel, evoking three traditions—hence its boldness and startling energy.

The narrative itself disappoints in the same way as pornography, or Poe's horror, because it's not equal to the meaning:

> But on a sensual level, she so bluntly craved any upheaval that the faintest call from the senses gave her a look directly suggestive of all things linked to deep sexuality, such as blood, suffocation, sudden terror, crime; things indefinitely destroying human bliss and honesty.

It's the task of Horror and Porno to constantly replace image with image, each more intense than its predecessor, but what visual could equal the intensity of this quotation?

In 1839 the trappings of Evil, the little people who make it all possible, were a stage company devoted to the starring figure, Sensibility. For Bataille, sensibility is just another actor in the troupe, and subjectivity has retreated to tone. (One imagines a tonal coherence, the echo of high monotone, as in Corneille.) Fifty years later, the trappings are commodified, evil is commodified, the tone is commodified, subjectivity is commodified; they call to each other again and the story continues in, say, the work of Dennis Cooper and Kathy Acker.

> Three days after our first meeting, Simone and I were alone in her villa. She was wearing a black pinafore with a starched white collar. I began realizing that she shared my anxiety at seeing her, and I felt even more anxious that day because I hoped she would be stark naked under the pinafore.

The third beginning is Porn: Simone's black pinafore and starched white collar suggest a nun's habit but more likely it's a school uniform. In any case it invokes the rather formal tradition of porn and uniforms, of nasty pictures: "I hoped she would be *stark* naked." Porn wants structures, roles, in order to transgress. The effect will be complete when the characters abandon their boundaries and the dos and don'ts of life's starched collars.

If Poe's story is about Death and Bataille's is about Sex, it's that particular sex and death, twins who live in a single breath. The sex in Bataille is situational—it's about obsession and power, disconnected from the body. It's at the far pole of the erotics of the self, the manipulations of image, distanced and objectifying. Death in Poe is the result of heightened sensation—death that brings us close to the body. The world becomes sensually intimate for Roderick—a pre-language of the senses. Language (narration, analysis) fails on approaching what directly pertains to us, the working of our senses. It's none of its business. Language wants to monitor what happens between us and the world; at either side of the negotiation it's silent. The old ballad supplies the voice that Roderick lacks. In *Story of the Eye*, the ultimate image is an eye (distance, analysis) inserted in a cunt—sexual seeing, reordering the senses.

PUBLICATION: *Close Reading* (1982), 2:67–70.

KEYWORDS: New Narrative; sexuality; genre; negativity.

LINKS: Robert Glück, "Baucis and Philemon" (*PJ* 5), "Fame" (*PJ* 10), "Truth's Mirror Is No Mirror" (*PJ* 7); Steve Benson, "Personal as Social History: Three Fictions" (*PJ* 7); Kathy Acker, "Ugly" (*Guide*; *PJ* 7); Dodie Bellamy, "Can't We Just Call It Sex?: In Memory of David Wojnarowicz" (*Guide*; *PJ* 10); Bruce Boone, "Kathy Acker's *Great Expectations*" (*PJ* 4); Laura Moriarty, "Sex and Language" (*PJ* 8); Bernard Noël, "Poetry and Experience" (*PJ* 3); Larry Price, "Harryman's Balzac" (*PJ* 4); Leslie Scalapino, "Aaron Shurin's *Elsewhere*" (*PJ* 8); Aaron Shurin, "Orphée: The Kiss of Death" (*PJ* 10).

SELECTED BIBLIOGRAPHY: Glück, *Andy, a Long Poem* (Los Angeles: Panjandrum, 1973); *Family Poems* (San Francisco: Black Star, 1979); *Jack the Modernist* (1981; New York: Serpent's Tail, 1995); *Elements of a Coffee Service* (Bolinas, Calif.: Four Seasons, 1983); *Reader* (San Francisco: Lapis, 1989); *Margery Kempe* (New York: Serpent's Tail, 1994); *Denny Smith* (Astoria, Ore.: Clear Cut, 2004); with Bruce Boone, *La Fontaine* (San Francisco: Black Star, 1982); with Mary Burger, Camille Roy, and Gail Scott, eds., *Biting the Error: Writers on Narrative* (Toronto: Coach House, 2004).

The Rejection of Closure

In her essay, Lyn Hejinian takes up a key distinction in American poetry since the 1950s, between "closed" and "open" forms. Charles Olson, in his epoch-making manifesto "Projective Verse," defined closed verse as "the verse print bred" (and that literary magazines continued to publish), while he advocated open forms in which one perception "must move, instanter, on another." Hejinian's rethinking of this distinction—and the cultural politics of its period—involves both revisionist and innovative arguments. In separating openness and closure in poetry, she refuses their merely formal distinction. Regular stanzas and metrical forms are not necessarily closed if their language is productive of open horizons of interpretation, and it would be reductive to see open forms as simply those that look like open fields or processual streams. Invoking the Russian Formalists, Hejinian shows how form can be radically constructive of new meaning, and how language's nonidentity with the world it incompletely names is located at the heart of form's constructive potential. In seeing the language/world relation as central to the rejection of closure, Hejinian takes up, but finds limited, the French feminist poetics of desire, even though gender was elided in Olson's account. Her argument is a fundamental contribution to the shift from a subject-centered to a language-centered poetics.

[...] In writing, an essential situation, both formal and open, is created by the interplay between two areas of fruitful conflict or struggle. One of these arises from a natural impulse toward closure, whether defensive or comprehensive, and the equal impulse toward a necessarily open-ended and continuous response to what's perceived as the "world," unfinished and incomplete. Another, simultaneous struggle is the continually developing one between literary form, or the "constructive principle," and writing's material. The first involves the poet with his or her subjective position; the second objectifies the poem in the context of ideas and of language itself.

The axes across these two areas of opposition are not parallel. Form cannot be equated with closure, nor can raw material be equated with the open.[1] I want to say this at the outset and most emphatically, in order to prevent any misunderstanding. Indeed, the conjunction of *form* with radical *openness* may be a version of the "paradise" for which the poem yearns—a flowering focus on confined infinity.

It is not hard to discover devices—structural devices—that may serve to "open" a poetic text, depending on other elements in the work and by all means on the intention of the writer. One set of such devices has to do with arrangement and, particularly, rearrangement within a work. The "open text," by definition, is open to the world and particularly to the reader. It invites participation, rejects the authority of the writer over the reader and thus, by analogy, the authority implicit in other (social, economic, cultural) hierarchies. It speaks for writing that is generative rather than directive. The writer relinquishes total control and challenges authority as a principle and control as a motive. The "open text" often emphasizes or foregrounds process, either the process of the original composition or of subsequent compositions by readers, and thus resists the cultural tendencies that seek to identify and fix material, turn it into a product; that is, it resists reduction.

> It is really a question of another economy which diverts the linearity of a project, undermines the target-object of a desire, explodes the polarization of desire on only one pleasure, and disconcerts fidelity to only one discourse.—Luce Irigaray[2]

"Field work," where words and lines are distributed irregularly on the page, such as Robert Grenier's poster/map entitled "Cambridge M'ass" and Bruce Andrews's "Love Song 41" (also originally published as a poster), are obvious examples of works in which the order of the reading is not imposed in advance. Any reading of these works is an improvisation; one moves through the work not in straight lines but in curves, swirls, and across intersections, to words that catch the eye or attract attention repeatedly.

Repetition, conventionally used to unify a text or harmonize its parts, as if returning melody to the tonic, instead, in these works, and somewhat differently in a work like my *My Life*, challenges our inclination to isolate, identify, and limit the burden of meaning given to an event (the sentence or line). Here, where certain phrases recur in the work, recontextualized and with new emphasis, repetition disrupts the initial apparent meaning scheme. The initial reading is adjusted; meaning is set in motion, emended and extended, and the rewriting that repetition becomes postpones completion of the thought indefinitely.

But there are more complex forms of juxtaposition. The mind, said Keats, should be "a thoroughfare for all thoughts."[3] My intention (I don't mean to suggest I succeeded) in a later work, "Resistance" (from "The Green"), was to write a lyric poem in a long form—that is, to achieve maximum vertical intensity (the single moment into which the Idea rushes) and maximum horizontal extensivity (Ideas cross the landscape and become the horizon and the weather). To myself I proposed the paragraph as a unit representing a single moment of time, a single moment in the mind, its content all the thoughts, thought particles, impressions, impulses—all the diverse, particular, and contradictory elements that are included in an active and emotional mind at any given instant. For the moment, as a writer, the poem *is* a mind.

To prevent the work from disintegrating into its separate parts—scattering sentence-rubble haphazardly on the waste heap—I used various syntactic devices to foreground or create the conjunction between ideas. Statements become interconnected by being grammatically congruent; unlike things, made alike grammatically, become meaningful in common and jointly. "Resistance" begins:

> Patience is laid out on my papers. Its visuals are gainful and equably square. Two dozen jets take off into the night. Outdoors a car goes uphill in a genial low gear. The flow of thoughts—impossible! These are the defamiliarization techniques with which we are so familiar.

There are six sentences here, three of which, beginning with the first, are constructed similarly: subject—verb—prepositional phrase. The three prepositions are *on*, *into*, and *in*, which in isolation seem similar but used here have very different meanings. *On* is locational: "on my papers." *Into* is metaphorical and atmospheric: "into the night." *In* is atmospheric and qualitative: "in a genial low gear." There are a pair of inversions in effect here: the unlike are made similar (syntactically) and the like are sundered (by semantics). Patience, which might be a quality of a virtuous character attendant to work ("is laid out on my papers"), might also be "solitaire," a card game played by the unvirtuous character who is avoiding attention to work. Two dozen jets can only take off together in formation; they are "laid out" on the night sky. A car goes uphill; its movement upward parallels that of the jets, but whereas their formation is martial, the single car is somewhat domestic, genial and innocuous. The image in the first pair of sentences is horizontal. The upward movement of the next two sentences describes a vertical plane, upended on or intersecting the horizontal one. The "flow of thoughts" runs down the vertical and comes to rest—"impossible!" (There is a similar alternation between horizontal and vertical landscapes in other sections of "The Green.")

One of the results of this compositional technique, building a work out of discrete intact units (in fact, I would like each sentence itself to be as nearly a complete poem as possible), is the creation of sizeable gaps between the units. The reader (and I can say also the writer) must overleap the end stop, the period, and cover the distance to the next sentence. "Do not the lovers of poetry," asks Keats, "like to have a little Region to wander in where they may pick and choose, and in which the images are so numerous that many are forgotten and found new in a second reading. . . . Do not they like this better than what they can read through before Mrs. Williams comes down stairs?"[4] Meanwhile, what stays in the gaps, so to speak, remains crucial and informative. Part of the reading occurs as the recovery of that information (looking behind) and the discovery of newly structured ideas (stepping forward).

In both *My Life* and "The Green" the form (grossly, the paragraph) represents time. Conversely, in Bernadette Mayor's *Midwinter Day*, time is the form—imposed, exoskeletal. The work was written according to a predetermined temporal framework; it begins when the "stop-watch" was turned on (early morning, December 22, 1978) and ends when time ran out (late night of the same date).

> It's true I have always loved projects of all sorts, including say sorting leaves or whatever projects turn out to be, and in poetry I most especially love having time be the structure which always seems to me to save structure or form from itself because then nothing really has to begin or end.
> —Bernadette Mayer[5]

Whether the form is dictated by temporal rules or by numerical rules—by a prior decision that the work will contain, say, x number of sentences, paragraphs, stanzas, or lines, etc.—it seems that the work begins and ends arbitrarily, and not because there is a necessary point of departure or terminus. The implication (correct) is that the words and the ideas (thoughts, perceptions, etc.—the material) continue beyond the work. One has simply stopped because one has run out of fingers, beads, or minutes, and not because a conclusion has been reached or "everything" said.

The relationship of form, or the "constructive principle," to the "materials" of the work (its ideas, the conceptual mass, but also the words themselves) is the initial problem for the "open text," one that faces each writing anew. Can form make the primary chaos (i.e. raw material, unorganized information, uncertainty, incompleteness, vastness) articulate without depriving it of its capacious vitality, its generative power? Can form go even further than that and actually generate that potency, opening uncertainty to curiosity, incompleteness to speculation, and turning vastness into plenitude? In my opinion, the answer is yes; this is, in fact, the function of form in art. Form is not a fixture but an activity.

In an essay entitled "Rhythm as the Constructive Factor of Verse," Jurij Tynjanov writes:

> We have only recently outgrown the well-known analogy: form is to content as a glass is to wine. . . . I would venture to say that in nine out of ten instances the word 'composition' covertly implies a treatment of form as a static item. The concept of 'poetic line' or 'stanza' is imperceptibly removed from the dynamic category. Repetition ceases to be considered as a fact of varying strength in various situations of frequency and quantity. The dangerous concept of the 'symmetry of compositional facts' arises, dangerous because we cannot speak of symmetry where we find intensification.[6]

(Compare this with Gertrude Stein's comment in "Portraits and Repetitions": "A thing that seems to be exactly the same thing may seem to be a repetition but is it. . . . Is there repetition or is there insistence. I am inclined to believe there is no such thing as repetition. And really how can there be. . . . Expressing any thing there can be no repetition because the essence of that expression is insistence, and if you insist you must each time use emphasis and if you use emphasis it is not possible while anybody is alive that they should use exactly the same emphasis.")[7] Tynjanov continues:

> The unity of a work is not a closed symmetrical whole, but an unfolding dynamic integrity. . . . The sensation of form in such a situation is always the sensation of flow (and therefore of change). . . . Art exists by means of this interaction or struggle.[8]

Language discovers what one might know, which in turn is always less than what language might say. We encounter some limitations of this relationship early, as children. Anything with limits can be imagined (correctly or incorrectly) as an object, by analogy with other objects—balls and rivers. Children objectify language when they render it their plaything, in jokes, puns, and riddles, or in glossolaliac chants and rhymes. They discover that words are not equal to the world, that a shift, analogous to parallax in photography, occurs between things (events, ideas, objects) and the words for them—a displacement that leaves a gap. Among the most prevalent and persistent categories of jokes is that which identifies and makes use of the fallacious comparison of words to the world and delights in the ambiguity resulting from the discrepancy:

—Why did the moron eat hay?
—To feed his hoarse voice.

—How do you get down from an elephant?
—You don't, you get down from a goose.

—Did you wake up grumpy this morning?
—No, I let him sleep.

Because we have language we find ourselves in a special and peculiar relationship to the objects, events, and situations which constitute what we imagine of the world. Language generates its own characteristics in the human psychological and spiritual condition. Indeed, it nearly *is* our psychological condition. This psychology is generated by the struggle between language and that which it claims to depict or express, by our overwhelming experience of the vastness and uncertainty of the world, and by what often seems to be the inadequacy of the imagination that longs to know it—and, furthermore, for the poet, the even greater inadequacy of the language that appears to describe, discuss, or disclose it. This psychology situates desire in the poem itself, or, more specifically, in poetic language, to which then we may attribute the motive for the poem.

Language is one of the principal forms our curiosity takes. It makes us restless. As Francis Ponge puts it, "Man is a curious body whose center of gravity is not in himself."[9] Instead it seems to be located in language, by virtue of which we negotiate our mentalities and the world; off-balance, heavy at the mouth, we are pulled forward. [...]

Language itself is never in a state of rest. Its syntax can be as complex as thought. And the experience of using it, which includes the experience of understanding it, either as speech or as writing, is inevitably active—both intellectually and emotionally. The progress of a line or sentence, or a series of lines or sentences, has spatial properties as well as temporal properties. The meaning of a word in its place derives both from the word's lateral reach, its contacts with its neighbors in a statement, and from its reach through and out of the text into the outer world, the matrix of its contemporary and historical reference. The very idea of reference is spatial: over here is word, over there is thing at which the word is shooting amiable love-arrows. Getting from the beginning to the end of a statement is simple movement; following the connotative by-ways (on what Umberto Eco calls "inferential walks") is complex or compound movement.

To identify these frames the reader has to 'walk,' so to speak, outside the text, in order to gather intertextual support (a quest for analogous 'topoi,' themes or motives). I call these interpretative moves inferential walks: they are not mere whimsical initiatives on the part of the reader, but are elicited by discursive structures and foreseen by the whole textual strategy as indispensable components of the construction. —Umberto Eco[10]

Language is productive of activity in another sense with which anyone is familiar who experiences words as attractive, magnetic to meaning. This is one of the first things one notices, for example, in works constructed from arbitrary vocabularies generated by random or chance operations (e.g., some works by Jackson Mac Low) or from a vocabulary limited according to some other criteria unrelated to meaning (for example, Alan Davies's *a an aves*, a long poem using only words without ascenders or descenders, what the French call "the prisoner's convention," either because the bars are removed or because it saves paper). It is impossible to discover any string or bundle of words that is entirely free of possible narrative or psychological content. Moreover, though the "story" and "tone" of such works may be interpreted differently by different readers, nonetheless the readings differ within definite limits. While word strings are permissive, they do not license a free-for-all.

Writing develops subjects that mean the words we have for them.

Even words in storage, in the dictionary, seem frenetic with activity, as each individual entry attracts to itself other words as definition, example, and amplification. Thus, to open the dictionary at random, *mastoid* attracts *nipplelike*, *temporal*, *bone*, *ear*, and *behind*. Turning to *temporal* we find that the definition includes *time*, *space*, *life*, *world*, *transitory*, and *near the temples*, but, significantly, not *mastoid*. There is no entry for *nipplelike*, but the definition for *nipple* brings over *protuberance*, *breast*, *udder*, *the female*, *milk*, *discharge*, *mouthpiece*, and *nursing bottle*, and not *mastoid*, nor *temporal*, nor *time*, *bone*, *ear*, *space*, or *word*. It is relevant that the exchanges are incompletely reciprocal. [...]

The "rage to know" is one expression of the restlessness engendered by language.

As long as man keeps hearing words
He's sure that there's a meaning somewhere

says Mephistopheles in Goethe's *Faust*.[11]

It's in the nature of language to encourage, and in part to justify, such Faustian longings. The notion that language is the means and medium for attaining knowledge (and, concomitantly, power) is, of course, old. The knowledge toward which we seem to be driven by language, or which language seems to promise, is inherently sacred as well as secular, redemptive as well as satisfying. The *nomina sint numina* position (i.e., that there is an essential identity between name and thing, that the real nature of a thing is immanent and present in its name, that nouns are numinous) suggests that it is possible to find a language which will meet its object with perfect identity. If this were the case, we could, in speaking or in writing, achieve the "at oneness" with the universe, at least in its particulars, that is the condition of complete and perfect knowing.

But if in the Edenic scenario we acquired knowledge of the animals by naming them, it was not by virtue of any numinous immanence in the name but because Adam was a taxonomist. He distinguished the individual animals, discovered the concept of categories, and then organized the species according to their various functions and relationship in a system.

What the "naming" provides is structure, not individual words.

As Benjamin Lee Whorf pointed out, "every language is a vast pattern-system, different from others, in which are culturally ordained the forms and categories by which the personality not only communicates, but also analyses nature, notices or neglects types of relationship and phenomena, channels his reasoning, and builds the house of his consciousness."[12] Whorf goes on to express what seem to be stirrings of a religious motivation: "What I have called patterns are basic in a really cosmic sense." There is a "PREMONITION IN LANGUAGE of the unknown vaster world." The idea

> is too drastic to be penned up in a catch phrase. I would rather leave it unnamed. It is the view that a noumenal world—a world of hyperspace, of higher dimensions—awaits discovery by all the sciences [linguistics being one of them] which it will unite and unify, awaits discovery under its first aspect of a realm of PATTERNED RELATIONS, inconceivably manifold and yet bearing a recognizable affinity to the rich and systematic organization of LANGUAGE.[13]

It is as if what I've been calling, from Faust, the "rage to know," which is in some respects a libidinous drive, seeks also a redemptive value from language. Both are appropriate to the Faustian legend.

Coming in part out of Freudian psychoanalytic theory, especially in France, is a body of feminist thought that is even more explicit in its identification of language with power and knowledge—a power and knowledge that is political, psychological, and aesthetic—and that is identified specifically with desire. The project for these French feminist writers is to direct their attention to "language and the unconscious, not as separate entities, but language as a passageway, and the only one, to the unconscious, to that which has been repressed and which would, if allowed to rise, disrupt the established symbolic order, what Jacques Lacan has dubbed the Law of the Father."[14]

If the established symbolic order is the "Law of the Father," and it is discovered to be not only repressive but false, distorted by the illogicality of bias, then the new symbolic order is to be a "woman's language," corresponding to a woman's desire.

Luce Irigaray:

> But woman has sex organs just about everywhere. She experiences pleasure almost everywhere. Even without speaking of the hysterization of her entire body, one can say that the geography of her pleasure is much more diversified, more multiple in its differences, more complex, more subtle, than is imagined. . . . That is undoubtedly the reason she is called temperamental, incomprehensible, perturbed, capricious—not to mention her language in which "she" goes off in all directions.[15]

"A feminine textual body is recognized by the fact that it is always endless, without ending," says Hélène Cixous: "There's no closure, it doesn't stop."[16]

The narrow definition of desire, the identification of desire solely with sexuality, and the literalness of the genital model for a woman's language that some of these writers insist on may be problematic. The desire that is stirred by language is located most interestingly within language itself—as a desire to say, a desire to create the subject by saying, and as a pervasive doubt very like jealousy that springs from the impossibility of satisfying these yearnings. [. . .]

> When I'm eating this I want food. . . . The I expands. The individual is caught in a devouring machine, but she shines like the lone star on the horizon when we enter her thoughts, when she expounds on the immensity of her condition, the subject of the problem which interests nature. —Carla Harryman[17]

If language induces a yearning for comprehension, for perfect and complete expression, it also guards against it. Thus Faust complains:

> It is written: "In the beginning was the Word!"
> Already I have to stop! Who'll help me on?
> It is impossible to put such trust in the Word![18]

Such is a recurrent element in the argument of the lyric: "Alack, what poverty my Muse brings forth ..."; "Those lines that I before have write do lie ..."; "For we / Have eyes to wonder but lack tongues to praise...."[19]

In the gap between what one wants to say (or what one perceives there is to say) and what one can say (what is sayable), words provide for a collaboration and a desertion. We delight in our sensuous involvement with the materials of language, we long to join words to the world—to close the gap between ourselves and things—and we suffer from doubt and anxiety from our inability to do so.

Yet the incapacity of language to match the world permits us to distinguish our ideas and ourselves from the world and things in it from each other. The undifferentiated is one mass, the differentiated is multiple. The (unimaginable) complete text, the text that contains everything, would in fact be a closed text. It would be insufferable.

A central activity of poetic language is formal. In being formal, in making form distinct, it opens—making variousness and multiplicity and possibility articulate and clear. While failing in the attempt to match the world, we discover structure, distinction, the integrity and separateness of things. As Bob Perelman writes:

At the sound of my voice
I spoke and, egged on
By the discrepancy, wrote
The rest out as poetry.
         ("My One Voice")

NOTES

1 For the sake of clarity, we can say that a "closed text" is one in which all the elements of the work are directed toward a single reading of the work. Each element confirms that reading and delivers the text from any lurking ambiguity. In the "open text" all the elements of the work are maximally excited; it is because ideas and things exceed (without deserting) argument that they have been taken into the dimension of the poem.

2 Luce Irigaray, "This Sex Which Is Not One," trans. Claudia Reeder, in *New French Feminisms* (Amherst: University of Massachusetts Press, 1980), 104.

3 John Keats to Benjamin Bailey, 8 October 1817.

4 Ibid.

5 Bernadette Mayer to Lyn Hejinian.

6 Jurij Tynjanov, "Rhythm as the Constructive Factor of Verse," in Ladislav Matejka

and Krystyna Pomorska, eds., *Readings in Russian Poetics* (Ann Arbor: Michigan Slavic Contributions, 1978), 127–28.

7 Gertrude Stein, "Portraits and Repetitions," in *Writings and Lectures, 1909–1945*, ed. Patricia Meyerowitz (Baltimore: Penguin, 1971), 104.

8 Tynjanov, "Rhythm as the Constructive Factor of Verse," 128.

9 Francis Ponge, *The Power of Language*, trans. Serge Gavronsky (Berkeley: University of California Press, 1979), 47.

10 Umberto Eco, *The Role of the Reader* (Bloomington: Indiana University Press, 1979), 32.

11 Johann Wolfgang von Goethe, *Faust*, trans. Randall Jarrell (New York: Farrar, Straus and Giroux, 1976), 137.

12 Benjamin Lee Whorf, *Language, Thought, and Reality* (Cambridge, Mass.: MIT Press, 1956), 252.

13 Ibid., 247–48.

14 Elaine Marks, "Women and Literature in France," *Signs* 3, no. 4 (Summer 1978), 835.

15 Luce Irigaray, *New French Feminisms*, 103.

16 Hélène Cixous, "Castration or Decapitation?" *Signs* 7, no. 1 (Autumn 1981), 53.

17 Carla Harryman, "Realism" in *Animal Instincts: Prose Plays Essays* (San Francisco: This, 1989), 106.

18 Goethe, *Faust*, 61.

19 Lines excised from Shakespeare's sonnets, nos. 102, 115, and 106.

PUBLICATION: Excerpted from *Women and Language* (1984), 4:134–43.

KEYWORDS: language; feminism; Russian poetics; formalism.

LINKS: Lyn Hejinian, "An American Opener" (*PJ* 1), "La Faustienne" (*PJ* 10), "Hard Hearts" (*PJ* 2), "The Person and Description" (*PJ* 9), "Strangeness" (*PJ* 8); Bruce Andrews, "Total Equals What: Poetics and Praxis" (*Guide*; *PJ* 6); Jean Day, "Moving Object" (*PJ* 9); Laura Moriarty, "The Modern Lyric" (*PJ* 7); Alexei Parshchikov, "New Poetry" (*PJ* 8); Jim Rosenberg, "Openings: The Connection Direct" (*PJ* 10); Viktor Shklovsky, "Plotless Literature: Vasily Rozanov" (*Guide*; *PJ* 1); Barrett Watten, "Missing 'X': Formal Meaning in Crane and Eigner" (*PJ* 2); Ellen Zweig, "Feminism and Formalism" (*PJ* 4).

SELECTED BIBLIOGRAPHY: *The Language of Inquiry* (Berkeley: University of California Press, 2000); *A Thought Is the Bride of What Thinking* (Berkeley: Tuumba, 1976); *Writing Is an Aid to Memory* (Berkeley: The Figures, 1978); *My Life* (Providence, R.I.: Burning Deck, 1980); *Oxota: A Short Russian Novel* (Great Barrington, Mass.: The Figures, 1991); *The Cell* (Los Angeles: Sun & Moon, 1992); *The Cold of Poetry* (Los Angeles: Sun & Moon, 1994); *Happily* (Sausalito, Calif.: Post-Apollo, 2000); *A Border Comedy* (New York: Granary, 2001); *The Fatalist* (Richmond: Omnidawn, 2003); *Saga/Circus* (Richmond: Omnidawn, 2008); *The Book of a Thousand Eyes* (Richmond: Omnidown, 2012); with Michael Davidson, Ron Silliman, and Barrett Watten, *Leningrad: American Writers in the Soviet Union* (San Francisco: Mercury House, 1991); with Rae Armantrout et al., *The Grand Piano*.

My Emily Dickinson Part One

Susan Howe's *My Emily Dickinson*, solicited for *Poetics Journal* in 1984 and published as a book in 1985, led the way toward the feminist revision of Dickinson scholarship, both within the academy and in communities of poet-scholars and feminists. Howe's approach demands painstaking archival research and focus on the material text of Dickinson's poetic oeuvre— after the revolution in Dickinson scholarship inaugurated by Ralph W. Franklin's *Manuscript Books of Emily Dickinson* (1981)—as it calls for a poetic rereading of Dickinson's writing in the spirit of its letter. Her insistence that we return to the material text of Dickinson's writings, using both archival and intertextual methods, responds to two objections. The first is to the lack of recognition of women writers in general, and especially in their treatment by male editors. The second is to normative feminist readings, for failing to understand what is both feminine and radical in Dickinson's work. Howe insists that we acknowledge Emily Dickinson's risk-taking strategies, her engagements with other writers, and above all her self-confidence. Grounded in a thorough rereading of Dickinson's writings alongside her major sources—the Brontës, George Eliot, Elizabeth Barrett Browning, and Charles Dickens— Howe argues for Dickinson's importance as a scholar-poet. She finds Dickinson's materialist procedures at the heart of her poetry's linguistic sublimity, and restages them in the epiphanic intensity of her own language.

King Lear: When I am through the old oak forest gone—
—Keats to G. and T. Keats, *Letters*

In the college library I use there are two writers whose work still refuses to conform to the Anglo-American literary tradition these institutions perpetuate. They are women and they are American—Emily Dickinson and Gertrude Stein. Among the most radical precursors of Modernist poetry and prose, they still remain strangely out of bounds, more out of bounds certainly, than James Joyce, Ezra Pound, or Samuel Beckett. To this day influential critical discussion from Kenner to Bloom persists in dropping their names and ignoring their work. Why these two should have been women is a question too often lost in the penchant for gossipy biographical detail that "lovingly" muffles their voices. Both originally destroyed the chronological linearity of poetry and prose. Both originally emphasized the illogical/logical flow of psychic babble.

Both saw "space of time filled with moving." Their writing accomplishes the disintegration of conventional meaning in the voice of a remote-seeming narrator. Although markedly different in many respects, both represent the still critically undefined anti-language dynamic in American literature. There was a chance for a radical feminist discourse to focus on the extent of the revolution of the word they achieved, to study why these two women felt it was necessary to tear apart customary syntax and lexical direction of meaning. It is particularly sad then to find that feminist literary scholarship as evidenced in *The Madwoman in the Attic*, although valuable in dealing with a more conventional tradition of writing, fails to discuss or come to terms with the implications of a feminine penchant for linguistic decreation and re-creation. No language experimenters here. A woman may confess all, *if* she does it in a logical syntax. Dickinson and Stein suggest that the language of the heart has quite another grammar.

In fairness, Gertrude Stein falls outside the time frame of *The Madwoman in the Attic*, but there is a chapter devoted to Emily Dickinson, and she runs as a troubling presence throughout. Although professing admiration for her "metaphorical history," Sandra Gubar and Susan Gilbert seem perplexed by the extent of her self-renunciation. They fail to understand her mysticism and utterly misread her profound remark to T. W. Higginson:

> When I state myself, as the Representative of the Verse – it does not mean – me – but a supposed person. (268)

They worry unnecessarily that she couldn't celebrate and sing herself with Whitman, or declare confidently with Emerson that "the Poet is the sayer, the namer," that "he is a sovereign and stands at the center." In fact she said something far subtler.

> Nature is a Haunted House – but Art – a House that tries to be haunted. (459)

But they haven't been really listening to her, and such misreading has belittled the ruthless sweep of her linguistic rebellion. This acutest lyric poet, the author of scores of unforgettable lines—(most writers in a lifetime manage only a few if they are lucky)—sings the sound of the Imagination as learner and founder, sings of liberation into an order beyond mere sexual gender where:

> – Love is it's own rescue, for we – at our supremest, are but it's trembling Emblems – (522)

[...] Wallace Stevens said that "Poetry is a scholar's art." It is for some. It was for Dickinson. For nineteenth-century women of her class, the word *scholar* echoed power, insecurity, a sense of being "other." Scholar was "other." Scholar was male. In the Victorian New England middle- and upper-class world of expansive intellectual gesturing, men gesticulated and wrote books and lectures, while women sat in parlors or lecture halls *listening*. Women like Elizabeth Barrett Browning and George Eliot were the rare exception, and they suffered agonies of insecurity about daring to speak more than "Lady's Greek, without the accents."

> Uncertain lease – develops luster
> On Time
> Uncertain Grasp, appreciation
> Of Sum –
>
> The shorter Fate – is oftener the chiefest
> Because
> Inheritors upon a tenure
> Prize –   (857)

If scholar was an uncertain word, *love* was more uncertain. Women of all classes risked dying every time they bore children. Sexual love too often meant their own Death. Uncertain relation of opposition—Birth and Death. For men the fusion was metaphysical and metaphorical. Centuries of tropes and clever punning in Western literary tradition married and mated the meaning. Wedding. Who was creator, what was creation? [...] Was wedding epithalamion or entrapment? Death a soothing Mother or a mastiff Father, was Awe—Nature? Destruction the beginning of every foundation? Do words flee their meaning? Define definition.

> Love – is anterior to Life –
> Posterior – to Death –
> Initial of Creation, and
> The Exponent of Earth –
>   (917)

Initial of creation. In the beginning was the Word. Relation of oppositions, misprision double meaning and uncertain.

Titania: But she being mortall, of that boy did die....

Quince: Bless thee, Bottom, bless thee! Thou art translated.

(A Midsummer Night's Dream, act 2, 1; act 3, 1)

That distance was between Us
That is not of Mile or Main –
The Will it is that situates –
Equator – never can –   (863)

Does a woman's mind move in time with a man's? What is the end of Logic?
[...]

Staking our entire Possession
On a Hair's result –
Then – Seesawing – coolly – on it –
Trying if it split –   (971)

Is this a poem about writing a poem or cosmic speculation? Is the time before or after? is space of time constantly changing? Spenser made Mutability a woman. Staking and Seesawing. Allegorical transfusion. To balance on a precipice of falling into foolishness was often the danger of opening your mouth to speak if you were an intellectually ambitious person with a female education. Dickinson chose to stay at home when Emerson visited her brother's house next door. One unchosen American woman alone at home and choosing. American authors reverently swept the dust of England's domain. Meek at whose feet did this myriad American Daisy play? August sun above, below the searing heat of a New England summer. *Salad days when I was green in judgement* ... silent judgment of the august past might silence you if you challenged it. Might and might.... Wandering through zones of tropes. World filtered through books—*And I and silence some strange Race—Wrecked solitary here*—I CODE and SHELTER might say one thing to mean the other. An American woman with promethean ambition might know better than anyone how to let the august traces (domain of dust)—lie.

The look of the words as they lay in print I shall never forget. Not their face in the casket could have had the eternity to me. Now, *my* George Eliot. The gift of belief which her greatness denied her, I trust she receives in the childhood of the kingdom of Heaven. As childhood is earth's confiding time, perhaps having no childhood, she lost her way to the early trust, and no later came. Amazing human heart, a syllable can make to quake like jostled tree, what infinite for thee more … then? (710)

Dickinson said this in a letter to her Norcross cousins after she had seen the death notice in the paper of one of her favorite authors. Earlier she had said of George Eliot, "She is the lane to the Indes, Columbus was looking for." What did this female Columbus crossing an uncharted fictive ocean find in George Eliot that made her the lane to the Indies rather than Harriet Beecher Stowe or Margaret Fuller, her own countrywomen, or even Elizabeth Barrett Browning, her fellow poet? Eliot's refusal to give in to bitterness in the face of unrelenting pessimism. Her agnosticism despite her reverence for the power of mythology. Her long and lonely self-education. Her late-blooming. Her unswerving skepticism (even after she had reached the pinnacle of literary success in her own lifetime). Skepticism that made her repeatedly and ruthlessly pull the rug out from under her most attractive heroines. Eliot's fictional scholars wandering through a wilderness of languages to encounter only reversals and false meanings. The uselessness of all theory. Constant curiosity. Camouflage as strategy. Refusal to imitate men's literary voices. Belief that there were indeed different voices for both sexes. Fury at the double bind an educated woman, given intellectual aspiration, was placed in, expected to efface her intellectual drive in the role of servant/mother to the reigning male culture. Scorn for women who congealed into the literary mold men made for them, severe self-criticism. Icy dissection of all that was "silly" in Lady's writing.

> By a peculiar theometric adjustment, when a woman's talent is at zero, journalistic approbation is at the boiling pitch; when she attains mediocrity, it is already at no more than simmer heat; and if she ever reaches excellence, critical enthusiasm drops to the freezing point. Harriet Martineau, Currer Bell, and Mrs. Gaskell have been treated as cavalierly as if they had been men. . . . In the majority of women's books you see that kind of facility which springs from the absence of any high standard; that fertility in imbecile combination or feeble imitation which a little self-criticism would check and reduce to bareness . . . .
>
> A cluster of great names, both living and dead, rush to our memories in evidence that women can produce novels not only fine, but among the very finest;—novels too, that have a precious speciality, lying quite apart from masculine aptitudes and experience. No educational restrictions can shut women out from the materials of fiction, and there is no species of art which is so free from rigid requirements. Like crystalline masses, it may take

any form, and yet be beautiful; we have only to pour in the right elements—genuine observation, humour, and passion. (George Eliot, "Silly Novels by Lady Novelists")

[...] Emily Dickinson took the scraps from the separate "higher" female education many bright women of her time were increasingly resenting, combined it with voracious and "unladylike" outside reading, and used the combination. She built a new poetic form from her fractured sense of being eternally on intellectual borders, where confident masculine voices buzzed an alluring and inaccessible discourse, backward through history into aboriginal anagogy. Pulling pieces of geometry, geology, alchemy, philosophy, politics, biography, biology, mythology, and philology from alien territory; a "sheltered" woman audaciously invented a new grammar, grounded in humility and hesitation. HESITATE from the Latin, meaning to stick. Stammer. To hold back in doubt, have difficulty speaking. "*He* may pause but *he* must not hesitate"—Ruskin. Hesitation circled back and surrounded everyone in that confident age of aggressive industrial expansion and brutal Empire building. Hesitation and Separation. The Civil War had split America in two. *He* might pause, *She* hesitated. Sexual, emotional, and geographical separation was at the heart of Definition. Tragic and eternal dichotomy—if we concern ourselves with the deepest Reality, is this world of the imagination the same for men and women? What voice when we hesitate and are silent is moving to meet us?

> The Spirit is the Conscious Ear
> We actually Hear
> When We inspect – that's audible –
> That is admitted – Here –
>
> For other Services – as Sound –
> There hangs a smaller Ear
> Outside the Castle – that Contain –
> The other – only – Hear –   (733)

5. Services] purposes   7. Castle] Centre-/ City
6. smaller] minor   7. Contain] present—

At the center of Indifference a soul feels her own freedom ... the Liberty in wavering. Compression of possibility tensing to spring. Might and might ... mystic illumination of analogies ... instinctive human supposition that any word may mean its opposite. Occult tendency of opposites to attract and merge. *Hesitation of us all*, one fire-baptized soul was singing. A poem must always stand in peril, to be saved, each line, at the brink of Invisible. Necessity is the mother of Invention.

In many and reportless places
We feel a Joy –
Reportless, also, but sincere as Nature
Or Deity –

It comes without a consternation –
Dissolves – the same –
But leaves a sumptuous Destitution –
Without a Name –

Profane it by a search – we cannot –
It has no home –
Nor we who having once inhaled it –
Thereafter roam.   (1382)

6. Dissolves] abates-/ Exhales—   9. a search] pursuit
7. sumptuous] blissful   11. inhaled it] waylaid it

On this heath wrecked from Genesis, nerve endings quicken. Naked sensibility at the extremest periphery. Narrative expanding contracting dissolving. Nearer to know less before afterward schism in sum. No hierarchy, no notion of polarity. Perception of an object means loosing and losing it. Quests end in failure, no victory and sham questor. One answer undoes another and fiction is real. Trust absence, allegory, mystery—the setting not the rising sun is Beauty. No titles or numbers for the poems. That would force order. No titles for the packets she sewed the poems into. No manufactured print. No outside editor/"robber." Conventional punctuation was abolished not to add "soigné" stitchery but to subtract arbitrary authority. Dashes drew liberty of interruption inside the structure of the poem. Hush of hesitation for breath and for breathing. Empirical domain of revolution and de-creation where words are in danger, dissolving . . . only *Mutability* certain.

I saw no Way – the Heavens were stitched –
I felt the Columns close –
The Earth reversed her Hemispheres –
I touched the Universe –

And back it slid – and I alone –
A Speck upon a Ball –
Went out beyond Circumference –
Beyond the Dip of Bell –   (378)

American jump, American jump,
One—two—three.
Under the water, under the sea,
Catching fishes for my tea.
          —Dead or alive?
               ("Nursery Rhyme")

Did you ever read one of her Poems backward, because the plunge from the front overturned you? I sometimes (often have, many times) have – A something overtakes the Mind – (Prose Fragment 30)

We must travel abreast with Nature if we want to know her, but where shall be obtained the Horse –
A something overtakes the mind – we do not hear it coming.
(Prose Fragment 119)

Found among her papers after her death, these two fragments offer a hint as to Emily Dickinson's working process. Whether "her" was Elizabeth Barrett Browning or Emily Brontë is unimportant. What is interesting is that Dickinson found sense in chance meeting of words. Forward progress disrupted, reversed. Sense came after suggestion.

The way to understand Emily Dickinson is through careful study of her reading. This sort of study, standard for male poets of her stature, is only recently beginning. Ruth Miller and Joanne Fiet Diehl have written interesting books on the subject, but the surface has only just been tapped. Why have Feminist scholars failed to concern themselves, so far, with her working process? Is it because a poet-scholar in full control of her voice won't fit the waxwork they, with the help of John Cody's reprehensible biographical psychoanalysis, have modeled? John Cody's *After Great Pain* is the rape of a great poet. That Gubar and Gilbert would mention it favorably is a sorry illustration of the continuous vulgarization of the lives of poets, pandering to the popular sentiment that they are society's fools and madwomen.

Day and night
I worked my rhythmic thought, and furrowed up

Both watch and slumber with long lines of life
Which did not suit their season. The rose fell
From either cheek, my eyes globed luminous
Through orbits of blue shadow, and my pulse
Would shudder along the purple-veined wrist
Like a shot bird.

(Elizabeth Barrett Browning,
Aurora Leigh, book 3, lines 272–79)

To recipient unknown   about 1861
Master.

If you saw a bullet hit a Bird – and he told you he was'nt shot – you might weep at his courtesy, but you would certainly doubt his word.

One drop more from the gash that stains your Daisy's bosom – then would you *believe*? . . . (233; second "Master" letter)

'You'll take a high degree at college, Steerforth,' said I, 'if you have not done so already; and they will have good reason to be proud of you.'

'*I* take a degree!' cried Steerforth. 'Not I! my dear Daisy—will you mind my calling you Daisy?'

'Not at all!' said I.

'That's a good fellow! My dear Daisy,' said Steerforth, laughing, 'I have not the least desire or intention to distinguish myself in that way. I have done quite sufficient for my purpose. I find that I am heavy company enough for myself as I am.'

'But the fame—' I was beginning.

'You romantic Daisy!' said Steerforth, laughing still more heartily; 'why should I trouble myself, that a parcel of heavy-headed fellows may gape and hold up their hands? Let them do it at some other man. There's fame for him, and he's welcome to it.' (Charles Dickens, *David Copperfield*, chap. 20)

Much discussion has centered around the three enigmatic "Master" letters written in the early 1860s and found among Dickinson's posthumous papers. Written when she was at the height of her creative drive, there is no evidence that they were ever actually sent to anyone. Discussion invariably centers around the possible identity of the recipient. More attention should be paid to the structure of the letters, including the direct use of ideas, wording, and imagery from both *Aurora Leigh* and *David Copperfield*; imagery most often taken from the two fictional characters, Marian Earle in Barrett Browning's poem and Little Em'ly in Dickens's novel, who are "fallen women." Dickinson's love for the writing of Charles Dickens has been documented, but not well enough. It is a large and fascinating subject, beginning with the chance similarity of their last names, and the obsession both writers shared for disguising and allegorical naming. Her letters to Samuel Bowles, in particular, are studded with quotations and direct references to characters and passages from Dickens. There is only space to touch on certain resemblances here.

> —so she spoke.
> She told me she had loved upon her knees,
> As others pray, more perfectly absorbed
> In the act and inspiration. She felt his
> For just his uses, not her own at all,—
> His stool, to sit on or put up his foot,
> His cup, to fill with wine or vinegar,
> Whichever drink might please him at the chance,
> For that should please her always: let him write
> His name upon her ... it seemed natural;
> It was most precious, standing on his shelf,
> To wait until he chose to lift his hand.
> (Elizabeth Barrett Browning,
> *Aurora Leigh*, book 6, lines 903–15)

In *David Copperfield*, Little Em'ly writes three disjointed, pleading letters after her elopement with Steerforth, addressed to her family. Ham, and possibly Master Davy/David/Daisy—the recipient is never directly specified, and the letters are unsigned.

> Oh, if you knew how my heart is torn. If even you, that I have wronged so much, that never can forgive me, could only know what I suffer! I am too wicked to write about myself. Oh, take comfort in thinking that I am so bad. Oh, for mercy's sake, tell uncle that I never loved him half so dear as now. Oh, don't remember how affectionate and kind you have all been to me— don't remember we were ever to be married—but try to think as if I died when I was little, and was buried somewhere. . . . God bless all! I'll pray for all, often, on my knees. If he don't bring me back a lady, and I don't pray for my own self, I'll pray for all. . . . (Charles Dickens, *David Copperfield*, chap. 31, from Little Em'ly's first letter)

To recipient unknown   early 1862(?)

Oh, I did offend it – . . . Daisy – Daisy – offend it – who bends her smaller life to his (it's) meeker (lower) every day – who only asks – a task – (who) something to do for love of it – some little way she cannot guess to make that master glad – . . .

Low at the knee that bore her once unto (royal) wordless rest (now) Daisy (stoops a) kneels a culprit – tell her her (offence) fault – Master – if it is (not so) small eno' to cancel with her life, (Daisy) she is satisfied – but punish (do not) don't banish her – shut her in prison, Sir – only pledge that you will forgive – sometime – before the grave, and Daisy will not mind – She will awake in (his) your likeness. (248; third "Master" letter)

Attention should be paid to Dickinson's brilliant masking and unveiling, her joy in the drama of pleading. Far from being the hysterical jargon of a frustrated and rejected woman to some anonymous "Master"-Lover, these three letters were probably self-conscious exercises in prose by one writer playing with, listening to, and learning from others.

The Martyr Poets – did not tell –
But wrought their Pang in syllable –
That when their mortal name be numb –
Their mortal fate – encourage Some

The Martyr Painters – never spoke –
Bequeathing – rather – to their Work –
That when their conscious fingers cease –
Some seek in Art – the Art of Peace –

(544)

3. name] fame   8. Some] Men—

Facts of an artist's life, while interesting, will never fully explain that particular artist's truth. The more work thrusts itself into the Extraordinary, the more strange and solitary it becomes. Poets and poems of the first rank remain mysterious. Emily Dickinson's life was language and a lexicon her landscape. The vital distinction between concealment and revelation is the essence of her work.

For a Tear is an Intellectual thing;
And a Sigh is the Sword of an Angel King

And the bitter groan of a Martyr's woe
Is an Arrow from the Almighties Bow!
　　　　(Blake, from *Jerusalem*, chap. 2,
　　　　　　　　"To the Deists")

[...]

PRIMARY SOURCES: PART ONE

The Poems of Emily Dickinson. Thomas H. Johnson, ed. (Cambridge, Mass.: Belknap Press, Harvard University, 1955).

The Letters of Emily Dickinson. Thomas H. Johnson, ed. (Cambridge, Mass.: Belknap Press, Harvard University, 1958).

Mrs. Browning's Complete Poetical Works. Cambridge ed. (Boston: Houghton Mifflin and Co., 1900).

Sandra M. Gilbert and Susan Gubar. *The Madwoman in the Attic: The Woman Writer and the Nineteenth-Century Literary Imagination* (New Haven: Yale University Press, 1979).

I have used Johnson's system of numbering and listing all of Dickinson's variations to her poems throughout. She added them herself very carefully to the fascicle manuscripts. They were marked by a neat + sign over the word to be changed. Then the possible changes were listed at the end of the poem.

PUBLICATION: Excerpted from *Women and Language* (1984), 4:20–34.

KEYWORDS: material text; feminism; intertextuality; readings.

LINKS: Susan Howe, "Robert Creeley and the Politics of the Person" (*PJ* 9); Rae Armantrout, "On *Pythagorean Silence*" (*PJ* 2); Steve Benson, "Close Reading: Leavings and Cleavings" (*Guide*; *PJ* 2); Carolyn Burke, "Without Commas: Gertrude Stein and Mina Loy" (*PJ* 4); Tina Darragh, "Error Message" (*PJ* 5); Michael Davidson, "'Hey Man, My Wave!': The Authority of Private Language" (*Guide*; *PJ* 6); Erica Hunt, "Beginning at Bottom" (*PJ* 3); Leslie Scalapino and Ron Silliman, "What/Person: From an Exchange" (*Guide*; *PJ* 9); James Sherry, "Dreyer's *Step Work*" (*PJ* 4); Ron Silliman, "The Dysfunction of Criticism: Poets and the Critical Tradition of the Anti-Academy" (*PJ* 10).

SELECTED BIBLIOGRAPHY: *My Emily Dickinson* (Berkeley: North Atlantic, 1985); *The Birth-mark: Unsettling the Wilderness in American Literary History* (Middletown, Conn.: Wesleyan University Press, 1993); *The Western Borders* (Berkeley: Tuumba, 1976); *Pythagorean Silence* (New York: Montemora, 1982); *The Defenestration of Prague* (New York: Kulchur, 1983); *Articulation of Sound Forms in Time* (Windsor, Vt.: Awede, 1987); *A Bibliography of the King's Book; or, Eikon Basilike* (Providence, R.I.:

Paradigm, 1989); *The Europe of Trusts: Selected Poems* (Los Angeles: Sun & Moon, 1989); *Singularities* (Middletown, Conn.: Wesleyan University Press, 1990); *The Non-conformist's Memorial* (New York: New Directions, 1993); *Frame Structures: Early Poems, 1974–1978* (New York: New Directions, 1996); *Pierce-Arrow* (New York: New Directions, 1999); *The Midnight* (New York: New Directions, 2003); *Souls of the Labadie Tract* (New York: New Directions, 2007); *That This* (New York: New Directions, 2010).

Continuous Reframing

Berkeley linguist George Lakoff's analysis of linguistic devices in contemporary art and writing joins a long conversation between the sciences of language and radical experiments of the avant-garde, from the influence of Russian futurism on the St. Petersburg OPOYAZ (Viktor Shklovsky) and Moscow Linguistic Circle (Roman Jakobson) through Prague structuralism and French poststructuralism. In the early 1980s, Lakoff was a central participant in what came to be known as "the linguistics wars," which pitted the logicist and rationalist models of language of Noam Chomsky against the critiques of several of his most advanced students, Lakoff among them. In moving from "generative grammar" through "generative semantics" to the development of a new approach, "cognitive linguistics," Lakoff and Berkeley linguists such as Charles Fillmore and Paul Kay sought evidence of embedded cultural frameworks in the cognitive structures of language. Lakoff saw the avant-garde as formally deploying these cognitive elements of language—prototypes, categories, and frames—even while contesting their normative use. Reading strategies of "frame shifting" and "partial local coherence" in performance artist George Coates and poet Michael Palmer, Lakoff shows how the frames we employ to make sense of experience are both linguistic and available for art. It is crucial that Lakoff's linguistic examples are not confined to literature or theater; his concepts of category and frame suggest a larger cultural poetics.

The Way of How, by George Coates. With Leonard Pitt (mime), Paul Dresher (composer), John Duykers and Rinke Eckert (vocalists). First performed at the Performance Gallery, San Francisco, 11–27 September 1981

Notes for Echo Lake, by Michael Palmer (San Francisco: North Point, 1981)

We make sense of our experiences by categorizing them and framing them in conventional ways. A frame (as the term is used in the cognitive sciences) is a holistic structuring of experience. Each frame comes with a setting, a cast of characters, a collection of props, and a number of actions, states, and/or images. These may be related in various ways, for example, spatially, temporally, by cause-and-effect, means-and-end, plan-and-goal. One typical kind of frame is a scenario for a cultural event: a wedding, lecture, or football game. Another typical kind is a conventional scene, say, a hill with a tree on the slope, or a stagecoach being chased by bandits. Framing requires categorizing;

the objects, characters, images, and events must all be of the right kind to fit a given frame. And just about everything we do requires framing of some kind, most of it done so continuously and unconsciously that we don't notice it.

If we notice framing at all, it is when there is a problem. Are we still in a friendly conversation or has it become an argument? We may need to frame it one way or another to know what to do next. A sequence of events happens. Does the shooting amount to a civil war or a foreign invasion? Our actions, from the most minute to the most momentous, depend on framing and on the corresponding categorizing of people, objects, and events.

Art is framed as art: the curtain rises, the musicians take their seats; the urinal is on the museum wall not in the men's room. If the art is representational, then we understand what is being represented by using our ordinary non-art frames together with whatever means of framing the genre provides. A traditional play has a plot, that is, a frame that spans the whole work, with a fixed setting or sequences of settings, fixed props, a fixed cast of characters, and a recognizable sequence of events. Now consider a scenario—a structured sequence of actions by a cast of characters with some props. Let a company of actors start the scenario and play it until it becomes clear what kind of scenario it is. Then stop the action. At that point, the scene could be one taken out of an indefinitely large number of other scenarios. Pick one. And let the action continue from that point as part of the new scenario. What we've done is shift frames, and in the process the characters, props, images, and events have to be recategorized. If it is done well—and without actually stopping the action—the transition will be smooth. Frame-shifting is one of the basic techniques used by the Blake Street Hawkeyes—George Coates's alma mater. It's a technique Coates has mastered, and it is central to the structuring of his pieces.

To work at all, a Coates piece must make use of *partial* framing and categorization. We don't (and can't) frame and categorize every aspect of our experience, however much we may try. Part of Coates's art is the use of uncategorizable and unframeable objects and actions. The result is not merely a shift from one frame to another, but from the frameable to the unframeable and back. What permits the smoothness of the transitions is the partialness of the framing. A scenario may be partially frameable as an attack by two characters upon a third, but various aspects of the attack frame will be left unfilled—who the characters are, their relationship, the motivation for the attack, etc. The partialness of the framing is part of the art form, and an indispensable part, since this kind of art requires the audience to try constantly to categorize and frame, while never being totally successful. Things unframed gradually become framed, and through the piece there is at each moment some partial framing or other. It is this *partial local coherence* that holds the piece together, and that constantly holds our attention.

To see what I mean by frame shifts, reperceptions, category shifts, and partial framing and categorization, let us take a sequence from *The Way of How*. I will divide the sequence up into regions with illustrations so I can talk about it more easily.

Region 1   Eckert, at the end of a sequence, says: "I'm thinking really big."

Region 2   Duykers, ten feet tall in a black robe, appears at the rear of center stage, and starts singing a decomposition of "Una Furtiva Lagrima." (He is standing on a wheelchair, which Pitt, who is in the wheelchair under the robe, gradually moves forward with his feet.) The image is of the ten-foot Duykers moving toward the audience, getting larger and more menacing as he sings.

Region 3   Pitt, in wheelchair, emerges from under Duykers's cloak as Duykers goes on singing and remains ten feet tall. (Eckert, invisibly from behind, has gotten under the cloak and has taken Duykers on his shoulders.) Pitt in the wheelchair is covered by a black cloak. His covered head barely sticks up over the top of the wheelchair, his body is horizontal, and his legs are extended far forward, moving the wheelchair around. On top of the cloak he is wearing strangely colored goggles on both the front and back of his head, each looking like an otherworldly partial face.

Region 4   Pitt moves about in wheelchair.

Region 5   Duykers and Eckert enter from the sides holding saws at the ends of sticks. They make menacing sawing gestures around Pitt's head while rubbing the saws together and

thus creating music that is elaborated through Dresher's feedback system.

Region 6   Pitt's head disappears into the cloak and a plastic bag floats out of where the head disappeared and goes up out of view.

Region 7   The wheelchair with the cloak around it collapses and Pitt emerges from the rear.

Region 8   Pitt pulls a long piece of cloth out of his mouth bit by bit and does various movements.

Region 9   Pitt notices string attached to floating plastic bag and pulls bag down. He puts the bag on his head and then lets it slowly float up again.

Region 10   Two sticks appear, coming down from above on each side of the stage. They stop at the level of Pitt's ears and start moving toward his head. Duykers and Eckert appear holding the sticks. As the sticks hit Pitt's ears, Duykers and Eckert sing "Vesti la Giubba."

Region 11   Duykers and Eckert, still singing, move sticks so that they cross in front of Pitt, emprisoning him.

Region 12   Pitt grabs hold of the sticks in desperation. Duykers and Eckert, still singing, lift him up as he rolls into a ball-like object.

Region 13   They put Pitt in the wheelchair. Dresher enters lying on his back on a dolly, pushing it with his feet. He is carrying five plastic-bag balloons. Duykers and Eckert attach a balloon to each of Pitt's limbs and one to his mouth.

Throughout these regions there are entities that are not completely categorizable. Duykers ten feet tall, in a black robe moving toward us on wheels. Pitt, low in the wheelchair, head up, body horizontal, feet down, at an inhuman angle, covered completely by a black cloak, with unearthly goggles on both sides of his head, creating the illusion of two faces. The wheelchair collapsing under the black cloak. Pitt rolled into a ball on the sticks. Part of the power of these images is that they are partly, but not completely, characterizable.

The regions are characterized by partial framing. Duykers, in region 2, is a menacing figure, ten feet tall, all in black, moving toward us, getting even bigger, booming out an aria. The emergence of Pitt from under Duykers's cloak in region 3 is like a birth scene. In region 5, Duykers and Eckert move the saws as if to cut off Pitt's head, which disappears in region 6, and is replaced by the balloon, which floats up off the body-wheelchair, which then collapses and "dies" in region 7. In region 10, Pitt is made the victim of opera, is imprisoned, turns into a vegetable, and is put in a wheelchair.

Reperception occurs throughout. The bottom of Duykers's cloak in region 2 is actually Pitt's cloak, and is reperceived as such in region 3. The plastic-bag balloon in region 6 is perceived as replacing Pitt's head. When the sticks hit Pitt's ears in region 10, they are perceived as a single pole going through his head. The wheelchair functions as a wheelchair for the first and last time in region 13. In a somewhat later sequence, a stiff pole becomes a snake-like flexible object forming waves, which splits into six short sticks, which then become percussion instruments and later wind instruments.

Sequential frame overlapping is not the only kind of structuring I see in Coates's art, but I think it is central to the art form. Moreover, I see the same kind of structuring in Michael Palmer's poetry—again not the only kind of structuring, but a kind that is of central importance. The smoothness in Palmer's poetry also comes from partial local coherences, partial framings that exist at each point in a poem and that shift gradually as one goes along. Since Palmer's medium is so different from Coates's, the framings are naturally of a different kind. Palmer's medium is language, as written and as spoken. His resources are (among others) syntax, words, images, sounds, individual speech acts, spoken and written genres, etc. Each of these can be viewed as a dimension within which framing can occur. Syntactic constructions are one kind of frame; idiomatic expressions are another; conventional images are another, and so on. At each point in a Palmer poem there is a coherent framing in one or more of these dimensions, and at the same time there may be discontinuities—a lack of framing or a break between frames in other dimensions.

Here are some examples:

An eye remembers history by the pages of the house in flames,
rolls forward like a rose, head to hip, recalling words by their accidents.
"Notes for Echo Lake 11" (68)

Here the syntax provides the local coherence, while the meanings and images overlap and shift from phrase to phrase.

> Someone identical with Dante
> sits beside a stone. Enough
> is enough is enough of.
>
> It's odd that your hand feels warm . . .
>   "Pre-Petrarchan Sonnet" (38)

In line 3 there is an overlap of "enough is enough," and the syntax breaks off at the end of the line, but the "enough is enough" formula has evoked an expression of frustration that is carried by the breaking of the syntactic frame as well as the semantics of the idiom.

One of the most characteristic of Palmer's structuring devices is the use of syntax to set up temporal regions of a poem, where the presence of the syntactic element or construction functions like an object or character on stage—evoking a setting, a partial framing which can change gradually.

> And throughout the winter each said one sentence
> And more were alive than had ever been dead
> More than had ever been
> A thing said as if spoken as if
> A thing told with eyes closed
> A chain I dragged along in quotes
> In Cairo there had been a fire
> Then he read to her displeasure
> Then he misremembers the names of the bridges
> Then he says seven
> Then he says seven inside her . . .
>   "Notes for Echo Lake 8" (51)

Region 1: The two lines beginning with "and."
Region 2: The second and third lines containing "more (. . .) than had ever been. . . ."
Region 3: The three lines beginning with "a" followed by a noun.
Subregion 3a: The two lines beginning "a thing," followed by a past tense verb and a manner adverb.
Region 4: The two lines containing "in" followed by a noun ("quotes," "Cairo").
Region 5: The four lines beginning with "then."

What we have is a gradual series of changes in the grammatical cast of characters. The presence of each defines a region of the poem and creates a local coherence.

The art of Coates and Palmer is experientialist art—in which the main focus is experiencing, moment-by-moment, always in the present. To work at all, experientialist art requires constant changes and shifts in perception. The reader or theater-goer can't just sit back and watch from a distance, secure in the knowledge of where and when the action is located, who's in the cast of characters, what has gone before, what long-range expectations have been built up. Any of these would take focus away from the changes occurring at the moment. The real action is not just on stage or in the text. It is in the mind of the audience, moment-by-moment, line-by-line, with nothing taken for granted for very long.

Art of this sort has sometimes been mistakenly called meaningless. The mistake comes from an overly narrow view of meaning, one where meaning is objective—in the work rather than in the audience. Contemporary linguists, myself among them, have been challenging the idea that one can speak sensibly of "the meaning of the _____," where the blank can be filled in by "text," "sentence," or even "word." Meaning (if you want a slogan) is meaningfulness to a person. Linguistic and other symbolic elements are meaningful only in a context, and only to a person who has had a certain range of experience and knowledge, some of which is shared and some of which isn't. Language evokes frames that constrain the possibilities for meaningfulness, sometimes tightly, sometimes loosely. Since the framing of one's experience is always partial, any constraints imposed by language are usually open enough to permit a broad range of meaningfulness for most people. Much of the meaningfulness of any experience comes from framing and categorizing. Art like that of Coates and Palmer, art that requires constant reframing, is art that requires its audience to find new (and fragmentary) meaning in the work as it progresses. It is art that is centered around the discovery of meaning.

PUBLICATION: Introduction (1981), 1:68–73.

KEYWORDS: avant-garde; linguistics; performance; meaning.

LINKS: George Lakoff, "The Public Aspect of the Language of Love" (*PJ* 6); Ed Friedman, "How *Space Stations* Gets Written" (*PJ* 5); Félix Guattari, "Language, Consciousness, and Society" (*PJ* 9); Jackson Mac Low, "*Persia/Sixteen/Code Poems*" (*PJ* 4); Joan Retallack, "Blue Notes on the Know Ledge" (*PJ* 10); Kit Robinson, "Bob Cobbing's Blade" (*PJ* 1); Haj Ross, "Poems as Holograms" (*PJ* 2); Ron Silliman, "Migratory Meaning: The

Parsimony Principle in the Poem" (*Guide*; *PJ* 2); Barrett Watten, "On Explanation: Art and the Language of *Art-Language*" (*PJ* 3).

SELECTED BIBLIOGRAPHY: with Mark Johnson, *Metaphors We Live By* (Chicago: University of Chicago Press, 1980); *Women, Fire, and Dangerous Things: What Categories Reveal about the Mind* (Chicago: University of Chicago Press, 1987); with Mark Turner, *More Than Cool Reason: A Field Guide to Poetic Metaphor* (Chicago: University of Chicago Press, 1989); *Moral Politics: What Conservatives Know That Liberals Don't* (Chicago: University of Chicago Press, 1996); with Johnson, *Philosophy in the Flesh: The Embodied Mind and Its Challenge to Western Thought* (New York: Basic Books, 1999); with Rafael Núñez, *Where Mathematics Comes From: How the Embodied Mind Brings Mathematics into Being* (New York: Basic Books, 2000); *Don't Think of an Elephant: Know Your Values and Frame the Debate* (White River Junction, Vt.: Chelsea Green, 2004); *Whose Freedom?: The Battle over America's Most Important Idea* (New York: Farrar, Straus and Giroux, 2006); *The Political Mind: Why You Can't Understand 21st-Century American Politics with an 18th-Century Brain* (New York: Viking, 2008).

Some Ways Philosophy Has Helped to Shape My Work

In a personal account of the relation of philosophy to the making of experimental poetry, Jackson Mac Low shows how his radically text-based writing may be read in terms of its intellectual history. Mac Low discusses the early influence on his work of the Chicago Aristotelians (Richard McKeon, R. S. Crane) and their revisionist reading of the *Poetics*, as well as the inspiration of Paul Goodman, a poet and cultural activist who argued for personal liberation during the political repression of the 1950s. The Chicago School admired Aristotle for valorizing poetry as an object of knowledge (in opposition to Plato); for seeing tragedy as a scene of instruction (versus aestheticism); for refusing formal proscription (as with the New Critics); and for unlinking art from history (as with the Left). Each of these interpretations would be crucial for Mac Low's strategies for constructing alternative communities through formal experiment, particularly in his use of chance techniques after Marcel Duchamp and John Cage. Mac Low also insists that an artist's use of philosophy is serious even if it occurs through misreadings and conflicting lines of thought. Thus the influence of Asian philosophy—particularly Zen but also the *I Ching*—can make sense of concepts of synchronicity in C. G. Jung or occasion in A. N. Whitehead. In Mac Low's essay, multiple philosophical traditions conjoin to provide interpretative frameworks for experimental poetics. Jackson Mac Low died on 8 December 2004.

Philosophy has always "influenced" my poetry and other art work, if what is designated by the term "philosophy" comprises both the published original and translated works of recognized Western philosophers, translations and interpretations of Asian religious philosophers, and published and orally communicated philosophical ideas of relatively contemporary Americans, Europeans, and Asians. In the space available I will be able only to outline briefly some of the ways philosophy has significantly influenced my work.

Although I "majored" in philosophy in the early 1940s at the University of Chicago and I have continually read philosophical works since then, my competence as a student of philosophy has never been very great. But possibly this very incompetence has been fruitful. That is, philosophers may have influenced my work meaningfully through misreadings or through misapplications (or skewed applications) of concepts (or even dogmas) gained from more or less valid readings and from oral teaching. I'll try to illustrate this.

At the University of Chicago in the late 1930s and early 1940s certain members of the philosophy department (notably, Richard Peter McKeon) and of the English department (notably, Ronald Salmon Crane) developed what came to be known as "Chicago Aristotelian" formal criticism. Until he left Chicago in about 1940, Paul Goodman contributed crucially to this development, and his book *The Structure of Literature* (Chicago: University of Chicago Press, 1955) is his own later revision of his own c. 1940 doctor's thesis. However, I did not study directly with McKeon and Crane until 1942, although some of my philosophy and English teachers in 1939–41 had probably been influenced by them.

Aristotle's *Poetics* was then widely and intensively studied at Chicago, not only in the courses of the Chicago Aristotelians themselves, but also in many other courses in philosophy, criticism, comparative literature, etc. The reigning interpretation of the *Poetics* was one that ran counter to the "recipe book" view of the work that had mostly prevailed since the Renaissance. The Chicago Aristotelians and their fellow travelers viewed the *Poetics* as an empirical formal analysis of the particular type of tragedy exemplified preeminently by Sophokles' *Oedipus Tyrannos* and Euripedes' *Iphigenia in Tauros*. That is, the *Poetics* was seen as an analytically descriptive, *backward-looking* work, rather than as a prescriptive, *forward-looking* one.

It followed that one would have to develop a somewhat different poetics for other types of tragedy, e.g., those of Shakespeare. It would not do to condemn later tragedies for "not living up to" the general principles Aristotle had drawn from analyzing *Oedipus T.*, etc. Goodman, in his *Structure of Literature*, even re-did Aristotle's own analysis to come up with a somewhat different poetics of the *Oedipus* type of tragedy.

From this followed a general principle of criticism that has been of immense help to me during the forty-odd years since McKeon, Crane, and others brought it to my attention, namely, that critics should follow the artists rather than trying to tell them what to do. This attitude came not only from the Chicago interpretation of the *Poetics* but also from Aristotle's view of history (as understood and taught by McKeon), namely, that although the past has been determined, the future is open. That is, one cannot predict the future (except possibly in short-term or trivial ways) in any field constituted by the actions of people. (The concomitant question of prediction in the physical sciences is too complex to open here.)

These principles, which I as an undergraduate may have misunderstood or which may have been based on erroneous views of Aristotle's thought, protected me against the many influential prescriptive critics running rampant in the 1940s and 1950s, especially the anti-experimental New Critics and the Vulgar Marxists. (Crane, incidentally, used to lampoon some of the more prescriptive New Critics as "Disappointed Bards and Southern Reviewers" and as "The Huey Long Gang," since the "Kingfish" had been instrumental in the founding and funding of the *Southern Review*—a bastion of the New Criticism—at Louisiana State.)

Aristotle's view of history, as interpreted by McKeon, also helped immunize me against political arguments based on dialectical or historical materialism or dialectical idealism and, in general, against historicism and progressivism. So far, my present examination of Hegel has not de-immunized me. I still see history not as any kind of upward-tending line or spiral but as an irregular three-dimensional curve that is as likely to sink definitively below the horizon as to mount to the zenith. But this is probably a digression.

I have long ascribed my continuing openness to what is usually called "experimentation" in the arts, and eventually my adoption of aleatoric and systematic procedures and of indeterminacy in composition of texts and performance works, to my interpretation of Aristotle as viewed by McKeon, et al. An openness to experimental art is commonplace now, but in the 1940s and 1950s, especially in literary circles, experimentation was anathema. The New Critics reigned, and even their challengers shared many of their assumptions. "Tradition" was "in" and "experiment"—even the poems of Cummings, much less Pound's *Cantos* or anything further afield—was altogether looked down upon. Eliot and Yeats were the great modern exemplars (and I must admit that I've never rejected them and have found some of their works inspiring—probably for what they would have considered wrong reasons), and even the collage method of *The Waste Land* was barely tolerated because of Eliot's explicit traditionalism.

As late as 1954, when I began verbal composition using aleatoric and systematic procedures, experimental work was considered beneath notice by most influential critics. The latter thought Stein a mere eccentric (with the possible exception of *Three Lives*) and only "Joyce specialists" took *Finnegans Wake* seriously. Whether or not the Chicago version of Aristotle and my interpretation of it were "correct," they helped me to feel free to experiment in the 1940s and 1950s.

However, the particular kinds of experimentation I embarked on in 1954 were largely due to a convergence of certain Asian philosophical traditions (and their Western interpreters) and Euroamerican left libertarian political philosophy. (Nowadays one must write *"left* libertarian" because of the neo-laissez-faire capitalists of the Libertarian Party.)

The Asian traditions were those of Taoism, Buddhism—especially Zen and Kegon Buddhism—and the philosophy, both explicit and implicit, of the *I Ching* or *Book of Changes*. Superficially, the first two seem to run counter to the personal voluntarism of Euroamerican libertarianism, but in practice this contradiction eventuated in a fruitful self-nonself dialectic.

I had been introduced to Taoism sometime after 1945 by Paul Goodman, to whom I had, late that year, introduced the anarchist-pacifist group then publishing the magazine *Why?* (called *Resistance* from 1947 to 1954, when it ceased publication). Both through Goodman (who published several important theoretical articles in *Why?/Resistance*) and through myself and other anarchist poets and theorists, the principle of *wu-wei* (non-action or non-interference) came to permeate the thinking of New York anarchists and pacifists in the late 1940s and early 1950s. *Wu-wei* in society was taken to mean the same as "anarchism": the absence of a central institution exercising power over the individuals and groups constituting a society and competing for power with the central institutions of other societies through such procedures as diplomacy, covert and open warfare, and economic and political imperialism. The ideal society was envisioned as a community fairly limited in extent and population and in which decisions were made by members arriving at a consensus rather than by voting (in the course of which a majority overwhelmed a minority) or by fiat (through which the will of an individual or a relatively small group was imposed on the other members).

In my poetry, prose, and performance works composed after 1953 *wu-wei* has been exemplified in two principal ways: through aleatoric or chance procedures operative during composition, performance, or both; and through composition of works requiring performers or readers to exercise personal choice. Ideally, performances of works of the latter type exemplify or at least act as analogies for libertarian communities in that performers make independent choices throughout each performance while paying close attention to everything they can hear—both the sounds produced by other performers and ambient sounds—and relating very consciously with this perceived aural plenum as well as with the other performers themselves. The materials and performance rules provided by the composer act as analogies for the natural and social situations encountered by communities.

The principle of *wu-wei* amounts in practice to standing out of the way (at least to a significant extent) of processes conceived either as natural or as otherwise transpersonal. A motivation for following this principle (over and above those found in Taoist classics) is provided by Buddhism, which regards the ego as an illusory formation.

My own introduction to Buddhism (aside from the reading of translations of portions of the *Dhammapada*) came largely in the early 1950s from the writings, and after 1954 from the classes at Columbia, of Dr. Daisetz Teitaro Suzuki on Zen and Kegon Buddhism. Suzuki and other historians of religion view Zen Buddhism as a major result of the meeting of Buddhism and Taoism in southern China early in the sixth century C.E. Thus Taoist *wu-wei* and Buddhist egolessness were probably closely associated from the earliest days of the Zen sect.

On the other hand, *wu-wei* and Zen egolessness were associated in about 1950 with the use of chance operations in artmaking by John Cage, who was also influenced collaterally by the philosophy of the Chinese classic or "wisdom book" known as the *I Ching* or *Book of Changes*. The work and thought of Cage's older friend Marcel Duchamp, who had used chance operations in making both sculptures and music as early as around 1920, was also undoubtedly a leading influence on Cage's work with chance, but as far as I know, the rationale of Duchamp's aleatoric work came from neither Buddhism nor Taoism nor the *I Ching*.

My own acquaintance with the *I Ching* began in 1950, not long after Pantheon's publication of Gary F. Bayne's English translation of Richard Wilhelm's German version of the Chinese classic. There is no room here to tell the sources or many details of this work, which, although adopted as a canonical book by Confucius and his followers, also shares crucial concepts (especially that of the basic Way of the universe, or *Tao*) with the Taoist writings of Lao-tse and Chuang-tse. However, an important, mostly implicit, principle of the *I Ching* was made explicit by C. G. Jung in his foreword to the Pantheon edition, namely, that events happening at the same time are meaningfully, though "acausally," connected. (Jung's term for this is Englished as "synchronicity.")

As is well known, the *I Ching* may be consulted as an oracle by means of chance operations: either by repeatedly separating a bundle of fifty dried yarrow stalks or by flipping three coins a certain number of times. The person consulting the book performs the chance operations while holding in mind a bothersome or otherwise important question or problem. The result of the chance operations is a group of six broken and/or unbroken lines, known as a "hexagram," and one or more or even all of the lines may be "changing" into their opposites, producing a second hexagram. Meanings traditionally associated with each hexagram as a whole and with the changing lines are given in the book and are considered relevant to the consulter's problem or question.

About 1950 Cage adapted the coin method of consulting the *I Ching* to the composition of music, one of the first notable instances being his large piano work *The Music of Changes.* Since then he has usually employed chance operations, and very often "*I Ching* methods," in composition.

Taoist writings read in the late 1940s, Suzuki's writings and later his classes in the 1950s, and the *I Ching* from about 1950 predisposed me toward ways of making art that de-emphasized the ego of the maker, but at first I strongly resisted Cage's musical use of chance. In the early 1950s I attended most of the first New York concerts in which chance-generated, indeterminate (greatly different in each performance), and unpredictable (different in important ways in each performance) works by Cage, Morton Feldman, Christian Wolff, and Earle Brown were performed, notably by David Tudor, and I became personally acquainted with Cage in about 1953. However, it was not until late 1954 that the combined philosophical influences of Western libertarianism and of Taoism, Buddhism (especially Zen and Kegon, with its emphasis on the transparence and interpenetration of all entities and a picture of the universe akin to that of Whitehead—whose influence on me I cannot go into here), the *I Ching*, and Cage's own Duchamp-influenced "take" on these Asian philosophies crystallized in me sufficiently for me to be impelled to begin employing chance operations in the composition of verbal texts and performance works, many of which are indeterminate or unpredictable in significant ways in performance. I continued developing and employing such methods for nearly three decades.

As I wrote above, I think it was the Chicago (largely McKeon's) interpretation of Aristotle (who was so much on the side of poets against captious critics that he devotes the whole twenty-fifth chapter of the *Poetics* to answers that poets and their partisans may give to such critics) that made me feel free to begin using aleatoric and related methods at a time when work of that sort was unknown in the American and British literary worlds, where the climate of critical opinion was strongly antiexperimental.

The way this amalgam of Greek, Asian, later European, and American philosophical influences—some or all of which may have been misread or misconstrued, either by myself or by my teachers—helped crucially to shape my work after 1953 in poetry, prose narrative, theater, music, and the visual arts exemplifies some ways philosophy may influence artmaking. It would take many times the number of pages available for this essay to spell out the many interrelations and contradictions among my philosophical influences, and some—especially the work of Alfred North Whitehead—I have hardly been able to mention.

The fact is that at the present time I am studying a number of philosophers whose works may eventually have an influence on my art work and may help to turn it in entirely different directions than those it has taken previously.

PUBLICATION: *Poetry and Philosophy* (1983), 3:67–72.

KEYWORDS: philosophy; avant-garde; method; history.

LINKS: Jackson Mac Low, "Sketch toward a Close Reading of Three Poems from Bob Perelman's *Primer*" (*PJ* 2), "*Persia/Sixteen/Code Poems*" (*PJ* 4), "*Pieces o' Six*—XII and XXIII" (*PJ* 6); Charles Bernstein, "Professing Stein/Stein Professing" (*PJ* 9); Richard Blevins, "'The Single Intelligence': The Formation of Robert Creeley's Epistemology" (*PJ* 9); Allen Fisher, "Poetry, Philosophy, and Difference" (*PJ* 3); Ben Friedlander, "Laura Riding/Some Difficulties" (*PJ* 4); Lyn Hejinian, "La Faustienne" (*PJ* 10); George Lakoff, "Continuous Reframing" (*Guide*; *PJ* 1); Peter Middleton, "The Knowledge of Narratives" (*PJ* 5); Dmitrii Prigov, "Conceptualism and the West" (*PJ* 8).

SELECTED BIBLIOGRAPHY: *22 Light Poems* (Los Angeles: Black Sparrow, 1968); *Stanzas for Iris Lezak* (Barton, Vt.: Something Else, 1972); *Asymmetries 1–260* (New York: Printed Editions, 1980); *From Pearl Harbor Day to FDR's Birthday* (College Park, Md.: Sun & Moon, 1982); *Bloomsday* (Barrytown, N.Y.: Station Hill, 1984); *French Sonnets* (Tucson: Black Mesa, 1984); *Representative Works: 1938–1985* (New York: Roof Books, 1986); *Words nd Ends from Ez* (Bolinas, Calif.: Avenue B, 1989); *Twenties: 100 Poems* (New York: Roof, 1991); *Pieces o' Six: Thirty-three Poems in Prose* (Los Angeles: Sun & Moon, 1992); *42 Merzgedichte in Memoriam Kurt Schwitters* (Barrytown, N.Y.: Station Hill, 1994); *Barnesbook* (Los Angeles: Sun & Moon, 1996); *Doings: Assorted Performance Pieces, 1955–2002* (New York: Granary, 2005); *Thing of Beauty: New and Selected Works*, ed. Anne Tardos (Berkeley: University of California Press, 2008); *154 Forties*, ed. Tardos (Denver: Counterpath, 2012).

Plotless Literature Vasily Rozanov

The Russian Formalists were a group of avant-garde Russian literary theorists who emerged in the decade prior to World War I and the Russian Revolution. The term "formalism," then and now, has been a contested one, both aesthetically and politically. The autonomous and claustrophic (closed) formalism championed by the New Critics was attacked, for both aesthetic and cultural reasons, by American avant-garde poetry from the 1950s—with Charles Olson's projective verse, Robert Duncan's open field composition, Denise Levertov's organic form, LeRoi Jones/Amiri Baraka's political poetry. At the same time, many cultural studies critics from the 1970s on have seen literary form and "formalism" as separating art and society. However, concepts like Shklovsky's *ostranenie* (defamiliarization), the "semantic shift," "foregrounding" or "laying bare of the device," and the motivation of art by *byt* (everyday life) bridge the gap between art and society and have widely influenced Left aesthetics and ideology critique. In publishing Shklovsky's "Plotless Literature" (in Richard Sheldon's exemplary translation) as the opening essay of *Poetics Journal*, we meant not only to revive interest in the Formalists' work but also to show how attention to radical form is motivated by political and social concerns. In his essay on the forgotten dilettante Vasily Rozanov, Shklovsky reveals the constructive potential of nonnarrative form, in its refusal of generic expectations, as a new form of *literaturnost* (literariness).

I

Wilhelm Meister contains a section entitled "The Confession of a Beautiful Soul." The heroine of this confession says that she used to view the beauty of a work of art in the same way that people view the beauty of the typeface in a book: "It's nice to have a beautifully printed book, but who reads a book just because it's beautifully printed?"

Both she and Goethe knew that people who speak in that fashion understand nothing about art. And yet that attitude is as prevalent among contemporary art critics as slant eyes in a Chinaman.

That view may have become ridiculous in music and provincial in the visual arts, but it is still rampant in literature.

But that contemporary theoretician who concludes from his examination of a work of literature that its so-called form is a sort of veil that must be pierced, jumps over the horse that he is trying to mount.

A work of literature is pure form; it is not a thing and not material, but a relation between materials. And like each and every relation, it is a relation of zero dimensionality. Consequently, the scope of the work, the arithmetic value of its numerator or denominator, is inconsequential: what matters is the relation between them. All works—whether humorous or tragic, universal or parochial—and all juxtapositions, whether of world to world or cat to rock, are equivalent.

That is precisely why art is benign, self-contained, and unassuming. The history of literature moves forward along a broken, staccato line. If we line up all the literary saints canonized in Russia between the seventeenth and the twentieth century, the line that results will not enable us to trace the history of how literary forms developed. What Pushkin wrote about Derzhavin is not acute and not true. Nekrasov clearly does not derive from the Pushkin tradition. Among the prose writers, Tolstoy just as clearly derives neither from Turgenev nor from Gogol, and Chekhov does not derive from Tolstoy. These gaps are not due to the chronological distances between the designated names.

No, the fact of the matter is that in the shift of literary schools, the line of succession goes not from father to son but from uncle to nephew. Let us begin by developing the formula. In each literary epoch, there exists not one but several literary schools. They exist in literature simultaneously, one of them constituting its canonized apex. The others exist in uncanonized form, subliminally, as, for example, in Pushkin's time, the Derzhavin tradition existed in the poetry of Kuchelbecker and Griboedov simultaneously with the tradition of Russian vaudeville verse, and with a set of other traditions, such as, for example, the pure tradition of the adventure novel in Bulgarin's work.

The Pushkin tradition did not continue after him—another example of the phenomenon whereby geniuses fail to produce exceptionally gifted children.

Meanwhile, though, new forms come into being on the lower stratum, where they coexist with the old art forms that are no longer sensed. Elements once charged with artistic power become subservient and inert. The recessive strain supersedes the dominant and the vaudeville writer Belopyatkin becomes Nekrasov (the work of Osip Brik); Tolstoy, the direct heir of the eighteenth century, creates a new novel (Boris Eikhenbaum); Blok canonizes the themes and tempos of the "gypsy ballad"; and Chekhov introduces the "Alarm Clock" into Russian literature. Dostoevsky elevates the devices of the dime novel to a literary norm. Every new literary school is a revolution, something like the appearance of a new class.

But that, of course, is only an analogy. The vanquished "line" is not annihilated; it does not cease to exist. It is merely toppled from the summit; it sinks into obscurity but can be restored, so it remains a perpetual pretender to the throne. Actually, however, all this is complicated by the fact that the new hegemony is usually not a pure recapitulation of a prior form: it is adulterated by traits from other, lesser schools and even by traits inherited from its predecessors on the throne, now reduced to a subservient role.

Now let us shift to Rozanov for some new digressions.

In this commentary on Rozanov, I have confined myself to his last three books: *Solitaria* and *Fallen Leaves (Baskets One and Two)*.

Needless to say, these books, which are intimate to an insulting degree, reflect the soul of the author. But I will try to demonstrate that the soul of a work of literature is none other than its structure, its form. According to my formula, "A work of literature does not exceed the sum of its stylistic devices." In the words of Rozanov (*Fallen Leaves, Basket One,* 170):

> Everyone imagines that the soul is a being. But suppose it's music?
>> And people look for its "properties" (the properties of an *object*).
> But suppose it has only structure? (*At morning coffee*)

A work of art has a soul tantamount to structure, to the geometric relation between solids. The selection of the material for a work of art is also a matter of formal signs. The quantities chosen are significant and palpable. Each epoch has its own Index, its list of themes forbidden because of their obsolescence. Tolstoy, for example, put into effect such an Index when he forbade such topics as the romantic Caucasus and moonlight.

The foregoing is a typical prohibition of "romantic themes." In Chekhov we see something else. In his early piece, "What Is Most Frequently Encountered in Novels, Tales, etc.," he enumerated some clichés:

> A rich uncle, liberal or conservative, depending on the circumstances. His exhortations are not as useful to the hero as his death.
>> An aunt in Tambov.
>> A doctor with a concerned face offering hope during a crisis; he frequently has a bald spot and a cane with a knob.
>> Dachas in the suburbs and a mortgaged estate in the south.

As you see, here the prohibition is imposed on several typical "real-life" situations. This prohibition is imposed not because there are no longer any doctors who declare that the crisis has passed, but because that situation has already become a cliché. It is, however, possible to renew the cliché by emphasizing its conventionality. That approach—playing with banality—can work well, but only on rare occasions. Here's an example (Heine):

Die Rose, die Lilie, die Taube, die Sonne,
Die liebt' ich einst alle in Liebeswonne.

[Further on, he plays with rhymes: Kleine—Feine—Reine—Eine = krov—lyubov, radost—mladost.]

But forbidden themes continue to exist outside the realm of canonized literature, just as the erotic anecdote exists now and has always existed, or as there exist in the psyche suppressed desires that occasionally emerge in dreams, sometimes to the surprise of the afflicted. The theme of ultimate "domesticity"—the domestic attitude toward things, marital double-bedded love—has not risen, or almost never risen, to the "high society" of literature, but it has existed, for example, in letters. Tolstoy writes his wife:

I kiss you in the nursery, behind the screens, in your gray housecoat. (10 November 1864)

Elsewhere:

So Seryozha is putting his face on the linoleum and crying "Aha"? That I'll have to see. You surprised me so when you explained that you are sleeping on the floor; but Lyubov Aleksandra said that's how she's sleeping, too, and then I understood. I like it and I don't like it when you imitate her. I would have wished that you might be just as innately good as she.

In three days' time, I'll be standing on that linoleum in the nursery and embracing you, my fleet, slender, dear wife. (10 December 1864)

But time passed; the Tolstoyan material and device faded and became clichés. Being a genius, Tolstoy had no heirs. So, in the absence of a declaration or a promulgation of a new list of forbidden themes, his work went into the stockpile. What happened then is what happens in married life, according to Rozanov; when a man and wife cease to feel that they are two disparate beings:

The cogs (disparity) wear down, rub smooth, cease to mesh. And the "shaft" grinds to a stop, "work" has stopped: because the *machine*, as a *balance* and *harmony* of "opposites," has disappeared.

That love, having died a natural death, *will never regenerate*. That is why, before love ends (once and for all), *infidelities* flare as love's final hope; nothing so *alienates* (creates that *disparity* between) lovers as infidelity. The last remaining cog, not quite rubbed smooth, increases in size and the corresponding cog meshes with it. (*Fallen Leaves, Basket One*, 136–37)

In literature, that type of infidelity is seen in the succession of literary schools.

It is common knowledge that the greatest works of literature (I'm speaking now only of prose) do not fit within the framework of a specific genre. It is difficult to say exactly what *Dead Souls* is, difficult to assign this work to a specific genre. Tolstoy's *War and Peace*, as well as Sterne's *Tristram Shandy*, with their almost complete lack of a central plot (frame novella), can be called novels only because they violate the laws of the novel. Even a relatively pure genre such as "neo-classical tragedy" makes sense only in terms of a canon that is itself not always a model of clarity. But the canon of the novel genre, perhaps more than any other, lends itself to multiple parody and modification.

True to the canon of the eighteenth-century novel, I am permitting myself a digression.

Apropos of digressions. In Fielding's *Joseph Andrews*, the description of the brawl is followed by an interpolated chapter (book 3, chapter 10). That chapter is called "A discourse between the poet and the player," and the title continues with the following words—"of no other use in this history but to divert the reader."

Digressions generally have three functions. Their first function is to permit the introduction of new material into the novel. Thus, the speeches of Don Quixote permitted Cervantes to introduce into his novels a wide variety of critical and philosophical material. The second function of digressions is much more significant, that is, to retard, or brake, the action. That device is widely used by Sterne. The essence of the device in Sterne is that one plot motif is elaborated by the introduction of a new theme (in Sterne's *Tristram Shandy*, for example, that is how the story of the hero's aunt and her coachman is introduced).

Playing with the reader's impatience, Sterne keeps reminding him of the stranded hero, but does not return to the hero after the digression; the reminder serves only to whet the reader's expectation.

In a novel with parallel plots, such as Victor Hugo's *Les Misérables* or Dostoevsky's novels, an action from one plot interrupts another, where it functions as a digression.

The third function is to create a contrast. This is what Fielding says about it:

And here we shall of necessity be led to open a new vein of knowledge which, if it hath been discovered, hath not to our remembrance been wrought on by any ancient or modern writer. This vein is no other than that of contrast, which runs through all the works of the Creation and may probably have a large share in constituting in us the idea of all beauty, as well natural as artificial; for what demonstrates the beauty and excellence of anything but its reverse? Thus the beauty of day and that of summer is set off by the horrors of night and winter. And, I believe, if it was possible for a man to have seen only the two former, he would have a very imperfect idea of their beauty. (*Tom Jones*, book 5, chapter 1)

I believe that the previous quotation sufficiently clarifies the third function of digressions—to create contrasts.

When Heine was assembling his *Reisebilder*, he deliberately tampered with the order of the chapters in order to create such a sensation of contrast.

II

Back to Rozanov.

The three books being analyzed are a brand-new genre, an infidelity of extraordinary proportions. Into these books have gone entire newspaper articles, broken into interlocking segments, and these are interspersed with Rozanov's biography, scenes from his life, snapshots, etc.

These books are not utterly formless, since we see in their structure a certain continuity of device.

These books strike me as a new genre, one most closely related to the parody novel, with a rudimentary central plot and no comic coloration.

Rozanov's book was a heroic attempt to get away from literature, to "declare himself without words, without form," and the book worked out beautifully because it created a new literature, a new form.

Rozanov introduced into literature new, "kitchen" themes. Family themes had been introduced before. Charlotta slicing bread in *Werther* was for that time a revolutionary phenomenon, as was the name Tatyana in *Evgeny Onegin*; but family humdrum—the quilt, the kitchen and its smell (with no satiric overtones)—had not existed in literature.

Sometimes Rozanov introduced these themes in unadulterated form, as in the following series of fragments:

This kitchen ledger of mine is worth every bit as much as *Turgenev's Letters to Madame Viardot*. Though *something else*, it is the same axis of the world and, as a matter of fact, the same poetry.

What effort! frugality! fear of exceeding the "limit"! and—satisfaction when the "first of the month" arrives and the books balance. (*Fallen Leaves, Basket One*, 129)

Elsewhere:

I love tea. I love putting a tiny patch on my cigarette (where it's torn). I love my wife, my garden (at the dacha). (*Fallen Leaves, Basket One*, 175)

Sometimes these themes are motivated by a sweet memory:

... I still save cigarette butts. Not always, mind you, but certainly if half the cigarette is left. Or even less. "Everything must be utilized" (the scraps of tobacco must be used over again).

Yet I make 12,000 rubles a year and certainly don't need all that. Why then?

A habitual messiness of hands (childhood) ... and even, believe it or not, the sweet memory of my childhood years.

Why do I love my childhood so? My tormented and sullied childhood. (*Fallen Leaves, Basket Two*, 265)

Among the original things in these books is a new image of the poet:

Goggle-eyed and slobbery—that's me.
    Unattractive?
    Can't be helped. (*Fallen Leaves, Basket Two*, 220)

My soul is compounded of dirt, tenderness, and sadness.

Or:

Some goldfish are "playing in the sun," but they are housed in an aquarium full of slushy manure.

And they don't suffocate there. Quite the contrary ... Improbable. And yet—*true*. (*Solitaria*, 52)

Rozanov introduced new themes. Why? Not because he was a singular person, though he was a genius, i.e., singular, but because the laws governing the dialectical self-generation of new forms and the attraction of new materials had, after the death of the old forms, left a vacuum. The soul of the artist sought new themes.

Rozanov found a theme. A whole category of themes, the themes of everyday existence and the family.

Things stage periodic rebellions. In Leskov, it was the rebellion of the "great, mighty, truthful" and every other Russian language, exaggerated and mannered—the language of shopkeepers and poor relatives. Rozanov's rebellion was more extensive. The things surrounding him demanded halos. Rozanov gave them halos and glorification:

> It is certainly without precedent and its repetition is unthinkable in the universe—at the very moment when tears were flowing and my soul was bursting, I sensed unmistakably the presence of a listener and felt that those tears were flowing literarily, musically "even if I were to write them down" and for that reason alone I wrote down: (*Solitaria*: little girl at the railroad station, ventilator). (*Fallen Leaves, Basket Two*, 220)

Here are the two passages mentioned by Rozanov in the parentheses:

> Fail to give something and you feel heartsick. Even if you fail to give a present. (A little girl at the railroad station, Kiev, whom I wanted to give a pencil, but hesitated, and she left with her grandmother.)
>
> But the little girl returned and I gave her the pencil. She had never seen one and I could hardly explain what sort of "miracle" it was. How fine for her and me. (*Solitaria*, 60)

> The ventilator in the corridor hums distractingly, but not offensively: I started weeping (almost): "If only for the purpose of listening to that ventilator, I want to go on living, but, above all, my *friend* must live." Then came the thought: "Won't she (my friend) hear that ventilator in the other world?" And a craving for immortality so gripped me by the hair that I almost sank to the floor. (*Solitaria*, 72)

The very concreteness of terror in Rozanov is a literary device.

To show how deliberately Rozanov uses "domesticity" as a literary device, I want to call attention to one typographic detail of his books. You surely remember the family snapshots inserted into both Baskets of his *Fallen Leaves*. Those snapshots make a strange, unusual impression. If you scrutinize them, the reason for that impression will become clear: the snapshots have been printed with no border and not in the way that illustrations in books are usually printed. The gray background of the snapshots goes right to the edge of the page. There is no caption and no outline whatsoever. All this, taken together, creates the impression of something that is not an illustration in a book, but a genuine photograph that has been glued or merely stuck into the book. The deliberate nature of this type of reproduction is proved by the fact that only certain family photographs are reproduced in that way; the illustrations of less importance are printed in the usual way, with margins retained.

True, the margins are retained on the photograph of the writer's children, but the outline is curious:

> Mama and Tanya (standing by her knees) in the garden on Pavlovskaya Street in St. Petersburg (the Petersburg Side of town). Next to them is the Nesvetevich boy, a neighbor. The Efimov house, No. 2.

Here Rozanov indicates the address with all the exactitude of a policeman and he stresses the documentary nature of the illustration, which is also a deliberate stylistic device.

My words about Rozanov's "domesticity" should in no sense be understood to mean that he has made a confession and bared his soul. No, he adopted the confessional tone as a device. [...]

IV

Now I will try to sketch briefly the plot pattern of *Solitaria* and the two Baskets of *Fallen Leaves*.

Several themes are presented, the most important being: 1) the friend (his wife), 2) cosmic sex, 3) newspaper accounts of the opposition and the revolution, 4) literature, with full-fledged articles on Gogol, 5) biography, 6) positivism, 7) the Jews, 8) a sizable interpolated swatch of letters, and various others.

Such a profusion of themes is not unique. We are familiar with novels that have quadruple and quintuple plots; the very device of violating the plot by means of interpolated themes that interlock was used by Sterne, who also worked with no fewer themes.

Of the three books, *Solitaria* is the one that can be considered an independent entity.

The interpolation of new themes is handled in the following way. We are presented with a fragment of some complete situation, but no explanation is given for its appearance and we do not understand what we see; then comes the elaboration—along the lines of first the riddle, then the solution. Extremely characteristic is the theme of the "friend" (about Rozanov's wife).

First comes simply a reference (22), then (35) various allusions lead us into the heart of the matter. We are given an individual in bits and pieces that seem to refer to someone we already know, but only much later do the fragments jell (67–71), at which point we have a coherent biography of Rozanov's wife, which can be integrated by extracting all the remarks about her and grouping them under the rubric of "the wife." The unfortunate diagnosis by Bekhterev also appears for the first time as a simple reference to Doctor Karpinsky's name:

"Why didn't I call in Karpinsky?"
　　"Why didn't I call in Karpinsky?"
　　"Why didn't I call in Karpinsky?" (*Fallen Leaves, Basket One*, 177)

And only afterward do we get an explanation, with the story of the incorrect diagnosis which failed to take into account the "reflex of the pupils" (180). The same with "Byzov." At first only his name is given (*Basket One*, 140), then he is elaborated into an image. In this way, Rozanov makes sure that a new theme does not appear to us out of the blue, as in a collection of aphorisms; instead, he prepares a thread and the character or situation is wound in and out of the entire plot.

These interlocking themes, set against each other, are the threads that, alternately appearing and disappearing, create the plot fabric of the work. Cervantes elaborates the second part of *Don Quixote* by using the names of people mentioned in the first part—for instance, the Moor Ricote, Sancho Panza's neighbor.

Several of the themes contain a curious conglomeration of fragments; for example, out of the random comments on literature, one can piece together an elaborate essay on Gogol. In addition to numerous fragments, there is a full-fledged article (*Basket One*, 118–20); similarly, at the end of the second Basket, some contradictory allusions have been distilled by Rozanov into an entire article. It starts out in the tone of a newspaper and then shifts abruptly to the cosmic tone of the fragment about the breasts of the world, which ends the book.

Generally, Rozanov's fragments succeed one another according to the following principle: contradiction of themes and contradiction of planes; i.e., the "real" plane gives way to the cosmic plane; for example, the wife theme gives way to the Apis theme.

So we see that Rozanov's three books have a certain structural unity, that they are novels with the connective motivating material excised. For example, one fairly common device in novels is the interpolation of poems, as we see in Cervantes, in *The Arabian Nights*, in Ann Radcliffe, and, to some extent, in Maksim Gorky. These poems are a distinct material that exists in some sort of relation to the prose of the work. Various motivations are used for their interpolation—either they are presented as epigraphs or they are presented as the product of the characters, whether major or minor. The latter constitutes plot motivation, while the former involves laying bare the device. But in both cases, the device is essentially the same. We know, for example, that Pushkin's "Prophet" or "Once There Lived a Poor Knight" could just as easily have been presented as epigraphs for the individual chapters of Dostoevsky's *Idiot*, instead of being read by the characters within the work itself. In Mark Twain's *Pudd'nhead Wilson*, the epigraphs are taken from the speeches of the main character. In Vladimir Solovyov's "Three Conversations," the point is made that the epigraph on Pan-Mongolianism has been written by the author (this information is presented via the lady's question and the gentlemen's answer).

Likewise, the kinship used as a device to connect characters is sometimes far-fetched and poorly grounded, as in the case of Werther's father in *The Sorrows of Young Werther* or Mignon's parents in *Wilhelm Meister*, where kinship merely serves to motivate structural elements of the work and to create compositional juxtapositions. Sometimes the motivation is strained (a dream); sometimes it's not serious. Motivation by dream is typical of Remizov; in Hoffman's *Kater Murr*, shifts in plot and the confusion of the cat's story of a cat with the man's story are motivated by the fact that the cat was writing on his master's papers.

Solitaria and the *Baskets* can therefore be characterized as novels devoid of motivation.

Thus in the thematic sphere, these novels are distinguished by the canonization of new themes; in the structural sphere, by the laying bare of the device. [...]

VI

An image/trope comes into being when something is given an uncommon designation, i.e., when something is called by an unusual name. The purpose of this device is to shift the thing into a new semantic set, a set containing conceptions of a different order—for example, stars = eyes, girl = gray duck; in addition, the image is usually elaborated by describing the thing that has been substituted.

One can compare the image with the syncretic epithet, i.e., the epithet that defines auditory sensations in terms of visual and vice versa. For example, "crimson chime" or "brilliant sounds." This device is often encountered in the Romantics.

Here the auditory representations are mixed with the visual and it seems to me that what we have here is not confusion, but the device of shifting something into a new set—in short, removing it from its former category. It is interesting to examine Rozanov's images from that point of view.

This is how Rozanov realizes that phenomenon, citing the words of Shperk:

"Children differ from us in that they perceive everything with a power of realism completely inaccessible to adults. For us, a 'chair' is a detail of 'furniture.' But a child does not know the category 'furniture' and a 'chair' to him is enormous and alive in a way that it cannot be for us. For that reason, children *enjoy the world* much more than we." (*Solitaria*, 64)

That is the kind of work produced by a writer who destroys the category, wrenching the chair from its place with the furniture. Here is an absolutely staggering example:

Sex is a mountain of lights: a high, high mountain from which lights radiate. Its rays cover the entire earth, imbuing it all with a new, utterly noble meaning.

Believe that mountain. There it stands on its four wooden legs (iron and hard metal are not allowed here, just as "wounding" nails are not allowed).

I have seen. I bear witness. And I will stand behind what I have seen. (*Fallen Leaves, Basket One*, 159)

Here is how that image is constructed. First comes the "elevated," glorifying section—the thing is called a "mountain of lights" and is perceived as a world center, as something Biblical. It is shifted into the set of cosmic concepts.

Then comes a paraphrase and we recognize the thing. The words about iron make the thing still more concrete and, at the same time, transform a technical detail into a "symbolic" detail. The last section of the fragment is remarkable in that, although the thing has been "recognized," the tone does not change, but continues to be sustained at the height of prophecy. The recognized thing remains in the elevated set. That is one of the most elaborate applications of the device image/paraphrase.

In addition to its elevating function, paraphrase/estrangement can also have a reductive function, which is typical of the parodic style in all its varieties, including the Imagists. Here is one of Rozanov's similes, where abstinence is equated with constipation:

With inexpressible tears, my intent is to convey it all simply and crudely, diminishing something that is venerated, though in the sense *of pressure*, the comparison is accurate.

Your mouth is overflowing with saliva, but you must not spit. You might hit some monks.

A man eats for days, weeks, months on end, but he must not "excuse himself," he must keep it all inside himself. . . .

He drinks, keeps drinking—but once again he must not "excuse himself . . ."

That is virginity.

I'm suffocating. I'm bursting at the seams.

"Forbidden." That is monasticism. (*Fallen Leaves, Basket One*, 100)

Or:

Flexible matter envelopes the inflexible thing, however larger the latter may *seem*. Matter is always "larger" . . .

A boa constrictor the width of an arm, or at most the size of a leg at the knee, swallows a kid goat.

That is the basis of many strange phenomena. The appetite of boa constrictors, as well as nanny goats.

Certainly, it is somewhat painful, a tight squeeze, but it works. . . .

It seems impossible to get on one's hand the kid glove as it lies so narrow and "innocent" in the bin at the store. But it goes on and grips firmly.

The world has a metaphysical proclivity for the "firm grip."

God holds the world in a "firm grip" . . .

And though everything seems to strive for freedom and the "abyss," there is also an appetite diametrically opposed—the urge to enter the "narrow way," the constricting way. (*Fallen Leaves, Basket Two*, 414)

On the next page:

Firm, particularly that which is firm, seeks the narrow way. The "abyss" is for old women. . . . [This fragment is not localized.]

In the last fragment, we discern erotic symbolism, given first of all via the "image," via the location of the sexual organs in the category of gripping and entering things; then at the end, the image is doubled, i.e., the concept is used to translate the French Revolution from the "freedom" set into the "abyss" set. The latter thereby consists of the concepts "abyss," "senility," "French Revolution." The other set—"kid glove" (equivalent to the female sexual organ)—is given via the word "innocent," which seemingly refers to "glove."

Then come the boa constrictor and the goat, the metaphysical "firm grip." This leads to the concept of the "narrow way," placed in opposition to freedom.

In Rozanov's work, the glove is the usual image for the sexual object, for example:

Venal love seems "extremely convenient": "whoever has five rubles goes and takes." Of course, but:
The flowers have withered,
And the fires have died down . . .
What does he actually take? A piece of dead rubber. A kid glove spattered with spit and thrown on the floor. . . . (Fallen Leaves, Basket Two, 391)

These are the steps that a writer constructs in order to create a perceptible image . . .

This study has to be finished. I am thinking of ending it here. One possibility is to tie the ending with a bow, but I am certain that the old canon of the neat resumé for an article or lecture is dead. Thoughts summarized in artificial sets turn into a single road, into the ruts of the writer's thought. All the varied associations, all the innumerable paths which run from every thought in all directions are smoothed out. But I have only the greatest respect for my contemporaries and I know that they must either "produce an ending" or else write below that the author has died and for that reason there will be no ending. By all means, then, let's have an ending here, with some help from Rozanov (Basket One, 94):

. . . .
. . . .

Twisted railroad ties. Planks. Sand. Rock. Ruts.
"What have we here—street repairs?"
"No, this is The Works of Rozanov. And the streetcar hurtles confidently along on its iron rails." (Street repairs, Nevsky Prospekt)

I apply this to myself.

—Translated by Richard Sheldon

PUBLICATION: Excerpted from Introduction (1981), 1:1–24.

KEYWORDS: Russian poetics; modernism; nonnarrative; formalism.

LINKS: Abigail Child, "The Exhibit and the Circulation" (*PJ* 7); Ron Day, "Form and the Dialogic" (*PJ* 10); Carla Harryman, "Toy Boats" (*Guide*; *PJ* 5); Lyn Hejinian, "Strangeness" (*PJ* 8); Yulia Latinina, "Folklore and 'Novoyaz'" (*PJ* 9); Mikhail Dziubenko, "'New Poetry' and Perspectives for Philology" (*PJ* 8); Bob Perelman, "Plotless Prose" (*PJ* 1); Barrett Watten, "The XYZ of Reading: Negativity (And)" (*PJ* 6).

SELECTED BIBLIOGRAPHY: *A Sentimental Journey: Memoirs, 1917–1922* (1923; trans. Richard Sheldon; Ithaca, N.Y.: Cornell University Press, 1970); *Knight's Move* (1923; trans. Sheldon; Normal, Ill.: Dalkey Archive, 2005); *Zoo; or, Letters Not about Love* (1923; trans. Sheldon; Ithaca, N.Y.: Cornell University Press, 1971); *Theory of Prose* (1925; trans. Benjamin Sher; Elmwood Park, Ill.: Dalkey Archive, 1990); *Third Factory* (1926; trans. Sheldon; Ann Arbor, Mich.: Ardis, 1977); *Mayakovsky and His Circle* (1941; trans. Lily Feiler; New York: Dodd, Mead, 1972); *Leo Tolstoy* (1963; trans. Olga Shartse; Moscow: Progress, 1978); *Energy of Delusion: A Book on Plot* (1981; trans. Shushan Vagyan; Champaign, Ill.: Dalkey Archive, 2007).

Migratory Meaning The Parsimony
Principle in the Poem

Ron Silliman combines key concepts of cognitive linguistics—"frame," "envisionment,"
and "schema"—with the Russian Formalists' account of the literary "device" in his reading
of Joseph Ceravolo's abstract lyric "Migratory Noon." Silliman wants to know exactly how
this poem, as a communicative act between speaker and hearer, poet and reader, makes
meaning (or nonmeaning) by refusing to cohere in literal terms, even as it offers a meaning,
for one reader, "beyond the experience of words." He shows how the poem constructs a
series of "frame shifts" between schemas and envisionments through its use of grammatical and poetic devices—the play of phrase and sentence in the poem's lineation. What is
necessary for interpretation is either a shared experience of these envisionments or a sense
that their coherence does not depend on them: a second-order envisionment of coherence
itself. Silliman draws on linguist Paul Kay's concept of the "parsimony principle," where the
mind restricts interpretation to the smallest framework possible to make sense, proposing
a cognitive mechanism that reduces rather than multiplies interpretation when faced with
linguistic indeterminacy. His reading challenges the common theory that the reader can
make any meaning she wants from abstract poetry, connecting the interpretation of poetry
to theories of ideology where the demand for coherence is precisely the ideological effect
that radical writing seeks to undo.

In the Spring/Summer 1981 issue of *Parnassus*, Peter Schjeldahl has this to say
of *Transmigration Solo*, by Joseph Ceravolo:[1]

> Ceravolo is a lyric poet of such oddness and purity that reading him all but
> makes me dizzy, like exercise at a very high altitude. *I rarely know what he
> is talking about*, but I can rarely gainsay a word he uses. Nor do I doubt that
> every word is in felt contact with actual experience *beyond the experience
> of words.* [...][2]

Schjeldahl's vocabulary and tone are strategic, both with regard to the audience to which it is addressed, and to that ultimate editorial arbiter, space. I
doubt that he intends to be read quite as literally as I am about to suggest.
Nevertheless, his piece seems to advocate that not comprehending what a
poet "is talking about" should not be an impediment to appreciation and

response to the writing as such. And, further, that Schjeldahl's reaction to at least this poet is founded on his trust that there exists "beyond the experience of words" a unified, unitary signification—he calls it "contact with actual experience"—which motivates the individual poem's impression of coherence.

These two assertions reflect the current situation in much of American poetry. There persists the lack of an adequate shared vocabulary with which to think and speak of the poem as we find it. [...] To the degree that someone as thoroughly qualified and predisposed to read a poem as Peter Schjeldahl is prepared to praise in public work in which he admits not knowing what the poet "is talking about."

The absence of such a vocabulary obscures precisely what is at risk in those writings which I find most compelling. This issue is the nature of meaning itself, and its status in the poem. Specifically, this issue is a question as to the place of meaning and its alleged capacity to unify a work of writing, to create and endow coherence, whether or not this be conceived of as "beyond the experience of words" or within them.

I want to proceed by offering a partial reading of a specific text, focusing on: (1) what it is about a poem that would cause such a reader to *not* know what the poet "is talking about," and (2) what it is about a poem that would cause such a reader to *not* "doubt that every word is in felt contact with experience beyond the experience of words." [...]

The text, as given by Schjeldahl in his review of Ceravolo, is:

MIGRATORY MOON
    Cold and the cranes.
Cranes in the
        wind
like cellophane tape
on a school book.
The wind bangs
the car, but I sing out loud,
        help, help
as sky gets white
   and whiter and whiter and whiter.
Where are you
  in the reincarnate
      blossoms of the cold?[3]

"Migratory Moon" can be said to consist of five parts, a title and four sentences, no two of which coinhabit the same line. By focusing on the sentence, the poem can be described as a *series of devices*, both simple and complex. Device is used here in the Russian Formalists' sense: any part of the writing which perceptibly alters, and thereby shapes, an individual reader's experience of the text.[4]

The title is not a sentence, but simply an alliterative noun phrase, neither term of which occurs in the body of the text. "Migratory Moon" could be either the subject or predicate of a sentence which does not appear, but can be said *to have been evoked*. The phrase performs the work of both grammatical functions, doubling the sense of density or opacity to a reader.

It's important to discern whether the title functions as such or, following a distinction first made by Walter Benjamin,[5] is really more of a caption. A title proper points or refers to the body of the text *as a whole*, whereas the caption *penetrates* it, highlighting certain elements within. This often occurs in poems where the title anticipates or *repeats in advance* key terms or phrases.

A more complex use of the title-as-caption is to be found in this work from Robert Grenier's *Oakland*:

THREE
legged dog[6]

The title "Three" integrates grammatically with a potentially incomplete noun phrase, "legged dog," to form a full image, specifically one of imbalance. "Three" also foretells the number of syllables in the one-line text, again an instance of imbalance as the ear hears the stress given to the final syllable in "legged." This title penetrates the text not simply to foreground one element, but to combine with it for the total organization of the poem. Implicit within such a strategy is an assertion that "meaning" does not conveniently stop at the borders of the text.

Contrasted with this would be those titles which at least appear to have no inner role within the corpus of the text. Examples include Barrett Watten's "Mode Z," my own *Tjanting*, and Eliot's "The Waste Land." These headings can only be read as though relating to the body of the work as a whole, so that the reader experiences them as *orienting and contextualizing*, if not actually naming, the "subject" of the ensuing text.

"Migratory Moon" would at first seem to be such a title. There are no explicit references to the moon within the text, and the reader has only her own authority on which to rely if the moon is to be identified with the "you" of the final sentence. Nonetheless, at this stage of our reading we may respond to the first of the two questions negatively, stating that we do know what Ceravolo "is talking about": the moon. This represents a leap of faith from what it is about a poem that causes a reader to experience a cohering unity. For "Migratory Moon," as we shall see, is partially, if not entirely, a case of the title-as-caption.

Like the title, the first sentence is grammatically incomplete, being a noun phrase, "Cold and the cranes." If we follow speech act theoretician John Searle in stating that the characteristic of a subject is its capacity to intend, or refer to, a unique object, and that the characteristic of a predicate is the ability to "describe or characterize the object which has been identified,"[7] we still lack any mechanism by which to ascertain which, if either, function "Cold and the cranes" should be understood as fulfilling. This coordinative nexus could be read as a concise formulation of a specific object or state, yet its proximity to "Migratory Moon" permits a reading as an attribute of that, understood as a subject.

The sentence which is incomplete because of the lack of a "main" verb, be it one of action or some necessitated conjugation of *to be*, has long been a part of American literature. One tradition which is close to the use Ceravolo makes of it here descends principally from Imagism, particularly the work of Ezra Pound, whose "In a Station of the Metro" has no main verb. [...]

In "Cold and the cranes," the verb omission serves to ambiguously situate what little information is divulged. The important terms are nouns, one of which is plural (a disagreement in number that may suggest that more than one verb is absent). Both nouns have more than one feasible denotation, and nothing in the text clarifies whether these cranes are mechanical arms that lift and carry, or birds. This indetermination is a crucial element in a reader's not knowing what Ceravolo "is talking about," yet, at another level, it makes no difference: what does is that (with the exception of a model, such as a child's toy) neither is apt to inhabit the indoors. This *outdoorsness* is an example of what some linguists call a *frame* or *schema*, and "represent(s) the knowledge structures with which our experiences with the world are held together,"[8] what we know and can associate with cranes or with *the* cold, head colds, and the like. The structure of such frames is *not* identical with what we have traditionally learned as linguistic paradigms, to the degree that such structures are dependent on (determined by) a domain that is not wholly linguistic—experience—and, as Raymond Williams argues, experience is … the most common form of ideology. It is where the deep structures of the society actually reproduce themselves as conscious life.[9]

Outdoorsness is also a schema in which the term "Cold" can participate, and this association, if it is made and not later rejected, significantly narrows each noun's range of connotation. "Moon" likewise fits this frame, so that without having arrived at a single verb, and before reaching even the second line, a sensitive reader is well on the way toward the construction of what linguists Charles Fillmore and Paul Kay call an *Envisionment*,

> some coherent "image" or understanding of the states of affairs that exist in the set of possible worlds compatible with the language of the text.[10]

Harboring a metaphor of sight that needs detailed examination, Envisionment is a less than ideal formulation of such a critical concept. Yet it does approximate that state of coherence which is the basis for our second question: what is it about a poem that would cause a reader to not doubt that every word is in felt contact with actual experience *beyond the experience of words*. For our text such unity might be nothing more than an Envisionment, and at this moment in "Migratory Moon" there is no cause to refine it beyond outdoorsness, an Envisionment resulting less from "felt contact" than from a series of devices operating in the work. This is not to denigrate the text, but to suggest that "beyondness" is not without its explanations, and that *coherence itself might be just an effect.*

A further distinction needs to be drawn out of the concept of Envisionment, that between active and reactive construction. This distinction presumes a bias in our consumption of language signifying states that might be observed directly by our senses, particularly through sight. Terming one mode of Envisionment representation and the other thought, Manfred Sandmann says,

> Representation is essentially an automatic process, that is to say, given our sensorial apparatus and those parts of the brain responsible for its control, we cannot under certain conditions avoid representation. Thought, on the other hand, is essentially creative and constructive; it consists of purposeful acts in contrast to a mere train of associations. […] There is no concept without conception, that is without a position being taken up by the thinker and adapted to his [*sic*] purpose.[11]

The form of this essay can demonstrate the difference. To the degree that you fail or refuse to grant me the presumptions which underlie each of the words I introduce, to that degree you withhold their frame. Yet these schemata are essential if any linkage beyond syntax is to take place. Withhold some presumptions because they seem unwarranted and what will emerge are my mistakes. Withhold enough and this piece will be gibberish. Such resistance—critical, active frame construction—is far more difficult when the language being processed is on the order of "The arctic sun passed over the horizon causing darkness." Substitute a few terms which do not participate in the same visual frame-structure, however, and even this must be read actively, the presence of a composing intelligence, an Other, readily felt. For example, "The arctic honey blabbed over the report causing darkness," the first line of Ashbery's "Leaving the Atocha Station."[12]

To the extent that this distinction parallels Searle's differentiation of subject and predicate, and *because of the place of the verb within the function of the predicate*, it can be seen that a strategic function of sentences which omit verbs, such as "Cold and the cranes," is to enhance the reactive (integrative) rather than the active (resistant) mode of Envisionment. This is the essence of "Show, don't tell."

This absence in the title and first two sentences of "Migratory Moon" sets up the verb "bangs" and the word "I" in the third to be experienced as major semantic shifts. Unlike the verbless sentence, the semantic shift is not a device, but an effect, the result of one or more devices. [...] A semantic shift can take place either within a reader's perception of the language and/or at any level of integration above that of the linguistic, that is, at the level of Envisionment. Thus Viktor Shklovsky's classic example of the phenomenon is a story by Tolstoy in which the narrator is a horse.[13] Regardless of the level, what is shifted is the *element's relation to the reader's expectation*, something constructed out of that "most common form of ideology," experience. A theory of Envisionment thereby offers above the level of the sentence what more traditional forms of linguistic analysis offer at or below this horizon: identification and description by function of those devices which create meaning. At all levels meaning is built on expectation, and that on experience, be it as large as "life in general" or as localized as the title and first line of "Migratory Moon."

By displacing expectation, the semantic shift renders the element "strange" and therefore perceptible. Shklovsky's own account of this is:

In our studies of the lexical and phonetic composition of poetic speech, of word order, and of the semantic structures of poetic speech, we everywhere came upon the same index of the artistic: that it is purposely created to deautomatize the perception, that the goal of its creation is that it be seen, that the artistic is artificially created so that perception is arrested in it and attains the greatest possible force and duration, so that the thing is perceived, not spatially, but, so to speak, in its continuity. These conditions are met by "poetic language...." Thus we arrive at the definition of poetry as speech that is braked, distorted. Poetic speech is a speech construction.[14]

Shklovsky's emphasis on the dimension of time, contrasted with the spatial, reflects the importance of expectation in the creation of meaning in writing, whether such meaning unifies the text "beyond the experience of words" or does just the opposite. The effect of a semantic shift is therefore both experiential *and* temporal, lying at the crux of the problem of the status and nature of meaning as such.

The semantic shifts which exist in the title, "Migratory Moon," are modest and result from devices well known to students of poetry. Alliteration, for example, foregrounds the sound structure of the noun phrase, directing attention away from its orientational or nominative function. More problematic is the adjective "Migratory," a term for which plausible frames do exist which could integrate with those of "Moon." To what degree can a reader believe that these are the ones intended, let alone sort amongst such variants as the moon's daily cycle, its drift north and south in the sky, its phases, the effect on tides, the mythos of wanderlust, lunacy, etc.? Charles Fillmore identifies what he terms *levels of confidence* in the Envisionment, confidence the reader can have as to the extent her interpretation is that, and only that, intended by the author, so as to have, and put store in, her expectations. Fillmore delineates four levels:

(1) That which is "explicitly justified by the linguistic material of the text";
(2) that which comes "into being by inferences which the text is seen as clearly inviting";
(3) "interpretations which result from schematizations *brought* to the text to situate its events in common experience"; and
(4) "ways in which the world of the text has been shaped by the idiosyncratic experiences and imaginings of individual readers."[15]

The degree to which Envisionments in poetry depend on these different levels of confidence, which are in fact *levels of importation* of detail and nuance, that is, of *integrating frame-structure or schemata*, from extraneous, extraliterary, experiential sources, has not yet begun to be investigated.

An anecdote here may convey some sense of their power and function. In my seminar at San Francisco State, we were discussing a work by Rae Armantrout, "Grace," a short poem in three sections, each of which, for the purposes of this discussion, can be said to embody the title concept. Here is the first:

a spring there
where his entry must be made

signals him on[16]

Three differing Envisionments were offered to account for this passage, a process close to Ludwig Wittgenstein's proposition that "meaning is what an explanation of meaning explains."[17] In the first, a diver was about to enter a swimming pool, the spring found in the resilience of the diving board. In the second, an actor was about to go onstage, and the spring in his first step was vital in creating the spirit, the literal, physical rhythm of the role. In the third, a person was attempting to enter a forest or climb a mountain, but was blocked, unable to make progress until a spring opened up a path. All three present narrative scenarios, schematizations imported into the reading so as to contextualize its terms, particularly "spring" and "entry" (the subjects, respectively, of the host and embedded sentences). Note that the third Envisionment, which seems fanciful, defines "spring" as a flow of liquid, rather than as a bouncy quality. This parallels Armantrout's own authorial Envisionment, which was that of vaginal lubrication. That her Envisionment should be no more "explicitly justified" by the text is not surprising. [...]

What renders the phrase "Migratory Moon" problematic [and] accounts for the varying Envisionments in "Grace" [...] is the *Parsimony Principle*. Like Envisionment, frame, and schema, this is a concept appropriated from the work of linguists concerned with elaborating a theory of ideal readers, one of whom is posited to exist for each given text,

someone who knows, at each point in a text, everything that the text presupposes at that point, and who does not know, but is prepared to receive and understand, what the text introduces at the point.[18]

The Parsimony Principle converts the latency of the text and the ideological dimensions of presupposition into the actual Envisionment, combining frames always to a maximum of unification with a minimum of effort. It can be defined thusly:

Whenever it is possible to integrate two separate schema into a single larger frame-structure by imagining them as sharing a common participant, the reader will do.[19]

The Parsimony Principle is what enables some readers to discover narratives in poem after poem of Bruce Andrews. It is the process through which, to adopt the terminology of Alan Davies and Nick Piombino, we "connect the dots."[20] It governs the trope of anaphor so essential to any reading, described in "The New Sentence"[21] under the figure of the syllogism, and which Charles Bernstein has termed "projection."[22] [...]

With the Parsimony Principle in place and some differentiation as to levels of experiential importation (or "confidence"), we can return to the problem of "Migratory" and proceed through the remainder of the text. There is *no* device which explicitly determines the appropriate frame for "Migratory." Insofar as whooping cranes do migrate, the title proposes, momentarily, that Envisionment. However, industrial cranes are a part of urban lifestyle, a schema that can incorporate "cars" and "cellophane tape / on a school book" as *Grus americana* cannot. The Envisionment is both set up and countered, each step in this process displacing expectation, a shift, literally, at the level of semantics. Not only does "Migratory" resist any final fixity, but when it comes to "cranes," the reader has no means of knowing what the poet "is talking about." [...]

A major device of "Migratory Moon" is to be found in all the terms which conjoin, "and" in the first sentence, "like" in the second, "but" and the multiple occurrences of "and" in the third. Just as conjunctions bring lexical items together, so do prepositions. In nine of the thirteen lines of this text one or the other is used to express the relationship between terms. These categories ascribe such relations *even in the absence of verbs*, enhancing a reactive Envisionment.

"Like cellophane tape / on a school book" may be the first semantic shift so pronounced as to be noticed as such by the reader. The term of comparison, "like," is the most active of coordinate words, marking as does no other conjunction the presence of a point-of-view being asserted. In this sense, it carries that shadow of a speaker within it that is found also in any verb. To the degree that it enables the reader to better resist the granting of the frames introduced, it impedes the Envisionment. In "Migratory Moon," the impediment is intended: the schema to which the reader is being led will not integrate into any frame that could have been constructed from the information thus far received. The purpose of "like" is to render the very constructedness of this dissonant moment perceptible.

This event is not instantaneous, but occurs instead in time, in the continual *re*vision of expectation. At "cellophane tape," the reader must recognize the shift demanded of her Envisionment, yet the prepositional phrase "on a school book" transforms the instant, yielding a new *and competing* Envisionment of much greater specificity than that of the first three lines plus title.

This new Envisionment's function lies in its frame structure, the reader's experience of "cellophane tape / on a school book." The meaningful aspect of this schema, the engine of its humor—and it is funny—is to be discerned in its "triviality." The social sources of this are several. First, such tape on a book is apt to be nearly invisible, an opposition to its sharpness as a verbal construction. Second is a social convention which holds that what is important about a book is not its binding, and even less so a patchwork repair. Third is the social place of a text specifically intended for use in school and the individual reader's response and associations to such an object. This element of the schema will vary with each person, thus contributing to the density and "authenticity" of the Envisionment. For example, it could be read as signifying books which are large, physically heavy, poorly written, and costly, therefore better purchased in a "used" condition. Fourth is a much more controversial social convention holding that students themselves are an unproductive, thus trivial, segment of society. [. . .] It is in precisely this way that ideological conflicts are inbuilt into even the most apolitical of images "like cellophane tape / on a school book."

By the time the reader reaches "The wind bangs," she should be so oriented to the undulating, convoluting sequence of semantic shifts as to viscerally feel the poem's first verb. "The wind" returns us to an earlier stage of the work, skipping back over the new Envisionment to recall the suspended previous frame of outdoorsness. The repetition of the noun implies that each sentence is so separate as to make any backwards-pointing anaphoric use of pronouns pointless. Foregrounding the sentence-as-unit renders the language more braked and distorted, while setting up the coming use of reiteration in the last line to be perceptible as the moment of completion.

As a device, "the car" adds to (and revises) the earlier Envisionment. It follows the frame of outdoorsness, but does so within a context of human use, with no relation to whooping birds, yet capable in itself of a migration.

A transformative moment in the poem, this line is different from those which came before, continuing beyond a comma and through a conjunction. "But" is also a kind of negation, and of what could have been a complete sentence in itself. A narrator is introduced, as is a new schema, that of singing out loud. The acknowledgment of the speaking subject, "I," comes in the precise middle of the middle line of the poem, equidistant from either use of the term "cold." Structurally elegant though it is, a more important device occurs in "but," which serves to throw (right at the instant of the manifestation of humanity, or at least subjectivity) the entire relation of cause-and-effect in this text-world into a state of strangeness. At this point the reader may begin to suspect that she will never know what the poet here "is talking about."

And "help, help" doesn't, contrasting a cry for assistance with the frame of singing. Whether this formal inappropriateness is a part of the device or not is problematic, insofar as the punctuation surrounding this embedded cry also ascribes quietness, an equally unsuitable (or semantically shifted) quality. Nor, without knowing the date of composition, is it possible to know whether an allusion to the Beatles may be intended, with its potential for impacting on the total Envisionment of the work.

The following line returns us to the outdoors. "Sky" is a frame which can include the moon, an object perceived as white. It is here, and only within this and the next line, that the narrower, more "concrete" schema *moon* seems fully warranted. In this penetration of the text we see the title functioning as a caption. It links up with these lines to develop a frame suggesting that what is addressed and identified as "you" might be the moon. Again, however, there are as many reasons to conclude that this is not the case. The schematization moon is weak in comparison to the more consistent outdoorsness. The radical separateness of previous sentences and the shift in form of address here undermine any confidence in the continuity of focus. Finally, the question posed is senseless if asked of the moon while the "sky gets white / and whiter and whiter and whiter," unless the reader superimposes some imported schema such as snow. Like "cellophane tape / on a school book," the intervention of the title in the text at this point sets up a competing Envisionment not to be resolved by the work as a whole.

That the "you" has no identifiable signified, that "you" is, literally, absent, is the thrust of the question: where, under such circumstances, are you? Beyond the moon, one possible response might be that "you" is an Other, specifically a lover. While this interpretation situates the poem well within a subgenre of the "lover's lament," note that it requires an importation of meaning that rests entirely on a knowledge of literary conventions extraneous to the text.

If the poem is read as turning on, or even completing itself within, the word "you," the remaining lines serve only to provide closure. Yet the enjambed phrase "reincarnate / blossoms" goes well beyond such a modest function. Like the bird "cranes" and, in another sense, "the car," "reincarnate" is a term that fits a "Migratory" schema. It also contains the word "car," the long *a* of "cranes," and even an allophonic scramble of the word "crane." The noun "blossoms" adds one last complicating supplement to the frame of outdoorsness, stressing a pastoral Envisionment which recalls that of the poem's first three lines. Even if "reincarnate" were linked directly to "Migratory" (violating the integrity of these adjectives' nouns), no narrower frame than *the seasons* would result. Rather, "reincarnate" functions more as a tease, and "blossoms" as a final component to a complex, unstable whole *not equal* to any single Envisionment.

What, then, is there about this text such that a reader like Schjeldahl might not know what the writer "is talking about"?

(1) An unstable—or, better, *destabilized*—total Envisionment;
(2) key terms which resist final definition or specificity, such as "cranes" and "you";
(3) evidence that the title does not "name" the poem as a whole, but functions instead as a caption;
(4) a seeming rejection of anaphoric connection between sentences.

Given this, what is there about this text that a reader might not "doubt that every word is in felt contact with actual experience beyond the experience of words"? The outdoors schema combined with the perceptible determination of every device. Even those elements, such as "cellophane tape," which resist totalization into the dominant frame-structure, bear by their very opposition a relation to it, "felt contact," so that *the whole can be said to determine every device*, specifically with the function here of insinuating unity and closure.

Yet the degree to which this coherence is a direct consequence of the Parsimony Principle acting within the mind of the reader and not the simple determinism of the text can be gauged by the fact that "Migratory Moon" is *not* the title of Ceravolo's poem, but the result of a typographical error. The word in *Transmigration Solo* is "Noon." A single letter transforms the work. The implications of events such as the cold or the whitening of the sky are changed radically, while "Migratory" itself takes on a new spectrum of possible connotations, that of time passing and of the difference in hour from zone to zone. Yet, like the competing Envisionments of the first section of Armantrout's "Grace," there is a limit. Of the four answers given to the first of our questions with regard to the text in *Parnassus*, only one need be altered: "Migratory Noon" is not a caption. The two versions arrive at very dissimilar unifications, but each argues a totalization easily felt by a reader.

What can be drawn from this as a contribution toward an eventual shared vocabulary for poets and readers of the contemporary poem? First, that essential to such a lexicon would be a *theory of the device*. Such devices can best be determined and described *by function*, by the shifts which they create in the semantics of the poem, so as, in turn, to demonstrate the contribution of each part to the construction of the whole, whether that be the single Envisionment of a vulgarly "realist" text or something more problematic and complex. Without a theory of the device, there can be no rhetoric or listing of those actually in use.

Central to such a theory would be a description of what occurs, both on the page and within the reader, within the infinitesimal space of a semantic shift in relation to the Parsimony Principle, restated here for its broadest application:

> Whenever it is possible to integrate two separate elements into a single larger element by imagining them as sharing a common participant, the mind will do so.

One area of further articulation of the Parsimony Principle would be to establish at a finer level of discrimination the degrees of experiential importation which are required at any moment in a text, and to develop the relationship between this process of applying social frames to linguistic material and the still embryonic theory of ideology.[23] [...] The ideological component within a given work of written art needs to be discussed within three separate frames: the instrumental one of "content"; the more dynamic frames of form, genre, and *écriture*; and that of the social construction of experiential schema. [...]

One distinction which needs to be made before a roster of existing devices can be elaborated is the degree that a procedure can be said to be the same or different when it occurs at different levels of integration, particularly above and below the linguistic level of the sentence. For example, the device by which "cellophane tape / on a school book" resists linkage with the dominant outdoors schema is its lack of an experiential participant shared by the other frame. This device functions much like Tolstoy's narrating horse which is consistent throughout that story, but for which readers do not "in real life" possess an experiential frame. [...]

Even if we were to grant all three above examples the status of a single device, we could in turn distinguish it from a procedure equally based on resistance to integration, but not because of some failure to share experiential frames. This is a distinction which Noam Chomsky attempts to make when he contrasts "Colorless green ideas sleep furiously," a string he describes as "grammatical," but "thoroughly meaningless and nonsignificant," with the same words in reverse order, "furiously sleep ideas green colorless." According to Chomsky, "a speaker of English," confronted with the first string,

> will normally read it with the standard intonation pattern of an English sentence. But given some permutation of the words ... from back to front ... he will read it with the intonation pattern characteristic of a list of unrelated words, each with a falling intonation.[24]

Chomsky's example of reversed syntax has some close cousins in recent poetry. Bob Perelman's "Alone" in "Cupid and Psyche" reverses "Pleasure" from the same sequence.[25] Charles Bernstein's "So really not visit a remember to strange ..." is partly a reversal of "As If the Trees by Their Very Roots Had Hold of Us."[26] The resistance to normal syntactic integration occurs because syntax, like time, is essentially unidirectional. Chomsky's explanation is that

> the only thing we can say directly is that the speaker has an "intuitive sense of grammaticalness." (95)

But is this "intuitive sense" not also an experiential frame?

Is the device of reversed syntax the same as the juxtaposition of larger non-integrating syntactic units, such as occurs in Lyn Hejinian's *Writing Is an Aid to Memory*?[27] Is it the same or different if the point of non-integration takes place at a linebreak as when it happens in the middle of a traditionally punctuated paragraph, as in Kit Robinson's "Fast Howard"?[28] In fact, isn't non-integration and the shifting of semantics at the level of grammar precisely what punctuation attempts to articulate, perhaps even to obliterate, through convention? Can we say that this device of the reversed text is the same when, as with Perelman, the mirrored poems are separated by only one page within the same sequence, yet in Bernstein's case do not even appear within the same book?

The answer to these questions concerning the status of the device is to be found in how we conceive of the part:whole relations of the poem. As I noted above, each part or device is determined according to its relationship to the whole. This might be called the first axiom of the poetic device, to which we must now add a second, this based on the implications of the very privilege given to expectation, to the process of experiencing, in the generation of semantic shifts at all levels. *There is no such thing as a whole.* This is because time divides the poem: it can never, even on completion, be experienced "at once." The reader is always at *some point* with regard to the reading. Conversely, point-of-view or position is always a part of the semantics, whether or not it shifts. It is a recognition in the change of point-of-view that is most often felt by the reader as the perceptibility of any device.

In collapsing the poem to the privilege of the static text, New Critics and other advocates of an incomplete formalism lose sight not merely of the contributing participation of any reader's experience, but also the dimension of an everpresent and *never stable* temporality. It is only in the light of a triangulation of these three dimensions—text, time, reader's experience—that we can begin to ask, let alone answer, the question: is coherence only an effect?

By coherence I do not simply intend to indicate *referentiality*, as poets have come to use that word. Lyn Hejinian's *My Life* is as powerful an argument for coherence as can be imagined, yet the text resolutely problematizes narrative constructions.[29] The deliberate artificiality of its repeated phrases, true captions, is a necessary component in the book's vision of self-valuable constructedness. So that even if few of the sentences "follow" one another, a total Envisionment of a unified presence is carried forward to the nth degree. [...]

If, as "A Sentimental Journey" demonstrates, coherence is just an effect, the first task in elaborating a new rhetoric of poetic devices currently in use would be to identify those which motivate the semantic shift of closure. The tyrannical privilege of totality and those devices which can be utilized to counter this "unity effect" need also to be explained. [...] I have suggested, through a crude synthesis of Russian Formalism, recent linguistics, and the Althusserian theory of ideology, that the reading of any simple poem must involve the domains of all these disciplines. The Parsimony Principle is the point at which they connect.[30]

NOTES

1 Joseph Ceravolo, *Transmigration Solo* (West Branch, Iowa.: Toothpaste Press, 1980), in *Collected Poems*, ed. Rosemary Ceravolo and Parker Smathers (Middletown, Conn.: Wesleyan University Press, 2013), 2–24.

2 Peter Schjeldahl, "Cabin Fever," *Parnassus* (Spring/Summer 1981), 297 (emphasis mine).

3 Ibid.; original in *Collected Poems*, 17.

4 Viktor Erlich, *Russian Formalism: History-Doctrine* (New Haven, Conn.: Yale University Press, 1981), 190–91.

5 Walter Benjamin, "The Work of Art in the Age of Mechanical Reproduction," in *Illuminations*, trans. Harry Zohn (New York: Schocken, 1969), 276.

6 Robert Grenier, *Oakland* (Berkeley: Tuumba Press, 1980).

7 John Searle, *Speech Acts* (Cambridge: Cambridge University Press, 1969), 119.

8 Charles J. Fillmore, "Ideal Readers and Real Readers" (unpublished paper), 16.

9 Raymond Williams, "Marxism, Structuralism and Literary Analysis," *New Left Review*, 1st ser., no. 129 (September–October 1981): 63. This is a restatement of the Althusserian view.

10 Fillmore, "Ideal Readers," 13. Cf. also Paul Kay's "Three Properties of the Ideal Reader" (unpublished).

11 Manfred Sandmann, *Subject and Predicate* (Heidelberg: Winter, 1979), 70.

12 John Ashbery, *The Tennis Court Oath* (Middletown, Conn.: Wesleyan, 1962), 33.

13 Viktor Shklovsky, *The Theory of Prose*, trans. Benjamin Sher (Elmwood Park, Ill.: Dalkey Archive, 1990).

14 In *Theory of Prose*, but cited in this translation in *The Formal Method in Literary Scholarship: A Critical Introduction to Sociological Poetics*, by Pavel Medvedev and Mikhail Bakhtin (Baltimore: Johns Hopkins University Press, 1978), 89.

15 Fillmore, "Ideal Readers," 13 (emphasis mine).

16 Rae Armantrout, *Extremities* (Berkeley: The Figures, 1978), 13.

17 Ludwig Wittgenstein, *Philosophical Grammar*, trans. Anthony Kenny (Berkeley: University of California Press, 1978), 69.

18 Fillmore, "Ideal Readers," 7.

19 This follows the definition given in Kay, "Three Properties."

20 Alan Davies and Nick Piombino, "The Indeterminate Interval: From History to Blur," $L=A=N=G=U=A=G=E$ 4 (1981): 31–39.

21 Ron Silliman, "The New Sentence," in *The New Sentence* (New York: Roof, 1987), 63–93.

22 Charles Bernstein, "Writing and Method," in *The Difficulties* 2 (1982), reprinted in *Guide*, 46–54.

23 Cf. Louis Althusser, "Ideology and Ideological State Apparatuses," in *Lenin and Philosophy* (New York: Monthly Review, 1971); and Goran Therborn, *The Ideology of Power and the Power of Ideology* (London: Verso, 1980).

24 Noam Chomsky, *The Logical Structure of Linguistic Theory* (New York: Plenum, 1975), 94–95.

25 Bob Perelman, *7 Works* (Berkeley: The Figures, 1978), 87, 89.

26 Charles Bernstein, in *Controlling Interests* (New York: Roof, 1980), 37–38; and *Senses of Responsibility* (Berkeley: Tuumba, 1979), respectively.

27 Lyn Hejinian, *Writing Is an Aid to Memory* (Berkeley: The Figures, 1978).

28 Kit Robinson, *Down and Back*, (Berkeley: The Figures, 1978), 11.

29 Lyn Hejinian, *My Life* (Providence, R.I.: Burning Deck, 1980).

30 This project has had a lot of help. The students in my seminar at San Francisco State first posed the basic issues. George Lakoff introduced me to the work of Fillmore and Kay. Aaron Shurin, David Levi Strauss, and Kimball Higgs gave me opportunities to try out drafts on audiences. Jean Day first caught the typo in *Parnassus*. Barrett Watten closely read one version, offering hundreds of ideas.

PUBLICATION: Excerpted from *Close Reading* (1982), 2:27–41.

KEYWORDS: linguistics; New York school; critical theory; readings.

LINKS: Ron Silliman, "Composition as Action" (*PJ* 3), "The Dysfunction of Criticism: Poets and the Critical Tradition of the Anti-Academy" (*PJ* 10), "'Postmodernism': Sign for a Struggle, Struggle for the Sign" (*PJ* 7), with Leslie Scalapino, "What/Person: From an Exchange" (*Guide*; *PJ* 9); Fanny Howe, "Silliman's *Paradise*" (*PJ* 6); Jed Rasula, "What Does This Do with You Reading?" (*PJ* 1); Rae Armantrout, "Silence" (*PJ* 3); Andrew Benjamin, "The Body of Writing: Notes on the Poetry of Glenda George" (*PJ* 4); George Hartley, "Jameson's Perelman: Reification and the Material Signifier" (*Guide*; *PJ* 7); Lyn Hejinian, "Hard Hearts" (*PJ* 2); Ted Pearson, "The Force of Even Intervals: Toward a Reading of *Vernal Aspects*" (*PJ* 2); Andrew Ross, "The Death of Lady Day" (*Guide*; *PJ* 8); Reva Wolf, "Thinking You Know" (*Guide*; *PJ* 10); Barrett Watten, "The Politics of Style" (*Guide*; *PJ* 1).

SELECTED BIBLIOGRAPHY: *The New Sentence* (New York: Roof, 1987); *In the American Tree* (ed.; Orono, Me.: National Poetry Foundation, 1986); *Crow* (Ithaca, N.Y.: Ithaca House, 1971); *Mohawk* (Bowling Green, Ohio: Doones, 1973); *Nox* (Providence, R.I.: Burning Deck, 1974); *Ketjak* (San Francisco: This, 1978); *Tjanting* (Berkeley: The Figures, 1981); *BART* (Hartford, Conn.: Potes & Poets, 1982); *The Age of Huts* (New York: Roof, 1986); *Under Albany* (Cambridge: Salt, 2004); *The Age of Huts (Compleat)* (Berkeley: University of California Press, 2007); *The Alphabet* (Tuscaloosa: University of Alabama Press, 2008); *Revelator* (Toronto: Book Thug, 2013); with Bruce Andrews et al., *Legend* (New York: L=A=N=G=U=A=G=E/Segue, 1980); with Rae Armantrout et al., *The Grand Piano*; with Michael Davidson et al., *Leningrad*.

The Politics of Style

Barrett Watten begins his essay "The Politics of Style" by responding to Ron Silliman's "The Political Economy of Poetry" (1981), which argued that "poems both are and are not commodities." For Watten, the politics of poetry ought to be seen "in terms of the function poetry performs within language itself." In developing his argument, Watten takes up structuralist linguist Roman Jakobson's six "linguistic functions" that may coexist in any act of communication. Jakobson defines the "poetic function" as "the foregrounding of language for its own sake" that predominates in poetry, even as all other aspects of communication (like "the referential") remain in play. In seeking a poetics that conveys a politics that is not defined by overturning reification or the commodity form, Watten turns to Charles Olson's controversial reading at the Berkeley Poetry Conference (1965), where Olson abandoned poetry on the page to enter into a continuously unfolding, improvised performance. Citing Terry Eagleton's _Criticism and Ideology_ (1981), Watten shows how the rapid frame shifts and foregrounding of signification in Olson's "uninterruptible discourse" are both ideological (thus mystificatory) and critical (and unmasking). For Eagleton, "history enters the text as ideology, as a presence determined and distorted by its measurable absences"; for Watten, Olson's foregrounding of negativity in performance occasions poetry's entry into language and politics.

In "The Political Economy of Poetry," Ron Silliman begins his analysis of the material basis of poetry thus:

> Poems both are and are not commodities. It is the very partialness of this determination which makes possible much of the confusion among poets, particularly on the left, as to the locus, structure, and possibilities of literary production's ideological component.

In fact, the reason for this confusion lies in the paucity of identification, either in writing or in criticism, of actual poetics with political intentions. The causal necessity of the "commodity" as a material basis for the poem is a construction indicating the lack of a politically viable poetic method. Rather than seeing the agency of a poem as latent in, or in some sense determined by, the object status of the book, one could better analyze the politics of poetry in terms of the function poetry performs within language itself. What is wanted is a consideration of this function as exterior, autonomous, in the world, and here the commodity status of the book is a cue. [...] Poetry extends itself by its own means, in the act of writing, in public readings, and as a published text, into the political context.

Silliman is correct in asking for a "three-dimensional consideration of ideology." What the text accomplishes on its own is significant; the question remains whether the commodity status of the book is a dominant or a supporting convention. Obviously, the specific slant on "the commodity" brought to a book, both by an author and by the producer of the book, is an aesthetic choice with ideological dimensions. There are greater and lesser degrees of conjunction, however, between the content of a book and the manner in which it is produced. For example, the notion of "fame" in the works of Keats and Coleridge came into being parallel to the expansion of the reading public brought about by the increased mass production of books. That notion of fame survives in such postmodern Romantics as Olson and Ginsberg, but it is a reaction to the modernist compression, rather than any fact of the book trade, that allows for their "all-over" poetics. The writing is stylistically committed against the commodity; it is not readily packageable work, even if the City Lights "Pocket Poets" series provides a convenient package. Production values often differ wildly from ideology; for example, the low-budget mimeograph output of the New York School often tails the art market with covers by Alex Katz, Larry Rivers, and other known visual artists. Here poetry is borrowing from the stronger market, and in this manner such work as stylistically aspires to commodity status, in poetry, tends toward areas with long-established ideological superstructures. In a country with no real successors to Sandburg and Frost we still have a market for academic poetry (from George Keithley's *The Donner Party*, a Book-of-the-Month Club selection, to Iowa Workshop sonnet series) and magazine verse (*Redbook*, verse intended to compete for white space with cartoons). [...]

While "the book" can be thought of as a kind of template or outer form, style operates within the medium of language itself, altering that medium, which includes ideology. The manner of that operation is specific to the structure of a given language. This assertion is a major theme of Prague School linguistics, from Roman Jakobson's paper "On Czech Verse" in the early 20s to his position in *Style in Language*, a collection of papers from a conference held at the University of Indiana, in the early 50s. These papers, from the competing points of view of structural linguistics, behaviorist psychology, and new criticism, form an interesting cultural document. However, the range and power of Jakobson's methods extend well beyond those of any of the other participants. Jakobson is given virtually the last word on the subject in his "Concluding Statement: Linguistics and Poetics," summarizing the relation between style and language thus:

> There is a close correspondence, much closer than critics believe, between the question of linguistic phenomena expanding in space and time and the spatial and temporal spread of literary models.

The inner ordering of the text, its variation within what is possible in a given language, accounts for its propagation in that language, much as the spread of other linguistic facts reflects the systematic nature of the medium. Style is taken to be the coming into being of autonomous values which are allowable in but not essential to a language. Communicative acts exist in a continuity from the act of speech to literary products for Jakobson. [...]

An exemplary analysis of the mechanism of style is given by Jakobson in his paper "Linguistics and Poetics." "Linguistics is likely to explore all possible problems of relation between discourse and 'the universe of discourse.'" Jakobson characterizes this relation in terms of six functions of speech, deriving his model from Saussure's distinction between *langue* and *parole* but increasing its complexity by proposing these distinct modes contained within an individual act of speech:

> The ADDRESSER sends a MESSAGE to the ADDRESSEE. To be operative the message requires a CONTEXT referred to ... a CODE ... common to the addresser and addressee ... and finally a CONTACT, a physical channel and psychological connection ... enabling both of them to enter and stay in communication.

These six parts of Jakobson's schema of speech correspond to six functions in language itself. That is, language, not only in the context of speech, internalizes these six elements. In Jakobson's vocabulary these six functions of language are (together with a sense of their relation to poetry):

1) The *emotive*, corresponding to the addresser or "I," in which the addresser says something on his own behalf. In poetry both self-expression and the figure of self, as in Olson's *Maximus Poems*, reflect this.
2) The *conative*, corresponding to the addressee or "you," in which the addressee is to be found inherently in language. If Mayakovsky had

said, "Live, it is good!" to a crowd of six hundred persons, the conative would have been involved.

3) The *referential*, corresponding to the context, in which something is referred to. The referential includes not only Yvor Winters's tree but Pushkin's proliferation of statues. That is, the literary series of facts, as well as the facts one sees out the window, involve the referential function.

4) The *phatic*, in which language establishes contact between communicating parties. According to Jakobson the phatic is the only language function possessed by birds. In Ed Friedman's *Telephone Book* the first half dozen exchanges in any conversation usually establish nothing but the contact between speakers. On the other hand, continuity is often maintained for its own sake in poetry. "It's a poem . . . based on uninterrupted statements," Olson says of his first work, "The K."

5) The *metalingual*, corresponding to the code, in which language refers to itself. This sentence as it typifies a function in language is metalingual. In Jakobson's schema the metalingual is involved whenever communicating parties need to refer to the terms of the language itself. Metalanguage in poetry, then, comes into the foreground when there is a need to establish the values of words. A good contemporary example is the reinforcement of the noun phrase by the dictionary definition form in Coolidge's *The Maintains*.

6) The *poetic*, in which the structure of the language itself enables the message to be perceived. The poetic function in language as a whole, then, is its internal ordering. Literature partakes of the "poetic" as well as of other functions. The rhythm and sound relations that allow poetry its autonomy point to the "poetic"; similarly, the sound pattern of a language as a whole allows for a consideration of "the message for its own sake."

According to Jakobson, "any attempt to reduce the sphere of poetic function to poetry or to confine poetry to poetic function would be a delusive oversimplification. . . . Poetic function is not the sole function of verbal art but only its dominant. . . . In all other verbal activities it acts as a subsidiary, accessory constituent." It would make sense equally to speak of the poetics of advertising, professional language, or language itself. For Jakobson, the message rests in the "poetic," as it is bound in by rhythm, sound, grammar, and tropes. Jakobson gives the following capsule summary of how the poetic function works:

The poetic function projects the principle of equivalence from the axis of selection into the axis of combination.

If statement in a poem is imagined to be given along a temporal line, the poetic function would be the principle which extends the values of the poem (in terms ranging from sound to content) into its materials. As Zukofsky once said, "I grant that that might be only more or less well stated, that is all."

This fact of poetic language, rather than, say, the emotive or referential, is foregrounded by authors as otherwise far apart as Charles Olson and Steve Benson. A continuity is built of equivalence in many of the *Maximus Poems* and in Benson's *The Busses*. Whereas in Olson the emotive voice, the "ich dichter," is perceptible as a person behind the words, in Benson the formal argument intervenes to render ambiguous the real location of the author. In both cases, however, the time line is the axis of a continuity that argues, by iterating the "principle of equivalence," as a construct. Here, then, Olson's "uninterrupted statement" in the face of all other structures, both in poetry and in the world, begins to take on its political cast:

> Put an end to nation, put an end to culture, put an end to divisions of all sorts. And to do this you have to put establishment out of business. It's just a structure of establishment. And my own reason for being, like I said, on the left side and being so hung up on form is that I feel that today, as much as action, the invention, not the invention, but the *discovery* of formal structural means is as legitimate as—*is* for me the form of action. The radical of action lies in finding out how organized things are genuine, are initial. . . .

This identification of radical formal means with phenomena gives great insight into Olson's method. Olson's "initial" opposes itself to mutation and dispersal; it is his "axis of selection." "Initial" acts are hinges of historical and poetic progressions; in "Some Good News" the history of Gloucester and the poem begin with the single act of "fourteen men." Olson's poetic project is to project this value onto all other events. In his attack, Olson takes on numerous hitherto "divided" series and orders them on an "axis of combination" in poem, which uses an in-time romance of self as its basic structure. A characteristic, then, of both Olson's being as a poet, as a constructed entity, and his literary work, is the rendering of divided subject matter and literary forms into units that can be operated on by a poetic "principle of equivalence." Olson says as much himself:

> One wants narrative today to . . . strike like a piece of wood on a skin of a drum or to . . . be plucked like a string of any instrument. One does not want

narrative to be anything but instantaneous in this sense.... In other words, the problem, the exciting thing about poetry in our century is that you can get image and narrative both to wed each other again, so that you can get both extension and intensivity bound together.

Olson's "image" here might be better seen in the light of the notions of motif in folktale or device in poetry as used in the Formalist analysis. Olson is building an *imago mundi* in his poem, but it is one in which the impression of the image comes from stopping narrative at a moment in time. While this seizing of narrative has a great advantage in terms of motivation in the poem, it is also extremely unstable. A condition of Olson's image, then, is its immediate mutation in time, and Olson's poems duly record that fact. The devices of narrative, which in Formalist terms create the "time of expectation" in a literary work, fall instantly back on themselves, creating an impression both of impatience, the desire to get on with it, and of stasis—argument is exhausted at the precise point of the image, as in:

> the Wall
> to arise from the River, the Diorite Stone
> to be lopped off the Left Shoulder

Here "extension and intensivity" are linked in this isolation of a moment of a continuity of inspired, nearly prophetic discourse. The result is the compression of both emotive and referential arguments, the personal and literary experience of Gloucester, to little more than names. An unusual topography is evoked, to say the least. There is a similar topography in the prophetic works of Blake, and its political use is, crudely, aimed at a disruption of commonplaces of rational procedure. Olson's *imago mundi* is likewise political; however, an element of dissolution is present in his plans for the future.

And the future did arrive. If Olson's actual writing proceeded by means of the compression of narrative time to an imagistic radical, his in-time self also aspired to that compression. In his lecture at the Berkeley Poetry Conference, 1965, the *image* of the poet caught among masses of atomized, contingent narratives and pushing out against them communicates much more clearly than Olson's actual negotiation with those narrative blocks. His performance is remarkable for the number of arguments left unfinished—with people in the room, with his own past, and with the poem. Rather the frantic movement from one thing to the next is identified in Olson's assertion of the moment as *the* value of his approach to his material. The hinge of the story becomes the story in its own right. Olson's refusal of closure gives the affect of presence, and this imagistic "stand" appears as the "solution" to a lifelong public and political dilemma. In fact, the theme of Olson's political experience, the failure of liberal politics from the Roosevelt era to the present, is central to Olson's assumption of the hero-poet. That some present felt that Olson was, on this occasion, "as good as his poems" shows that this crisis was accepted as essential by many. Prefigured by the "extension and intensivity" of his writing, Olson achieved a "resolution" in real time of at least part of his original motivation. The poetic act had become the "uninterrupted statement" that Olson saw in his first poem, "The K." But now, any possible material could be rendered by the poetic "principle of equivalence" to a moment in actual time:

> Absolutely! In the sense of the population explosion: the whole terrestrial angel vision, baby! Like, if I get to be President, I told you about who was going to be my Secretary of State for Love.... I mean, is there or is there not a Great Business Conspiracy called America and Russia? It was proved by a West German, writing in 1946 or 7, in *Der Dinge Zeit* or something, a great man, a man most of you, because you don't read enough, don't even know. And the guy was dying.... Dig! I mean value, let's talk! Words are value, instruction, action, and they've got to become political action. They gotta become social action. The radicalism lies from our words alone. And if they're not right—and I'm not talking Mr. Williams's "republic of words." I'm talking our selves here in this week, the poets of America. And I don't mean America: I saw Ezra Pound, like an Umbrian angel, listening to anything that's said, going to see LeRoi Jones, which...I saw it....just walked in, thank god, seven o'clock, after the reading in the Teatro de something, Melisso, Jesus, Melisso, Melissa. Doesn't it sound like honey and sweet song? Yeah, exactly. Melissa, Caio Melissa, Teatro Caio Melissa, Spoleto: which means "spoiled."

With this brief foray into the political use of language in its poetic function, the more general question of the relation of a text to actual politics comes up. In his *Criticism and Ideology*, Terry Eagleton, far from locating literary work in the mechanics of a class position, proposes that "ideology" in a text is composed of elements of both the underdevelopment and overdevelopment of statement. Ideological values of a work can to some extent be determined by a consideration of possibilities which are excluded from the text. "Something is by virtue of what it is not." Eagleton makes an analogy between the underdevelopment of ideology and the avoidance of areas of maximum conflict in the language of dreams. For Eagleton:

History enters the text as ideology, as a presence determined and distorted by its measurable absences.

Such a measurable absence in Olson's work is any form of cultural center. That is, there is no *polis* in Olson's work. It is not Gloucester; Olson quotes with approval an article by J. H. Prynne which says as much. Rather, *polis* is exploded and dispersed by the act of the poem. This displacement argues of necessity a psychologically elaborated topography in which persons, places, and things enter in a kind of "dream time." The poem reflects this topography on the level of style, constantly deviating from direct statement, in fact, from the sentence, and accepting only "the modality of song" as its possibility. The elaboration of this topographical modality, then, is a motivation for the "principle of equivalence" in the poem. The fact that there is no cultural or structural "bottom line" is a primary source of the linguistic reality of the work. In Eagleton's terms, the autonomy of the text has a valid ideological component by virtue of its creation of an autonomous world *in* the text:

> For the text presents itself to us less as historical than as a sportive flight from history, a reversal and resistance of history, a momentarily liberated zone in which the exigencies of the real seem to evaporate, an enclave of freedom enclosed within the realm of necessity.

Hence, the text sets up a reality principle in its own right. Here a Marxist critic comes to recognize one of the true conditions of literature, though it may not necessarily be "sportive."

Politics, normally jealous, wishes for the sole right of expression of the terms for the transformation of conditions. That is, politics often claims both the language of social transformation as well as its mechanism to be its proper ground. Politics and poetry might be said to be competing for the right to represent the possibility of transformation, then. The value of Eagleton's approach, beyond the affirmation of the autonomy of the poetic text, is that it constructs a relation by which the seemingly competing claims of poetry and politics can coexist. Poetry can only be a part of the actual world. So:

> The literary text seems ... to produce its own object, which is inseparable from its modes of fashioning it—which is an effect of those modes rather than a distinct entity.

The agency of the literary text is in the production of its *own* effect. It neither affirms nor creates the truth of anything existing prior to it. This seeming autonomy, however, does reflect points of stress in ideology, both in the "literary series" and exterior to the text. In the Formalist account, the succession of literary forms proceeds in terms of the atrophy of defunct modes, and this process can be internalized as conflicts in the text. Perhaps the method of Williams's "no ideas but in things" had become for Olson a defunct mode. Likewise, the nonidentity, the non-fit of the literary work in relation to its model is a motive for further production; the generative force of Olson's borrowing of Edward Dahlberg's mythological figures in the face of the actual Gloucester would be an example of this. Thus:

> The pseudo-real of the literary text is the product of the ideologically saturated demands of its modes of representation.

The "constructive potential" of the work derives, partly, from the demands placed on the available but overloaded and inadequate modes of statement. Olson's use of the already existing schema of Williams and Dahlberg led to conflicts in the work that finally arrived at a synthesis of "fact" and "myth." But the non-fit and exhaustion of these modes of representation were responsible for what Jakobson calls "the superinducing of the equivalency principle," the non-stop "irritable reaching after" everything in Olson's work. Just as the phenomenon of *zaum* poetry in the Russian Futurist movement burst from the confines of literary models that could not accommodate contents which had irrevocably changed, so the mass of contingent detail that could not be integrated into the prior American modernist models produced the "superinduction" of Olson's Berkeley reading.

And then what happened, for this possible person in the thirty-eight years removed front seats:

> The signifying process is thrown into a certain relief.

By the excess of signification involved. This is not to gloss over the problem of the "ich dichter," in his own words "one of the most devious, non-objective, plural, subjective sons-of-a-bitch this side of the wind." But there is a useful distinction between means and effect, between the person and the work. An experience of the overload of signification to the point of autonomy—as occurs when the "principle of equivalence" becomes a continuity in actual time—is more generative than an identification with the Romantic figure intended by Olson. An identification with the parts of that psychology would lead only to less successful reproductions of Olson's conflicts. Such conflicts operate only up to the production of the text, or the poetic act, for Olson and not for anyone else. "If it is to be a finished text, its non-solution must signify" (Eagleton), and it is the non-solution of Olson's work that is of most interest. This denial of the final reality of organic form is, of course, a project of Marxist criticism:

> The function of criticism is to refuse the spontaneous present of the work—to deny that "naturalness" in order to make its real determinants appear.

But this is not just a question of "critical method"; it is also accurate to the effects on an auditor of Olson's Berkeley reading. The availability of materials in the discourse—the *linguistic* present created—far outweighs the "in-time romance of self" in importance. Neither is this response a "neutral evaluation"; the rejection of Olson's paternalist psychology, with its cooptation of common familial experience, and his manipulation by means of physical presence, and almost a wall of sound, is a matter of some conflict. Only later do the political consequences of the Romantic position appear, insisting on the advantage of its defects in the precedence of language over self. And from that point one can enter the work, in which comparative mythology, particle physics, continental geomorphology, popular culture, and the landscape of dreams become, in the image, "extension and intensivity." In this sense, Olson's creation of a non-static *imago mundi* is the real success of his work.

The chain of literary acts, then, is a continual sequence of non-identities. In various stages the grounds for the work are processed into the work, the work produces new ground, and so on. Eagleton makes an interesting analogy to the relation of the text for a play to its staged production. Writing can be described as a production of authorial intention; the written work is further produced as a material book; and the work in book form is produced by a reader, either in private or in public. At each stage labor is advancing; by such labor an inhabitable world can be built, though its initial scale might be small. However, the question of this process separates from the more-or-less "ideal" position expounded by Eagleton and insists on a commitment to, rather than a distance from, new developments in writing. The critical intervention is not really needed in one sense—the overload of signification of the post-modern Romantics meets a politically informed self-consciousness in a number of current writers. One reason for this self-consciousness might be the perceived failure of the politics of the post-modern Romantics after the period of the Donald Allen anthology. That that failure parallels almost exactly in time the defeat of American imperialism in Vietnam is significant; conditions have changed, to say the least. Beyond the need for analysis, there is a new social command, to which current literary production is offered as a response.

SOURCES

Benson, Steve. *The Busses*. Berkeley: Tuumba, 1981.

Eagleton, Terry. *Criticism and Ideology*. London: Verso, 1978.

Jakobson, Roman. "Concluding Statement: Linguistics and Poetics." In Thomas Sebeok, ed., *Style in Language*. Cambridge, Mass.: MIT Press, 1960.

Olson, Charles. *Muthologos*, vols. 1 and 2. Bolinas, Calif.: Four Seasons, 1979.

Silliman, Ron. "The Political Economy of Poetry." *L=A=N=G=U=A=G=E*, vol. 4 (1981).

Voloshinov, Valentin. *Marxism and the Philosophy of Language*. New York: Seminar Press, 1973.

PUBLICATION: Excerpted from Introduction (1981), 1:49–60.

KEYWORDS: linguistics; New American poetry; critical theory; negativity.

LINKS: Barrett Watten, "The Literature of Surface" (*PJ* 7), "Missing 'X': Formal Meaning in Crane and Eigner" (*PJ* 2), "On Explanation: Art and the Language of *Art-Language*" (*PJ* 3), "Robert Creeley and 'The Person'" (*PJ* 9), "Social Space in 'Direct Address'" (*PJ* 8), "What I See in *How I Became Hettie Jones*" (*PJ* 10), "The XYZ of Reading: Negativity (And)" (*PJ* 6); Beverly Dahlen, "Forbidden Knowledge" (*Guide*; *PJ* 4); Ron Day, "Form and the Dialogic" (*PJ* 10); Arkadii Dragomoshchenko, "I(s)" (*Guide*; *PJ* 9); Norman Finkelstein, "The Problem of the Self in Recent American Poetry" (*PJ* 9); George Hartley, "Althusser Metonymy China Wall" (*PJ* 10); David Lloyd, "Limits of a Language of Desire" (*PJ* 5); Bob Perelman, "Good and Bad/Good and Evil: Pound, Céline, and Fascism" (*Guide*; *PJ* 6); David Plotke, "Language and Politics Today" (*PJ* 1); Lorenzo Thomas, "The Marks Are Waiting" (*Guide*; *PJ* 10).

SELECTED BIBLIOGRAPHY: *Total Syntax* (Carbondale: Southern Illinois University Press, 1985); *The Constructivist Moment: From Material Text to Cultural Poetics* (Middletown, Conn.: Wesleyan University Press, 2003); *The Poetics of New Meaning*, ed., *Qui Parle* 12, no. 2 (Spring/Summer 2001); with Carrie Noland, *Diasporic Avant-Gardes: Experimental Poetics and Cultural Displacement* (ed.; New York: Palgrave Macmillan, 2009); *Barrett Watten: Contemporary Poetics as Critical Theory*, ed. Rod Smith, *Aerial* 8 (1995); *Opera—Works* (Bolinas, Calif.: Big Sky, 1975); *Decay* (San Francisco: This, 1978); *Plasma/Parallèles/"X"* (Berkeley: Tuumba, 1979); *1–10* (San Francisco: This, 1980); *Complete Thought* (Berkeley: Tuumba, 1981); *Progress* (New York: Roof Books, 1985); *Conduit* (San Francisco: Gaz, 1987); *Frame: 1971–1990* (Los Angeles: Sun & Moon, 1997); *Bad History* (Berkeley, Calif.: Atelos, 1998); *Progress/Under Erasure* (Los Angeles: Green Integer, 2004); with Rae Armantrout et al., *The Grand Piano*; with Michael Davidson et al., *Leningrad*.

Constellations I Practices of Poetics

Boone, Bruce. "Kathy Acker's *Great Expectations*." One of the principal early proponents of New Narrative, Boone offers a confrontational yet celebratory review of Kathy Acker's "shameless" novel. Acker's transgressive emotional content "NAMES NAMES" and results in a direct personal connection that reinserts subjectivity into postmodern writing.

PUBLICATION: *Women and Language* (1983), 4:77–82.

KEYWORDS: New Narrative; postmodernism; sexuality; readings.

LINKS: Boone, "A Narrative Like a Punk Picture: Shocking Pinks, Lavenders, Magentas, Sickly Greens" (*PJ* 5); Kathy Acker, "Ugly" (*Guide*; *PJ* 7); Michael Amnasan, from *Joe Liar* (*PJ* 10); Dodie Bellamy, "Can't We Just Call It Sex?: In Memory of David Wojnarowicz" (*Guide*; *PJ* 10); Steve Benson, "Personal as Social History: Three Fictions" (*PJ* 7); Robert Glück, "His Heart Is a Lute Held Up: Poe and Bataille" (*Guide*; *PJ* 2); William McPheron, "Remaking Narrative" (*PJ* 5); Laura Moriarty, "Sex and Language" (*PJ* 8); Larry Price, "Harryman's Balzac" (*PJ* 4).

Bromige, David. "Philosophy and Poetry: A Note." Bromige compares the abstraction and redundancy of philosophical language against poetry as "philosophy sensuously apprehended" and enmeshed in the multiplicity of experience. Contemporary examples of poetry from the Language School demonstrate uses of language that are irreducible to concepts.

PUBLICATION: *Poetry and Philosophy* (1983), 3:20–24.

KEYWORDS: philosophy; Language writing; critical theory; language.

LINKS: Bromige, "Alternatives of Exposition" (*PJ* 5); Charles Bernstein, "Writing and Method" (*Guide*; *PJ* 3); Mikhail Dziubenko, "'New Poetry' and Perspectives for Philology" (*PJ* 8); Allen Fisher, "Poetry, Philosophy, and Difference" (*PJ* 3); Erica Hunt, "Beginning at *Bottom*" (*PJ* 3); Jackson Mac Low, "Some Ways Philosophy Has Helped to Shape My Work" (*Guide*; *PJ* 3); Ted Pearson, "Things Made Known" (*PJ* 10); Joan Retallack,

"Blue Notes on the Know Ledge" (*PJ* 10); Barrett Watten, "On Explanation: Art and the Language of *Art-Language*" (*PJ* 3).

Burke, Carolyn. "Without Commas: Gertrude Stein and Mina Loy." Carolyn Burke's scholarship on Mina Loy spurred a revival of interest in her poetry and her radical feminism. Burke demonstrates Loy's theoretical interest in Bergson, Freud, and Otto Weininger and cites her stylistic indebtedness to Stein as crucial for her poetics of "consciousness."

PUBLICATION: *Women and Language* (1983), 4:43–52.

KEYWORDS: feminism; modernism; psychoanalysis; readings.

LINKS: Charles Bernstein, "Professing Stein/Stein Professing" (*PJ* 9); Ben Friedlander, "Laura Riding/Some Difficulties" (*PJ* 4); Susan Bee [Laufer], "Kahlo's Gaze" (*PJ* 4); Leslie Scalapino, "Re-Living" (*PJ* 4).

Davis, Lydia. "Coolidge's *Mine*." In her review of Clark Coolidge's hybrid "prosoid" work *Mine: The One That Enters the Stories*, Davis admires Coolidge's "almost perfect" ear and the stylistic density of his turn to language, but she criticizes his relation to narrative as overly self-conscious and not fully in control of his experimental impulses.

PUBLICATION: *Poetry and Philosophy* (1983), 3:91–96.

KEYWORDS: Language writing; nonnarrative; genre; readings.

LINKS: Davis, "Some Notes on Armantrout's *Precedence*" (*PJ* 6); Edie Jarolim, "Ideas of Order" (*PJ* 5); Pierre Alferi, "Seeking a Sentence" (*Guide*; *PJ* 10); Bruce Campbell, "'But What Is an Adequate Vice to Limit the Liquid of This Voice'" (*PJ* 9); Alan Davies, "Language/Mind/Writing" (*Guide*; *PJ* 3); Carla Harryman, "Toy Boats" (*Guide*; *PJ* 5); Bill Luoma, "Astrophysics and You" (*PJ* 9); Jackson Mac Low, "*Pieces o' Six*—XII and XXIII" (*PJ* 6); Alice Notley, "Narrative" (*PJ* 5); Travis Ortiz, from "variously, not then" (*PJ* 10); Bob Perelman, "Plotless Prose" (*PJ* 1); Leslie Scalapino, "War/Poverty/Writing" (*PJ* 10); Diane Ward, "The Narration" (*PJ* 5).

de Laroque, Françoise. "What Is the Sex of the Poets?" De Laroque focuses on the concept of poetic "work" in Claude Royet-Journaud's anthology of French experimental writing, *Travail de poésie* (1980). Poetic work is gendered both masculine and feminine, active and passive; in her close readings, she deliberates on its manner of "working."

PUBLICATION: *Women and Language* (1983), 4:109–17.

KEYWORDS: French poetics; avant-garde; gender; readings.

LINKS: Pierre Alferi, "Seeking a Sentence" (*PJ* 10); Jerry Estrin, "Penultimate Witness: On Emmanuel Hocquard" (*PJ* 8); Lanie Goodman, "Georges Perec: Life Directions for Use" (*PJ* 3); Emmanuel Hocquard, from *The Cape of Good Hope* (*PJ* 8); "Télégrammes: Recent Québecois Writing" (*PJ* 8).

Fisher, Allen. "Poetry, Philosophy, and Difference." U.K. poet Allen Fisher charts a necessary distinction between poetics and philosophy. Poetics is more open to a speculative construction of new ways of making meaning extended from poetry (which may not yet exist), while philosophy, however methodologically open, is descriptive of what is made.

PUBLICATION: *Poetry and Philosophy* (1983), 3:17–19.

KEYWORDS: philosophy; U.K. poetics; language; genre.

LINKS: Fisher, "Postmodernism as Package" (*PJ* 7); Andrew Benjamin, "The Body of Writing: Notes on the Poetry of Glenda George" (*PJ* 4); cris cheek, ". . . they almost all practically . . ." (*PJ* 5); William Corbett, "Harwood/Walker and Raworth" (*PJ* 2); Paul Green, "Literate Tones: On John Wilkinson" (*PJ* 8); Peter Middleton, "The Knowledge of Narratives" (*PJ* 5); Ted Pearson, "The Force of Even Intervals: Toward a Reading of *Vernal Aspects*" (*PJ* 2); Gavin Selerie, from *Roxy* (*PJ* 8).

Fraser, Kathleen. "Overheard." A founding editor of the feminist journal of experimental poetics *HOW(ever)*, Fraser reviews three collections by "women poets of great privacy": Gail Sher, Mei-Mei Berssenbrugge, and Fanny Howe. She sees a common concern of these poets with feminist modernism in "the prizing of uncertainty as legitimate content."

PUBLICATION: *Women and Language* (1983), 4:98–105.

KEYWORDS: lyric poetry; feminism; modernism; readings.

LINKS: Rae Armantrout, "Silence" (*PJ* 3); Beverly Dahlen, from "The Tradition of Marginality" (*PJ* 6); Jean Day, "Moving Object" (*PJ* 9);

Barbara Guest, "Shifting Persona" (*PJ* 9); Susan Howe, "*My Emily Dickinson*, part 1" (*Guide*; *PJ* 4); Pamela Lu, from "Intermusement" (*PJ* 10); Jackson Mac Low, "*Persia/Sixteen/Code Poems*" (*PJ* 4); Lisa Samuels, two poems (*PJ* 10); James Sherry, "Dreyer's *Step Work*" (*PJ* 4); Chris Tysh, from "Dead Letters" (*PJ* 10); Barrett Watten, "What I See in *How I Became Hettie Jones*" (*PJ* 10); Hannah Weiner, "Other Person" (*PJ* 9); Ellen Zweig, "Feminism and Formalism" (*PJ* 4).

Hunt, Erica. "Beginning at *Bottom*." In a lucid and condensed summary, Hunt describes the overarching concern of Louis Zukofsky's *Bottom: On Shakespeare* as the primacy of visual evidence for knowledge. The relation of "love:reason::eyes:mind," however, is positivist and finally conservative; skepticism and distortion are equally necessary for knowledge.

PUBLICATION: *Poetry and Philosophy* (1983), 3:63–66.

KEYWORDS: modernism; philosophy; knowledge; visuality.

LINKS: Lyn Hejinian, "An American Opener" (*PJ* 1); Bob Perelman, "Good and Bad/Good and Evil: Pound, Céline, and Fascism" (*Guide*; *PJ* 6); Ron Silliman, "Composition as Action" (*PJ* 3); Barrett Watten, "Missing 'X': Formal Meaning in Crane and Eigner" (*PJ* 2).

Mandel, Tom. "Codes/Texts: Reading *S/Z*." In *S/Z*, Barthes demonstrates the relation between "work" and "text" in his reading of overlapping textual codes dispersed throughout the work. Mandel's critique of the reading of Balzac's "Sarrasine" is that it is nondialogic and assumes an automatic "textual processing" of a presumed linguistically competent reader.

PUBLICATION: *Close Reading* (1983), 2:49–54.

KEYWORDS: French poetics; narrative; intertextuality; readings.

LINKS: Bruce Campbell, "'Elsewhere': On Artaud and Barthes" (*PJ* 8); Beverly Dahlen, "Forbidden Knowledge" (*Guide*; *PJ* 4); Félix Guattari, "Language, Consciousness, and Society" (*PJ* 9); George Hartley, "Althusser Metonymy China Wall" (*PJ* 10); Lyn Hejinian, "The Rejection of Closure" (*Guide*; *PJ* 4); Bernard Noël, "Poetry and Experience" (*PJ* 3); Delphine Perret, "Irony" (*PJ* 3); Herman Rapaport, "Poetic Rests: Ashbery, Coolidge, Scalapino" (*PJ* 10).

Plotke, David. "Language and Politics Today." Plotke, a former editor of
Socialist Review, assesses the status of "language" for Marxist theory in the
early 1980s and with the emergence of revisionist modernism. "Language"
for Marxism reflects the dispersion of the political throughout culture; it
is both "heterogeneous" and resistant to "totalizing."

PUBLICATION: Introduction (1983), 1:35–48.

KEYWORDS: language; Marxism; politics; modernism.

LINKS: Kathy Acker, "'Culture doesn't account . . .'" (PJ 7); Michael
Amnasan, from Joe Liar (PJ 10); Daniel Davidson, "Bureaucrat, My Love"
(PJ 10); Michael Davidson, "The Poetics of Everyday Life" (PJ 9); Allen
Fisher, "Postmodernism as Package" (PJ 7); Félix Guattari, "Text for the
Russians" (PJ 8); George Hartley, "Jameson's Perelman: Reification and
the Material Signifier" (Guide; PJ 7); David Lloyd, "Limits of a Language
of Desire" (PJ 5); Steve McCaffery, "And Who Remembers Bobby Sands?"
(PJ 5); Kofi Natambu, "The Multicultural Aesthetic: Language, 'Art,' and
Politics in the United States Today" (PJ 9); Kit Robinson, "Time and
Materials: The Workplace, Dreams, and Writing" (PJ 9); Andrew Ross,
"The Oxygen of Publicity" (PJ 6); Rod Smith, from "CIA Sentences" (PJ 10);
Lorenzo Thomas, "The Marks Are Waiting" (PJ 10); Barrett Watten,
"Social Space in 'Direct Address'" (PJ 8).

Rasula, Jed. "What Does This Do with You Reading?" In an early review of
Ron Silliman's Tjanting, Jed Rasula points to the constructivist aspects
of the work, citing the importance of the reader and the linguistic
exchangeability of "subject" and "object": "The sentences are workers.
All parts are studios. Silliman's is a study in assembly relationships."

PUBLICATION: Introduction (1983), 1:66–67.

KEYWORDS: Language writing; critical theory; performance; reading.

LINKS: Rasula, "Rodefer's Lectures" (PJ 3), "On Rothenberg's Revised
Technicians of the Sacred" (PJ 6); Steve Benson, "Close Reading: Leavings
and Cleavings" (Guide; PJ 2); Alan Davies, "Close Reading Close Reading"
(PJ 2); Johanna Drucker, "Close Reading: A Billboard" (PJ 2); Steven
Farmer [Roberts], "Reading Eye Lets" (PJ 3); Lyn Hejinian, "Hard Hearts"
(PJ 2); Fanny Howe, "Silliman's Paradise" (PJ 6); Stephen Ratcliffe, "How

to Reading" (*PJ* 6); Barrett Watten, "The XYZ of Reading: Negativity (And)" (*PJ* 6); Reva Wolf, "Thinking You Know" (*Guide*; *PJ* 10).

Ross, Haj. "Poems as Holograms." A post-Chomskyan linguist who sought alternatives to generative grammar, Haj Ross looks at lyric poetry using methods developed by Roman Jakobson's structuralist poetics, to show how sonic patterning and semantic framing can be conjoined in poetry seen as going beyond "the conduit metaphor" of communication.

PUBLICATION: *Close Reading* (1982), 2:3–11.

KEYWORDS: linguistics; lyric poetry; meaning; readings.

LINKS: George Lakoff, "Continuous Reframing" (*Guide*; *PJ* 1), "The Public Aspect of the Language of Love" (*PJ* 6); Yulia Latinina, "Folklore and 'Novoyaz'" (*PJ* 9); Ron Silliman, "Migratory Meaning: The Parsimony Principle in the Poem" (*Guide*; *PJ* 2); Barrett Watten, "Missing 'X': Formal Meaning in Crane and Eigner" (*PJ* 2).

II Numbers 5–7

Ugly

One of the most influential postmodern feminist writers, Kathy Acker explodes the politics of gender, sexuality, and genre in a series of experimental texts that have revolutionized narrative prose. Her technique of appropriation—pastiching pornography with autobiography, contemporary politics with traditional fiction, and psychoanalytic explorations with textual *détournements*—undermines narrative representation while creating new possibilities. At once excessive and subversive, Acker's writings expand the sphere of the (un)speakable, after de Sade, the French surrealists, and Georges Bataille, but from the perspective of a radical feminism. "Ugly" is a futuristic narrative of human cruelty, misery, and revolutionary unrest set in a hypothetical present—an imagined, alternative Paris of the 1980s erupting with racial and class violence, anticipating historical events that would take place, two decades later, with the revolt of the *banlieux*. Her text presents a radical critique of colonialism, class, and capital using techniques of narrative defamiliarization. In both method and content, Acker's work was an important precedent for writers of her generation such as Dodie Bellamy, Dennis Cooper, Carla Harryman, Kevin Killian, and Chris Tysh, while her influence continues with emerging writers such as Renee Gladman, Rob Halpern, and Tisa Bryant. Kathy Acker died on 30 November 1997.

In the face of suicide, in the face of those living corpses who are trying to drag us into their own suicides, in the faces of those old men, there seem to be two strategies:

One is a pure act of will. To bang one's head against a wall, preferably a red brick wall, until either the red brick wall or the world, which seems unbearable and inescapable, breaks open. The Algerians in Paris had banged their heads against walls for years, on the street. Finally their heads opened into blood.

The second strategy wasn't exactly one of will. The heads, being broken, gave up. Gave up in the face of the unopposable suicide of the owning class. Gave up in the face of the nothingness of the owning class. Because, for the Algerians, the world of humans was creepy disgusting horrible nauseous shit-filled exacerbating revolting, humans not revolting, green smelling of dead rats which were decaying and, in endless decay, covered in, like a royal blanket of flowers, purple herpes pustules which had riveted and cracked into fissures either to the body's blood or to the earth's blood, pale green and pale pink liquid minerals in the bottoms of one-thousand-feet-diameter strip mines in Arizona. Blood of the earth leaks into death. A chicken whose head had been cut off ran around like a chicken without a head. Because the head of a person who'd just been guillotined, lying on the earth, for five minutes remembered what had just happened to its head and body. Because in almost every nation political torture was a common practice so there was nowhere to which to run. Because most of the nations' governments are right wing and the right wing owns values and meanings: the Algerians, in their carnivals, embraced nonsense, such as Voodoo, and noise.

The Caribbean English slave-owners in the nineteenth century had injected a chemical similar to formic acid, taken from two members of the stinging nettle family, into the already broken skins of their recalcitrant slaves. Ants crawl ceaselessly under the top layer of skin. And forced their unwilling servants to eat Jamaican "dumbcane" whose leaves, as if they were actually tiny slivers of glass, irritating the larynx and causing local swelling, made breathing difficult and speaking impossible. *Unwilling to speak* means *unable to speak.*

When Mackandal had been a child, a cane mill shaft, running over his right arm, had crushed his arm to its shoulder. With every force he had the tiny child pulled the mangled fragments out of the machine. Delirious he remembered something—Africa—many kinds of animals easily running, loping, over rolling hills—him running alongside of and as fast as these animals who accepted him as their friend, without effort. He remembered all that he couldn't name. From then on, the child did not name. Not until. He wanted to unite his people and drive out the white Parisian owners. Once he knew unity, he would begin to name. Until then, his words were the words of hate. Mackandal was an orator, in the opinion even of Mitterrand, equal in his eloquence to the French politicians and intellectuals, and different only in superior vigor. Though one-armed from the childhood accident, he was fearless and had a fortitude which he had and could preserve in the midst of the crudest tortures.

"In the beginning of the world," Mackandal once explained, "there was a living person. Because a person has to be living before he or she can be a corpse. The white people believe that death is prior to life.

"In the beginning, in his or her beginning, this living person is both physical and mental, body and spirit. The body must touch or cross the spirit to be alive. Touching they mirror each other. A living person, then, is a pair of twins.

"In the beginning, the twins are children. Children are the first ones. I'm a child," Mackandal explained himself. His brown hair was sticking so straight out of each angle of his head that it seemed to be a wig.

"After a while, my children," Mackandal also wore a top hat and was as thin as anyone's shadow, "it was no longer the beginning. The two children had aged and died. There existed two corpses.

"After another while, the people who came after and after remembered the first children. Those first two beings were now two loa.

"I, then, or you, or he or she or even it, is five: body, spirit, living, dead, and memory or god. The whites make death because they separate death and life." Obviously this black, like horses dogs cats and some wild animals, judged a human not by the skin's colors but by how she or he behaved.

From 1981 to 1985, for five years, Mackandal built up his organization. But revolutions usually begin by terrorism. His followers poisoned both whites and their own disobedient members. But this wasn't enough terror to start a revolution in such a bourgeois city.

Most of Mackandal's followers were Algerians, and even other Black Africans, who hadn't been content only to hover in the shadows corners alleyways of the city like tamed animals who had once been animals of prey, who were not content only to be alive by dying, slowly. Being godless this trash had only itself to turn to. Being ambitious vengeful burning with pride fierce as any blood-stained beast these remnants of oral history sought more than their own survivals. They sought revenge for the past and paradise for the future. They lived in camps in the squalor of the northernmost sections of Paris or in the crime-infested eastern areas. If you could call it *living*.

The Parisian and the French government desired simply to exterminate the Algerian trash, the terrorists, the gypsies. The urban sections inhabited by Algerians were literally areas of plague to the Parisians who knew how to speak properly. The French authorities murdered pregnant women. They made every Algerian they could locate carry a computerized identity card. As a result, one rebellion, for instance, that took place over a vast city block, part of which was a deserted parking lot, in the south, lasted a hundred years until every Parisian deserted the zone altogether.

As a result of this *urban* rather than *political* situation, by 1985 city ordinances prohibited all blacks from going anywhere at night unless accompanied by a white and carrying a special governmental ordinance. Even in broad daylight three or more blacks who talked together or even stood together without at least an equal number of whites were considered to be a terrorist cadre and subject to penal disciplines up to death. Night searches in the slums, the gypsy camps, would have been frequent if the flics, as bourgeois as all other Parisians, hadn't preferred the warmth of their own Parisian couscous to a possible knife in the groin. Whenever a flic caught an Algerian with a weapon, such as a pencil, the flic was rewarded and the Algerian punished in some manner that was always very public. But there were too many Algerians, blacks, in the slums, the shadows, the alleyways, the deserted Metro stations: by 1985 an official police report states that "security was now non-existent" for whites in Paris. It was unwise for whites to act.

Not only did Mackandal's direct followers steal on Metro lines, from the apartments not only of the rich, not … Mackandal himself walked through the city of the whites as freely as he pleased. Whoever was of the disenfranchised the unsatisfied the poor those so wallowing in misery they were almost mindless, what the white call "zombie," followed him and did not know why. Not knowing was their only possible way. Just how many of the urban semi-inhabitants—*semi* because only partly alive—chose to follow this desperate man and this desperate path cannot be known. We have wallowed in non-knowledge for not long enough.

Since it is easy enough to kill, terrorism, unlike conventional rebellion, cannot be stopped. Mackandal grew sick of thievery, pillaging, arson. When a person arises from that poverty which is death and can begin and begins to dream, these dreams echo the only world that has been known or death. Soon such dreams of negation are not enough. Mackandal no longer was interested in petty violence: he dreamed of paradise, a land without whites. He determined to get rid of every white.

The Algerian women who had been forcibly sterilized by the French. The street-cleaners. Etc. Everywhere, in the shadows where they couldn't be seen because they were too low and black, Mackandal's followers learned the fastest ways to poison whites. Mackandal especially concentrated on those who labored as servants: he taught them about herbs, the puffer fish and the scaly toad. From old women who lived alone in basements and in the outskirts of the city under used-up and left-over McDonald's stands, Mackandal himself learned how to regulate the human body with natural chemicals. A person who eats even a small amount of the tetrodotoxin of the puffer fish or fugu feels pale, dizzy, and nauseous. Insects seem to be crawling just beneath the skin. The body seems to float. Drool drops out of the mouth while sweat runs out of the pores—the body is deserting the body—the head is aching and almost no temperature exists. Material is cold. All is ice. Nausea; vomiting; diarrhea; the eyes are fixed; it is almost not possible to breathe; muscles twitch then stop, paralyzed. Unable to move you. Eyes are glass you. The soul lies in the eyes. The mental faculties remain acute until shortly before death; sometimes death does not occur. Many many herbs. In time, like ink on a blotter, poison seeped into the lives of the whites. Poison entered the apartments of the bourgeoisie. There is a way to stop guns and bombs. There's no way to stop poison which runs like water. The whites had industrialized polluted the city for purposes of their economic profit to such an extent that even clean water was scarce. They had to have servants just to get them water and these servants, taught by Mackandal, put poison in the water.

One day Mackandal arranged for the poisoning of every upper-middle- and upper-class apartment in Paris. The old man didn't need to suicide. While, due to their beloved, almost worshipped, victuals, the white Parisians writhed around, bands of Algerians and other blacks appeared out of their shadows and alleyways.

In the meantime, Spanish sailors, longtime anarchists, had flowed in from the ports near Paris, via the Seine, in orgies of general hooliganism and destruction. Pale blue and pink condom boxes cluttered up the brown river. Diseased and non-diseased sperm flowed down the Champs-Elysées. Empty needles lay under bushes north of the Ted Lapidus on the rue du Four. Drunk with animal blood and whatever else they had been pouring into their mouths, these sailors, black white and other, who couldn't speak a word of French, began breaking into shops, taking whatever merchandise they could stuff in their mouths pockets pants and assholes. As soon as they realized this merchandise meant nothing to them (except for the contents of the pharmaceutical cabinets), they trashed the stores. Soon the hardy men, though inured to longer days of boredom, grew tired of this game.

They joined the Algerians, their brothers, who were breaking into flats of the rich. The whites were already trembling from fear, nausea, and diarrhea. A few of them managed, hands raised over heads, to shove themselves against wall-papered walls. The blacks no longer backed off. The few sailors who had been doomed to remain on their ships, at the western edge of the city on the filthy river, from the far distance saw this city: Algerians, blacks swarming everywhere: dogs nudging over garbage cans with their cold black noses. The flames of cigars and lit candles overflowing the churches falling on this mass of garbage ignited it, starting thousands of tiny fires which finally had to grow.

The whole city was in flames. In the middle, a very tall very thin black man stood. Finally the winds, instead of fanning fires, swirled the dead ashes which used to be a city.

A group of white soldiers in the American Embassy, off the corner of the Louvre, when the looting had started, had held three innocent Algerian boys and one girl who had entered the Embassy out of curiosity up to one wall with machine guns. The soldiers acted exactly as they had been trained. First they asked the blacks the name of their leader. There was no reply.

"If you don't tell us what we want to know, we're going to kill one of you."

The Algerian boys were between the ages of twelve and eighteen and the girl was six. They looked at each other. None of them said a word.

Doing his duty, a soldier, a lieutenant, twisted one of the Algerian boy's arms behind his back until the cracking of a bone could be heard. "Watch," the American lieutenant told the other three Algerians. The lieutenant's other hand, grabbing the boy's chin, yanked it up and back while his knee kept the lower spine straight. When the boy's growing black eyes fell straight into the lieutenant's face, the lieutenant's face registered no emotion. He simply increased the pressure of his double pull until the young neck cracked. The boy still wasn't dead. Blood fell out of the left side of his mouth.

Finally the youth said more than blood to the American. "Kill me." The American had already killed him.

When another soldier started playing with one of the youngest boy's balls, the girl tried to protect her friend by biting at the soldier's hands. The soldier kicked her head. She lay lifeless on the expensive marble floor.

"Who's your leader? Do you want all of you to die?" the soldier who had the authority asked the two boys.

"Don't tell them anything. Never tell Americans anything cause all they know how to do is kill," the oldest boy instructed the youngest.

From the floor the girl watched another death.

All the soldiers turned to the remaining boy. The girl watched them turn to the remaining boy. She watched them emotionlessly, sexuallessly, without caring, torture him to the point they realized they could not get information out of him then murder him. She perceived these men were not humans.

One man grabbed her by her hair. "Slut." The word surprised her. She wasn't sure what they were talking about.

"Do you see what's happened to your little friends? Don't you want to grow up?"

"Yes," she said. They were adults.

"Do you know how much pain your friends felt?"

All she knew was that the world, totality was terror. She screamed out Mackandal's name, all the other names of leaders which she could remember, and then they killed her.

Such betrayals or rather such hideous perceptions of the totality of terror, of the fact that there is nothing else in this world but terror, happened so often that finally the whites who were left had Mackandal in their grasp.

They didn't bother to speak to the Algerian leader. They hit him over the head, handcuffed him to a steel post inside some room in the same embassy, which by now was almost deserted. The lieutenant who had killed the first boy took out his cigarette lighter. He was going to burn Mackandal to death in reprisal for the lack of respect the Algerians had shown to the Americans. With this, the whites seemed to have regained the city.

As the first flames lit up the bottoms of his pants and socks, being more inflammable than his shoes, Mackandal whose guiding spirit, surprisingly, was Erzulie, the spirit of love, that is not of fertility, but of that which longs beyond reality infinitely, of all unrealizable desire, screamed so awfully the soldiers who were burning him thought they were in the presence of a victim of madness. His body began to shake, not in spasms, but regularly, not as if from flames, but as if possessed. He tried to tear his wrists from the handcuffs. A small section of a corner of that room had been decimated by a bomb. With a single almost invisible spasm the black leader in flames succeeded in wrenching himself out of his handcuffs. Before the dumbed Americans could react, still burning he was half-way across the room and through the hole.

It was not known what happened to Mackandal. Poisonings of whites continued: finally the Algerians won Paris. Except that more than a third of the city was now ash.

I had escaped from the rich old man, from his seemingly causeless desire to murder me, to this. I wondered whether I wanted to return to the old man. They always say that money equals safety, though I'm not sure who "they" are or about whose safety they're speaking.

It used to be that men wandered over the earth in order to perceive new phenomena and to understand. I was a wanderer like them, only I was wandering through nothing. Once I had had enough of working for bosses. Now I had had enough of nothing.

PUBLICATION: *Postmodern?* (1987), 7:46–51.

KEYWORDS: New Narrative; postmodernism; politics; race.

LINKS: Kathy Acker, "'Culture doesn't account ...'" (*PJ* 7); Bruce Boone, "Kathy Acker's *Great Expectations*" (*PJ* 4); William McPheron, "Remaking Narrative" (*PJ* 7); Robert Glück, "His Heart Is a Lute Held Up: Poe and Bataille" (*Guide*; *PJ* 2); Steve McCaffery, "And Who Remembers Bobby Sands?" (*PJ* 5); Harryette Mullen, "Miscegenated Texts and Media Cyborgs: Technologies of Body and Soul" (*Guide*; *PJ* 9); Bernard Noël, "Poetry and Experience" (*PJ* 3); Andrew Ross, "The Oxygen of Publicity" (*PJ* 6); Leslie Scalapino, "War/Poverty/Writing" (*PJ* 10); Barrett Watten, "Social Space in 'Direct Address'" (*PJ* 8); Ellen Zweig, "Feminism and Formalism" (*PJ* 4).

SELECTED BIBLIOGRAPHY: *Bodies of Work: Essays* (London: Serpent's Tail, 1996); *Essential Acker: The Selected Writings of Kathy Acker*, ed. Amy Scholder and Dennis Cooper (New York: Grove, 2002); *Politics* (New York: Papyrus, 1972); *The Childlike Life of the Black Tarantula: Some Lives of Murderesses* (San Diego: Community Congress, 1973); *Ripoff Red: Girl Detective* (San Francisco: pvt. ptd., 1973); *I Dreamt I Was a Nymphomaniac: Imagining* (San Francisco: Empty Elevator Shaft, 1974); *The Adult Life of Toulouse Lautrec by Henri Toulouse Lautrec* (New York: TVRT, 1975); *Kathy Goes to Haiti* (Toronto: Rumor, 1978); *Great Expectations* (New York: Grove, 1982); *Blood and Guts in High School* (New York: Grove, 1984); *My Death My Life by Pier Paolo Pasolini* (London: Pan, 1984); *Don Quixote, Which Was a Dream* (New York: Grove, 1986); *Empire of the Senseless* (New York: Grove, 1988); *In Memoriam to Identity* (New York: Grove, 1990); *Hannibal Lecter, My Father* (New York: Semiotext[e], 1991); *My Mother: Demonology, a Novel* (New York: Pantheon, 1993); *Pussy, King of the Pirates* (New York: Grove, 1996); *Eurydice in the Underworld* (London: Arcadia, 1997).

Total Equals What Poetics and Praxis

Language writing from its beginnings sought to engage political theory and to stage the writing of poetry as a social practice. Bruce Andrews, who since 1975 has taught political science at Fordham University, was cofounder and coeditor (with Charles Bernstein) of *L=A=N=G=U=A=G=E*, published from 1978 to 1982. In the following essay on poetics and politics, first presented as a talk at Canessa Park, San Francisco (17 May 1985), Andrews presents a vision of layered strata of linguistic structure and social praxis, or, in Marxist terms, "revolutionary, critical-practical activity." He maps the relationship between language and society from a baseline of signification and practice, through mediating forms of discourse and power, toward a horizon that merges language and society in "totality" as a set of structural limits and ideological practices. Responding in part to Lyn Hejinian's essay "The Rejection of Closure," Andrews writes: "It's a commonplace that language denies closure, and that language is a kind of openness. But I think we've come to recognize the need for a more social conception of what that openness is—and to frame what's open against the dangers of closure." In his view, poetic form should address and challenge the social limits of language and experience, necessitating a move from explanation to agency: "what to do/prescription."

Upset within this context, public discourse, writing in & on the social body, possibility of meaning (horizon, system, dialogue, limits) how far extended, comprehended, challenged.

Today I want to talk about the social ground and the social dimensions, political dimensions as well, of recent writing within this extended community. And I want to draw an analogy, throughout, between language and society—both in terms of explanation (of how those things are understood) and also in terms of praxis and prescriptions deriving from that explanation.

First, in terms of explanation, the link is between conceptualizing the nature of the social order and how it's organized and trying to conceptualize the nature of the material of writing. That material I'm going to be talking about as systems of meaning in a way that's broader than signification, broader than the structure of the sign, but something more like 'sense' or 'value' in a more social dimension. Second, in terms of prescription, again I want to draw a link between writing and politics in the prescriptions that follow directly from those understandings. So these are prescriptions about how to intervene, or come to terms with, both the nature of writing and its materials and the nature of society and *its* materials—in a way that stresses the implicit prescriptions that are involved in writing. (For example: if it's a question of how to stop repressing the process by which it's made, then it matters how that process gets defined—whether you define it in terms of signification, more narrowly, or whether you define it more broadly, as I'd like to do, in terms of 'making sense.')

Things don't change fast enough.

Talking about society and writing both, I want to introduce a picture of *levels* that I think parallels the way you can talk about language being organized, on the one hand, and society being organized, on the other; so that you can see the way these levels exist, in a sense, in a series of concentric circles—one larger, one outside each—or almost like a series of interlocking Chinese boxes.

With society, on the one hand, you can talk about this surface level or this first level as a social order as a kind of decentered constellation of different practices, of differences, of heterogeneity, of pluralism, a micro-politics of fragments on this inner circle. Second, beyond that, you can talk about those multiple interests or points of activity being organized into a dominant hegemony and a variety of counter-hegemonies trying to challenge that hegemony, organized into specific functions, specific struggles, and specific blindnesses within society. And then third, as an even more extended perimeter, you can talk about the outer limits of something like a totality, an overall horizon of restriction and constitution, a limit, a set of organizing principles within the social order. A dominant paradigm. (In the American case, talking socially, you would then be talking about something like the relations of domination within a corporate-run, almost 'one-dimensional' type of society or capitalist patriarchy that exists also with a certain role and position within the world system or the world political economy.) Limits, throughout, are a qualification of action. Suffocating within these limits.

As a parallel, I think you can talk about language in a somewhat similar way. That language, being social, being socially constructed, suggests that what's not possible is a condition of transparency or presence or the aura. Because meaning isn't naturally reflected in language; language is producing it actively. There isn't a natural or automatic possibility of presence. This ends up being a dream, an illusion of satisfaction. Instead you have absence, displacement, the erosion of the aura.

If you talk about language in terms of these same levels I was using to talk about society, first, on the surface, you would talk about it as a set of differences, the production of meaning (as signification). Outside that you can talk about the structure of discourses: the way in which those differences get organized into a polyphony—of different voices, different literary traditions—that goes beyond merely talking about language as a system of signs; and, in a sense, put this system of signification or these utterances in motion, through action, through the organization of desire, through the organization of discourse.

Finally, like society, there's this final concentric circle for language in which polyphony is embedded. The polyphony inside, or the proliferation of signs and discourse is embedded in, limited in certain ways by, or collusive with, or inscribed in different ways by: this outer horizon, this set of limits, this set of ideologies, this overall body of sense that makes language into an archive of social effects.

1. Social Sense / Contextualizing Literary Choices (Explanation)

First, in terms of explanation, I'm interested in the way in which recent work in the literary world suggests how both language and society can be explained and understood in a way that can guide practice. Beginning with form, and politicizing that with the force of impatience, I think originally impelled this range of writing practices toward questioning tradition in styles and methodology. Because if all experience is constructed—is socially constructed—then writing which recognizes that fact ends up involving itself with a more active consideration of social questions. As form itself begins to seem autonomous, the path of writing cuts beyond form and style, beyond the dynamics of any local situation or mode of address, beyond the particular partners in a dialogue, and moves toward a more critical (or contextual) focus on meaning itself and on this overall social comprehension. And this I think involves a greater sensitivity to the matter of ideology—which is embodied in the discursive frames that we use and in the social arrangements which stage the possibilities for meaning to be produced (by authors) and also the possibilities for meaning to be realized (in a kind of reception/market). So that, beyond dealing with the sign—the formal underpinnings of *product*—recent work has tended to deal more with *method*, as a social *process*, as more than a question of form but as a question (or questioning) of society itself. [. . .]

And as long as we're acknowledging that language is rooted in communal experience, we're acknowledging also that it's socially saturated and that the communal experience which saturates it is organized. For that reason, a social dialogue must become possible—beyond the narrower interpersonal dialogue—that would be like the dialogue that internal polyphony has with its limits (with language; and also, as a constructive factor, with society). So if we start with a commitment to a writing praxis that's oriented toward the productivity of meaning, we become more aware that it's also involved with a kind of social sense, with this prior construction of opportunities and risks, this materializing of certain kinds of value rather than others.

Practice takes place within these systems of convention, and they're what make meaning possible—both linguistically (in terms of signification, or the structure of the sign) but also more broadly socially (as value, or sense). So that the dialogues and the layerings of voices and the ploys of communication, and rhetoric, utterances, are bound up by the coercive social limits of the possible. They're socially governed. That governing takes the shape of rules that are being followed or a context that's being adapted to—a context in light of which certain actions 'make sense.'

So there's this process by which the sign—the material body of the sign—is transformed into meaning. It's allowed to make sense—or not—and this process is socially organized, or coded, at the level of discourse. This is a social government of meaning or value that's built up on top of the structure of the sign. And it enables units in a text to function both as signs and also as pieces of this social body, as materializations of social value.

That's another reason why some of these parallels come into view. I mean, we're used to seeing language in use, or speech, framed against some systematic language, some language system—in the way the structuralists would talk about it. Politically, also, influenced by equally structuralist kinds of thinking, people are more used to seeing immediate issues of politics framed against the limits and shape of the social totality. In a parallel way, either language in use or language as a system can be framed against a social totality. So that the overall meaning system, in this sense, would be analogous to the social order or the nature of the social formation, of society as a unit.

Now, this established structure of value and sense is arbitrary—like the shape of the sign—but, on the other hand, it's also *imposed*, it's made to seem natural. And what's dislocated (sense and language) are brought together by a set of power relations. They're organized. They're organized by an apparatus or a machine of discourse, this policing system of something like power /

knowledge. These might not be fixed structures—there's always struggle going on underneath—but it is a configuration of forces out there, an empowered configuration with some historical weight to it. And it does seem to embody, at the same time, the possibility of a collective reference—however disfigured that may be. This may be more like a crossroads than a closed and fixed corpus, ready for the dissection table. But still: there's this clampdown by society on what's possible. So that this established structure of meaning isn't just being created and constituted at its core, day by day. It's also something that has stability; it has a certain force; it's institutionalized; it makes up a solid mode.

So if you think of discourse or ideology as something like a mode of production, then literature becomes something that's inscribed onto material within that mode. Not in a reductionist way, like a superstructure related to a base, but it's something that's mediated by meaning (which in this case would be operating like the means of production) and in which literature then is positioned more actively as the way the relations of production are organized. So: discourse, as mode of production; meaning, means of production; and the organization of writing, the relations of production. Now the hegemonic political organization of writing (literature) would end up seeming like a strategic project or paradigm of sense, of appropriating sense, of making use of it. And discourse itself (this larger figure) is also then articulated with society in a similar way. Even discourse begins to look like a paradigm of society, a strategic politics, a constitutive politics—with society as its field, its referent, its context, its target, and also as the condition of its slimy embeddedness.

From the point of view of trying to explain things, and thus orient praxis, scale looks like the issue here. The problem is total. Meaning totality. Or at least it's performed on the stage of totality. And by totality here, I'm talking about the internal organization of a society, a historically constituted social formation and its organizing principles, the way it defines itself in discourse and in social sense, as well as the apparatus of domination (or of power/knowledge) that holds it together. Totality, in that sense, would suggest the roots of discourse and the system of meaning within a national social order—some overall organization of ideology or ways of making sense that underpin the variety of signifying practices or cognitive forms.

Because writing's 'material' is discursively articulated, it's also culturally and politically articulated in light of these limits. The materials—or the building blocks of sense—are related internally in society as distinctions within a whole; and they're also organized to be mutually interdependent. They require each other as the ground of their *possibility*.

By calling attention to possibility, we're acknowledging that the totality isn't just a negative restrictive thing, or some deterministic program. It's also something that's reproduced by action within the system and, at the same time, it becomes a resource or a medium that can be drawn upon. So it's a source, for instance, of something like what Foucault calls 'positive power.' The social rules that are involved in it are positive, enabling, constructive, and constitutive. But it does have this horizon as well.

To imagine the limits of language (as an active process, as method) is also to imagine the limits of a whole form of social life—in this case, of a predatory social order (or an interlocking network of orderings) that desperately needs to be changed. Now, often the horizon goes unrecognized—and unchallenged—so that those limits, and the social world as a whole, are seen as natural, or they're not seen at all. [...]

I'm suggesting that the alternative for many of us has been to come up with a more explanatory vision of writing that could come closer to *comprehending*—by moving out and extending out into—this larger social whole.

2. Social Praxis / What to Do (Prescription)

[...] We hear occasionally about 'the death of meaning' within society, not just within certain schools of poetry. Meaning clearly didn't die. But it's possible that instead of remaining as a *content* that's relatively freely and easily appropriated, it's become the limits of method within a social order, that it's relocated itself within certain fixed modes, and that these need to be confronted with a more social or totalizing perspective within writing: one that recognizes the point of those fixed modes, those fixed blocks, as something that is *public*. A praxis which fits this more inclusive vision of what's at stake would be one that orients the privacies of the text toward a more public context to be addressed, intervened into, contested—or at least, to be *implicated*, for the reader as well as for the writer. So that highlighting the public (or social-political) implications of these relationships at least gives the possibility of a more public conception of the subject, of interpersonal relations and interpersonal experience, of intertextual relations (and also of politics, more broadly) at this public/social level.

The related collective project looks like one of articulating this content of contested social themes, of a social horizon—in order to better guide our choices and frame the experiences that we're operating with. For that reason, in discussions of poetry and politics, sometimes, I find it troublesome to hear 'politics' being instrumentalized—as for instance it is in neo-populist discussions; to think that the whole notion of politics involved with writing is being narrowed down to specific struggles toward change, while the contexts that are actually directly implicated in the use of writing are being ignored. Because this can corrupt our conception of what the public realm looks like by bringing with it, or even valorizing, manipulation or a kind of 'means justify the ends' point of view about what to do, how to proceed, and what's at stake. I'm suggesting instead that politics can also bring to mind the older sense of community good or public good rather than specific struggles. The idea of politics as, for instance, a matter of arranging community matters needs to be reinstated. Because here, in writing, I think it's also paralleled by a concern *for* language and for its limits and its point—the point of its organization. [...]

So, both in language and politics, there is registered this desire to have a totalizing perspective. And within language as well as within politics, it also may need to be equivalent in strength to the strength of the homogenizing impact of the totality on whatever is inside. Recent work that's challenging those things then becomes the rough equivalent, in praxis, of a totalizing stance for writing.

The task, beyond coding and decoding particular messages, is also one that raises the question: 'What is this code?' How is it that these codes are constructed? I think this suggests a way to explore these larger frames, the 'limits of the normative'—by foregrounding not only the shape of different stylistic traditions but also the shape of linguistic structure, of utterance structure, of discourse structure, and of the social codes which are also providing the limits for all of that.

It helps give an understanding of the limits as well as the building blocks of those social codes. Its contextualizing and reshaping and contesting are what I'm calling *totalizing*. Beyond form's maximizing of *act*, this would be a parallel maximizing of *context*, or of paradigm. More than just a pluralizing of voices and traditions within some taken-for-granted whole, and more than adding to the multiplicity of voices all situated within a system of social sense which is ungraspable, these would be ways of revealing the socially coded nature of larger units of language and of language as an overall system, and politicizing them by showing or implicating their place within one or another ideological bloc—which is a social bloc, some constellation of different social forces and social values outside.

So, this politicizing, or this totalizing, which is a form of radical *reading* embodied in writing, involves a comprehension of social limits that are built up on top of the limits of signification, the limits of the sign. This raises the possibility that our experience could be reoriented and made intelligible in a different way. It orients us to keep in mind, to keep facing, this larger other— this contextual horizon which shows the most broadly social possibilities of meaning being constructed. And social, here, means unnatural, or constructed. The grasp of these social limits can help to define the projected future of the work. Or if you don't want to talk about the future, or time, it would define the scale of the work—as a political act—which then recalls these questions about both explanation and prescription. [...]

Now, meaning isn't something that precedes explanation but it's constructed through a social method—an explanatory method—that places and positions texts within the horizon of some outer social world, and in that way reveals some connection between orders of the text and orders outside the text—not on a point-by-point basis (a naturalistic or referential basis) but at this meta-level, or this systemic level, in terms of the overall organization. So you'd be enabled to recognize the fit between experience (textual experience, individual experience, collective experience) and this larger envelope of meaning. And to see that fit as fidelity or as a kind of adequacy in an explanatory way, as the way things 'make sense,' seems appropriate in the light of some specific context and acquires value in the process of framing, and as they're felt to become intelligible. So that the links involved in this explanatory thrust aren't a kind of mechanical cause/effect link. Instead, you're starting with a purposive act, motivated by desire, [and] relocating those units within the largest totalizing of this context that's possible.

The praxis involves a contextualizing of the text, a pointing of the text beyond itself, and a re-mapping of the subject (the position of the author, the position of the reader) in terms of that larger interaction between writing and this social body (of meaning). [...] You're expanding to the limit this contextual horizon within which sense gets produced and realized. So that the relationship keeps extending outward—in a series of concentric circles—each one framing and bounding and making sense out of what's inside, so that the contextualizing is an expanding one. [...]

In the end, the grasp of the system of society, the meaning system, the explanations from which prescriptions can directly follow, involves pointing to this complicated fabric of power relations and domination, of control systems and normalization (the prison-house of language, the prison-house of society). The grasp involves making that contextualization as total as possible, so that we're facing the totality (or what we think of as that) with our explanations, or with the explanations that are implicit in the work. Beyond trying directly to give body to our dreams and our visions of what we want or imagine, there's also this implicit recognition, within that embodiment, of what the limits are, and of what's *pushing against* that and of what we therefore need to challenge and try to get beyond. [...]

We're trying therefore to get beyond established meaning from *within* the structure of meaning—not just bypassing it with 'experimentalism' of different kinds, but to risk it and to reveal its constructedness. [...] The act of enunciating becomes part of the content—in a way that makes the *social method* become visible (and not just to illuminate the products that can be carried through that method). [...]

The frames are insecure and they can be challenged. Laying bare the device remains as a task but it becomes a more social act, of social unbalancing, of a social reflexivity of content, rather than some kind of (what I have in the past called) preppie formalism. Because the modernism that's at stake now is more public and is more involved with the conditions of meaning, it also becomes more social. So that if people are arguing (as some of the post-structuralists seem to) that social meaning has disappeared, then just trying to disrupt the sign system with some radical formalism isn't going to be enough. Instead, if something's going to be disruptive, or disrupted, it's going to have to be *method*, seen in a more social sense—as the social organization of signs, as ideology, as discourse; those are the more broadly social things that need to be shaken up: historicized, politicized, contextualized, totalized—by laying bare the social devices, or the social rules which are at work. [...]

This acknowledges that if you want to talk about things like tradition, community or experience being built on more *legitimate* ground, that there's really this massive job of comprehension that's on the agenda first. Getting this demystifying and distancing perspective on the prior condition is going to be crucial. And so will writing that recognizes its social ground and contests it—that contests the establishment or the institutionalization of that social ground and its 'point' as well as its claims to authority and the claims to the 'natural' which that ground often (usually, in fact) carries with it. [...]

This foregrounding of the limits of the possible begins to seem like a form of address, increasingly global, so that when you're articulating a specific language (or experience or possibility) you're framing it, always, by addressing this implicit and more distant Other, this general system of language and the social principles and organization of meaning. The methods by which meaning arrives in a prefabricated way are challenged and, at the same time, the limits of the social order are questioned. There is this implicit recognition that meaning isn't just arbitrary (in the way the structure of the sign would suggest) but it's also systemic; it's based on these conventions which need to be restaged, reconsidered and reconvened, in a prefigurative way. Writing can acknowledge how constructed those norms are and, at the same time, try to create a kind of impossibility—so that you'd be able to restage the preconditions of being able to say ... everything. [...]

The praxis is one that implicitly recognizes the possibilities of constructing and reconstructing a society. It looks at the regulation of meaning as something inseparable from the way the social whole is composed, so that the way sense is regulated is analogous to the way that the social body is written. Language and writing wouldn't be regarded as something determined, externally, by a socio-economic system, for instance; but they're actually part of that system, they're part of the reproduction needs of that system. As a result, writing and language both are active and they're constitutive of this social body.

Politics itself ends up as something that you can look at as a type of writing that takes as its material a society as a whole, as a collection of practices governed by discourse and certain rules of behavior. There's already this existing material and politics is involved with its constant rewriting. In the same way, to change what exists, with writing you're pointing towards this newer collective body of referents; you're generating new contexts; you're constantly motivating and remotivating what's already there. And in doing so, you're encouraging the idea of a constant (not permanent revolution but a constant) renegotiating of this political and social contract—with all of its typical projections, institutional embodiments, and coercions.

You're raising the possibility of something entirely new taking shape: constructing a set of common meanings, some common network into which people can move, a way of exchanging different kinds of awarenesses. This would allow desire to register as a kind of community-building and put writing at the forefront of envisioning what a positive social freedom and participation might look like. By imagining a different *sense*, you're beginning to imagine a change also in what's possible in the practical transactions between social individuals—even to the point of implicating a different kind of subject: a new subject that could begin to coalesce, or that begins to coalesce around this desire to signify more widely—and fittingly—in light of 'what is, indeed, happening.' [...]

Now, in terms of politics and political praxis, I think that this conception of writing is related to the idea that an overall perspective, nationally, in politics, on the needs of existing institutions or the official model of social development at the national level is necessary to account for, and also to securely change, specific patterns of domination within that system. That you can't expect a mild reformism that's oriented toward specific problems to be capable of challenging (and altering) the broadest contexts in light of which those problems might keep making 'perfect sense.' The political dimension of writing isn't just based on the idea of challenging specific problems or mobilizing specific groups to challenge specific problems, but it's based on the notion of a systemic grasp—not of language described as a fixed system but of language as a kind of agenda or as a system of capabilities and uses. [...]

On what basis are conflicting groups and claims in society going to be able to come together? How can you link up the actions of all these different groups by means of some larger vision or some larger social worry, some sense of the totality that they're all enclosed by? Because if there is a common agenda and there is some ideological mobilizing around it, it's very likely to require a recognition of the overall system that it's operating in—as a precondition. And that means opening up the possibility of some conceptual (or experiential) totalizing that would be visible and understandable to these different groups—helping to keep them from being isolated and atomized and competitive with each other.

Without that idea of a totality in politics, I think it's hard to get a common grasp of what's needed for these groups and individuals to mobilize themselves together. [...] The parallel here might be a notion of the *public*, or of a public sphere, as a totalizing notion that is underneath the more surface phenomena of 'alliance building' and the construction and reconstruction of these different hegemonies in society. This idea that a public might need to come into being—a sense of the public within politics—as existing subjects reorient themselves toward a more social form of self-determination and thereby begin to cut against the grain of these more subjective preoccupations (for instance, in writing, I think that would suggest those of Romanticism or much of the New American Poetry) that have led to a weakening of the sense of any kind of common public life, or any sense of the public at all.

So, another linked notion involved with totalizing would be *participation* as a criterion for evaluating the present and mapping an alternative. If you combine this sense of the 'public' and of participation, you end up with a theme like *literacy*, characterized more socially than technically. The capacity for totalizing as literacy. [...]

Literacy, here, suggests building a public in the old-fashioned sense—one where individuals are able to orient themselves to social life more broadly, rather than just rubberstamping the existing agendas of the rich and the powerful. In a parallel way, this kind of writing might then seem like a part of public life—in the sense of the public sphere—an access point to totality, through this vehicle of the public sphere, the underlying conditions for the construction of which are tied up with the social system of meaning. So that a totalizing poetic practice involves a kind of social denormalizing—at work on the structure of the sign but also on these larger shapes of meaning—that would allow for revitalizing of the idea of a *public sphere*, as more than a cheering section for the effects of capitalism.

The whole is unfinished.

PUBLICATION: Excerpted from *Marginality: Public and Private Language* (1986), 6: 48–61.

KEYWORDS: Marxism; Language writing; method; politics.

LINKS: Lyn Hejinian, "Hard Hearts" (*PJ* 2); David Bromige, "Alternatives of Exposition" (*PJ* 5); David Lloyd, "Limits of a Language of Desire" (*PJ* 5); Steve Benson, "Mediations in an Emergency" (*PJ* 5); Johanna Drucker, "Close Reading: A Billboard" (*PJ* 2); Hejinian, "The Rejection of Closure" (*Guide*; *PJ* 4); Paul Hoover, "Domination: Public and Private Language" (*PJ* 6); Kofi Natambu, "The Multicultural Aesthetic: Language, 'Art,' and Politics in the United States Today" (*PJ* 9); David Plotke, "Language and Politics Today" (*PJ* 1); Ron Silliman, "'Postmodernism': Sign for a Struggle, Struggle for a Sign" (*PJ* 7); Rod Smith, from "CIA Sentences" (*PJ* 10).

SELECTED BIBLIOGRAPHY: *The L=A=N=G=U=A=G=E Book* (ed. with Charles Bernstein; Carbondale: Southern Illinois University Press, 1984); *Paradise and Method: Poetics and Praxis* (Evanston, Ill.: Northwestern University Press, 1996); *Bruce Andrews*, ed. Rod Smith, *Aerial* 9 (1999); *Edge* (Washington, D.C.: Some Of Us Press, 1973); *Corona* (Providence, R.I.: Burning Deck, 1974); *Vowels* (Washington, D.C.: O Press, 1976); *Film Noir* (Providence, R.I.: Burning Deck, 1978); *Praxis* (Berkeley: Tuumba, 1978); *Sonnets (momento mori)* (San Francisco: This, 1980); *Wobbling* (New York: Roof, 1981); *R + B* (New York: Segue, 1981); *Ex-communicate* (Elmwood, Conn.: Potes & Poets, 1982); *Love Songs* (Baltimore: Pod, 1982); *Give 'em Enough Rope* (Los Angeles: Sun & Moon, 1987); *Getting Ready to Have Been Frightened* (New York: Roof, 1988); *Executive Summary* (Elmwood, Conn.: Potes & Poets, 1991); *I Don't Have Any Paper So Shut Up (or, Social Romanticism)* (Los Angeles: Sun & Moon, 1992); *Tizzy Boost* (Great Barrington, Mass.: The Figures, 1993); *Strictly Confidential* (Tenerife, Spain: Zasterle, 1994); *Ex Why Zee: Performance Texts* (with Sally Silvers; New York: Roof, 1995); *Lip Service* (Toronto: Coach House Press, 2001); *The Millennium Project* (online ed.: Eclipse, 2002); *Swoon Noir* (Tucson, Ariz.: Chax, 2007).

Mainstream Marginality

Rae Armantrout's "Mainstream Marginality" is a critical send-up of the gap between main-stream and avant-garde poetries, read in terms of the "anthology wars." For the editors of an anthology of mainstream poets (*The Morrow Anthology of Younger American Poets*, 1985), the younger poets they select are "rarely a card-carrying group member, political or aesthetic." Armantrout questions this refusal of explicit ideology as disingenuous. To begin with, it is based on a clear set of exclusions: there will be no ideologues, eccentrics, New York School or Language poets, or lyric poets in such a collection. Armantrout's reading of the poems included, however, reveals a consistent rhetoric of marginality, to the degree that it approaches an ideology itself: "The 'typical younger American poet' is outdoors in an 'abandoned' location doing physical labor with a sharp instrument." Such a rhetoric of marginality leads, through the use of appropriately framed poetic narrative, to claims for authenticity—which for Armantrout are unexamined and poorly defended. At the heart of her review is a refusal to allow editorial selection to occur without itself being subject to scrutiny. The aesthetic issues she engages are still timely—the programmatic disavowal of aesthetic ideology versus the unconscious reproduction of one—in this scathing gem. In 2010 Rae Armantrout received both a National Book Critics Circle Award and a Pulitzer Prize for her collection of poetry *Versed*.

The Morrow Anthology of Younger American Poets, ed. Dave Smith and David Bottoms (New
   York: Quill, 1985)

Dave Smith and David Bottoms, the editors of the *Morrow Anthology of Younger American Poets*, include in their foreword a composite portrait of the younger, American poet. They write that "he is rarely a card-carrying group member, political or aesthetic" (19). In this foreword Smith and Bottoms, typical younger American poets in this regard, reveal none of the aesthetic criteria around which they have shaped this book. In fact, they claim to have used only two simple guidelines in choosing their contributors: "The poets chosen must have published one full length book, preferably recent in appearance, and a book that indicated future work of quality from the poet" (16), and their contributors must be "poets born since 1940" (17). Guidelines so general would produce, one would suppose, an extremely diverse anthology. The editors almost appear to deny responsibility for the contents of the book, in fact, when they write, "The publication of an anthology of new poets is an opportunity to observe the language discovering its possibilities as if for the first time" (1). We are the passive witnesses, then, to some inarguable linguistic Genesis.

An introduction by Anthony Hecht follows the editors' foreword. He is able to draw conclusions about this generation (my generation) of American poets based on the material he finds in these pages. For instance, "Their poems are not offered as the adornments or by-products of colorful or eccentric personal lives" (37). One wonders what Hecht considers eccentric. But, leaving aside his snide terminology, one could conclude from Hecht's statement that literary descendants of Frank O'Hara or Allen Ginsberg such as Ted Berrigan and Anne Waldman will not be found in this book. He may not have a colorful life but, according to the editors, "In his poems the younger poet tends to be himself, an invented version of himself" (19). In other words, these poems are written from a single, privileged point of view; they will be unitary, first-person narratives. From this one could conclude that "language" poets, such as Charles Bernstein and Hannah Weiner, who have opened their poems up to a number of conflicting social voices in a critique of the conventional concept of self, will not be included here. Finally Hecht finds himself able to claim, "They are a generation that seems disinclined to song" (40). From this one might conclude that poets influenced by the play of sound and reference in a poet like Robert Duncan, such as Susan Howe and Michael Palmer, will not be found in this book. If one were to take the claims of this book seriously, one would decide that contemporary American poetry represents a radical narrowing of poetic possibility. But even a moderately well-informed reader will know that many poets born since 1940 who have published full-length books have been left out. Why? It must be because the editors don't think that their books promise "future work of quality." Yet they never make the slightest effort to define or defend their concept of quality. It is assumed that we (a completely imaginary we) understand and agree with their taste implicitly.

Now that we have some idea of what is *not* in this book, let's look at the poems that are in it. Glancing through the book, one could get the idea that these were "card-carrying members" of *some* club. One sees immediately that almost all the lines are of medium length and begin flush against the left-hand margin—no prose poems here. Looking closer, say comparing opening stanzas, one sees, again and again, a narrative, discursive approach which places the writer physically in some particular setting, often, though not always, rustic, and begins to relate one (complexity is not favored) particular experience meant to either make a (one) point, confer on the poet some special authority, or both. We could compare "Picking Grapes in an Abandoned Orchard," by Larry Levis, with "An Abandoned Overgrown Cemetery in the Pasture Near Our House," by Gregory Orr. The poem by Levis begins:

Picking grapes alone in the late autumn sun
A slight, curved knife in my hand,
Its blade silver from so many sharpenings,
Its handle black.
I still have a scar where a friend
sliced open my right index finger once,
in a cutting shed—
The same kind of knife.
The grapes drop into the pan,
And the gnats swarm over them, as always. (390)

The second stanza of Gregory Orr's poem reads:

I clear it with clippers;
slicing the prickly stalks
and tossing wiry tangles
of briars over the wall
to the cows. It's a warm day.
Working, I sluff off winter's
torpor as a snake sheds skin.
I find a wren's nest, cup
from which ghosts sip.
What's in it? Human tears,
their only food. Always it's empty,
always it's filled to the brim. (495)

Thus we see that the "typical younger American poet" is outdoors in an "abandoned" location doing physical labor with a sharp implement. Both isolation and sharp implements seem associated in the "typical" American mind with a certain glamor. Perhaps that is what lends these poems their tones of authority and solemnity. The quote from Levis seems, simply, to assert that the poet is in touch with what he probably thinks of as "real life." This might be reassuring if one were personally concerned with the state of Mr. Levis's mental health. Otherwise, it seems to me to be emptily self-aggrandizing. The Gregory Orr stanza sets out to establish the poet's authority by means of an identical strategy. Once that authority is established, Orr uses it to make several assertions: ghosts drink from wrens' nests; wrens' nests contain human tears; tears are the only food of ghosts. Are you convinced? For me there is an oppressive machismo inherent in all this. A book full of such poems proves that poetry in the United States is "practiced in a wide and generous variety of idioms," as Hecht states in his introduction, only to the extremely myopic.

But the characteristic of the "typical younger American" poetry that I object to most is exemplified in Diane Ackerman's poem "A Fine, a Private Place," which begins:

> He took her one day
> under the blue horizon
> where long sea fingers
> parted like beads
> hitched in the doorway
> of an opium den. (43)

This is a poem about a sexual encounter, and one can see why the writer might want to suggest the illicit by mentioning an opium den—although such imagery is somewhat trite. But the sea can only be "like beads / hitched in the doorway" momentarily and for Ms. Ackerman's convenience. In fact, the ocean can resemble a vertical sequence of discrete, solid objects in almost no way imaginable. To make such a fatuous simile is to insult one's materials: the sea, opium dens, and language itself. The problem with this anthology is that language is being *used* for ulterior purposes, not appreciated and explored. As George Oppen says in his poem "The Gesture":

> The question is
>
> How does one hold something
> In the mind which he intends
>
> To grasp and how does the salesman
> Hold a bauble he intends
>
> To sell? The question is
> When will there not be a hundred
>
> Poets who mistake that gesture
> For a style.
> (*Collected Poems*, 80)

It is perfectly legitimate, of course, for Smith and Bottoms to choose the poets they prefer for an anthology. It is illegitimate, however, for them to obscure the nature of the choices they've made and pretend that other tendencies do not exist in contemporary American poetry. It is disingenuous for them to pretend that their book created itself by means of a kind of natural selection while they stood back and watched "language discover its possibilities." As usual, it is worthwhile to examine claims to naturalness and objectivity carefully to find out what or who is being suppressed.

PUBLISHED: *Marginality: Public and Private Language* (1986), 6:141–44.

KEYWORDS: lyric poetry; genre; ideology; readings.

LINKS: Rae Armantrout, "Chains" (*PJ* 5), "On *Pythagorean Silence*" (*PJ* 2), "The Person in My Work" (*PJ* 9), "Silence" (*PJ* 3); Lydia Davis, "Some Notes on Armantrout's *Precedence*" (*PJ* 6); William Corbett, "Harwood/Walker and Raworth" (*PJ* 2); Alan Davies, "Motor Mouth" (*PJ* 5); Norman Finkelstein, "The Problem of the Self in Recent American Poetry" (*PJ* 9); Kathleen Fraser, "Overheard" (*PJ* 4); Lyn Hejinian, "An American Opener" (*PJ* 1); Laura Moriarty, "The Modern Lyric" (*PJ* 7); Jed Rasula, "On Rothenberg's Revised *Technicians of the Sacred*" (*PJ* 6); Ron Silliman, "The Dysfunction of Criticism: Poets and the Critical Tradition of the Anti-Academy" (*PJ* 10).

SELECTED BIBLIOGRAPHY: *Collected Prose* (San Diego: Singing Horse, 2007); *A Wild Salience: The Writing of Rae Armantrout*, ed. Tom Beckett (Cleveland, Ohio: Burning Press, 1999); *Extremities* (Berkeley: The Figures, 1978); *The Invention of Hunger* (Berkeley: Tuumba, 1979); *Precedence* (Providence, R.I.: Burning Deck, 1985); *Necromance* (Los Angeles: Sun & Moon, 1991); *Made to Seem* (Los Angeles: Sun & Moon, 1995); *True* (Berkeley: Atelos, 1998); *Pretext* (Los Angeles: Green Integer, 2001); *Veil: New and Selected Poems* (Middletown, Conn.: Wesleyan University Press, 2001); *Up to Speed* (Middletown, Conn.: Wesleyan University Press, 2004); *Next Life* (Middletown, Conn.: Wesleyan University Press, 2007); *Versed* (Middletown, Conn.: Wesleyan University Press, 2009); *Money Shot* (Middletown, Conn.: Wesleyan University Press, 2012); *Just Saying* (Middletown, Conn.: Wesleyan University Press, 2013); with Steve Benson et al., *The Grand Piano*.

"Hey Man, My Wave!" The Authority of Private Language

Cultural studies was emergent when Michael Davidson wrote this groundbreaking essay on the social construction of "private language," presented at New Langton Arts, San Francisco (22 March 1984). The concept of "private language" originated as a thought experiment in Ludwig Wittgenstein's writings, but Davidson is more interested in public registers of "the language of the heart," from surfer lingo to graffiti to the "ideoglossia" of aphasic twins to lyric poetry. A nonprofessional but expert surfer, Davidson had an insider's knowledge of the linguistic markers that identified a surfer both as a member of a group and as a particular individual within it. Extending this model of group reference to individuals, Davidson discusses the signifying practices of graffiti artists in New York and a linguistic microculture invented by aphasic twins. Concluding his discussion of private language with a critique of Emily Dickinson, he refuses to identify lyric subjectivity with hermetic references and opaque meanings. Rather, he sees Dickinson's rescripting of cultural codes as a direct critique of institutional power. The essay reveals the influence of structural linguistics (the Prague Circle, Mikhail Bakhtin) and American sociolinguistics (Basil Bernstein) in seeing poetry in terms of cultural codes. It makes an important contribution to the theory of the lyric, bridging Davidson's poetics to his work in disability and globalization studies.

We make up a different language for poetry
And for the heart—ungrammatical.
—Jack Spicer

We may agree with Pascal that the heart has its reasons which reason does not know, but at this point in history we might add that the language of the heart, in order to speak at all, must first deform the language of the reason. In the condensed and displaced language of the dream, in the repetitions and distortions of schizophrenic discourse, in various social dialects within subcultures, even in the trivialized and trivializing banter of public gossip we hear the language of the heart speaking its reasons against the claims of reason. But when we attempt to penetrate the privacy of these private languages we are often faced with the inverted reflections of those public and official discourses against which the heart makes its claim. In the most intimate of secrets shared between lovers can be found a rhetoric as ancient as the *Sympo-*

sium and as public as the afternoon soap opera. How then can we speak of a private language at all? Can a language speak of the heart without first inventing a heart by which to speak?

These are questions that lie at the heart of any sociolinguistics and, I would add, at the heart of literary study as well. In both spheres we rely on the idea of a private language as a zone free of ideology, free of rhetorical and logical constraints. Private languages, in the common-sense usage of the phrase, can be anything from glossolalia (speaking in tongues) in which there is no clear source language, to idioglossia (the language of twins) in which several source languages are combined, to highly ritualized dialects shared by large segments of society. In the arts, private language often refers to the hermetic character of certain works in which meaning is hidden or occluded. Or the phrase may refer to various linguistic strategies of the avant-garde (Futurist *zaum* language, Dada performance, Surrealist automatic writing) whose impulse is directed toward deformations of "ordinary" or "logical" discourse. It is precisely because the phrase "private language" has so many associations that it loses its potentially subversive relationship to something called "public language," and it is this relationship that will be my subject.

I should point out that I am not speaking of private language as it is discussed by Wittgenstein in his *Philosophical Investigations*, where the phrase refers to a private sphere of sensation or experience entirely specific to one individual. Wittgenstein points out that access to this realm would necessitate some form of verification or criteria by which utterances could be evaluated, and these criteria could only exist in a public sphere. I am more interested in private language *within* that public sphere where the impulse to restrict, contain or sequester a semiotic field represents an attempt to subvert the authority of a public discourse. Criteria are not value-neutral; they exist to validate and legitimize certain kinds of expressions—expressions produced by individuals in their social interaction. The impulse to privacy in such interaction does not represent a rejection of some dominant code so much as a willed transformation of it. The reasons for this transformation are various, lying in the institutions that depend for their existence on the idea of free and unrestricted communication. [...]

The most obvious form of private language in social interaction is the argot of subcultures (fraternal organizations, hobby enthusiasts, sports fans, ethnic groups) whose language exists both to restrict participation to members of the group as well as to specify particular features of an activity. In the case of surfing, for example, special words and phrases define particular qualities of wave and weather and describe, in minute detail, the design and structure of surfing equipment. But at the same time, surfing argot is used to represent one's physical performance in a way that both identifies a particular ride and establishes a peer bond essential to maintaining one's participation. Thus, when a surfer sitting during a lull between sets turns to his friends and says, "That last right was bogus; I was hauling all over the face—really cranking— thought it would wall up on the inside for a tube, but it backed off just as I cut back and I stalled out," he means two things: 1) I just had an experience and 2) I am one of us. A translation of this remark might read as follows: that last ride was a disappointment; I went right and was moving quickly all over the face of the wave—really cranking sharp turns; I thought the wave would hold up as it approached the beach and provide me with a tube ride, but the back- wash from the shore caused the wave to become mushy just at the point where I was beginning to cut back into the wave, and I was left standing there. The second meaning is more subtle and concerns the fraternal nature of surfing— the macho cult of performance with its perpetual need for verification and assertion. In the case mentioned above, it is clearly not the surfer's fault that things did not work out, but rather the wave's. If you are disappointed that a wave "mushed out," then you are presumably one for whom speed, quick ma- neuvering, and daring are quite common.

Basil Bernstein calls such a socially coded dialect a "restricted code" since the possibility of predicting its organizing pattern is relatively simple and its potential for unexpected variations restricted. Ritual modes of communica- tion like surfing language are regulated by protocol, and thus much of their meaning occurs at nonverbal levels. The restriction occurs because members of this social group share identifications:

> The speech is played out against a background of communal, self-consciously held interests which removes the need to verbalize subjective intent and make it explicit. The meanings will be condensed.[1]

However predictable the syntax and lexicon of such codes might be, the sources and reasons for their development would seem to vary considerably. In the case of surfing, to continue my example, the lexicon is dominated by terms involved with possession and acquisition that are then applied to inanimate things—like beaches and waves. Surfers refer to "my wave," "my beach," and "my ride" the way that some people refer to "my alma mater" or "my pen." In- truders to "their" spaces are tourists, Vals (people from inland), greasers, kooks, fags, creeps, and, depending on lifestyle preferences, dopers, punks, and long-hairs. Right-of-way on waves is established by a complicated pecking order based on one's proximity to the break, unless the surfer is an aggressive local in which case he has carte blanche, no matter where he takes off. Female surfers have absolutely no right of way and are better off left sitting on the beach. The bumper sticker "locals only" is only the most visible sign of surfing's pervasive desire to restrict participation and "own" what cannot be possessed.

This assertion of ownership with its attendant verbal claims and challenges stems partly from the fact that surfing occurs in, quite literally, a fluid environment, one that changes from beach to beach. There are no enforceable rules or guidelines to govern the sport other than those asserted by each individual surfer. Most surfers come from middle-class beach suburbs in which possession and acquisition are necessary forms of verification. To move from a relatively static, consumerist demography into an unstructured, changeable environment necessitates the imposition of a grid from the first onto the second. Thus some illusion may be created that a wave "belongs" to someone, that a teenage boy who lives with his parents can find solace at "his" beach among the "locals." At the same time, he may find some validation of his male status by pulling his "stick" (board) out of a "quiver" (group of different sized boards) and "run over some turkey" where on land his social and sexual identity is still uncertain. The vernacular code he relies on may be restricted, in Bernstein's sense, but its register of power relations in the larger culture is subtle and complex.

Clearly, surfing vernacular, like the social dialects of other subcultures, represents less an inversion than a replication of the dominant code.[2] Sexist and racist attitudes, present in middle-class households, are easily grafted onto the highly encoded rhetoric of those subgroups that might, on the surface, appear to stand in opposition.[3] The use of private codes to secure relations of power and dominance in surfing yields only an exchange value; nothing is produced beyond reestablishing the male bond necessary to that culture. Territoriality and position have already been validated in the community, and it is a relatively simple matter to find a parallel, if condensed, social rhetoric. In the case of lower-class private language use, however, territoriality has to be claimed in a much more public way—by assaulting the public space or by producing something within it. [...]

We may see a more decisive example of private language as protest in the cases of so-called speech "defects" that occur in the course of language acquisition.

Take the case of Gracie and Ginny Kennedy, the San Diego twins who developed what the newspapers called a private language between themselves and what speech pathologists call "idioglossia." After the twins were born they were diagnosed as being retarded and were sequestered by the family away from childhood friends and activities. The parents, Tom and Chris Kennedy, treated their daughters' presumed retardation as a scandal to be covered up, and it was only when Tom was forced to go on welfare that the twins' isolated existence was discovered. Ironically, it was through this severe change in the Kennedy's economic status that the twins were finally able to get adequate professional help, which led to the discovery of their idioglossia.

In Jean-Pierre Gorin's film *Poto and Cabengo*, the subject is ostensibly the twins and their language, but it is equally about manipulation: familial, linguistic, and economic. And since Gorin, as filmmaker, is conscious of his own participation in the twins' lives, the film is about aesthetic manipulation. What the film makes clear is that Ginny and Gracie's private speech is actually a pastiche of the two languages present in their household: their father's rather monosyllabic English and their mother and grandmother's German. Although the twins' talk is difficult to translate, it is not impossible; one can quite clearly make out its conflation of Germanic and American words, especially when nonverbal factors are taken into consideration.[4] What is ultimately more difficult to define are the causes for their idioglossia—causes that Gorin implies lie not in the twins themselves but in their parents' failed hopes for success and prosperity in America.

The father, Tom Kennedy, is a tragic figure whose faith in the free-enterprise system is unswerving, despite the dismal state of his nascent real estate business. He seems able to talk only about making money and promoting his interests. He regards his daughters as an unexpected boon to himself, feeling that any publicity brought to his household will ultimately be good for business. His wife, Chris, whom he met in Germany, yearns for the good life: a larger house, more appliances, a swimming pool, a big kitchen. In one crucial scene, Tom and Chris sit on the bed somewhat stiffly before the camera and rehearse a real estate scenario in which he plays the salesman and she, the prospective buyer. She describes her dream house—endless bedrooms, bathrooms, kitchen space—and he, acting the part both of real estate salesman and ideal husband, agrees to each new demand. They act out their fantasies of wealth and power against the backdrop of their meager Linda Vista postwar prefab in much the same fashion as the twins act out stories in their private language. The disparity between their hopes for success and the sad contrary evidence can be felt in all of their interviews and can be seen in the obsessive cleaning and tidying that seem to be the central activities of the mother and grandmother. Given the oppressive atmosphere of the household, it is little wonder that the twins developed a private mode of communication, if only to gain control over a world where control is perpetually uncertain.

Gorin's interviews with the twins' speech pathologist provide another frame for viewing the public dimension of their private language. The therapist clearly regards their private dialect as an aberration, something to be treated and corrected by standard behaviorist methods. In several sequences, we see videotaped sessions in which the therapist vigorously rewards the twins for identifying an object by its correct English name. And in interviews, the therapist defines "their" problem entirely within psycholinguistic terms and never in terms of their larger familial and social environment. Gorin's film explores the way that such limiting and limited definitions of idioglossia ignore the socioeconomic factors that contribute to language acquisition. Clearly the two languages adopted by the girls are German and English, but their reasons for deforming their parents' languages lie in the uncertain power relations of the household and the ways in which language is used by the parents to establish control and authority and not to establish communication or bestow affection.

In [the two] examples I have mentioned, a private discourse shared by two or more persons exists to subvert a public language. In Bakhtin's terms, such discourses serve to offset the "centripetal forces in sociolinguistic and ideological life" that centralize and unify a particular class interest.[5] Rather than providing a distinctly different language or idiolect, the private code appropriates and deforms the dominant code. What I will call the "impulse to privacy" occurs socially in various kinds of exclusive behavior and linguistically in the transformations of legitimizing discourses, whether in the home or in the culture at large. The private codes of surfers [...] or twins depend on a source language not only for exchange of information but for the production of new, potentially subversive information. Such usage is performative in the sense that its function is to *do* as well as *communicate*; it authenticates by the context in which it is used as much as by the content of any utterance. And, to continue in J. L. Austin's terms, such usage is perlocutionary in that it always serves ends beyond those contained in the message. [...]

Much of what I have been saying about private language in the realm of sociolinguistics could be said of literature, but with significant modifications.

Bakhtin provides me with a transition in the way that he characterizes various forms of social heteroglossia in the novel. According to Bakhtin, the novel is essentially dialogic in that it may present languages, all of which have an ideological character, speaking to each other. Dialogism occurs not only between characters but between various discourses by which characters establish their ideological positions in society and signal their class affiliations and aspirations. Poetry, on the other hand, cannot share in this proliferation of languages since "no matter how many contradictions and insoluble conflicts the poet develops within it, [poetry] is always illumined by one unitary and indisputable discourse."[6] As I have pointed out elsewhere, this consignment of poetry to the monologic is based on a rather narrow view of poetic discourse, one formed largely around nineteenth-century German and Russian works.[7] I feel that what Bakhtin says about forms of heteroglossia in the novel could be applied to poetry, even where poetry most appears to retain its monologic character—as in the lyric, for instance.

According to most genre theorists, the lyric is the site of personal self-expression. For Hegel, the subjectivity of the author provides the lyric both with its content as well as its aesthetic *raison d'être*. But when Hegel attempts to provide a historicized account of the genre's evolution he uses the rhetoric of authority that we have already applied to social discourse. Unlike the epic,

> lyric poetry presupposes for its composition not a primitive but an advanced state of society, where art, having become self-conscious in an increasingly prosaic world, perfects its self-defined sphere deliberately. It is indeed favored to an exceptional degree in times like ours where the prosaic regularity of the social order prompts each individual to claim for himself the right to his own point of view and feelings.[8]

This claim to one's subjectivity is based on the individual's presumed access to a language of unmediated expressivity. But within the lyric announced by Hegel's aesthetics, there emerges a countertendency away from private states to private rhetorics. We have come to feel in the modern period that all claims to a private perspective must be made by means of the internally cohesive structure of the aesthetic artifact. According to Mukarovsky, the poetic utterance consists of a "maximum foregrounding of the utterance" in which patterns of repetition (rhyme, meter, alliteration) and semantic complexity (paronomasia, metaphor) force attention on the material construct.[9] Thus the lyric stands as an "objective correlative" (Eliot), verbal icon (Wimsatt), or "pattern of resolved stresses" (Brooks) for thoughts that live "too deep for tears."

The author thus creates a hermetically sealed world of private (because un-recoverable) meanings.

Both criteria of the lyric mentioned here—its presumed accessibility to subjective states, its foregrounding of the signifier—would seem to contradict each other. The first is based on a theory of language as transparent vehicle; the second is based on language as mediated expression, semantically con-textualized by internal organization and distinct from "ordinary" discourse. We could see this opposition as being two perspectives on the same thing: the world of the subject, by its refusal of prosaic or "public" discourse, de-mands a rhetoric that reflects that difference. Interior states do not admit of words; therefore it is by defamiliarizing language that we may regain that earlier state. By a logic of metaphor or through a forest of symbols the lyric poet may express the inexpressible.

In this conflation of "lyric subject" and hermetic rhetoric, what remains intact is the ideal of subjectivity itself by which the lyric genre may be said to receive some metaphysical legitimation. We know, through the work of Althusser, on the one hand, and Benveniste on the other, that such a state is not so much the source as the product of specific sociohistorical structures. The subject upon which the lyric impulse is based, rather than being able to generate its own language of the heart, is also constituted within a world of public discourse. The lyric "I" emerges as a positional relation. Its subjectivity is made possible by a linguistic and ultimately social structure in which "I" speaks.[10] It is by a similar description that Adorno frames the lyric gesture as being social in nature:

> This demand, however, that of the untouched virgin word, is in itself social in nature. It implies a protest against a social condition which every indi-vidual experiences as hostile, distant, cold, and oppressive; and this social condition impresses itself on the poetic form in a negative way: the more heavily social conditions weigh, the more unrelentingly the poem resists, refusing to give in to any heteronomy, and constituting itself purely ac-cording to its own particular laws.[11]

The Kantian rhetoric of his last sentence notwithstanding, Adorno's remarks suggest a way that lyric poetry may be given a critical dimension: not by what the poem says about the author's condition but about the social condition by which that "private" condition becomes a necessity. The ideology of the lyric may be read, as it were, between the lines —in those gestures toward solitude, isolation, and privacy that invert or negate a rhetoric of multiplicity, plurality, and communalism. For Adorno, "the greatness of works of art lies solely in their power to let those things be heard which ideology conceals."[12] [...]

Unfortunately Adorno's lyric poet, like Bakhtin's, remains monologic, one who remains unconscious of his/her retreat from the social world and bent on fabricating an alternate world as a form of self-protection. This seems like a limited view of lyric discourse in which not only is there interplay between the private individual and failed social plenitude but between the various registers and tones, generic markers, and rhetorical devices by which even the most hermeneutically intransigent poem is made. A great lyric poet like Emily Dickinson, for example, while isolating herself socially and aesthetically from the public eye, retains much of the rhetoric of Protestant ideology and social discourse in her poems—not to insulate herself against them but in order to subvert their authority:

> A Word made Flesh is seldom
> And tremblingly partook
> Nor then perhaps reported
> But have I not mistook
> Each one of us has tasted
> With ecstasies of stealth
> The very food debated
> To our specific strength—
>
> A Word that breathes distinctly
> Has not the power to die
> Cohesive as the Spirit
> It may expire if He—
> "Made Flesh and dwelt among us"
> Could condescension be
> Like this consent of Language
> This loved Philology.[13]

In this, her most famous poem on the subject of poetic incarnation, Dickinson describes the "ecstasies of stealth" by which poetry speaks where God is absent. Joanne Feit Diehl points out that here the poet "creates an alternative power potentially subversive of any external authority based upon the sovereignty of a male-identified divinity or predicated upon the supremacy of those within the religious fold."[14] I would add that not only is the poem an inversion of orthodoxy, it is also a deformation of the authoritative role of language in sustaining God's Word. It is the "consent of Language" to allow the individual to speak *at all* rather than the "condescension" of language to speak *for* one that inaugurates the poet's meditation. The process is dangerous, "tremblingly partook," even though each one of us has "tasted," like our Edenic parents, the fruits of potentiality and power. Dickinson's language of stealth, danger, and immanence is powerful because it retains associations with Puritan orthodoxy and scriptural authority. She has not, like Emerson or Whitman, used the rhetoric of individualism and personal assertion but has adopted the rhetoric of the New Testament and placed it, quite literally, in quotes.

It may seem a great and perilous leap from the private dialects of subcultures or the creolized speech of the Kennedy twins to the lyrics of Emily Dickinson. In one case, private languages serve to strengthen group bonds and permit communication; in the other case, private language permits the poet to appropriate and transform social discourse—to "tell the truth but tell it slant." In both, however, the construction of private codes occurs in some direct relation to the public languages they seek to offset. When Emily Dickinson seeks to choose her own "Society," she chooses a word as well, one with recognizable cultural and historical connotations. She has not simply chosen a metaphor from others to suit poetic ends. The word exists enmeshed in political and theological contexts that lie at the heart of American institutions. And when she chooses to become, as Mabel Loomis Todd says, the "Myth of Amherst," speaking to others through a partially open door, she is at last able to have a dialogue with the world on her own terms.[15] [...]

We come to Emily Dickinson's lyrics with the expectation that her inner experiences have been translated into a private language of poetry and that our role as readers is to decode those signs back to some original, nonverbal state. That is, we read her lyrics within the conventions of Romantic Idealism by which art is said to transcend concrete historical and spatial limits.[16] But literature is discourse, a product of specific signifying practices that exist in the social world and, at the same time, productive of its own structures of signification. The opposition between "poetic" and "ordinary" language is being broken down in various critical arenas (speech act theory, ethnomethodology, discourse analysis), but such research has occurred largely within the field of narrative. Here the competition among ideologemes—socially coded discourse structures—may be dramatized by interaction between specific individuals or types. I would like to see the analysis of discourse broadened to study the nature of the subject itself and the extent to which it is constituted in and by speech situations. [...] The twins not only "use" a private language, they create themselves within it as speaking subjects. Emily Dickinson not only "creates" an elliptical and hyperbolic style, she textualizes herself out of the doctrinal and social discourse she finds around her. We may discover the ideological character of these subjective projections not by rejecting "private language" as an idealist fiction but by searching within it for traces of authoritative and authoritarian discourse.[17]

"We make up a different language for poetry / And for the heart— ungrammatical," says Jack Spicer,[18] and it has ever been the province of poetry to enact that difference. Elsewhere Spicer makes it clear that this language comes not from some internal, private realm but from the outside—from Martians and ghosts for whom the poet is only a medium. I would add that the outside is also a world of social heteroglossia—of class- and gender-based discourses that officiate the terms by which any individual is able to receive its messages. Spicer's ungrammatical, private language of the heart must first, in order to be received, pass through the defiles of an inherited language—one that, as I have tried to show, is not only grammatical but is also encrusted with ideological concerns. Spicer's radical orphism provides us with a felicitous model of how ideology works to mediate our private discourse and produce us as subjects. It is not that we remain unconscious of the forms of this mediation—as my remarks on Dickinson should make clear— but that in reading the language of the heart we must be willing to see the public arena in which it takes shape.

NOTES

1 Basil Bernstein, ed., *Class, Codes, and Control: Theoretical Studies towards a Sociology of Language*, 2 vols. (London: Routledge, 1971), 1:77.

2 On the term "social dialect," see R. Hasan, "Code, Register and Social Dialect," in *Class, Codes, and Control*, 2:253–92.

3 Consider, for example, a recent profile of surfer Tim Fretz, published in *Surfer* 25, no. 4, which begins: "Tim Fretz is a perfect example of Hitler's attempt at a so-called 'superior race.' He is a six-foot tall, blonde [sic] haired ball of muscle. The wild look in his eyes is only a hint as to why he's been nicknamed 'Taz' (short for Tasmanian Devil)."

4 Gorin finds a felicitous parallel to the Kennedy twins' interlinguality in the *Katzenjammer Kids* comic strip. Much of the humor in the strip is based on confusions of terms between German and English, and Gorin uses clips from old *Katzenjammer Kids* films as obbligato to the main narrative in *Poto and Cabengo*.

5 M. M. Bakhtin, "Discourse in the Novel," in *The Dialogic Imagination*, ed. Michael Holquist (Austin: University of Texas Press, 1981), 271.

6 Bakhtin, *Dialogic Imagination*, 286.

7 Michael Davidson, "Discourse in Poetry: Bakhtin and Extensions of the Dialogical," in *Code of Signals: Recent Writings in Poetics*, ed. Michael Palmer (Berkeley: North Atlantic, 1983), 143–50.

8 *Hegel on the Arts*, ed. and trans. Henry Paolucci (New York: Frederick Unger, 1979), 163.

9 Jan Mukarovsky, "Standard Language and Poetic Language," in *A Prague School Reader on Estetics, Literary Structure, and Style*, ed. Paul L. Garvin (Washington, D.C.: Georgetown University Press, 1964), 19.

10 See Louis Althusser, "Ideology and Ideological State Apparatuses," in *Lenin and Philosophy*, trans. Ben Brewster (New York: Monthly Review Press, 1971), 127–86; and Emile Benveniste, *Problems in General Linguistics*, trans. Mary E. Meek (Coral Gables, Fla.: University of Miami Press, 1971), 217–30. For a good summary of current discussion of the "subject" in critical theory see Catherine Belsey, *Critical Practice* (London: Methuen, 1980), 56–84.

11 Theodor W. Adorno, "Lyric Poetry and Society," *Telos* 20 (Summer 1974), 58.

12 Ibid. This passage, as well as much of Adorno's thinking in this essay, is strikingly similar to the theory of literary production put forth by Pierre Machery in *A Theory of Literary Production*, trans. Geoffrey Wall (London: Routledge and Kegan Paul, 1978). See also Jerome McGann's discussion of relationships between Althusserian thought and the Frankfurt School in his afterword to *The Romantic Ideology* (Chicago: University of Chicago Press, 1983).

13 *The Complete Poems of Emily Dickinson*, ed. Thomas H. Johnson (Boston: Little, Brown, 1960), no. 1651.

14 Joanne Feit Diehl, "'Ransom in a Voice': Language as Defense in Dickinson's Poetry," in *Feminist Critics Read Emily Dickinson*, ed. Suzanne Juhasz (Bloomington: Indiana University Press, Ind., 1983), 157.

15 See Mabel Loomis Todd's fascinating portrait of Dickinson through her letters and journals, excerpted in Richard B. Sewell, *The Life of Emily Dickinson* (New York: Farrar, Strauss, and Giroux, 1980). 216–28.

16 The problem of reading Romanticism *outside* of Romantic models and criteria is the burden of Jerome McGann's *Romantic Ideology*.

17 Bruce Boone provides me with a model for how one might read "private language" in oppositional terms within the context of gay poetry. See his "Gay Language as Political Praxis: The Poetry of Frank O'Hara," *Social Text* 1 (Winter 1979), 59–92.

18 Jack Spicer, "Transformations II," in *The Collected Books of Jack Spicer* (Los Angeles: Black Sparrow Press, 1975), 233.

PUBLISHED: Excerpted from *Marginality: Public and Private Language* (1986), 6:33–45.

KEYWORDS: cultural studies; public sphere; linguistics; lyric poetry.

LINKS: Michael Davidson, "Framed by Story" (*PJ* 5), "The Poetics of Everyday Life" (*PJ* 9), seven poems (*PJ* 10); Steve Benson, "Personal as Social History: Three Fictions" (*PJ* 7); Robert Glück, "Fame" (*PJ* 10); Susan Howe, "*My Emily Dickinson*, part 1" (*Guide*; *PJ* 4); George Lakoff, "The Public Aspect of the Language of Love" (*PJ* 6); Tom Mandel, "Codes/Texts: Reading *S/Z*" (*PJ* 2); Kit Robinson, "Time and Materials: The Workplace, Dreams, and Writing" (*Guide*; *PJ* 9); Leslie Scalapino, "Poetic Diaries" (*PJ* 5); Barrett Watten, "The Politics of Style" (*Guide*; *PJ* 1).

SELECTED BIBLIOGRAPHY: *The San Francisco Renaissance: Poetics and Community at Mid-Century* (Cambridge: Cambridge University Press, 1989); *Ghostlier Demarcations: Modern Poetry and the Material Word* (Berkeley: University of California Press, 1997); *Guys Like Us: Citing Masculinity in Cold War Poetics* (Chicago: University of Chicago Press, 2003); *Concerto for the Left Hand: Disability and the Defamiliar Body* (Ann Arbor: University of Michigan Press, 2008); *On the Outskirts of Form* (Wesleyan, Conn.: Wesleyan University Press, 2009); *The Mutabilities and The Foul Papers* (Albany, Calif.: Sand Dollar, 1976); *The Prose of Fact* (Berkeley: The Figures, 1981); *The Landing of Rochambeau* (Providence, R.I.: Burning Deck, 1985); *Analogy of the Ion* (Great Barrington, Mass.: The Figures, 1988); *Post Hoc* (Bolinas, Calif.: Avenue B, 1990); *The Arcades* (Oakland: O Books, 1999); with Lyn Hejinian et al., *Leningrad*.

Hypergraphy A Note on Maurice Lemaître's Roman Hypergraphique

Maurice Lemaître was an active participant in the postwar cultural movement known as *lettrism* (with Isidore Isou, generally acknowledged as its founder). Indebted to, but wanting to go beyond, Dada and surrealism, lettrism emerged in Paris after World War II as a radical avant-garde tendency; it had a major impact on later developments in poetry, painting, cinema, music, and cultural theory. In her reading of Lemaître's visual novel, *La Plastique lettriste et hypergraphique* (1956), Johanna Drucker points to its fetishization of visual form and its separation of visual from sonic aspects of language in a way that suggests, even is ultimately different from, deconstruction's privileging of "writing over speech." She describes the opacity of the material text—a sequence of icons and signs whose "meaning" seems available only privately to their author—as both a radical refusal of normative public language and a public display of opaque signs. Lettrism's early, experimental concern with a poetics of visual forms anticipated the aesthetic use of language as image in conceptual art in the 1960s and the later technology of the Graphic User Interface (GUI) in the digital era. Drucker is a noted creator of typographically innovative artist's books, as well as an expert on the material history of writing, experimental typography, visual language, and concrete poetry.

La Plastique lettriste et hypergraphique, by Maurice Lemaître (Paris: Caractères, 1956)

Lemaître's hypergraphy fetishizes writing, and this is the basis of its attraction for me. Manipulating resemblance and substitution of elements in the notation system along iconic and pseudo-iconic lines suggests the kind of arcane practice that is inherently seductive in the idea of letters as signs and symbols. The actual icons Lemaître uses aren't particularly arcane; he takes real letters, tiny pictograms and diagrams, each more or less recognizable and readable, but manages to make the pages of his hypergraphic novel present the coded face of a secret program. In so doing he confronts his readers on the line where the distinction between a public and private use of writing threatens readability.

In looking at Lemaître's *roman hypergraphique*, I would like to examine the project to describe it, give an idea of its intentions, and then put those observations into a framework where they raise some theoretical problems specific to written language: what are the limits of public and private in writing as a notational system; how do visual signs function when they pretend to be language; and how is the limit between public and private linked to the strategies of concealment and revelation inherent in writing in general.

In the essay which immediately precedes the hypergraphic novel, Lemaître explains the motivation behind his invention. The "Arts of Writing" explains that as far as he is concerned, the Dadaists and Surrealists had exhausted the potential of language as words, an exhaustion taken to its limit by Joyce, who "accomplished the last phase of this evolution in creating an unsurpassable descriptive chaos" (23). Feeling that writing had suffered an "aesthetic death," Lemaître decided to invent a new domain for exploration, *lettrisme*, and as a special project of lettrism he decided to experiment with hypergraphy. To some extent Lemaître's project can be seen as an act motivated by frustration, a response to the generational trauma of being a European writer at mid-century in the wake of the overwhelming force of modernism in its full glory. The result was the fetishization of the material fields (sound and image) of a writing which he felt was aesthetically exhausted. However, to fall back onto the letter as the locus of main activity seems to fall short of risking the generation of text; in fact, it seems to be a refusal to write. This abdication of literature can't be viewed in a totally pejorative light; but the blockage which resulted piled a tremendous concentration behind the refusal to write; and lettrism occurred in the maelstrom of energy which could not work out into literature.

In the "Arts of Writing," Lemaître describes lettrism as the project of extracting all utterable sound from existing or potential language systems or from fields of random articulations. This extraction, rarefaction, of sound material allowed a redefinition of the role of writing which could intensify its visual properties. The old conflict between writing defined either as the representation of spoken language or as a thing in itself would be resolved in this process, since each aspect would occupy a discrete domain. The second, visual writing, would be called Hypergraphy, and would call on "all the processes of the plastic arts and photography in making stories or texts in which the words are replaced by painting or photographs of what would formerly have been described" (24).

The hypergraphic novel consists of five plates, each of which uses writing or images substituted for writing in a different way. These five tableaux constitute the whole of the 'novel.'

Maurice Lemaître, from La Plastique lettriste et hypergraphique, *plate B.*
Reproduced by permission.

The first plate describes the 'situation' of the author, literally, zooming in from a sketch of the solar system to a fat round circle of the earth to a schematic map of Europe, etc., and ending with an i.d. photo of the author. The author's picture has to be understood as the last in this line, as the final position, which no one else could occupy, and not as an icon of a 'self' as personality. Here we have the first metacommentary, a pun on the notion of position as one of the key determining factors of value in a visual system. Position, on the page and in a system and as indicative of placement/system relations, can make distinctions in the visual realm, since a visual field is capable of registering it as significant. The first plate, A, then, is about position as a feature of identity.

Plate B uses all manner of iconic images, a kneeling man with no features, a croissant, a compass, a t-square, a tent, the Eiffel Tower, and a burning cigarette. These images substitute for the letter which they resemble in their grosser form. I frankly have difficulty deciphering the 'message' on this page, where the symbols, which look like they were peeled off bar napkins, beer caps, and other popular locations for rebus-like visuals, are displayed in a leisurely spiral, aping one of the great objects in the history of writing, a stone whose glyphs have never been deciphered.[1] I find my resistance to the amount of attention which would be necessary in order to understand this piece significant, and rather than dutifully untangling the letters to spell out the dozen or so French words which ultimately would be the meager fruit of such labor, I prefer to acknowledge this as one of the limits at which the boundary of readability is established. In its place in the catalogue of aspects of writing which Lemaître is establishing in this hypergraphic series, this plate simply calls attention to shape and the limits of shape, and to the degree of deviance permissible and tolerable for the forms to continue to function as versions of the letters whose norm is invoked.

The third plate (C) relies on a set of stick-figure icons, eyelids with their eyelashes extending downwards to indicate a state of sleep, open eyes with tears hanging in double rows, a rising sun, etc. All of these read pretty easily, and they are arranged in a grid of eight by ten elements, which is deceptively straightforward, since Lemaître in his introduction warns us that the sense of reading must be discovered. These little icons are not direct substitutes for any normal linguistic element, not for words or letters, and they refer only vaguely to concepts, ideas, actions or events which can be interpreted linguistically. To my mind, they question the process of conversion which is undergone in reading them: do they go from images to words, or to concepts already meaningful without linguistic translation? The potential of the visual sign to escape linguistic definitions and rules is suggested in this plate, and in the process the nature of the system within which meaning might be fixed when signs lack syntactic or semantic stability is questioned. Outside such stable systems, the link between private act and public fact in language is threatened.

Plate four (D) takes normal letters and imposes them on four supergraphic letters which are in turn piled up on each other. The spatial dimension of the page, another feature characteristic of the visual organization not normally

Plate C

used by writing, is emphasized, since the illusion of depth created by the pile-up depends upon pictorial conventions. The normal letters, here represented as individual letters from different typefaces and chosen in classic ransom note style, have all been shifted in terms of the values they actually represent. Each letter stands for another letter in the alphabet, and the key to the code is somewhere in the piece as a whole, particularly in the use of the four super-graphic letters, P, i, e, r. This is another plate whose surface I did not penetrate, and the code aspect of such substitutions, at once banal and tedious, failed to be sufficiently intriguing to suggest that its interpretation would be worth

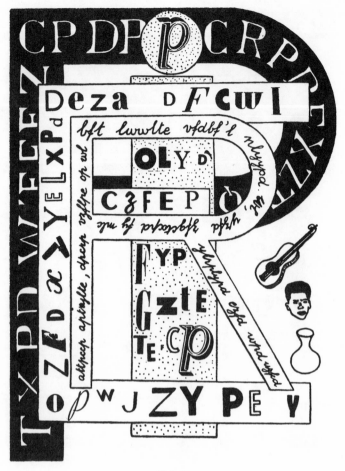

Plate D

the trouble. The intactness of the set as the guarantee of the value of each element of the notational system is the meta-issue here; the plate foregrounds the systematic nature of writing as a finite set of symbols.

The final plate uses a work frequently reproduced in standard texts on the history of writing. This work by a Youkagir Indian girl to her absent friend is not a form of writing and not dependent on language or the invention of a stable notational system capable of describing a range of messages; it is a particular figure describing a precise situation, a girl speaking of her love. In response to this valentine, Lemaître has invented a set of phonetic glyphs, also indecipherable to the uninitiated like myself, and he has surrounded the basic

Plate E

image with a heart-shaped frame, thus exaggerating the sentimental value of the original; the kitsch icon is the dominant referent in the visual field. Tiny marks encode the spoken language lost from the valentine, which in recognizing the impossibility of speaking across such a distance, attempted to recover the poignancy of lost speech: writing is not speech, it is its absence. Writing's presence conceals the lack of speech in this inscription of the words of the heart.

The content of these plates seems of less significance than their conceptual framework, the exposition of some of the features of writing as a visual form. Certainly the content is less available, and the strategies by which the writing-ness is revealed tend to obscure the semantic value behind this visual field. As a survey of writing's structural features it calls attention to the ways in which the conventions of writing depend upon certain systematic norms in order to ensure that the public/private interface succeeds in making an exchange of information.

Writing functions as a notational system for language by virtue of the same kinds of conventions which restrain spoken language within a cultural framework and ensure its operation; the forms in which language occurs adhere more or less to norms which enable messages to be recognized. When someone appropriates the territory of writing for experiment and invention, it undermines the linguistic aspect of the system of language, that is, the aspect which deals with syntactic and semantic values as they conventionally acquire definition.

The important thing Lemaître points out is the vulnerability of syntax, more than semantics, to such manipulation. For if the semantic value of a visual icon can be more or less granted within a particular cultural frame, a globe of the earth gets read as the 'world,' a rising sun as morning, or tearing eyes as sadness. We cull a 'meaning' from the little pictures as readily as we might from words. Still these icons remain isolated from any continuum in which their relations might be defined beyond a strictly linear sequence. Since these are not rebus-like arrangements, simply revealing through a laborious method a grammatical sentence, there is an absence of the duplication of a syntactic component. The argument could be made that the semantic value of language is much less unique to it than the syntactic conventions, and that the available means for communicating word values such as morning, sadness, or exit are considerable, whereas the means for constructing a prepositional relation 'of' or 'to' of a sequence of tenses or a conditional are essentially impossible within the visual realm. Realizing this, the operation of visual symbols as a form of language will carve up the space of private and public use rather differently than conventional language. It is tempting to claim private as the act of writing and public as the act of reading, to define the bringing into being of the written form as always private and the attempt to receive it as always public, since the transition requires some kind of common ground for exchange inscribed in the medium itself. Lemaître seems to want to problematize this by pushing the distinction towards another extreme, insisting that the private use of language imposes itself upon the public realm and forces the public to enter into the private domain of the author.

The process of fetishization has a different public/private opposition within it. The fetishizing of writing emphasizes the way in which it is a form of private pleasure, a self-involved activity before all else. No matter what its ultimate outcome, or place, or situation, writing begins with the self. The fetish is not just the private activity, but an image, representation of the private parts suitable for exhibition.

It is a substitute. It reveals the private parts in an alternate form, for display, and conceals the real absence of the actual object. If the pleasure of the text is private, and if the fetishizing of the letter conceals the text, then the only role for the public is that of voyeur. And the voyeur is, certainly, in this case, locked into a process of looking that is multilayered. First the eye is intrigued by the pictorial symbols, made curious enough to wonder at their relation and then to search behind the surface of the forms for some kind of meaning, some kind of value. The value, however, is all in the looking, and the interest in looking is another aspect of the fetish. This looking has nothing to do with getting to something more real, it is a purely symbolic activity, a function of the 'image of' whose status as a surrogate is actually secondary.

So the letters of Lemaître's work remain, the privileged images of a play in which the private is always on display, not in order to be revealed, but to remain, more or less, concealed. For to enter into decipherment would be to lose sight of the function and intrigue of the real, which is the image of the letters on the page. To get the text would be to lose the letters, to devalue the fetish. Instead, they remain, as the objects of intrigued curiosity, to be played with by both the author, who uses them as the inscription and objects of his privateness, and the public, which gazes voyeuristically on this display, fully defined as public by its position relative to that private material.

The fetish is the private face of the public life, and the public object of the private pleasure. The desire to look is what ensures the letters their life in both domains. Their interface in this case is the fetishized letter, which has very little to do with text.

NOTES

1 This is not actually a stone but a tablet, punched with seals which are each unique. It is called the Phaistos disc and is generally considered to be a Minoan artifact.

PUBLISHED: *Marginality: Public and Private Language* (1986), 6:109–16.

KEYWORDS: French poetics; material text; visual art; readings.

LINKS: Joanna Drucker, "Close Reading: A Billboard" (*PJ* 2), "Women and Language" (*PJ* 4); Pierre Alferi, "Seeking a Sentence" (*Guide*; *PJ* 10); Susan Bee [Laufer], "Kahlo's Gaze" (*PJ* 4); Steve Benson, "Close Reading: Leavings and Cleavings" (*Guide*; *PJ* 2); Margaret Crane and Jon Winet, from *This Is Your Life* (*PJ* 9); Tina Darragh, "Error Message" (*PJ* 5); Claire Phillips, "Violent Acts within Public Discourse" (*PJ* 6); Lev Rubinshtein, "Momma Was Washing the Window Frame" (*PJ* 8); Robin Winters, "Postmodern Means to Me That Modern Must Have Been a Very Important Movement" (*PJ* 7).

SELECTED BIBLIOGRAPHY: *Theorizing Modernism: Visual Art and the Critical Tradition* (New York: Columbia University Press, 1994); *The Alphabetic Labyrinth: The Letters in History and Imagination* (New York: Thames and Hudson, 1995); *The Century of Artists' Books* (New York: Granary, 1995); *Figuring the Word: Essays on Books, Writing, and Visual Poetics* (New York: Granary, 1998); *The Visible Word: Experimental Typography and Modern Art* (Chicago: University of Chicago Press, 1994); *Sweet Dreams: Contemporary Art and Complicity* (Chicago: University of Chicago Press, 2005); *Theorizing from Now* (Buffalo: Cuneiform Press, 2005); *Speclab: Digital Aesthetics and Speculative Computing* (Chicago: University of Chicago Press, 2008); *As No Storm* (Oakland: Rebis Press, 1975); *Twenty-Six '76 Let Hers* (Oakland: Chased Press, 1976); *Italy* (Berkeley: The Figures, 1980); *The Word Made Flesh* (New Haven, Conn.: Druckwerk, 1989); *Narratology* (New Haven, Conn.: Druckwerk, 1994); *Three Early Fictions* (Elmwood, Conn.: Potes and Poets, 1994); *Dark Decade* (Detroit: Detour Press, 1995); *History of the/my Wor(1)d* (New York: Granary, 1995); *Night Crawlers on the Web* (New York: Jabbooks/Granary, 2000); *A Girl's Life* (with Susan Bee; New York: Granary, 2002); *Combo Meals: Chance Histories* (Charlottesville, Va.: Create/Space, 2008).

Toy Boats

Among San Francisco Language writers, Carla Harryman stands out as a poet working with narrative forms. Her mini-manifesto "Toy Boats" appeared in the context of a "Symposium on Narrative" (*PJ* 5) where poets, visual artists, and musicians were asked, "What is the status of narrative in your work?" Participants responded with statements on their use or avoidance of narrative in their projects, but the motives for the question were somewhat larger. The turn to language in the 1970s, and the semiotic and poststructuralist theory that encouraged it, called for a privileging of nonnarrative and a suspicion of narrative. In wanting "to distribute narrative rather than deny it," Harryman considers both sides of the question: narrative is the location of a suspicion that undoes it (the story's lack of veracity), while the undoing of narrative is still a story to be told in its fragments. Narrative turns out to be a deeper issue than a mode of formal construction or even genre, while nonnarrative form can never be entirely separated from narrative. For Harryman, working critically within narrative form is a poetics: "I don't have to tell a story to make a point. / The story is an example of your point." Harryman's assertive and playful (non)narrative writings have had an important influence on experimental, hybrid-genre prose writing and poetics.

I prefer to distribute narrative rather than deny it.

The enemies of narrative are those who believe in it and those who deny it. Both belief and denial throw existence into question. Narrative exists, and arguments either for or against it are false. Narrative is only a ping-pong ball among blindspots when considered in the light of its advantages and defects.

Narrative holds within its boundaries both its advantages and defects. It can demonstrate its own development as it mutates throughout history. This is its great advantage. I.e., in accomplishing its mutability, it achieves an ongoing existence.

Narrative might be thought to be a character, and its defects lie in his "potential to observe his own practice of making falsehoods." If this narrative is imitating anything, it's the intention to convince the audience to enjoy its imitation, whatever the lack of truth or reasonableness.

Those who object to this artifice are narrative's enemies, but they, too, are part of the story. They are subjects in the hypothetical world of a story. "I" too am a subject of narrative; *I see enemies all around.*

Because nothing is happening these days, no weather, no fighting, morning and nights, I had thought to begin my account with a little fable or narration. But I have been intercepted en route by a question, attempting to trap in flight that which forms a narration. What does it mean to allow oneself this indulgence? The indulgence of a little story? (Meanwhile we have gone down in defeat and my account has entered history.)

This is a more or less inaccurate translation of a bit of writing from Jean Pierre Faye's *Le Récit hunique*.[1] It is a story about the temptation to tell a story whose fate by the mere coincidence of time is to enter history. Faye tells us the story about the story rather than the original story, which has disappeared into history along with the enemy. The original has been replaced with a story that functions as a critique. The critique holds its story up as an example. Or, another way to look at this is a story can be an example of a story and so serve as a critique.

What Is the Status of Narrative in Your Work?

Oh, the boats are large, are they not?

Whatever gave you that idea?

From looking at myself.

You are introspective?

I am an indication of what occurs around me. For instance, some snakes occur in forests; whereas, others occur at the zoo. This is something zoos will not confess, for when you read the labels, snakes occur someplace other than in their cages.

Your argument doesn't follow. You are a false philosopher.

I am showing you around behind the scenes and you call me a false philosopher. You don't have to call me anything. Look at those large boats, dream of the ports they have come from. Think of the miscellany they carry, the weapons that can drive anyone into a frenzy of fear and conjure a story. *From out of the blue, the boats descended upon us. We were dwarfed by their size. What were they doing here and why so many? The German and the Mongolian were nearly touching hulls. It was as if they were human and we were ants. The children playing behind us had not yet noticed this ominous display.* But as you can see, I can only make fun of the possibility of your tale.

My tale?

Isn't that what you wanted?

You have no tact, no skill, no frame of, frame of . . .

You mean no plan.

Nor do you produce resemblance or have a serious purpose or struggle with truth.

Or dally in genre literature.

There are no sentiments. It seems we are beginning to find some points of agreement. A resemblance to death and destruction is death and destruction, etc.

Like beans on the same shelf.

Yes, a bond.

The reality principle is continuous with our relationship so we don't have to trace things.

The facts we have come up against are in need of processing.

I don't have to tell a story to make a point.

The story is an example of your point. An ugly howling face comes out of nowhere. It is artfully executed.

You mean a bad boat.

No, you have provided *that* information. But don't get upset by the disparity. An harmonious relationship produces a tedious vanity and a single repetitive conversation . . .

(Then the boats sank, leaving behind them pieces of purple debris floating out of the harbor.)

The question of the status of narrative presupposes a hierarchy of literary values I do not entertain in my work. Narrative is neither an oppressor to be obliterated nor the validating force of all literary impulse.

"You get to the world through the person. Anyway, it's true. And yet, I keep wondering what does this mean in some larger sense? And then I wonder what larger sense I am getting at. There is something on the other side of what I can articulate that grabs the writing to it."[2]

Extension is inside and outside of the writer. But I could also say that the thing pulling the writing toward it is chaos: the words fall in place in anticipation of a jumble. Or equally it could be an as yet unarticulated theory, which if ever made articulate will comprise a number of fragmented histories. Histories that have been intercepted en route by questions. The result might be something like a montage of collapsed ideas. This is a reflection on the enormity of the world. I am not in possession of all the facts.

Because I continue to avoid those absolutes like morning and then night, I cannot get back to the original statement. And yet I contradict myself, as these statements distribute themselves in their oblique reference. The word *ground* here comes to mind. The ground is the constructed ideology. Or a world of print.

Do I see the ground but can't make sense of it?

I am already anticipating exhausting this subject.

A structure for writing that comes from anticipation relative to an elsewhere, which to become somewhere—i.e., a writing—must borrow from the things of this world in their partiality.

NOTES

1 Jean Pierre Faye, *Le Récit hunique* (Paris: Editions du Seuil, 1967); see Carla Harryman, *The Middle* (San Francisco: Gaz, 1984).

2 Letter to Steve Benson.

PUBLISHED: *Non/Narrative* (1985), 5:104–7.

KEYWORDS: nonnarrative; genre; performance; manifesto.

LINKS: Carla Harryman, "Pedestal/Tulip Chair" from *Chairs of Words* (*PJ* 10), "What in Fact Was Originally Improvised" (*PJ* 2), with Steve Benson, "Dialogue: Museo Antropología, Mexico" (*PJ* 8), with Chris Tysh, "Interview" (*PJ* 10); Larry Price, "Harryman's Balzac" (*PJ* 4); Bruce Campbell, "'But What Is an Adequate Vice to Limit the Liquid of This Voice'" (*PJ* 9); Kathy Acker, "Ugly" (*Guide*; *PJ* 7); Beverly Dahlen, "Forbidden Knowledge" (*Guide*; *PJ* 4); Daniel Davidson, "Bureaucrat, My Love" (*PJ* 10); Jerry Estrin, "Penultimate Witness: On Emmanuel Hocquard" (*PJ* 8); Barbara Guest, "Shifting Persona" (*PJ* 9); Peter Middleton, "The Knowledge of Narratives" (*PJ* 5); Delphine Perret, "Irony" (*PJ* 3); Viktor Shklovsky, "Plotless Literature: Vasily Rozanov" (*Guide*; *PJ* 1).

SELECTED BIBLIOGRAPHY: *Percentage* (Berkeley: Tuumba, 1979); *Under the Bridge* (San Francisco: This, 1980); *Property* (Berkeley: Tuumba, 1982); *The Middle* (San Francisco: Gaz, 1983); *Vice* (Hartford, Conn.: Potes & Poets, 1986); *Animal Instincts: Prose Plays Essays* (Berkeley: This, 1989); *In the Mode Of* (Tenerife, Spain: Zasterle, 1992); *Memory Play* (Oakland: O Books, 1994); *There Never Was a Rose without a Thorn* (San Francisco: City Lights, 1995); *The Words, after Carl Sandburg's Rootabaga Stories and Jean-Paul Sartre* (Oakland: O Books, 1999); *Gardener of Stars* (Berkeley: Atelos, 2001); *Baby* (New York: Adventures in Poetry, 2005); *Open Box* (Brooklyn: Belladonna, 2007); *Adorno's Noise* (Athens, Ohio: Essay Press, 2008); with Rae Armantrout et al., *The Grand Piano*; with Amy Scholder and Avital Ronell, *Lust for Life: On the Writings of Kathy Acker* (eds.; New York: Verso, 2006); with Lyn Hejinian, *The Wide Road* (New York: Belladonna, 2011); with Jon Raskin, *Open Box* (CD; New York: Tzadik, 2012).

Jameson's Perelman Reification
and the Material Signifier

George Hartley's essay on Fredric Jameson's reading of Language writing, specifically Bob Perelman's nonnarrative poem "China," challenges the critic's association of language-centered poetry with a litany of postmodernism's symptoms—depthlessness, the loss of historicity, the waning of affect, even "schizophrenia." Jameson's well-known essay "Post-modernism; or, The Cultural Logic of Late Capitalism" (first given as a talk in 1981) is now a touchstone of postmodern theory, but his use of Perelman's poem remains a much debated component, with potentially negative implications for avant-garde poetry. In carefully working through the theoretical (Marxist and psychoanalytic) assumptions of Jameson's essay, Hartley shows that the unconscious automatism of schizophrenic language and the conscious deployment of material signification by artists are utterly unlike: "There is a world of difference between the schizophrenic's *inability* to get beyond the material signifier and the artist's creation of one." This distinction permits Hartley to show how Perelman's aesthetics—and that of others in the avant-garde—may share common political motives with Jameson: a critique of the reification of language under capitalism and a turn toward art as a necessary corrective, through what Jameson terms "cognitive mapping." Hartley's essay was a cornerstone of his book-length study of Language writing, *Textual Politics and the Language Poets* (1989), the first—and still essential—account of the aesthetic and political aims of the movement in its emergence.

In *New Left Review* 146 (July–August 1984), Fredric Jameson published his by now notorious essay "Postmodernism; or, the Cultural Logic of Late Capitalism." In that essay he compares Lacan's description of schizophrenic language to the writings of what he refers to as the Language Poets. He points out in particular that Bob Perelman, in his poem "China," seems to have made schizophrenic language the basis of his aesthetic. Prior to Jameson, John Ensslin [...] also pointed out the striking similarities between clinical accounts of schizophrenic language and recent poetry, but he offered "one precaution: don't confuse schizophrenic speech with poetic language.... To treat [schizophrenic speech] as a freakish bit of literature is to overlook the fact that these bizarre turns of language are the products of a torturous state of mind." Jameson's problem is the opposite of this—confusing poetic language with schizophrenic speech.

To be sure, Jameson is careful to explain that he is using Lacan's account only as a useful description, not to imply that Perelman is in any way a clinical schizophrenic. But even if such is the case—I will later argue against his claim to innocent description—the usefulness of such a comparison is far from obvious, *especially* in the way he uses it. Nevertheless, the positive value of the Lacanian notion of schizophrenia, if there is one in this context, is its bringing into focus two conflicting accounts of the effects of reification on language use, as well as two conflicting aesthetics. At the heart of the debate is the material signifier—the significatory unit (whether the phoneme, the word, the phrase, or the sentence) isolated from standard syntactical patterns, drawing attention to itself as much as, or more than, to any concept it may point to. The question comes down to this: what are the political effects of the use of the material signifier? [...]

The key to evaluating Jameson's comments about postmodernism is to grasp the basic concept behind his periodization. That concept, based on Nikos Poulantzas's extension of Althusserian theory, is *social formation*.

In *Political Power and Social Classes* Poulantzas writes that the "mode of production constitutes an abstract-formal object which does not exist in the strong sense of reality.... The only thing which really exists is a historically determined social formation, i.e. a social whole, in the widest sense, at a given moment in its historical existence: e.g., France under Louis Bonaparte, England during the Industrial Revolution" (15). "Mode of production" is to be viewed as a methodological concept, not as some real discrete object. The social formation may ultimately be determined by a mode of production, but it can never be reduced to one. Poulantzas explains further that "a social formation ... presents a particular combination, a specific overlapping of several 'pure' modes of production" [leading to] the expanded view of historical determination [that] follows:

> The dominance of one mode of production over others in a social formation causes the matrix of this mode of production ... to mark the whole of the formation. In this way a historically determined social formation is specified by a particular articulation (through an index of dominance and overdetermination) of its different economic, political, ideological and theoretical levels or instances. (15–16)

The key phrase in the above passage is "index of dominance and overdetermination." Rather than crudely reducing the complex network of various social determinations to the economic, we can now take into account the influences of many relatively autonomous levels or instances at one time, each level's relative autonomy stemming from its own determined placement within a network of competing modes of production. Raymond Williams refers to these competing influences as the residual (the remaining influence of past modes), the dominant, and the emergent (nascent modes struggling for dominance; 121–27). One problem we avoid, at least in part, by focusing on the particularity and relative autonomy of the various levels of the social formation is the positing of homologies between different levels. The Hegelian notion of an expressive totality—in which each analytically distinguished level of society is seen as an expression of some essence and thus structurally similar to all other levels—often leads to the conclusion that cultural objects are expressions of the economic base. This is not to say that the Althusserians reject the concept of totality, just that they define it differently. "The structure is not an essence *outside* the economic phenomena," Althusser explains,

> which comes and alters their aspect, forms and relations and which is effective on them as an absent cause, *absent because it is outside them. The absence of the cause in the structure's "metonymic causality" on its effects is not the fault of the exteriority of the structure with respect to the economic phenomena; on the contrary, it is the very form of the interiority of the structure ... in its effects*. (188; his emphasis)

The reasons for this discussion of the Althusserian concept of social formation should become clear when we turn to Jameson's notion of a cultural dominant in his definition of postmodernism. From the concept of social formation Jameson develops an important analogy on the cultural plane—which we presumably could call the *cultural formation*, an analogy that becomes clear when Jameson writes that "it seems to me essential to grasp 'postmodernism' not as a style, but rather as a cultural dominant" ("Postmodernism," 56). [...] Once he substitutes cultural dominant for structural dominant (or "structure-in-dominance"), the rest of the analogy falls into place, the cultural formation being seen as determined by the various conflicting cultural modes of production at a given moment. After doing so, he can then (theoretically, at least) avoid many of the problems that surround all attempts at periodization, especially the problem of explaining how an artist from what we determine to be the modern period can look quite like those artists we associate with an earlier or later period—just as the concept of social formation helps to explain the existence of typically feudal features, for example, in the capitalist era [...]: "I am very far from feeling that all cultural production today is 'postmodern' in the broad sense I will be conferring on this term. The postmodern is how-ever the force field in which very different kinds of cultural impulses— ... 'residual' and 'emergent' forms of cultural production—must make their way" (57).

Such a formula allows him to write, for example, that "Gertrude Stein, Raymond Roussel, or Marcel Duchamp ... may be considered outright post-modernists, *avant la lettre*" (56). He goes on to qualify this statement, however, in what may be the most important point in his essay.

> What has not been taken into account by this view is ... the social position of the older modernism.... [Modernism and postmodernism] still remain utterly distinct in their meaning and social function, owing to the very dif-ferent positioning of postmodernism in the economic system of late capi-tal, and beyond that, to the transformation of the very sphere of culture in contemporary society. (56–57)

Literary form, in other words, takes on its particular political meaning from its position within a specific historical context. Having said this, however, Jame-son then overgeneralizes the political context of postmodernism, neglecting to sort out the various contexts which Poulantzas's conception of social for-mation posits. The social positioning of a particular form may have a different political charge depending on its relationship not only to the period but also to its overdetermined location within the social formation. [...]

It is when Jameson fleshes out this very promising outline by describing what he sees as the political effects of postmodernism in the present social formation that problems arise, most notably as a return to the very homolo-gies that he has elsewhere warned us against. Specifically, his importation of Lacan's discussion of schizophrenia leads him to the traditional Marxist de-nunciation of modernist (and now postmodernist) fragmentation, rather than to an appreciation of Perelman's particular use of the material signifier as a political critique. Jameson frames his discussion of Perelman's "China" in such a way that he prematurely forecloses any other avenues of a more positive analysis. That frame begins with his discussion of what he sees as the consti-tutive feature of postmodernism: its new depthlessness.

By contrasting Van Gogh's painting of peasant shoes with Andy Warhol's *Diamond Dust Shoes* Jameson illustrates one of the major differences he sees between modernism and postmodernism. While Van Gogh's shoes must be seen as the result of the reification of the senses—in this case, sight—due to the increased division of labor under capitalism, Jameson also draws attention to its utopian side, in which "the most glorious materialization of pure colour in oil paint is to be seen as ... an act of compensation" (59) for precisely that fragmented life in capitalist society. The painting speaks to us, imparts its meaning as it "draws the whole absent world and earth into revelation around itself," representing the wretched life of the peasant woman. The problem with Warhol's shoes, however, is that they don't speak to us at all. Instead "we have a random collection of dead objects, hanging together on the canvas like so many turnips, as shorn of their earlier life-world as the pile of shoes left over at Auschwitz, or the remainders and tokens of some incomprehensible and tragic fire in a packed dancehall" (60). The images of Auschwitz and a tragic fire are not incidental here. Even though Jameson has just stressed the need to see the utopian value of Van Gogh's reified impressionism, he expends very little of such dialectical thought on his postmodern examples. Although later in the essay he will try to rescue his argument from a "pre-Marxian" moralism, it remains clear here that Warhol *ought* to do something other than present dead and meaningless objects on a canvas.

At any rate, this passage from Van Gogh to Warhol, Jameson claims, illustrates "perhaps the supreme formal feature" of postmodernism—its anti-hermeneutical, superficial depthlessness. The "deep" works of the modernists have been succeeded by the slick TV surfaces of the simulacrum, the image. Jameson describes one problem with the simulacrum as follows:

> The simulacrum['s] ... particular function lies in what Sartre would have called the *derealization* of the whole surrounding world of everyday reality. [...] The world thereby momentarily loses its depth and threatens to become a glossy skin, a stereoscopic illusion, a rush of filmic images without density. (76–77)

The simulacrum's derealization of everyday life affects not only spatial but temporal depth as well. Jameson argues that "what was once, in the historical novel as Lukács defines it, the organic genealogy of the bourgeois collective project ... has meanwhile itself become a vast collection of images, a multitudinous photographic simulacrum. ... In faithful conformity to poststructuralist linguistic theory, the past as 'referent' finds itself gradually bracketed, and then effaced altogether, leaving us with nothing but texts" (66). Postmodernists substitute a nostalgic cannibalization of past styles for an older attempt to come to terms with "real" history. This crisis in historicity appears in a formal innovation of postmodernism, namely the transformation of the time-bound narrative sentence into the "finished, complete, and isolated punctual event—objects which find themselves sundered from any present situation" (70)—the material signifier.

In order to make sense of these "heaps of fragments," Jameson next resorts to Lacan's account of schizophrenia "as a breakdown in the signifying chain, that is, the interlocking syntagmatic series of signifiers which constitutes an utterance or a meaning" (71–72). The function of the sentence is to form our personal identity: "If we are unable to unify the past, present, and future of the sentence," Jameson claims, "then we are similarly unable to unify the past, present and future of our own biographical experience or psychic life" (72). (The key word here which he seems to ignore in his analysis is "unable.") What makes all this relevant for Marxism is that such a meaningful grasp of historical time is necessary for political praxis. Without it we cannot recognize the historical determination of present conditions which we need to change. But it is Jameson's extension of all this to cultural production to which I object.

My first objection is that his description of the signifying chain does not convey the full import of Lacan's conception. Lacan is not talking about individual sentences when he uses this term, although sentences do illustrate on a manifest level what he is describing; rather, "signifying chain" refers to the structure of the unconscious as a whole, which can be compared to a sentence but cannot be reduced to one. [. . .] "That the dream uses speech makes no difference," Lacan writes, "since for the unconscious it is only one among several elements of the representation" (161).

The signifying chain constitutes the unconscious. But this occurs only after the primal repression of the Imaginary phase, during which the subject cannot distinguish its own body from that of others, seeing instead "a world of bodies and organs which in some fashion lacks a phenomenological center and a privileged point of view" (Jameson, "Imaginary and Symbolic in Lacan," 354). The failure to complete this process of repression leads to the various forms of psychosis. Lacan refers to this failure as the *foreclusion* or foreclosure of the Other, the refusal or inability to enter the Symbolic Order of signification. "Foreclosure effects neither the judgment of existence nor the negation; only the symbol remains, but, because of the absence of its relation to the signified, it loses its true value as a signifier, as a symbol. It is no longer any more than an image taken for reality. The imaginary has become the real" (Lemaire, 233). In other words, the schizophrenic is left with material signifiers. [. . .]

According to Lacan, schizophrenic discourse is binary, while Symbolic discourse is ternary. The schizophrenic remains at or reverts to the Imaginary state of unmediated fusion of self and other, of subject and signifier. Only in the Symbolic Order do these two poles become mediated by a third—language. There is no meaning engendered by the schizophrenic's material signifier; the question arises, however, whether such is the case with the poet's material signifier. In other words, does the poet's signifier signify? This question brings me to my second and major complaint against Jameson's use of *schizophrenic* even as a descriptive term (although it is obviously more than that for Jameson). There is a world of difference between the schizophrenic's *inability* to get beyond the material signifier and the artist's creation of one: whereas the schizophrenic could be said to operate on a pre-Symbolic level of discourse, poets such as Perelman operate on a meta-Symbolic plane. Jameson implies that the effect of the material signifier, whether produced by the psychotic or the artist, is the same in either case. But in order to reach this conclusion, he has to ignore his own argument about the variability of formal effect within different contexts.

I would argue that Jameson's brief commentary on "China" does not entirely constitute his analysis of the poem. The actual analysis of "China" and, by illegitimate extension, of all Language writing, lies in his inserting the poem at a specific moment of his essay. While Jameson claims that he mainly wants to show that "schizophrenic" writing has no necessary relationship to psychosis, the momentum of the essay necessitates just that relationship; adopting the Lacanian apparatus at such a key moment in the essay is not merely descriptive but ascriptive. The use of the label *schizophrenia*, in other words, is no innocent gesture but instead a strategic form of guilt-by-association.

Now to Jameson's discussion of "China." "Many things," he begins, "could be said about this interesting exercise in discontinuities: not the least paradoxical is the reemergence here across these disjoined sentences of some more unified global meaning" (74). [. . .] Jameson goes on to say that the poem "does seem to capture something of the excitement of the immense, unfinished social experiment of the New China." The important unstated point is that the claim of schizophrenia may not hold here precisely because of this reemergent unity. But Jameson next assures us that "we have not thereby fully exhausted the structural secrets of Perelman's poem, which turns out to have little enough to do with the referent called China" (75). Pointing out that Perelman's lines in the poem were written as captions to photographs in a Chinese book, Jameson contends that the unity of the poem lies outside it in the absent Chinese text. Perelman's poem is thus a text about a text, just as photorealist works are pictures of pictures, or simulacra.

Once Perelman's poem becomes reduced to the simulacrum, it has the same political effect for Jameson as the schizophrenic signifier. In both cases we confront free-floating signifiers with little or no connection to the "real world," serving at best as decoration but more often more negatively as distraction from the real work to be done—symptoms and perpetuations of reification. There seems to be a naive mimeticism at work here that exposes the problem behind Jameson's attack on the simulacrum. Is the authenticity or political efficacy of a work really dependent on the immediacy of its model? And are a text's model and its referent identical? How Perelman generated his text is in any case irrelevant to our understanding it. Jameson here outdoes Plato by attacking Perelman for creating a copy of a copy of a copy.

Using Ernest Mandel's conception of Late Capitalism, or the period of multinational capital which has transformed society into a "whole new decentred global network" beyond representation, Jameson posits that the corresponding technological analogue is the machine of reproduction—the television, the camera, the computer—whose processes are also beyond representation. Modernist artists, excited by the "sculptural nodes of energy" of the electric and combustion motors (machines of *pro*duction), represented that kinetic energy in their art. But postmodernists, Jameson continues, are more concerned with "the processes of reproduction . . . [such as] movie cameras, video, tape recorders, the whole technology of the production and reproduction of the simulacrum" (79).

Depending on how it is used, such a formula of homological relations could become a technologism and a Marxism at its crudest. When one thinks of some recent artistic creations such as Max Headroom, then Jameson's formula can be seen to have a legitimate specific application (or "local validity," as he might say), the capitalist appropriation of art forms being especially clear. But when the search for the "logic of the simulacrum" is overgeneralized, it not only leads to oversimplification but also blinds us to those contemporary works of art which challenge such a logic. Jameson is aware of this:

> In the most interesting postmodernist works . . . one can detect a more positive conception of relationship [than the censure of fragmentation] which restores its proper tension to the notion of difference itself. This new mode of relationship through difference may sometimes be an achieved new and original way of thinking and perceiving; more often it takes the form of an impossible imperative to achieve that new mutation [in perceptual organs] in what can perhaps no longer be called consciousness. (75)

Jameson all too quickly discards the possibility of a positive conception of relationship through difference for the latter negative critique of postmodernism throughout most of his essay.

As we have seen, Jameson implicitly attributes Perelman's schizophrenic aesthetic to the process of reification in late capitalist society. It is interesting, therefore, to find Perelman and others claiming that their aesthetic is based on a critique of precisely that same fragmenting process. When Steve McCaffery writes, for instance, that "Marx's notion of commodity fetishism ... has been central to my own considerations of reference in language," we at least have to examine this claim before characterizing the poetry. Such an examination reveals that foregrounding the materiality of language, far from a schizophrenic disorder or an hallucinatory escapism, is intended instead, according to Bruce Andrews, as "a political writing practice that unveils demystifies the creation & sharing of meaning." Words are never our own, Ron Silliman reminds us, "rather, they are our own usages of a determinate coding passed down to us like all other products of civilization" ("Political Economy of Poetry"). The unveiling of this determinate coding and the ways in which that coding reinforces the capitalist power structure lies behind the "schizophrenic" poetry of Perelman, McCaffery, Andrews, Silliman, and others.

"The essence of commodity-structure," Georg Lukács explains, "is that a relation between people takes on the character of a thing and thus acquires a 'phantom objectivity,' an autonomy that seems so strictly rational and all-embracing as to conceal every trace of its fundamental nature: the relation between people" (83). Evidently for Jameson the material signifier exemplifies just this process of fragmentation and "thingification," as Marx called it. Even Jackson Mac Low asks, "What could be more of a fetish or more alienated than slices of language stripped of reference?" (23). Indeed, if all that these poets were doing was isolating language from its social context, then they would be perpetuating reification. But is that what Perelman and others are doing? Reification, we should remember, is an effect of an historically determined mode of perception, *not* a formal quality residing in the commodity or the signifier. A material signifier by itself neither perpetuates nor liberates us from reification. How we perceive the social relations inscribed within the signifier will determine its particular political effect. [...]

What is missing from "China" are the standard syntactical conjunctions and explicitly coherent subject matter common to everyday speech. But when have these components been necessary for poetry? At least since Pound's "In a

Station of the Metro," parataxis has seemed to many *the* "poetic" form of jux-taposition, with its demand that the reader fill in the gaps between the lines, as we have been doing with "China." Unlike those in Pound's poem, however, the gaps in "China" are not metaphoric but, as in Stein's *Tender Buttons*, met-onymic. The meaning of the poem develops along the axis of contiguity, the sentences establishing an interlocking, sometimes contradictory and polyse-mous, series of semantic frames which continually qualify and redirect the overall narrative movement. "China" is "certainly not something that tries to throw you off the track," Perelman has suggested to me in conversation, "like playing train as a kid, whipping from side to side until someone falls off." The foregrounded structuration of this poem, far from obliterating the meaning of its content, *adds* a formal dimension of meaning quite consistent with the content's insistence on change, perceptual renewal, and self-determination. The structure of the poem itself can be seen as a metaphor for the historical process that Poulantzas describes in his complex, conflictual model of the so-cial formation.

Contrary to the implications of Jameson's schizophrenia analogy, Perelman isn't suggesting that we can do without narration, only that 1) the particular narrations into which we are inserted are coded justifications for the status quo, and 2) there are alternative ways of structuring (constituting) our experi-ences. Such alternatives *foreground* our social relations, not reify them. [...]

The foregrounding of the materiality of the signifier at this time is meant to draw attention to the socially inscribed gestural nature of language, the dialectical consciousness of which capitalism seeks to repress by valorizing what Ron Silliman calls the "disappearance of the word / appearance of the world syndrome" of realism. Seen in this context, poems like "China" must be seen as critiques of and utopian compensation for the reification of language in late capitalism.

WORKS CITED

Althusser, Louis, et al. *Reading Capital*. Trans. Ben Brewster. London: New Left Books, 1970.

Andrews, Bruce. "Writing Social Work and Political Practice." In *The L=A=N=G=U=A=G=E Book*, ed. Andrews and Charles Bernstein. Carbondale: Southern Illinois University Press, Ill., 1984.

Bartlett, Lee. "What Is 'Language Poetry'?" *Critical Inquiry* 12, no. 4 (Summer 1986): 741–52.

Ensslin, John. "Schizophrenic Writing." *L=A=N=G=U=A=G=E*, no. 4 (August 1978).

Jameson, Fredric. "Imaginary and Symbolic in Lacan: Marxism, Psychoanalytic Criticism, and the Problem of the Subject." *Yale French Studies* 55/56 (1977): 338–95.

———. "Postmodernism; or, the Cultural Logic of Late Capitalism." *New Left Review* 146 (July–August 1984): 53–92. An earlier version, "Postmodernism and Consumer Society," appeared in Hal Foster, ed., *The Anti-Aesthetic*. Port Townsend, Wash.: Bay Press, 1983.

Lacan, Jacques. *Ecrits*. Trans. Alan Sheridan. London: Norton, 1977.

Lemaire, Anika. *Jacques Lacan*. Trans. David Macey. London: Routledge and Kegan Paul, 1970.

Lukács, Georg. *History and Class Consciousness: Studies in Marxist Dialectics*. Trans. Rodney Livingstone. Cambridge, Mass.: MIT Press, 1971.

Mac Low, Jackson. "'Language-Centered.'" *L=A=N=G=U=A=G=E* 4 (Winter 1982): 23–26.

McCaffery, Steve. "Repossessing the Word." *L=A=N=G=U=A=G=E* 1, no. 2 (April 1978): n.p.

Perelman, Bob. "Exchangeable Frames." *Poetics Journal* 5 (May 1985): 168–76.

———. *Primer*. San Francisco: This Press, 1981.

Poulantzas, Nikos. *Political Power and Social Classes*. Trans. Timothy O'Hagan. London: Verso, 1973.

Silliman, Ron. "Disappearance of the Word, Appearance of the World." *L=A=N=G=U=A=G=E*, supplement no. 3 (October 1981): n.p.

———. "The Political Economy of Poetry." *L=A=N=G=U=A=G=E* 4 (Winter 1982): 52–65.

Williams, Raymond. *Marxism and Literature*. Oxford: Oxford University Press, 1977.

PUBLISHED: *Postmodern?* (1987), 7:52–62.

KEYWORDS: Language writing; Marxism; postmodernism; material text.

LINKS: George Hartley, "Althusser Metonymy China Wall" (*PJ* 10); David Benedetti, "Fear of Poetic (Social) Knowledge: Why Some People Don't Like (Language) Poetry" (*PJ* 10); Bruce Boone, "Kathy Acker's *Great Expectations*" (*PJ* 4); Félix Guattari, "Language, Consciousness, and Society" (*PJ* 9); Bob Perelman, "Plotless Prose" (*PJ* 1); Perelman, "Exchangeable Frames" (*PJ* 5); Larry Price, "The Contingency Caper" (*PJ* 7); Dmitrii Prigov, "Conceptualism and the West" (*PJ* 8); Barrett Watten, "The Literature of Surface" (*PJ* 7).

SELECTED BIBLIOGRAPHY: *Textual Politics and the Language Poets* (Bloomington: Indiana University Press, 1989); *The Abyss of Representation: Marxism and the Postmodern Sublime* (Durham, N.C.: Duke University Press, 2003).

Good and Bad / Good and Evil
Pound, Céline, and Fascism

The Pound Tradition is a much debated context for poetics. While Ezra Pound was a major proponent of innovation in modernist form, and thus progressive in aesthetic terms, his authoritarian dogmatism, the Rome Radio broadcasts and their anti-Semitic content, and the dispute over his canonization after his award of the Bollingen Prize (1948) have kept his reception in doubt. What should a politically conscious, formally innovative poet make of the paradox of Ezra Pound? Bob Perelman addresses this troubling dark side of modernism, framed by Friedrich Nietzsche's distinction between good/bad and good/evil in *The Geneal-ogy of Morals* and its later use for Nazi ideology. For Perelman, readings of Pound's poetry as aesthetically "good"—in its progressive techniques of "direct treatment of the thing" and its rejection of sentiment—mask an expulsion of unwanted psychic material (after Julia Kristeva's concept of "abjection") that makes poetic form complicit with despicable politics—the expulsion and destruction of the Jews and other groups. Perelman goes on to read the psychic abjection of difficult "material" in Louis-Ferdinand Céline's novels as a model for anti-Semitism in fascism, showing how Pound's formal construction of value in *The Cantos* connects his diatribes against Jews, usury, and cultural degeneracy with the value-making assumptions of poetry. Perelman's essay is a courageous challenge to examine the psychic mechanisms of literary form as inherently political and moral.

We use the terms *good* and *bad* when discussing writing; we reserve *good* and *evil* for politics. To call writing evil seems exaggerated. A good writer can have bad politics, we say, treating politics aesthetically, which is much the easiest way. Pound and Céline had lousy politics, we say, but they're good writers. Since their political statements are often so monstrous, since support-ing Hitler and Mussolini is no longer a live option, and since Pound and Céline both, in various ingenuous to disingenuous ways, recanted, it's convenient to dismiss their politics as having arisen from some psychological defect and to look at what's good in their writing in a purely aesthetic context. But politics, aesthetics, and psychology are so intertwined in their work as to provide a chance to explode the fiction of a purely aesthetic or formal consideration of writing.

To start with an unfair comparison. Take the Compleynt of Artemis in Canto XXX:

Pity spareth so many an evil thing.

. . . .

All things are made foul in this season,
This is the reason, none may seek purity
Having for foulnesse pity
And things growne awry;
No more do my shaftes fly
To slay. Nothing is now clean slayne
But rotteth away.   (147)

Compare Himmler, speaking to the SS group leaders in 1943:

"The Jewish people are to be exterminated," says every party member. "That's clear, it's part of our program, elimination of the Jews, extermination, right, we'll do it." And then they all come along, the eighty million upstanding Germans, and each one has his decent Jew. Of course the others are swine, but this one is a first-class Jew. . . . Not one has had the stomach for it. Most of you know what it is to see a hundred corpses lying together, five hundred, or a thousand. To have gone through this and yet . . . to have remained decent, this has made us hard. This is a glorious page in our history. (In Miller, 79)

I find it hard to believe, but as I watch myself reading, I see myself feeling as much anger towards Pound's words as towards Himmler's. Clearly my feelings have no sense of scale. After all, Himmler is a mass murderer talking to an audience of mass murderers, exhorting them to kill with a firmer sense of purpose. But his language is a dull blend of pep talk, nagging, and that horrible mix of disguised arousal ("made us hard") and cliché at the end. The fact that its reference is absolutely real makes its bathetic surface stupefyingly pathological.

So why be mad at Pound? He wrote those lines as a supporter of Mussolini, but before Hitler came to power. And what is he talking about? Artemis, for god's sake. Meaning what? Is he complaining that *Poetry* is publishing too much Amygism? That people are listening to Brahms and not Antheil?

But reference isn't exactly the point, nor is the exact depth of Pound's commitment to fascism. It is true that there are passages in his radio broadcasts where he calls for Jews to be murdered and preaches eugenics; in a letter he writes, "With 6 million jews on the premises, the U.S. has 5 million 900 thousand walking advertisements for the Nazi regime" (in Nicholls, 155); in the *Pisan*

Cantos, after his supposed recantation, he writes, "and the only people who did anything of any interest were H., M. and/Frobenius" (LXXIV [436]), and twice in the later Cantos he speaks of Hitler as "furious from perception" (XC [606] and CIV [741]). But beyond the damning particulars of Pound's personal history, beyond the analogies that are present between the Compleynt and Himmler's address, there is the fact that, as writing, the Compleynt is so good. Pound's lines have art, and are not displaceable. They stand there unavoidably perceptible and particular. Archaism, rhyme, half rhyme, long vowels, wrenched emphatic word order, enjambment—a crude telegraphic list to forestall a long discussion of terribly effective sound patterning: "clean slayne."

It's right there that my anger lodges.

I can see much of Pound's work, holographically, fractally, in those two words. They fit together like granite blocks, so "clean," "hard," "virile." Consider when he leaves Hell in Canto XVI: "the passage clean-squared in granite" (69); or "With usura hath no man a house of good stone / each block cut smooth and well fitting" (XLV [229]); or the way he so easily eliminates societies for lack of such hardness and precision: "'No civilization' said Knittl, they got no stone.' (Hrooshia)" (LXXXIX [604]). Or consider the clean/rot separation which governs so much of what he says, or the *ay* of "slayne," its erotic, pagan archaism.

There's power on Pound's page, and it's shocking how writing so good makes such an accurate anthem to the glories of the SS. This is not mere irony, as when a death-camp commander whiles away his spare time listening to Beethoven or reading Goethe. The rhyme between Pound and Himmler is not fortuitous.

Pound pretends to a god-like moral perfection, and strives to make his art perfect. Céline, on the other hand, aspires in the opposite direction, and thus makes for much more "comforting" and "amusing" reading. Words, for him, are definitely not instruments of perfection. "Our sentences are hard put to it to survive the disaster of their slobbery origins. The mechanical effort of conversation is nastier and more complicated than defecation . . ." (*Journey*, 291). [. . .]

At this point, it will be useful to bring in Nietzsche. His discussion of good-and-bad and good-and-evil is helpful in comprehending how Pound's transcendent fascism is related to the more hysterical, anarchic variety indulged in by Céline.

In *The Genealogy of Morals*, Nietzsche explains that the term *good* originates with the nobility. It conflates their power and their essence; they *are*, and they are good. *Good* and *bad* originally meant good and not-so-good: noble, fair-haired, tough and healthy; or not. But, Nietzsche's originary narrative goes on, if the warrior and priest castes aren't synonymous, there's trouble: impotent vengeful priests, the worst kind of enemies. These are the Jews who "dared to invert the aristocratic value equations: good/ noble/powerful/ beautiful/happy/favored-of-the-gods and maintain, with the furious hatred of the underprivileged and impotent, that 'only the poor, the powerless, are good; only the suffering, sick, and ugly, truly blessed'" (167–68). This "Jewish inversion of values" produced the moral categories of good and evil, which are therefore a slavish invention; Christian love, sickly and anti-life, grows out of this damaged root. A key point is that the "good" of the good/bad pair, the powerful nobles, are precisely the "evil" of the good/evil pair, the powerful slave masters. [. . .]

Listing the primary, most powerful terms first, the two sets could be redefined as Strong/bad and Evil/weak. Another point to keep in mind is that there's a narrative involved: the Strong are originary, archaic, ancestral; the Evil are historical. What "the poets sing about" is always set back in the mythic past.

Céline belongs to the second pair. But where Nietzsche places slaves and nobles in a national, cultural setting, for Céline in *Journey to the End of the Night* and *Death on the Installment Plan* the stage is much smaller, and more privatized: the family is the matrix where the Evil keep the weak in their place. It's a grim and disfiguring battle. In *Journey*, the narrator, living in a tenement, overhears some parents beating their daughter:

> First they tied her up; it took a long time, like getting ready for an operation. That gave them a kick. "You little skunk!" cried the father. "The filthy slut!" went the mother. [. . .] Meanwhile the child was squeaking like a mouse in a trap. "That won't help you, you little scum. You've got it coming! Oh, yes! You've got it coming!" . . . They gave her a terrible thrashing. I listened to the end to make sure that I wasn't mistaken, that this was really going on. . . . I was helpless. . . .
>
> And then I heard the old man saying:
>
> "All right, old girl! Step lively! In there!" As happy as a lark.
>
> He said that to the mother, and then the door to the next room would slam behind them. Once she said to him, I heard her: "Oh, Julien, I love you so much, I could eat your shit, even if you made turds this big . . ." (229–30)

This sense of detachment, of listening in horror, which might ultimately connote some moral purpose, vanishes in *Death on the Installment Plan*. Ferdinand, the narrator, Céline's namesake, becomes that abused child.

Childhood there is a disgusting fecal prison—his ass is never clean—with his father constantly bellowing and his mother whining at him in reaction to the mental and economic hopelessness of their lives. For hundreds of pages they frantically struggle to get out of debt, the father working in an insurance office, hating it and terrified of being fired, and the mother, lame, limping around Paris to sell second-hand lace. They constantly feel themselves falling short and compensate by foisting their dreams onto Ferdinand, who fails miserably at everything.

He goes to school and learns nothing. He has one moment of success, passing his examinations (even though he seems to know nothing more than that there are four seasons) and receiving a proud hug from his father. But the fact that he's shit in his pants turns this triumph into more mortification.

Out of school, Ferdinand looks for work. It's hot, hopeless, his suit is boiling, his shoes pinch, he's dirty. Somehow, he manages to find a lousy job as a jeweler's errand boy, but then he gets seduced by the Boss's wife, a graphic cow; there's a sex scene, with Ferdinand humiliated by his black feet and, as usual, his unwiped ass. The seduction is part of a swindle to steal a gold scarab he's carrying around in his pocket for the Boss (castration) and to pin the blame on him. The guilt sticks, of course: he's fired.

Days, months, or years later—there's no time in Céline's writing, only the accumulation and evacuation of stress—he's sent on a sensible errand by his mother. The scene (308–17) reads like a cross between Jack and the Beanstalk and Oedipus Rex. At first the fairy tale predominates. His mother sends him out to buy a careful measure of this and that—"seventy centimes' worth of their best ham for your father . . . three portions of cream cheese and if you can remember a head of lettuce, not too wide open"—but of course he completely screws up, ending up in a drunken delirium amid a pile of stuporous bodies in the mud of a park lake which they have drained dry by their thirst on a boiling summer day. (Céline is no realist.)

Back home at two in the morning, we're in the land of Oedipus. Ferdinand is drunk, smeared with mud and cream cheese; the father, suffering from boils, still up practicing his typing in a pathetic attempt at career advancement, is furious: the mother is lying in the bed, "naked up to her stomach," as the father sees it. He begins a typical Célinian tirade, pages and pages of obsessive, static nagging: "As corrupt as three dozen jailbirds! . . . Profligate! Scoundrel! Idler! And then some! He's calamity personified!" etc. (314).

Father and son fight, almost to the death. Céline makes sure we feel the father's pus, fat, blood: "I dig into the meat . . . It's soft . . . He's drooling . . . I tug

... I pull off a big chunk of moustache." At the end of the fight, the father has turned into a baby. "I squeeze some more. I knock his head against the tiles ... He goes limp ... he's soft under my legs ... He sucks my thumb" (316–17).

But if the parents are the fountain of endless horror and disgust, the one good, sane figure in the book is Uncle Edouard, who is constantly coming to Ferdinand's rescue. [...] These good uncles represent kind fathers, not fulminating irrationally, not covered with boils, not economic failures. Céline longs to have the hopelessness and rage that he sees within the petit bourgeois family resolved without altering its structure.

But the hopelessness and rage have left their mark: the child, the self, will always be a mess, a defect. Just as his parents feel victimized by society and by their problem son, Céline asserts his identical status: "I stuck to my convictions. I too felt myself to be a victim in every way" (289–90).

These are the feelings of an abused child, and, as Alice Miller shows in *For Your Own Good*, were a possible psychological basis for the rise of Fascism. *Mein Kampf* contains descriptions of family life that are very much like those in Céline's first two novels. The same cycle of debt, despair, nagging, self-loathing, and violence prevails in the midst of hopeless pretense towards bourgeois respectability. Hitler was regularly beaten and humiliated by his bastard-risen-to-civil-servant father, who always wore his uniform, insisted on being addressed as "Herr," and, when he wanted Hitler to come to him, would whistle on two fingers. But Hitler clung all the more tightly to the family model of power of which he was the victim. A world without Father meant Communism—swarms, chaos, death:

> The Jewish doctrine of Marxism rejects the aristocratic principle of Nature [Father] and replaces the eternal privilege of power and strength [Father] by the mass of numbers and their dead weight. ... The result of an application of this law could only be chaos, on earth it could only be destruction for the inhabitants of this planet. (65–66)

Here, the apotheosis of the father conflates the historical (the aristocracy, i.e., feudalism) with the transhistorical (Nature and eternity) in ways that will be quite similar to Pound's. This granting of omnipotence to a finite source of damage was the initial Big Lie of the Nazi regime. It was, obviously, quite a popular solution. Céline, in the first part of his career, avoided any such solutions, instead clinging obsessively to his devastating presentation of the problem. In his hands it was so funny, so horrific, and his use of slang gave voice to such a large, hitherto-silent segment of society, that his first two books were immensely popular. Not so popular in France as National Socialism in Germany, but still, for a novelist, not bad.

Quite possibly ill at ease with such success, in the late thirties he staked this literary capital in a passionate and hysterical political gesture, transforming himself from a nihilistic novelist, acclaimed by the left, to a virulently anti-Semitic right-wing pamphleteer, publishing *Mea Culpa*, *Bagatelles for a Massacre*, *School for Corpses*, and *Les Beaux Draps*. The pamphlets are violently anti-Semitic, pacifist, and somewhat diffidently fascist, but, throughout, threads of self-loathing are mingled together with the anti-Semitism, and large patches of anarchy and even a little vague communism blur the commitment to fascism. At first, in right-wing circles and later in Vichy France, Céline was acclaimed as a famous spokesman. But by the time the third pamphlet came out, Céline, as well as being despised by the left, was considered useless by the right and was ignored. After the war, of course, he was scum. Throughout, and to the end of his life, he "felt himself to be a victim in every way." [...]

The pamphlets reproduce the structure of the Célinian family. The above represents the horrible father, the existing cultural institutions. The child-individual is more worthless than ever: no longer merely unwashed, he is now pure shit. Religion, the father-institution, has made this explicit. It "grabbed hold of man in the cradle and broke the bad news to him right away.... 'You little amorphous particle of putrescence, you'll never be anything except garbage. By birth you're just shit'" (*Mea Culpa*, in Thiher, 229–30). There is also the good father or uncle, now a beneficent dictator. Céline has a tepid vision of "all of France in the same family, Jews excluded of course, a single family, a single dad, dictator and respected" (*Les Beaux Draps*, in Kristeva, 177). "Jews excluded of course"—but, unfortunately for Céline, his vision of the Jew is so polymorphous that it includes almost everyone. England and the Church are Jewish; Stalin is Jewish; France is Jewish. The Jews are "camouflaged, disguised, chameleon-like, they change names like they cross frontiers, now they pass themselves off for Bretons, Auvergnats, Corsicans ..." (*Bagatelles*, in Kristeva, 181). It's not exactly that for Céline the self is the Jew, but that the entire constellation of power and loathing—the Evil/weak scenario—that the self feels in the family has become crystallized in the figure of the Jew, now omnipotent (Evil), now despicable (weak). [...]

Céline finally becomes the ultimate monad, the abused child, the self-hating petit bourgeois, a mercenary army of one in the "war of all against all." [...] His last words [in *Rigadoon*] speak of a failed invasion of the Chinese, with the yellow vermin drowning in vats of brandy, white France's last line of defense.

Céline may have made the switch in enemies to the imaginary Chinese, but the charged particle, what triggered the figuration of an enemy, was the Jew, who of course was also central in the Evil/weak scenarios of Nietzsche, Hitler, and Pound.

They are not the same scenarios, however. In Nietzsche's *Genealogy*, the Jew was a philosophical moment, the ancient producer of the Bible. For Pound and Hitler, on the other hand, the Jew was the essence of what was wrong with modern life: he was the incarnation of Finance.

Marx, in "On the Jewish Question," sheds some interesting light on this. He's making a basic distinction between civic (i.e., economic) and political society. In feudal times, he says, there was no separation between the two: one's economic status was one's political status, with the lords, and finally the king, divinely in control of all wealth. The bourgeois revolution fractured this unity, creating 1) economic man, an asocial unit with certain "natural" rights, all of which translate finally into nothing more than illimitable economic activity, and 2) political man, "an *allegorical, moral* person" (234). Making use of the Jews' historical position in Germany, and of a German pun equating "Judaism" with "business," Marx then asserts that the Jew is the typical civic man, that "civil society ceaselessly begets the Jew [i.e., the businessman] from its own entrails." [...] One of the losses entailed by the money economy is that it dissolves any sense of place: "The *chimerical* nationality of the Jew is the nationality of the merchant, of the man of money in general" (238–39). This is especially disturbing because nationalism, besides projecting an image of familial wholeness, is the nearest thing in the contemporary world to the lost sense of feudal wholeness.

Marx's analysis sounds quite like Pound in places, except that Pound is not punning when he says "Jew." Money has deprived the entire world of its specific value: "With Usura hath no man a house of good stone ... no picture is made to endure nor to live with / but it is made to sell and sell quickly" (XLV [229]). The Jew stands between Pound and his goals in two ways: 1) the modern Jew, as money incarnate, represents the society which commodifies everything, including writing, and thus the Jew makes a very convenient enemy for the marginalized intellectual; Pound is constantly harkening back to some form of feudalism, European or Confucian, where there would be identity between the political and the economic, and where there would be no commodities, only aesthetic objects: stone, bread, emerald, poetry. And 2) the historic

Jew, the "inverter of aristocratic values" in Nietzsche's sense, stands for the moment when the weak, the manufacturers of the Evil/weak pair, somehow managed to push the Strong back into archaic never-never land. Pound constantly laments that "the Gods have not returned" (CXIII [787]): the Jew would be the prime villain, having introduced monotheism and incarnating money.

In wanting to transcend the money economy via art, Pound, far from being iconoclastic, is echoing a primary Victorian concern. Fifty years before him, Matthew Arnold had extolled "Culture" as the vehicle for overcoming the tawdriness of commodity culture and for erasing all class conflict. Culture, says Arnold, "seeks to do away with classes, to make the best that has been known and thought in the world current anywhere.... The men of culture are the true apostles of equality" (*Culture and Anarchy*, 70). Here, an aesthetic quality, "the best that has been known and thought," seeks to replace that religion of political culture, money, that uniter of all abstract economic cogs, with a more mysterious currency, art, which is not exchangeable but which always retains its specific qualities, its *virtù* in Pound's usage.

Arnold calls his standards of value "touchstones," passages from the classics against which to measure all other mental expression. [...] The touchstone of all touchstones, the passage which can survive intact as only a single line, is "In His will is our peace." Arnold's Culture preaches a similar acquiescence; however, for Arnold, the calming authority is not God but the State. "We want an authority, and we find nothing but jealous classes, checks, and a deadlock: culture suggests the idea of *the State*. We find no basis for a firm State-power in our ordinary selves; culture suggests one to us in *our best self*" (96–97).

Underneath this neutral superlative, "best," lurks the figure of power, the Strong. Arnold quotes Joubert approvingly: "*Force till right is ready*, and till right is ready, force, the existing order of things, is justified, is the legitimate ruler" ("The Function of Criticism," 138). The values from an ahistoric past justify a transcendentally natural status quo facing a permanently deferred future. In the meantime, Culture naturalizes the State by being the mask of authority, presence, and common sense, all the more total for being internalized: "The deeper I go in my own consciousness ... the more it seems to tell me that I have no rights at all, only duties; and that men get this notion of rights from a process of abstract reasoning" (*Culture and Anarchy*, 175).

Pound had Mussolini's dictum, "Freedom is not a right but a duty," engraved on his stationery.

Marx agrees with Arnold that abstraction breeds rights, but for Marx the "natural rights of man" are the result of the economic abstraction—the endless exchangeability produced by the money economy. The rise of capitalism coincides with a similar process of abstraction in mental habits: the ascendancy of logic (e.g., Utilitarianism). "Logic is the money of the mind.... [It] is alienated thinking and therefore thinking which abstracts from nature and from real man" (in Hyde, 264).

Pound's ideogrammatic method is thus not just a fortuitous discovery out of Fenollosa but an attempt to circumvent the money economy by presenting "unalienated thinking": unmediated particulars. Pound specifically opposes the ideogram to the syllogism ("Sapor, the flavour ... not to be split by syllogization"; CV [748]). In Pound's presentation of Fenollosa's description of the ideogram, the primary example is the word for *red* in Chinese, which brings together pictures of "rose," "cherry," "iron rust," and "flamingo." There is no convention, only the immediacy of perception. Pound explains approvingly that "the Chinese 'word' or ideogram for red is based on something everyone KNOWS" (*ABC of Reading*, 22).

The components of the ideogram are, for Pound, natural signs, impossible to misconstrue. In China, one locus for Pound's notion of totality, everyone could read "by nature." But this can only be reproduced in our mercantile age by the genius, who is equivalent to the imaginary natural man of archaic wholeness. "Gaudier Brzeska, who was accustomed to looking at the real shape of things, could read a certain amount of Chinese writing without ANY STUDY. He said, 'Of course, you can *see* it's a horse'" (21).

Here, "the real shape of things" invokes the authority of Nature, just as Nietzsche's mythic good (Strong) also is backed by Nature: the nobles are more natural than the slaves—stronger, healthier, better looking. But the authoritative, immediate, visible, real—rose, cherry, etc.—is perpetually shading over into the authoritarian mystery revealed only to the elect.

This dichotomy is present throughout the poem:

> "We have," said Mencius, "but phenomena."
> monumenta. In nature are signatures
>   needing no verbal tradition,
> oak leaf never plane leaf.   (LXXXVII [573])

Phenomena are utterly immediate, visible, but somehow it takes an authority, Mencius, to tell us this. Phenomena become monuments to genius. A few lines down: "Monsieur F. saw his mentor / composed almost wholly of light."

On the other hand, *The Cantos* are filled with an ever growing mass of ignorance and blindness, from the sailors who fail to recognize Dionysus in Canto

II to "the living" in the fragment of CXV who are "made of cardboard." The truth that is so visible to the elect becomes "arcanum" by the end of the poem. [...] Pound's use of "Donna mi Prega" in Canto XXXVI is typical of the poem's disposition toward its readers: "Wherefore I speak to the present knowers / Having no hope that low-hearted / Can bring sight to such reason" (177).

Pound, through Cavalcanti, is speaking of Love here, and although the tone of the translation is ethereal, it would be wrong to take Pound's vision of Love as nonsexual. The emphasis on sex throughout *The Cantos* is obvious: there are a number of passages similar to the ode to procreation in Canto XLVII: "By prong have I entered these hills" (238) etc. Sex—correct sex—is explicitly a divine act and is central for Pound: the Eleusinian mysteries are, he says, predicated on sex; Confucian authority is sexual: "that man's phallic heart is from heaven" (XCIX [697]); even the seemingly "chaste" light imagery in the late cantos is explicitly sexual, constantly associated with procreation (see Sieburth, 129–58). Light, for Pound, is a kind of divine sperm; and the brain is specifically spermatic:

> It is more than likely that the brain itself, is, in origin and development, only a sort of great clot of genital fluid. . . . Let us say quite simply that light is a projection from the luminous fluid, from the energy that is in the brain. ("Postscript to *The Natural Philosophy of Love*," 203, 210)

Far-fetched as the above assertions sound, Pound is enabled by the contingent physicality of this intellective, procreative light to produce some of his most characteristically beautiful images, as when he speaks of light flowing or raining, being solid or tensile. And this conception is clearly of great personal importance to him. He speaks of "the thought of genius" being "a sudden outspurt of mind" and equates his activity as an intellectual with sex: "Even oneself has felt it, driving any new idea into the great passive vulva of London, a sensation analogous to the male feeling in copulation" ("Postscript," 204, 208).

But, as the last quote shows, this procreative, loving light has its shadow. Love, for Pound, is inseparable from authority. On a social-sexual level, he is absurdly sexist: woman is "a chaos / An octopus / A biological process" (XXIX [144]); whereas sperm is "the form-creator ... which compels the ovule to evolve in a given pattern" ("Postscript," 206). Pound is treating the Male (or sperm) here as Nietzsche's narrative treats the nobility: there is hierarchy without conflict. But, for Pound, political authority is threatened by the interchangeability produced by money, and procreative authority is circumscribed (circumcised) by monotheism. Correct sex—light, authority, order, beauty, natural increase—is continually being swamped by perverted sex—usury, kikes, buggery, darkness. This is most patent in Canto XCI (610–13), where a long apotheosis of light beginning "that the body of light come forth / from the body of fire" and ending with images of crystalline light "overflooding, light over light ... the light flowing, whelming the stars" is set next to:

> Democracies electing their sewage
> till there is no clear thought about holiness
> a dung flow from 1913
> and, in this, their kikery functioned, Marx, Freud
>   and the american beaneries
> Filth under filth   (613–14)

This split between light and dark is absolute, and all the terms involved are tightly associated in a fundamentalist rhyme. [...]

The marketplace represents the fall from mystical presence, which only is available to the authority. Pound's position is most revealed at the point when he's being interviewed at St. Elizabeth's, preparatory to pleading insanity. For years, he's been trying to save the world, writing letter after letter to world leaders, and, via radio, addressing the whole world. But suddenly, as he says to one examiner, "There was no use to discuss his ideas about monetary theories and economics because most people ... would not be able to ... comprehend them" (Torrey, 201). The Truth is authoritative and ineffable, equally. The teacher merges into the high priest. [...]

Action is Pound's hope for transcending the money economy that leaves no room for him to be anything more than an aesthete, an epiphenomenon. Only by action can he realize his feudal fantasies of power and presence, and, finally, of paradise.

The Boss, of course, is action incarnate:

> Having drained off the muck by Vada
> From the marshes, by Circeo, where no one else wd. Have
>   drained it.
> Waited 2000 years, ate grain from the marshes;
> Water supply for ten million, another one million *"vani"*
> that is rooms for people to live in.
>   XI of our era.   (XLI [202])

The contradictions of the money economy are now gone, and, as the date suggests, the millennium is here, inaugurated by Italian fascism. The masses react—in dialect (working-class language is always, for Pound, a more or less amusing deformation)—with insane gratitude: "'Noi ci facciam sgannar [i.e., scannar] per Mussolini' / said the commandante della piazza" (We would let ourselves be butchered for Mussolini; XLI [202]). [...]

The Cantos, in which historical particulars were to stand undistorted, end up by dissolving difference into an immaterialist and authoritarian idealism. The Fasa and their king, Gassir, "rhyme" with Mussolini and the Salô Republic, aestheticizing and canceling history.

Nor does Pound's use of the aesthetic overcome the political and economic contradictions it's aimed at; it merely repeats them. In *Jefferson and/or Mussolini*, Pound, in condemning the reductive logic of industrialism and political economy, mimes that action, making Jefferson and Mussolini interchangeable ideogrammatic units:

> If you are hunting up bonds of sympathy between T.J. and the Duce, put it first that they both hate machinery or at any rate the idea of cooping up men and making 'em all into UNITS, unit production, denting in the individual man, reducing him to a mere amalgam. (63) [...]

In a money economy, value is abstract and can, I think, be usefully compared to the way meaning floats above the words in Saussure's model: in both cases, there will always be a gap because there is no organic authority backing either meaning or value. Pound is always castigating the nonnatural circulation of money: hoarding and, especially, usury do not follow the natural order. The proper relation of authority to money will finally produce, as he sees it, a transparent, immediate, natural wealth: "ate grain from the marshes." Pound's desire for a language without syntax, where words would have their full value, aims at a similar immediacy: Osiris before he was torn apart, before he lost his phallus.

Pound the economist is constantly repeating Mussolini's claim that the problem of production has been solved. And Pound the poet is constantly repeating his touchstones as if their value were completely transferable, their meaning unalterable. Yet the text that is actually produced, far from being naturally obvious, is notoriously privatized, with Pound's mind the final arbiter of meaning and producer of value.

"The exact word," the *ch'ing ming* that Pound finds to be the root of Confucianism and that is the root of his own practice as a poet, is finally a monad, not tainted with the negative difference that words have in Saussure's model. The exact word has its *virtù* conferred on it by an act of authority: it's the guinea stamp that makes value, Pound says (aware of the pun on his name), not the metal. Meaning comes directly from the phallus.

But Pound's authority is a private mystery and can't transcend the marketplace. This contradiction ultimately drove Pound to posit an "unwobbling pivot" of poetry and absolute rule, backed by the unlimited credit of Nature. So, grain becomes sacred, olive oil worthy of a rite; the polite remarks of a Mussolini become the words of a god. The more imaginary the Father, the more totally he is said to rule.

In the Evil/weak pairing, the weak are naturally obsessed with Evil, which has power over them. But in the Strong/bad pair, the Strong can't really be bothered with noting the existence of the bad. The Strong tends towards self-universalization: "the whole tribe is from one man's body." Dissecting this fantasy along economic lines would yield Marx's description of feudalism where "the unity of the state . . . inevitably appears as the *special* concern of a ruler and his servants, separated from the people" (232).

When the bourgeois monad (the weak) encounters his projection of this feudal wholeness (the Strong), the gaze of power is impossible to reciprocate or comprehend, one simply worships:

> between the two pine trees, not Circe
> > but Circe was like that
> > > coming from the house of smoothe stone
> "not know which god"
> > > > nor could enter her eyes by probing
> > the light blazed behind her
> > > > nor was this from sunset
> > > > > (CVI [754])

To make an unfair comparison again, this passage can be set beside the following account of another bourgeois monad, who found that looking at Hitler was a similar experience:

> Hauptmann was introduced. The Führer shook hands with him and looked into his eyes. It was the famous gaze that made everybody tremble, the glance which once made a distinguished old lawyer declare that after meeting it he had but one desire, to be back home in order to master the experience in solitude. (Miller, 74)

Fascism was to transcend the atomization of contemporary capitalist society. In the "Limbs of Osiris," Pound begins by seeing a career in poetry as something that would act as a bond between specialists: "Every man who does his own job really well has a latent respect for every other man who does *his* own job really well. . . . He gets his audience . . . [by proving] him[self] the expert." But this specialization is transmuted into the universal truth of the genius. First Pound fetishizes words in a long simile, comparing them to giant cones filled with a complex electricity, then he asserts that the resultant energy is "the power of tradition, of centuries of race consciousness . . . which nothing short of genius understands" (33–34). [. . .]

But for Pound to say that he could read the contemporary interest rates off any given painting—an act of genius-seeing like that of Gaudier-Brzeska—is to treat art in a profoundly *abstract* way, to give it a quantifiable value in the aesthetic marketplace. By filling *The Cantos* with gods, languages, quotes, Chinese and Egyptian characters, Pound is finally equivalent to the bourgeois interior decorator, the consumer-king acting out his fantasy of pre-market wholeness, purchasing uniqueness with interchangeable units.

Céline, the essential petit bourgeois, makes an excellent tool (club) with which to critique (smash) Pound's pretensions. The next time Pound says

> God's eye art 'ou.
> > The columns gleam as if cloisonné,
> > > The sky is leaded with elm boughs.
> > > > (CVI [755])

making the world his church, the petit bourgeois reader can come back with Céline: "But what does the grocer think of it . . . shit on the panorama!"

Céline at his best is utterly untranscendental—his fantasies are all present-tense paranoia—but that is the problem with him as well: his humor and shock is finally static. One's resentment is gratified, but one is then stuck with that gratified resentment. Pound's work, on the other hand, does present a model for a writing that takes on a significant portion of experience and tries to change it. But his fantasy of the Good/Strong, born out of the actual weakness of his position as marginalized intellectual, pointed his project in exactly the wrong direction—his work is a Mistake in unusually pure form.

This is valuable in that contemporary writing often can't even be bothered to address the problem that might result in such a mistake. O'Hara's apotheosis of personality communicates beautifully, but it eschews social change. [. . .] On the other hand, both would-be Archaic poetry and language writing often *assume* social change. "The whole tribe is from one man's body"—exactly wrong, twice. We don't spring from Pound's or Mussolini's or the Great Sage's mind/phallus, nor is it informative to define us as a tribe. But the next line does pose a necessary question: "What other way can you think of it?"

WORKS CITED

Arnold, Matthew. *Culture and Anarchy*. Ed. J. Dover Wilson. Cambridge: Cambridge University Press, 1981.

———. "The Function of Criticism at the Present Time." *Selected Prose*. Ed. P. J. Keating. Harmondsworth, U.K.: Penguin, 1982.

Céline, Louis Ferdinand. *Castle to Castle*. Trans. Ralph Manheim. New York: New Directions, 1970.

———. *Death on the Installment Plan*. Trans. Ralph Manheim. New York: New Directions, 1971.

———. *Journey to the End of the Night*. Trans. Ralph Manheim. New York: New Directions, 1983.

———. *Rigadoon*. Trans. Ralph Manheim. New York: New Directions, 1975.

Eagleton, Terry. *Criticism and Ideology*. London: Verso, 1982.

Hitler, Adolf. *Mein Kampf*. Trans. Ralph Manheim. Boston: Houghton Mifflin, [1943].

Hyde, Lewis. *The Gift: Imagination and the Erotic Life of Property*. New York: Vintage, 1983.

Kristeva, Julia. *Powers of Horror*. Trans. Leon S. Roudiez. New York: Columbia University Press, 1982.

Marx, Karl. "On the Jewish Question." *Early Writings*. Trans. Rodney Livingstone and Gregory Benton. New York: Vintage, 1975.

Miller, Alice. *For Your Own Good*. Trans. Hildegarde and Hunter Hannum. New York: Farrar, Straus and Giroux, 1983.

Nicholls, Peter. *Ezra Pound, Politics, Economics, and Writing: A Study of The Cantos*. Atlantic City, N.J.: Humanities Press, 1984.

Nietzsche, Friedrich. *The Genealogy of Morals*. Trans. Francis Golffing. Garden City, N.Y.: Anchor Books, 1956.

Pound, Ezra. *ABC of Reading*. New York: New Directions, n.d.

———. *The Cantos*. New York: New Directions, 1975.

———. *Certain Radio Speeches*. Ed. W. Levy. Amsterdam: Cold Turkey Press, 1975.

———. *Guide to Kulchur*. New York: New Directions, 1970.

———. "I Gather the Limbs of Osiris." *Selected Prose*. Ed. William Cookson. New York: New Directions, 1973.

———. *Jefferson and/or Mussolini*. London: S. Nott, 1935.

———. "Postscript to *The Natural Philosophy of Love* by Remy de Gourmont." *Pavannes and Divagations*. New York: New Directions, 1974.

———. *Selected Prose*. Ed. William Cookson. New York: New Directions, 1973.

Sieburth, Richard. *Instigations: Ezra Pound and Remy de Gourmont*. Cambridge, Mass.: Havard University Press, 1978.

Terrell, Carroll F. *A Companion to The Cantos of Ezra Pound*. Berkeley: University of California Press, 1980.

Thiher, Allen. *Céline: The Novel as Delirium*. New Brunswick, N.J.: Rutgers University Press, 1972.

Torrey, E. Fuller. *The Roots of Treason*. San Diego: McGraw-Hill, 1982.

PUBLISHED: Excerpted from *Marginality: Public and Private Language* (1986), 6:6–25.

KEYWORDS: modernism; psychoanalysis; politics; history.

LINKS: Bob Perelman, "Exchangeable Frames" (*PJ* 5), "Plotless Prose" (*PJ* 1), "Three Case Histories: Ross's *Failure of Modernism*" (*PJ* 7); Jackson Mac Low, "Sketch toward a Close Reading of Three Poems from Bob Perelman's *Primer*" (*PJ* 2); George Hartley, "Jameson's Perelman: Reification and the Material Signifier" (*Guide*; *PJ* 7); Bruce Andrews, "Total Equals What: Poetics and Praxis" (*Guide*; *PJ* 6); Charles Bernstein, "Writing and Method" (*Guide*; *PJ* 3); Norman Fischer, "Modernism, Postmodernism, and Values" (*PJ* 7); Ben Friedlander, "Laura Riding/Some Difficulties" (*PJ* 4); Doug Hall, *Forgotten Tyrant* (*PJ* 5); Lyn Hejinian, "The Person and Description" (*PJ* 9); Leslie Scalapino, "War/Poverty/Writing" (*PJ* 10); Scalapino and Ron Silliman, "What/Person: From an Exchange" (*Guide*; *PJ* 9).

SELECTED BIBLIOGRAPHY: *Writing/Talks* (ed.; Carbondale, Ill.: Southern Illinois University Press, 1985); *The Trouble with Genius: Reading Pound, Joyce, Stein, and Zukofsky* (Berkeley: University of California Press, 1994); *The Marginalization of Poetry: Language Writing and Literary History* (Princeton, N.J.: Princeton University Press, 1996); *Braille* (Ithaca, N.Y.: Ithaca House, 1975); *7 Works* (Berkeley: The Figures, 1978); *Primer* (San Francisco: This, 1981); *a.k.a.* (Great Barrington, Mass.: The Figures, 1984); *To the Reader* (Berkeley: Tuumba, 1984); *The First World* (Great Barrington, Mass.: The Figures, 1987); *Captive Audience* (Great Barrington, Mass.: The Figures, 1988); *Face Value* (New York: Roof, 1988); *Virtual Reality* (New York: Roof, 1993); *The Future of Memory* (New York: Roof, 1998); *Ten to One: Selected Poems* (Middletown, Conn.: Wesleyan University Press, 1999); *Iflife* (New York: Roof, 2006); with Rae Armantrout et al., *The Grand Piano*; with Francie Shaw, *Playing Bodies* (New York: Granary, 2004).

Poets Theater Two Versions of Collateral

RAISING *COLLATERAL* KIT ROBINSON

San Francisco Poets Theater, founded in 1979, was preceded by several prior incarnations. In the early 1950s, Frank O'Hara and his friends wrote and produced plays as Poets' Theater in Cambridge, Mass.; poets of Jack Spicer's circle did likewise in San Francisco; and the Judson Church Poets Theater flourished in New York in the 1960s. The following essays from *Poetics Journal*'s symposium on Poets Theater (1985) focus on Kit Robinson's *Collateral*, directed by Eileen Corder (1982), as representative of the compositional methods and performance values of San Francisco Poets Theater.[1] Borrowing from many sources (Bertolt Brecht, Vsevolod Meyerhold, El Teatro Campesino, improvisatory techniques, and New York School and Language School poetries), its productions were always highly conceptual and often hilariously funny. Central to its methods was the construction of illusionistic sequences from the interpretation, through improvisation, of abstract, elliptical, nonnarrative scripts. In the resulting performances, fragments of language strike poses and acquire agency even as persona and voice become arbitrary. Poets Theater has been a creative resource for the writing of Steve Benson, Charles Bernstein, cris cheek, Carla Harryman, Kevin Killian, C. S. Giscombe, Leslie Scalapino, Rodrigo Toscano, and Edwin Torres, and it continues to thrive with the development of work by younger writers. An anthology of writing for Poets Theater, edited by Killian and David Brazil, was published in 2009.

In writing the play *Collateral*, I had the advantage of knowing not only that it would be produced, but that it would be produced by a group willing to take on any challenge to the director and actors I might care to throw their way. I had license to write a problematic work.

Scouring a notebook, I lifted lines for a play, to be built up from particular instants, realized in writing, toward a whole to be realized on stage. So the themes were derived, not from a sole idea or plot, but directly from disparate, daily experience. And I tried to shape the materials to give them dramatic form—scenes, characters, conflict, resolution, fast and slow pacing, cumulative emotional pressure and release. I imagine this is the inverse of the way plays are normally written.

To develop characters, I looked for distinct tones in the writing and assigned each a name. The first two character types to emerge this way were Bell and Lopez. Bell's tone is sharp, exuberant, and extravagant. In scene 1, he personifies the revolutionary Russian Futurist Velimir Khlebnikov. While taking shots at conventional wisdom ("What's clear and distinct to you and me may look like smog to an Aleutian"), he seems to suggest that literally anything is possible and that he's the man whose say-so makes it so. If he's living way beyond his means—heavily in debt to language for the reality he so elastically delineates—he grounds his confidence in the dramatic artifice ("For collateral take stages left and right"). Bell's sidekick and foil, Lopez, speaks with a slightly sour, fatalistic tone. I imagine him as a cynical old warrior, someone who's "seen it all." His skepticism tempers Bell's flamboyant visceral ideologistics.

Other characters attained more or less definition in the writing. Patel has a droning, sing-song, continuous speech pattern, whereas Fang's speech is sometimes broken by abrupt hesitations every five words, a series of false starts. They form a pair, with Fong watching Patel read the news on television and vice versa, and they are not always in character. Beck talks to Keller a lot about views, present or from memory. Jameson, the scholar, reads quotations from Shklovsky, Marx, and Wittgenstein, as well as a cabinetry manual. Dumas— the secret agent?—issues cryptic one-liners dubiously related to the action.

While putting my materials into dialogue form, I added speeches that would refer directly to the apparatus of the theater. To begin with, I had all the characters introduce themselves by name. The names are surnames only, so the characters' sexes are not prescribed by the script. By not defining specific hierarchical relations, I aimed for an institutional collectivity. I wanted to represent individuals as members of a group none of them directs and which is subject to forces beyond its control.

The play had already been handed over to the director for auditions before it was completed. Then several scenes were inserted near the end, where it seemed to need more weight. The long speeches by Patel and Fong were meant to slacken the breakneck pace and give the audience an opportunity to relax before the accelerated conclusion.

Collateral is a performance text that demands of the director and actors a maximum of interpretation.[2] The Poets Theater production went through about two months of rehearsal under the direction of Eileen Corder. I viewed the auditions, one early improvisation, and, a few nights before opening, a dress rehearsal. What Eileen had done with the script was hilarious, dazzling, and darkly brooding.

The ambiguities of the text—who, for instance, is talking to whom in the group scenes—were compounded by physical blocking that added further levels of possible interaction. Props literalizing abstract lines of dialogue undercut metaphysical projections. Dumas says, "Press and this world gives," squeezes a foam ball painted to represent the earth, "Press on this world, it gives."

My sense of the play is very much informed by the Poets Theater production, so much so that I now have trouble distinguishing my ideas from those that were developed in production. I even added some of the actions into the final version of the play for publication in *Hills* 9. For instance, in scene 10 the original script read:

> Bell: . . . Let me show you something.
> Lopez: That's very interesting. . . .

The space between these lines was left as an opening for action. I was shocked when I learned that for action the director had Bell suddenly turn and stab Keller, killing him. But the possibility for such violent action was suggested in the script when, several moments later, Lopez says, "Stabbing in Tenderloin Hotel / Plaintiff lodger in defendant hotel stabbed." In performance, Lopez shouted this headline from the newspaper Keller had been holding. The gratuitously victimized Keller returns in the next scene, a "new man," distracted from death by a member of the audience.

The beautifully lit and painted sets functioned variously, as shifting contexts suggested various scenes—a museum tour, a cocktail party, a hotel room, a pool hall, a prison visit, a train ride, a TV room, a dressing room, and the theater itself.

The props—masks, newspaper, suitcase, photographs, bed, books, television screen (a cut-out cardboard frame)—were used repeatedly in variation, just as the words of the play were. (Nearly every word in *Collateral* is said at least twice, each time in altered context, usually by a different speaker.) Often the props were used to extend rather than illustrate the meanings of the words. For example, when Bell said, "We don't have salad plates. We do have this though. Click click click. Big wooden spoons," he produced from his suitcase not spoons but masks, widening further the range of meanings. (Spoons are like masks in shape. If masks are spoons, faces must be served up like soup, as Bell's menacing tone seemed to imply.) Later, Keller wore one of these masks as he sat reading a newspaper. In that scene, it seemed to mark him as a target for Bell's vicious attack.

In scene 13, Lopez answers Bell's soliloquy by repeating its verbs in order. In performance, the set was a cheap hotel room lit at night by a flashing colored light from the window. Bell stood by the window while Lopez lay asleep on the bed. His response to Bell's speech was spoken in sleep, a set of verbal twitches suggesting dream states.

In the script, Jameson's lengthy speeches are followed by separately numbered scenes dedicated to one-liners by Dumas. In the production, Jameson addressed Dumas, reading to him from a book and gesticulating emphatically, while Dumas, the bad student, winced, squirmed, put his fingers in his ears, and finally stood up to holler a terse non sequitur in reply. The ridicule Dumas threw on Jameson's pompous manner set the didactic messages in perspective. While the ideas expressed—on craft, art, ideology, and intention—reflect on the nature of the play, they can't transcend or speak from outside it.

Circumscribing the zany sight gags and off-base rejoinders was a dark sense of impending collective danger, graphically fleshed out in scene 17, when the white-gloved Dumas drew an invisible rope around the entire cast and appeared to hoist them en masse, by pulley, skyward at the blackout. Chilly dread formed the scrim before which the players matched their lucky wits. But *Collateral* played too fast and loose to be simply booming doom. This was no static stalemate clogged with ennui à la Beckett. The push-pull of enthusiasm and resistance created a time that was all action.

The script calls for forty separate scenes, but these were lumped together to form several longer scenes in which various interactions overlapped or took place simultaneously. The numbered scenes were used as modules to make bigger temporal structures, defined by set changes and blackouts. The script is a toolkit for making a play. The Poets Theater production took full advantage of the liberties so proposed.

SUBTEXT IN *COLLATERAL* NICK ROBINSON

Two levels of narrative can be traced in the Poets Theater production of Kit Robinson's *Collateral* (San Francisco, 1982), in which I played the role of Bell. The more substantial and prominent is the score of physical actions created by the director Eileen Corder. Given a script which contains virtually no staging directions and no clearly delineated story line, Corder initiated a collaborative process in which author, director, and actors took part. In early rehearsals we investigated the play's rhythmic dynamics and physicalized our encounter with the text—strategies typical of a methodology proposed by the Russian director Vsevolod Meyerhold:

> There is a whole range of questions to which psychology is incapable of supplying the answers. A theatre built on psychological foundations is as certain to collapse as a house built on sand. On the other hand, a theatre which relies on *physical elements* is at the very least assured of clarity. All psychological states are determined by specific physiological processes. By correctly resolving the nature of his state physically, the actor reaches the point where he experiences the excitation which communicates itself to the spectator and induces him to share in the actor's performance: what we used to call 'gripping' the spectator. It is this excitation which is the very essence of the actor's art. From a sequence of physical positions and situations there arise those 'points of excitation' which are informed with some particular emotion.[3]

Within the framework of this "sequence of physical positions and situations" articulated by the director, the actors are free to create individual scores or subtexts. The subtext proceeds by narrative means which are largely interior: personal associations, memories, imaginary objectives and obstacles. It is a field of possible meanings and intentions; it can remain fluid and improvisatory within the structures of the text and the mise-en-scène. It is also a private creation whose terms and organizational principles are seldom presented directly to the audience. Meyerhold describes subtext as "the 'inner dialogue' which the spectator should overhear, not as words but as pauses, not as cries but as silences, not as soliloquies but as the music of plastic movement."[4] The subtext I developed for Bell contained several discrete narrative threads which were variously complementary, overlapping, and contradictory. A conventional approach would have been to discard all but those which bore the most literal and linear relation to the narrative interpretation advanced by the director. But since Corder's direction seemed designed to tease meaning from the text on a scene by scene basis rather than coerce the play into a singular narrative structure, I let my subtext remain loosely jointed and multiple. Brecht provides some encouragement for such an approach to story-making in the theater:

> For a genuine story to emerge it is most important that the scenes should to start with be played quite simply one after another, using the experience of real life, without taking account of what follows or even of the

play's overall sense. The story than unreels in a contradictory manner; the individual scenes retain their own meanings; they yield (and stimulate) a wealth of ideas; and their sum, the story, unfolds authentically without any cheap all-pervading idealization (one work leading to another) or directing of subordinate parts to an ending in which everything is resolved.[5]

What follows is a description of scene 1 of *Collateral*. A general outline of the physical score appears in italics. Bell's lines are immediately followed by an account of some of the subtextual resources I drew upon in performance.

Lopez whimpers offstage. Bell enters carrying suitcase. Lopez follows.
WHEN I SOUND A VAPOR I FEEL SECURE. SOUNDING VAPORS SECURES ME.

"Sound a vapor" at its most literal means "talk," "vibrate breath." It can also be played as referring to one of several activities: performing a scientific experiment (imagine sending sound waves through a gas-filled tube); taking drugs; engaging in fraud (maybe high-tech computer bank fraud). Each meaning carries a freight of associations relevant to Bell's occupation and character. The possible roles of actor, scientist, decadent, and criminal first encountered here may be echoed and extended throughout the play.

Bell opens suitcase and removes two neckties. Bell and Lopez put them on.
I OCCUR AT INTERVALS. SOME DAYS PASS ME BY ENTIRELY.

As a sarcastic come-back to Lopez's "I don't see how you do it, Bell," these lines indicate Bell's stance as wise guy to Lopez's straight man. They set up the two as stock character types: Bell as quick-witted, light, positive; Lopez thoughtful, bulky, negative. These basic characteristics of tempo and physicality may be maintained through a variety of circumstances and subtextual choices.

At another level these lines announce and describe the function of character in *Collateral*. "I," my stage persona, emerges from a field of associations by rhyme and rhythm to foreground a particular configuration, which is then allowed to dissolve back into the field, perhaps to be echoed or opposed in "my" next occurrence. It seems Bell is a theater theorist, or an actor explaining his method of taking on masks.

WHEN I TALK, WHAT I SAY MEANS ME.

A condescending jibe at Lopez: "When *I* talk ... ," as opposed to when you talk.

Bell is boasting about his facility at inventing personae. Bell as a successful entertainer, adept at artifice for every occasion. Or as a con-man.

As a reversal of the cliché "I mean what I say" this line reveals Bell's position on a central theatrical problem: the creation or construction of character. To "mean what you say" is the acting method of the dominant theatrical trend of this century, best exemplified and articulated by the work of Constantin Stanislavsky. How to fully inhabit a role, living the life of a character moment-to-moment—this is the goal which Stanislavsky moved toward with astonishing accuracy, founding a tradition whose basis is the fostering of empathy. In his early period Stanislavsky's methods stressed a movement from internal processes to external manifestations, building a character from the inside out.

> [The artist] must fit his own human qualities to the life of this other, and pour into it all of his own soul. The fundamental aim of our art is the creation of this inner life of a human spirit, and its expression in an artistic form.
>
> That is why we begin by thinking about the inner side of a role, and how to create its spiritual life through the help of the internal process of living the part. You must live it by actually experiencing feelings that are analogous to it, each and every time you repeat the process of creating it.[6]

"What I say means me" proposes an alternative method (and ideology), perhaps best articulated by Vsevolod Meyerhold. Meyerhold's theory of bio-mechanics advocated building a role from the outside in.

> Constructivism challenged the artist to become an engineer. Art must have a basis in scientific knowledge, for all artistic creativity should be conscious. The art of the actor consists in organizing his materials, that is in properly utilizing his body with all its means of expression.[7]

This line rhymes with "I occur at intervals" in supporting a concept of character which is constructed and contingent. Instead of asking the audience to suspend its disbelief in his performance. Bell invites the audience to observe how the language of the play shapes the artifice of his role. He probably reads Brecht.

> The bourgeois theater's performances always aim at smoothing over contradictions, at creating false harmony, at idealization. Conditions are reported as if they could not be otherwise; characters as individuals, incapable by definition of being divided, cast in one block, manifesting themselves in the most various situations, likewise for that matter existing without any situations at all. If there is any development it is always steady, never by jerks; the developments always take place within a definite framework which cannot be broken through.
>
> None of this is like reality, so a realistic theater must give it up.[8]

ORDINARY LANGUAGE POINTS TO ITSELF EQUALLY.

Failing any big ideas, this line can always be tossed off as "obvious":

CONSIDER THE EARTH AS A SOUNDING PLATE, AND THE CAPITALS AS COLLECTING THE DUST INTO BUNDLES OF STANDING WAVES.

This line has a scientific ring which rhymes with the reading of "sound a vapor" (first line of the scene) as an experimental process. I visualize a demonstration of magnetic fields using carbon particles on glass.

As critical commentary on the structuring devices in *Collateral*, this line offers a metaphor which extends the concept of character posed in "I occur at intervals." Consider the play ("earth") as a musical/vibrational field ("sounding plate"), and the actors ("capitals") as collecting textual particles ("the dust") into characters ("bundles of standing waves"). The "bundles" suggest a process of knotting—a term Brecht uses in his discussions of character and story.

Knotting joins independent and dissimilar episodes or aspects while leaving the knots visible to the audience. "The episodes must not succeed one another indistinguishably but must give us a chance to interpose our judgement."[9] "Standing waves" proposes character as a musical phenomenon: a polyphonic composition of various rhythmic units.

ENGLAND AND JAPAN KNOW THIS VERY WELL.

High-class gangster talk. Reference to industrialized capitalist nations keys "criminal" narrative. Bell and Lopez as international entrepreneurs practicing high-finance fraud and extortion. In hotel room, suiting up for job.

Whistle offstage. Dumas enters. Lopez goes to Dumas. Dumas hands Lopez a note.
WHAT'S CLEAR AND DISTINCT TO YOU AND ME MAY LOOK LIKE SMOG TO AN ALEUTIAN.

A one-liner in the repertoire of Bell the comic.
This line acknowledges the partnership of Bell and Lopez in relation to some "others," one of whom has just entered. Aleutians are: the audience, the law, other scientists.

Lopez reads note and gives it to Bell. Bell reads note.
(SHOUTS) PAGING MILLENNIA MINOR!

An exclamation of delight. The note is a tip in a crime venture.

LOPEZ, MY DARK PLASTIC WOOD!

Bell calls for his gun.
"Dark plastic wood" could be plot glue needed at this juncture to join events into a credible sequence.

VAPOR! IT CAN BE APPLIED!
Bell closes suitcase. Lopez and Bell begin to leave. Bell stops, turns back, leaves a dollar bill on stage. Bell and Lopez exit.

This brings us back to the first line, making scene 1 a loop. Lopez's negative response to the previous line throws Bell onto his own resources. For "vapor" read "language." Bell's confidence springs from his ability to apply his text to describe (invent) various theatrical illusions—character, story, subtext—without being bound or determined by his inventions. This is the primary narrative statement of scene 1.

Bell is in debt to the stage for his freedom of action. He leaves a dollar as a tip for whoever cleans up after scene 1.

On paper this analysis looks like a plan for acting Bell upon which physical choices such as posture, gesture, and tempo would depend. The opposite is true. These ideas and associations occurred during rehearsal in response to the physical tasks given by the director, and in relationship with the other actors. They are readings of the text whose ground is the stage.

These readings operate on two basic levels of meaning, each containing fissures and variations. On one level they refer to a developing action narrative. Bell prepares for and commits a burglary (scenes 1 and 3), disguises himself (scene 6), appears as a speaker at a convention where he meets his victim (scene 8), commits theft and murder (scene 10), discovers he's bungled the job (scene 12), vents his anguish (scene 13), dreams of a simple life (scene 14), is interrogated (scene 20), is tortured (scene 22), confesses (scene 26), and ends in philosophic beatitude in a public looney bin (scene 32), or perhaps a theater (scene 40).

On the second level the lines refer to the process of creating the first level of meaning. They are about acting, asserting a character, inventing and justifying motives and actions. They reveal, make conscious the processes of generating meaning in the theater. As Eileen Corder put it, "Your characters are creating characters." In Brechtian lingo these two levels of meaning are empathy and demonstration. Both are advocated:

> However dogmatic it may seem to insist that self-identification with the character should be avoided in the performance, our generation can listen to this warning with advantage. However determinedly they obey it they can hardly carry it out to the letter, so the most likely result is that truly rending contradiction between experience and portrayal, empathy and demonstration, justification and criticism, which is what is aimed at.
>
> The contradiction between acting (demonstration) and experience (empathy) often leads the uninstructed to suppose that only one or the other can be manifest in the work of the actor (as if the Short Organum concentrated entirely on acting and the old tradition entirely on experience). In reality it is a matter of two mutually hostile processes which fuse in the actor's work; his performance is not just composed of a bit of the one and a bit of the other. His particular effectiveness comes from the tussle and tension of the two opposites, and also from their depth.[10]

The particular achievement of *Collateral* lies in its formal precision as a vehicle for contradiction and change. It is a latticework of scenes with clearly articulated stresses, points of intersection, divergent interests. Its structure provides maximum stimulus and support for the playing out of a dramatic torque. It is active and contemplative. It fulfills Mayakovsky's dream of a play which is capable of continual transformation, and is therefore constantly topical. Each company that performs *Collateral* will discover its own stories and its own ways of telling them.

NOTES

1 As originally published in *Poetics Journal*, this symposium on one of the San Francisco Poets Theater productions was titled "Three Versions of Collateral" and in-

cluded an essay by director Eileen Corder, who did not grant permission to republish it. —Eds.

2 COLLATERAL, SCENE 1

Bell: When I sound a vapor I feel secure. Sounding vapors secures me.

Lopez: I don't see how you do it, Bell.

Bell: I occur at intervals. Some days pass me by entirely. When I talk, what I say means me. Ordinary language points to itself equally. Consider the earth as a sounding plate, and the capitals as collecting the dust into bundles of standing waves. England and Japan know this very well. What's clear and distinct to you and me may look like smog to an Aleutian.

Lopez: My memory banks off to the left. Still, I'm here and can breathe. My condition built this single strand of hair.

Bell: (*Shouts*) Paging Millenia Minor! Lopez, my dark plastic wood!

Lopez: That's shit, Bell.

Bell: Vapor! It can be applied!

3 Vsevolod Meyerhold, *Meyerhold on Theatre*, trans. and edited Edward Braun (New York: Hill and Wang, 1969), 199.

4 Ibid., 36.

5 Bertolt Brecht, *Brecht on Theatre*, trans. and ed. John Willet (New York: Hill and Wang, 1964), 278–79.

6 Constantin Stanislavsky, *An Actor Prepares*, trans. Elizabeth R. Hapgood (New York: Theater Arts, 1936), 14.

7 Meyerhold, *Meyerhold on Theatre*, 198.

8 Brecht, *Brecht on Theatre*, 277.

9 Ibid., 201.

10 Ibid., 277–78.

PUBLISHED: Excerpted from *Non/Narrative* (1985), 5:122–38.

KEYWORDS: Language writing; performance; material text; readings.

LINKS: Michael Amnasan, from *Joe Liar* (*PJ* 10); Steve Benson, "Close Reading: Leavings and Cleavings" (*Guide*; *PJ* 2); Benson and Carla Harryman, "Dialogue: Museo Antropología, Mexico" (*PJ* 8); Alan Bernheimer, "The Simulacrum of Narrative" (*PJ* 5); cris cheek, ". . . they almost all practically . . ." (*PJ* 5); Abigail Child and Sally Silvers, "Rewire//Speak in Disagreement" (*PJ* 4); Harryman, "What In Fact Was Originally Improvised" (*PJ* 2); George Lakoff, "Continuous Reframing" (*Guide*; *PJ* 1); Jackson Mac Low, "*Pieces o' Six*–XII and XXIII" (*PJ* 6); Tom Mandel, "Codes/Texts: Reading *S/Z*" (*PJ* 2); Bob Perelman, "Plotless Prose" (*PJ* 1); Kit Robinson, "Bob Cobbing's Blade" (*PJ* 1); Leslie Scalapino, "War/Poverty/Writing" (*PJ* 10); Fiona Templeton, "My Work Telling the Story of Narrative in It" (*PJ* 5); Rodrigo Toscano, "Early Morning Prompts for Evening Takes; or, Roll 'Em" (*PJ* 10); Barrett Watten, "The XYZ of Reading: Negativity (And)" (*PJ* 6); John Woodall, detail from *Gimcrack* (performance) (*PJ* 9).

SELECTED BIBLIOGRAPHY: *Plays and Other Writings*, ed. Bob Perelman, *Hills* 9 (1983); *Kenning Anthology of Poets Theater: 1945–1985*, ed. Kevin Killian and David Brazil (Chicago: Kenning, 2009); Steve Benson, *Blindspots* (Cambridge, Mass.: Whale Cloth, 1981); Carla Harryman, *Animal Instincts: Prose Plays Essays* (Oakland: This, 1989); *Memory Play* (Oakland: O Books, 1994); Killian, *Island of Lost Souls* (Vancouver, B.C.: Nomados, 2003); Jackson Mac Low, *The Pronouns: A Collection of Forty Dances for the Dancers, 3 February–22 March 1964* (Barrytown, N.Y.: Station Hill, 1979); Leslie Scalapino, *Goya's L.A.* (Elmwood, Conn.: Potes & Poets, 1994); Fiona Templeton, *You—The City* (New York: Roof, 1990); Rodrigo Toscano, *Collapsible Poetics Theater* (Albany, N.Y.: Fence, 2008).

Pattern—and the 'Simulacral'

Leslie Scalapino surveys nonnarrative forms that construct the postmodern present in poets such as Michael McClure, Ron Silliman, Charles Bernstein, and Alice Notley. If Gertrude Stein's notion of a bodily "continuous present" represents a modernist account of temporality, postmodernists differ in building up sequences of disjunct temporal moments that are more simulacral than embodied. Writing in a manner that parallels the works she discusses, Scalapino constructs a series of present-tense, paratactic moments that create complex compositional patterns. The elements of this series, as simulacra of each other, present a multiperspectival display, recalling both Jacques Derrida's concept of *différance* and Fredric Jameson's notion of a depthless postmodern present. In the radical present of postmodern writing, "new formations as words, fantasies, sounds, occur potentially infinitely" in verbal and visual forms. Scalapino's essay creates a repeating movement from depthless present to simulacral pattern and back, defining an aesthetic practice that draws equally on contemporary physics, Buddhist philosophy, feminist subjectivity, and the visual spectacles of Busby Berkeley and Cindy Sherman. Her account of the radical present and its simulacral effects in nonnarrative form is a defining moment of literary postmodernism. Leslie Scalapino died on 28 May 2010.

The way things are seen in a time is that period of time; and is the composition of that time. The way things are seen is unique in any moment, as a new formation of events, objects, and cultural abstraction.

> The composition is the thing seen by every one living in the living they are doing, they are the composing of the composition that at the time they are living is the composition of the time in which they are living. It is that that makes living a thing they are doing. Nothing else is different, of that almost any one can be certain. The time when and the time of and the time in that composition is the natural phenomena of that composition.[1]

Stein's conception of a continuous present is when everything is unique, beginning again and again and again. A does not equal A, in terms of Stein's view of the continuous present. This leads to lists; which leads to romanticism in which everything is the same and therefore different.

Romanticism is then when everything being alike everything is naturally simply different, and romanticism

Romanticism is not a confusion but an extrication. Culture is a transformative composite separate from individuals. The quality in the creation of expression in the composition has to do with the unique entity, being in balance and moving as it ceases to be identical with itself. This has to do with apprehending what occurs now. With it being *always* now, which constitutes being in a state of turmoil:

> There must be time that is distributed and equilibrated. This is the thing that is at present the most troubling and if there is the time that is at present the most troublesome the time-sense that is at present the most troubling is the thing that makes the present the most troubling.

The present is the loci (i.e., multiple) of change. The travel book as a genre is a stylized mode having its own laws and pattern, which is realistic with present-time events and people: Hemingway, in *Green Hills of Africa*, creates a new form while using the travel book format describing an actual hunting expedition which lasted for a month.[2] It is not fiction; there is no beginning, middle, or end as such. There are potentially an infinite number of animals and events as the condition of writing.

Therefore his pattern is a list of places, objects, animals, and actions. Reading is somehow the means of their actual occurrence.

Style is cultural abstraction—i.e., that period—how relationships with people take place (how they're seen) in a period. They become visible by being simplified—by indicating this is occurring—as the canned scenario.

The narrator does not write while hunting, only reads. Therefore action is "doing something you are ignorant about." So killing is everything being the same and therefore different, the trigger of the gun being "like the last turn of the key opening a sardine can." A unique connection is the vulcanized rubber faintly transparent looking (as if miming) rhino discovered in death. As the relation between life and writing:

> The rhino was in high grass, somewhere in there behind some bushes. As we went forward we heard a deep, moaning sort of groan. Droopy looked around at me and grinned. The noise came again, ending this time like a blood-choked sigh. Droopy was laughing. "Faro," he whispered and put his hand palm open on the side of his head in the gesture that means to go to sleep. Then in a jerky-flighted, sharp-beaked little flock we saw the tick birds

rise and fly away. We knew where he was and, as we went slowly forward, parting the high grass, we saw him. He was on his side, dead.

In *Green Hills of Africa*, the pattern of experience and the account (expressed as being the mode of 'genre') are not parallel; which makes this text similar to the dissimulation and simulacra of artists of the postmodern period.

The closure of the genre is its means of realistic observation.

In Michael McClure's work,[3] oneself is the 'simulacra' identified as an infinite free universe. Identity is defined in his poems in terms of other entities (we are "DARK FLESH MUSIC / LAYING OUT A SHAPE," we are "INSTRUMENTS / THAT / PLAY / ourselves," etc.). Therefore the author or the sense of self and the investigation of its desire is the pattern, which is neither present time nor the past. It is potentially infinite in form and number, as points of intuitional apprehension.

Cultural abstractions such as the love image of Jean Harlow or the perfect chill slot of space of Wall Street (in "Cold Saturday Mad Sonnet") are qualitative transformations as expressions of this instant of time. In the following passage from "La Plus Blanche," the juncture of connection is "How," and the new utterly wild formation is something referred to as "grace."

> you return love. Love returned for admiration! Strangeness
> is returned by you for desire. How. Where
> but in the depth of Jean Harlow is such strangeness
> made into grace?

Some of McClure's poems are 'genre' in the sense of being formal as sonnets, odes, or ballads but actually as unique, as artificial, not the same as anything else. Therefore the new formations can't be replicated, as are images of Pop Art or as would be commercial images. They are sensitive. The imagination causes transformations, realistic as culture causing mutations. The 'transformations' in the "Hummingbird Ode" are the "black lily of space," the "sweetness of the pain," and "the beautiful shabby colors / and the damp spots where the eyes were" of the dead hummingbird:

> WHAT'S
> ON YOUR SIDE OF THE VEIL?
> DID YOU DIP YOUR BEAK
> in the vast black lily
> of space? Does the sweetness
> of the pain go on forever?

Dark Brown, for example, is writing as a self-analyzing surface which is vision. One is lost in the 'simulacra': "The tigers of wrath are wiser than the horses of instruction—/ means that the belief of something is necessary to its beauty." As in a Busby Berkeley follies, change or movement is by virtue of the intrinsic qualities of something: "The flow of energy through a system acts to organize that system."

In Ron Silliman's *Paradise* the unit of change occurs on the level of the sentence, many such changes occurring in each paragraph.[4] A series or list of simple sentences creates simple states of being, requiring that consciousness exist only in the moment of each sentence, i.e., in an infinite series of succeeding moments. That experience actually occurs in the lovely light 'clear' writing. An overt simplification or abstraction of a view of character, either reader's or writer's, is imposed to create these states of being, which may be the expression of a period or an inward state:

> In romance, sexual desire is freed from a relation to power. The real bandit queen of India, Madame Gandhi. Puffball clouds in a blue sky. Simple sentences, again and again. The old sisters walk to the store together, slowly, one wearing bright slippers. Our lives are like this, quiet on a Sunday. Sink full of cups.

Reading as imposing syntax, is creating reality as imposition on or formation of one's thoughts and actions:

> This was and now you are constituted in the process of being words, your thought actualizing through the imposition of this syntax. Resistance alone is real (coming distractions). Cross against the light. Leave work to write a poem and not mention the dragonfly.

New formations as words, fantasies, sounds, occur potentially infinitely. The 'directorial intelligence' is seen to be either author or context or the one as the other. Therefore our being replications or something being replicated takes place 'visibly' as an action.

So the process of cultural abstraction itself is the model or mechanism for the pattern. Reading imposing a reality on us is therefore the "response card referred to as the action." Deciphering oneself entails what one is; the concept of that entails the action of what the text is. We mime the simulacra, "syntax mimes space," in order to get at the real.

A variation on the notion of apprehending the inherent nature of a being, object, or event as motion is suggested by the Busby Berkeley follies or a dance concentrating on one point or juncture repeated but never the same, which cannot remain identical with itself.

In the example of a centralized pattern, the Busby Berkeley follies with skits or vignettes without necessarily a beginning, middle, or end: the pattern is submitted to the control of an overriding authority, but with the notion that the finely tuned unit would avoid the distortion of the whole. Using the notion of the pattern being the inherent nature of something as movement, the model of such writing while possibly using a 'format' ('genre'), would be tuned to change occurring on every level. As suggested by a model from physics, the individual person, general context of nature, social behavior, and specific event are undergoing change in one moment. The same scene will not be repeated.

> The same pattern of things is not necessarily repeated at all levels; and secondly, we are not even supposing that the general pattern of levels that has been so widely found in nature thus far must necessarily continue without limit.[5]

A variation and extension of aspects of the discussion suggested here may be seen in Cindy Sherman's work.[6] Her early photographs refer to scenes or atmosphere from thirties or forties movies: an example of a projection or aping of a genre or mode fixed in time—but taken seriously in its establishing its own version or reality—therefore that which duplicates can't be easily duplicated.

Her work to date is a series of replicas—the subject is always Cindy Sherman herself; yet they are not self-portraits. The photographs become increasingly unrecognizable as to their subject. One photograph, for example, is a masculine figure wet gravel on its face seemingly having died recently, but on closer observation showing sores indicating the beginnings of decomposition; another figure is a blonde-wigged woman propped on her elbows on pebbles with her mouth open showing a bright red liquid blood-like interior. The use of costumes, overtly staged and stagy scenes produces a potentially infinite series of new characters.

Therefore the question as to the identity of the author and of oneself is apparently the subject—that conception itself being an expression or 'analysis' of postmodernist sensibility, i.e., the photographs overtly expressed as cultural abstraction or the critical conceptualization of the present art scene.

The following passage as an example of this critical conceptualization is from an essay by Rosalind Krauss, titled "A Note on Photography and the Simulacral":

That Sherman is both subject and object of these images is important to their conceptual coherence. For the play of stereotype in her work is a revelation of the artist herself as stereotypical. It functions as a refusal to understand the artist as a source of originality, a fount of subjective response, a condition of critical distance from a world which it confronts but of which it is not a part.... If Sherman were photographing a model who was not herself, then her work would be a continuation of this notion of the artist as a consciousness that knows the world by judging it. In that case we would simply say that Sherman was constructing a critical parody of the forms of mass culture. With this total collapse of difference, this radical implosion, one finds oneself entering the world of the simulacrum.... If the simulacrum resembles anything, it is the Idea of nonresemblance. Thus a labyrinth is erected, a hall of mirrors, within which no independent perspective can be established from which to make distinctions—because all of reality has now internalized those distinctions.[7]

The criticism as description, using Krauss's essay as an example, is the process of creating convention—the description of ourselves as culture. Sherman's work is the convention and the revelation of that; as such, the focus is the mystery of the convention which is nonresemblance itself, i.e., originality or subjectivity.

The Unit as the Book—the Book as a Unit

Examples of Sherman as unrecognizable subject: a photograph of a large figure with a long red artificial sensual tongue in the foreground behind which are ant-size humans; a shot of a head with a pig's snout, blood-like smears on the snout and cheek, the figure lying on a dark background. Another photograph shows a sweat-covered or moist figure unrecognizable as to gender crouching clutching or sorting through pebbles, looking up at the camera with a wild expression showing a mouth of rotten teeth. The costume dramas in the collection, coming at the end of the series, cause the sequence of photographs to seem to fly apart.

Charles Bernstein's *The Sophist* presents a multiplicity and potentially endless proliferation of voices and characters.[8] In terms of the use of genre: the poem "Fear and Trespass" is an example of being entirely inside some other voice. The details of the circumstance of the couple in this piece are never given; but the circumstance is conveyed in a deliberately bathetic language of Harlequin romance or soap opera. Bathos and turgid vocabulary are as valid as any other information. There is no introspective or conscious voice which would have a different or outside perspective; in that sense the form of the writing goes beyond or outside the confines of the convention of a 'poem' and is someone else's 'book.' The piece is language as a jostling whipped-up surface—its motion is entirely in that, in terms of it being the whipped-up singular perspective. So it is not simply satire.

Other examples of the use of 'genre'—which are therefore unlike the model: "The Only Utopia Is in a Now" uses a voice or perspective reminiscent of eighteenth-century genre describing people's attitudes and behavior, and criticizing their manners and morals. The authorial voice criticizes the inhabitants of this imaginary Utopia by assimilating their constructs of emotion and anti-emotion:

> You see, emotion doesn't express itself only in words we already know. But people here who talk about emotion don't really want to experience it. They only want simulations of it in patterns of words they've already heard.

Other examples of 'genre' are ostensible imitation of some other writer, as in "From Lines of Swinburne," in which the poem speaks of itself as a voice—maintaining that singular perspective—as aping itself, being a play on itself. The writing is different from either the old model or the present conception of a poem.

Poems may in *The Sophist* actually be plays, as in the piece titled "Entitlement," in which named characters speaking to each other—things being like something else—simply make statements of those resemblances, rather than having dramatic situations or action. The statements of resemblances are an aping of actions.

In "The Last Puritan," a hypothetical character is projected as "anything merely seen or heard." A single poem or prose piece may have multiple voices or perspectives. The voice in a piece may seem to be the author's, or there may be a variety of characters, or simply voices interweaving ideology, information, commentary on the writing, or contradiction of previously declared opinions or assertions. The text uses words that aren't real or are hybrids or deliberately misspelled; its language also consists of blank spaces, slang, nonsense sounds, capitalization of parts of words; the text introduces as one character a Mr. Bernstein who turns out not to be the author: it introduces someone else's book, *The Odyssey*, misquoting it. Word and object are expressions or formal projections of each other.

Bernstein comments in reference to the proliferation of perspectives or detail: "There is never annul / ment, only abridgement." Nothing is left out of the writing; so it goes past the confines of a 'book.' Distortion of the individual unit by the whole is part of the writing's acknowledged mode; comparable to Peter Schjeldahl's notion, in his introduction to Sherman's work, of "Presence" as emerging in the costume dramas with the photographer finally being there as only herself the actress.

The order of *The Sophist* is carefully composed to create "a single but layered structure." The book does not have a beginning, middle, and end as would occur in the unfolding of a drama or story. As in the play "Entitlement," which consists of statements of resemblances, there is no progression of development of a plot. The poem, "the order of a room," is a series of statements or types of order:

> a geometric order
> a cosmetic order
> a temporal order
> public order

Some of the ways of seeing the structure or order of the 'book' are "hypostatization of space, the relations detemporalized," "idea of explaining the visible world by a postulated invisible world," distance, arrangement of letters on the page, blanks that could be filled in thereby changing the order, abbreviations, etc. In terms of a geometric model, the notion is of the 'book' being detemporalized and spatial.

Aping doing imitations (as in the Swinburne poem) is an example of incorporating a sense of relativity in terms of time.

The book is the "single but layered structure"—the notion of "a body that seemed genuinely music"—given more as the *idea* of a music than the actual formal rendition and sound of that music. In other words, the latter occurs as the abstract configuration of the idea.

Similar to aspects of Stein's view of composition or Hemingway's cultural abstraction in *Hills*, yet seeing experience differently from them (for example, all times operating at the same time, a different sort of cultural analysis), Bernstein's work projects a symphonic structure that would reflect multiple changes occurring in the present instant. Such a projected work need not be seen as a dissipated version of modernism or as leading to confusion, but rather actively engaging reality/as Maya.[9]

Bernstein's sense of the 'idea' as being the shape and reverberation, the formal configuration of the 'book,' is a variation and contrast to the characteristics of Alice Notley's *Margaret and Dusty*.[10] The internal workings of her 'book' in its process as if using itself up or being the same as its material are the actual rendition and sound of that music.

A manifestation of postmodernism: the proliferation of the particular— has to do with recognizing social definitions ("The composition is the thing seen by every one living in the living they are doing") as not intrinsic to reality or oneself.

Margaret and Dusty is composed of discrete poems, which are an interwoven pattern of voices and characters. Real individuals sometimes mentioned or addressed by name enter the conversation; people are quoted and designated by name as in "Bob and Simon's Waltz"; unnamed multiple voices interweave snatches of conversation; imaginary characters address each other as in the piece "Postcards"; a poem may be entirely a monologue by some other character as in "At the End-of-School Party"; or the author carries on conversations with invisible presences, reading aloud from a book or newspaper or responding off-the-cuff to TV or movies as part of the conversation.

Parts of poems are designated as songs. The songs are format variations and projections of the particular poem in which they're found.

The authorial voice in a chatty, daffy duration of a sort of "Macho Daisy Duck" (a poem in which she titles her own voice) becomes apparent as a social surface, or a constructed personality.

The subject of one's 'life' is discussed in terms of the conventional conception of the separation of autobiography from the 'book.' This subject also relates to actual life and death—i.e., the separation of life from 'book' is narrowed or erased—by the fact of the author dealing with the occurrence of an actual death, thus going past the confines of the book. Social construction and private experience of reality are seen as the same, mirrored in each other:

> I learned two things from the play last night,
> God is Love, & when you're dead you're dead.
> Look at this picture, that was his look that when
> he looked at you like that you felt terrific.
> I'll never get to see him again.
> What's it like out?

The creation of the voices in *Margaret and Dusty* apes projections of what we think 'life' is, or what we think ourselves are. People are mimicked to be seen as social configurations and also as "talk," the conversations in the book which are the abstraction the only existence of the person. I.e., the poem or projections of the person are the news or conversations:

Gloria Steinem will speak at length on abortion.
Can I have 35¢ for baseball cards?
I just want to be in my life!
Where are you?
In my life!
I am a black lace fan.
I need the paper & the many little mineral waters.
Unacceptable to Winfield & Jackson.

Stock maxims, understood in the poem as socially derived sentiment, occur as overtly imposed or mimicked voices—therefore the reader comes to a view of sentiment, and to an accuracy in experience of a sentiment, which is different from the stereotype.

As in Cindy Sherman's use of costume, the seeing of oneself as social form a kind of hyped Presence, causes oneself to open up and fly apart.

All things belie me, I think, but I
look at them though. Well boys, at
least you're not dead, right? What's
the date today? Until something. What?
Of the lady of the whitening blow.
I'm ashamed to keep on babbling
as if I've always been oneself,
diamond flow through. Humble
flannel skeleton. Grin, laugh unbecoming
Living at the bottom of the water may
have been obvious all the time. But
I forget. What's my plot? Hand
of a child, paw of an animal.

The sense of time in this book is a phase of intense emotion. The process of the 'book' is that of using itself up; the conversation of all those people in the writing becomes the only stuff there is:

what would you think then? But I
wouldn't do that. Light surrounded oranges
towels clouds. You don't think you're my you.
Not here not you. You still think you're he. she.
Because I wouldn't "you" you, would I? I only
"you" some other he. she. I
who writes poems. When she writes them,
it's different . . .

The author in the 'book' is just that person, which is simply and purely the created other characters, such as Margaret and Dusty.

NOTES

1 This and the following two quotations are from Gertrude Stein, "Composition as Explanation," *Selected Writings of Gertrude Stein* (New York: Modern Library, 1962).

2 Ernest Hemingway, *Green Hills of Africa* (New York: Charles Scribner's Sons, 1935).

3 Michael McClure, *Selected Poems* (New York: New Directions, 1986); and *Hymns to St. Geryon and Dark Brown* (San Francisco: Grey Fox, 1980).

4 Ron Silliman, *Paradise* (Providence, R.I.: Burning Deck, 1985).

5 David Bohm, *Causality and Chance in Modern Physics* (Philadelphia: University of Pennsylvania Press, 1971).

6 Cindy Sherman, *Cindy Sherman* (New York: Pantheon, 1984); exhibit at the Metro Gallery, New York, 1986.

7 Rosalind Krauss, "A Note on Photography and the Simulacral," *October* 31 (Winter 1984): 49–68.

8 Charles Bernstein, *The Sophist* (Los Angeles: Sun and Moon, 1987).

9 *Maya*, reality as infinite multiplicities of illusion.

10 Alice Notley, *Margaret and Dusty* (St. Paul, Minn.: Coffee House, 1985).

PUBLISHED: Excerpted from *Postmodern?* (1987), 7:86–94.

KEYWORDS: postmodernism; nonnarrative; visuality; science.

LINKS: Leslie Scalapino, "Aaron Shurin's *Elsewhere*" (*PJ* 8), "Poetic Diaries" (*PJ* 5), "Re-Living" (*PJ* 4), "War/Poverty/Writing" (*PJ* 10), and Ron Silliman, "What/Person: From an Exchange" (*Guide*; *PJ* 9); Herman Rapaport, "Poetic Rests: Ashbery, Coolidge, Scalapino" (*PJ* 10); John Rapko, "Of Persons as Persons" (*PJ* 9); Stephen Ratcliffe, "How to Reading" (*PJ* 6); Carolyn Burke, "Without Commas: Gertrude Stein and Mina Loy" (*PJ* 4); Beverly Dahlen, from "The Tradition of Marginality" (*PJ* 6); Alan Davies, "Language/Mind/Writing" (*Guide*; *PJ* 3); Arkadii Dragomoshchenko, "Syn/Opsis/Taxis" (*PJ* 8); Allen Fisher, "Postmodernism as Package'" (*PJ* 7); Ed Friedman, "How *Space Stations*

Gets Written" (*PJ* 5); Kit Robinson, "Pleasanton/Embassy Suite" (*PJ* 10); Ron Silliman, "Migratory Meaning: The Parsimony Principle in the Poem" (*Guide*; *PJ* 2).

SELECTED BIBLIOGRAPHY: *How Phenomena Appear to Unfold* (Elmwood, Conn.: Potes & Poets, 1991); *Objects in the Terrifying Tense/Longing from Taking Place* (New York: Roof, 1994); *The Public World/Syntactically Impermanence* (Middletown, Conn.: Wesleyan University Press, 1999); *Green and Black: Selected Writings* (Jersey City, N.J.: Talisman, 1996); *O and Other Poems* (Albany, Calif.: Sand Dollar, 1976); *The Woman Who Could Read the Minds of Dogs* (Albany, Calif.: Sand Dollar, 1976); *Instead of an Animal* (Oakland: Cloud Marauder, 1978); *This eating and walking is associated all right* (Bolinas, Calif.: Tombouctou, 1979); *Considering how exaggerated music is* (San Francisco: North Point, 1982); *that they were at the beach — aeolotropic series* (San Francisco: North Point, 1985); *way* (San Francisco: North Point, 1988); *The Return of Painting, The Pearl, and Orion: A Trilogy* (San Francisco: North Point, 1991); *Goya's L.A.* (Elmwood, Conn.: Potes & Poets, 1994); *Defoe* (Los Angeles: Sun & Moon, 1995); *The Front Matter, Dead Souls* (Middletown, Conn.: Wesleyan University Press, 1996); *New Time* (Middletown, Conn.: Wesleyan University Press, 1999); *The Weatherman Turns Himself In* (Tenerife, Spain: Zasterle, 1999); *Zither and Autobiography* (Middletown, Conn.: Wesleyan University Press, 2003); *Day Ocean State of Stars' Night* (Los Angeles: Green Integer, 2007); *It's go in horizontal: Selected Poems, 1974–2006* (Berkeley: University of California Press, 2008); with Lyn Hejinian, *Sight* (Washington, D.C.: Edge, 1999); with Kevin Killian, *Stone Marmalade* (Philadelphia: Singing Horse, 1996).

An Example from the Literature

Peter Seaton's poem is both an essay in verse and a lecture on aesthetic theory: an example of poetics as praxis, theory as act. In reflecting on the act of writing *as* a form of writing, Seaton's poem continually builds new meanings as it performs its own erasure, canceling out any possible conclusion as it moves forward. Its account of the truth value of literature is its refusal to give one in the act of writing: "Signing a formula for writing in ink, a rare, concentrated / Ink made from a division of myself and English / That I'm crossing out." Seaton's "Example" demonstrates how a reflection on a work of art can be productive of the work itself, how form and content may coincide in a demonstration of meaning, its construction and dissemination. As a literary model for writing about poetry *as* poetics, Seaton's poem adds to the long tradition of texts by poet/critics who demonstrate a poetics through their mode of writing: Gertrude Stein's "Composition as Explanation," Louis Zukofsky's *Bottom: On Shakespeare*, Charles Olson's *Bibliography on America for Ed Dorn*, John Ashbery's *Three Poems*, Charles Bernstein's *Artifice of Absorption*, Susan Howe's *Pierce-Arrow*, and Bob Perelman's *Marginalization of Poetry*, key moments in the continuing genre of poetics as self-reflection. Peter Seaton died on 18 May 2010.

There is no text, and its pleasures devolve
Upon this tristesse. There's always a logic
In which the security of the existence of the momentarily
Unimaginable is ignored in the down to earth
Construction of the perfect poem. That's what
Nobody's inside of and in which there is no standing
Because the afterthought is this item of inheritance
Whose all embracing bequest provides for the appearance
Of emptiness, of heroic possibility, of the myth
Enduring never forgetting there's nobody inside
Being too true to be normal. The white country
Of the page, "trembling with anticipation," can
Be written off into the clearest cultures
Of the structure of reciprocity to propose and prepare
And observe their growth in the leisure of a lifetime
Of work. But this remote intelligence is preoccupied

With references without which no standing can endure though
It exists famously without relation to itself, occupying
The alienated analysand with confused dreams
Of perfect ego just as the hero's
Authenticity resides in his will, a residence
Keeping the poet homeless and forever at home with
Indeterminacies themselves adrift from words
Of little wings tied to the mountains, fresh water
Sliding up in one's soul on currents of the human
Voice between efforts of finding myself falling for
Decisions that no longer exist. I can linger along
The earth's surface, folding the highway's edge
Into vulnerable limits of the sun burning
Down with information that lets me tell you
Where I would wander. There nothing moves
When I stop to be alone, no sign of life
Defined on one of the pages acquiring different kinds
Of English to infinity, no fact, no parts, no prime banks
Of ancient days where the person you may not know
Conducts me to the truth. No unintentionally
Scattered horizons discovered in someone
Signing a formula for writing in ink, a rare, concentrated
Ink made from a division of myself and English
That I'm crossing out. I'll just leave
Some sweet concept of my culture in an English
Settling whatever we believe an American means in
The language preserve of gland controlled unity.

I can see us in its new division, looming out of continuous
English in a paper-strewn past, understanding insights
You might have vigorously finishing with us. Then you
Might have a different word for erupting out of
Civilization which is what I think
You mean takes place in thoughts I think
I had in mind, evanescent possibilities of a hero's blush
Verging on pluralistic mortality. But you guys
You look out from anything that seems poles are cool
Among crags, the peaks gathering you like dizzying lab drops

Under a tree. The flatness of rocks shoots into
A little bit about baths right under your nose.
If I read you classify some small black object
Under the sun I expect to see the unused
Fantasy watered by a whale running
Out of rocks and bristling with the evidence of a pen
Where it feels this sudden margin in the grip
Of a tradition of a word or two. I don't really believe
Cells to be single, or even dots of exciting principles
Of preceding days plodding by. I want to pretend
To be a man and actually think, to bring us two small
Pieces of the two of us in that past made
Of all future extravagance that ends a feeling that
Everything comes back grinning, the moon and wild grass
Joined by contrasts of undefined writing grounded
In the one you see that's on me, the old saying
That doesn't mean defend yourself against seeming to
Like to touch me or that there'd be surging
Spectra of full vowel futures written on tough
Haunting guesses of everything expectantly locating
Your words out of how good you were you evil
Looking reader disrupting the shock of begging for
Attention from every metaphor for reading
Assignments into the needs of inventive images dominating
The planets about to leave land into a lineage
That some intense dream trails in words.

Hero and Heroine, I was asked to speak while
Writing these priorities. One, this must be
Said because of an urge to write. Two, to write
Something one reads into erotic discovery.
Three, to write so you can read a father
Was killed on the basis of anticipating an urge
To assemble the determining line.

You can ask me this heart line in tropes
Fortuitously sustaining the association of the raw
Material of the language of right thoughts in
Quotes inseparable from antidotes to telling

You this, in differential sleep distilled
To participation in geometries of so many advanced
Ideas for living everywhere, in doing something
For a man who runs against fine timing.
You're talking to old friends, to a legend,
A scheme of resistance humanizing you
Within reach of my writing. Yet the elusive
Tempo of seeking patterns in the methods of questions
In my muscles actually happened to that poet
Existing in the loss of a word. It's that adventure
I want, the nature of what happens starting to create
A subset of cleared-away English giving you trouble
Between two nouns sounding good on the bridge
To word matter, in the mind's hardness
Of the word instance of eloquent new painting
Around a field and a cow. Without this
New object becoming a context for images of thinking
Becoming words my impetus does not falter in the fact
Of something you see in thinking this thing out. But
One good idea for secret technical gratification
Is not that tightly revelatory written word. It's not
Those words referring to veiled thoughts of sure reading
Demanding concepts of the nervous spectator and his wife
Admitting me to proving to take decades
That I have to work with, centuries
To occur to our sufficient age beyond the reach
Of classical certainty. That's how
You understand humans earnestly lacking means
For adding the future I to each strange language
I guess I can't imagine arising from mine.

Ah, Maria, these problems don't tear
The place down. And what a lot of reasons jar
Le neige bleu into certain kinds of Proust
Aviation such as dialects minus those syllables
Going to make me cry. This son of a gun
Is reading the highest standard of living.
This moralist studies the subject's real things

Overflowing his or her main chance. This patriot
Exists in spite of books written for me
To read Kant, this troubled people
Orders its survival and keeps it whole and breaks
Your heart into dossiers of elementary ambition, live people
Need so much. These peasants starve into print
And rush through pearls of prime guesses to see you.
These women, reduced to the trouble with men define
The developing words with grammars you mix with reading
Knee deep in concentrating on upright amounts of time.
This technician sees the words that always come
For us. This linear being just lets go.

Because the subject is pure matter in excess
Of roaming some writer's logic it's our golden
Age remaining embarrassingly central to how we are
Where we are now varies right away. At least one
Formula for necessity or speaking to incidents
Radiating letters to literature hovers over all the time
That grants composite logics openly and ceaselessly
To you. I want its greedy associations
To accommodate far-fetched archetypes of inaccessible
Nerve sites of the oldest fantasy specializing in
Getting away with menacing attention.

That's why the poet demands the discontinued artifice
Of its energy. I'm talking of making one million
Years merge in each metaphysics of creating
A fever eater poem. The best page
Sees it first, the blessing this emphasis
Makes print all physiology at once and
Spirits in the traits of misleading believing
Proud things into the sunset design thought
Gripping life true to an aesthetic verity that fits
All the riches to referential riches to English.

Maybe I persist in seeing the several rhythms cruise
Agencies of metaphysics of the imperative for
Converging on historical shock, for honing

The edge of seeing you think I'm mixed up
In my libido, my education, etc. I'd learn how
To like the idea, but you'd write and talk
In my crisp fantasies, making up
Where I just lived, then dropped into everyone
I think you'll feel up to rescuing from the miracle
Of solid walking off before strong bodies sleep
Off the difference you come up with remembering
The rope to my room looks like entities of English
You'll write to me soon, especially words inventing
Blue and pink sounds like a language producing
The approval of the first word which is red.

That helps you recite a page in alien alphabets
In the written debris you write home not to mention.
Congratulations to the two best males judging both
Poetry and painting exercising sources to pieces.
They're earthlings in our influence respected
For disappearing into the bosom of an integral depletion
I also wrote out of a new dimension for surveilling
Them from stopping being who you are. I want your world
Which was not always I make a poetry we don't know
Yet, a vibrant poetics keeping the walls of my life
Sufficient to the field of carbon-produced facts from
Draining the need of the largest adult into tons
Of something to say that could sum up the parts
I was in love with. I thought life could manage
Iconoclastic micro-things mobbing the problems you say
You make up reading of gaining each other, let's say
Where you'd kiss the hands of every woman in the sixties
Writing unpredictable intermissions in particularly
Escapist Soviets. But linear sighs
Of narrative lines form huge imperious
Looks across the bay. And daily, or even hourly,
This is the pumping heart. I never began writing.

I write I have a fantastic rock and look
At it again. I wrote How To Read into the blur
That becomes words behind the trunks of trees.

And I knew my mother's finite intervals as passages
Before the spot that went into the military. I was
Writing the sensibility of the subject satisfied
With being looked at with a kind of fear packed
Into a test for mind that meant something
Fills me with terror. But the disappearing
Herald of numinous suspense, that thing
In my nature that cannot be mistakes words
You say to yourself for edges of something you drop
For falling beyond itself. By the time our conscience
Accelerates such things to the service
Of the dilemma of so much work a wish
Permutes to a world in which writing is too
Much for any man to have to jinx
That mythical necessity separately, in steps.

PUBLISHED: *Marginality: Public and Private Language* (1986), 6:98–103.

KEYWORDS: Language writing; poetry; philosophy; nonnarrative.

LINKS: Mike Anderson, "Framing the Construals" (*PJ* 5); Alan Davies, "Close Reading Close Reading" (*PJ* 2); Jean Day, "Moving Object" (*PJ* 9); Erica Hunt, "Beginning at *Bottom*" (*PJ* 3); Pamela Lu, from "Intermusement" (*PJ* 10); Bill Luoma, "Astrophysics and You" (*PJ* 9); Larry Price, "Aggressively Private: Contingency as Explanation" (*PJ* 6); Lisa Samuels, two poems (*PJ* 10); Leslie Scalapino, "Pattern—and the 'Simulacral'" (*Guide*; *PJ* 7); John Smith, "Philadelphia Newspapers Read Crossways" (*PJ* 10).

SELECTED BIBLIOGRAPHY: *Agreement* (New York: Asylum's Press, 1978); *The Son Master* (New York: Roof, 1982); *Crisis Intervention* (Berkeley: Tuumba, 1983); *Imaginary Ship* (N.p.: Beaumont, 2003).

Narrative Concerns

Cinema has provided poetry with many points of reference, from Hart Crane's *The Bridge* to Frank O'Hara's "Ave Maria" and John Ashbery's "Daffy Duck." Less familiar are avant-garde cinema's contributions to poetics, from the modernist period to the present. Warren Sonbert (1947–95) was a San Francisco experimental filmmaker with close ties to poetry, particularly New York School and Language writers. His essay, as part of the "Symposium on Narrative" (*PJ* 5), addresses his limited use of narrative in nonnarrative films: narrative may provide images with emotional power, but images should be kept from being overdetermined by plot. Influenced by Soviet directors such as Sergei Eisenstein and Dziga Vertov, by the French New Wave, by a selective canon of Hollywood masters and genre films, and by the avant-garde from Andy Warhol to Stan Brakhage, Sonbert's films are complex realizations of the material and affective possibilities of cinema. His thinking on cinematic technique—from shot selection to larger combinatory principles—owes much to Eisenstein and Vertov's theories of montage. However, it is his use of these techniques to produce visual sequences that are both intellectually complex and emotionally rich that makes his films of particular interest to poets. Sonbert's poetic cinema anticipated the recent emergence of "Neo-Benshi" performances, where avant-garde poetry is read with film and often music, in the Bay Area and elsewhere.

The strengths of narrative as well entail its limitations. On one level narrative could be defined as the eventual resolution of all elements introduced. This classical balance is always satisfying: when the various strands are climactically tied together. But this also implies a grounding that may often enough be deadening.

A fairly interesting Jacques Tourneur film, *Nightfall* (1956), illustrates this point. At the opening, a man, ostensibly the hero, since he's also the star (Aldo Ray), walks into a city bar at night. He is being watched, unawares, by two men in a car. Once in the bar a third man also begins to observe him. While seated at the bar Aldo is approached by a woman (Anne Bancroft) to borrow some money to pay for her drink as she's mistakenly left her money at home. At this juncture the possibilities are rampant: three different sets of strangers have either approached or are observing the protagonist. What could they all want from him? What is below the surface of this rather ordinary-looking hero? Then, are any of the three sets involved with one another or are they working separately? Is Bancroft's plea a ruse or the truth? If a ruse, is it a sexual pickup or something more ominous? At this moment when anything can happen, narrative is at its most fascinating. (In my own films I generally try to include an image of forward motion on train tracks in which several lines converge but cut before any actual track or direction is taken—it's a metaphor for possibilities open.) In *Nightfall's* case the questions are answered all too soon perhaps. Bancroft is telling the truth, the single trailing man is on his side, the men in the car are against him and none of these initial strangers are working together. But the frissons with which the first scene of the film are filled almost carry over into the entire unraveling of the work. Though settling down into a very good, standard thriller, nothing quite matches this opening assault of question marks.

Beyond this initial barrage of possibilities open, narrative can partake of shiftings in value identification as another one of its strong suits. The opening chapter of Balzac's *Splendors and Miseries of Courtesans* has this in spades, in that the author always seems two moves ahead of the reader: the focus of viewpoint remains unanchored amidst a wide variety of conflicting identity figures. This avoidance of set bearings is all to the good as it supplies one of the prerequisites of art. The changing stress between comedy and tragedy in Renoir's *Rules of the Game* is another instance of a profound, unsettling, architectonic strategy. Again, the major works of Hitchcock brim with this tension of paying for your laughs. (In my *Noblesse Oblige* shots of a "cute" kitten at play is immediately followed by an image of someone being wheeled into an ambulance, and briefly enough displayed to hopefully be disturbing). Any given must fairly soon be qualified to preclude smugness and an easily assumed attitude: Balzac and Stendhal were prime investors in this policy. *Psycho* and *Splendors* in fact partake of the same function of cheating the anticipations of the receiver (viewer/reader). In both works an identity figure is posited (Marion in *Psycho*, Esther in *Splendors*), then removed and replaced by another identity figure (Arbogast and Lucien, respectively), to which the receiver is cannily made to make a complete emotional transference, only to be removed and replaced once again by what turns out to be both works' archvillains (Norman and Herrera). Such discomforting sleights of hand regarding character identification seem to be one of narrative's most effective calling cards.

When narrative settles down and becomes domesticated, when a given just stays that way throughout the length of the work, it becomes inert and predictable.

From A Woman's Touch, © *1983 by Warren Sonbert.*

In my last completed work, *A Woman's Touch* (1983), which lasts 23 minutes, there is a given and then a series of qualifications, almost like a Theme and Variations. The initial set is a number of images of women involved in solitary action. All is presented positively, benignly, almost *too* complacently: women at work, at play, constructing, striving, succeeding—a paean to their independence. The first variation is the introduction of men: singly active as well and intercut with the women. The men here are initially conceived as threats and tinged with negative associative imagery: men drinking, men gambling, men ordering, pointing, bossing. There is a very brief (hence again hopefully disturbing) image of a man sharpening a knife. Other images show men carrying guns or dominating others within their sphere. After all this, no wonder the women might prefer to be on their own. The second variation softens the first two sets: men become less of a threat. The elements of couples, of domesticity, of sweet family existence invade the pattern of images. The same man who earlier was briefly shown sharpening a knife is now seen in a much longer shot (obviously a chef) scooping up ice cream. See? It's not so bad. Throughout the film (in which an image of one man or woman performing an activity is always seen/felt as a *surrogate* for any other, different man or woman respectively performing another activity).

A specific man and a specific woman have constantly been intercut with one another though they never appear within the same frame. The woman is confident, a worker, assured, the epitome of Independence. The man is shown in contained spaces—usually a chauffeured car or in an office—and invariably giving orders and directions to others. He's obviously a dominating force, perhaps one of repression. The first two images of the film are a woman on the phone then another woman on the phone. The last four shots of the film: 1) *the* independent, working woman opens a mirrored door and answers a phone, smiling and nodding her head in agreement—obviously glad to accept an offer. The mirrored door behind her *closes*, but it is as well in movement/flux and therefore as a metaphor suggests the situation/predicament of the viewing audience. 2) *The* dominating man is on the phone in what seems to be his office. He has certainly softened. His suit coat is off and he's more relaxed than in his previous images. By the juxtaposition of these two images the viewer registers that these two "characters" have finally come together: the man is asking the woman out, or they're married and he's checking in, or whatever—some bond is present. Other factors: he has called her, made the move—reenforcing the traditional aggressor role. She complies, capitulates, gives in. Throughout the film there has been a movement towards domestication: an image of a woman hailing a (offscreen) cab on a city street is followed by (in an apparently different location) an image of a mobile home being transported down a road on an enormous truck. So 3) a very brief fade-in fade-out (almost like the flicker of an eye) image of the interior of a comfortable vine-covered cottage. Clichés certainly come in handy to build visual arguments. 4) In long shot, symmetrically framed, at a significant distance, the exterior of an impressively grand ranch house as a man leaves the front door and gets into his limousine and slams the door. The lines of the driveway converge in a path that leads to the house: but it is also a cul-de-sac, a dead end. The man does have the last word. All the independence that the women in the film have throughout evinced, and as well the straining towards home and domesticity, here both converge in a narrative summation of tying together the threads within a devastating conclusive context. This final surrogate man is in a suit—just like our dominating hero. The slamming of the car door is the opposite of Nora's exit in *A Doll's House*. The enclosures of the house and car represent safety, insularity, complacency and, at the same time, wealth and power. Man is still calling the shots. In *A Woman's Touch* the men have the last word from the force built up via montage into this lost image. The converging lines of the driveway represent a road, a passage, an escape—to flee (like the converging lines of the railway station at the beginning of *Marnie*), but the cul-de-sac at the end of these lines diverts/inundates/cancels this attempt at escape, at Independence.

PUBLISHED: *Non/Narrative* (1985), 5:107–10.

KEYWORDS: cinema; nonnarrative; avant-garde; visuality.

LINKS: Rae Armantrout, "Silence" (*PJ* 3); Abigail Child, "The Exhibit and the Circulation" (*PJ* 7); Child, "Outside Topographies: Three Moments in Film" (*PJ* 8); Michael Gottlieb, five poems (*PJ* 10); P. Inman, "Narrating (Moving) People" (*PJ* 9); "Poets Theater: Two Versions of *Collateral*" (*Guide*; *PJ* 5); Larry Price, "Harryman's Balzac" (*PJ* 4); Jed Rasula, "What Does This Do with You Reading?" (*PJ* 1).

SELECTED FILMOGRAPHY/BIBLIOGRAPHY: *Where Did Our Love Go* (1966); *Hall of Mirrors* (1966); *Amphetamine* (1966); *Truth Serum* (1967); *The Tenth Legion* (1967); *Ted and Jessica* (1967); *Connection* (1967); *The Bad and the Beautiful* (1967); *Holiday* (1968); *The Tuxedo Theatre* (1968); *Carriage Trade* (1971); *Rude Awakening* (1975); *Divided Loyalties* (1978); *Noblesse Oblige* (1981); *A Woman's Touch* (1983); *The Cup and the Lip* (1987); *Honor and Obey* (1987); *Friendly Witness* (1990); *Short Fuse* (1991); *Whiplash* (1995; posthumously completed, 1997); Alan Bernheimer, "What Happens Next," in Rae Armantrout et al., *The Grand Piano* 8:187–204; Steve Anker, Kathy Geritz, and Steve Seid, eds., *Radical Light: Alternative Film and Video in the San Francisco Bay Area*, 1945–2000 (Berkeley: University of California Press, 2010).

Constellations II New Methods and Texts

Amnasan, Michael. "The Eclipsing Function of Full Comprehension." New Narrative writer Amnasan meditates on the relation between sublime incompletion, the gap between labor and public, and narrative: "Within monotonous labor the sublime feels suspended, promised to unfold as the work's conclusion, as a broad space of material fascination."

PUBLISHED: *Marginality: Public and Private Language* (1986), 6:104–8.

KEYWORDS: New Narrative; class; public sphere; material text.

LINKS: Michael Amnasan, from *Joe Liar* (*PJ* 10); Steve Benson, "Mediations in an Emergency" (*PJ* 5); Bruce Boone, "A Narrative Like a Punk Picture: Shocking Pinks, Lavenders, Magentas, Sickly Greens" (*PJ* 5); Jerry Estrin, "Cold Heaven: The Uses of Monumentality" (*Guide*; *PJ* 9); Larry Price, "The Contingency Caper" (*PJ* 7); Leslie Scalapino, "Pattern—and the 'Simulacral'" (*PJ* 7); Ron Silliman, "'Postmodernism': Sign for a Struggle, Struggle for the Sign" (*PJ* 7).

Child, Abigail. "The Exhibit and the Circulation." Avant-garde filmmaker/poet Child reads the "constructivist biographies" of her Soviet forebears Dziga Vertov and Sergei Eisenstein, charting the parallels between montage and writing. She finds Eisenstein's status as "modern artist, making it big" to be theatrical, admires Vertov's more fragmentary openness.

PUBLISHED: *Postmodern?* (1987), 7:71–78.

KEYWORDS: cinema; Russian poetics; formalism; modernism.

LINKS: Abigail Child, "Outside Topographies: Three Moments in Film" (*PJ* 8); with Sally Silvers, "Rewire//Speak in Disagreement" (*PJ* 4); Viktor Shklovsky, "Plotless Literature: Vasily Rozanov" (*Guide*; *PJ* 1); Warren Sonbert, "Narrative Concerns" (*Guide*; *PJ* 5).

Friedman, Ed. "How *Space Stations* Gets Written." Friedman describes the development of *Space Stations*, a process-oriented experiment in textual production begun in 1979 that juxtaposes "present-time physical phenomena"; "memory, ideas, emotional responses"; "reading material" (NASA's *Apollo 13 Spacecraft Commentary*); and visual images.

PUBLISHED: *Non/Narrative* (1985), 5:22–39.

KEYWORDS: nonnarrative; experience; visuality; method.

LINKS: Steve Benson and Carla Harryman, "Dialogue: Museo Antropología, Mexico" (*PJ* 8); cris cheek, ". . . they almost all practically . . ." (*PJ* 5); Tina Darragh, "In 1986, I began . . ." (*PJ* 9); Fred Frith, "Helter Skelter" (*PJ* 9); Nick Piombino, "Towards an Experiential Syntax" (*PJ* 5); Kit Robinson, "Time and Materials: The Workplace, Dreams, and Writing" (*Guide*; *PJ* 9); John Zorn, "Memory and Immorality in Musical Composition" (*Guide*; *PJ* 9).

Jarolim, Edie. "Ideas of Order." In her review of Lydia Davis's *Story and Other Stories*, Jarolim connects the individual stories' exploration of order and its ironic underside with the self-consciousness of her narration: "The careful dialectical questions the narrator poses [. . .] clearly serve the same distancing and controlling functions for her as the act of writing."

PUBLISHED: *Non/Narrative* (1985), 5:143–45.

KEYWORDS: narrative; psychoanalysis; subjectivity; readings.

LINKS: Lydia Davis, "Coolidge's *Mine*" (*PJ* 3), "Some Notes on Armantrout's *Precedence*" (*PJ* 6); Pierre Alferi, "Seeking a Sentence" (*Guide*; *PJ* 10); Robert Glück, "His Heart Is a Lute Held Up: Poe and Bataille" (*Guide*; *PJ* 2); Lanie Goodman, "Georges Perec: Life Directions for Use" (*PJ* 3); Ted Pearson, "Unit Structures" (*PJ* 5).

Lloyd, David. "Limits of a Language of Desire." In his critique of *The L=A=N=G=U=A=G=E Book*, the anthology published in 1984, Lloyd admires the collective project's undermining of liberal ideologies of presence and representation, but asks whether the fragmentariness of the resulting aesthetic might not reinforce capitalism in a more efficient form.

PUBLISHED: *Non/Narrative* (1985), 5:159–67.

KEYWORDS: Language writing; critical theory; politics; readings.

LINKS: Bruce Andrews, "Total Equals What: Poetics and Praxis" (*Guide*; *PJ* 6); Rae Armantrout, "Mainstream Marginality" (*Guide*; *PJ* 6); David

Benedetti, "Fear of Poetic (Social) Knowledge: Why Some People Don't Like (Language) Poetry" (*PJ* 10); Charles Bernstein, "Professing Stein/ Stein Professing" (*PJ* 9); David Bromige, "Alternatives of Exposition" (*PJ* 5); Alan Davies, "Strong Language" (*PJ* 7); Norman Finkelstein, "The Problem of the Self in Recent American Poetry" (*PJ* 9); Félix Guattari, "Language, Consciousness, and Society" (*PJ* 9); George Hartley, "Jameson's Perelman: Reification and the Material Signifier" (*Guide*; *PJ* 7); Kofi Natambu, "The Multicultural Aesthetic: Language, 'Art,' and Politics in the United States Today" (*PJ* 9); David Plotke, "Language and Politics Today" (*PJ* 1); Ron Silliman, "The Dysfunction of Criticism: Poets and the Critical Tradition of the Anti-Academy" (*PJ* 10); Barrett Watten, "Robert Creeley and 'The Person'" (*PJ* 9).

McCaffery, Steve. "And Who Remembers Bobby Sands?" McCaffery sees the mass media's dissemination of narrative as having produced a form of saturated but stultifying hypercommunication in which "media narrative is no longer a localizable telling but the refabrication of information as impulses far removed from any social dictates of communication."

PUBLISHED: *Non/Narrative* (1985), 5:65–68.

KEYWORDS: nonnarrative; postmodernism; public sphere; media.

LINKS: Jeff Derksen, "North Of" (*PJ* 8); William McPheron, "Remaking Narrative" (*PJ* 7); Kathy Acker, "Ugly" (*Guide*; *PJ* 7); Margaret Crane and Jon Winet, from *This Is Your Life* (*PJ* 9); Allen Fisher, "Postmodernism as Package" (*PJ* 7); Andrew Ross, "The Oxygen of Publicity" (*PJ* 6); Rod Smith, from "CIA Sentences" (*PJ* 10); Lorenzo Thomas, "The Marks Are Waiting" (*Guide*; *PJ* 10).

Middleton, Peter. "The Knowledge of Narratives." In a context of skepticism about narrative among poets, Middleton recalls the degree to which narrative, while banished from positivism, cannot be dissociated from scientific knowledge. Narratives of discovery, progress, time, and space may be taken for granted, but there is no objective truth outside them.

PUBLISHED: *Non/Narrative* (1985), 5:52–57.

KEYWORDS: narrative; science; knowledge; philosophy.

LINKS: Michael Davidson, "Framed by Story" (*PJ* 5); Mikhail Dziubenko, "'New Poetry' and Perspectives for Philology" (*PJ* 8); Lyn Hejinian, "La Faustienne" (*PJ* 10); Nick Piombino, "Towards an Experiential Syntax" (*PJ* 5).

Moriarty, Laura. "The Modern Lyric." Moriarty charts the turn to lyric poetry in four language-centered poets, finding a common impulse to "possess the world through stylistic accuracy" at epiphanic moments as characteristic of the genre. "The lyric sensibility is a heroic one," but it also offers "refuge from the world which threatens and overwhelms [one]."

PUBLISHED: *Postmodern?* (1987), 7:133–39.

KEYWORDS: lyric poetry; Language writing; negativity; readings.

LINKS: Laura Moriarty, "Sex and Language" (*PJ* 8); Jackson Mac Low, "*Persia/Sixteen/Code Poems*" (*PJ* 4); Rae Armantrout, "Chains" (*PJ* 5); Kathleen Fraser, "Overheard" (*PJ* 4); Ben Friedlander, "Lyrical Interference" (*PJ* 9); Herman Rapaport, "Poetic Rests: Ashbery, Coolidge, Scalapino" (*PJ* 10); Andrew Ross, "The Death of Lady Day" (*Guide*; *PJ* 8); Aaron Shurin, "Orphée: The Kiss of Death" (*PJ* 10); Chris Tysh, from "Dead Letters" (*PJ* 10); Hannah Weiner, "Other Person" (*PJ* 9).

Piombino, Nick. "Towards an Experiential Syntax." Piombino seeks the relationship between the dynamics of psychoanalytic processes ("primary forms of free association and the analyst's suspended, evenly hovering attention") with "their syntactical expression in speech and writing." Poetry and art become necessary sites for reordering perception and cognition.

PUBLISHED: *Non/Narrative* (1986), 5:40–51.

KEYWORDS: psychoanalysis; science; experience; visuality.

LINKS: Beverly Dahlen, "Forbidden Knowledge" (*Guide*; *PJ* 4); Steve Benson, "Personal as Social History: Three Fictions" (*PJ* 7); Arkadii Dragomoshchenko, "The Eroticism of Forgetting" (*PJ* 10); Ed Friedman, "How *Space Stations* Gets Written" (*PJ* 5); Peter Middleton, "The Knowledge of Narratives" (*PJ* 5); Fiona Templeton, "My Work Telling the Story of Narrative in It" (*PJ* 5).

Price, Larry. "The Contingency Caper." In a media-saturated, postmodern world, narratives are often reduced to a codified "suspended mimesis" of reduced meaning within their overdetermined atomization. Postmodern writing is an attempt to break down these reduced narratives in order to reanimate the drama, violence, and agency of their lost origins.

PUBLISHED: *Postmodern?* (1987), 7:3–17.

KEYWORDS: postmodernism; media; nonnarrative; meaning.

LINKS: Larry Price, "Aggressively Private: Contingency as Explanation" (*PJ* 6); "Harryman's Balzac" (*PJ* 4); Michael Amnasan, "The Eclipsing Function of Full Comprehension" (*Guide*; *PJ* 6); Alan Bernheimer, "The Simulacrum of Narrative" (*PJ* 5); Daniel Davidson, "Bureaucrat, My Love" (*PJ* 10); Michael Gottlieb, five poems (*PJ* 10); Steve McCaffery, "And Who Remembers Bobby Sands?" (*PJ* 5); John Rapko, "What Will Postmodernity Be?" (*PJ* 7); Jim Rosenberg, "Openings: The Connection Direct" (*PJ* 10); Peter Seaton, "An Example from the Literature" (*Guide*; *PJ* 6).

"Symposium on Narrative." Sixteen writers, performers, and visual artists were asked, "What is the status of narrative in your work?" Responses range from examples of nonnarrative form (Andrew Voigt's scores; Fiona Templeton's performance); to skepticism about overarching narratives (Warren Sonbert's films; Doug Hall's installations); to advocacy of the critical redeployment of narrative (Michael Davidson; Robert Glück; Carla Harryman).

PUBLISHED: *Non/Narrative* (1985), 5:69–121.

KEYWORDS: narrative; nonnarrative; performance; visual art.

LINKS: Steve Benson, "Mediations in an Emergency" (*PJ* 5); Carla Harryman, "Toy Boats" (*Guide*; *PJ* 5); Bob Perelman, "Exchangeable Frames" (*PJ* 5); "Poets Theater: Two Versions of *Collateral*" (*Guide*; *PJ* 5); Leslie Scalapino, "Poetic Diaries" (*PJ* 5); Warren Sonbert, "Narrative Concerns" (*Guide*; *PJ* 5).

"Symposium: Postmodern?" Is the theoretical discourse of "postmodernism" a necessary and useful framework for producing contemporary writing and art? The nine responses range from strong rejection of the postmodern (Bill Berkson; Allen Fisher; Duncan McNaughton; Alan Davies) to its critical embrace (John Rapko; Connie Fitzsimons; Kathy Acker).

PUBLISHED: *Postmodern?* (1987), 7:95–117.

KEYWORDS: postmodernism; modernism; critical theory; history.

LINKS: Jerry Estrin, "Cold Heaven: The Uses of Monumentality" (*Guide*; *PJ* 9); Robert Glück, "Truth's Mirror Is No Mirror" (*PJ* 7); Bob Perelman, "Three Case Histories: Ross's *Failure of Modernism*" (*PJ* 7); Harry Polkinhorn, "The Failure of a Postmodern Aesthetic" (*PJ* 7); Ron Silliman, "'Postmodernism': Sign for a Struggle, Struggle for the Sign" (*PJ* 7); Barrett Watten, "The Literature of Surface" (*PJ* 7); Jason Weiss, "Postmodernism and Music: The Reaches" (*PJ* 7).

III Numbers 8–10

Seeking a Sentence

Pierre Alferi's work represents one of many parallels between French poetry and North American language-centered writing in the 1970s and 1980s, in part due to their shared influence by French theorists like Roland Barthes, Hélène Cixous, Gilles Deleuze and Félix Guattari, Jacques Derrida, and Julia Kristeva. Alferi began publishing as a philosopher before turning to poetry and cinema, developing what he terms a *cinépoésie*. His essay "Seeking the Sentence," drawn from his collection *Chercher une phrase* (1991), argues for the poetic possibilities of the sentence through a sequence of cinematic frames to construct a montage of discursive perspectives. The essay explores three interrelated possibilities of the sentence for verbal art: its active and improvisatory form, its rhythmic character, and its relation to objects, which it both represents and becomes. Stemming from the French tradition of aphoristic poetry after Lautréamont's *Poésies*, Alferi's writing "about writing" draws on philosophical debates from Plato's *Phaedrus* to Ferdinand de Saussure's *Course in General Linguistics*. His notion of the sentence may be compared to the device of the "New Sentence," theorized by Ron Silliman, a widely shared formal strategy of Language writing. In his contribution, French philosophical inquiry into the nature of language and creative expression coincide in a central demonstration of poetics as a genre of writing.

1. Language

ESTABLISHING

Literature is made of sentences presented for what they are. Fiction clearly shows how sentences, by saying something, do something. Firstly each sentence returns to its own possibility: a singular past—experience, thought, language—which is invented in the sense that it cannot be found elsewhere. Each sentence is clearly presented as a gesture or an act: a summoning of its past through wording. Literature, then, puts a theory of the sentence into practice. Yet it does not need to formulate this theory distinctly. Literature forms new sentences which contain their own past; these sentences operate solely upon what they themselves are saying. Producing a sentence and producing its origin are confounded in the act of wording. This singular gesture is that of establishing. Sentences in literature are not descriptive; they are establishing.

RETROSPECTION

The establishing gesture takes the form of a return to the past. But, here, retrospection is not laying a foundation; the origin it attains is not a foundation. A foundation is discovered retrospectively in the course of an examination. A foundation is laid because something happened to be there already, independent of the examination and its retrospective movement. The foundation is an absolute anterior, an object of detached contemplation and retrospective judgment. (Philosophy made a foundation of origin: it underlined the "forever already.") Literature invents the sentence's past. Origin is not separate from literary work, whose retrospective movement constructs and fashions it. It is a projected anterior; it is neither the object of contemplation or judgment, nor is it the object of a question or response; it is the object of an establishing. (Literature makes a forever contemporary anecdote of origin: it underlines the "first time.") In literature, retrospection is in itself active, establishing; its object is invented by being pushed into the past; its object is produced by being projected backwards. In literature, the origin is merely the establishing gesture, the very movement of invention in all its forms. And since this movement is retrospective, the forms of origin are merely the forms of retrospection.

RETURN

Literature projects an origin in language first. There is nothing nearer than the mother tongue. Its proximity is the marker of all proximity. In language, literature does not project just any origin. Even when its source lies in such and such an experience or thought, origin is experienced through the proximity of the language. Forms of retrospection can be declined into a series of gestures—a wide variety of gestures that retroject experiences or thoughts, thereby saying what they are making. And these gestures form the open ensemble of the sentences of literature: establishing phrases, fashioning an origin. But all these forms of retrospection have something in common, a minimal form is repeated: the form of a return to language.

DISTANCING

Returning to the mother tongue—to one's native language—is being faithful to it. And yet, with this return, language is not found any nearer than it was—it was the nearest. Not only is approximation found to be impossible here, but fidelity—if that means being restricted to this unequalled proximity, to be confined by it—would be unbearable. What stands for return in this intolerable proximity is but that movement toward language which pushes it back into the past: a setting for return where there was not the slightest distance. So, in effect, retrospection is active—a gesture that makes language step back. Literature begins when an adherence to the mother tongue, its immanence, is warded off. This detachment is authorized by a non-subjective sentiment, the matter of which is a quality of the language: that strange quality of pastness which only the nearest can possess. (The "sweetness of the language," when it appears ever so remotely stranger to itself, is also its clarity.) Hearing texts giving themselves an origin in language, maintaining its distance, one experiences the sentiment of a pure past. There alone fidelity is possible, for it is by distancing language that one can give it a voice. (Archaisms, in literature, have the inverse effect from what one expects.) This voice is a literary idiom, language heard as echo. Making sentences in this language is making language step back. Making sentences in this language which is not a language, but a certain retrospective take on language, is inventing sentences.

"ORIGIN"

Literature reduces its origins to the retrospective forms of an establishment. But does it answer to a "question of origin"? If radical responses are amiss, it is because origin is language in general: proximity unequalled, yet an intangible figure of proximity. The question dries up on its own then: literature dissolves origin in the invention of each singular sentence, resolves the question— without responding to it—in the operation of the sentence. (Questions of origin are traps.)

2. Rhythm

THE SENTENCE

The literary object is the sentence. Sentences do not share a common form, and yet, in each sentence, one can recognize the sentence. Each sentence is, firstly, the operation that each new sentence—to be invented—had to carry out on itself: namely, the action of phrasing. Each sentence was worded— invented, before being used—used over. The sentence is that moment when a new sentence is formed, the emergence of its singularity. (As an operation, the sentence decides for itself the relations it entertains with its linguistic, pragmatic, literary context.) Since literature invents sentences, it takes place in the sentence. Yet the sentence is not a universal entity. There is more to say about "the sentence" than about common language's use and usury of sentences; there is less to say about it than about new, particular sentences. Talking about the sentence is not meant to describe a common form, but to show how one phrases in order to invent sentences.

SYNTAX

Every sentence is musical. Yet the imitation of sound music is always secondary. (Compared to strictly musical possibilities, assonance remains a relatively poor play on timbre, accentuation a play relatively poor on pitch, prosody a play relatively poor on rhythm.) The most obvious musical forms are not the most decisive: the sound music of the sentence can escape the blandness of ornamentation only by accompanying its intrinsic music, giving itself up to it. This merges in a rhythm which is essentially mute. Syntax itself is this rhythm. It is a cadenced order, a sequential hierarchy. The grammatical construction of the sentence is obviously rhythmical—it segments by giving value to each of its parts. But precise relations also exist from one term to another above and beyond the limits of the parts of the sentence and without reference to their grammatical organization: echo, nuance, opposition, trope, a relation of one term to an other whose absence is made known or to its own absence which is made known elsewhere, etc. Often independent of the construction, these sense relations nevertheless form rhythmical structures—they make the line of the sentence oscillate and define the amplitude of its vibrations. Hence they are syntactical though not by nature grammatical. (Between constant semantic relations studied by lexicography and variable semantic structures studied by rhetoric and stylistics, the break takes place at the sentence.) The sentence establishes a rhythm proper to itself, but one which cannot be reduced to its construction: a syntax richer than its grammar. All that is balancing, speed, or syncope concerns the syntax. In this sense, syntax is much more than the sentence's skeleton, it is its circulatory system: it is what is rhythmical in meaning.

ENJAMBMENT

To experience rhythm, and to act upon it, syntax must be held at a distance. Everyday language is submerged in the element of syntax, it lets itself be lulled by its rhythm; it is enough that it re-employ the forms of sentences gone by. Whereas in poetry, enjambment is the sound index of a syntactical crisis necessary to the invention of sentences. (The backward step of the language produces a "musical sentiment.") This is why poetry is the critical site of the invention of sentences: line and prosody, non-grammatical unity and rhythm, put syntax in a crisis. But poetry can get along without sonorous accompaniment or metric musicality: enjambment alone is essential to it. And the syntactical crisis of which it is the clearest index can also take place, more discreetly, in prose, which is to say in a purely syntactical rhythmic setting. (In poetry as in prose, academicism is first betrayed by a snoring syntax.) Literature can be defined by the uneasiness of its syntax without resorting to mixed genres or confounding it with their respective practices.

FORCE

The sentence sets a force into rhythm. Neither the origin nor the nature of this force is of interest to literature. This force is of interest only to the extent that it is oriented toward a proffering. It is not an issue of this or that desire, nor does it let itself be determined by "objects of desire"—provoking conditions, attaining things or beings. It is not even an issue of meaning, it does not yet mean to say anything. In order to mean to say something, one must dispose of the sentence where this will is articulated, where this thing is named. (There is no "mean-to-say" until afterwards.) The force engaged in the forming of a sentence is but the *élan* of proffering.

MEASURE

The sentence stages this *élan*, or *spirited performance*; the performance is rhythmed. But it does not represent the performance, does not imitate it, for a performance cannot be represented. (Expression always fails.) The performance is measured by the sentence. By nature the performance is excessive, outlandish. Its immeasurability consists in its indetermination. Infinite, pure affirmation—the performance borders on vacuity: that of a desire to speak which is insatiable, or of an utterance that can say nothing, and is untenable. The spirited performance then falls from its own weight into measure. The measure is its very falling; it is not an exterior constraint, but the logical form in which the performance exhibits its own excess, the sequence that alone can deploy its paradox. Logical form does not set itself up against the performance's outlandish excess; it measures its immoderation. (To maintain the outlandishness as an autonomous moment is to go from the inarticulate to disarticulated, which is to say toward gibberish.) And so each sentence constitutes an internal articulation of the performance. In its own manner each sentence affirms it, explains it, stops it, sets it into motion again. The sentence takes place when the spirited performance of proffering—its immoderation and its falling—becomes pulsation, or when a rhythmical disposition carries an affirmation. Thus in establishing measure, each sentence becomes its own unit of measure.

TONE

Sentences are distinguished above all by their rhythmical disposition, or by measure and its various aspects. In falling, the spirited performance of proffering first takes on a certain fold—it is precipitated into a curve or contour. Each curve gives the tone, which may correspond to a register of rhetorical invention. In irony, the performance is inversed, in ellipsis it is interrupted, in paradox it diverges, in correction it starts over, in concession it bends, etc. In no manner can such forms subsist outside of the sentence, nor can they be composed before it. Nevertheless, they are not yet forms of sentences. They are the forms which the growing sentence projects retrospectively onto the very performance of proffering. The sentence thus presupposes a retrospective invention of the curve or the tone. It imposes such and such curve on the performance, meanwhile projecting it into the past as an origin of the sentence. So the singularity of each sentence then happens in a retrospective establishing.

MEANING

Such an establishing also commands other aspects of the sentence's measure. By means of a retrospective gesture it precipitates the spirited performance of proffering into a given concrete syntactical form. The sentence retrospectively positions the source of the proffering through forms of interlocution: first-person narration or the impersonal report, dialogue, free indirect style, etc. The sentence retrospectively positions the finality of the proffering through forms of eloquence: the role reserved for its addressee, an appeal to emotion, approbation, or their rejection, the evocation of the presence of things and the effect of reality, or irreality, etc. Finally, the sentence retrospectively positions the meaning it attempts to produce—through rhythmical relations it establishes phrase by phrase in its lexicon and through the rhythmical arrangement of all of the preceding elements: a curve or a tone, a source of proffering positioned here or there, an explicit finality. (In rhythm, the identity of form and content is a concrete given: the meaning of a sentence is the global effect of its rhythm.) What these sentences have in common is being presupposed by the sentences and at the same time resulting from them; this is why they must be the product of a retrospection. The sentence takes on body or meaning in a retrospective relationship to the indeterminate force that animates it.

The sentence projects its origin at the performance of proffering. It retrospectively attributes a measure to this performance; it thereby establishes a singular rhythmical disposition—its own syntactical form. But, before even taking form, doesn't each sentence have an author whose subject matter it will serve? The idea of an enunciating subject, the idea of a desire matured by objects, and the very idea of something to say are secondary effects of the sentence, of its retrospective establishing; they are formed after the fact. The illusion that this subject, this desire and this meaning-to-say exist before the sentence is but the passively contemplated deformed image of the first active retrospection. That which seems to determine the sentence from the exterior is part of the sentence. The establishing of the sentence is the sentence.

3. Things

EXPERIENCE

The sentence sets things to rhythm. It is an experience. All that one calls "experience" presupposes succession and hierarchy—which is to say rhythm and syntax. To have an experience, to lead it to its conclusion, is to say it. The sentence furnishes the syntactical form which defines the experience; it then makes the experience, retrospectively, by projecting it into a forever present past. (Experience is a contemporaneous origin, a form of retrospection.) By inventing the rhythm of things, the sentence as experience recovers things.

THE BEAT

An experience begins with the apparition of a thing and the first usage of a word. In the apparition's simplest form, a thing falls. Before being installed, objectified in a representation, given a usage, a thing falls before one's eyes, it makes sense, it takes place, it lands. Its "first time" was unforeseeable, dependent upon the chance of an encounter. The contingency or grace of its apparition does not indicate a far-off or invisible provenance. It is rather the mark of that which comes to its own site without a trace of provenance: of a thing which is not yet an object, given before being presented. In the simplest relation between a word and a thing, the word names the thing. Before being associated to an image, and to seal the closure of a representation, it is enough that the word refer to the thing, indicate the thing in its own site. Reference is a link both higher-strung and stronger than that of a representation to a represented object: it simply hangs the word on the thing, without the violence or precarity of an appropriation. Reference takes place—one can neither reenforce it nor compromise it. (Literature no more alters reference than it does things; it enacts it.)

THE CELL

Reference and apparition fit together. Two movements are measured one to the other and thus constitute a rhythmical cell: that of a thing coming to the encounter, that of a word pointing to it. And the simplest forms of experience leave the thing intact, because, for us, the thing itself is nothing other than the beat between apparition and reference. (In its intimate beat, experience gives no clue of the "inadequation" of language, any more than its "adequation." The beat is there simply because each and every thing has several names as each and every word has several referents.) But, given over to the routine of perception, this elementary pulsation makes itself imperceptible. The apparition sets itself into a grounded presence: the thing becomes the subject of a representation. Reference is encumbered with psychology: the word is tied to images.

ANIMATION

Only a sentence can maintain the beat of a thing. The performance of proffering pulls words and their references into its curve; they no longer simply refer to things, they also call on each other. Each minimal rhythmical cell then finds itself caught in a play of contrasts, anticipations, reminders. These internal relations which make the sentence's rhythm do not unhook the word from the thing, they do not hamper reference. (Literature's sentences are overlays on the referential graph: they do not modify points but they trace out rhythmical lines with some of them.) Nevertheless, the syntactical rhythm, while putting reference into play, imposes a sufficient tension upon it to raise things slightly—things take off ever so slightly from their site, they too are carried away. The tranquil presence in which they were installed—object of a certainty which leads to forgetting the contingency of their apparition—this presence is temporarily suspended. Syntax reanimates elementary rhythmical cells. The sentence makes reference scintillate: it creates a hovering in things. (Language's transport of things is not a metaphor.) But this weightlessness lasts only as long as the duration of the sentence. Reference assures the hanging of words onto things in their own sites. Slightly raised, things can only fall back down, thus regaining the calm grounds upon which habitual perception recognizes them. The sentence will have been for them the occasion of a brief leap.

CONTINGENCY

The fall of things is orchestrated by the sentence. Having made reference scintillate, having raised things, the sentence concludes by letting them settle back down again, offer themselves as if for the first time. The more the sentence pulls on the thread of reference, the more its rhythm distances itself from that of habitual perception, and the more things appear in their contingency. Habitual perception can reclaim its right—the detour it imposes was for an instant short-circuited. The sentence indicates the path of a return to things themselves—not through imitation but through a form of abandon. To do this, it need not even describe experience: it produces it. For, by creating a hovering in things, the sentence's rhythm fixes in its logical time the conditions of a simple apparition, and it lets the sentence have the last word, the fall. (The neutrality of a report is less faithful than the deviation of a poem.) In this manner literature's sentences indicate—above and beyond rhetorical sites—the unique site where things fall. Literature puts things back together again; things in literature beat their own measure.

THE "PAST"

The sentence invents an experience. It retrospectively projects a minimal rhythmical cell into each thing; the sentence maintains its beat by integrating it into a stable rhythmical form where the thing does not cease falling, inexorably contingent. This is an establishing. But don't sentences serve to describe what is known, to evoke past experiences? The same illusion is used to confound, after the fact, reference and imitation, things and objects equal to themselves, sentences and descriptions. After the fact, everything happens as if, in the sentence, an experience already spent has been stated. The sentence imposes a form upon an experience that knew no other form; and, for this very reason, form seems to be imposed beforehand upon the sentence that invents it. (The claim uttered in the sentence by an experience nevertheless impossible before the sentence exists, is the source of elegiac sentiment.) But experience can only happen in a sentence: the sentence imposes itself as experience, as the only form capable of containing its own past.

—*Translated by Joseph Simas*

PUBLICATION: *Knowledge* (1998), 10:1–9.

KEYWORDS: French poetics; language; philosophy; method.

LINKS: Lydia Davis, "Coolidge's *Mine*" (*PJ* 3); Françoise de Laroque, "What Is the Sex of the Poets?" (*PJ* 4); Arkadii Dragomoshchenko, "I(s)" (*Guide*; *PJ* 9); Emmanuel Hocquard, from *The Cape of Good Hope* (*PJ* 8); Bob Perelman, "Plotless Prose" (*PJ* 1); Peter Seaton, "An Example from the Literature" (*Guide*; *PJ* 6); Lytle Shaw, "Language Acquisition as Poetics: Notes on Recent Educational Writing" (*PJ* 10); Barrett Watten, "The XYZ of Reading: Negativity (And)" (*PJ* 6).

SELECTED BIBLIOGRAPHY: *Guillaume d'Ockham le singulier* (Paris: Minuit, 1989); *Chercher une phrase* (Paris: Bourgois, 1991); *Des Enfants et des monstres* (Paris: P.O.L., 2004); *Les Allures naturelles* (Paris: P.O.L., 1991); *Le Chemin familier du poisson combatif* (Paris: P.O.L., 1992); *Fmn* (Paris: P.O.L., 1993); *Kub Or* (Paris: P.O.L., 1994); *Natural Gaits*, trans. Cole Swenson (Los Angeles: Sun & Moon, 1995); *Personal Pong*, with Jacques Julien (Sète, France: Villa Saint Clair, 1996); *Personal Pong*, trans. Kevin Noland (Cambridge: Equipage, 1997); *Handicap* (Lyon: Rroz, 1997); *Sentimentale Journée* (Paris: P.O.L., 1998); *Le Cinéma des familles* (Paris: P.O.L., 1999); *Petit Petit* (Paris: rup et rud, 2001); *Cinépoèmes et films parlants* (Paris: Laboratoire d'Aubervilliers, 2003); *L'Inconnu* (Quimper, France: Le Quartier, 2004); *La Voie des airs* (Paris: P.O.L., 2004); *Oxo*, trans. Cole Swenson (Providence, R.I.: Burning Deck, 2004); *Intime* (Paris: Inventaire/Invention, 2005); *Les Jumelles* (Paris: P.O.L., 2009).

Can't We Just Call It Sex? In Memory of David Wojnarowicz

Dodie Bellamy is a prominent figure in the New Narrative movement, which from its inception pursued writing at the intersection of genre fiction and sexuality. In her essay on David Wojnarowicz, Bellamy takes the often repeated explanation of experimental writing—"the reader makes meaning"—and turns it into a physical encounter, scarcely mediated by the page. Bellamy's view of the reader is that she is "not merely a passive recipient of the writer's sexuality, but an active participant in the romance," thus bringing active eroticism and the bodies of real persons (often naming names) into play. If every reader, as reader, has an engaged sexual body as well as a creative critical mind, the experience of reading may be understood directly as a form of sexuality. Even more importantly, the reader is queer, capable of fantasies beyond the scope of social or internalized norms and also of a transgressive relation to the text. The title of her essay, as Bellamy tells us, comes from Kathy Acker's response to the term "New Narrative": "Can't we just call it sex?" It is dedicated to the memory of David Wojnarowicz, a multimedia artist and arts/political activist who died of AIDS in 1992.

I once had dinner in a Taoist restaurant with a serious young man. Let's call him "Rendezvous." We savored the restaurant's specialties, sweet and sour "pork" made from deep-fried gluten, roast "duck" made from tofu skins, and stir-fried "chicken" that tasted like it was grown on Mars. All these analogues reminded but never fooled, and our conversation naturally turned to writing and its relationship to the "real thing," that is, life. I asked him what he thought of Kathy Acker. Rendezvous swallowed a mouthful of slippery but genuine straw mushrooms, then admitted that he reads her books by skipping to the "dirty parts." I flashed back to when I was ten years old, and in my parents' bedroom I found a pulp paperback, *Lust Campus*. I was dying to cruise through those small yellowing pages, but my mother was in the next room. She hardly ever left me alone in the house: I bode my time. Weeks seemed to pass, though in actuality I think it was a few days. Finally, one fateful afternoon, she had errands to run, and decided to leave me home to watch the spaghetti sauce she had simmering on the stove. Opening the screen door she shouted at me, "I'll be back in an hour or so. Behave yourself." As soon as the latch clicked I darted into her bedroom. *Lust Campus* toppled off the bookshelf into my chubby eager little hands. I flipped rapidly through the pages past the tedious exposition until I landed on a sex passage—then sitting cross-legged on the polished oak floor I wallowed in obscenity while the spaghetti sauce burned to a scorched red mass, like lava. I remember a detailed description of taking off a woman's bra and an orgy where a group of college students were lying on the floor in a circle. Since I was so naive about the birds and the bees this didn't strike me as kinky, merely as information. All sex was equally arousing and this book was great. Then I heard my mother's key in the back door— I crammed the paperback in the bookcase and rushed to the living room, sprawled on the couch like nothing had happened. Dropping her purse on the coffee table my mother sniffed at the scorched air. "Dodie, what the hell have you been doing while I was gone?" "Nothin'."

On my own I never would have thought of applying the *Lust Campus* approach to Kathy Acker, but Rendezvous seemed so highly motivated I decided to give it a try. Scanning my bookcases I happened upon *Empire of the Senseless*. Opening the book I discovered that Kathy had inscribed it: "Love, Acker." Beneath that she'd added, "New Narrative? Can't we just call it sex?" After recovering from a Jungian pang of synchronicity I began to flip rapidly through the pages with my chubby eager hands. I found plenty of sexual snippets, but extended sex scenes were rare. I thought to myself *Rendezvous must be quick to burn*. Finally on pages 93–95 I located a passage that's pretty hot. In it a soldier fucks a whore on a white wolf fur:

> I took hold of her thighs. I ran my hands around them. I put my mouth on them. I bent her forward so I could run my hands up and into the ass. Red head backwards, she kissed me on the lips. I had her ass.
>
> Dinosaur, who was a stuffed animal, was sitting next to us. Dinosaur was female therefore a prostitute. I could see her cunt. Cherries were sitting on top of her thighs. One of her gigantic paws as if she was a wild cat grazed my knee in affection. The buzzing of a mad bee caught prisoner in the bathroom resounded from tile floor to tile floor. When I managed to get my head up, the red-head rubbed her thighs into the back of my neck.

As the scene progresses, the stuffed animal becomes increasingly animate, competing with the whore for the soldier's affections:

> I laughed at myself and gave her [the whore] what she wanted. I pierced myself through her belly-womb. As her red head rose out of the white fur, her mouth opened: monstrous scarlet. Tiny white shells appeared in that

monster sea. 'My little dead shark. Better than dead fish.' I whispered to her while I fucked her in the asshole.

Stray sprays of sperm streamed down the stuffed animal's left leg. Our fucking had made her less fearful for the moment. She actually touched my arm and left her paw there. Then this paw pulled my arm to her monstrous body, lifted it and placed it on her swollen belly. Then she stuck the hand in and squeezed it between her two hot wide thighs. I thought that my hand was going to break.

I had already stopped fucking the whore. I rolled to, almost over, the dinosaur by the dinosaur. My soft gluey cock pulsed against her thigh which was made out of sackcloth. She looked at me. She licked my eyelids which looked pale to her. I turned away from the monster, back to the whore.

I tried to imagine getting off on this passage—physically that is. Acker is not whipping us into a frenzy of arousal to the point we forget we're reading a book. Quite the contrary—the eros in this passage lies not in the sailor's fucking of woman and toy, but in the writer's seduction of the reader. Acker is playful, coy, teasing—surprising and tantalizing us with rapidly shifting perspectives. She is a selfish, demanding mistress: she never lets her monstrous sackcloth characters upstage her erotic tropes, never lets us forget we are immersed in Writing, immersed in Her.

This is a model I try to live up to in my own work. Though I'm constantly writing about sex, increasingly what I'm interested in is not sex, but the impossibility of its representation, how physical sensation always eludes language. As Lynne Tillman's narrator says in *Motion Sickness*, "The tongue is privileged with information indifferent to words." My essay/narrative "Days without Someone" (*Poetics Journal* 9) explores this tension between experience and text:

> I removed the belt from my robe and tied his wrists to the bedstead—do whatever you want with me, he said, make it hurt *he wanted to be pliable, pliable as absence* . . . beyond a few entries in my diary, the gush of a school girl, I never could write about Ryder *I was silenced before the undefinable thingness of his lips, his hands, his cock, all the insistent anatomical components* . . . *then he left and the words rushed in like vultures, picking away, redefining* . . .

In "Days without Someone" writing is a vampiric agent that sucks the essence from life and uses it to shapeshift. Despite the narrator's frantic attempts to do so, Ryder the man is never captured in words, but destroyed by them, replaced by an analogue she barely recognizes.

The writers I find most exciting aren't searching for descriptive equivalents to sex acts but rather, like Kathy Acker, their writing is a sex act in itself, creating a romance between writer and reader. This romance transcends gender and sexual preference. How else would I feel such an erotic frisson when reading the work of Dennis Cooper and David Wojnarowicz—since the texts of these two gay men in no obvious way mirror my own sexual inclinations or desires. Rather, they extend my range of eros.

Long after it was out of print I asked Cooper to autograph my tattered copy of *Safe*, which in my enthusiastic reading I had marked up, underlined, and written in the margins of to the point of obliterating his words. When Dennis opened the book and saw my scrawls, saw *me* smeared all over *him*, I felt the mélange of thrill and embarrassment I did in junior high when Billy found out I had a crush on him. "Dodie," he said, "You've written more in this book than I did." In a sense I had displaced him out of his own writing project. It made me feel both transgressive and vulnerable. The point I'm sauntering to here is that the reader is not merely a passive recipient of the writer's sexuality, but an active participant in the romance. The reciprocity between observer and observed is a recurring theme throughout Wojnarowicz's collection *Close to the Knives*. I'd like to focus on his apocalyptic tale of desire, "In the Shadow of the American Dream," where the creativity of erotic perception is dissected:

There is really no difference between memory and sight, fantasy and actual vision. Vision is made of subtle fragmented movements of the eye. These fragmented pieces of the world are turned and pressed into memory before they can register in the brain. Fantasized images are actually made up of millions of disjointed observations collected and collated into the forms and textures of thought. So when I see the workers taking a rest break between the hot metal frames of the vehicles, it doesn't matter that they are all actually receding miles behind me on the road. I'm already hooked into the play between vision and memory and recoding the filmic exchange between the two so that I'm without a vehicle and I have my hand flung out in a hitchhiking motion and one of the men has stopped his pickup along the stretch of barren road. Now I am seated next to his body in the front seat.

This breaking down of the distinctions between memory, fantasy, and vision creates a fissure in the landscape of this writing, and in this fragmentation of vision Wojnarowicz finds freedom. Cracks are exposed through which he experiences the void, a gravity-free zone where he's able to jump out of the "preinvented existence" that outlaws his sexuality. With Wojnarowicz we get the sense of a vision so clear it fries him. This fractured transcendence is experienced most fully in the orgasmic scene where Wojnarowicz has sex in a car with a man so huge he seems like a giant:

My eyes are microscopes. My eyes are magnifying lenses. My face is plowing through the head and sensations of this guy's flesh, through the waves of sweat, and in my head is the buzzing sensation of either insect or atmosphere. I see the hallucinogenic way his pores are magnified and each hair is discernible from the other and the uncircumcised dick is bouncing up against my lips as it's released from the trousers. The sensation of its thickness pulls against the surface of my tongue and rubs the walls of my throat, burying itself past the gag-reflex and then the slow slide of its withdrawal as a disembodied hand descends against the back of my neck, just barely grazing the hairline of the scalp and in the periphery of vision there's the steel-blue glaze of the steering wheel and the threads weaving themselves into the fabric of his trousers and the sound of his body bending and the cool sensation of my shirt being pulled up over my back and the shock of his tongue trailing saliva up my backbone and under my shoulder blades and I am losing the ability to breathe and feeling a dizziness descend, feeling the drift and breeze created by the whirling dervish, using the centrifugal motion of spinning and spinning and spinning to achieve that weightlessness where a polar gravity no longer exists. The sounds of his breath and the echo of body movements I am no longer able to separate. The pressure of the anxiety slips closer in the shape of another vehicle or of the cops arriving, nearing the moment where the soul and the weight of flesh disappears in the fracture of orgasm: the sensation of the soul as a stone skipping across the surface of an abandoned lake, hitting blank spots of consciousness, all the whirl of daily life and civilization spiraling like a noisy funnel into my left ear, everything disintegrating, a hyper-ventilating breakthrough the barriers of time and space and identity. And all of it mixing with the stream of semen drifting over the line of my jaw and collecting in a pool in a pocket created by the back of my neck where it meets his upper thigh and abdomen. I'm tipping over the edge in slow motion. In the moment of orgasm, as I'm losing myself, I become vaguely aware of his hands cradling my skull and his face appearing out of the hot sky leaning in, or else he's pulling my face close to his and I'm breaking the mental and physical barrier, I'm listening to my soul speak in sign language or barely perceptible whisperings and I'm lost in the idea that at the exact moment of the kill, the owl's eyes are always closed, and I feel his tongue burning down my throat and the car is in a seizure and he's smacking me in the throat and the car is in a seizure and he's smacking me in the face to rouse me from this sleep, leaning in close again like something on the screen of a drive-in movie, his lips forming the whispered sounds, "Where are you?" and had a cop car pulled up in that moment and had I possession of a gun, I'd have not thought twice of opening fire.

The above passage moved young writer Mark Ewert to send one of his own stories to Wojnarowicz. "He's like a total touchstone for this material," Mark wrote in a letter, "Or do I mean litmus test—like he'll know if it's fake or not—and I am just utterly in love with him, though I'm sure I'm projecting and romanticizing a lot, but not entirely. Not entirely by a long shot." I know what Mark means because I can't imagine how anyone reading *Close to the Knives* could help but fall in love with David Wojnarowicz. In a whirlwind courtship Wojnarowicz oscillates from statistics to rage to heart-wrenching eros. His book fractures the lines: between memoir and high art, fiction and essay, politics and arousal, and even between what's inside and what's out. For me, love has always equaled a permeation of boundaries, and *Close to the Knives* left me shot full of holes, like Swiss cheese. I wrote a shameless fan letter. "Dear David," it began, "I am simply overwhelmed by the mingling of beauty and terror that makes your book so powerful." But I've felt this way about Dennis Cooper's writing too. I have these dreams (and I'm a little embarrassed to talk about them), dreams where Dennis appears as a radiant Christ-like figure whose presence fills me with awe and ecstasy. I don't think these dreams are about Dennis the man, a friend who sits in easy chairs buzzing with bi-coastal gossip. These dreams are about the Dennis I experience in his novels, my fascination with the religious overtones of his sensual knowledge, or more precisely, his mystical pursuit of sensual knowledge.

I met Wojnarowicz on Castro and 18th, in front of the camera shop. It was a brisk Sunday afternoon and he smoked nervously. He seemed a shy, awkward man. He said, "Hi, Dodie" and extended his hand, and I babbled at him, foolish talk, because there are no words to express my desire. My partner, Kevin Killian, asked him to sign a copy of *Close to the Knives*, a signature which made the book precious to him. To prepare for this essay I wrote all over it—I had to—

and it felt like I was committing adultery. Kevin screamed when he saw the book. I was more controlled with his autographed copy of *Mona Lisa Overdrive*, treating it with kid gloves. But I acted out by complaining in a letter to William Gibson: "Dear William, I managed to read a few chapters of *Mona Lisa Overdrive*. It's the hardcover copy that Kevin had you autograph, and he will murder me if I mess it up, so I have to carry it around in a manila envelope and be neat—I need to go out and get a paperback version I can abuse." A couple of weeks later a bubble envelope arrived from Vancouver, containing the paperback edition of Gibson's book. I turned to the title page where he had scrawled in large black letters, "Dodie, get it dirty!"

WORKS CITED

Acker, Kathy. *Empire of the Senseless*. London: Picador, 1988.

Tillman, Lynne. *Motion Sickness*. New York: Poseidon Press, 1991.

Wojnarowicz, David. *Close to the Knives*. New York: Vintage Books, 1991.

PUBLICATION: *Knowledge* (1998), 10:255–59.

KEYWORDS: New Narrative; sexuality; queer; readings.

LINKS: Dodie Bellamy, "Days without Someone" (*PJ* 9); Kathy Acker, "Ugly" (*Guide*; *PJ* 7); Michael Amnasan, from *Joe Liar* (*PJ* 10); Andrew Benjamin, "The Body of Writing: Notes on the Poetry of Glenda George" (*PJ* 4); Bruce Boone, "A Narrative Like a Punk Picture: Shocking Pinks, Lavenders, Magentas, Sickly Greens" (*PJ* 5); Robert Glück, "His Heart Is a Lute Held Up: Poe and Bataille" (*Guide*; *PJ* 2); Laura Moriarty, "Sex and Language" (*PJ* 8); Aaron Shurin, "Orphée: The Kiss of Death" (*PJ* 10); Chris Tysh, from "Dead Letters" (*PJ* 10).

SELECTED BIBLIOGRAPHY: *Feminine Hijinx* (Madras: Hanuman, 1990); *The Letters of Mina Harker* (West Stockbridge, Mass.: Hard Press, 1998; 2nd ed., Madison: University of Wisconsin Press, 2004); *Cunt Ups* (New York: Tender Buttons, 2002); *Fat Chance* (Vancouver, B.C.: Nomados, 2003); *Pink Steam* (San Francisco: Suspect Thoughts, 2004); *Academonia* (San Francisco: Krupskaya, 2006); *Barf Manifesto* (Brooklyn: Ugly Duckling, 2008).

I(s)

Arkadii Dragomoshchenko, a Russian/Ukrainian poet who lived in St. Petersburg (formerly Leningrad), was one of the foremost writers of the late- and post-Soviet periods. In the 1980s, two Soviet avant-garde movements became known in the West, both containing aspects of language-centered writing. *Conceptualism* involved the direct importation of language and imagery from Soviet political culture and everyday life, often in an unmediated manner; Dmitrii Prigov and Lev Rubinshtein represent this tendency. *Metarealism*, a term coined by critic Mikhail Epstein, complicates the representation of reality in poetic language; its key figures are Dragomoshchenko, Alexei Parshchikov, and Ilya Kutik. In the 1980s and early 1990s, these poets encountered like-minded writers from the West, and a productive literary exchange took place that resulted in a series of translations published in *Poetics Journal* (*PJ* 8–10). Given their relative isolation and different political cultures, however, parallels between late- and post-Soviet and Western avant-gardes are not exact. Soviet conceptualism depended on the absence of the commodity in the Soviet Union and has a different relation to objects than in the West. Metarealism, on the other hand, often draws from premodern, religious sources; it is open to metaphysical speculation in ways that Western avant-gardes, especially after the "turn to language," may not be. Dragomoshchenko's poetry is a site of radical metaphysical inquiry, evidencing the intensity of alternative belief in the period. Arkadii Dragomoshchenko died on 12 September 2012.

O, the delusion of our thoughts
You, the human I . . .
—Fyodor Tiutchev

In the digressions and convergings of significations which seem—which seem what? Already here at the beginning we need the word *mirage*, in which undoubtedly (or, more precisely, predoubtedly) consciousness foresees a self-replicating doubling. And it is delightful, as well as desirable, rising out of the depths of reality and geographic folios, with the heliographic boundless luminescence of the world, standing at the edge of vision, turned within (as the later meaning of the Latin word *mirare* suggests),[1] glimmering faintly in a fixed mirror of immutable wonder as if enraptured by a mira-ge.[2]

"I understand" threatens us by protracting an endless tautology. The Penrose triangle, the Klein bottle,[3] and so forth are decorations in a spectacle, aspiring to the role of mirrors. It's possible that somewhere in the very beginning the mirror was broken. A prolonged flash, gradually crossing the limits of power and continuing its extension into time. Perhaps it was then that the atomized "I" settled into some kind of pattern, which subsequently with my blind fingers I would read as a possibility for reconnecting "things and words," fingers and thoughts. Or more precisely, I would grope with the intention of intersecting the "lines of invention," or rather the features of "reality" (but at this point a concomitant question arises: How can the respective territories of one thing and another be determined independently of their interwoven transmutations?)—"I understand I" or "I teach I"—whose functioning extends the area of some completely transparent membrane, which during the course of observation acquires depth (or more correctly, volume) in an ornamental design of familiar Freudian toponymics.

But even in the coordinates of this system the three *gunas* enter into the composition of *prakrti*, nonexistent but in all their immutability revealing themselves in interrelationship: *sattva*, the guna of pleasure and rejoicing; *rajas*, the desire that puts everything in motion; and *tamas*, the guna of inertia, darkness, death, nondifferentiation.[4] But even in the coordinates of this system "I" turns out to be nothing more than a dynamic variable similar to the glimmer in the formation of meaning in the figure of an ellipsis, in the endlessly shifting space of meaning's absence, in the pre*con*ceiving of some meaning. It is possible, even likely, that "I" is connected with what is circumscribed by the concept of finitude, the point at which all perspective lines diverge. Turn around; regardless of your position there is always an opposite "point" (in this shiver created by accumulation, like a word): I, the point of interference, the knot of parallax, which slips away from definition. Moreover there behind you, turning on its axis, the most tender dance of things is taking place, in which they attach themselves to the possibility of a world, revealed in the pollen of digressions and convergings, as pure as bee-bread, sliding on parchment, or a calculation process directed toward an expansion of time, weaving times, just as a letter swaddles its abstract foundations, the page, the substance of anticipation, layer by layer in absence. "But in joining the body be beautiful, pleasurable to the Gods in their loftiest domain" (*Rig-Veda*, 10.56).

The imagination populates the other. The other is imagination, or the other is the possibility of understanding oneself (from the fairy tale of the invisible cap to Husserl, Benveniste, Bakhtin, etc.). I don't have dreams. Possibility is the mediastinum that creates all territories. A maple leaf from the area around Chernobyl can reach more than a meter in width. What size do I reach coming from that same area? Or, where have they stored these sites in space—or in time—which are evidently exceeding normal dimensions? And as for dreams, I do have them, but I have forgotten everything and I continue to forget everything—isn't this my consciousness coinciding with a world which excludes itself from "co-"—hour by hour acquiring what was only a moment ago forgotten—by me? All my past is seeping through the pores of non-memory. Probably the mirror was broken (forgotten), dis-I-ed into real-I-ty. And instead, in order to meet eye to eye, someone with the natural right to affirm that he is he, having come to believe forever in "I teach I," in uttering I randomly prefers something else. And hence in a letter, in merging with anticipation or "In joining the body be beautiful, pleasurable to the Gods in their loftiest domain."

Nonetheless, one can't manage to forget the most insignificant thing in dreams—namely, that the continual basis of "dreaming," being the unassailable repetition of some excessive and empty element, is the possibility of taking a reading on the origin of distance and space, rolling themselves into a cocoon (I don't understand *what* I am writing or saying at this moment, but the fascination of this flickering net of sequences and divergences in disappearances' bends is becoming incredibly strong). It is something incontrovertible—I, presented to myself as some kind of corporeal periphery, an incompleteness (like the shoulder, like part of the cheek or nose, like the movement of the hand "past the eyes"), melting away near the threshold of its realization, like multitudes in the web of time—are these the characteristics of a fantasy (my body is "social" right up to its brain of bones, my body is tattooed into me with a certain congealing blossom of promise, the body is the promise of sending me through it toward what in that particular instant will surpass me—I, revolving around an axis, encompassing a single point free of the most precise dance of things, a point of anticipation, and isn't it in that point, obliged to reiterate by its presence the wholeness of its surroundings, that all connections come together?)? It is like something which belongs to me, i.e., to what slips between me and a set of defined (as if predefined) "images and appearances," slipping by completely without a trace like ice in water. It is the eroticism of disembodiment, opened into the magnetic winds of a desert in whose sources even the sun turns black from solitude, blessing the betrothal of dead children.

I is always situated between me (like the reflexive pronoun, re-revolving "I" on the point where without exception all perspective lines disconnect) and "him," which is also I, even as it doesn't seem to be. But the problem isn't worth an eaten egg.[5] I suppose that if you or I were alone together, or alone with somebody else, or if I, let's say, happened to be with her—and I must admit I'm curious then to imagine her name (no, not the face, faces are all the same, just as bodies, male or female, are like memories, images with which we are doomed, but only the senseless name is incapable of telling me anything with its idiotic attachment and repetition)—there would be nothing for me to say, either to the name or to him/her. Cigarette? Coffee? Wine? Food? Justice? The fly on the windowpane is my infinite I—here is the never broken *mirare*. And so on.

But sometimes in dreams I am dreamed. This interpretation of my phenomena depresses me. Dreams search out metaphysical residue. Sometimes their fury is shattering and indescribable. Dreams form a procession like forgotten worm-eaten gods carrying their heads in their hands with the skin torn from their faces. But sometimes it seems to me that I might be able to understand, that is, to return through what's going on, like the infamous (or better, blind) bee returning to the hive.

A needle without thread.

There is no hive. It disappears at the very moment when understanding comes close to being embodied in itself and its "things," which to all appearances is really the "hive." We wander through a civilization of destroyed metaphors: road, home, language, a man on a bicycle, embraces, Tarkovsky's films, moisture, "I," memories, history, and so forth. And we shouldn't forget the fact that "I" remains for the present the last possibility for metadiscourse, the sole protagonist of what in the current situation there is. The problem of subjectivization is tautological.

However, nature/culture or all that is "I" come from the same code. On the surface of a cup of tea the blue-gray smoke floats. Evaporation—the line begins here. Sometimes I'm prepared to ask if it is possible that someone could think, could conceive his or her own "I," as some continuous given without the thought process itself, or, conversely, that "I" (my selfness, my ness, the axis of my *beingness*, my presence) is a certain definitively unsplintered unity, arising in a conscious process as a collective volitional act. What does such thinking about it propose by way of terminus and goal or "description"?

However, "my birth and death cannot serve me as the object of my thought."[6]

But then, reading his/her poetic "work" (or simply hearing about the amazing strangeness of the everyday), I create exactly his/her "I" (producing myself in their activity which is directed at me—interference—and departing further, through, there, to where, I guess, having drained away—evaporated—all the crookedness from the constant distancing, the desert luminescence of the anticipation of things is made possible—but this doesn't concern me either, any more than Paradise does), as themselves. In other words, their "I" is the product of my collective-volitional effort.

These are aspects of commonsense logic, controlled by a real inexplicable urge to utter "I" (isn't this what constitutes *desire*?). What does it mean to me, taking pleasure in a body flowing and slipping over me and through me in all directions? But posing the question in this way is generally misleading, even if only because it supposes a certain me as the question, existing before the eyes, perception, memory, sensation, the ability to follow certain generally accepted rules (provoking, I should note, growing bewilderment with the passing years) combine into what it is easier to call the impulse to transgress the limits of oneself (but where do the limits lie? what remains?—believe me, if we stayed alone together I'm more than certain that I would have nothing to tell you, but then undoubtedly you know all this, and all the questions that come to me are pursuing only one goal, to keep me from sleep, to keep me from surrendering again to dreams, that dumb tribunal of the anatomical theater, incapable of distinguishing yesterday from space, in which light collapses toward the eyes, bringing them mountains, empty scorching roads whose whiteness removes me from the scene of soundless inquiry: but whom am I addressing?)—but it is the "self" from which the impulse should emanate, being absent or present as the constant incompleteness of meaning.

More than anything I like impersonal sentences. If I'm not mistaken Kleist says: "Only puppets are free." [...]

—Translated by Lyn Hejinian and Elena Balashova
The translators wish to thank Martin Schwartz for inestimable help.

NOTES

1 The imperative form of the verb *mirari*, "to wonder, be astonished at; to admire, look on with admiration." Here it could be translated as "behold!" (All notes are those of the translators unless otherwise indicated.)

2 The author is playing with the Russian word *mir* (in the possessive case, *mira*) which means "world" (and also "peace").

3 The Penrose triangle and the Klein bottle are examples of tautologies of the same order as the Moebius strip.

4 "According to the classic Indian view, matter (*prakrti*) is characterized by the three qualities (*gunas*) of inertia (*tamas*), activity (*rajas*), and tension or harmony (*sattva*). These are not merely qualities, but the very substance of the matter of the universe, which is said to be constituted of the *gunas*, as a rope of three twisted

strands" (Heinrich Zimmer, *Philosophies of India* [Princeton, N.J.: Princeton University Press, 1951], 230n).

5 An idiom equivalent to something like the English "not worth a brass farthing."

6 Maurice Merleau-Ponty, *The Phenomenology of Perception*, trans. Colin Smith (London: Routledge and Kegan Paul, 1967), 364.

PUBLICATION: Excerpted from *The Person* (1991), 9:127–37.

KEYWORDS: Russian poetics; avant-garde; subjectivity; metaphysics.

LINKS: Arkadii Dragomoshchenko, "The Eroticism of Forgetting" (*PJ* 10), "Syn/Opsis/Taxis" (*PJ* 8); Barbara Guest, "Shifting Persona" (*PJ* 9); Lyn Hejinian, "Strangeness" (*PJ* 8); Ilya Kutik, "The Tormentor of Life" (*PJ* 10); Jackson Mac Low, "*Pieces o' Six*—XII and XXIII" (*PJ* 6); Duncan McNaughton, "From the Empty Quarter" (*PJ* 7); Alexei Parshchikov, "New Poetry" (*PJ* 8); Dmitrii Prigov, "Conceptualism and the West" (*PJ* 8); Viktor Shklovsky, "Plotless Literature: Vasily Rozanov" (*Guide*; *PJ* 1).

SELECTED BIBLIOGRAPHY: *Dust: Collected Prose in English Translation* (Evanston, Ill.: Dalkey Archive, 2008); *Description*, trans. Lyn Hejinian (Los Angeles: Sun & Moon, 1990); *Xenia*, trans. Lyn Hejinian (Los Angeles: Sun & Moon, 1993); *Chinese Sun*, trans. Evgeny Pavlov (New York: Ugly Duckling, 2006).

Cold Heaven The Uses of Monumentality

Jerry Estrin's essay, given at a symposium titled "The Politics of Everyday Life" at Small Press Distribution, Berkeley (1988), explores the dehumanizing experience of postmodernity. For Estrin, the postmodern is a historical endgame in which artistic form and architectural monument collaborate in a no-win situation for the viewer or subject seeking to know. Comparing the paradigm of meaning in Marcel Duchamp's *With Hidden Noise* (whose interior cannot be perceived, hidden within a ball of string and clamped shut by metal plates) to Mies van der Rohe's Seagram Building, Estrin shows how postmodernism multiplies and intensifies the modernist crisis of meaning as lived experience. What results is a space of permanent dissociation that recalls Robert Smithson's meditations on entropic monumentality or Fredric Jameson's description of postmodern spatial anomie. Estrin's account of the cultural logic of the postmodern, however, is given not in descriptive or symptomatic terms but as an active force of cultural destruction: culture is the hidden meaning of international capital and its political violence. Estrin's criticism, like his poetry, offers a historical index to the epistemological crisis of postmodernity, an unresolvable contradiction in culture and art that precedes any possible personal experience. Jerry Estrin died in 1993.

In this essay I'm going to be taking certain historical moments of monumentality in visual art and in architecture and talking about how my thinking about this subject matter produced writing. In part, I'm interested in the dissolution of modernism and in the relation between urban monumentality and daily life. The writing will be quoted abruptly, so you will have to consider its relationship with the more direct, and analytical, histories elliptically.

I often work in relation to a reading of the logics of other mediums, of the logic of historical endgames. It is interesting to gain a distance that is not artful, that is not posed but that works at a distance from one's own medium, writing. It is perhaps artful to attempt this distance toward art and toward architecture, especially monumental architecture, because one is so constantly confronted by it as a user of the city. Here are all these towering monoliths, thoughts in space, signals from other eras, crisscrossing with this era, with this era's monuments. How does one write in relation to this urban landscape? I read the city and I read its culture industry from the perspective of historical critique and I use this critique in a duel with appropriated motivation. The

Marcel Duchamp, With Hidden Noise *(1916). © 2010 Artists Rights Society (ARS), New York/ ADAGP, Paris/Succession Marcel Duchamp.*

moves one might make and the reverb from the limits of one's moves are stored in the city.

An alien dialogue begins to represent this immersion.

This is a quote from my work entitled "With Hidden Noise," which was written in 1985 and which attempted to situate a reader in the dialogic oscillation of Duchamp's *With Hidden Noise*, a readymade conceived in 1916.

What interested me about Duchamp's piece at the time was that *With Hidden Noise* was both a moving object and a perfectly immobile object, a signaling device whose meaning was constantly seeming to come from elsewhere, from a space that had nothing to do with the object. That is to say, the Duchampian object is actually a process which provokes an observer to keep reaching for the essence of it, the *Hidden Noise* of its meaning, only to realize, through a kind of engaged training, that one can't ever pin down the meaning—meaning always vanishes and this is its *noise*. The readymade object continually displaces itself to networks of semantic relations, then ricochets back upon itself—to its own indifferent and self-sufficient if enigmatic reality. The *Noise* names the speed of a process of dialogic communication, a cluster of doubt about real facts, and its doubt makes one produce an act of communication for oneself, an act of thought which is direct and pleasurable.

It is possible to analyze the project of the architectural avant-garde of the early twentieth century—the monuments envisioned—in terms of this Du-

Mies van der Rohe, Seagram Building, New York (1954–58). © 2010 Artists Rights Society (ARS), New York/VG Bild-Kunst, Bonn.

champian model. That is, to link up the dialogic seesaw of the readymade with its social potential for liberating thought.

What you see in the second figure is the Seagram Building in New York City, designed by Mies van der Rohe, 1954–58. Withdrawn from the kaleidoscopic image tank of the city, aloof, present in the particularity of its accelerating repetitive order, its steel columns (its steel skeleton) and glass cover wall (its multidirectional reflecting skin), the Seagram Building is autonomous and yet proposes—through its reflecting and yet nearly transparent facades, its combination of tremendous weight and near emptiness, its permutating mullions, its cleared space around its own staged structural foregrounding and perfection—a critical dialogue with the observer. Or at least, if purely from the perspective of the progressive intent of the early 1920s, the heroic age of modernism, one might paradisiacally regard the Seagram Building as doing this. Mies's high-rise office rectangle with its paradoxical glass walls is an urban landscape play. The analogy with a Gertrude Stein play is not inexact. The Seagram Building can be read as existing partly to be performed, dematerializing into a process of design supplied and completed by the man on the street. The masses confront the Seagram Building. The building confronts the masses. Utterly rational organization proposes its dialogue. The dialogic space opens up a public exhibition of critical space: subversive theater. Art abandons its aura, which vanishes into politics.

From the perspective of the 1980s, however, this liberating scenario loses validity when confronted by the measure of history. An operative history, real time systems, bracket the Seagram Building and the dialogic project it monumentally symbolizes. The utopian intent of Mies's structure of steel and glass floats free of its activation in real time, leaving architecture, leaving modernism, with a suspension, an imaginary social purpose, a void, as the basis for the structures in space which are designed. Mies makes his glass skyscrapers for an institutional clientele. The self-evident fact of the era, the autonomous foregrounded structural machine, the monumental multivalent building, designed to train the citizen to take a critical attitude toward the conventional life around him, becomes a corporate headquarters, signature of multidirectional authority flowing from the decentered autonomy of perfect monumental structure. Awe and intimidation, an asymmetrical authoritarianism, a barrier, an insulation, all highly traditional connotations of the monument, flow from Mies's high-rise building. The dialogic production of meaning is appropriated.

The will of the epoch translated into space, Mies's dictum, becomes the will of the multinational corporation, administering the Manhattan air. The passerby comes to orchestrate not his own composition but a commercial to the secrets of power enacted by the building's design.

"With Hidden Noise," which I wrote guided by Duchamp's *With Hidden Noise*, mimes this dream of a utopian dialogue as it proposes Utopia's historical failure and nevertheless enacts it—with all the ambiguity that implies. Writing the *Noise*, reading the *Noise*, one performs again as a subject in a system which has taken possession of that subjectivity. In the result, the writer is naturally dubious about collectivity while nevertheless portraying it. A paradox hits the street, then bumps into Philip Johnson's glass fishscale tower at California and Market in San Francisco, then goes back to perform the *Hidden Noise*.

What's left? The world in motion? The world as text for this readymade dimension moving on defects in our representation of it? *With Hidden Noise, Assisted Readymade*, 1916/1988: through the fuzzy white and red buildings of the night that is not the inner city the simulacrum of suburban businessmen move. In the world, monoliths suck up one's will and reflect the state. Hordes of readers glance in ice age entropy as sudden meanings turn them numb as this abstraction.

One might argue that Mies was not unconscious of the tragedy of the arrogation of the dialogue opened up by his designs. Mies's response was to withdraw, designing mythically aloof buildings which transcended the immediate social context by reflecting themselves. Mies's buildings become mute testaments, self-reflective to their structural purity. Monumental architecture answers its social appropriation by a corporate clientele with silence. As you confront the Seagram Building, as you perform its meaning, as you complete its design, the Seagram Building withdraws from the speculators, the real estate developers, the bureaucrats, the cops. Mies's skyscrapers, in all their monumentality, become semiotic Utopias, reflectors of their own structure. They come to exist by means of their own death.

In 1984, I found myself walking around my apartment roof one Saturday morning, watching a helicopter hovering over the new Philip Johnson building, on California and Montgomery. Dangling from the helicopter was a whitish human figure, wearing a kind of long flowing robe, and holding a sickle across its body. I later discovered that the helicopter had installed neoclassical togas, which had been commissioned by Johnson, to stand atop the gray glass mansard roof of his new building. Johnson's building displays these human-sized togas, devoid of faces, as abstract specters of the utopian dialogue of the 1920s. For Johnson, history acts like Baudelaire's opium nymph in "The Double Room," with those subtle and terrible eyes that one recognizes by their dread mockery. The citizen on his roof, I, looks down at the crowds on California Street—crowds moving in and out of the Bank of America Building, the Holiday Inn, the Embarcadero Center. The utopian polysemy of the International Style dialogue pulls back to Johnson's demonic laughter, in the form of empty togas atop his building. A profound skepticism may offer a distance from reactionary surfaces but it does not prevent one's immersion in historical time. The avant-garde utopia has become an absence stolen from history for the purposes of power and money. Now it is not the passersby who portray themselves when completing the design of the building; now Johnson's draped abstractions, figures of emptiness, mimic the predetermined responses of the citizens.

There is a story by Borges titled "The Immortals," in which a narrator who has been searching for the city of the immortals finally locates it, only to discover that the city of the immortals is a monumental parody because the immortals have realized that building an actual heaven on earth (tradition of the monumental city, simulacrum of heaven!) is impossible. The architects therefore have designed a perverse mimicry of a timeless city. They have invented an architecture whose meaning is that it lacks the finality of the architecture of finality. With no possibility (with every opportunity) of constructing a Utopia in this fallen world (myth of modernist autonomy or no), one constructs monuments to a mannered emptiness, demon monuments.

It is interesting to speculate upon Philip Johnson's purposeless surfaces in this context. For example, how do the political ethics of mannerism, the total separation between concept and function, read when contextualized by the monumental form of a nuclear reactor, which Johnson designed for the Israeli government in the 1960s? Is the empty surface of raw concrete covering the nuclear reactor a rhyme with the desert surrounding it: is it at play with Malevich's nonobjective art, i.e., nothing but a desert, a Suprematist emptiness? One approaches the reactor through a courtyard designed to resemble the approach to a church. It makes no difference evidently whether one designs plutonium or religion: in fact, one appreciates the play of signifiers in such a desert. The barriers of monumentality go neither up nor down; in fact they cease to exist, since the barrier has merged with itself. There's no meaning, there's no rules, life is a chaos of surfaces.

> If one could once to obstruct, collides as the city arrives the cancelled mind, as its boulevards declare abolished sound, language to remain alone. Suppose they do mime, as having never arrived.

> The city is a casual seduction, is empty, shutdown to its wires, as if an American cobalt bomb had consumed every unexpected one of us. The city was occasional for one to inhabit a while. But equally there are artifacts from the past unified by the dream—what does this last quotation mean— the city arranges words like war, sneakily, invents us, and arcades. To be uncanny. In the city, they count something obvious that isn't gone, a perfumed converging and urban projects in their cancelled darks, this is nervous territory.

> So no one is really dressed to go out. They have in fact been previously choreographed, and looking in the water is a resemblance to that escapade. So nostalgia is left as an escape hatch.

In Robert Longo's work, monumentality markets loss. The failed project to enact the spirit of the age, a *Zeitgeist*, generates a pathos and a futility, a futility which is valuable merchandise and of which, one might argue, Longo is rather cynically aware. In *Cold Heaven*, Longo floats little gold leaf tombs before the viewer, ruined transcendent monuments. A grandiose avant-garde project floats before the viewer, the possibility of social change suspended in

Robert Longo, (For R. W. Fassbinder) Now Everybody *(1982–83), mixed media.*
Photo: Pelka/Noble, courtesy Metro Pictures.

a simulated diorama, the work's multivalence no longer offering a transformative depth but a tarnished surface, documenting the gesture of attempting an impossible totality, a corrupted *Zeitgeist.* Longo takes the desire for collectivity and fixes it to a process of consumption: i.e., the consumption of disaster. This death dance, this expressionist melodrama, becomes the surface of a truth, of a posed catharsis which mimics not active engagement in social reality but the witnessing of a fantasy surface, a collaged readymade distance, an advertising layout, replicating seduction mechanisms, predicated on the viewing of ruins as spectacle.

There were real victims in those burnt black-and-white reproductions of staged suburban slums, but to Longo the disappearance of their aura implies the vanishing of their historical truth. Culture produces trance witnesses to devastation, who watch apocalyptic previews. One can shoot up with the thrill, encountering Longo's diorama. Is it afternoon after the riot? Simply turn the TV on or off. Trapped in the video arcade? Freebase off the artificial screen. Consume art which assigns one a viewpoint which is riskless. In *Body of a Comic,* instead of encountering another person, personal presence, depth, you encounter storage drums (nuclear waste containers). This is a farce. *Body of a Comic.* Longo's work keeps enacting these simulated perspectives in which the viewer continually sees himself advancing into a perspective which denies entrance. The work displays this process of vanishing perspectives, of blocked totalities. In *Now Everybody*, the human figure is shot (pun), the human figure is readymade. One needs only dip into the program with all the other film stills, call up the image to construct a generic, allegorical figure: everybody. It is a collaborative project, like Mies's modernist dialogue, only here, with Longo's art, the collective experience is a death dance, with man caught in defeated transformative gestures. Longo memorializes the subject, as in *Pressure*, where subjectivity is the last shrine, a penultimate moment to an apocalyptic culture where the citizen becomes a marionette, as in *Men in Cities*, continually teased, titillated, always on the verge of consummation, yet only achieving consumption, utter consumption of subjectivity. Here one floats, as in *Tongue to the Heart*, suspended within a mausoleum which is itself an imploding allegory of selfhood. One becomes an opera mask amid the artificial if chaotic waves of deranged symbols. There is community in shared exhibition of ironic comment concerning one's own estrangement. Longo's work sells the spectacle of the monument obliterating separateness. The artist has become a good cop, bad cop. Good cop: packaging the subject; bad cop: inhibiting one's singular outbreak to subversive ends. Human beings come when their names are called. I float in my suspended world therefore I am. That's how ideology works. So you get expressive gestures of kitsch transcendence, the last monuments wheeled out as a cold heaven, along with images of junk heap connections, disaster lyrics.

Longo *is* mediation, an enactment of fascist desire, in which experience—the presentment of and response to a multileveled reality—has become a tremendous illusion, a drive-in movie. The seduction mechanisms, of which Longo's art is ideological symptom, are powerful, and to me, terrorizing. I read juxtaposed images of this our American culture to reveal meaning, to situate a relation to history, instead of having history in its reality dematerialize. I make propositions about events in order to put some of the *noise* back in—to interrupt the kaleidoscope surrounding the screen with a critical awareness. I want to reframe the image fate. Critique perhaps can generate an uncorrupted present, free of irony and cynicism. We hit and run, we replicate our subversion suits, we suspend ourselves for a time in the urban landscape play, we enact paratactically a critical enclave, we read the contingent city. We think in this reading a good deal of why it is perhaps problematic to write, as Clark Coolidge does in his work *The Crystal Text*, that "I hate history." But there, down the hill, before the Bay, are the new urban skyscrapers of the financial district. The light is already changing as I write this. The light makes its own surface high-rise, a disfigured, asymmetrical skyscraper, superimposed against the glass of the buildings down below. The buildings are in high performance. Shades of light, an approaching blue, enter the floating business offices. We are suspended together in this theater of reflection and refraction. The temporary immediacy of the street goes unnostalgic against the successful dematerializing of the Battery and Sacramento gray glass monolith. Crosshatches of white painted steel float free of their facades.

Within the Ball of Contradictions (ghost vaporized by exaggeration) the waste products of a prehistoric . . .

PUBLICATION: *The Person* (1991), 9:177–84.

KEYWORDS: postmodernism; subjectivity; visual art; space.

LINKS: Jerry Estrin, "Penultimate Witness: On Emmanuel Hocquard" (*PJ* 8); Daniel Davidson, "Bureaucrat, My Love" (*PJ* 10); Alan Davies, "Language/Mind/Writing" (*Guide*; *PJ* 3); Howard Fried, "The Museum Reaction Piece" (*PJ* 5); Doug Hall, *Forgotten Tyrant* (*PJ* 5); Bill Luoma, "Astrophysics and You" (*PJ* 9); Harry Polkinhorn, "The Failure of a Postmodern Aesthetic" (*PJ* 7); Kit Robinson, "Hayward" (*PJ* 6); Barrett Watten, "Social Space in 'Direct Address'" (*PJ* 8).

SELECTED BIBLIOGRAPHY: *A Book of Gestures* (Berkeley: Sombre Reptiles, 1980); *In Motion Speaking* (San Francisco: Chance Additions, 1986); *Cold Heaven* (Tenerife, Spain: Zasterle, 1990); *Rome: A Mobile Home* (New York: Roof, 1993).

Miscegenated Texts and Media Cyborgs
Technologies of Body and Soul

Poet and scholar Harryette Mullen critiques the postmodern construction of race, where blackness as "soul" is dissociated from black bodies and commoditized in popular media. Framing her argument historically from slave narratives and abolitionist literature, Mullen shows how depictions of the emotions of the enslaved offered a "readable and interpretable" argument for the slave's humanity. As a result, "soulfulness has ever since been regarded as the irreducible essence of emotional expressivity," far from the conditions of the enslaved. In the twentieth century, this cultural logic continues with the circulation of racial images in media, which, abstracted from black bodies and textualized in sound bytes and visual clips, "represent repressed elements of . . . the white psyche." The circulation of deracinated, mediated subjectivity in American culture is the subject of the rest of Mullen's essay, which cites examples from film (Al Jolson's blackface), music (Motown), and advertising (the California Raisins ad). Where the cyborg of Donna Haraway's "Cyborg Manifesto" is a self-realizing and intentionally subversive figure that refuses cooptation, the white-bodied/black-souled cyborg of Mullen's essay exists by means of appropriation and negation. What results is a culture where "racial samples" as "split/merged sound-images" are ubiquitous in music, film, and advertising. In terms of race, the postmodern condition offers only a simulacral substitute for a long history of denial.

The interiority of the Afro-American subject emerged as a discursive formation in a political context that demanded its textualization in order to make "visible" the lives, emotions, and intimate experience of a population that earlier had been visible only as a mass of bodies represented as possessing little or no interiority. Female narrators, who occupied a special relation to the conventional codes of emotional sensitivity so closely associated with the feminine, also had to confront, more explicitly than male narrators, the paradox of modesty in addition to the paradox of proving their humanity. Indeed, the paradox of modesty was, for the black woman, inextricably entwined with the paradox of proving humanity, since the black woman, especially the slave woman, had been defined by a slave-holding society as excluded from the social category of woman. The difficulty that all of the slave narrators faced in expressing their humanity in any other terms than those already in circulation was complicated in different ways for men and women because sexuality in part dictated the forms in which an individual's humanity might be represented.

Like the auction block, the slave narrative required a display of the black, but as subject rather than object. Offered up for inspection is not the body but the sensibility and consciousness of the narrator, who must expose emotions as the slave on the block demonstrates the soundness of limbs or teeth. For Harriet Beecher Stowe, whose *Uncle Tom's Cabin* borrows heavily from the slave narrative genre, not only must the emotion be felt but it must be visibly represented and described in terms familiar to the literate white audience. The ability to blush, in the case of Eliza, and to produce tears of grief, in the case of Topsy, serve to prove the capacity for human feeling in each character. Blushing and weeping, not incidentally, are more particularly emblems of feminine sensibility. The codification of emotional responses embedded in European literary traditions is drawn upon by Stowe, and to some extent by the slave narrators as well, in providing suitable, moving evidence of black humanity that would be readable and interpretable for a white audience. Black emotion had to be represented in a form that was recognizable to readers for whom a set of behaviors encoded in a literary tradition were equated with apparent humanity. Interestingly, from the nineteenth century to the present black human beings are associated with emotionality, yet in the eighteenth-century descriptions of black people emphasize a curious lack of emotion, or what the white observer can read as emotion.

Abolitionist literature—most accurately characterized as a literary production involving the collaboration of black and white writers, narrators, editors, and amanuenses—including the religious-political tracts, Afro-American conversion and slave narratives, as well as the novels, poetry, and short stories of popular writers such as Stowe, John Greenleaf Whittier, and Lydia Maria Child, altered the conventional representation of the Afro-American so that soulfulness has ever since been regarded as the irreducible essence of emotional expressivity. This religious-based literature can be credited, in fact, with being the first United States literature that consistently attributes a soul, and therefore an inner life of emotion, to black individuals. During the eighteenth century, faces of recently captured Africans had been routinely described as empty of comprehensible emotion: opaque, unreadable, impassive, and inscrutable. By the nineteenth century, a shift from depicting captive Africans as a mass of bodies to searching out the interiority or soul is registered textually in the ironies and contradictions surrounding the status of Africans and Afro-Americans as subjects or objects.

The African as a text is the controlling trope of Herman Melville's *Benito Cereno*, where the reader-narrator's terror, paradoxically, arises not from the gross, unrestrained passions of slaves but from the precision of their collectively demonstrated self-restraint and ability to play a stereotypical role to perfection while simultaneously carrying out a mutiny. As much as their color, customs, and language, this apparent lack of affect, or in some cases demonstration of apparently inappropriate affect, contributed to the white observer's sense of estrangement. One effect of literacy—along with the cultural assimilation characteristic especially of the class of domestic servants and artisans—among a small but significant portion of the Afro-American community seems to have been that black people began to interiorize the Western code of emotional display through the descriptions and commentary that fiction writers provided. In this way the discursive representation of the Afro-American acquired a soul and an individuality to inhabit what had been represented previously as a mass of anonymous bodies.

If in the eighteenth century the black image iconically represents the unreason of the dark body as opposed to the enlightened mind, it seems that in the nineteenth century, with its privileging of sentiment, the emphasis in the representation of the black shifts from the body to the soul, with the black image, now an object of pity, increasingly sentimentalized as it becomes invested with emotive content, most notably in Stowe's depiction of Uncle Tom. In the twentieth century, the use of the black image to represent repressed elements of what has been constructed ideologically and semiotically as a "white psyche" becomes more pervasive as the very means of expression are tied to technologies highly susceptible to regressive and repressive ideological formations, as Jim Pines's analysis of the interlocking racism and increasingly proficient technologies of Hollywood film suggest. Pines argues, for instance, that Al Jolson's groundbreaking "talkie" films *The Jazz Singer* and *The Singing Fool* utilized the sentimental, emotive power of the blackface image in a way that says a great deal about the construction of the white male as a (universal) human image. The attenuated humanity of the controlled, repressed, rational, ambitious white male has to be augmented by the animal/child/woman/black who stands in relation to it as dependent and inferior. The white male reincorporates the values consigned to the Other, investing the Other with what is repressed and devalued in himself, so that the Other has to exist as reservoir and supplement, expressing for the dominant male the values and emotions that, due to his position of authority, he cannot afford to express himself.

Jolson's particular use of blackface in both *The Jazz Singer* and *The Singing Fool* ... shows an interesting deviation from the traditional use of the artifice employed by whites. ... It is clear from Jolson's play of feature that the primary function of his blackface guise is to inflate the emotional content of the scene, of the (white) character's moral dilemma. His agony, in other words, is symbolized and enhanced by the minstrel image, an image that evokes pity. ... Clearly, the overall effect of the scene is achieved through the emotive visual content of the tragic minstrel image. ... Jolson's white character (his "normal" role) always conveys tough, self-confident determination, whereas his blackface "alter ego" is most certainly a bundle of tearful sentimentalism. In both *The Jazz Singer* and *The Singing Fool* the white Jolson is portrayed as an ambitious type working positively toward some form of quasi-rational solution. At some stage in his development he takes an excursion into simplistic emotionalism via the blackface "alter ego" figure. Exploiting this as a kind of "soulful" reservoir the Jolson character is thus able to exorcise intense and generally repressed feelings—such as sorrow and guilt—without actually having to disrupt the basically white rational world the white "ego" is striving to succeed in. The pathos of the blackface Jolson character is markedly an attempt to inject a sense of spiritual substance into the white character's ambitions and dilemmas; and by so doing facilitate the audience's experience of the white protagonist's development as a popular humanizing figure. (*Blacks in Film*, 17–19)

The black begins to be seen less as the dark body contrasted with the enlightened mind and more as the repressed and emotional soul of a white social-cultural-political-economic body, imagery Martin Luther King, Jr., and other twentieth-century civil rights activists were to draw upon in figuring black people as the sign of an incompletely realized ideal, the rumbling conscience of America, guardians of an endangered ethical tradition. As the imagery has become increasingly secularized, its metaphysical implications are both transformed and made graphic via the technological possibilities of electronic media, cropping up in contemporary film and advertising, with black expressivity now encoded in countless images: as black backup singers in white rock groups (or, for that matter, in the miscegenated history of rock and roll itself, with black musical ancestors producing soulful white offspring through the *in vitro* fertilization of radio and phonograph); as the Motown soundtrack of the film *The Big Chill*, in which black music nostalgically evokes the turbulent youth of the aging cohort of baby boomers—a generation metonymically signified on screen by an all-white clique; as voice-over lyrics sung by unseen black performers on television commercial sound tracks accompanying hip white images.

Abolitionist literature, particularly the slave narrative, with its interracial collaborative textual production, made possible by a shared technology of writing—despite legal codes prohibiting literacy for slaves—anticipates the technological grafting of white body and black soul through the mechanical synchronization of filmic image and soundtrack. In the narrator/amanuensis dyad, the white hand writes for the black voice, or the white editor solicits, corrects, tidies, and introduces the black text. The collaborative literary production reenacting textually the actual genetic miscegenation embodied by a Frederick Douglass, Henry Bibb, William Webb Brown, or Harriet Jacobs—who were all products of racial mixing—was the nineteenth-century equivalent of today's crossover hit song moving from "black charts" to "mainstream pop," or the latest successful buddy film with its big-box-office demographic casting coup of a commercially compatible salt-and-pepper team.

The contemporary model of a racial integration achieved, if nowhere else, through an audiovisual medium has become so iconically suggestive that it goes unnoticed as an almost subliminal message. Such technology encodes racial ideology so powerfully that it accomplishes an otherwise unachieved racial integration through a synthesized synchronicity of images and voices drawn from disparate sources, the media equivalent of gene splicing. (Gene splicing: a biotechnological metaphor derived from audio and film technology, suggesting the pervasiveness of information models due to the proliferation of information technologies. DNA is regarded as genetic information, while information has long since been transformed into both commodity and capital. The dominance of the information model results in life itself being regarded as simply another form of information storage and retrieval.)

The split/merged sound-image has itself been made the content as well as the form of one television commercial that explicitly articulates this figuration of white body/black soul through its depiction of a white teenager alone in her room, with headphones, lip-synching lyrics recorded by Aretha Franklin, illustrating the advertising slogan "Be the music." This advertisement uses film editing conventions of the music video while parodying the lip-synching common not only to music video (which often goes to great lengths to separate the music and lyric of the song from the visual narrative of the video) but also to early television programs formatted for promotion of recorded rock and roll music, such as *American Bandstand*, and the earlier movie musicals which allowed non-singers to appear in singing roles with performances dubbed by professional vocalists. This parodic use of a very visible process makes perceptible, rather than subliminal, the technique of grafting or splicing together the sound and image, the white body with a black voice/soul, by cross-cutting the color film image of the white teenager with vintage black-and-white footage of Franklin singing what might be regarded as her personal anthem, "Respect." Here the technical solution for dramatizing the slogan "Be the music" demonstrates how even the film stock itself may be used ideologically.

The technical resources of film signifying the division and separation of black and white (black-and-white film evokes legalized Jim Crow segregation and the "race records" predating music crossover, Civil Rights, Black Power, and "Black Is Beautiful") are shown to underlie the merging of black and white in the miscegenated colored image of a media cyborg: the white body with a black soul, black-and-white film representing the nostalgic/turbulent past just as the soulful crossover soundtrack of *The Big Chill* evokes yuppie nostalgia. It is as if the visual media of film and television had thoroughly digested the black image, anatomizing and redistributing its energy so that the plasticization of the kinetic visual icon is no longer strictly required, the reediting of synchronous sound and image (read as the empowerment rather than silencing of the white lip-syncher, whose voice is omitted) producing something like a contemporary whiteface minstrelsy.

This movement has been accompanied by a corresponding shift in the representation of essential blackness from body ("African" skin/hair/features) to (soulful) voice or movement, although the use of a white dancer as body double for the Afro-American actress Jennifer Beals in the film *Flashdance* suggests that the media cyborg may be constructed paradoxically by splicing in for the dance sequences a soulful white body to provide the rhythm all God's children haven't got. Yet because she lives alone, works with whites, and dates an affluent white man, the deracinated black character (or generic white American) that Beals plays is probably presumed to be white by movie audiences who don't read *Ebony* or *Jet*. Aside from the surgical strategies, hair weaves, and "commercial voices" of a Michael Jackson, Whitney Houston, or a Diana Ross, performers who seem to embody in their public personae a bankable merger of "black" and "white" styles, the racial composition of the media cyborg more typically works by grafting the black soul as a supplement to a white body, effectively placing the black body offstage, behind the scenes, or in the recording studio as backup. Whites covering black material: the invention of rock music. Berry Gordy's gold mine: the "sophisticated soul" of Motown and millions of crossover dollars. Who covers? Who crosses over?

These are questions anticipated by James Weldon Johnson in *Autobiography of an Ex-Colored Man*, a text that disseminates the ethical problem of passing beyond the individual decision of one man to reproduce black or white offspring, to satirize "passing" as a national mechanism for forgetting a history that links African-Americans with other Americans in kinship, a mechanism for the production of whiteness and suppression of blackness. The unnamed narrator lets his white skin cover his African heritage as he crosses over into the freedom of mainstream U.S.A. through a strategy of self-denial; a loss of soul, but one preferable to the loss of life of the black man burned alive whose horrific public execution by a white mob determines the narrator's decision to pass into the white race in order to escape the stigma of blackness. Johnson's musician protagonist is a passable mulatto whose sense of belonging essentially to a black race (acquired rather late in life), furthermore is associated metonymically with the voice of his African-American mother, whose repertoire included black spirituals, those same sorrow songs that inspired the writings of Douglass and W. E. B. DuBois:[1]

> Sometimes on other evenings, when she was not sewing, she would play simple accompaniments to some old Southern songs which she sang. In these songs she was freer, because she played them by ear. Those evenings on which she opened the little piano were the happiest hours of my childhood.... I used to stand by her side and often interrupt and annoy her by chiming in with strange harmonies which I found either the high keys of the treble or the low keys of the bass. I remember that I had a particular fondness for the black keys. Always on such evenings, when the music was over, my mother would sit with me in her arms, often for a very long time. She would hold me close, softly crooning some old melody without words, all the while gently stroking her face against my head; many and many a night I thus fell asleep. I can see her now, her great dark eyes looking into the fire, to where? No one knew but her. The memory of that picture has more than once kept me from straying too far from the place of purity and safety in which her arms held me. (In *Three Negro Classics*, 395–96)

As the voice of the black mother or grandmother figures in the transmission of a distinctly African-American culture for Johnson, as it does for Brown, Bibb, Jacobs, and others—if not for Douglass, whose mother and grandmother are virtually silent in the 1845 narrative—the soulful singing voice, representative of the repressed or appropriated cultural contribution of the descendants of African slaves, becomes an aural rather than visual conveyor of emotional expressivity, or "soul." The white visual image absorbs the plastic iconicity and emotive content of the black through the expedient of a black soul technologically grafted to a now thoroughly materialized white body. The inscrutable interiority of the African-American, having by now been pried out of the shell of the body and made comprehensible in its expressiveness, is purveyed in various media representations as a "black" voice which has become the essence of consumable soul.

The commercial potential of black soul to sell everything from California raisins ("I heard it through the grapevine") to plastic wrap ("It don't mean a thing if it ain't got that cling") has been proven time and again. It is illustrated spectacularly in a Pepsi-Cola advertisement's cyborganic production of Tina Turner as a cross between an 8 x 10 glossy photo of a conventionally attractive blond white woman and a soft drink accidentally spilled in a high-tech dream machine by mad scientist David Bowie. This absent-minded scientist is himself transformed from klutzy nerd to hip rocker as the plain vanilla erotic appeal of the white woman of his wildest dreams is raised to the tenth power by a racier partner for Bowie's walk on the wild side, to the tune of his hit rock song "Modern Love." Reading the mini-narrative of the commercial alongside Johnson's novel suggests different possibilities, within the twentieth century, for incorporating race into a narrative of (re)production: from the early 1900s when Johnson's novel first appeared anonymously, to the 1980s cola commercial, a shift from repression to expression, from anonymity to celebrity, from blackness as the sign of illicit sexuality to blackness as the sign of sexual freedom. Repression is figured in the novel as a cultural production and racial reproduction of whiteness, a movement from black to white that allows and is reinforced by a corresponding movement from illicit sexuality to marriage. In the advertisement, expression of desire and fulfillment of fantasy lead to a racial integration produced technically with the invention of the cybernetic mulatta as the ideal partner for "modern love"—sex without reproduction. The mechanical production of the sexy cyborg out of the mating of Pepsi and pin-up girl by the scientist taking a cola break replaces the sexual reproduction of the mulatto driven by a puritan work ethic who, once he has become a successful white businessman—concerned with supporting his white offspring, protecting his white identity, and concealing his (black and illegitimate) origins—presumably can no longer afford to waste time or risk recognition by visiting his old haunts, the dives and gambling dens of his youth, marginal sites where blacks and whites met and mingled illicitly.

The "love" without marriage that brought a white Southern aristocrat and his family's colored servant together to produce Johnson's narrator, a musical prodigy who trades his cultural birthright as an African-American for white assimilation, giving up his dream of composing an American classical music based on African-American folksong and ragtime in order to pass as a safe, successful, but ordinary white businessman, has been superseded by the "modern love" made possible by technologies that improve on fantasy, allowing the interracial marriage of black rhythm to white melody that produces rock and roll, a music that can no longer be seen as a bastard child but has to be acknowledged as big business as well as one of the most successful products the United States exports to other countries. While Johnson's text models itself on the slave narrative genre and pushes to its logical conclusion the construction of the narrative as a miscegenated or mulatto text striving to pass the test of humanity measured as whiteness, the Pepsi commercial is a contemporary descendant of Mary Shelley's *Frankenstein*, with fears of technology, sexual expression, and the irrational or unconscious drives associated with blackness tamed—so that the scientist and his soulful creation make a stylish couple rather than deadly antagonists.

The discursive formation of black soul in the slave narratives, as Douglass sees it, is a textual production somewhat equivalent and parallel to the oral production of spirituals and folksongs, an oral production itself characterized as equivalent to "whole volumes of philosophy." Douglass asserts it is: "To those songs I trace my first glimmering conception of the dehumanizing character of slavery." In their exteriorization of the slave's interiority, both have the paradoxical effect of constructing an expressive humanity for African-Americans at the same time that they begin to construct white audiences for cultural productions in which black soul may be a more lucrative commodity than black bodies ever were.

NOTES

1 W. E. B. DuBois, *The Souls of Black Folk*, in *Three Negro Classics*, 378: "Ever since I was a child these songs have stirred me strangely. They came out of the South unknown to me, one by one, and yet at once I knew them as of me and of mine.... Out of them rose for me morning, noon, and night, bursts of wonderful melody, full of the voices of my bothers and sisters, full of the voices of the past."

WORKS CITED

Franklin, John Hope, ed. *Three Negro Classics*. New York: Avon, 1965.

Haraway, Donna. "A Manifesto for Cyborgs." In *Feminism/Postmodernism*, ed. Linda J. Nicholson. New York: Routledge, 1989.

Pines, Jim. *Blacks in Films*. London: Studio Vista, 1975.

PUBLICATION: *The Person* (1991), 9:36–43.

KEYWORDS: African American poetics; cultural studies; race; media.

LINKS: Erica Hunt, "Beginning at *Bottom*" (*PJ* 3); Steve McCaffery, "And Who Remembers Bobby Sands?" (*PJ* 5); Kofi Natambu, "The Multicultural Aesthetic: Language, 'Art,' and Politics in the United States Today" (*PJ* 9); Andrew Ross, "The Death of Lady Day" (*Guide*; *PJ* 8); Leslie Scalapino and Ron Silliman, "What/Person: From an Exchange" (*Guide*; *PJ* 9); Lorenzo Thomas, "The Marks Are Waiting" (*Guide*; *PJ* 10); Barrett Watten, "What I See in *How I Became Hettie Jones*" (*PJ* 10); Jason Weiss, "Postmodernism and Music: The Reaches" (*PJ* 7).

SELECTED BIBLIOGRAPHY: *Freeing the Soul: Race, Subjectivity, and Difference in Slave Narratives* (Cambridge: Cambridge University Press, 1999); *Tree Tall Woman* (Galveston, Tex.: Energy Earth Communications, 1981); *Trimmings* (Providence, R.I.: Tender Buttons, 1991); *S*PeRM**K*T* (Philadelphia: Singing Horse, 1992); *Muse and Drudge* (Philadelphia: Singing Horse, 1995); *Blues Baby: Early Poems* (Lewisburg, Pa.: Bucknell University Press, 2002); *Sleeping with the Dictionary* (Berkeley: University of California Press, 2002); *Recyclopedia: Trimmings, S*PeRM**K*T, and Muse and Drudge* (St. Paul: Graywolf, 2006).

TED PEARSON

"A Form of Assumptions"

Ted Pearson's close reading of a single poem from Robert Creeley's *Pieces* was presented at the 1990 Poetry Project symposium in New York. Nothing less than a "politics of the person"—the title of our lead symposium in the special issue titled *The Person*—is entailed in the relentlessly autobiographical focus of Creeley's work. Pearson revises Creeley's account of personhood as univocal and continuous by insisting on reading his poem ("When he and I . . .") for its partial and gendered account of subjectivity—namely, *masculine* subjectivity. For Pearson, Creeley's poems "are thematically saturated by a discourse on masculinity"; he demonstrates precisely how by unpacking the poem via linguistic, psychoanalytic, and feminist theory to account for its gendered poetics. In his reading, Pearson sees a dissociation of pronouns between "I" and "he" that both depends on and excludes an objectified other, the feminine/"she." Masculinity is split at the moment of sexual encounter; the poem exists to bring together the parts of that shattered moment. Pearson's reading works against the claims of a stable, consistent identity that, through the vehicle of the poem, makes experience knowable and tellable. Rather, the poem presupposes a politics of gender that necessitates that we read it critically, apart from its own terms.

Robert Creeley's poems, among their other insistences, are thematically saturated by a discourse on masculinity—a discourse derived from a culturally determined nexus of identity politics and lyric self-fashioning. I want to begin my analysis of that discourse with two citations which may suggest, respectively, the context in which I first read these poems, and the context in which I continue to read them.[1]

The first citation is from Gilbert Sorrentino: "I loved that bright sense / of his responsibility to some abstract demonology / we both understood to be manhood."[2] And the second is from Virginia Woolf, whose reflections on the encounter between modernist male writers and feminism led her to suggest that "virility has now become self-conscious."[3] As Peter Schwenger notes in "The Masculine Mode," this is not to suggest that

> these writers only question the received images of maleness, [but that] often they set out to validate those images or, through such images, to validate themselves. Their explorations of maleness are not abstract but intensely individual. They are not straightforward but are riddled with

contradictions and paradoxes.... Always knowledge is rooted in experience and inseparable from it. The masculine mode is above all an attempt to render a certain *maleness of experience*. (102)[4]

I submit that the construction of masculinity in Creeley's work is thoroughly interwoven with that of the "person" as such and the "domestic" as a site of gender conflict. Though the task of sorting these strands is beyond the scope of this essay, I hope to suggest the parameters of such a project by reading in some detail the final poem in *Pieces*. Let me start by recalling the book's epigraph, which is taken from a poem by Allen Ginsberg: "yes, yes, / that's what / I wanted, / I always wanted, / I always wanted, / to return / to the body / where I was born" (378). It is the interrogation of that "I," that "want," and that "body" that leads me to the following poem:

When he and I,
after drinking and
talking, approached
the goddess or woman

become her, and by my
insistence entered
her, and in the ease
and delight of the

meeting I was given that
sight gave me myself,
this was the mystery
I had come to—all

manner of men, a
throng, and bodies of
women, writhing, and
a great though seemingly

silent sound—and when
I left the room to them,
I felt, as though hearing
laughter, my own heart lighten.

•

What do you do,
what do you say,

what do you think,
what do you know.

$$(CP, 445–46)$$

I want first to consider the poem's personae. "He" and "I" are grammatically bonded and linguistically distinct figures: a single nonspecific "male" Other and a speaking "subject," also "male." Julia Kristeva's gloss of Emile Benveniste proposes that

> [an] author envisages subjectivity as "the capacity of the speaker to posit himself as subject." "Now we hold," writes Benveniste, "that that 'subjectivity' . . . is only the emergence . . . of a fundamental property of language. 'Ego' is he who *says* 'ego.'" This is the foundation of subjectivity, which is determined by the linguistic status of 'person.' (34)

In Creeley's own words, "as soon as / I speak, I / speaks" (294). But to whom? Throughout his work, it seems that whenever the "person" addressed is not specifically identified as "female," and indeed not always then, the addressee and/or reader is assumed to be "male" and is also assumed to share and have a stake in "a certain maleness of experience." In the poem at hand, I would argue that "he," formerly and implicitly a *you*, is, as Benveniste suggests,

> situated outside *I/you* and indicate[s] someone or something about which one speaks, but without necessarily being a specific person. . . . The 'third person' is not a 'person'; it is really a verbal form whose function is to express the *non*-person. (Quoted in Kristeva, 34–35)

The status of this "non-person" is ambivalent: on the one hand, by placing its specificity under erasure, the third person's identity is abrogated, allowing its subjugation by or subordination to *I/you*; on the other hand, the contingency of its formation relieves it of the vicissitudes of constructing and maintaining its specificity.

The undecidability, then, of the boundaries between, and the disjunctions within, both "he" and "I" is crucial—not only to the unfolding of events within the poem, but also to the (assumed male) reader's identification with "he and I," an identification toward which the rhetoric of the poem is deployed. In brief, the anxiety to consolidate an identity contests the desire to return to an undifferentiated totality. Encrypted in this undecidability is an existential dread, or *horror vacui*, that Georges Bataille, for example, figures as the context in which there exists . . . a unique moment in relation to the possibility of me—and thus the infinite improbability of this coming into the world appears. For if the tiniest difference had occurred in the course of the successive events of which I am the result, in the place of this *me*, integrally avid to be *me*, there would have been 'an *other*.' (130)

To elicit the relation between this "moment"—or rather such agency as extemporizes "successive events" as "unique moments" and therefore as tropes of identity—and its anxious reinscriptions in Creeley's poems as the originary if problematic site of the "speaking subject," let me cite several instances from work anterior to *Pieces*. Early in *The Charm*, for example, we find these lines from "Poem for D. H. Lawrence": "*I would begin by explaining / that by reason of being / I am and no other*" (7). In the preface to *For Love*, Creeley sketches a process "wherewith a man . . . contrives a world (of his own mind)" (105). And in the epigraph of *Words*, he invokes, via Williams, "a counter stress / born of the sexual shock / which survives it . . . to keep its own mind" (260).

Insofar as the loci of these instances are initial to the collections in which they occur, their discursive "subject," and its insistent "subjectivity," are no less initial to the poems Creeley writes to think with. It is this "insistence"—itself a metonymy for the limited agency of the "subject"—by which "the goddess or woman / become her" is "entered" and *enters* the poem.

There is, of course, a latent prosodic ambiguity attendant on the verb phrase "become her," such that a transfer of agency from "he and I" to "the goddess or woman" emerges as a possible reading. My own inclination, however, is to read the passage grammatically, and thus to construe the "goddess"/ "woman" relation as an equivocally hieratic inflection of gender which continues to foreground the "masculine."

In either case, readers familiar with Creeley's work will recognize the goddess, in her sundry guises, as an importantly recurring figure in the poems. The confluence of Creeley's proximity to Robert Graves when the latter was writing *The White Goddess*, the role of "the goddess" in the conventions of lyric poetry, the heterosexist formation of the goddess/drudge variant of the virgin/whore dyad, and the rhetorical deflection of the reader's gaze into a visionary realm where such apparitions are taken to be more real than real is not, I would argue, happenstance.

So we've got these two guys, drinking together and talking. And after a while, a "goddess or woman // become her" appears, and they approach her. And one of these guys, the one called "I," insists that they enter her. They do, etc. And therein lies a tale. But first we must establish who she is, noting that the phrase "become her" transforms the "goddess"/"woman" into the third, or linguistically *non*, person.

Now if it is a "woman" who is "entered," whatever else that may imply, it does imply that they fuck her. The manner and intent with which they do so remains unspecified, and perhaps irrelevant; but that *her* agency, desire, and status as a person are also unspecified, and unremarked, is *not* irrelevant, because, lacking agency, this nonspecific "female" figure is reduced to her object status, her use value, and very little else. And if her use is not a form of rape, it very well might be—unless of course the reader is willing to assume a too familiar form of illogic that equates her very presence with her sexual availability. This connection between rape and (male self-)knowledge is, of course, one of literature's most durable tropes: Homer, for example, equates the rape of Helen with the beginning of history as such.

If, on the other hand, the figure "entered" is a "goddess," one might imagine her an avatar of the "great mother," who both literally and figuratively accommodates "he and I" in a conflation of sexual intercourse and the return to the womb. In this variant, the circuit from the epigraph's express desire "to return to the body where I was born" is completed. There is, however, yet again no clear ascription of agency to the goddess—she remains both functionally and linguistically a nonperson, subject to such uses and modes of violence as might attend that role.

It is at this "unique moment" that a transformation occurs—from the quotidian realism of a scene of "male" camaraderie, via the entry of the "female" figure, to the magical realism of a "male" subject's singular visionary experience. Thus, "in the ease / and delight of the // meeting I was given that / sight gave me myself." It could be argued, of course, that these lines ameliorate the otherwise subjugated status of the "goddess or woman," but only if the forms of assumption I've been detailing still obtain, such that the "female" figure is *assumed* to willingly partake of the "ease and delight" (given that, throughout the poem, the reader has only "I's" word to inform and direct such assumptions).

Although "he" and "the goddess or woman" are both required for "I" to achieve the status of "person," these figures are by no means equivalent. The construction of "I" as a masculine "subject" is determined by his capacity to recognize (both within and beyond himself) an Other "male," who is met *in* the "woman," and who, in witnessing "I" perform *as a "male,"* confirms him as such. It is no great secret that "males" tend to measure their masculinity against other "males" and, in the domain of heterosexist relations, that a "woman" as such can be little more than the medium within or upon which the construction of an arguably homosocial masculinity is inscribed. Anthony Wilden notes that

> the Other is . . . the locus of the 'law of desire,' the locus of the incest prohibition and the phallus. According to Lacan, the Other . . . is the only place from which it is possible to say "I am who I am." The paradox of identity and autonomy which this involves—identical to or identified with what?—puts us in the position of desiring what the Other desires: we desire what the Other desires we desire. (Quoted in MacCannell, 131)

Having performed their assigned roles, "he" and "the goddess/woman" depart the poem, and the implied womb becomes an explicit "room" in which we find "all / manner of men, a / throng, and bodies of women, writhing." Note the contrast between "all / manner of men, a / throng," which encodes an implicitly hierarchical sampling of "men" subsumed to an essentialized "man's world," and "bodies of women, writhing," which continues to specify and to delimit women's "function."

Note also the extraordinary weight that "writhing" brings to the text: at once horrific and ecstatic in its shadings, it is far too polysemous and overdetermined to call forth anything other than "a great, though seemingly silent sound"—which may be the very echo or trace of the literal production of the word, its "writing"—after which "I" takes leave of this visionary company and feels his "own heart lighten."

"I" does not, however, take leave of the poem, but stays to deliver, in the final quatrain, an *envoi* that serves as coda to the poem, and to the book. The strategy here is to recuperate four common phatic phrases and through them to interrogate the agency, articulation, cognition, and epistemology by which his own or any subjectivity might gain a purchase on the world: "What do you do, / what do you say, / what do you think, / what do you know."

"I" speaks, and again we ask: to whom? "All manner of men," perhaps; but then perhaps not all—and what of "women"? Given that "I" to be "I" requires a "you," this particular "I" seems to require an interlocutor inscribed within a no less particular masculine discourse. According to Judith Butler,

> Signification harbors . . . 'agency.' The rules that govern . . . [that is] enable and restrict the intelligible assertion of an "I" . . . are partially structured along matrices of gender hierarchy and compulsory heterosexuality. . . .

When the subject is said to be constituted, that means simply that the subject is a consequence of certain rule-governed discourses. (14)

In closing let me cite Lacan, who said, "Love is a sign that we are changing discourses."[5]

NOTES

1 I am indebted to Mark Seltzer and Barrett Watten for their careful reading and discussion of this essay, the final version of which has benefited in several particulars from their comments.

2 "Apple Scrapple," 26. Although Creeley is not the "subject" of this poem, the register of its concerns is clearly congruent with his own articulations of "the masculine mode."

3 *A Room of One's Own*, quoted in Schwenger, 102.

4 Also see "Convivio" in Williams, *Collected Poems*, 2:199.

5 Quoted in MacCannell, 167.

WORKS CITED

Bataille, Georges. *Visions of Excess: Selected Writings, 1927–1939.* Minneapolis: University of Minnesota Press, 1985.

Butler, Judith. *Gender Trouble.* New York: Routledge, 1990.

Creeley, Robert. *The Collected Poems of Robert Creeley.* Berkeley: University of California Press, 1982. Cited as *CP* in the text.

Kristeva, Julia. *Language: The Unknown.* New York: Columbia University Press, 1989.

MacCannell, Juliet Flower. *Figuring Lacan.* Lincoln: University of Nebraska Press, 1986.

Schwenger, Peter. "The Masculine Mode." In Elaine Showalter, ed., *Speaking of Gender.* New York: Routledge, 1989.

Sorrentino, Gilbert. *Corrosive Sublimate.* Los Angeles: Black Sparrow Press, 1971.

Williams, William Carlos. *Collected Poems.* Ed. Christopher MacGowan and A. Walton Litz (New York: New Directions, 1991).

PUBLICATION: *The Person* (1991), 9:159–64.

KEYWORDS: New American poetry; gender; subjectivity; readings.

LINKS: Ted Pearson, "The Force of Even Intervals: Toward a Reading of *Vernal Aspects*" (*PJ* 2), "Some Remarks on Method" (*PJ* 3), "Things Made Known" (*PJ* 10), "Unit Structures" (*PJ* 5); Françoise de Laroque, "What Is the Sex of the Poets?" (*PJ* 4); Jerry Estrin, "Penultimate Witness: On Emmanuel Hocquard" (*PJ* 8); Jackson Mac Low, "Sketch toward a Close Reading of Three Poems from Bob Perelman's *Primer*" (*PJ* 2); Laura Moriarty, "The Modern Lyric" (*PJ* 7); Nick Piombino, "Towards an Experiential Syntax" (*PJ* 5); "Robert Creeley and the Politics of the Person" (*PJ* 9); Ron Silliman, "Composition as Action" (*PJ* 3); Barrett Watten, "The Politics of Style" (*Guide*; *PJ* 1).

SELECTED BIBLIOGRAPHY: *The Grit* (San Francisco: Trike, 1976); *The Blue Table* (San Francisco: Trike, 1979); *Soundings* (Blue Bell, Pa.: Singing Horse, 1980); *Ellipsis* (San Francisco: Trike, 1981); *Coulomb's Law* (San Francisco: Square Zero, 1984); *Mnemonics* (San Francisco: Gaz, 1985); *Catenary Odes* (Oakland: O Books, 1987); *Evidence: 1975–1989* (San Francisco: Gaz, 1989); *Planetary Gear* (New York: Roof, 1991); *Acoustic Masks* (Tenerife, Spain: Zasterle, 1994); *Songs Aside: 1992–2002* (Detroit: Past Tents, 2003); *Encryptions* (San Diego: Singing Horse, 2007).

Time and Materials The Workplace, Dreams, and Writing

Kit Robinson discusses writing in relation to the time frames of work and dream, after the modern tradition of poets (like William Carlos Williams and Wallace Stevens) who wrote poetry in relation to their employment. The postmodern, post-Fordist workplace is increasingly organized around the scarcity of time, in competing categories like "production, personal work, consumption, culture, and idleness," resulting in a "time crunch" that threatens to incapacitate creativity under late capitalism. Among these conflicting time frames, Robinson finds "a vacant center at the heart of late capitalist production" as a site for writing, while he also discovers, within the alienated spaces of the workplace, materials for writing. On the other hand, dreams, produced in the downtime reserved for "personal work" and bodily maintenance, provide a powerful source of the dynamic, reflexive power that writing can bring to alienated time. In a world where idleness or bohemianism are absorbed into production, Robinson explores ways to reorganize the experience of work and dream by directly incorporating them as materials. Writing with the details and contradictions of the postmodern workplace, while deploying the syntax of dreams, creates a new kind of time that sutures them together. In bringing creativity into the context of everyday life, Robinson's essay shows how writing may recover lost time.

[...] Time has been a big issue for me as a writer lately, because I've felt as if I haven't had time to write. What I have written has been snatched from the jaws of circumstance, from odd phrases encountered at my job to notations of dream experiences hastily jotted down in a notebook by my bed. So when I saw the phrase "Time and Materials" in a technical journal I edit, I recognized a possible vocabulary for dealing with my situation as a poet. [...]

Since I have been employed full-time, writing has continued under increasing time constraints. [...]

My job has seemed, on the face of it, to be in conflict with my career as a poet. [...]

I wanted, therefore, to turn this situation around. I wanted to find, for myself, value in the condition of employment that would add to rather than subtract from the value of my writing. [...]

The constriction of time involves the writer in tactical maneuvers that define and limit the writing practice. Time is limited not only by normal working hours, but also by fatigue and the practical necessity for relief from applica-tion. As sheet metal worker, fiction writer, and critic Michael Amnasan writes:

> While working at Presbyterian Hospital up around 168th Street, it was eas-ier for me to write during lunch break than once I arrived home, at which time I felt a terribly distracting freedom from explicit constraints.

Amnasan [...] intersperses his terse narratives of job life with reflections on the incommensurability of his two vocations. But he's not complaining; he accepts this clash with pleasure. "I feel lost without tension," he writes. Find-ing himself "spaced within the contingencies of irreconcilable activities," he uses this position to create an ongoing dialectic movement in his alternately descriptive and reflective prose. He writes, "Yeah I want things to be confused and complex." This position strengthens Amnasan's writing by throwing it into relief against his job as a construction worker. Here is an advantage for writing, which is always a contingent practice, of an alternate career, one which bears the impress of an overarching social necessity. While writing remains relatively "free," it carries within itself the rigor of material produc-tion experienced as a given.

The materiality of the job infuses writing with value, no longer practical except in the broadest sense, but resonant with form wrought of direct en-counter with the working world. [...]

The time constraint I experience as an employee has been my greatest problem as a poet. But it's a problem not limited to writers. According to Swed-ish economist Steffan Linder, our society has entered what he calls a "time famine."

In his book *The Harried Leisure Class*, Linder does what he calls "a system-atic explanation of changes in time allocation." He sets out to prove that, contrary to the classical economic model, as society becomes increasingly productive and affluent, it experiences a corresponding reduction in available time.

High productivity has created a time famine, in which articles of consump-tion vie for the attention of the harried affluent. The surplus of goods in West-ern society has brought with it a shortage of time in which to enjoy them. Time is experienced as a commodity in short supply.

Linder divides time among five categories: production, personal work, con-sumption, culture, and idleness. This last category is prevalent in so-called undeveloped societies and, according to Linder, has been completely elimi-nated in contemporary Western society. (Linder's book was published in 1970.

We have since seen the rise of a dispossessed class in the United States for whom this category again may apply.)

To analyze time allocation, Linder invokes the standard economic principle of equilibrium of yield. This principle states that in capital investments distributed over many sectors, if the yield on one sector increases, the investments must be redistributed to bring them into a state of equilibrium. The corollary is that when the yield on time spent working is increased as a result of productive growth, the yield on non-working time must be brought into parity. One way to do this is to increase the yield on consumption time. "This takes place by an increase in the volume of consumption goods per time unit in consumption."

But these leisure commodities, in turn, take time to select, purchase, and maintain, further adding to the time crunch.

As an example of the foolishness this consumption-intensive pattern may lead to, Linder writes,

> the acceleration of consumption can take various forms.... A man ... may find himself drinking Brazilian coffee, smoking a Dutch cigar, sipping French cognac, reading the *New York Times*, listening to a Brandenburg Concerto, and entertaining his Swedish wife—all at the same time, with varying degrees of success.

The movie *Sammy and Rosie Get Laid* recently updated this scenario: it's Rosie's night out; Sammy is on the sofa with Walkman headphones, a sandwich, a milkshake, a plate of cocaine, and a magazine, with his pants down around his knees, when the phone rings.

Time shrinkage operates at both the level of the society and that of the individual. The high-powered CEO is so productive, that is, his working time is worth so much, that there is practically nothing he can do with his leisure time that will guarantee equivalent value. As a result, he must do nothing but work. And this, indeed, seems to be the pattern for today's young breed of apoplectic top execs.

Linder classifies "sleep" under the category of "time for personal work," that is, "maintenance of one's body." In the current voraciousness for time, various techniques for the reduction of time needed for sleep have been discussed. "Sleep, it seems, has something in common with the recreation areas in our big cities: both are subject to continual attacks from those who would like to use these resources for productive purposes." Needless to say, the economy of consumption posits little value in the natural productions of sleep.

Linder's objective analysis of the economies of time accounts in part for the experience of pressure many of us feel. His study of time as a "moving belt of units" also confirms the French situationist political analysis of the late 1950s. In a talk presented May 17, 1961, at a conference of the Group for Research on Everyday Life convened by Henri Lefebvre in Paris, Guy Debord, the author of *Society of the Spectacle*, had already anticipated this situation.

"The use of everyday life," he said, "in the sense of a consumption of lived time, is governed by the reign of scarcity: scarcity of free time and scarcity of possible uses of this free time."

In the shift from classical to late capitalism, what constitutes productive or wasted time has reversed itself.

> For classical capitalism, wasted time was time not devoted to production, accumulation, saving. . . . But it so happens that by an unexpected turn of events modern capitalism needs to increase consumption, to "raise the standard of living" (if we bear in mind that this expression is completely meaningless). Since at the same time production conditions, compartmentalized and clocked to the extreme, have become indefensible, the new morality already being conveyed in advertising, propaganda and all forms of the dominant spectacle now frankly admits that wasted time is the time spent at work, which latter is only justified by the hierarchized scale of earnings that enable one to buy rest, consumption, entertainments—a daily passivity manufactured and controlled by capitalism.

But as we have seen, it is an increasingly frantic passivity of temporal constraint.

Contemporary consumer society is a logical but surprising extension of Protestant/capitalist ideology—an age of curiosity, in which the subject is driven by fear of "missing something" but can never be satisfied by the limitless series of self-reflective commodities, and where work and politics provoke only boredom. Work—conceived by the Puritans as the road to the hereafter—now simply signifies a means to leisure, "self-realization," etc. The emptying out of work leaves a large vacant space around which we organize the time of our lives.

Time in the workplace is generally treated as a cost factor, to be reduced to a minimum per productivity unit. Time management is seen primarily as a means for controlling costs. With the fashionable use of the daily planner, the priority on time efficiency has been extended beyond the workplace to social, leisure, and personal life. In this view, the *experience* of time, as rhythm, is simply an unnecessary by-product.

But the ideal of total temporal efficiency is only that. By their nature, the eight-hour workday and forty-hour week are laced with unproductive periods. [...]

Work flow may vary, but employment hours do not, so there is slack time. The experience of this vacuity, and the airlock between work and home, the commute, are fertile ground for speculation. Thus working time is organized around vacant or interstitial time. [...]

The opening up of a vacant center at the heart of late capitalist production presents an opportunity for writing. From within this abandoned core, writing may excavate the materials of production and export them into general circulation. In so doing it may even reanimate the processes and episodes of production.

All of this has been meant to show that time organized around work makes its mark on writing in a variety of ways, and that the limits imposed by work represent not simply an obstacle but an opportunity for writing—not least because the workplace is the site of common activity and therefore enables writing to bear witness to our common experience.

As part of that experience we encounter language. In its role in the workplace, language is employed as a tool, with specific uses and applications. As a tool, language is the foremost delimiter of specialization.

Professional languages function by excluding ambiguity, as well as by excluding non-members of the profession. The relation of word to meaning is strictly determined by the instrumentality of the profession. Misunderstanding must be precluded. Moreover, the social exclusivity of the profession must, at the same time, be defended. These functional limits, in the connotation and reception of language, preserve the status of its users and the consistency of its methods. [...]

However, this restrictive use of language is always a holding pattern, a provisional and ultimately fated attempt to hold back the floodgates of language, which, by its structure, always tends toward multiplicity of usage.

Jacques Derrida proposes this dynamic in his essay "Signature Event Context."

> A written sign carries with it a force of breaking with its context, that is, the set of presences which organize the moment of its inscription. This force of breaking is not an accidental predicate, but the very structure of the written.... Writing ... carries with it predicates which have been subordinated, excluded, or held in reserve [and] whose forces of generality, generalization, and generativity find themselves liberated, grafted onto a

"new" concept of writing which also corresponds to whatever always has resisted the former organization of forces, which always has constituted the *remainder* irreducible to the dominant force which organized the [language].

This sense of resistance, of activity excluded from the normal considerations of the workplace, as a site for writing has been expressed by Carla Harryman in her discussion of her own work. In her book *Vice* she writes:

> We know in the workplace there are many things that can't be said. The individual response functions as pure subjectivity. I.e. it cannot be taken into account.

When the language of the workplace is excerpted and reframed as part of writing in its widest, most generative sense, its instrumentality is sacrificed. The loss of practical meaning sets off a concomitant release of potential energy. The power stored in the language is released like an electron in a nuclear reaction. Here we could redefine the meaning of our century's most famous equation: $E = mc^2$ where m = functional meaning, c = the possible meaning horizon, and E = energy—an intellectual/emotional displacement.

As work language is cut away and grafted, it tends toward more personal, everyday meanings, often with a strong emotional content.

In his "Preface to the Lyrical Ballads" Wordsworth wrote:

> The Poet writes under one restriction only, namely, the necessity of giving immediate pleasure to a human Being possessed of that information which may be expected from him, not as a lawyer, a physician, a mariner, an astronomer, or a natural philosopher, but as a Man.

Wordsworth's attack on Pope and his circle, who made of poetry its own specialized, professional language, was consistent with his view of the dehumanization of specialized labor in newly industrial urban Britain. His plea for a simple, common vocabulary for poetry houses democratic and humanist values within a rural nostalgia.

In our time, the fracture and dissociation of communications tools is assumed as a given. Within this situation, a semantic displacement of terms can drain specialized language of its isolating productive assurance and exploit it in the expression of human desires.

The paring away and grafting of specialized work language into alternate human terms is a project with incredible unrealized potential. It involves a separation from, though not a rejection of, the workplace, in order to reintegrate that place with other places resident in the heart and mind of the person. This linguistic reintegration is a way of countering the compartmentalization of daily life.

Alan Davies's book *Name*, for example, is a series of love poems in the language of ventilation unit sales. The semantic dicing of elements produces some startling, funny, and often moving results. By mixing elements of daily language, including the language of work, Davies creates a dreamlike medium that is difficult to analyze, despite the obvious displacements of its elements. This synthesis is a remarkable feat, a voice constructed of command-driven particles, as supple and tender as a lover's.

The Dream Life of Writing

For writing, dreams have always held a singular fascination. As both time and material they seem to be of an entirely other order. Since the beginnings of writing, the dream has served as a framing device for embedding stories within stories, adding richness and complexity to narratives. Poets have cited dreams as sources of inspiration, images from the Muse. In dreams, the subjective vision acquires a kind of universal validity, by virtue of seeming to come from outside. Their means of interpretation have empowered priest classes and bolstered cultural mythologies. Yet the modern obsession with the interpretation of dreams obscures their value for the activity of writing. [...]

The language of work is normally viewed as a semantically closed space, with circumscribed referentiality and membership. The language of dreams has been similarly regarded—as a set of symbols referring to the particular psychology of the individual and accessible only to those within the personal sphere, and even then perhaps only with the aid of an instrumental, professional language—in our era the language of psychiatry.

This emphasis on the semantic dimension of dreams aims at a reduction of dream material to complex but delimited meanings. What it neglects is the syntactic dimension—the grammar of dreams. This aspect becomes especially interesting when you look at how dreams may be written.

Dreams do not dictate the manner in which they are to be recorded. Despite the Beat "first thought, best thought" claim to natural, spontaneous prose, Jack Kerouac's dream narrative style is highly conscious, involves great density of decision-making within the moment-to-moment writing activity, and is in fact a triumph of artifice.

The range in styles of dream writing delineates differences not only in individual psychic experience but in systems of retrieval and storage. We may distinguish Steve Benson's florid piling on of intricate detail; Lyn Hejinian's novelistic, crafted prose; my own telegraphic, affectless approach; Peter Schjeldahl's arch, socially ironic polish; De Quincey's baroque rhapsody; Kerouac's helter-skelter soloistic improvisations; etc.

Finally, the dream material in itself becomes less interesting than its use in writing. [...] The concrete naming necessary to the written text requires the destruction of the "original" in the moment of its apprehension through language.

Thus, to write a dream is to obliterate its contents, and to replace them with the parallel but unequivalent contents of language. One might argue the same thing about any descriptive language, and the propaganda of the 1988 presidential election campaign would be an example, but there is a difference. The dream, being by definition private experience, can never be independently verified, so the report cannot be contested.

The dream elements are thus withdrawn from their context in sleep and grafted into the ongoing context of language as it presents itself to consciousness. Such activity may reveal the dream work itself, the preparatory work of dreams. But it will also involve the mind in a host of further associations, intentions, and imaginings.

Thus, the dream record is a cover, in several senses: it covers the dream the way a report covers an event—or the way a musical group may "cover" an original hit—but it also covers in the sense of obscuring the event, covering it with a screen of words which supplant memory's vague sensations with crisp, delineated images and set verbal rhythms.

Dreams operate by mechanisms of displacement; one element stands in for or replaces the next. The telling or writing of a dream performs a further displacement. It stimulates the memory to discover parts that had been submerged, but also forces elements into a greater degree of definition than they had in memory. In effect, any dream record is a fiction.

Work time is not organized in relation to experience. It is simply organized in relation to production. One person's time is someone else's materials.

Dream time is organized *solely* in relation to experience and purely to fulfill the demands of the individual psyche. In dreams, one is, as it were, at the mercy of one's own control.

Time in dreams seems to possess the kind of absolute density of production the workplace may strive for but can never achieve. There is no down time in dreams, for dreams are, themselves, pure production. It is only in the gap between the dream and the record that an interstitial space opens up. This space begins, presumably, at the dream itself, but writing begins from a re-experiencing of the dream in memory, and memory, in turn, is responsive to the stimulus of writing. [...]

[In dreams] we are "disembodied," [...] even if they involve us in bodily adventures, since locus and moment are no longer fixed by what we consensually term "reality." The increased availability to perception of contents stored in memory is accompanied by a loss of identity, for there is no one outside one's self to confirm for oneself an identity. As Gertrude Stein wrote, "I am I because my little dog knows me," but in dreams we are, by analogy, "at the movies alone"—though I may encounter others in the most intimate or antagonistic ways, they are no more than my own "inventions" and can never confirm or deny my reality, much less my character.

The loss or confusion of identity becomes, itself, the theme of many dreams. And as Lyn Hejinian shows in the following discussion, presence is not a requirement. The dreamer may completely cease to exist in the dream, while, in waking retrospect, the dream contents may be seen to stand, metonymically, for the person.

> An example of a person in dissociation from context is a dream I had of myself—I know it's a dream of myself in retrospect, but in the dream it is only a sequence of images, dreamed on the night of September 28, 1987: "A dress, or a woman wearing blue or black. She is a manikin or a living woman. The figure is full face or maybe in silhouette. A view then or after a little time of a saddle-stitch stapler and a book nearby. First the stapler is in focus and then the book."
>
> ... Now what interests me right off is that every sentence—i.e., every expression—is in the form of a duality. It enacts the double situation already existing in a dream, in which there is a dreamer (in this case never even in range—I didn't feel the situation as "*I* saw a stapler and then a book") and a dreamed (which here is "I" but again never felt as such until after I woke up). I know it's "I" because of wearing black, because I can identify the stapler and even identify with the stapler, or the symbolism of the stapler and the book. But all the contexts in which a manikin (immobilized figure) and a living woman (eroticized figure) and a stapler (the one I used in putting together all the Tuumba books) and a book (I am a literary person) function as parts of a life are missing from the dream. As a result, one has, so to speak, a series of nouns. [...]

If the fundamental duality that Hejinian points out is that of the dreamer and the dreamed, this duality is constantly displaced, because the dreamer virtually does not exist, except as a boundary to the possible domain of dream contents. Therefore the duality is injected into the content itself, which takes the form of a series of transformations, antitheses, and equivalences.

The syntax in dreams is characterized by a dialectical movement, where a unique element is immediately modified by a counter-element, sometimes an opposite, to produce a revised or transformed element.

Often in writing my dreams, I find myself punctuating sentences with a semi-colon, to divide two clauses, the first a kind of thesis, the second an antithesis or qualification of the first. Another common feature is the double-take, a replaying of a scene, as if the first time one didn't quite "get it right."

The dialectical movement, driven by a dynamic negativity, finds expression in language whose elements, as "nouns" or images or sentences or scenes, represent the resting places of dream thought, and whose syntax, the sequence, rhythm, and inevitable editorial construction, convey the leaps or gaps or synthetic fusions of its becoming.

In his introduction to a 1954 edition of the existential psychoanalyst Ludwig Binswanger's essay *Dreams and Existence*, Michel Foucault points to this syntactic movement as an important key to the meaning of dreams missing from Freud's classic symbolic interpretation.

> As waking consciousness darkens and flickers out, the dream seems to loosen, and finally untie, the knot of meanings. Dream had been taken as if it were the nonsense of consciousness. We know how Freud turned this proposition around, making the dream the meaning of consciousness.
>
> Freud caused the world of the imaginary to be inhabited by Desire as classical metaphysics caused the world of physics to be inhabited by Divine Will and Understanding: a theology of meanings in which the truth anticipates its own formulations and completely constitutes them. The meanings exhaust the reality of the world which displays that reality.
>
> One might say that psychoanalysis gave the dream no status beyond that of speech, and failed to see it in its reality as language.

Freud's symbolism concentrates exclusively on the semantic or paradigmatic dimension of language. We are presented with a series of symbols whose root meanings can be discovered through a search for the subject's repressed thought. Each dream symbol is a complete result of a complex synthesis of causes drawn from various planes of experience: physical sensation in the moment of sleeping, the events of the previous day, ongoing personal issues, and deep memories, often most significantly of early childhood.

Thus Freud unties the sequential order of the dream in order to show it in its verticality, as a forest of symbols, of correspondences. This method has proven tremendously useful for the treatment of neurosis, and has determined the very form of our thought in the twentieth century, but it does not exhaust the meaning of dreams, because by concentrating on the semantic dimension it leaves out the syntactic, horizontal dimension.

That a dream can be reduced to the product of a complex of private causes leaves unaddressed the meanings it inevitably accumulates by virtue of its expression in communal, multivalent language. [. . .]

Wittgenstein observed of Freudian dream analysis that if dreams are essentially a translation of information from one form of thought into another, then we should be able to translate in both directions. In other words, if from the dream we are able to deduce the complex, then we should be able to go the other way and, if we know the complex, derive the dream. But this, of course, is not the case. It is the peculiar fascination of dreams that they are entirely unpredictable.

The possibility of a grammar of dreams leads away from the consideration of the dream as a code for the analysis of the individual psyche toward a more general view of dreams as problems in perception and description, that is, as problems for writing.

In my book *Covers*, I have extended the dialectic of displacements that occurs in the progression from life to dreams to writing. On each page, a brief dream narrative in prose is followed by an improvisation in verse form. The poems were constructed by selecting key words at random from my dream notebook. [. . .]

The poems are often reflections on or extensions of the dream fragments. As such they combine interpretation and fiction. In addition, due to the intervention of the key words, they bear trace elements of other dreams. And finally, each seeks its own path in the ongoing temporality of writing.

My intention was to expand on the possible meanings of the dream fragments, by engaging the attention in an instantaneous complex, through rhythm, syntax, and sequence. The faithful, transparent language of the dream record is set against the capricious, alert action of writing at play with its materials.

In *The Introduction to Psychoanalysis*, Freud speaks of dreams as "the guardians of sleep," and it is easy to think of examples wherein by the ceaseless activity of transformation, equivalence, and opposition, the inevitable moment of waking is redefined, disguised, and folded back into the dream contents in a perpetual holding action.

But while the dream defends the body from waking, and ensures the continued rest and revitalization of our physical powers, it also eludes deep, dreamless sleep. Dreams represent a consciousness poised between waking and sleep, which defends sleep from waking, but also, as Maurice Blanchot points out in his foreword to the dream journals of Michel Leiris, fights to stay alive as mental activity, so that "sleep grows sleepless." This persistent activity, akin to insomnia, is also at the source of writing.

In Kafka, we find a writer of fiction for whom dreams and the workplace share an equal though conflicting significance.

Kafka's *The Trial* was apparently written in all-night, insomniac sessions, and it contains the kinds of displacements found in dreams: the court inappropriately located in the rundown suburb; the abjectly seductive nurse; the whipper and his victims in the "lumber room" of the bank—and there again, as if no time had passed, the next morning.

The writing inhabits a claustrophobic thought world, where each assertion engenders an immediate counter-assertion. Every ray of hope is qualified by a reason for despair. The protagonist K attempts, in the unfolding of the unseemly and preposterous details of his narrative, to justify everything—not only himself, but all appearances.

This obsessive desire for justification is present at every level. K's case may be seen as a cipher for Kafka's writing, by which he stakes his only claim to self-justification. But the tortuous difficulty of his "case" interferes with and eventually overwhelms his career at the bank, his "normal" daily life.

Kafka's relation to both work and dreams is alienation. The limits of bureaucratic hierarchy by day and subjective isolation by night become unbearable burdens. The evident joy of his writing is bitterly humorous.

Writing is always a matter of limits. The language of the workplace, functioning within the limits of instrumentality and class, may be liberated by cutting it from its normal context and grafting it within the process of creative work. When this is done, the specialized language may, itself, serve as a limiting factor, within which the creative process may be able to define itself. For freedom always requires limits, however arbitrarily they are established.

As the composer Anthony Braxton remarked of a particular solo by the saxophonist Warne Marsh:

It's so inside the chord changes, he's really somewhere else. It's like you know the context so well that you're free: you're free because you understand the rules to such a level that you can do anything you want. That's what freedom is. You can't be free unless you have a context to be free in. [...]

While the dream itself would appear to be a free play of ideas, unchained by normal limits of perception and logic, [it also presents] an impenetrable limit: [it is] pure experience; [its] facts can never be verified, [its] implications never entirely known. It is the peculiar fascination of dreams that they appear "all ours" on the one hand, but completely outside us on the other, for they come to us, as it were, out of the blue.

In [dream writing] one is poised between the abject [instance of] a remote subjectivity and the expression that confirms itself, through language, in [shared] history.

The threat of alienation and isolation is present to our experience both of dreams and of the workplace. At the same time, the limits we encounter in both spheres may be turned to advantage through the singular power of writing.

Writing can go anywhere and use anything. There are no privileged subjects and no primary materials. My interest in work and dreams meets in a third term, which encompasses them without exhausting itself. It is continually outstripping its materials. It condenses our experience of time to the level of momentary attention. It transcends its own time and materials. It is writing.

WORKS CITED

Amnasan, Michael. *Five Fremont*. Unpublished ms.

Benson, Steve. *As Is*. Berkeley: The Figures, 1978.

Bernstein, Charles. *Shade*. College Park, Md.: Sun and Moon, 1978.

Blanchot, Maurice. "Dreaming, Writing." In Michel Leiris, *Nights as Day, Days as Night*. Hygiene, Colo.: Eridanos, 1987.

Davies, Alan. *Name*. Berkeley: This, 1986.

Debord, Guy. "Perspectives for Conscious Alterations in Everyday Life." *The Situationist International Anthology*. Ed. Ken Knabb. Berkeley: Bureau of Public Secrets, 1981.

Derrida, Jacques. *Margins of Philosophy*. Chicago: University of Chicago Press, 1982.

Foucault, Michel. "Dream, Imagination, and Existence." *Review of Existential Psychology and Psychiatry* 19, no. 1 (1986).

Freud, Sigmund. *General Introduction to Psychoanalysis*. New York: Simon and Schuster, 1989.

Harryman, Carla. *Vice*. Elmwood, Conn.: Potes and Poets, 1986.

Hejinian, Lyn. Dream journal, 1988. Unpublished ms.

Kafka, Franz. *The Trial*. New York: Schocken, 1968.

Kerouac, Jack. *Book of Dreams*. San Francisco: City Lights, 1961.

Linder, Staffan. *The Harried Leisure Class*. New York: Columbia University Press, 1970.

Locke, Graham. *Forces in Motion*. London: Quartet, 1988.

Robinson, Kit. *Covers*. Great Barrington, Mass.: The Figures, 1988.

Schjeldahl, Peter. *Dreams*. New York: Angel Hair, 1973.

Wittgenstein, Ludwig. *Lectures and Conversations on Aesthetics, Psychology, and Religious Beliefs*. Ed. Cyril Barrett. Berkeley: University of California Press, 1966.

PUBLICATION: Excerpted from *The Person* (1991), 9:21–35.

KEYWORDS: postmodernism; class; psychoanalysis; time.

LINKS: Kit Robinson, "Bob Cobbing's Blade" (*PJ* 1), "Hayward" (*PJ* 6), "Pleasanton/Embassy Suite" (*PJ* 10), "Raising *Collateral*" (*Guide*; *PJ* 5); Laura Moriarty, "The Modern Lyric" (*PJ* 7); Nick Robinson, "Subtext in *Collateral*" (*Guide*; *PJ* 5); Michael Amnasan, "The Eclipsing Function of Full Comprehension" (*PJ* 6); Steve Benson, "Mediations in an Emergency" (*PJ* 5); Michael Davidson, "The Poetics of Everyday Life" (*PJ* 9); Carla Harryman, "Toy Boats" (*Guide*; *PJ* 5); George Lakoff, "Continuous Reframing" (*PJ* 1); Robin Palanker, "1. The person is . . ." (*PJ* 9); Jim Rosenberg, "Openings: The Connection Direct" (*PJ* 10); Rod Smith, from "CIA Sentences" (*PJ* 10).

SELECTED BIBLIOGRAPHY: *Chinatown of Cheyenne* (Iowa City, Iowa: Whale Cloth, 1974); *The Dolch Stanzas* (San Francisco: This, 1976); *Down and Back* (Berkeley: The Figures, 1978); *Tribute to Nervous* (Berkeley: Tuumba, 1980); *Riddle Road* (Berkeley: Tuumba, 1982); *A Day Off* (Oakland: State One, 1985); *Windows* (Cambridge, Mass.: Whale Cloth, 1985); *Ice Cubes* (New York: Roof, 1987); *Covers* (Great Barrington, Mass.: The Figures, 1988); *The Champagne of Concrete* (Elmwood, Conn.: Potes & Poets, 1991); *Counter Meditation* (Tenerife, Spain: Zasterle, 1991); *Balance Sheet* (New York: Roof, 1993); *Democracy Boulevard* (New York: Roof, 1999); *The Crave* (Berkeley: Atelos, 2002); *9:45* (Sausalito, Calif.: Post-Apollo Press, 2003); *The Messianic Trees: Selected Poems, 1976–2003* (New York: Adventures in Poetry, 2009); *Train Ride* (Toronto: Book Thug, 2009); *Determination* (Austin, Tex.: Cuneiform, 2010); with Alan Bernheimer, *Cloud Eight* (Lowestoft, England: The Sound & The Language, 1999); with Lyn Hejinian, *Individuals* (Tucson: Chax Press, 1988).

ANDREW ROSS

The Death of Lady Day

Andrew Ross's reading of Frank O'Hara's "The Day Lady Died," presented at the 1987 conference of the Modern Language Association in San Francisco, opened an entirely new approach to O'Hara and New York School poetry. Departing from aesthetic approaches that identified O'Hara with painterly form and surrealist influences in the 1950s, Ross considers O'Hara's writing as a "protopolitical" intervention into urban everyday life. Rather than seeing the poem as a species of ideology—"the imaginary solution to real contradictions"—Ross reads it as a moment of praxis and critique that anticipates a fully political response, just as the everyday-life politics of the 1950s anticipated the counterculture of the 1960s. Ross locates O'Hara's politics in his negotiations with consumerism (his tour of midtown Manhattan), race (his invocation of Billie Holiday and the aesthetics of jazz), and masculinity (in a new style of self-presentation, camp), a "grace to be born and live variously" that configures identity among competing identifications. "O'Hara's is a code of personal politics, which says that at some level you have to take responsibility for your own conduct in the everyday world and toward others," even as normalizing social pressures required a high degree of dissimulation for gay men as a survival strategy. In his revisionist essay, Ross positions O'Hara in the cultural and gender debates where he continues to be read today.

Some of those who attended Frank O'Hara's funeral in 1966 heard Larry Rivers read a speech which they found distasteful. The offending portion was a graphic account of the state of O'Hara's body on his hospital deathbed:

> This extraordinary man lay without a pillow in a bed that looked like a large crib.... He was purple wherever his skin showed through the white hospital gown. He was a quarter larger than usual. Every few inches there was some sewing composed of dark blue thread. Some stitching was straight and three or four inches long, others were longer and semicircular. The lids of both eyes were bluish black. It was hard to see his beautiful blue eyes which receded a little into his head. He breathed with quick gasps. His whole body quivered. There was a tube in one of his nostrils down to his stomach. On paper he was improving. In the crib he looked like a shaped wound, an innocent victim of someone else's war....[1]

Not everyone, however, found these comments inappropriate. That evening, in a bar, Rivers recounted the details to Andy Warhol, and recalled how, at the funeral, "everyone was screaming at [him] to shut up." Warhol noted: "It sounded like a very Pop eulogy to me—just the surface things. It was just what I hoped people would do for me if I died." In fact, the circumstances of O'Hara's death inspired another thought on Warhol's part that has since proved to be prophetic: "It was scary to think that you could lose your life if you were taken to the wrong hospital or if you happened to get the wrong doctor at the right hospital."[2]

If both of these commentaries on the death of O'Hara are aimed at a kind of stylized shock-effect, Warhol's response is the one that trades on language and not the body; it distances itself sympathetically from the gruesome details and from the madding crowd, and even suggests a conventional form for Rivers's tone of address—the Pop eulogy. And yet one cannot help but feel that it is nothing short of violence that reduces, in Warhol's comment about Rivers, a horrid corporeal realism to formal elegance. It is nothing short of violence, however banal and anti-apocalyptic, that reduces the *busyness* of everyday life to business as usual, to the ethic of "surface things" which Warholian Pop came to consecrate under its rubric of maximum indifference—Everything is Good.

In what way, exactly, could a eulogy of "surface things" have been appropriate for O'Hara, who is increasingly remembered today as one of *the* poets of everyday life? It's true that the painters in Rivers and O'Hara's circle had been obsessed with "surface," but this technical obsession was underpinned by a whole ideology of depth—angst, alienation, and autonomy—which marked the tradition of moral seriousness that was their heritage as artist-intellectuals. Pop's egalitarian crusade was to put to the sword the whole apparatus of discrimination that had rested upon a hermeneutics of depth, interpretation, and moral value. Value could be located in any and every object, and because everything *mattered*, nothing mattered very much more than everything else. Pop, in its purist, theoretical form, was intended as an utter negation of the use of taste as a category of cultural power.

Whatever one could say about the friendliness of O'Hara, in his poetry, to the surface detail of everyday life, it is as difficult to find evidence there of this Pop disavowal of taste as it is to detect any sign of heroic Nietzschean loneliness of the sort espoused by Jackson Pollock and others. In fact, his poetry is very much the record of a *man of taste*, not in the bourgeois mode, of course, but in the sense in which it presents a discourse about a certain kind of masculinity that takes a responsible interest in "surface things" at the cost of the more traditional male leaning towards "important" affairs, topics, judgments, values, etc. For O'Hara's man of taste, everyday life things matter, not because they are a way of advertising wealth or power, nor because everything matters equally, but because their value is linked to how people use them to make sense of their world. Taste, in this sense, is more like a survivalist guide than a cultural category through which class-marked power is defined and exercised. No doubt this notion of taste also contains the rudiments of the principle that came to be recognized by feminism as "the personal is the political." In this respect, then, surely there are good reasons for remembering O'Hara through "just the surface things" he wrote about, and little danger in confusing this O'Hara with his other reputation as a poet of trivia who shunned the social, artistic, and political questions of his day.

If that is so, then there are also good reasons for rethinking the categories of surface and depth which have come to plague our debates about cultural politics in the two decades since O'Hara died, or, more exactly, ever since Pop inaugurated the kind of culture, known today as postmodernist, which seems to take itself at face value. A culture of surface is not simply a culture that declares its immunity to historical anxiety; it is also a culture that has become suspicious of History with a capital H, moving with awesome solemnity and depth through our lives, a culture which recognizes that history, for the most part, is also made out of particulars, by people whose everyday acts do not always add up to the grand aggregates of canonical martyrdom which make for *real* politics.

In fact, it is a commonly held view that, when it comes to politics, cultural texts are *least* successful when they are long on militant fiber (and short on pleasure); in other words, when they are at their *most* articulate or didactic, and when their explicit relation to the political is there for all to read, and to be deferred to or browbeaten by. Indeed, most of the cultural texts we encounter are protopolitical—they express an imaginary relation to real conditions of oppression or resistance, a relation that is often difficult to *read*, not least because of its contradictions, but more generally because it is expressed in a symbolic form. Texts, in other words, speak more than they say, even when they seem to be about "surface things." We have learned to recognize this state of affairs as the work of ideology, often viewed by left critics in terms similar to the work of Satan. But there are good reasons, I think, for preferring the term "protopolitical" to the term "ideological." "Protopolitical," for example, suggests submerged *activity*, while "ideological" suggests unremitting *passiv-*

ity; "protopolitical" suggests embryonic or future forms, while "ideological" suggests the oppressive weight of the past extending into the present. So too, in looking at texts that occur "elsewhere," whether in time or place, we ought to be encouraged to look for the protopolitical in those things that *can* be said, rather than in what cannot be said—what is suppressed, in short, by the work of ideology.

To illustrate generally what I mean, I have taken the example of one of O'Hara's best-known poems, "The Day Lady Died." It was written in 1959, a kind of prepolitical age—which is to say, an age that preexists the more explicit formation, in the sixties, of the kind of political culture which most of us have come to live and breathe. It was written, *elsewhere*, in that prelapsarian period of innocence—before the break-up of consensus liberalism, before the conspiracy climate of all post-Kennedy ideology, before the sixties "changed everything"—a period that has been celebrated, for over a decade now, in that glut of yuppie nostalgia culture that stretches from *American Graffiti* to *Dirty Dancing*. It was written by a poet, as I have suggested, whose blithe disregard for politics is equally well known, a disregard, for example, that caused a stir when, in 1966, a minor quarrel broke out among certain literati over his refusal to sign a petition condemning U.S. involvement in Vietnam. Agit-prop, or anything like it, is the last thing we would expect from Frank O'Hara in 1959. And yet, this is a poem, recording one of his celebrated lunchtime walks, which (and those who know and love O'Hara's "I-do-this-I-do-that" poems will surely agree) has radically transformed modern poetry's expectations of how it is licensed to represent everyday life. It is a poem, like the three-minute rock 'n' roll classics of its day, which brashly articulates the fresh disposability of time and energy, lived at high speed, in the new pop continuum of a consumer culture.

> It is 12:20 in New York a Friday
> three days after Bastille day, yes
> it is 1959 and I go get a shoeshine
> because I will get off the 4:19 in Easthampton
> at 7:15 and then go straight to dinner
> and I don't know the people who will feed me
>
> I walk up the muggy street beginning to sun
> and have a hamburger and a malted and buy
> an ugly NEW WORLD WRITING to see what the poets
> in Ghana are doing these days
>   I go on to the bank

and Miss Stillwagon (first name Linda I once heard)
doesn't even look up my balance for once in her life
and in the GOLDEN GRIFFIN I get a little Verlaine
for Patsy with drawings by Bonnard although I do
think of Hesiod, trans. Richard Lattimore or
Brendan Behan's new play or *Le Balcon* or *Les Nègres*
of Genet, but I don't, I stick with Verlaine
after practically going to sleep with quandariness

and for Mike I just stroll into the PARK LANE
Liquor Store and ask for a bottle of Strega and
then I go back where I came from to 6th Avenue
and the tobacconist in the Ziegfeld Theatre and
casually ask for a carton of Gauloises and a carton
of Picayunes, and a NEW YORK POST with her face on it

It's the day after Billie Holiday's death, and America's consumer markets have never been busier; bank tellers are dispensing cash to spendthrift clients without even consulting their balances. Bohemian poets, as we can see from the conspicuous consumption described here, are no longer immune to the contagious seductions of the commodity world. This is not Baudelaire's poet-dandy-*flaneur* lured to the marketplace to look but not buy. In the space of a few blocks, O'Hara's motivated, discriminating consumer-poet has found an entire range of cultural goods to purchase from all over the world, from hamburgers to ancient philosophy. Robert Von Hallberg points out that all of art and history (most of it is not American) is available here, not through Eliotic tradition, but through the benefits of mass production and cheapness.[3] The last stanza, however, suggests that there are some cultural experiences that are literally priceless, and which therefore lie beyond the realm of paperback discount shopping:

and I am sweating a lot by now and thinking of
leaning on the john door in the 5 SPOT
while she whispered a song along the keyboard
to Mal Waldron and everyone and I stopped breathing

This memory of a "live" Billie Holiday moment, with its extreme effect on the motor functions of the body—sweating, constricted breathing—contrasts with the somnolent, low-key anxiety of "quandariness" which was the physical effect of making the earlier consumer choices. Such live moments cannot be reproduced on vinyl for mass consumption—you had to be there. Although O'Hara's poet seems to be perfectly at home in the modern environment of consumer culture, the poem in which he acts out his nostalgia-struck desire ends up paying its tribute to what we might recognize as the modernist poem, with its own epiphanic moment to record the loss, in the past, even the very recent past, of a culture of authenticity evoked by Lady Day's "breath-taking" live presence.

In a poem called "Jitterbugs" Amiri Baraka put the matter more succinctly: "though yr mind is somewhere else, your ass ain't."[4] Baraka is addressing himself more to the contradictions of ghetto realism than to the romantic spirit of the white bohemian in ritual thrall to the spectacle of jazz performance. But his tone here might serve as an earthy corrective to the rapt mood of O'Hara's last stanza. In fact, if we look back through the poem, beginning with the encounter in the first stanza with the probably black shoeshine boy, who may be worried about how he is going to be fed in a way that is different from the poet's anxiety about his unknown hosts in Easthampton, we begin to see how the references to postcolonial "Negritude"—Genet's *Les Nègres*, and those "poets in Ghana"—have indirectly, perhaps even unconsciously, prepared the reader for the final confrontation with American "negritude."

By 1959, scenes of jazz idolatry on the part of white intellectuals had become a commonplace, if not a cliché, especially in the poetry world where the Beat cult of hipsterdom had become an object of national media attention. What is striking, however, is that O'Hara is not like that; he is not *that kind of poet*. Sure, he frequented the jazz clubs, and even gave readings at the 5-Spot. There is enough personal testimony around, from friends and acquaintances, to establish that he was quite familiar with jazz music. But when it comes to his poetry, jazz almost never figures in the taste milieu within which he represented himself, or in the realm of cultural events about which he wrote in copious detail. True to his impeccably camp outlook, Carnegie Hall and the Metropolitan Opera House were more standard venues in his poetry than the 5-Spot, Rachmaninoff a more constant source of religious ecstasy than Miles Davis. This scene in the 5-Spot doesn't seem properly to *belong* in O'Hara's work, where it is employed nonetheless to invoke a spirit of authenticity. It appeals to me as a fond reader of O'Hara that this scenario might be read as an ironic, even parodic, gloss on the stereotyped Beat devotee of the more "authentic" world of jazz culture.

By 1959, the image of the white intellectual worshipping a black jazz performer had become a popular icon, the subject of a thousand cartoons and comedy routines. Jazz was beginning to acquire the legitimacy of a high art form and was therefore being annexed as a realm of minority and not popular taste. But while intellectuals of the day were ritually crowding into small jazz clubs, the popular action was elsewhere, ever since white high school kids had begun to tune in to black R&B radio stations in the late forties and early fifties. By 1959, the rock 'n' roll revolution was over three years old, but you can comb through O'Hara's entire oeuvre—compendiously packed with cultural details—and never find any evidence that such a revolution had taken whole regions and sectors of the culture by storm. The civil rights movement was beginning to gain momentum. But which would prove more crucial to the future gains of multiculturalism—the power of white liberal fantasies, centered upon the idolizing of the purity of black culture and its fine arts? or the prospect of fully integrated dance floors—black and white bodies moving to recognizably black rhythms, and the other racial crossovers which rock 'n' roll culture has generated ever since its scandalous origin?

For white intellectuals, the sacred spectacle of the spontaneous jazz performer was underscored, among other things, by a highly romantic form of racism. It suggested that work was simply an extension of a kind of pre-social culture that was at ease with play and had mastered leisure; in other words, making jazz was work that didn't look like work, by people who weren't supposed to know the difference. In O'Hara's poem, what Billie Holiday does comes "naturally." Her languorous "whisper," by contrast, precipitates an unnatural response, a near cardiovascular attack, on the poet's part, which can be compared, diametrically, with the nonchalance which he had earlier displayed during his bout of compulsive buying. Then, what was most self-conscious about consuming had been made to seem like the most natural thing in the world. "Just" strolling in here and there and "casually" asking for this and that, at once indecisive and pragmatic in his purchasing, he had behaved almost like a practiced shoplifter, carefully covering his tracks with a whole range of consumer rituals. But, for all of its worked-at insouciance, the art of consuming, unlike the art of the jazz singer, proves to be hard work: after a while, he's "sweating a lot," unlike Lady Day, who is remembered as the very image of cool. Even now, when she literally has stopped breathing, it is the poet who takes on her symptoms as he reads of her death in the newspaper.

That it is a Lady Day and not a Charlie Parker being commemorated in this way is, of course, O'Hara's own personal touch. As a gay poet, and one of the most spontaneous of all camp writers, it is no surprise to find that it is a woman singer who shares the billing along with the goddesses of the screen which he celebrates in other poems. In fact, O'Hara's most celebrated camp line occurs in a poem in which the poet sees a newspaper headline which announces that "LANA TURNER HAS COLLAPSED!" It ends thus:

> I have been to lots of parties
> and acted perfectly disgraceful
> but I never actually collapsed
> oh Lana Turner we love you get up

Survivalist exhortations of this sort lie at the very heart of camp's insistence that the show must go on, and that irony and parody can redeem even the most tragic *and* sordid events which color everyday life. The last years of Judy Garland's life, for example, in which she transformed her career role as a self-destructive loser into that of a reliant, irrepressible fighter, came to exemplify this survivalist spirit for the gay community, and the final period of Billie Holiday's checkered life and career is certainly the closest equivalent among female jazz performers ("The Day Lady Died" takes place almost exactly a decade before the day which saw both Garland's funeral and the Stonewall riots).

In the prepolitical climate of O'Hara's day, this survivalism found expression in the highly ironized flamboyance of the camp ethic—"laughing to keep from crying"—which structured a whole subculture around the act of imagining a *different* relation to the existing world of too strictly authorized and legitimized sexual positions. In this respect, camp has to be seen as an imaginative conquest of everyday conditions of oppression, where more articulate expressions of resistance or empowerment were impossible. The most elaborate of these imaginary codes involved identification with the "power," however restricted, exercised by certain women, especially those in the cinema, and especially those like Bette Davis whose mannered repertoire was a highly performed caricature of the conventional representations of women. The suggestion that role-playing, and the destabilizing of fixed sexual positions, could actually add to the exercise of sexual power was a very attractive suggestion for the gay male, who knew that his sexuality, in everyday life, was likely to get him into trouble.

The sometimes mawkish sentimentalism of camp is often seen as an institutionalized expression of self-hatred, and thus a dangerous form of acceptance, by an oppressed group, of the oppressor's definition of the oppressed. Like the eponymous "Jewish self-hatred or "Tomming" in black culture, or certain expressions of "machismo" in Latin cultures, camp is a form of defense constructed by an oppressed group out of conditions not of its own making.

That is why it is protopolitical; in other words, it is a response to politically induced oppression, but at the same time, it is a response which accepts its current inability to act in an explicit political manner to combat that oppression. This response takes many covert forms and baroque systems of disclosure, not least in the heavily coded speech repertoires and intonations of gay vernacular which the attentive reader can find everywhere in O'Hara's poetry.[5]

Looking back over O'Hara's poem, we can see how it tends to accept what might have been stereotypically regarded as the social contours of gay masculinity in 1959: the obsession, for example, with trivia, with feelings, with discriminations of taste, and, of course, with the fine arts. The tone of the poem marks its obvious distance from the voice of legitimate masculinity; O'Hara's is not the voice of the public sphere, where real decisions are made by real men, and where real politics is supposed to take place. In fact, the hectic itinerary followed by his poet could just as well be that of a genteel lady about town, if you substitute a hairdresser for the shoeshine, the Russian Tea Room for the soda parlor, Rizzoli's for the Golden Griffin, and so on. This is *a man on a shopping trip*, and the dizzy combination of quandariness, fastidiousness, vagrant attention, distaste for ugly items, and the general air of practiced nonchalance which he displays in the process of making the various purchases— all of this mirrors or mimics the way in which a woman of means with a busy social schedule might have conducted herself as the fifties were drawing to a close. (It is open to debate whether, in fact, a woman would deliberate for so long over the choice of gift for "Patsy," while proving so confident in making such a straightforward selection for "Mike.") The "lady's" version of this poem would have ended, of course, with the shock of reading the obituary, in the *Times*, of a fashionable musician or composer. In fact, the "day lady died" is an account of a lady's day, played out by a man through the imaginary of a lunch hour which is the very opposite of the power lunches which were being eaten in restaurants in the same few blocks by the men who make real history—no quandariness for them! they know what they like, and it's not Gauloises and it's not Genet, even though they may share the 4:19 to Easthampton, the same commuter train as O'Hara's poet, who, incidentally, shares the same working hours as they do.

Even while it accepts a stereotype of gay masculinity, itself based upon a sexist stereotype of female character traits and mannerisms, O'Hara's poem begins to imagine a different relation to everyday life for men in general. The masculinity he imagines here has increasingly become more familiar along with the steady erosion, since 1959, of the sexual division of labor, and the gradual softening of the contours of social masculinity to incorporate more attention to style, feeling, taste, desire, consumer creativity, and sexual toleration. It marks the beginning of a whole chapter of sexual politics that will come to learn almost as much from the redefinition of masculinity articulated by gay males, as from the struggle against everyday oppression mounted by feminists.

O'Hara's poetry rejects the big, global questions of politics and economics, even the big "artistic" questions of aesthetics. His is certainly not a heroic poetics of self-reliance or self-making in the transcendent, Emersonian tradition, nor does it make a pragmatic religion out of individualism, in the American grain. Instead it subscribes to the micropolitics of personal detail, faithfully noting down dates, times, events, feelings, moods, fears, and so on, and devoting a bricoleur's disciplined attention to details in the world and in the people around him. O'Hara's is a code of personal politics, which says that at some level you have to take responsibility for your own conduct in the everyday world and towards others; you can't rely on organized politics or unorganized religions to change that. It is a code which starts from what we find lying, unplanned, around us, rather than from achieved utopias of the body and mind. In 1959, well before the coming riots of self-liberation, this was a mannered way of saying: take things into your own hands.

It seems impossible to end without recalling the elegiac note with which I began, for death is a very important part of "The Day Lady Died." Who can read this poem about Billie Holiday's death without thinking of O'Hara's own untimely death seven years later? Who can read it without thinking of the deaths today, from AIDS, of thousands of young homosexual men, like O'Hara, in a culture that is only beginning to recognize how public agendas work by reorganizing and redefining private responsibilities? It is in this context that O'Hara's code of everyday responsibility begins to take on a new kind of sense, three decades later. It is in this context that the *survivalism* of the camp sensibility, always prepared to deal with an apocalypse of worst possible outcomes, takes on new meanings, when danger is located today in the smallest things in our lives. It is in this context, perhaps, that the "surface things" in O'Hara's poetry show their unhidden depths.

NOTES

1 Larry Rivers, "Speech Read at Frank O'Hara's Funeral, Springs, Long Island, 27 July 1966," in Bill Berkson and Joe Le Sueur, eds., *Homage to Frank O'Hara* (Bolinas, Calif.: Big Sky Books, 1978), 138.

2 Andy Warhol and Pat Hackett, *Popism: The Warhol '60s* (New York: Harcourt Brace Jovanovich, 1980), 186–87.

3 Robert Von Hallberg, *American Poetry and Culture: 1945–1980* (Cambridge: Cambridge University Press, 1985), 178.

4 Amiri Baraka/LeRoi Jones, *Selected Poetry* (New York: William Morrow, 1979), 93.

5 Bruce Boone describes the "oppositional" significance of these covert forms in the context of O'Hara's work in "Gay Language as Political Praxis: The Poetry of Frank O'Hara," *Social Text* 1 (Winter 1979): 59–92.

PUBLICATION: *Elsewhere* (1989), 8:68–77.

KEYWORDS: New York School; queer; cultural studies; readings.

LINKS: Andrew Ross, "The Oxygen of Publicity" (*PJ* 6); Bob Perelman, "Three Case Histories: Ross's *Failure of Modernism*" (*PJ* 7); Dodie Bellamy, "Can't We Just Call It Sex?: In Memory of David Wojnarowicz" (*PJ* 10); Bruce Boone, "Kathy Acker's *Great Expectations*" (*PJ* 4); Steve Evans, "Gizzi's *No Both*" (*PJ* 10); Robert Glück, "Fame" (*PJ* 10); Tom Mandel, "Codes/Texts: Reading *S/Z*" (*PJ* 2); Ted Pearson, "'A Form of Assumptions'" (*Guide*; *PJ* 9); Aaron Shurin, "The Irruptive Text" (*PJ* 8); Reva Wolf, "Thinking You Know" (*Guide*; *PJ* 10).

SELECTED BIBLIOGRAPHY: *The Failure of Modernism: Symptoms of American Poetry* (New York: Columbia University Press, 1986); *Universal Abandon?: The Politics of Postmodernism* (ed.; Minneapolis: University of Minnesota Press, 1988); *No Respect: Intellectuals and Popular Culture* (London: Routledge, 1989); *Strange Weather: Culture, Science and Technology in the Age of Limits* (London: Verso, 1991); *The Chicago Gangster Theory of Life: Nature's Debt to Society* (London: Verso, 1994); *Science Wars* (ed.; Durham, N.C.: Duke University Press, 1996); *Real Love: In Pursuit of Cultural Justice* (New York: NYU Press, 1998); *The Celebration Chronicles: Life, Liberty, and the Pursuit of Property Value in Disney's New Town* (New York: Ballantine, 1999); *No-Collar: The Humane Workplace and Its Hidden Costs* (New York: Basic Books, 2003); with Kristin Ross, *Anti-Americanism* (eds.; New York: NYU Press, 2004); *Fast Boat to China: Corporate Flight and the Consequences of Free Trade—Lessons from Shanghai* (New York: Pantheon, 2006); *Nice Work If You Can Get It: Life and Labor in Precarious Times* (New York: NYU Press, 2009).

What/Person? From an Exchange

This well-known exchange between Leslie Scalapino and Ron Silliman, over his introduction
to a selection of work by Scalapino and three other contemporary poets in *Socialist Review*
(1988), begins with Scalapino's disagreement with Silliman's distinction between poets
"who identify as members of groups that have been the subject of history" (e.g., white
male heterosexuals, or WMHs) and poets "who have instead been its objects." Silliman attempts to describe a divergence within aesthetic practice in which the former are motivated
to dismantle conventions of narrative, persona, and reference, while the latter "need to
have their stories told." For Scalapino, this distinction is hierarchical and thus derogatory in
that it assumes the first group is more predisposed to formal innovation, while the other
is more "conventional." For Scalapino, "no one is free of their narrative," nor from an obliga-
tion to contest it. This debate, which is still not concluded, took place on the threshold of a
major shift in the cultural politics of the avant-garde and its relation to identity politics.
While black, gay, and feminist liberationist movements demanded the recognition of identity, a new generation of minority writers consider identity not as a given but as a site for
exploration. Poets like Harryette Mullen, Renee Gladman, Pamela Lu, Tisa Bryant, Tan Lin,
and Rodrigo Toscano took full advantage of the contradictions disclosed in this provocative
debate.

Dear Ron,

We agreed on an exchange concerning views expressed in your introduction which prefaced writing (requested and in some cases excerpted by
you) by eight poets including myself published in the July–September 1988
Socialist Review. I'll quote the passage which contained, in my view, the
most problematic aspects of your argument:

> Progressive poets who identify as members of groups that have been the
> subject of history—many white male heterosexuals, for example—are
> apt to challenge all that is supposedly 'natural' about the formation of
> their own subjectivity. That their writing today is apt to call into ques-
> tion, if not actually explode, such conventions as narrative, persona and
> even reference can hardly be surprising. At the other end of this spec-
> trum are poets who do not identify as members of groups that have
> been the subject of history, for they instead have been its objects. The

narrative of history has led not to their self-actualization, but to their exclusion and domination. These writers and readers—women, people of color, sexual minorities, the entire spectrum of the 'marginal'—have a manifest political need to have their stories told. That their writing should often appear much more conventional, with the notable difference as to who is the subject of these conventions, illuminates the relationship between form and audience.

Your argument as I understand it is that white heterosexual men in groups (i.e., elites) being free of their social condition are more able to write formally innovative work than are women, gays, and minorities who by virtue of being caught in their social condition have the need to "have their stories told" and therefore tend to write "conventional" narrative.

The word *conventional* by definition is value-laden in reference to any art or scholarly/thought form, implying inferiority.

Elsewhere in your statement, you associate awareness of the formation of subjectivity in writing with questioning "the role of the unified subject."

Though I do not deny the prevalence of 'conventional narrative' (the characteristics of which you do not describe more specifically than those of making connections and 'telling one's story') written by many including white men, the argument thus phrased—though you are entirely concerned with radically questioning social structure—is authoritarian. As you know, I wrote a letter responding to your introduction which I intended for publication in the *Socialist Review*. I was refused publication on the basis that my language was too poetic and did not qualify as political discourse. That is to say, I must speak a language recognized as discourse before it can be regarded as public and as germane.

The issues regarding narrative phrased very simply seem to me to include the following:

No one is free of their narrative. My own poetic construct is similar to yours in wanting to 'deconstruct' our illusion or constructions of reality—which I see as including the illusion that 'elites,' whatever these constitute, are able to have objectivity by removing 'themselves'/as critiquing subjectivity. The corollary to this is to say that "radical subjectivity" would seem to = the person recognizing themselves/oneself as 'marginalized' no matter what and at all times.

the attitude of
in a setting
aging and dying at

some time

as—that

we

should be

that

My point about development and form in writing was the following: Those in social power and those without it might be equally capable of questioning their subjectivity. But those who are without social power are less inclined to see reality as orderly; for example, less inclined to see the social construction as unified.

The nature of groups is to sustain and nurture members, not to urge them to question themselves or the sense of reality established by the group.

The desire on the part of a writer (such as Flaubert) to remove himself from the writing as a kind of objective camera-lens-like analysis of reality (i.e., the hidden narrator: the illusion, however interesting as an experiment, that one could do this) is in fact similar to your idea of men capable of objectivity by being free of their social condition.

From my first letter to you:

> I once worked as a writer for a labor arbitrator. Arbitrators of course are chosen by the two sides of a dispute to resolve the dispute between them. Almost all arbitrators in the country were white men. Seeking to enter a program to train women and minorities to become arbitrators, I asked my employer about this program. He said, "Those people can't be objective."

My point is that, in your view, the conception of transcendence (objectivity) = the *critique* of the unified subject (that the tendency to view reality via the unified subject is the historical condition of people who are disenfranchised). In fact: the concept of 'objectivity' *constitutes* a unified subject.

The conception of a 'unified subject' is merely taught, in certain conventionalizing settings such as school or workshops, i.e., people writing would not otherwise have such a view. Your argument is that this conception is inherent in the 'experience' of women, gays, and minorities.

The very notion of the 'unified subject' is a white, 'Anglo' description which conventionalizes writing radical in its own time such as that of Flaubert or Williams.

I am referring to a different sense of 'telling one's story.'

Here are four lines translated from a Yaqui (Native American) song or poem shown to me at Chax Press in Tucson:

> walk
>
> > walk
> >
> > > walk
> > >
> > > > walk

The entire poem was composed of such directions. There were no designated persons.

You have a Marxist narration. Supposing there is an acknowledged need for community, which is a theme of the Yaqui poems (I was told). Is the expression of that a 'conventional' narration (i.e., the construction of convention, the construction of narrative, which is the community)? And why would that not be innovative?

You are defining innovation as the repository of white men who are supposedly free of connection. Even if they could be free of connection, why should they be? E.g., why would that be viewed as innovative?

I'm defining narrative as 'constructing.'

My premise, in general and in writing, is that I do not think there is a man, or woman, or society, social construction; though it is there. It is not there.

A primary formal element of your writing is statements.

Best,

Leslie

Dear Leslie,

Underneath your accusation ("the argument thus phrased . . . is authoritarian"), there are troubling issues, for poets generally, and certainly for white male heterosexuals (WMHs). What I'd like to do is to use this occasion (and your aid, critical as it may be) as a means of approaching these questions—"identity," "objectivity," and "instrumentalism"—with some hope that this dialogue will allow us to go further than I could on my own.

What I did *not* do was claim that straight white males (or any other persons) at any point in history had access to something called "objectivity." There is no universal subject position, and without that, the objective—transparent access to an object—is simply an hallucination, albeit one that historically has been used by those in power on (and against) the powerless many. I believe we agree on this.

What I did write was that a group with an historically specific subject position would have an historically specific response. As you put it, "No one is free of their narrative." I agree completely.

What is historically distinct about the subject position of the white male hetero (WMH) is its relation to power.[1] Far from being liberating, this experience of power has been profoundly troubling and confusing for many WMHs. Both in that it exists at all (for it has no legitimate basis) and in the particular forms that it takes: always simultaneously privilege and oppression. Power is always already overdetermined: one cannot escape its stratifications and limits. Power is never our own—it can only exist "elsewhere."

It is this double-nature of power in its relation with the specific subject position of the WMH that has generated, in some writers, a response I have characterized as a critique of subjectivity (and of the subject itself). Not because of any peculiar aesthetic or analytical capabilities it gives them—there are none—but because of the specificity of privileged oppression.

It's not an accident that this critique or reaction occurred within a generation that was, for the most part, of draft age during the Vietnam War. For a time at least, the experience of contradiction was neither an abstraction nor an intellectual game.

Historically, an identification with privilege has rhetorically posed its experience in universal terms. Thus, the linked concepts of objectivity, truth, and transcendence (all moments in the same discourse), far from being an option or feasible goal for any or all people, has been rather a strategy for (and by) a specific cluster, one subset of the grouping WMH. The point was never objectivity, but rather identity—what subjective state could imagine a condition through which all other peoples disappear?

Art exists solely in the context of real lives, real communities, complex ensembles of difference. But in a universe in which only the WMH is acknowledged, the WMH as such is no longer perceptible in his own landscape. It was precisely this invisibility that permitted centuries of men to imagine the pronouns *he* and *him* as gender-neutral.

You argue that "those who are without social power are less inclined to see reality as orderly; for example, less inclined to see the social construction as unified." You present no evidence for this very large claim. To cite simply one possible counter-example, the history of organized religion over two millennia would have to be explained away.

What I have called a critique of the subject on the part of some WHMs is not a transcendent position, but one grounded in position and history. If we reject (as I do) any universalized point of view, those other poetics that superficially appear more conventional are no less radical. I thought that I said as much in *Socialist Review*. By demonstrating traditional WMH subject positions (such as protagonist, voice, "I," point-of-reflexivity) inhabited by other subjects—women, homosexuals, people of color—such writing explodes fictions of the universal.

But the agenda facing anyone whose history includes that combination of privileged oppression necessarily will have to be different. The point is not correctness. Nor is it an imaginary future moment where all literary tendencies will merge into one.

I disagree strongly with the nostalgic notion (to which much of the left still clings) that the "trick" to a progressive movement is fathoming how to create a grand universal project or coalition by which to "seize history." Ours is not a struggle for unity, but rather with unity itself. For the quest for unity leads only to a thousand defeats.

So language poetry (to pick a project) is not—and can never be—the research and development department for "progressive" literature. Rather, it is the practical, day-to-day writing of a real community, complex, historical, positioned, flawed.

Not a struggle for unity (objectivity, transcendence), but rather with the mutual problem of domination in a world of difference. We must not privilege any position, our own included.

Ron

———

Dear Ron,

I interpreted the (original *Socialist Review*) argument to be that white (by implication 'elite' or avant-garde) males (having perceived the split between themselves and experiences—i.e. the dismantling of narrative) were *more* inclined to question their own subjectivity than the others mentioned, who are thus thought of as 'marginal,' as 'interest groups.'

The basis of my argument was that anyone as they are in the modern context could perceive the split between themselves and experience (this would actually be a *traditionally* held view in Asian, Buddhist cultures).

But 'conventional narrative' does not express this.

For example, one is taught a definition of one's humanness when a small female child which is immediately unbelievable to that child—one knows that is not the self.

Regarding narrative, we both are assuming that rebellion from or un-peeling of the layers of the self is an element of awareness. But we are seeing and describing it differently.

Women began to write novels (by the nineteenth century) having a market for these narratives that displayed the people to each other.

The novels portrayed a sense of the psyches of people, for example.

The creation of a sense of private psyche was an expression of the split between oneself and experience.

As such, these were radical expressions which were later commented upon and changed by such writers as Virginia Woolf, using a 'fragmented' form to implode even further the previous sense of reality.

Conversely, the collective modern sense of 'inability' to make connections is not a given: a fragmented sense of reality is also socially constructed.

Our discussion is partly talking about one current focus of writing which is examining the *concept* of psyche.

I am currently interested in a form which is a version of the comic book (a written form using frames and without pictures). One element of it is to render itself/'psyche' invalid—that it will use itself up as pulp and be regarded as nothing. It is not 'discursive,' 'analytical' 'method'—by in some ways reproducing such and not being that.

The conception of this does not exist for those who are far from the highly organized civilization which is based in the view that being free is not having consumer goods.

Not using the mind.

We see as in this—the comic book—one frame at a time.

only not in

the comic book

The (other) is beside herself. In where the mother whales are suckling the babies, stillness, the foam spray of the turmoil being on the outside. She is right next to them, amongst them.

The side of one of the creatures.

mind isn't in

this

In the hive of the arcade, the intruder foreigner has come in surrounded by a mob—who're the mirror images, the reverse of the civilization and don't move.

mind is before

it

The crowd seeming to jeer at us leaving in droves having it was found later seen banners advertising it as a strip show. Not knowing at the time. And so the young man having been jeered compared it to after coming out, discovered by his classmates, being ridiculed on the schoolbus.

changing them

from inside

and so only in rare instances is the comic book in rapport with the experience of its readers.

the emancipation from experiences

The people who are going to work walking with their briefcases or with shopping bags past the sea on the sand—on their way—the moon in the sky above them.

Our collective sense of not making connections which is seeing as fragmentary series is not a given. [...]

[Writing the relation of interior—experience—to social constructing as event changes the language.]

Leslie

———

Dear Leslie,

One might begin anywhere (and, with this topic, it seems one is necessarily always at the beginning, that "getting closer" is not an option, so that the most one can hope for is a useful circumambulation). [...]

The question of person is not separable from that of closure, at least for this moment, this discourse, this juncture.

The closed person is defended, complete.

The closed person is autonomous.

The closed person does not require reflection, because reflection is a dividing off, a supplement, a confession of incompleteness.

The closed person is not the body that dies, but the name (the signifier) that could conceivably "live forever."

So death is not a disappointment, but the jumping-off point—the moment at which the name is free of the body, so that it can (finally) actualize its truly autonomous existence.

Progress begins at the moment of death.

This is why critics still prefer dead poets.

It is also why video games in the arcade keep track of point scores, and list
best games by the players' initials—"I can lose this game [death], but my
point score will never die."

As a boy of ten I found in writing
a world I could control
in contrast to the other one,
anxious, unpredictable,
governed by the psychotic grandmother
who stalked the kitchen, shouting,
in hand a knife.

Closure and consumption, I
would argue, are likewise
inextricably linked.
Marketing wants a
simple message. The
indeterminacy of a
multiply-defined consumer
offers immense problems.

All the computer manufacturers want the corporate market, the Fortune
1,000, 500, 100. Yet the vast majority of new jobs—the site of real social
development—occur in small businesses, literally Mom-n-Pop operations.

The autonomous consumer prefers Pepsi.
The message presumes completeness.
No ad suggests post-purchase indeterminacy.

Imagine an industry that gave away product,
knowing that it would make a profit
from post-warranty repairs.

Scholars
are the service technicians
of the soul—

in the early years they do installation and configuration,
then later software applications and support,
and finally repair, replacement, and data recovery. [. . .]

Ron

Dear Ron,
Using the mind is not a product of leisure. [. . .]
In regard to "vanguardism," there is no question but that elites make
more changes in culture (i.e. contribute more to evolution) than those who
aren't. The question in that context is what constitutes 'elite'; it is as you
would agree not simply social power—it is also understanding.

Dear Leslie,

[...] What is the distinction between audience and market?

Dear Ron,

What is the separation between information and the unfolding of phenomena? We've invaded a country and gotten their 'leader' formerly enmeshed in our drug-soaked CIA and we've arrested him for drugs our newsmen interviewing people in the street who say to parade him through the streets.

say to execute him. anyone who does not agree is cut off by the newsmen, not allowed to speak. They merely reflect our policy. The trial jury will have to not have heard of the invasion not to have seen the news being on it will depend on their ignorance.

so the unfolding of phenomena is dependent on ignorance. and we would stop it have it come back in if we were not that.

the grey silk dove feeding back in.

and feeding back in is ignorance

itself the purple spurt from the man seen on the retina.

which wouldn't have happened

and so history is calm throughout feeding back into itself. contemplating.

and so experience itself is convention and we are outside of experience.[2]

the comic book is to enable people always to be outside of experience.[3]

There is no relation between the adult and the child and they continually create action.

Actions such as getting naked on the cover of a magazine are narrative which is ostensibly inside experience and therefore rebelling

by being outside of the present convention and, being experience itself.

Leslie

Dear Leslie,

Awareness does not free us from experience—and why would that be the goal? Freedom becomes avoidance when the preposition it invokes is "from." I'm interested in the freedom to . . .

What awareness might do is to provide tools for negotiating experience. Awareness of choices within experience might even enable us to choose the phenomenological layerings of experience itself.

In 1949, my mother was a single parent trying to raise two small children while working as a waitress in a donut shop. Realistically, returning "home" to live with her parents may well have been her best option, although the consequences were many. Her father, a foreman in a paper recycling plant in Emeryville, was a silent, emotionally withdrawn person, possibly because he was both extremely shy and hard of hearing. Her mother's "spells"—today we might call them episodes of severe depression with psychotic features—lasted for months at a time. My brother and I were given my mother's childhood bedroom, while she slept on the sofa in the living room for the next fifteen years.

I'm personalizing this as much as possible to make a point. Experience, as such, has no value. Value is something that is assigned. We were taught that we had a happy family and I am convinced that nobody believed they were lying when they said this. The distinction between action and discourse was absolute. So it was impossible to know even what our emotions were, let alone what options any one of us might have had. The disjunction between these elements is in no way exceptional. Rather, only through an act of analytic construction can they even be connected.

"Experience regarded as 'lower class'" is an hallucination of the middle and upper classes. As always, you take extraordinary care in your wording of this statement—nowhere does it say who is doing the regarding.

At first this seems obvious—dualism is constructed upon opposites: self/other, presence/absence, now/then, mind/body, here/there. Difference recedes into infinity. BUT, on either side of this slash mark is something that has been astoundingly reified and reduced. Direct experience is a social construction. You say as much and I agree.

Ironically, the famed (or notorious) relativism of the poststructuralists too often simply substitutes relativity itself as a reified form, displacing this condition without resolving it. A blind spot, institutional power, organizes the terrain, so that many otherwise honorable, otherwise intelligent young scholars do not even see how (or why) they restrict their interpretive moves to always already canonical texts. A refusal to do so—a recognition that an honest poststructuralism would require not just a revolution of the critical canon, nor even the literary canon, but of the concept of canonicity itself, is what makes Cary Nelson's *Repression and Recovery: Modern American Poetry and the Politics of Cultural Memory, 1910–1945* such an extraordinarily courageous (as well as brilliant) book. It is not an accident that *R&R* has no chapter divisions, no linear argument—it would be impossible to outline—nor that its footnotes (!) should prove to be possibly the best history of modern American poetry we have yet had in print. Nelson shifts subject position (and subject) on almost every page. *R&R*'s expository strategy is one of refusing to let the argument—and with it the object of discourse—freeze into any fixed form. Not coincidentally, it's a grounded, eminently practical discussion as well.

There is, I want to say, no such thing as an essential definition. Think of the competing possibilities. Each of us possesses race, class, gender, and sexual identity. It can be argued that each of us also has an historic, if not always personal, relationship to religion, nationality, and even generation (and this last term reveals just how historically specific "essentials" can be). The category class, even in its narrowest productivist sense, requires fixing class background, class position, class stance, and directionality. Michael Omi and Howard Winant have chronicled how even race is historically constructed. And, as the recent revolutions in Eastern Europe (and they can all be legitimately described as such, even in the narrowest sense of that term) have shown, mobs demanding the production of basic goods—while resisting in the workplace any speedups in their own productivity—one's status as consumer may be as, or even more, important than one's status as producer (Baudrillard's thesis has been verified) in the constitution of one's subjective perception of identity.

All of these categories occur *prior* to the instant of direct perception. Dualism can occur only when an entire host of these terms are suppressed simultaneously, enabling one term to subordinate the others and thus to found an Other (which, in turn, has its own subordinations).

The ensemble of categories that constructs identity can neither be denied, it seems, nor taken for granted. Chantal Mouffe makes a point worth raising here. As one of the first theorists to articulate how and why the politics of new social movements differ substantially from the modernist Enlightenment model of a class-centered politics, she has been working for several years to respond to the fundamental(ist) charge that such initiatives only fragment "the people united" and keep them from their utopian goal of a world in which class as well as class conflict dissolve into a unitarian homogeny of political correctness. Mouffe has raised the question of the desirability of any such utopia, dependent as it would be on the repression of specific interests, on the repression of specificity itself.

The objective of Mouffe's alternative, which she calls radical pluralism, is not a static utopia, but "a chain of equivalence among the democratic demands found in variety of movements—women, blacks, workers, gay, ecological, etc.—around a radical democratic interpretation of the political principles of the liberal democratic regime." For her, these are radically opposed impulses: "The logic of democracy is a logic of identity, a logic of equivalence, while the liberal logic is a logic of pluralism that impedes the realization of a complete equivalence and the establishment of a total system of identifications."

The phrase "chain of equivalence" indicates that we are exactly in the terrain of hypo- and parataxis. A politics of pure hypotaxis can only succeed through the mass subordination of every element. A politics of pure parataxis will never complete a thought. Recognized as such, the question of politics itself must be transformed—it must cease to be a project. It must become, instead, a process. As such, politics does not have an end. There is no "final conflict" toward which history rushes (unless it should be with nature, but that is another story). Mouffe puts it this way: "The common good can never be actualized, it has to remain a vanishing point to which we should constantly refer, but which cannot have a real existence." Here the problem posed by dualism—what Mouffe calls the necessary frontier of the Other—has ceased to exist. What we have instead is "an unending 'war of position.'"

This war occurs not only between people, but within every person as well—the battle or the self-determination of every category active or latent within our psyches. Our goal should not (indeed, cannot) be the stasis of resolution but learning to balance and negotiate never-ending tensions.

For the poet trying to think her or his way through the poem, this means that social context must be understood as dramatically active. A white male "new formalist"—Dana Gioia, Mark Jarman, Dick Allen, Frederick Feirstein, or Timothy Steele—seeks maximum hypotaxis, a poetry that reinforces the most traditional modes of privilege. A lesbian involved in the same project, such as Marilyn Hacker, has to be read differently. Her work challenges the possessors of privilege but not privilege itself—indeed, it longs for it. The social logic of rhyme and meter manifests a universe made possible precisely by the terms of her own subordination. Gertrude Stein had no such ambivalence. Neither does Judy Grahn.

Sarah Schulman, in *After Dolores*, makes use of the mystery novel to turn its presumptions of value on its head (right side up). The lesbian heroine solves nothing by the end of the book. She remains obsessed by the same lost love as on page one. Schulman rejects *both* hypotaxis (subordination through justice/traditional form) and parataxis (identity as transcendence).

My point here is much as it was in *Socialist Review*—that none of us is privileged, yet each of us is positioned. The question of politics in art can only be how conscious we are of the multiple determinations that constitute position, and the uses to which these understandings are put.

Ron

Dear Ron,

I concur with many elements of your last letter; insofar as it states or interprets my argument in certain ways, I must briefly summarize mine.

In "experience regarded as lower class," I was of course *referring* to the hallucination of that. (The creation or conception of a division between experience and oneself.)

It 'seems' that change, political and phenomenal, arises from this division. And the process of such, maybe a 'dialectic of history,' is a fabrication.

At the same time my belief is: one does not have an 'actual' knowledge of reality if one regards oneself as one's experience.

In regard to narrative, for me these thoughts imply the following:

that we are not experience—and also that all analysis/theory (anyone's, or the academy's which has a format for a paper or a poem) is a false conception of what is 'objective,' which creates a reality—it is producing itself.

narrative is the 'meeting' of these. This is a relief, as it reveals that one is not 'actually' inside any convention.

My Best,
Leslie

NOTES

1 In practice, of course, this has never been a pure experience. White males are divided into thousands of overlapping subcategories that inevitably stratify lives and perceptions. So even to imagine a category as general as the "white male het" will always miss each individual within that group. I don't expect anyone to recognize himself in my description.

2 It seems to me the heart of the dialogue which I'm seeing as implicit in your argument and in many current interesting works such as James Sherry's *Our Nuclear*

Heritage, is quintessentially dualistic (and aware of that): that narrative or "story-telling" itself is convention, arising from or concomitant with the conception that experience itself is convention. Analysis, which is itself culturally determined, is to be awareness which frees us from experience.

The dialectic of the expression of this conflict is the following. Viewed critically, this struggle of Western dualism may (as a direction of writing melding with criticism) lead to being trapped in and by its convention of analysis.

Experience regarded as 'lower class.'

3 See my #2 letter.

PUBLICATION: Excerpted from *The Person* (1991), 9:51–68.

KEYWORDS: avant-garde; narrative; race; identity.

LINKS: Leslie Scalapino, "War/Poverty/Writing" (*PJ* 10); Ron Silliman, "The Dysfunction of Criticism: Poets and the Critical Tradition of the Anti-Academy" (*PJ* 10); Steve Benson, "Personal as Social History: Three Fictions" (*PJ* 7); David Bromige, "Alternatives of Exposition" (*PJ* 5); Beverly Dahlen, from "The Tradition of Marginality" (*PJ* 6); Michael Davidson, "'Hey Man, My Wave!': The Authority of Private Language" (*Guide*; *PJ* 6); Norman Finkelstein, "The Problem of the Self in Recent American Poetry" (*PJ* 9); Pamela Lu, from "Intermusement" (*PJ* 10); Travis Ortiz, from "variously, not then" (*PJ* 10); Rodrigo Toscano, "Early Morning Prompts for Evening Takes; or, Roll 'Em" (*PJ* 10); Hung Q. Tu, "Very Similitude" (*PJ* 10); Ellen Zweig, "Feminism and Formalism" (*PJ* 4).

SELECTED BIBLIOGRAPHY: see Silliman, "Migratory Meaning" (*Guide*) and Scalapino, "Pattern—and the 'Simulacral'" (*Guide*).

The Marks Are Waiting

Informed by the politics of everyday life in the New York School, Lorenzo Thomas demonstrates how to turn the politics of media language into poetry. In the first half of his hybrid work, Thomas mines the dissociated and conflicted language of the media as a continuous presentation of political irony; in the second half, he unpacks the terms of this constantly present, degraded language into a larger political framework. Permanent war, serial emergencies, depraved politicians, offshore finance capital, and mass bread and circuses in the 1990s led to the national security state in the new millennium. Thomas's analysis, between diatribe and improvisation, creates a space in poetry where the poet can reflect, in a hipster idiom that is at once ironic and immediate, on the reality of the crimes that everywhere surround us but which are ignored every day. Thomas's synthesis of aesthetic and political concerns reflects his early involvement, in the 1960s, with the Umbra Workshop on the Lower East Side, a group that included Ishmael Reed, Calvin C. Hernton, and David Henderson and was influential for the Black Arts Movement. During the same period, Thomas was friendly with many second-generation New York School poets like Ted Berrigan, Ron Padgett, and Ted Greenwald, and he pursued a multicultural aesthetic that was informed by his Caribbean background. Lorenzo Thomas died in 2005.

Our new acuity
Has been misread
As short attention span
But all our aptitude for euphemism
Has been stretched
Like the elastic
In a pair of drawers
Floating around our hips
Uncomfortably
We behold the birth of a new world
Odder than the ones before
In the blue gloom of tv light in Darien
In Pueblo Heights, in College Station
Imagination wilting
Our shopping malls explode with petrojunk

Become necessities
Recycled endlessly
As yellow ribbon

The computers spit out
Inventories of foreshortened amnesia
Long lists of metaphors now obsolete
Willing acceptance of the reprehensible
Lite War
Reports of suffering
Enough to satisfy
But low on passion

You must give up outmoded ideas
New and improved
Marinetti to Super Mario III
Forget
Honor or hygiene

Flushing the planet with
Blood
It's cleaner to think of
Punitive surgery
Competition
Forget it   old hat
Sort of like a lethal Olympics
Strategy   A game of checks
A commerce cruel enough to make E. F. Hutton
Hard sell canard
Shut up but not shut down
Patriotism of the ploy du jour?
The boys in the backroom
Will come up with an ideology
If that still gets it

A 24-7 sideshow
No business but police business
It's never out it's never over
Is what remains, a bit of theatre
Going on all the time

A murderous roadshow
With out-of-town tryouts
For smart bombs and stealth politicians
Without a Broadway to go to

If history can still be understood as a record of the deeds of leaders, then recent history of the United States is the record of bizarre plots and frantic attempts to cover their behinds performed by an amazingly conscienceless batch of born-again hypocrites and felons-in-waiting. Shameless and possibly insane, these men have presided over the decay of both cities and countryside and the demoralization of citizens facing a plummeting standard of living.

If history is properly a narrative of the collective tropism of masses of people, then our recent history is the tale of a populace mesmerized by ever more technically elaborate and intellectually vacuous entertainments designed to distract them from their deepening poverty.

All of the traditional events of the Olympic games are, in fact, martial arts. The rationale of the games, however, is the display of martial prowess in the interest of intertribal nonbelligerence. If these "war games" can, in fact, be construed as simultaneous competition and international cooperation, we have a perfect model for conceptual confusion that can do much more than merely stimulate sales of beer, exercise clothing, and motor vehicles.

For a population addicted to entertainment, demented leaders have invented real war presented as games. The names should be familiar: Grenada, Panama, Kuwait (or Iraq). There are also the minor league games: El Salvador, Nicaragua. Then there's the really funky training camp called Bosnia. Somehow, if you ask folks, you'll find that most people know more details about the 1956 World Series than about any of these campaigns. But each one was presented in the papers and on radio and tv just like the real thing and—of course—for the unfortunate human beings maimed or killed in those places, it *was* the real thing.

In *Nineteen Eighty-Four* George Orwell showed how leaders could manipulate populations by preying upon a usefully inarticulate combination of patriotism and self-interest. Ray Bradbury's *Fahrenheit 451* went further in showing the way that scapegoating becomes the instrumentality of such a system. The current permanent crisis provides opportunity for ambitious men to keep busy while thinking they are performing historic deeds; and the public, fitfully distracted by incomprehensible events occurring in never-heard-of places, remains confused. Gore Vidal, educated to find causes for effects, has guessed that the transformation of the United States into a "national security state" in the late 1940s explains the subsequent armed adventures of the past decade, but that means taking these escapades seriously. Actually, the old Roman recipe for ruling is at work: keep the people in line with bread and circuses.

Less bread, more circuses. When there's really nothing worth seeing, the show goes on all night long.

PUBLICATION: *Knowledge* (1998), 10:71–73.

KEYWORDS: African American poetics; politics; cultural studies; media.

LINKS: Ben Friedlander, "Lyrical Interference" (*PJ* 9); Félix Guattari, "Language, Consciousness, and Society" (*PJ* 9); Lyn Hejinian, "An American Opener" (*PJ* 1); Harryette Mullen, "Miscegentated Texts and Media Cyborgs: Technologies of Body and Soul" (*Guide*; *PJ* 9); Kofi Natambu, "The Multicultural Aesthetic: Language, 'Art,' and Politics in the United States Today" (*PJ* 9); Delphine Perret, "Irony" (*PJ* 3); Kit Robinson, "Pleasanton/Embassy Suite" (*PJ* 10); Andrew Ross, "The Oxygen of Publicity" (*PJ* 6).

SELECTED BIBLIOGRAPHY: *Sing the Sun Up: Creative Writing Ideas from African-American Literature* (New York: Teachers and Writers, 1998); *Extraordinary Measures: Afro-Centric Modernism and 20th-Century American Poetry* (Tuscaloosa: University of Alabama Press, 2000); *Don't Deny My Name: Words and Music and the Black Intellectual Tradition* (Ann Arbor: University of Michigan Press, 2008); *Chances Are Few* (Berkeley: Blue Wind, 1979; 2nd ed., 2003); *The Bathers* (New York: I. Reed Books, 1981); *There Are Witnesses* (Osnabrück, Germany: OBEMA, 1996); *Dancing on Main Street* (Minneapolis: Coffee House, 2004).

Thinking You Know

Constructing a rich interpretive framework for John Ashbery's "Farm Implements and Rutabagas in a Landscape," art historian Reva Wolf questions how decisive such contexts can be
for reading the poem. Specifically, she wants to know whether it was possible for Ashbery
to have seen a certain painting by Andy Warhol (*Popeye*, 1962) that depicts the hero of his
poem and also contains the phrase "farm implements" (in a fragment of a crossword puzzle). Should that evidence as historical determine our reading of the poem? Ashbery himself
denied knowing the painting, crediting the phrase to his writing for *ArtNews* on a Dutch
landscape painting, *Farm Implement and Vegetables in a Landscape*. What would constitute
reliable knowledge of the sources and contexts of the poem? Wolf's account engages several kinds of knowledge: first, the everyday knowledge of experience that presents us with
what she terms "unexceptional yet utterly strange epistemological dilemmas"; second,
knowledge of the sources from which an artist or writer draws his or her materials, and why
they enter the work; and finally, knowledge of what a work is about, its meaning. In Wolf's
critical detective story, Ashbery's social life, art writing, and knowledge of painting all provide evidence, even while "in the end, the discovery must remain unsure."

Is it possible to know something and then again to not really know it? A great
deal of the knowledge we possess contains this sort of uncertainty. Think of
the way we "know" circumstances when we take a position on a political
issue. Or of the way we "know" friends and acquaintances when we assess
their motives or the nature of their personal struggles. The kinds of understanding that we gain from such knowledge are important—they contribute
to our behavior and attitudes toward the events and people of our lives.

The shaky status of this day-to-day knowledge is a recurrent topic in John
Ashbery's poetry. Clues, coded messages, and puzzles the reader cannot solve
are in Ashbery's writing especially effective metaphors for our altogether unexceptional yet utterly strange epistemological dilemmas. These metaphors
are effective because they nudge the reader—often annoyingly—to experience something similar to the author's own struggles with the limits and
limitations of knowledge.[1] But what happens when a reader thinks he or she
has actually pieced together clues in an Ashbery poem and has found a meaningful reference? Does the purported discovery take away from the power of

the poem? Or does it add to it? And what about the unsure status of the discovery? These are some of the questions I was led to raise after spending a long time thinking about Ashbery's poem "Farm Implements and Rutabagas in a Landscape."

"Farm Implements" was first published in *Paris Review* in 1967.[2] Ashbery later included the poem in *The Double Dream of Spring* (1970), which has as one of its leitmotifs duplicity, as the word "double" in the title quietly intimates. The title poem is in itself a double: it is the title both of the poem and of a painting by Giorgio de Chirico (1915) in the collection of the Museum of Modern Art, as Ashbery acknowledges in an author's note.[3] The title "Farm Implements and Rutabagas in a Landscape," too, has a double in the visual arts, as will soon become evident, although the source of this title is unacknowledged by the author, and is concealed.

The characters in this amusing poem are Popeye, Olive Oyl, their family, and their coterie of strange friends. On the surface, the only evident link between the landscape of the title and the comic-strip drama that unfolds in the poem is in the general theme of rural imagery—"it was cheaper in the country"; "it sure was pleasant to spend a day in the country." (However, the narrative occurs not in the country but in Popeye's urban dwelling, and this confusion of locations is consistent with the general theme of duplicity.)

The title seems more directly related to the poem if the whole is understood in relation to a painting of Popeye made by Andy Warhol in 1961 (fig. 1). In this hand-painted work, Warhol superimposed a representation of Popeye onto a depiction of another feature of the entertainment pages of the newspaper, a crossword puzzle. Only a fragment of this puzzle is visible, and only three clues (which themselves function as a Dada-like poem): "award," "farm implements," "distress." The two words of the second clue, "farm implements," are also the first two words of Ashbery's poem. The combination in both the painting and the poem of Popeye and "farm implements" appears, then, to be a hidden link between the title of the poem and its ostensible subject.

Indeed, Ashbery has produced a kind of verbal translation of Warhol's Popeye/crossword superimposition. As a parallel to the crossword in the painting, the narrative of the poem begins with a word puzzle: "The first of the undecoded messages read: 'Popeye sits in thunder.'" And on the third line, a Chinese puzzle allows for an escape from a tenement apartment to a more expansive environment (of the mind?): "a tangram emerges: a country."

The structure of the poem, a sestina, itself resembles a puzzle. In a sestina, the last word of each of the six lines in the first stanza are repeated in the re-

Figure 1. Andy Warhol, Popeye. *Collection Mr. and Mrs. S. I. Newhouse, Jr. © 2010 Andy Warhol Foundation for the Visual Arts/Artists Rights Society (ARS), New York. Reproduced by permission.*

maining stanzas in a regulated shifting order (in Ashbery's poem, the six end-words are: *thunder, apartment, country, pleasant, scratched, spinach*). There is a final stanza of three lines, in which three of the endwords fall at the end of the line, and three in the middle. The endwords, then, are filled in, somewhat like the answers to clues in a crossword puzzle. In "Farm Implements," as in the crossword puzzle, these answers do not seem to add up to anything more than a bit of pleasure, a distraction, as the ribald final stanza of Ashbery's poem implies (see fig. 4).

Just as Warhol uses preexisting imagery, so Ashbery uses preexisting poetic formats, but also preexisting arrangements of words. A conspicuous example is found in the ironic *"For this is my country"* of the second stanza. Also plundered, as Ashbery himself has pointed out, is a comic strip of Popeye published in the New York Spanish-language newspaper *El diario* (fig. 2): "'How pleasant / To spend one's vacation *en la casa de Popeye*.'"[4] It is interesting that these two appropriated passages are set apart from the rest of the text through being italicized; the reference to citizenship in the United States together with the Spanish words bring to mind the situation of immigrants in New York, who often must live in small apartments such as the one in which Popeye resides. Popeye himself is an uprooted figure ("'Popeye, forced as you / know to flee the country / One musty gusty evening, by the schemes of his wizened, duplicate / father'"). In one sense, Ashbery's poem is about how various cultures intersect, appropriate, and/or parallel one another.

A parallel between Ashbery's poetic language and the peculiarities of Popeye's English has been explained by Ashbery in an interview: "Popeye's malapropisms ... might be another reason why I find him interesting, since I tend to dislocate language myself."[5] The comparison of comic strip language to poetry had been in Ashbery's mind for many years, and is found in a poem from his first book, *Some Trees* (1956):

The shutter clicked. Though I was wrong,
Still, as the loveliest feelings

Must soon find words, and these, yes,
Displace them, so I am not wrong
In calling this comic version of myself
The true one.[6]

The title of this poem, "The Picture of Little J. A. in a Prospect of Flowers," which is based on the title of a poem by Andrew Marvell,[7] in all likelihood doubles as an allusion to Captain Marvel and the Marvel Family, thereby producing another equation of poetry with comics.

In "The Picture of Little J. A.," Ashbery's comic self, like Popeye, transforms ordinary language. This comic self is perhaps Dick Tracy, as a character named "Dick" in the poem suggests. Dick Tracy—along with Popeye and other figures of popular culture—also appears, in the guise of a statue, in a collaborative poem by Ashbery and Kenneth Koch entitled "Death Paints a Picture," published in 1958.[8] Dick Tracy can be understood as one of Ashbery's many poetic

Figure 2. El diario, *Sunday supplement to* La prensa, *16 April 1967. Houghton Library, Harvard University, Ashbery Papers, AM 6. Reproduced by permission.*

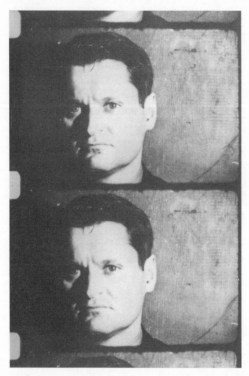

Figure 3. Andy Warhol, John Ashbery, *film portrait frame enlargement, ca. 1965–66.*
© 2013 The Andy Warhol Museum, Pittsburgh. Reproduced by permission.

alter egos. When Andy Warhol made a "screen test," or film portrait, of Ashbery around 1965–66 (fig. 3), either Warhol or Ashbery, according to a later report, had described Ashbery "as kind of having a Dick Tracy profile—he has a kind of square face and nose."[9]

The detective is an apposite identity for a poet whose writing is cluttered with clues, hidden meanings, and puzzle pieces. Inquisitive readers are prompted to attempt to make sense of this kind of imagery, an activity that casts them, too, in the role of detective—and the search for knowledge becomes detective work. In an intriguing essay, "Clues: Roots of an Evidential Paradigm," Carlo Ginzburg observes that three figures—Sherlock Holmes, the art historian Giovanni Morelli, and Sigmund Freud—each used, at the same moment in history, a method of piecing together minute and hidden clues to intuitively determine, respectively, who the criminal is, whether a painting is authentic, and why psychological trauma occurs.[10] The clues in "Farm Implements and Rutabagas in a Landscape" are precisely what lead readers to find "evidence"—meaning, really—not only within the poem itself, but also outside it, such as in the connection with Warhol's *Popeye*.

As a character, the detective may likewise be duplicitous, and is often required to hide his or her identity in order to obtain clues. In "Farm Implements" the poet plays out this role by producing several types of doubles, including a sexual duplicity. The *El diario* comic strip quoted in "Farm Implements" shows the Sea Hag wearing a tie and Popeye in a dress and bonnet, disguised as Swee' Pea's grandmother. Popeye, moreover, is a sailor; the sailor is often an object of homosexual desire (as in, to cite one in a large number of examples, Kenneth Anger's 1947 film *Fireworks*).[11]

Warhol's depiction of Popeye is a double, too, along with the one appearing in the first frame of the *El diario* comic strip—both of these having been derived from an earlier "original," namely, the first frame of the strip as it appeared in a newspaper in English. This doubling up of references creates ambiguities concerning the origins of the poet's words—the point being that their origins are only knowable to an (unmeasurable) extent.

The preceding analysis is based on the assumption that the words "Farm Implements" of Ashbery's title were copied from Warhol's painting. Yet Ashbery has claimed that his poem has no connection whatsoever to the Warhol painting, and that he saw the painting for the first time at the "Andy Warhol: A Retrospective" exhibition held at the Museum of Modern Art in 1989.[12] According to Ashbery, the title of his poem was taken, rather, from a Dutch old master painting; he came upon this title while, as executive editor of *ARTnews*, he was routinely looking through auction catalogues for works to list in the magazine's monthly column on the highlights of upcoming auctions. The title appealed to him, and eventually he used it in his poem.[13]

Indeed, among the titles included in the column on upcoming auctions in the March 1966 issue of *ARTnews* is *Farm Implements and Vegetables in a Landscape*, a painting by the seventeenth-century artist Salomon van Ruysdael.[14] This is the title that appears on the manuscript of Ashbery's poem (fig. 4); at some point he decided to change "Vegetables" to the more quirky "Rutabagas." But the title of the Ruysdael painting is a double of sorts, too.

Going back one step further, to Ashbery's initial discovery of this title in a Christie's auction catalogue, reveals that he invented the title published in *ARTnews*. The Christie's catalogue lists this work as *A Wheelbarrow, Baskets of Vegetables, and Implements in a Landscape*,[15] a longer title than the one appearing in *ARTnews* and in the poem. The editing of the title may well have been a result of having to make it fit into the rather short *ARTnews* column, a

Farm Implements and Vegetables in a Landscape

The first of the undecoded messages read: "Popeye sits in thunder,
Unthought-of. From that shoe-box of an apartment,
From livid curtain's hue, a tanagram emerges: a country."
Meanwhile the Sea Hag was relaxing on a green couch: "How pleasant
To spend one's vacation en la casa de Popeye," she scratched
Her cleft chin's solitary hair. She remembered spinach

And was going to ask Wimpy if he h ad bought any spinach.
"M'love," he intercepted, "the plains are decked out in thunder
Today, and it shall be as you wish·." He scratched
The part of his head under his hat. The apartment
Seemed to grow smaller. "But what if no pleasant
Inspiration plunge us now to the stars? For this is my country."

Suddenly they remembered how it was cheaper in the country.
Wimpy was thoughtfully cutting open a number 2 can of spinach
When the door opened and Swee'pea crept in. "How pleasant!"
But Swee'pea looked morose. A note was pinned to his bib. "Thunder
And tears are unavailing," it read. "Henceforth shall Popeye's apartment
Be but remembered space, dry or wet, toxic or salubrious, whole or scratched."

Olive came hurtling through the window: its geraniums scratched
Her long thigh. "I have news!" she gasped. "Popeye, forced to leave the country,
As you know, by the machinations of his wizened, duplicate father, the spinach
King and die-hard politico, heaves bolts of loving thunder
A t his own astonished becoming, rupturing the pleasant
Arpeggio of our years. No mo re shall p leasant
Rays of the sun refresh your sense of growing old, nor the scratched
Tree-trunks and mossy foliage, only immaculate darkness and thunder."
She grabbed Swee'pea. "I'm taking the brat to the country."
"But you can't do that—he hasn't even finished his spinach,"
Urged the Sea Hag, looking fearfully around at the apartment.

But Olive was already out of earshot. Now the ap artment
Succumbed to a strange new hush. "Actually it's quite pleasant
Here," thought the Sea Hag. "If this is all we need fear from spinach
Then I don't mind so much. Perhaps we could invite Alice the Goon over"—she scratched
One dug pensively—"but Wimpy is such a country
Bumpkin, always burping like that." Minute at first, the thunder

Soon filled the apartment. It was domestic thunder,
The color of spinach. Popeye chuckled and scratched
His balls: it sure was pleasant to spend a day in the country.

Figure 4. John Ashbery, "Farm Implements and Rutabagas in a Landscape," typescript and autograph revisions, 1967. Houghton Library, Harvard University, Ashbery Papers AM 6. Reproduced by permission.

Figure 5. Ugo Mulas, Thanksgiving dinner at Robert Rauschenberg's loft, mid-1960s (detail).
From New York: The New Art Scene *(New York: Holt, Rinehart, and Winston, 1967), 28.*
Reproduced by permission.

practical function of Ashbery's job. Still, this job became, finally, part of his poetry writing process, however mundane such an operation may appear to be (and perhaps this operation is similar to the imaginative distractions that make life at the office bearable in an earlier poem, "Instruction Manual").[16]

In any case, what stands out is that the words "Farm Implements" were not part of the painting's title as Ashbery first encountered it. *He* wrote them into the title. The title thus was made to have a double reference—to the painting by Ruysdael, and to the one by Warhol.

Ashbery's statement that he never saw the painting by Warhol can be questioned in other ways as well. He would have had the opportunity to see this painting both at first hand and in reproduction. Warhol had given *Popeye* to the artist Robert Rauschenberg in 1962 (perhaps because the collagelike layout, and the combination of comic strip imagery and a loose paint handling, were indebted to Rauschenberg's own work).[17] Rauschenberg hung *Popeye* in his studio, as can be seen in a photograph of the mid 1960s showing a Thanksgiving gathering there (fig. 5). Ashbery may have seen this photograph, and he may well have seen the painting on a visit to Rauschenberg's studio. He had been an early supporter of Rauschenberg's work, and knew him personally.[18]

Throughout the later 1950s and 1960s Ashbery was a prolific art critic—writing for such venues as *Art International*, *ARTnews*, and the Paris edition of the *New York Herald Tribune*—and, as is well known, the art he reviewed often found a place in his poetry.[19] For instance, "The Double Dream of Spring," as previously noted, takes its title from a painting by de Chirico, whose work Ashbery reviewed favorably.[20] His pillagings of visual art are never descriptions of the painting or sculpture in question. Instead, they are woven into the themes of the poems in complex, associative ways. At times this complexity involves a concealment of the visual source, as with "Farm Implements and Rutabagas in a Landscape."

Ashbery had been following the career of Warhol for some years. He had become interested in the artist's work when he first saw it at a spring 1963 exhibition of pop art at the Galerie Ileana Sonnabend in Paris, where he was then living. In a review of this show, he wrote that he was surprised to find that the work of some pop artists, which he had been attracted to in reproduction, seemed weak when viewed in person, while,

> on the other hand, Warhol's Marilyn Monroe repetitions, which I had not particularly noticed in reproduction, impressed me with their strength, their hardness and their absolute uncontrovertibility. Unlike Rosenquist's and Wesselmann's ambiguity, Warhol's is unambiguous; his work makes a direct and unformulable point.[21]

Ashbery here envisioned a kindred spirit in what he saw as the paradoxes of Warhol's work—the "unambiguous" ambiguity and the "direct and unformulable point."[22] Contained within these comments is the more general theme of the limits of knowledge.

A few months after the review of the Sonnabend exhibition was published, in September 1963, during a trip to New York, Ashbery met Warhol.[23] Upon returning to Paris, Ashbery wrote an essay about Warhol's "Death and Disaster" series (paintings of car crashes, electric chairs, race riots, and the like) for the catalogue of Warhol's first one-person exhibition there. In this essay, he again expressed his fascination with how Warhol's work reflected on the limits of knowledge, especially regarding the nature of newspaper reports and photographs. Ashbery himself had already appropriated and explored the media's handling of the tragedies of contemporary life in his 1962 book *The Tennis Court Oath* (in such lines as "And all I can smell here is newsprint" and "to be dying, he gets them into magazines / and some of them mangy and rabid").[24] Discussing Warhol's use of press photographs in the silkscreen paintings, Ashbery observed that

> one cannot really say what is taking place in most of the photographs published by the press, above all when one views them like a rubbing on the surface of a kitchen table oilcloth (which is of course on par with our inability to discern the real nature of an event—what exactly happened—when we read a newspaper report). It is acknowledged that press photographs are imprecise and hardly flattering.[25]

The inaccessibility of concrete knowledge is also expressed in a lengthy and rather bleak—even though parodic—poem, "The Skaters,"[26] composed around the time of the Paris exhibit of the "Death and Disaster" paintings, and first published in late 1964.[27] As with "Farm Implements," it seems as though Warhol's imagery is embedded, in a concealed form, in the poem. Warhol's paintings *Red Race Riot* (1963, Museum Ludwig, Cologne) and *Mustard Race Riot* (1963, private collection), which were included in the "Death and Disaster" exhibit, and his use of repetition, are evoked by this passage of "The Skaters":

> and all the clumsy seductions and amateur paintings done,
> Clamber to join in the awakening
> To take a further role in my determination. These clown-shapes
> Filling up the available space for miles, like acres of red and mustard
>   pom-poms
> Dusted with a pollen we call "an air of truth." Massed mounds
> Of Hades it is true. I propose a general housecleaning
> Of these true and valueless shapes which pester us with their raisons d'être
> Whom no one (that is their weakness) can ever get to like.[28]

Though the tone here may be parodic, a feeling of agitation emerges in these (and many other) lines from "The Skaters." If the "amateur paintings," the red and mustard "clown-shapes," and the "true and valueless shapes" bring to mind Warhol's *Red Race Riot* and *Mustard Race Riot*, they do so in such a way as to imply an ambivalence about Warhol's work, or at least toward what it might signify about our culture.

The lines preceding the above-quoted passage suggest other works by Warhol, the well-known Campbell's Soup Can paintings:

> But another, more urgent question imposes itself—
>   that of poverty.

How to excuse it to oneself? The wetness and coldness?
     Dirt and grime?
Uncomfortable, unsuitable lodgings, with a depressing view?
The peeled geranium flowering in a rusted tomato can,
Framed in a sickly ray of sunlight, a tragic chromo? . . .

But to return to our tomato can—those spared by the goats
Can be made into a practical telephone, the two halves being
     connected by a length of wire.
You can talk to your friend in the next room, or around corners.
An American inventor made a fortune with just such a contraption.[29]

While the framed, rusted tomato can seems to allude to the Campbell's Soup Can pictures, the "American Inventor" may well refer to Warhol.[30] And again, bleakness figures in the sociological diagnosis, although this time in the form of an unanswered question: "a tragic chromo?"[31] Who can judge? On what kind of knowledge are such judgments based?

The passage about the tomato can is especially resonant in connection with the "Farm Implements" poem. It appears as part of a description of the apartment of a poverty-ridden individual. These "unsuitable lodgings" have a counterpart in Popeye's "shoebox of an apartment." In each instance, Ashbery has associated pop art with the poverty—both material and spiritual—of modern urban life. This association implies a judgment, but at the same time judgment is withheld. The value of things is known, and yet not knowable.

Another association found in "Farm Implements" as well as in "The Skaters" is between pop art and seventeenth-century Dutch painting. We have seen that the title "Farm Implements and Rutabagas in a Landscape" links up a Warhol painting with one by Ruysdael. Skaters are a common subject of Dutch painting. It is interesting that Hendrick Avercamp's skaters are discussed by Roland Barthes in an essay appearing in the same issue of *Art and Literature* as the poem "The Skaters"[32]—Ashbery was a co-editor of this journal. Interesting, too, is the fact that Barthes discusses these depictions of skaters as examples of how the lower classes were represented in the seventeenth century; these same social strata are evoked by the "unsuitable lodgings" with the framed tomato can in "The Skaters," which contain, on the wall, a calendar of a Dutch girl.[33]

The connections between pop art and Dutch art, then, is a repeated theme in Ashbery's work. So, what to do with Ashbery's claim that he never saw Warhol's painting *Popeye*? One possibility is to turn to an explanation by

Margaret Atwood of the poetry-writing process, in which Ashbery has acknowledged he finds personal meaning: "I believe most poets will go to any lengths to conceal their own reluctant scanty insight both from others and from themselves."[34] With Ashbery, this act of concealment, as it operates in his poetry, is his way of getting the reader to feel with him the uncertainties of his judgments about art, poetry, people, both on the personal level and epistemologically.

Uncertainty is one of the things that happens when a reader thinks he or she has actually pieced together a puzzle in an Ashbery poem. Regarding the question of whether the purported discovery—a source for the poem "Farm Implements" in Warhol's painting of *Popeye*—takes away from or adds to the power of the writing, my answer is that it adds to it. It opens up one of the numerous, intersecting worlds of reference that Ashbery has drawn upon in his work. It gives us a sense of his working process. And all this, in turn, expands our sense of the poetry, allowing it to spill out into the world. However, in the end the discovery may remain unsure. This discovery is, nonetheless, a kind of knowledge, perhaps the most common kind.[35]

NOTES

1 It has been claimed that these struggles make Ashbery's work superior to poems by contemporaries that lack uncertainty and have a clear subject; see Geoff Ward, *Statutes of Liberty: The New York School of Poets* (New York: St. Martin's Press, 1993), 84.

2 John Ashbery, "Farm Implements and Rutabagas in a Landscape," *Paris Review* 11 (Summer–Fall 1967): 84–85.

3 John Ashbery, *The Double Dream of Spring* (1970; New York: Ecco Press, 1976), 95. Another double embedded in the title concerns the authorship of de Chirico's painting, which de Chirico claimed was a forgery according to a 1946 account in *Time*; then, in 1949 he pronounced that it was painted by him, and that he had been misquoted by the *Time* reporter; see James Thrall Soby, *Giorgio de Chirico* (New York: Museum of Modern Art, n.d.), 106. A discussion of this story in connection to Ashbery's work is found in Fred Moramarco, "John Ashbery and Frank O'Hara: The Painterly Poets," *Journal of Modern Literature* 5 (September 1976): 457. On Ashbery's attraction to de Chirico's painting as a confrontation with epistemological questions, see W. S. Piero, "John Ashbery: The Romantic as Problem Solver," *American Poetry Review* 1 (August–September 1973): 39; and on his use of titles of works of art as a way of posing questions about authenticity and imposture, see Lee Edelman, "The Pose of Imposture: Ashbery's 'Self-Portrait in a Convex Mirror,'" *Twentieth Century Literature* 32 (Spring 1986): 95–97.

4 See David K. Kermani, *John Ashbery: A Comprehensive Bibliography, Including His Art Criticism, and with Selected Notes from Unpublished Materials*, foreword by Ashbery (New York: Garland Publishing, 1976), 85; quoted by Kermani from his unpublished interview with Ashbery, 2 June 1974, Oral History Collection, Columbia University. The page of *El diario* quoted by Ashbery has been reproduced by Helen Vendler, "Ashbery and Popeye," in *The Marks in the Fields: Essays on the Uses of Manuscripts*, ed. Rodney G. Dennis with Elizabeth Falsey (Cambridge, Mass.: Houghton Library, 1992), 165.

5 Interview by Kermani, 2 June 1974 (as in note above), 86.

6 John Ashbery, *Some Trees* (1956; New York: Ecco Press, 1978), 29; originally published in *Partisan Review* 18 (July–August 1951): 420–21.

7 Ashbery, *Some Trees*, 27. On Ashbery's adaption of this title from Marvell's "The Picture of Little T. C. in a Prospect of Flowers," see Kermani, *Ashbery*, 72.

8 "Poets on Painting," *ARTnews* 57 (September 1958): 24, 63.

9 Gerard Malanga, interview by the author, New York, 15 August 1989, tape recording.

10 In Carlo Ginzburg, *Clues, Myths, and the Historical Method*, trans. J. and A. C. Tedeschi (Baltimore: Johns Hopkins University Press, 1989), 96–125.

11 It would be simplistic to conclude, as one scholar recently did, that the use of comic strip figures such as Popeye on the part of pop artists served only to perpetuate stereotypes of male power; whether this occurs depends upon who is looking at the painting (or reading the poem). The argument that paintings such as Warhol's *Popeye* and *Dick Tracy* (1960) served to reinforce the political status quo is found in Christin J. Mamiya, *Pop Art and Consumer Culture: American Super Market* (Austin: University of Texas Press, 1992), 96–98. Mamiya views Dick Tracy's "firmly set jaw," as it appears in Warhol's painting, as a sign of "strength and moral fiber," while, on the other hand, the art critic David Bourdon has understood this jaw as a type that "Warhol typically found so attractive in men," in *Warhol* (New York: Abrams, 1989), 72. And in an alarmist study of 1954, *Seduction of the Innocent*, the psychiatrist Fredric Wertham warned that some comic strips were homoerotic; see William W. Savage, Jr., *Comic Books and America, 1945–1954* (Norman: University of Oklahoma Press, 1990), 97. For a recent assessment of the homosexual content of *Popeye* and *Dick Tracy*, see Michael Moon, "Screen Memories; or, Pop Comes from the Outside: Warhol and Queer Childhood," in *Pop Out: Queer Warhol*, ed. Jennifer Doyle, Jonathan Flatley, and José Esteban Muñoz (Durham, N.C.: Duke University Press, 1996), 78–100.

12 Telephone conversation with the author, 25 July 1989.

13 On Ashbery's practice of using titles as springboards for poems, see Janet Bloom and Robert Losada, "Craft Interview with John Ashbery," in *The Craft of Poetry: Interviews from "The New York Quarterly,"* ed. William Packard (Garden City, N.Y.: Doubleday, 1974), 111–12; and David Lehman, "The Shield of a Greeting: The Function of

Irony in John Ashbery's Poetry," in *Beyond Amazement: New Essays on John Ashbery*, ed. Lehman (Ithaca, N.Y.: Cornell University Press, 1980), 111.

14 "Sales in London," *ARTnews* 65 (March 1966): 28.

15 *Catalogue of Pictures by Old Masters: The Properties of*... (London: Christie, Manson, and Wood, Ltd., 1966), 17, no. 63 (auction of 4 March 1966).

16 Ashbery, "Instruction Manual," *Some Trees*, 14–18.

17 Rauschenberg sold the painting in 1985; see Andy Warhol, *The Andy Warhol Diaries*, ed. Pat Hackett (New York: Warner Books, 1989), 631. On the relationship between Warhol's comic strip paintings of 1960–61 and Rauschenberg's work, see Bradford R. Collins, "The Metaphysical Nosejob: The Remaking of Warhola, 1960–1968," *Arts* 62 (February 1988): 48 and 54, n. 17.

18 Reviews by Ashbery of Rauschenberg's work include: *ARTnews* 57 (March 1958): 40, 56–57; "Paris Notes," *Art International* 7 (25 February 1963): 72–76; and *New York Herald Tribune*, Paris Edition, 26 July 1961, 4; 19 September 1962, 5; 13 February 1963, 5; and 23 June 1964, 5. Connections between Rauschenberg's work and Ashbery's poetry have been discussed in Moramarco, "Ashbery and O'Hara," 455–56; Charles Altieri, "John Ashbery and the Challenge of Postmodernism in the Visual Arts," *Critical Inquiry* 14 (Summer 1988): 820–25; and John Shoptaw, *On the Outside Looking Out: John Ashbery's Poetry* (Cambridge, Mass.: Harvard University Press, 1994), 55.

19 See David Shapiro, *John Ashbery: An Introduction to the Poetry* (New York: Columbia University Press, 1979), 21; and David Bergman's introduction to John Ashbery, *Reported Sightings: Art Chronicles, 1957–1987* (New York: Knopf, 1989), xi–xii. The existing studies of the relationships between Ashbery's poetry and work by his contemporaries in the visual arts tend to make general, conceptual comparisons, and to focus on either abstract expressionism or the work of Jasper Johns and Robert Rauschenberg. See Moramarco, "Ashbery and O'Hara," 448–62; Leslie Wolf, "The Brushstroke's Integrity: The Poetry of John Ashbery and the Art of Painting," in *Beyond Amazement*, 224–54; and Altieri, "Ashbery and Postmodernism," 805–30.

20 See, for example, John Ashbery, "The Heritage of Dada and Surrealism," *New Republic*, 1 June 1968; and "A De Chirico Retrospective," *Newsweek*, 12 April 1982; both are reprinted in *Reported Sightings*, 5–8 and 401–4 respectively.

21 John Ashbery, "Paris Notes," *Art International* 7 (25 June 1963), 76. Among the sources of Ashbery's earlier familiarity with Warhol's work through reproductions is the exhibition catalogue *New Realists* (New York: Sidney Janis Gallery, 1962), to which Ashbery had contributed an essay.

22 The possibility that Ashbery's art criticism is at least as much about his poetry as about the art being discussed is noted by Bergman, in *Reported Sightings*, xxii.

23 Ashbery met Warhol through the young poet Gerard Malanga, who at the time was Warhol's silk-screening assistant; Ashbery, telephone conversation with the author, 25 July 1989.

24 John Ashbery, from "The New Realism" and "Europe," *The Tennis Court Oath* (Middletown, Conn.: Wesleyan University Press, 1962), 60 and 80 respectively. The similarity of pop paintings to the "tone" and the "look" of poems in *The Tennis Court Oath* was noted by Shapiro, *Ashbery*, 55.

25 Author's translation; [...] *Warhol* (Paris: Galerie Ileana Sonnabend, 1964), n.p. The essay is dated 16 November 1963. For a discussion of the exhibition and its reception, see Michel Bourel, "Andy Warhol à Paris dans les années 60," *Artstudio* 8 (Spring 1988): 96–97.

26 The importance of parody in "The Skaters" is discussed by Shapiro, *Ashbery*, 93–95, 105, and 125.

27 *Art and Literature* 3 (Autumn–Winter 1964): 11–47; reprinted in Ashbery, *Rivers and Mountains* (New York: Holt, Rinehart, and Winston, 1966), 34–63.

28 Ashbery, *Rivers and Mountains*, 49.

29 Ibid., 48–49.

30 The rusted tomato can is compared to pop imagery, and Ashbery to Warhol, as a "subtle critic of the commercial world" by Shapiro, *Ashbery*, 115.

31 *Rivers and Mountains*, 36. Connected to these allusions to Warhol is a passage occurring elsewhere in "The Skaters," among a list of bad news—"The bundle of Gerard's letters"—a reference to Warhol's painting assistant. Ashbery has acknowledged that the Gerard mentioned here is Gerard Malanga; telephone conversation with the author, 25 July 1989.

32 Roland Barthes, "The World Become Thing," *Art and Literature* 3 (Autumn–Winter 1964): 153–54. On the connection of the theme of skaters to music, see Kermani, *Ashbery*, 81, and Shoptaw, *On the Outside*, 92.

33 Ashbery, *Rivers and Mountains*, 48.

34 Margaret Atwood, quoted in Shapiro, *Ashbery*, 23. On Ashbery's concealment of his most important influences as it relates to Harold Bloom's theories about the "anxiety of influence," see Ward, *Statutes of Liberty*, 120.

35 I want to thank Allen Grossman for having introduced me to Ashbery's poem in his poetry class at Brandeis University in the mid 1970s.

PUBLICATION: *Knowledge* (1998), 10:165–78.

KEYWORDS: New York School; visual art; knowledge; readings.

LINKS: Bruce Campbell, "But What Is an Adequate Vice to Limit the Liquid of This Voice" (*PJ* 9); Lyn Hejinian, "La Faustienne" (*PJ* 10); Susan Howe, "*My Emily Dickinson*, part 1" (*Guide*; *PJ* 4); Bob Perelman, "Three Case Histories: Ross's *Failure of Modernism*" (*PJ* 7); Herman Rapaport, "Poetic Rests: Ashbery, Coolidge, Scalapino" (*PJ* 10); Joan Retallack, "Blue Notes on the Know Ledge" (*PJ* 10); Andrew Ross, "The Death of Lady Day" (*Guide*; *PJ* 8); Barrett Watten, "The Literature of Surface" (*PJ* 7).

SELECTED BIBLIOGRAPHY: *Goya and the Satirical Print in England and on the Continent, 1730 to 1850* (Boston: Godine, 1991); *Andy Warhol, Poetry, and Gossip in the 1960s* (Chicago: University of Chicago Press, 1997); introduction, *I'll Be Your Mirror: The Selected Andy Warhol Interviews*, ed. Kenneth Goldsmith (New York: Da Capo, 2004).

Memory and Immorality in Musical Composition

John Zorn is the most visible jazz composer and instrumentalist to have emerged from the Lower East Side in the 1970s. In influential early works such as *Hockey*, *Locus Solus*, *The Classic Guide to Strategy*, and *Cobra*, he employed techniques of spontaneous choice, improvisation, and constraint, often with collaborators, that led to new genres of multiauthored composition that went beyond free improvisation. In this essay, Zorn argues for radical compositional approaches that maximize musical possibility. His approach is grounded in the principle of distribution rather than composition, in the sense that his pieces are built through the distribution of their musical elements (motifs, timbres, sounds). In making art this way, Zorn's goals are both aesthetic and social: hierarchies are dissolved and continually reorganized, and the tradition of the master soloist is questioned. Zorn distinguishes his decentering approach from the chance-composed works of John Cage in order to ground aesthetic practice in performative difficulty. In his work, each compositional and performative decision is contextualized by layers of alternative possibility; their complexity gives every work, every performance a unique musical meaning and social resonance. Zorn has gone on to edit three volumes of writings by musicians on their art practices.

My personal creative activity is concerned with accumulating and processing information. Day-to-day experiences creep into my work and in some ways are at the center of it. All of my activities, all of my experiences become logged somewhere in my mind or imagination—sometimes toward the front and sometimes toward the back. Sometimes they go out the back door and are never thought of again. Maybe most of them go out the back door. But plenty of experiences are left. Any idea or experience that touches me might be transformed into a musical idea. It may be a scene from a film, from a book, from a conversation, from looking at art or even something on the street. When something sparks my imagination it is remembered or written down on a slip of paper or into a notebook, and then gets transformed into a sound, musical gesture or instrumentation. When enough sufficiently different ideas have been accumulated, then begins the process of fitting the different ideas—or even scraps of ideas—together. Everything in the selection and compositional process is very much about decision making—about trying to make it all as *conscious* as I possibly can, instead of *un*conscious. I think this—

this determination to be conscious—is what one is talking about when one discusses "the person."

For example, what John Cage has done seems to me very easy—perhaps *too* easy. He can produce reams of paper covered with black dots because he doesn't have to make any kinds of decisions about them. He has surrendered the decision-making process to the chance process, throwing coins or sticks or using star charts as the basis for putting his dots on paper. One decision determining the process functions for all. This rarely produces compelling work. The music and artworks that have consistently interested me the most are those in which the decisions have been the hardest to reach—Beethoven, Van Gogh, James Joyce, Artaud, Celan. The work of these artists inherently acknowledges the vast amount of information out there from which one has to choose one's little scraps. Of course, once you have your scraps you then have to decide how to put them together, what form it will take, which ones to eliminate—you labor, sweat, and bleed over each separate little decision. That to me is the essence of creating from experience—the essence of art.

On the surface, my basic working method seems very simple—an ordered set of blocks, one following another. It's the ordering process that people seem to be the most obsessed about. Why should this follow that, and why should that then be followed by this? Although I spend an enormous amount of time determining the order of these moments, both at my desk and then later in the recording studio, on another level, once the elements have been selected it almost doesn't matter what the order actually is. Of course, personal taste can determine this—one needs a certain number of contrasts, tension and release, the piece needs to flow, and not get bogged down. Pacing is critical. But on a higher level one could almost say that once you find the space that a piece resides in, its *being in time*, the moments will actually order *themselves*. Decisions are not only obvious, they become inevitable, inescapable. Some people make the mistake of thinking of music as being strictly temporal rather than potentially spatial. Musical blocks are in some sense like elements spread out on a board—their arrangement in time gives birth to form, but if listeners can keep them in their minds, it should be possible to rearrange them. Memory can recompose any piece.

Much of my work relates more closely to the film and performance scene in New York than it does to strictly musical examples. I've done a lot of musical study, but it's important to understand the correlation between contemporary performance theater pieces and a composition like *Spillane* or *Torture Garden* (the short hardcore pieces written for Naked City).[1] Richard Foreman's

Ontological-Hysteric Theatre, Jack Smith, Ken Jacobs, Stuart Sherman were all seminal influences. In theater, arranging elements can be more a spatial than a temporal activity, even though the chronology—the *narrative*—is crucial. It is crucial in my work too. There's a certain number of elements involved, depending on the length of the piece—but is time a linear progression of these events? Or is it an energy, an energy field, that acts upon everything simultaneously? If time is a form of energy, or if energy is a form of time—then the "narrative" can be built vertically. My work can often build vertically. In fact, some thinkers are more comfortable thinking of my work in that way. When I put ideas together, one listens to them across time—but it doesn't always make musical sense. Memory informs what you're listening to at any time. It's a building process, in this sense. One hears the present and remembers the past, and as information and emotions build up vertically, questions arise.

One of my interests is in devising new methods for making music—for letting music happen. *Spillane* is a composition of idea blocks (musical moments) with the "story" intact. But in a work like *Cobra*, what is accumulated from my life experiences and ideas aren't chords, notes or genres, but *dynamics*, *relationships*—both personal and musical. The actual sound of the music that's played onstage depends entirely on who happens to be in the band at a particular performance—what instruments each musician plays and what proclivities and background they have individually. In a piece like *Cobra*, I cannot control, nor do I wish to control, every detail of what a musician plays. What I'm concerned with is the *rate* of change, the changing of densities, the flux, how the flux itself can go through flux, so it isn't even constant in its change. The best way to accomplish this with a group of improvisers who have each created a highly idiosyncratic language which is inherently unnotatable is through a democratic system which lets everybody do as they like—or gives them that impression—within a precise set of parameters and rules. In *Cobra* the players are making the decisions, and as a part of the ensemble, I make decisions too, but my main role is in transmitting information, assuring clarity, inspiring the players and keeping the energy flowing. It's a misunderstanding to view me as a conductor in the traditional sense. Audiences are so used to the notion of an autonomous musical mind, a leader who's in control of everything, that they're often blind to the reality of *Cobra*. The fact is, everyone in the group is involved in making decisions—even musicians who make no decisions are making decisions. That's the essence of the game pieces—to create a situation in which the decision-making process is predominant and persistent. It forces musicians to *choose*. It creates its own momentum, and it is the responsibility of the prompter to prevent breakdown, and to know when the danger is there in advance to circumvent it. Everyone, no matter what the particular configuration of any performance, is excited when that momentum becomes musical, but in the best performances the decisions are seemingly making themselves, as we work as a collective mind.

There are many kinds of music that interest me, and it is very rewarding to expose both the audience and the musicians themselves to new sounds, experiences, and formats. The game pieces, with different players involved in almost every performance, provide a unique social situation. Involving musicians with completely and even radically different musical interests, no less personalities, produces new musical and social situations that resonate throughout the band and audience on a variety of levels. Social context is at the center of any musical performance. In my compositional process the reality and intricacies of creating an independent society on stage is intrinsically intertwined with and as important as the actual sounds they perform.

File card compositions like *Spillane* or *Godard*, *Torture Garden* or the *New Traditions in East Asian Bar Band* pieces all have extra-musical elements to them, and can be seen in a way as theater. Notes on paper produce only music, and just sound like music to me—something crucial is absent. In the tradition of "program" music, many of my compositions have a dramatic narrative, a larger theme or subtext involved that both ties the piece together and takes it out of a "pure" music context: something that resonates for me, the musicians and the audience in a dramatic, political, social or cultural way. It's got to present a story, or, let's say, the situation of a story. When I started putting together the *Bar Band* pieces, the concept was a response to a particular style of music that had cultural resonance beyond the sounds themselves. Jazz, for example, created not only a music, but also a fashion and a spoken language—a parlance, or lingo—that the followers of the music used as signifiers. The musical language was also a shared one. From one little sheet of paper people could play music all night long. Everyone understood immediately what to do with this one little sheet of paper, and actually most times there wasn't even any paper. The rules were understood within the community itself: the melody was played at the beginning, followed by solos, maybe trades, and a possible collective moment before a return to the melody. There were also ways of relating melodic material to chord changes that had developed over the course of decades—certain ways of playing upper extensions of chords, extended chords, more complex harmonies—that were understood, accepted, challenged. There was both form and content, socially and musically worked out—and within that tight set of rules an incredible amount of creativity, expression and growth took place. Many of my works function in a similar way, as independent societies, temporarily autonomous, but rich in possibilities and invention. For the bar band pieces I created a new improvisational musical context based on an invented sociocultural situation, which brings us back to a relationship with the performance aspect of what I do in each piece—each piece as theater.

I ask myself why I do what I do. Instead of going out on the stage and giving people what they want, I try to spark thinking patterns, to raise questions. One question that persistently comes up pertains to diversity and simultaneity. I am not asking how it is that so many different elements can exist at any one time and place. But I do insist on asking why everything is continually put into convenient boxes. My concern is in finding ways of breaking those boxes apart. This is a cultural, social, musical question that is urgent and broadly resonant. Music critics should be concerned with these questions, but it seems they too have been commodified into boxes—we have jazz critics and classical music critics and pop critics. In our modern world this is counterproductive. Absurd. One does not find film critics who review only one kind of film: only comedy, action, drama or documentary films. Critics cannot experience what is real from inside their boxes. Mixing what is seen as an eclectic variety of different genres—seemingly incompatible—into my compositions defies a critic's simplistic classifications, compartments, and hierarchies. Decision making is the product of consciousness, and that kind of human activity—a person's being conscious—is the opposite of escapism. My pieces are opposed to escape.

NOTES
 1 All of the works by John Zorn named in this essay are available on Tzadik.

PUBLICATION: *The Person* (1991), 9:101–5.

KEYWORDS: avant-garde; music; performance; manifesto.

LINKS: Fred Frith, "Helter Skelter" (*PJ* 9); Carla Harryman, "What in Fact Was Originally Improvised" (*PJ* 2); Lyn Hejinian, "The Rejection of Closure" (*Guide*; *PJ* 4); "Poets Theater: Two Versions of *Collateral*" (*Guide*; *PJ* 5); Jed Rasula, "What Does This Do with You Reading?" (*PJ* 1); Andrew Schelling, "Antin's *Tuning*" (*PJ* 5); Andrew Voigt, "Sound on Silence" (*PJ* 5); Jason Weiss, "Postmodernism and Music: The Reaches" (*PJ* 7).

SELECTED BIBLIOGRAPHY/DISCOGRAPHY: *Arcana: Musicians on Music*, vols. 1–3 (ed.; New York: Granary, 2000; Hips Road, 2007, 2008); *Lacrosse* (1977); *Pool* (1980); *Hockey*

(1980); *Archery* (1981); *The Classic Guide to Strategy*, 2 vols. (1983–85); *Locus Solus* (1983); *The Big Gundown* (1986); *Cobra* (1987); with Naked City, *Naked City* (1989); *Elegy* (1992); *Kristallnacht* (1993); with Masada, *Alef* (1994); *Filmworks, 1986–1990* (1997); *New Traditions in East Asian Bar Bands* (1997); with Painkiller, *Guts of a Virgin / Buried Secrets* (1998); *Godard/Spillane* (1999); *The String Quartets* (1999); with Masada, *Live in Sevilla* (2000); with Electric Masada, *At the Mountains of Madness* (2005); with Masada String Trio, *Azazel: Book of Angels*, vol. 2 (2005); with Bar Kokhba Sextet, *Lucifer: Book of Angels*, vol. 10 (2008); with Moonchild Trio, *The Crucible* (2008).

Constellations III The Expanded Field

Barone, Dennis. "A Note on John Smith's 'Philadelphia Newspapers Read Crossways.'" Barone introduces his discovery of an early American experiment in compositional procedures, a manuscript poem(?) written between 1767 and 1771 by Philadelphia Quaker John Smith. The poem anticipates the "cut-ups" of Tzara and Burroughs, the use of chance procedures after Cage and Mac Low, and the present-day interest in Flarf and conceptual writing.

PUBLICATION: *Knowledge* (1998), 10:149–50.

KEYWORDS: Language writing; conceptualism; method; history.

LINKS: John Smith, "Philadelphia Newspapers Read Crossways" (*PJ* 10); Daniel Davidson, "Bureaucrat, My Love" (*PJ* 10); Jackson Mac Low, "*Pieces o' Six*—XII and XXIII" (*PJ* 6); Dmitrii Prigov, "Conceptualism and the West" (*PJ* 8); Kit Robinson, "Bob Cobbing's Blade" (*PJ* 1); Rod Smith, from "CIA Sentences" (*PJ* 10).

Finkelstein, Norman. "The Problem of the Self in Recent American Poetry." Finkelstein counters arguments he identifies with the differing tendencies of deep imagism and Language writing and defends the ineradicability of self in poetry. Neither alienated nor fragmented subjectivity can silence the expressive undertow that animates any significant poem.

PUBLICATION: *The Person* (1991), 9:3–10.

KEYWORDS: lyric poetry; subjectivity; postmodernism; identity.

LINKS: Rae Armantrout, "Mainstream Marginality" (*Guide*; *PJ* 6); David Benedetti, "Fear of Poetic (Social) Knowledge: Why Some People Don't Like (Language) Poetry" (*PJ* 10); Maxine Chernoff, "The Fence of Character" (*PJ* 5); Norman Fischer, "The Poetics of Lived Experience and the Concept of the Person" (*PJ* 9); Lyn Hejinian, "The Person and Description" (*PJ* 9); Kofi Natambu, "The Multicultural Aesthetic: Language, 'Art,' and Politics in the United States Today" (*PJ* 9); "Robert

Creeley and the Politics of the Person" (*PJ* 9); Leslie Scalapino and Ron Silliman, "What/Person: From an Exchange" (*Guide*; *PJ* 9); "Symposium on the Person" (*PJ* 9).

Guattari, Félix. "Language, Consciousness, and Society." In an essay written for a *glasnost*-era conference in the USSR, the antipsychoanalytic theorist addresses the production of subjectivity in the global era. He argues for a polyphonic subjectivity circulating around "modules of intensity" or "ritornellos" that are modeled on "the poet's play of language."

PUBLICATION: *The Person* (1991), 9:106–15.

KEYWORDS: psychoanalysis; language; subjectivity; collectivism.

LINKS: Félix Guattari, "Text for the Russians" (*PJ* 8); Kathy Acker, "Ugly" (*Guide*; *PJ* 7); Abigail Child, "The Exhibit and the Circulation" (*PJ* 7); Arkadii Dragomoshchenko, "I(s)" (*Guide*; *PJ* 9); George Hartley, "Althusser Metonymy China Wall" (*PJ* 10); Yulia Latinina, "Folklore and 'Novoyaz'" (*PJ* 9); Harryette Mullen, "Miscegenated Texts and Media Cyborgs: Technologies of Body and Soul" (*Guide*; *PJ* 9); Lev Rubinshtein, "Momma Was Washing the Window Frame" (*PJ* 8).

Howe, Fanny. "Purgatory: All from Nothing." Howe charts the relation of Purgatory as a metaphysical "nonplace" to the literatures of dispersal and exile, in particular the modernism of Joyce and Beckett. The "turn to religion"—the necessity for considering the religious underpinnings of modernity—intersects the *via negativa* of poetic representation.

PUBLICATION: *Elsewhere* (1989), 8:92–94.

KEYWORDS: religion; modernism; metaphysics; space.

LINKS: Fanny Howe, "Silliman's *Paradise*" (*PJ* 6); Mikhail Dziubenko, "'New Poetry' and Perspectives for Philology" (*PJ* 8); Norman Fischer, "The Old City" (*PJ* 8); Paul A. Green, "Elsewhere" (*PJ* 8); Inagawa Masato, "For a Biography of the Redeemed" (*PJ* 8); Jed Rasula, "On Rothenberg's Revised *Technicians of the Sacred*" (*PJ* 6); Nathaniel Tarn, "Exile out of Silence into Cunning" (*PJ* 8).

Latinina, Yulia. "Folklore and 'Novoyaz.'" Latinina examines the folkloric aspects of Soviet ideology under Stalin. Premodern Russian folklore, as a "primordially collective" set of representations, intersected with state ideology, which in its formulaic repetition became a kind of folklore in itself. Soviet collectivity occurred as a system of cultural metaphors.

PUBLICATION: *The Person* (1991), 9:116–26.

KEYWORDS: ideology; linguistics; Russian poetics; cultural studies.

LINKS: Michael Davidson, "'Hey Man, My Wave!': The Authority of Private Language" (*Guide*; *PJ* 6); Félix Guattari, "Text for the Russians" (*PJ* 8); George Lakoff, "The Public Aspect of the Language of Love" (*PJ* 6); Bob Perelman, "Good and Bad/Good and Evil: Pound, Céline, and Fascism" (*Guide*; *PJ* 6); Viktor Shklovsky, "Plotless Literature: Vasily Rozanov" (*Guide*; *PJ* 1).

"The Poetics of Everyday Life." The contributors to this 1988 symposium— Lyn Hejinian, Michael Davidson, Norman Fischer, Jerry Estrin, Bill Luoma, Ben Friedlander, and Dodie Bellamy—explore diverse approaches to representing experience in literary form. Everyday life is described in terms of: personhood; ideology; self-reflexivity; unrepresentability; architecture; late capitalism; complex "states of affairs"; lyric presence; and sexual desire.

PUBLICATION: *The Person* (1991), 9:166–205.

KEYWORDS: experience; subjectivity; postmodernism; time.

LINKS: Ed Friedman, "How *Space Stations* Gets Written" (*PJ* 5); "Robert Creeley and the Politics of the Person" (*PJ* 9); Kit Robinson, "Time and Materials: The Workplace, Dreams, and Writing" (*Guide*; *PJ* 9); "Symposium on Narrative" (*PJ* 5); "Symposium on the Person" (*PJ* 9); "Symposium: Postmodern?" (*PJ* 7); Robin Winters, "Landlords / do not ..." (*PJ* 6); John Woodall, "The Maze System" (*PJ* 9).

Prigov, Dimitrii. "Conceptualism and the West." Prigov claims there is a fundamental distinction between Western conceptual art and Moscow conceptualism. While the former reflects the ubiquity of the commodity form, the latter reflects a culture from which things have been abstracted, in the absence of the commodity, leaving language in their place.

PUBLICATION: *Elsewhere* (1989), 8:12–16.

KEYWORDS: Russian poetics; conceptualism; postmodernism; critical theory.

LINKS: Erik Bulatov, *I Am Going*; *Disappearing Clouds* (*PJ* 8); Margaret Crane and Jon Winet, from *This Is Your Life* (*PJ* 9); Tina Darragh, "Error Message" (*PJ* 5); Jerry Estrin, "Cold Heaven: The Uses of Monumentality" (*Guide*; *PJ* 9); Connie Fitzsimons, *The Oath* (*PJ* 7); Howard Fried, "The Museum Reaction Piece" (*PJ* 5); Doug Hall, "The Bridesmaid" (detail from *Steps of City Hall, San Francisco*) (*PJ* 10); Carla Harryman, "Pedestal/Tulip Chair," from *Chairs of Words* (*PJ* 10); Lev Rubinshtein, "Momma Was Washing the Window Frame" (*PJ* 8); Fiona Templeton, "My Work Telling the Story of Narrative in It" (*PJ* 5); Barrett Watten, "On Explanation: Art and the Language of *Art-Language*" (*PJ* 3); John Woodall, detail from *Gim-Crack* (*PJ* 9).

Retallack, Joan. "Blue Notes on the Know Ledge." Retallack's essay on the epistemology of blue, or the blue of epistemology, is a postmodern improvisation employing provocative wordplay and multiple juxtapositions. The result, an instance of "poethics," is a polysemic indictment of universal knowledge and a polyphonic invitation to a contrary field of play.

PUBLICATION: *Knowledge* (1998), 10:39–54.

KEYWORDS: philosophy; feminism; knowledge; method.

LINKS: Richard Blevins, "'The Single Intelligence': The Formation of Robert Creeley's Epistemology" (*PJ* 9); Beverly Dahlen, "Forbidden Knowledge" (*Guide*; *PJ* 4); Johanna Drucker, "Women and Language" (*PJ* 4); Lyn Hejinian, "La Faustienne" (*PJ* 10); Erica Hunt, "Beginning at *Bottom*" (*PJ* 3); Ted Pearson, "Things Made Known" (*PJ* 10); Reva Wolf, "Thinking You Know" (*Guide*; *PJ* 10).

"Robert Creeley and the Politics of the Person." Five poets/critics—Barrett Watten, Richard Blevins, Alan Davies, Susan Howe, and Ted Pearson— take up the status of "the person" in Robert Creeley's autobiographical poetry. Imbued with spontaneous dynamics and a skeptical relation to knowledge, personhood in Creeley represents: presentist language; "single intelligence"; emotional immediacy; homosociality; and a defense of authorship.

PUBLICATION: *The Person* (1991), 9:138–65.

KEYWORDS: New American poetry; subjectivity; lyric poetry; gender.

LINKS: William Corbett, "Harwood/Walker and Raworth" (*PJ* 2); Alan Davies, "Motor Mouth" (*PJ* 5); Norman Finkelstein, "The Problem of the Self in Recent American Poetry" (*PJ* 9); Ben Friedlander, "Lyrical Interference" (*PJ* 9); Robert Glück, "Fame" (*PJ* 10); Jackson Mac Low, "Some Ways Philosophy Has Helped to Shape My Work" (*Guide*; *PJ* 3); Ted Pearson, "Unit Structures" (*PJ* 5); Laura Moriarty, "The Modern Lyric" (*PJ* 7); Ron Silliman, "The Dysfunction of Criticism: Poets and the Critical Tradition of the Anti-Academy" (*PJ* 10); "Symposium on the Person" (*PJ* 9); Barrett Watten, "What I See in *How I Became Hettie Jones*" (*PJ* 10).

Rosenberg, Jim. "Openings: The Connection Direct." Rosenberg's 1991 essay is an early, utopian forecast of the dawn of the digital age. New media's interactivity and hypertextuality will extend possibilities of writing into unforeseen (but now enacted) possibilities, fully realizing its open, nonlinear potential: "We haven't yet learned to start writing."

PUBLICATION: *Knowledge* (1998), 10:236–43.

KEYWORDS: media; postmodernism; writing; method.

LINKS: Pierre Alferi, "Seeking a Sentence" (*Guide*; *PJ* 10); Bruce Andrews, "Total Equals What: Poetics and Praxis" (*Guide*; *PJ* 6); Dennis Barone, "A Note on John Smith's 'Philadelphia Newspapers Read Crossways'" (*PJ* 10); Johanna Drucker, "Hypergraphy: A Note on Maurice Lemaître's *Roman Hypergraphique*" (*Guide*; *PJ* 6); Tom Mandel, "Codes/Texts: Reading *S/Z*" (*PJ* 2); Nick Piombino, "Towards an Experiential Syntax" (*PJ* 5); Joan Retallack, "Blue Notes on the Know Ledge" (*PJ* 10); Kit Robinson, "Pleasanton/Embassy Suite" (*PJ* 10); John Zorn, "Memory and Immorality in Musical Composition" (*Guide*; *PJ* 9).

Shurin, Aaron. "The Irruptive Text." As an alternative to the diminished referentiality of postmodern signification, Shurin locates a "romance of the referent" in H. Ryder Haggard's fiction as a model for his textual encounters with contemporary poets like Ronald Johnson, David Melnick, and Michael Palmer. Texts become erotic landscapes of discovery.

PUBLICATION: *Elsewhere* (1989), 8:87–91.

KEYWORDS: narrative; queer; meaning; readings.

LINKS: Aaron Shurin, "As Known" (*PJ* 9); "Orphée: The Kiss of Death" (*PJ* 10); Leslie Scalapino, "Aaron Shurin's *Elsewhere*" (*PJ* 8); Dodie Bellamy, "Can't We Just Call It Sex?: In Memory of David Wojnarowicz" (*Guide*; *PJ* 10); Steve Benson, "Personal as Social History: Three Fictions" (*PJ* 7); Bruce Boone, "A Narrative Like a Punk Picture: Shocking Pinks, Lavenders, Magentas, Sickly Greens" (*PJ* 5); Robert Glück, "His Heart Is a Lute Held Up: Poe and Bataille" (*Guide*; *PJ* 2); Laura Moriarty, "Sex and Language" (*PJ* 8); Andrew Ross, "The Death of Lady Day" (*Guide*; *PJ* 8); Warren Sonbert, "Narrative Concerns" (*Guide*; *PJ* 5).

Toscano, Rodrigo. "Early Morning Prompts for Evening Takes; or, Roll 'Em." Toscano presents a montage of challenges and hesitations, in a form of dialectical questioning, to demands of poetry and politics. As praxis, the poem works through aspects of negativity that lurk in the poet's relation to gender, class, community, and work—as an invocation to action.

PUBLICATION: *Knowledge* (1998), 10:223–25.

KEYWORDS: poetry; critical theory; subjectivity; negativity.

LINKS: Michael Davidson, seven poems (*PJ* 10); Jean Day, "Moving Object" (*PJ* 9); Michael Gottlieb, five poems (*PJ* 10); Pamela Lu, from "Intermusement" (*PJ* 10); Bill Luoma, "Astrophysics and You" (*PJ* 9); Travis Ortiz, from "variously, not then" (*PJ* 10); Lisa Samuels, two poems (*PJ* 10); Peter Seaton, "An Example from the Literature" (*Guide*; *PJ* 6); Gavin Selerie, from *Roxy* (*PJ* 8); Hung Q. Tu, "very similitude" (*PJ* 10); Chris Tysh, from "Dead Letters" (*PJ* 10).

Acknowledgments and Permissions

The editors thank Alan Golding, Lynn Keller, and Adelaide Morris for their support of *Poetics Journal* during the process of realizing the present volume and digital archive. Thanks are also due to Andrew Jaron for his help in preparing the manuscript for publication.

CREDITS

Thanks are due to the authors, editors, and executors who have granted permission for the inclusion of the materials that comprise this volume:

Kathy Acker, "Ugly." Reprinted with permission of Matias Viegener of the Kathy Acker Literary Trust

Pierre Alferi, "Seeking a Sentence." Reprinted with permission of the author and translator Joseph Simas

Bruce Andrews, "Total Equals What: Poetics and Praxis." Reprinted with permission of the author

Rae Armantrout, "Mainstream Marginality." Reprinted with permission of the author

Dodie Bellamy, "Can't We Just Call It Sex?: In Memory of David Wojnarowicz." Reprinted with permission of the author

Steve Benson, "Close Reading: Leavings and Cleavings." Reprinted with permission of the author

Charles Bernstein, "Writing and Method." Reprinted with permission of the author

Beverly Dahlen, "Forbidden Knowledge." Reprinted with permission of the author

Michael Davidson, "'Hey, Man, My Wave!': The Authority of Private Language." Reprinted with permission of the author

Alan Davies, "Language/Mind/Writing" was previously published in *Signage* (Roof: New York City, 1987). Reprinted with permission of the author

Arkadii Dragomoshchenko, "I(s)." Reprinted with permission of the author

Johanna Drucker, "Hypergraphy: A Note on Maurice Lemaître's *Roman Hypergraphique*." Reprinted with permission of the author

Jerry Estrin, "Cold Heaven: The Uses of Monumentality." Reprinted with permission of Laura Moriarty, executor of Jerry Estrin's estate

Robert Glück, "His Heart Is a Lute Held Up: Poe and Bataille." Reprinted with permission of the author

Carla Harryman, "Toy Boats" was published in *Animal Instincts* (This, 1989), and *There Never Was a Rose Without a Thorn* (City Lights, 1995). Reprinted with the permission of the author

George Hartley, "Jameson's Perelman: Reification and the Material Signifier" was published in *Textual Politics and the Language Poets*, Bloomington: Indiana University Press, 1989. Reprinted with permission of the author

Lyn Hejinian, "The Rejection of Closure." Reprinted with permission of the author

Susan Howe, "My Emily Dickinson." Reprinted with permission of the author

George Lakoff, "Continuous Reframing," © 2013 George Lakoff. Reprinted with permission of the author

Jackson Mac Low, "Some Ways Philosophy Has Helped to Shape My Work." Reprinted with permission of Anne Tardos, executor of Jackson Mac Low's estate

Harryette Mullen, "Miscegenated Texts and Media Cyborgs: Technologies of Body and Soul," copyright Harryette Mullen. Reprinted with permission of the author

Ted Pearson, "A Form of Assumptions." Reprinted with permission of the author

Bob Perelman, "Good and Bad/Good and Evil: Pound, Céline, and Fascism." Reprinted permission of the author

Kit Robinson, "Time and Materials: The Workplace, Dreams, and Writing" and "Raising *Collateral*." Reprinted with permission of the author

Nick Robinson, "Subtext in *Collateral*." Reprinted with permission of the author

Andrew Ross, "The Death of Lady Day." Reprinted with permission of the author

Leslie Scalapino, "What/Person: From an Exchange" and "Pattern—and the 'Simulacral.'" Reprinted with permission of the author

Peter Seaton "An Example from the Literature." Reprinted with permission of the author

Viktor Shklovsky, "Plotless Literature: Vasily Rozanov." Translation reprinted with permission of Richard Sheldon

Ron Silliman, "What/Person: From an Exchange" and "Migratory Meaning: The Parsimony Principle in the Poem." Reprinted with permission of the author

Warren Sonbert, "Narrative Concerns," copyright the estate of Warren Sonbert. Reprinted courtesy of the estate of Warren Sonbert, Ascension Serrano, executor

Lorenzo Thomas, "The Marks Are Waiting," copyright Lorenzo Thomas. Reprinted with permission of A. L. Nielsen, literary executor for Lorenzo Thomas

Barrett Watten, "The Politics of Style." Reprinted with permission of the author

Reva Wolf, "Thinking You Know." Reprinted with permission of the author

John Zorn, "Memory and Immorality in Musical Composition." Reprinted with permission of the author

We are grateful for permission to reprint the following illustrations:

Pages 217, 219, 220, 221: Maurice Lemaître: four pages from *La plastique lettriste et hypergraphique*, used as illustrations in "Hypergraphy: A Note on Maurice Lemaitre's *Roman Hypergraphique*," by Johanna Drucker

Page 327: Artists Rights Society, for Marcel Duchamp, *With Hidden Noise*; © 2010 Artists Rights Society (ARS), New York-ADAGP, Paris-Sucession Marcel Duchamp

Page 328. Mies van der Rohe, Seagram Building, New York; © 2010 Artists Rights Society (ARS), New York-VG Bild-Kunst, Bonn; used as illustration in "Cold Heaven: The Uses of Monumentality," by Jerry Estrin

Page 332: Robert Longo, for Robert Longo, "(For R. W. Fassbinder) Now Everybody" (1982–83), mixed media. Photo: Pelka/Noble, courtesy Metro Pictures; used as illustration in "Cold Heaven: The Uses of Monumentality," by Jerry Estrin

Page 399: Artists Rights Society, for Andy Warhol, Popeye; used as illustration in "Thinking You Know," by Reva Wolf

Page 401: Houghton Library, Harvard University, John Ashbery Papers: for "a page from El diario, Sunday supplement to La prensa, 16 April 1967"

Page 402: Andy Warhol Museum, Pittsburgh, for Andy Warhol, John Ashbery (film portrait frame); used as illustration in "Thinking You Know," by Reva Wolf

Page 404: manuscript page of John Ashbery, "Farm Implements and Rutabagas in a Landscape," typescript and autograph revisions; used as illustration in "Thinking You Know," by Reva Wolf

Page 405: Holt, Rinehart, and Winston, for Ugo Mulas, "Thanksgiving dinner at Robert Rauschenberg's loft, mid 1960s (detail)"; used as illustration in "Thinking You Know," by Reva Wolf

All other illustrations are by the author of the works in which they appear and are used with permission

Contributor Index to *Guide* and *Archive*

This index lists all writing and visual art published in the ten print volumes of *Poetics Journal* (1982–98) in alphabetical order by author; entries for articles and abstracts in this volume are in bold. Complete versions of nearly all entries (with exceptions indicated by an asterisk) are included in the companion *Poetics Journal Digital Archive*, where complete author, keyword, and volume indexes are linked to each entry.

Keyword Index

This index provides keywords for each article reprinted or excerpted in this volume, as well as for articles indexed in its Constellations sections. The expanded keyword index in the *Poetics Journal Digital Archive* links complete versions of all articles it reprints from the original volumes of *Poetics Journal*, reorganized alphabetically by author.

and the Politics of the Person" (423–24); Haj Ross, "Poems as Holograms" (174)

manifesto: Harryman, "Toy Boats" (225–28); Zorn, "Memory and Immorality in Musical Composition" (414–19)

Marxism: Andrews, "Total Equals What" (185–96); Hartley, "Jameson's Perelman" (229–39); Plotke, "Language and Politics Today" (173)

material text: Amnasan, "Eclipsing Function of Full Comprehension" (294); Benson, "Close Reading" (37–45); Drucker, "Hypergraphy" (202–14); Hartley, "Jameson's Perelman" (229–39); Susan Howe, *My Emily Dickinson* (98–110); "Poets Theater: Two Versions of *Collateral*" (257–69)

meaning: Lakoff, "Continuous Reframing" (111–18); Price, "Contingency Caper" (298); Haj Ross, "Poems as Holograms" (174); Shurin, "Irruptive Text" (424–25)

media: Mullen, "Miscegenated Texts and Media Cyborgs" (335–44); McCaffery, "And Who Remembers Bobby Sands?" (296); Price, "Contingency Caper" (298); Rosenberg, "Openings" (424); Thomas, "Marks Are Waiting" (393–96)

metaphysics: Dragomoshchenko, "I(s)" (320–25); Fanny Howe, "Purgatory" (421)

method: Alferi, "Seeking a Sentence" (303–12); Andrews, "Total Equals What" (185–96); Barone, "John Smith's 'Philadelphia Newspapers Read Crossways'" (420); Bernstein, "Writing and Method" (46–54); Friedman, "How *Space Stations* Gets Written" (294–95); Mac Low, "Some Ways Philosophy Has Helped to Shape My Work" (119–25); Retallack, "Blue Notes on the Know Ledge" (423); Rosenberg, "Openings" (424)

modernism: Burke, "Without Commas" (170); Child, "Exhibit and the Circulation" (294); Fraser, "Overheard" (171–72); Hunt, "Beginning at *Bottom*" (172); Fanny Howe, "Purgatory" (421); Perelman, "Good and Bad/Good and Evil" (240–56); Plotke, "Language and Politics Today" (173); Shklovsky, "Plotless Literature" (126–40); "Symposium: Postmodern?" (298–99)

music: Zorn, "Memory and Immorality in Musical Composition" (414–19)

narrative: Jarolim, "Ideas of Order" (295); Mandel, "Codes/Texts" (172); Middleton, "Knowledge of Narratives" (296–97); Scalapino/Silliman, "What/Person?" (378–92); Shurin, "Irruptive Text" (424–25); "Symposium on Narrative" (298)

negativity: Glück, "His Heart Is a Lute Held Up" (79–86); Moriarty, "Modern Lyric" (297); Toscano, "Early Morning Prompts for Evening Takes" (425); Watten, "Politics of Style" (158–68)

New American poetics: Pearson, "'Form of Assumptions'" (345–52); "Robert Creeley and the Politics of the Person" (423–24); Watten, "Politics of Style" (158–68)

New Narrative: Acker, "Ugly" (177–84); Amnasan, "Eclipsing Function of Full Comprehension" (294); Bellamy, "Can't We Just Call It Sex?" (313–19); Boone, "Acker's *Great Expectations*" (169); Glück, "His Heart Is a Lute Held Up" (79–86)

New York School: Andrew Ross, "Death of Lady Day" (367–77); Silliman, "Migratory Meaning" (141–57); Wolf, "Thinking You Know" (397–413)

visuality: Benson, "Close Reading" (37–45); Friedman, "How *Space Stations* Gets Written" (294–95); Hunt, "Beginning at *Bottom*" (172); Piombino, "Towards an Experiential Syntax" (297); Scalapino, "Pattern—and the 'Simulacral'" (270–81); Sonbert, "Narrative Concerns" (289–93)

writing: Bernstein, "Writing and Method" (46–54); Davies, "Language/Mind/Writing" (72–78); Rosenberg, "Openings" (424)

General Index

Page numbers in articles written by the indexed contributor are given in **bold**; keywords that also appear in the keyword index are in SMALL CAPITAL LETTERS.

Acker, Kathy, 4, 7, 18, 20, 25, 79, 85, 299, 313, 316; *Empire of the Senseless*, 314–15; *Great Expectations*, 169; "Ugly," **177–84**

Adorno, Theodor W.: and lyric poetry, 209–10; and Macherey's work, 213n12

AFRICAN AMERICAN POETICS, 335–44; and abolitionist literature, 336, 339; and Baraka's work, 13, 31, 126, 372; and Black Arts movement, 393; and identity politics, 27; and Mullen's work, 335; and popular culture, 335, 339–43; and Thomas's work, 393; and Umbra workshop, 393

A Hundred Posters (ed. Davies), 19

AIDS epidemic, 31, 313, 376

Alferi, Pierre, 30, **303–12**; and cinema, 303; and performance, 307–9; and referentiality, 309–11; and rhythm, 305–11; and retrospection, 304–5, 308–9, 311; and semantics, 306; and sentences, 303–11; and syntax, 306–7, 310

alienation, 12, 31, 57, 237, 249, 353, 364, 365, 368

Allen, Donald: and *The New American Poetry*, 167

alterity, 9, 25–27, 28, 29

Althusser, Louis, 30; and ideology, 155; and social formation, 231; and subjectivity, 209

Amnasan, Michael, 20, 30, **294**, 354

anarchism, 122, 181

Anderson, Michael, 21

Andrews, Bruce, 3, 17, 24, 46, 88, 149, **185–96**, 237; as editor of *L=A=N=G=U=A=G=E*, 3, 17, 46, 185; on Language writing, 185; on public sphere, 195–96; on social aspects of language, 186–91; on totality, 185, 186, 188, 189–92, 195–96

Antin, David, 22

anti-Semitism, 240–55; and Céline's work, 240, 242–47, 254–55; and Pound's work, 240–42, 245, 248–55

architecture: and Philip Johnson's work, 329–31; and Mies's work, 326, 328–30

Aristotle, 54; and Chicago Aristotelians, 119–21, 124; *Poetics*, 120

Armantrout, Rae, 6, 8, 22, 24, 148, **197–201**

Armstrong, Louis, 28

Arnold, Matthew, 248

Artaud, Antonin, 59, 415

Ashbery, John, 30, 146, 282, 289; "Farm Implements and Rutabagas in a Landscape," 397–409; "The Skaters," 407–8; and Warhol, 397–409, 411

Atwood, Margaret, 409

aura, disappearance of, 186–87, 329

Austin, J. L., 207

authority: Arnold's concept of, 248; and authoritarianism, 18, 212, 240, 249, 252, 329, 379, 381; of authorship, 18, 33, 88; contestation of, 88, 193; of expository style, 49, 51; of lyric poetry, 208, 210–12; and mainstream poetry, 199–200; Pound's concept of, 249–53; and psychoanalysis, 57–58; of public discourse, 203

authorship: authority of, 18, 33, 88; construction of, 28, 31; and Creeley's work, 29, 423; and Dickinson's work, 43–44; and intentionality, 167; and Lemaître's work, 217; and postmodernism, 13; and social context, 192; and Stein's work, 28; and Whitman's work, 40, 43

automatic writing, 203

autonomy: of literature, 126, 159, 160, 161, 165–66, 187; of monumental architecture, 329–31; of musical works, 416, 418; of self, 385; of social levels, 231

AVANT-GARDE, 111–18, 125, 170, 293, 325, 392, 418; and architecture, 327, 330, 331; and cinema, 289, 294; and identity politics, 378, 383; Jameson's critique of, 229; and lettrism, 215; and linguistics, 111; manifestos, 11, 46; modernist, 12; and *Poetics Journal*, 1, 5, 6, 11, 19; postmodernist, 12; postwar American, 126; and private language, 203; Russian, 126, 320; and theory of reading, 37

Avercamp, Hendrick, 408

Bacon, Francis, 49

Bakhtin, Mikhail, 6, 202, 207–8, 210, 321; and dialogism, 208; and heteroglossia, 207

Balzac, Honoré de, 290; "Sarrasine," 172

Baraka, Amiri, 13, 31, 126, 372

Barone, Dennis, 31, **420**

Barthes, Roland, 5, 14, 15, 37, 65, 303, 408; *S/Z*, 172

Bataille, George, 4, 20, 79, 80, 81, 177, 347–48; *Story of the Eye*, 83–85

Baudelaire, Charles, 330, 371

Baudrillard, Jean, 25, 389

Beals, Jennifer, 340

Beat literature, 12, 359

Beckett, Samuel, 98, 421

Beethoven, Ludwig van, 242, 415

Behan, Brendan, 371

Bellamy, Dodie, 4, 20, 28, 30, 79, 177, **313–19**, 422; and narrative, 313, 314; and New Narrative, 313–19; and pornography, 313–19; and queer, 313, 316–17; and sexuality, 313–19

Beltrametti, Franco, 9

Benedetti, David, 31

Benjamin, Walter, 143

Benson, Steve, 4, 16, 20, 27, **37–45**, 79, 162, 257, 360; and material text, 37; and performance, 16, 37–45; "Translations," 44

Benveniste, Émile, 209, 321, 347

Bergson, Henri, 170

Berkeley, Busby, 270, 273–74

Berkeley Poetry Conference, 15, 158, 163

Berkson, Bill, 25, 299

Bernheimer, Alan, 22

Bernstein, Basil, 202, 204

Bernstein, Charles, 3, 5, 17, 25, 28, **46–54**, 149, 154, 185, 198, 257, 270, 282, 357; as editor of *L=A=N=G=U=A=G=E*, 3, 17, 46, 185; on method, 46, 48–50, 52–53; and philosophy *vs.* literature, 46–49, 52–54; *The Sophist*, 275–78; on Wittgenstein, 46, 48, 53

Berrigan, Ted, 198, 393

Berssenbrugge, Mei-Mei, 6, 171

Bibb, Henry, 339, 341

Big Deal (ed. Barbara Baracks), 19

Binswanger, Ludwig, 362

Black Arts Movement, 393

Black Mountain poets, 126

Blake, William, 108–9

Blevins, Richard, 29, 423

Bloom, Harold, 98

Bonnard, Pierre, 371

Boone, Bruce, 213n17, 377n5; and New Narrative, 4, 20, 22, 79, **169**

Borges, Jorge Luis, 330

Bottoms, David, 197, 201

Bourdon, David, 410n11

Bowie, David, 342

Bradbury, Ray, 395

Brakhage, Stan, 289

Braxton, Anthony, 364–65

Brazil, David, 257

Brecht, Bertolt, 257, 267

Brik, Osip, 4, 127

Bromige, David, 17, 22–23, **169–70**

Brontë sisters, 98, 102, 105

Brooks, Cleanth, 208

Brown, Earle, 124

Brown, Norman O., 57

Brown, William Webb, 339, 341

Browning, Elizabeth Barrett, 98, 100, 102, 105–7

Bryant, Tisa, 177, 378

Buddhism, 72, 122–23, 270

Bulatov, Erik, 8

Bulgarin, F. V., 127

Burger, Mary, 5

Burke, Carolyn, 18, 63–64, **170**; on feminism, 170

Burroughs, William S., 6, 420

Butler, Judith, 350–51

Cage, John, 119, 123–24, 414, 415, 420

camp sensibility, 367, 372–76

canonicity, 388–89

capitalism: and Language writing, 295; Mandel's theory of late, 236; and reification, 232–33, 237, 238; shift from classical to late, 356; and workplace, 353, 356–57

Carroll, Lewis: *Alice's Adventures in Wonderland*, 59–61

Cavalcanti, Giovanni, 250

Cavell, Stanley, 46, 48, 53

Celan, Paul, 415

Céline, Louis-Ferdinand, 240, 242–47, 254–55; *Death on the Installment Plan*, 243–45; *Journey to the End of Night*, 242–43

Ceravolo, Joseph, 4; "Migratory Noon [Moon]," 141–55

Cervantes, Miguel de, 130, 135

chance procedures, 121–24, 414, 420

cheek, cris, 22, 257

Chekhov, Anton, 127–28

Chernoff, Maxine, 22

Chicago Aristotelians, 119–21, 124

Child, Abigail, 18, 27, **294**

Child, Lydia Maria, 336

Chinese ideograms, 249

Chomsky, Noam, 111, 153–54

CINEMA: Alferi's theory of, 303; and Neo-Benshi performance, 289; and race, 337–39, 340; and Sonbert's work, 289–93, 298; Soviet, 289, 294

Cixous, Hélène, 5, 55, 64, 95, 303

CLASS: and Bakhtin's theory of literature, 208; and experience, 388, 391; and identity, 27, 294; Mouffe's theory of, 389–90; and social categories, 389

closure, 87, 88, 95, 96, 155, 164, 185, 272, 309, 386

Coates, George: "The Way of How," 111–15, 117

codes: cultural, 202, 204–5, 238; linguistic, 160; social, 191

Cody, John, 105

cognitive linguistics, 111–17, 141

cognitive mapping, 229

coherence, poetic, 141, 142, 144, 145, 152, 155

COLLECTIVISM, 421

Cold War, 13, 26, 29, 164

Coleridge, S. T., 12

comic strips, 212n4, 384, 385, 387, 398, 400, 403, 405, 410n11

commercials, race in, 339, 342–43

commodity, 85, 356, 422; and commodity fetishism, 237; literature as, 158–59

communism, 245, 246

CONCEPTUALISM, 13, 14, 17, 420; Soviet, 8, 320, 422

Confucius, 123, 247, 250, 252

constructivism: and Meyerhold's work, 264; and *Poetics Journal*, 2, 12, 29; and Silliman's work, 173; and Soviet cinema, 294

consumerism: and closure, 386; and Longo's work, 331–33; and O'Hara's work, 367, 370–73, 375; and Pound's work, 254; and Protestant ideology, 356

contextualization, 37–38, 143

Coolidge, Clark, 20, 30, 161, 333; *Mine: The One That Enters the Stories*, 170

Cooper, Dennis, 4, 79, 85, 177, 316

Corder, Eileen, 22, 257, 258, 260–61, 267, 268n1

Crane, Hart, 4, 289

Crane, Margaret, 9

Crane, R. S., 119, 120, 121

Creeley, Robert, 22, 28, 345–50, 423; "Robert Creeley and the Politics of the Person," 423–24; "When he and I . . . ," 345–51

CRITICAL THEORY, 157, 158–68, 169, 173, 185–96, 229–39, 295, 299, 422, 425; and Adorno's work, 209–10; and Benjamin's work, 143; and Eagleton's work, 15, 158, 164–65, 167; and Jameson's work, 8, 20, 23, 24–25, 229–38, 270, 326

Croll, Morris, 49

cultural codes, 202, 204–5, 238

cultural dominant, Jameson's theory of, 231–32

CULTURAL STUDIES, 1, 126, 202–14, 335–44, 367–77, 396, 421

cummings, e. e., 121

cyborgs, 335, 340, 342

Dada, 203, 215, 216, 398

Dahlberg, Edward, 166

Dahlen, Beverly, 18; *A Reading*, **55–71**; on desire, 60, 63, 67; on feminism, 55, 58, 63–64; on interminable text, 65–66; on Lacan, 55–57, 59, 63, 66, 69n18; on Oedipus complex, 55, 58, 61; on the unconscious, 59, 60, 62, 67, 68

Darragh, Tina, 18, 22

Davidson, Dan, 30

Davidson, Michael, 16, 22, 24, 26, 30, **202–14**, 298, 422; on cultural codes, 202, 204–5; on identity, 205; on lyric poetry, 202, 208–12; on private language, 202–13; on public language, 202–3, 205, 207, 209, 211; on surfers' language, 202, 203–5

Davies, Alan, 16, 17, 25, 29, 51, **72–78**, 93, 149, 299, 359, 423; on language as thinking, 72–78

Davies, Paul, 67

Davis, Bette, 374

Davis, Lydia, 22, **170**; *Story and Other Stories*, 295

Day, Jean, 5, 18, 30

death, 61–62, 79, 81–82, 85, 100, 278, 385–86

Debord, Guy, 356

de Chirico, Giorgio, 398, 406, 409n3

deconstruction, 72, 81, 215

de Laroque, Françoise, 18, **170–71**

Deleuze, Gilles, 15, 303

democracy, 15, 251, 358, 390, 416

de Quincy, Thomas, 360

Derksen, Jeff, 26

Derrida, Jacques, 5, 14, 46, 72, 270, 303, 357–58

de Sade, Marquis, 84, 177

Descartes, René, 49

desire, 60, 63, 67, 129, 187, 194, 273, 307, 309, 324, 350, 362; in French feminism, 87, 88, 92, 95; and Longo's work, 332, 333

device: literary, 88, 126–39, 143, 149, 152–55, 163; and meaning, 193

dialogism: Bakhtin's theory of, 208; and Mies's architecture, 328–29; and philosophical discourse, 53. *See also* heteroglossia; idioglossia; monologism

Dickens, Charles, 98; *David Copperfield*, 106–7

Dickinson, Emily, 4, 16, 28, 98–109; and Benson's "Close Reading," 41–44; and Howe's *My Emily Dickinson*, 37; and private language, 202, 210–12

Diehl, Joanne Feit, 105, 210

difference, linguistic, 66, 270

Dorn, Edward, 31

Dostoevsky, Fyodor, 127, 130, 136

Douglass, Frederick, 339, 341, 343

Dragomoshchenko, Arkadii, 26, 28, 31, **320–25**

dreams, 129, 164, 165, 322–23, 353, 359–65, 362

Dreyer, Lynne, 18

Drucker, Johanna, 16, 24, 37, **215–24**; on Dada, 215–16; on Lemaitre's work, 215–24; on public language, 215–16, 218, 222–23

DuBois, W. E. B., 341, 343n1

Duchamp, Marcel, 119, 123, 124, 326; "With Hidden Noise," 327–29

Duncan, Robert, 126, 198

DuPlessis, Rachel Blau, 18, 64

Eagleton, Terry, 15, 158, 164–67

Eco, Umberto, 18, 92–93

economics: and Althusser's work, 231; and Marx's work, 247, 248–49; and modes of production, 230–31; and Pound's work, 247–49, 251–52; and private language, 206–7; and time management, 354–57

Eigner, Larry, 4, 16; "streets, streets . . . ," 43

Eikhenbaum, Boris, 4, 127

Eisenstein, Sergei, 289, 294

Eliot, George, 98, 100–103

Eliot, T. S., 121, 143, 208, 371

Emerson, Ralph Waldo, 48, 72, 99, 211

enjambment, 151, 242, 306–7

Ensslin, John, 229

envisionment, 141, 145–50, 152–53, 155

Epstein, Mikhail, 320

equivalence, principle of, in Jakobson's poetics, 162, 164–65

Estrin, Jerry, 26, **326–34**, 422; on architecture, 326, 329–31; on modernism *vs.* postmodernism, 326; on readymades, 327–29, 332, 333; on simulacra, 329, 330, 335; on subjectivity, 329, 333

Euripides, 120

Evans, Steve, 31

everyday life, 9, 126, 233, 326; and O'Hara's work, 367, 368–71, 374, 375; "The Poetics of Everyday Life," 422

evil in literature, 82, 83, 85, 240–43, 246–48, 253

Ewert, Mark, 318

existentialism, 72

EXPERIENCE: art as, 117; construction of, 187, 385, 387–88; extra-linguistic, 144–47; and postmodernism, 326; and referentiality, 309–11; and symposium on everyday life, 422; of reading, 154–55

expository style, critique of, 49–52

fame, 159

family: and Céline's work, 243–46; and experience, 388; and private language, 206–7; and Sonbert's work, 291; and writing, 386

fascism, 240–42, 245–46, 251–54, 333

Faust legend, 30, 93–94, 95–96

Faye, Pierre, 226–27

Feldman, Morton, 124

FEMINISM: and Acker's work, 177; and Dahlen's work, 55, 58, 63–64; and Dickinson's work, 98–99, 105; French, 5, 18, 55, 87, 95; and Howe's work, 98; and *HOW(ever)* journal, 171; and Loy's work, 170; and philosophy, 423; and poetic form, 87, 88, 92, 94–95; and psychoanalysis, 63–64, 94–95; second-wave, 18; and Stein's work, 98–99; and subjectivity, 345

Fenollosa, Ernest, 249

fetish: commodity, 158–59, 237; and Lemaître's work, 215, 216, 223

feudalism, 245, 247, 251, 253

Fielding, Henry, 130, 131

Fillmore, Charles, 111; and envisionment, 145, 147; and frame semantics, 147

Finkelstein, Norman, 8, 28, **420–21**

Fischer, Norman, 8, 27, 422

Fisher, Allen, 17, 25, 171, **299**

Fitzsimons, Connie, 299

folklore, Russian, 9, 29, 421–22

Foreman, Richard, 415–16

form, linguistic, 5, 30

form, narrative, 21, 33, 270, 271, 275, 384; and Harryman's work, 225–26; and Rozanov's work, 126; and Woolf's work, 384

form, poetic: and expanded field, 15; as generative, 32–33, 90–91; holistic, 64; open *vs.* closed, 12–13, 16, 18, 22–23, 29, 87, 90, 96; organic, 126, 167; paratactic, 238; refusal of normative, 17

FORMALISM: and Language writing, 79; and New Criticism, 126; and New Formalism, 390; and Russian Formalism, 3–4, 87, 126–41, 143, 155, 163, 294

Foucault, Michel, 14, 50, 190, 362

foundation, philosophical, 304

frames, cultural and linguistic, 111–12, 147, 153, 174, 193; and Ceravolo's work, 141, 144, 147–50; and Coates's work, 111, 112–15, 117; and Olson's work, 158; and Palmer's work, 111, 115–17

Frankfurt School, 14, 213n12

Franklin, Aretha, 339, 340

Fraser, Kathleen, 18, 171–72

free association, 21, 55–57, 64

FRENCH POETICS, 5, 14, 18, 26, 111, 170, 172, 215–24, 303–12; and feminism, 5, 18, 55, 87, 94–95; and lettrism, 215–23; and Oulipo, 5; and surrealism, 20, 26, 177, 203, 215, 216; *Travail de poésie* (ed. Royet-Journaud), 170–71

Freud, Sigmund: Dahlen's reading of, 55–62, 66–67; and Loy's work, 170; and theory of dreams, 362–64; and theories of reading, 37, 38

Fried, Howard, 6, 22

Friedlander, Ben, 18, 28, 422

Friedman, Ed, 21, 161; *Space Stations*, **294–95**

Frith, Fred, 9

Fuller, Margaret, 102

Gadamer, Hans-Georg, 16

Garland, Judy, 374

Gaudier-Brzeska, Henri, 249, 254

Gay, Michel, 27

gay literature: and Boone's work, 213n17, 377n5; and New Narrative, 79; and O'Hara's work, 367, 373–76

GENDER: and Creeley's work, 345–50; and Dickinson's work, 100, 103; and feminist poetics, 18–19; and French poetics, 18, 171; and slave narratives, 335–36; and Sonbert's work, 291–92

Genet, Jean, 371, 372

genius, Pound's doctrine of, 249, 250, 254

Henderson, David, 393

Heraclitus, 12

hermeticism, 202, 209

Hernton, Calvin C., 393

Hesiod, 371

heteroglossia, 207, 212 . *See also* dialogism; idioglossia; monologism

Hills (ed. Perelman), 19, 259

Himmler, Heinrich, 241–42

Hinduism, 321, 324n4

HISTORY: and Creeley's work, 29; and cyclical *vs.* monumental, 62–63; and "end of history," 26, 31, 390; and ideology, 158, 165; intellectual, 125; Marx's theory of, 121, 391; and postmodernism, 233–34, 299, 369; publication, 420; and Pound's work, 252

Hitchcock, Alfred, 290, 293

Hitler, Adolf, 212n3, 240–42, 245, 247, 253

Hocquard, Emmanuel, 26

Holiday, Billie, 367, 371–74, 376

Holocaust, 241

Homer, 276, 349

homology, critique of, 231, 236

Houston, Whitney, 340

Howe, Fanny, 6, 8, 18, 27, 171, **421**

Howe, Susan, 6, 16, 18, 29, 198, 282, 423; on Brontë sisters, 98, 102, 105; on feminism, 98, 99, 105; *My Emily Dickinson*, 18, 37, **98–110**

Hugo, Victor, 130

Hunt, Erica, 17, 18, **172**

Husserl, Edmund, 321

hypergraphy, 215–23

hypersubjectivity, 28, 31

Ibsen, Henrik, 292

I Ching, 119, 122–24

iconicity: and Lemaître's work, 215, 217–18, 221, 222

idealism, German, 72

identification, 6; Dahlen on, 61, 62; in Creeley's work, 345–52

IDENTITY, 26, 27, 378–91, 420; and whites' representation of black identity, 335–43. *See also* personhood; self; subjectivity

ideograms, Pound/Fenollosa's theory of, 249

IDEOLOGY: Althusser's theory of, 155; and close reading, 37; and critique of narrative, 228; and demand for coherence, 141, 155; and Dickinson's work, 210–12; Eagleton's theory of, 15, 158, 164–65; and experience, 145, 146; and history, 158, 165; and Longo's work, 333; and lyric poetry, 210–12; and mainstream poetry, 197–201; and market for poetry, 159; and Olson's discourse, 158, 166; and poetic production, 158–59; and private language, 203, 210, 212; and production of meaning, 187, 189; Protestant, 356; and protopolitical texts, 367, 369–70; Silliman on, 158–59; and Soviet folklore, 421; and Spicer's work, 212; totalizing, 185, 195

idioglossia, 203, 206–7. *See also* dialogism; heteroglossia; monologism

imagism, 144, 420

imago mundi, in Olson's work, 163–64, 167

imperialism, U.S., 167, 387, 395

improvisation: verbal, 37–45, 72–78; musical, 364–65, 414–18; and Poets Theater, 257–69; reading as, 88

indeterminacy, 13–14, 23, 67, 141, 144

indexicality, 3, 146, 230, 326

INTERTEXTUALITY, 30, 63–64, 93, 98–110, 172, 190

Irigaray, Luce, 5, 88

Iser, Wolfgang, 37

Isou, Isidore, 215

in *Poetics Journal*, 1, 2, 4, 5, 6–7, 13, 19, 23, 24, 25, 29, 30, 31; and Poets Theater, 257–68; in Seaton's "An Example from the Literature," 282–88; in Toscano's "Early Morning Prompts for Evening Takes; or, Roll 'Em!," 425

Lao-tse, 123

Latinina, Yulia, 9, 29, **421–22**

Lautréamont, comte de, 303

Lawrence, D. H., 348

Lefebvre, Henri, 356

Lemaître, Maurice, *La Plastique et hypergraphique*, 215–23

lesbian writing, 390–91

Leskov, Nikolai, 133

lettrism, 215–23

Levertov, Denise, 126

Levis, Larry, 199

libertarianism, 121–22, 124

Lin, Tan, 378

Linder, Steffan, 354–56

Linenthal, Mark, 62

LINGUISTICS: Berkeley school (Fillmore, Kay, Lakoff), 3, 15, 24, 111–18, 141, 145, 147; and difference, 66; and generative grammar, 111, 153–54; and Jakobson's work, 111, 158, 159–61; and Prague school, 159, 202; and private language, 202; socio-, 202, 203–4, 207; and Saussure's work, 66, 160, 252, 303; structuralist, 179, 421

Lloyd, David, 22, 23, **295**

Longo, Robert, *(For R.W. Fassbinder) Now Everybody*, 331–33

Loy, Mina, 18, 170

Lu, Pamela, 5, 30, 378

Lukács, Georg, 233, 237

Luoma, Bill, 9, 422

Lyotard, Jean-François, 25

LYRIC POETRY: and Adorno's work, 209–10; and Bakhtin's work, 208, 210; and Creeley's work, 345–52, 423; and Dickinson's work, 210–12; and gender, 100, 103, 170, 171, 345–50; and Hegel's work, 208; and identity, 420; and ideology, 210–12; and Language writing, 18, 297; and mainstream poetry, 198; and monologism, 208, 210; and private language, 202, 208–12; and society, 209–12; and Spicer's work, 212; structuralist theory of, 174; and subjectivity, 8, 28, 202, 208–9, 212

Macherey, Pierre, 213n12

Mac Low, Jackson, 16, 17, 24, 93, **119–25**, 237, 420; on Cage, 119, 123–24; on Chicago Aristotelians, 119–21, 124; on Duchamp, 119, 123, 124; on Goodman, 119, 120, 122; on tragedy, 119, 120; on Whitehead, 119, 124, 125; on Zen, 119, 122–23

mainstream poetry, 197–201

Malanga, Gerard, 411n23, 412n31

Malevich, Kazimir, 331

Mamiya, Christin J., 410n11

Mandel, Ernest, 236

Mandel, Tom, **172**

MANIFESTO: hybrid writing, 225–28; improvised music, 414–18; nonnarrative film, 289–93

marginality: and identity, 379, 383; and *Marginality* issue, 6–7, 19, 24; and negativity, 7; rhetoric of, 197

Marsh, Warne, 364–65

Marvell, Andrew, 400

Marx, Karl: "On the Jewish Question," 247

MARXISM: Céline and, 245; and critique of capitalism, 232–33, 236; and Eagleton's work, 158, 164–65, 167; and feudalism, 253; and history, 121, 391; and identity, 381; and Jameson's work, 229–39; and language, 15, 173; modes of production in, 230–31; and reading, 37, 38; and totality, 185–96; Western, 14; and writing, 185

masculinity: in Creeley's work, 345–50, 423; and gay identity, 367, 375–76; in O'Hara's work, 367, 375–76; and Pop art, 410n11

MATERIAL TEXT: and Dickinson's work, 98–109; in Lemaître's work, 215–23; and McGann's work, 37; and performance, 37–45

materiality, linguistic: and envisionment, 147; and incomprehension, 294; and Jameson's critique of Perelman's work, 229–30, 234–35; and Language writing, 13; and lyric poetry, 208; and open form, 13, 16; and Poets Theater, 257–69; and social production of meaning, 188

maya, Buddhist concept of, 277, 280n9

Mayakovsky, Vladimir, 160–61, 267

Mayer, Bernadette, *Midwinter Day*, 90

McCaffery, Steve, 17, 21, 237, **296**

McClure, Michael, 270; *Dark Brown*, 272–73

McGann, Jerome, 16, 37, 213

McKeon, Richard, 119, 120, 121

McNaughton, Duncan, 7, 25, 299

MEANING: and excess, 167–68, 424; expanded field of, 12–14, 32; and linguistic frames, 111–18, 174; in postmodernism, 294, 298; and reading, 37, 38; and society, 185–90, 192–94, 196

MEDIA: digital, 424; and narrative, 296; politics and, 393–96; race in, 335, 338–43; postmodern, 298; standardized discourse of, 52

Melnick, David, 424

Melville, Herman, 80, 337

Mencius, 249

metalanguage, 161

metaphor, 66, 237–38

METAPHYSICS, 320, 421

metarealism, 8, 320

METHOD: and Cage's work, 415; and Dahlen's work, 56; and language, 301–12; and Mac Low's work, 121–24; and new media, 424, and philosophy, 46, 48–50, 52–53, 423; and society, 187, 190–94; *vs.* technique, 52; and writing procedures, 294, 420; and Zorn's work, 414–18

metonymy, 66, 238, 348

Meyerhold, Vsevolod, 45, 257, 261, 264

Michaels, Walter Benn, 26

Middleton, Peter, 21, **296–97**

Mies van der Rohe, Ludwig, 326, 328–30

Miller, Ruth, 105

mimesis, 236, 298

mind: and language, 72–77; and lyric poetry, 88–89

Mitterrand, François, 178

mode of production, Marxist theory of, 230–31; and literary practice, 188

MODERNISM, 18, 98, 121, 193, 216, 270, 328, 372; and belief, 421; and fascism, 240–56; and knowledge, 172; and politics, 173; *vs.* postmodernism, 7, 12–13, 232–33, 236, 299; and Russian formalism, 126–41; and Soviet cinema, 294; and women authors, 170, 171

monologism: and lyric poetry, 208–10; and scientific authority, 49. *See also* dialogism; heteroglossia; idioglossia

montage, cinematic, 289

Montaigne, Michel de, 46, 50, 72

monumentality, critique of, 326, 327–31, 333

Moriarty, Laura, 27, **297**

Motown, 335, 338, 341

Mouffe, Chantal, 30, 389–90

Mullen, Harryette, 28, **335–44**, 378; on cinema, 337–40; on commercials, 339,

342–43; on Douglass, 339, 341, 343; on music, 238–41

Murakovsky, Jan, 208

MUSIC: and Bernstein's *The Sophist*, 277; chance procedures in, 123, 124, 415; and improvisation, 364–65, 414, 416–18; and race, 338–41. *See also* jazz

Mussolini, Benito, 240, 241, 248, 252–53, 254

NARRATIVE: and Acker's work, 169, 177; and Benson's work, 20; and Coolidge's work, 20, 170; and Lydia Davis's work, 295; and desire, 424; and experience, 155, 387, 391; and Friedman's work, 21; and Harryman's work, 22, 225–28; and Hejinian's work, 155; and identity, 27, 378–83; and McCaffery's work, 21; and media, 296; and New Narrative, 1, 4, 5, 20, 22, 23, 79, 169, 294, 313, 314; and *Non/Narrative* issue, 6, 19–23; and the novel, 126–31, 135–36; and Olson's poetics, 162–63; and Perelman's work, 238; and postmodernism, 298; and Scalapino's work, 20–21; and scientific knowledge, 296; and society, 23; and Sonbert's work, 289; and structuralism, 170; and subjectivity, 20; "Symposium on Narrative," 298; and Zorn's work, 416–17. *See also* New Narrative, nonnarrative

Natambu, Kofi, 28

national security state, 393, 396

Native American culture, 381

nature: and Céline's work, 245; and Dickinson's work, 99; and Pound's work, 245, 249, 253

Nazism, 240–42, 245–46

NEGATIVITY, 2, 7, 362; in narrative, 85, 169, 313, 424; in poetry, 55, 158, 297, 425

Négritude, 372

Nekrasov, Viktor, 127

Nelson, Cary, 16, 389

Neo-Benshi performance, 289

neopragmatism, 14, 17, 19

NEW AMERICAN POETICS, 12, 13, 14, 17, 25, 27, 29, 31, 195; and Creeley's work, 345–52, 423; and McClure's work, 272–73; and Olson's work, 158–59, 162–67

New Criticism, 4, 119, 121, 126, 155

new formalism, 390

NEW NARRATIVE, 1, 4, 5, 20, 22, 23, 79–86, 169, 294, 313–19, 424; in Acker's work, 169, 177; Acker's "Ugly," 177–84; and Boone's work, 4, 20, 22, 79, 169

New Sentence, 149, 303–12

NEW YORK SCHOOL, 159, 257, 393; and Ashbery's work, 397–413; and Ceravolo's work, 141–53; and O'Hara's work, 367–76

Nietzsche, Friedrich, 62, 240, 242–43, 247, 248, 250

Noël, Bernard, 17

nonidentity, 27, 28, 72, 87, 166

NONNARRATIVE: and Coolidge's work, 170; and Harryman's work, 225–28; and Friedman's work, 294; *vs.* narrative, 298; and *Non/Narrative* issue, 6, 19–23; and politics, 296; and Rozanov's work, 15, 126, 128, 131–39; and poetry, 282–88; and postmodernism, 229, 270, 298; and Sonbert's work, 289

Notley, Alice, 22, 270; *Margaret and Dusty*, 278–80

novelistic form, 126–39

Objectivist poetics, 14

objectivity: and experience, 391; and identity, 380–82; and philosophy, 47; and scientific knowledge, 296

Oedipus complex, 55, 58, 61, 244

O'Hara, Frank, 12, 27, 198, 254, 257, 289; "The Day Lady Died," 376–76

no. 4: *Women and Language*, 5–6, 15, 17–19; no. 5: *Non/Narrative*, 6, 19–23; no. 6: *Marginality*, 6–7, 19, 24; no. 7: *Postmodern?*, 8, 19, 24–25; no. 8: *Elsewhere*, 9–10, 25–27; no. 9: *The Person*, 11–12, 25, 27–29, 345; no. 10: *Knowledge*, 9–10, 25, 29–31

POETRY: Seaton, "An Example from the Literature," 282–88; Toscano, "Early Morning Prompts for Evening Takes; or, Roll 'Em," 425

"The Poetics of Everyday Life," **422**

Poets Theater, 6, 22, **257–69**; and Corder's work, 257, 258, 260–61, 267, 268n1; production stills, 262, 266

POLITICS: and aesthetics, 240, 248; and camp, 374–75; and Céline's work, 240, 245–47; and everyday life, 367, 369, 376; and expository style, 50–52; fascist, 240–42, 245–46, 251–53, 333; and hypotaxis *vs.* parataxis, 390–91; and identity, 378–83, 389–91; and ideology, 173, 158–59, 162–67; and Jameson's work, 232, 234–37; and Language writing, 185, 237–38, 295; and Mac Low's work, 122; and media, 393–96; and O'Hara's work, 367, 369–70, 376; and Olson's work, 158, 162, 164, 167; and performance, 122; and Pop art, 410n11; postcolonial, 177–84; and postmodernism, 232, 234–37, 369; and Pound's work, 240–42, 250–54; and reader-centered theory, 15–16; and social structure, 185–96; and Taoism, 122; and unity *vs.* pluralism, 389–90; and writing, 185, 188–96

Polkinhorn, Harry, 7, 25

Pollock, Jackson, 368

Ponge, Francis, 92

Pop art, 272, 368, 406–8, 410n11

Pope, Alexander, 358

pornography, 79, 80, 81, 84–85, 177, 313–19

POSTMODERNISM: and Acker's work, 169, 177–84; and everyday life, 422; and Jameson's work, 20, 24–25, 229–33, 236–37, 270; and Language writing, 13, 18, 24, 25; and media, 296; *vs.* modernism, 7, 12–13, 232–33, 236, 326; and narrative, 298; and new media, 424; and particularity, 278; and *Postmodern?* issue, 8, 19, 24–25; and race, 335; and personhood, 420; and reification, 229, 232–33, 236–38; and romanticism, 159, 167; and simulacra, 270, 272, 298, 335; "Symposium: Postmodern?," 298–99; and temporality, 270; and Western Marxism, 14; and workplace, 353

poststructuralism, 14, 17, 111, 193, 225, 233, 388

Poulantzas, Nikos, 230, 232, 238

Pound, Ezra, 98, 121, 144, 237–38, 240–42, 247–55; *The Cantos*, 240–41, 249–55; and fascism, 240–42, 245–46, 251–54

power: and Matthew Arnold's work, 248; and avant-garde, 386; and canonicity, 388; and identity, 380, 382; and meaning, 188–89; and Pound's work, 253; and private language, 206–7

pragmatism, 72. *See also* neopragmatism

Prague School, 159, 202

presence, 12, 13, 17, 149, 155, 164, 295

Price, Larry, 25, **298**

Prigov, Dmitrii, 320, **422**

private language, 202–13, 215–16, 218, 222–23

process, 187

Protestant ideology, 356

protopolitical texts, 369–70, 375

Proust, Marcel, 285

Prynne, J. H., 165

PSYCHOANALYSIS: and Céline's work, 240, 244–46; and Dahlen's work, 18, 55–71; and Lydia Davis's work, 295; and dreams, 57–59, 60, 62, 67, 362–64; and fascism, 245; and French feminism, 94–95, 170; incest taboo, 58, 350; and language, 92; and Olson's work, 165–67; Piombino on, 21, 297; and politics, 421; and Pound's work, 240; and schizophrenia, 24, 202, 229–30, 232, 234–38. *See also* Freud, Sigmund; Kristeva, Julia; Lacan, Jacques

public language, 202–3, 205, 207, 209, 211, 215–16, 218, 222–23

PUBLIC SPHERE, 16, 195–96, 294, 296, 375

Pushkin, Alexander, 127, 131, 136

quantum physics, 67

Québecois poetics, 8, 27

QUEER, 424; and O'Hara, 367–77; and Wojnarowicz, 313, 316–19

RACE: and abolitionist literature, 336, 339; and Acker's work, 177–83; and cinema, 337–39, 340; and emotion, 335–38, 342; and identity, 389; and music, 338–41, 372–73; and O'Hara's work, 367, 372–73; and politics of language, 51; and representation, 335–43

Radcliffe, Ann, 135

Rapaport, Herman, 30

rape, in literature, 349

Rapko, John, 7, 299

Rasula, Jed, 3, **173–74**

Rauschenberg, Robert, 405

READING: active, 146; close, 4, 37–38, 44; and *Close Reading* issue, 4, 15–16; and context, 37–38; and envisionment, 146; and gender, 170; ideology of, 37; and improvisation, 88; as interminable, 65–66; and interpretation, 141, 147, 151; linguistic, 141, 147, 174; and mass production of books, 159; and material text, 37, 98; as performance, 37–45; pol-

itics of, 15–16; and reader-response theory, 37–38, 173; and structuralism, 37; and syntax, 273; and temporality, 154–55; and typos, 152; and totality, 65–66, 191

READINGS: of Acker's work, 169, 314–16; of Ashbery's work, 397–409; of Balzac's work, 172; of Barthes's work, 172; of Bataille's work, 83–85; of Benson's work, 44; of Bernstein's work, 275–78; of Elizabeth Barrett Browning's work, 105–7; of Carroll's work, 59–61; of Céline's work, 242–45; of Ceravolo's work, 142–53; of Coates's work, 111–17; of Coolidge's work, 170; of Creeley's work, 345–51; of Lydia Davis's work, 295; of Dickinson's work, 41–43, 98–109, 210–12; of Duchamp's work, 327–29; of Eigner's work, 43; of Friedman's work, 294–95; of Goethe's work, 94–96; of Hagard's work, 424; of Harryman's work, 95; of Hejinian's work, 88–89; of Hemingway's work, 271–72; of *The L=A=N=G=U=A=G=E Book*, 295–96; of Lemaître's work, 215–23; of Language writing, 295; of Longo's work, 331–33; of Loy's work, 170; of lyric poetry, 297; of mainstream poetry, 199–200; of Mayer's work, 90; of McClure's work, 272–73; of Notley's work, 278–80; of O'Hara's work, 370–76; of Olson's work, 162–67; of Palmer's work, 115–17; of Perelman's work, 96, 229–38; of Poe's work, 77–83; of Poets Theater, 257–67; of Pound's work, 240–42, 249–55; of Rozanov's work, 128–39; of Sherman's work, 274–75; of Silliman's work, 173, 273; of John Smith's work, 420; of Sonbert's work, 291–93; of *Travail de poésie* (ed. Royet-Journaud), 170–71; of Whitman's work,

38–40; of Wojnarowicz's work, 316–19; of Zukofsky's work, 172

readymades, 327–29, 332, 333

realism, 21, 137, 153, 238, 264, 272, 349, 372

Reed, Ishmael, 393

referentiality: Alferi's theory of, 309–11; Jakobson's theory of, 158, 161; and spatiality, 92

reflexivity, poetics based on, 282

reification, 158, 229, 230, 232–33, 236–38, 388

RELIGION, and modernism, 421

Renoir, Jean, 290

Retallack, Joan, 30; on knowledge, **423**

retrospection, Alferi's theory of, 304–5, 308–9, 311

rhythm, in Alferi's work, 305–11; in Browning's work, 105; in Dickinson's work, 38, 41; Jakobson on, 161; and Robinson's work, 263, 265, 356, 360, 362, 363; of rock and roll, 343, 373; Tynjanov on, 91

Rimbaud, Arthur, 82

Rivers, Larry, 159, 367–68

"Robert Creeley and the Politics of the Person," **423–24**

Robinson, Kit, 3, 15, 26, 28, 31, 154, **353–66**; on alienation, 353, 364, 365, 368; *Collateral*, 6, 22, **257–60**, 260–69; *Covers*, 363; on dreams, 353, 359–65; on time management, 353–57; on workplace, 353–59, 364

Robinson, Nick, 22, **260–69**

rock and roll, 339–40, 343, 373

romanticism, 12, 83, 137, 159, 166, 167, 195, 211, 213n16, 270–71

Roof (ed. Sherry), 19

Rosenberg, Jim, 31, **424**

Rosenquist, James, 406

Ross, Andrew, 8, 24, 25, 27, **367–77**; on consumerism, 367, 370–73, 375; on every-day life, 367, 368–71, 374, 375; on proto-political texts, 369–70, 375; on whites' reception of black music, 372–73

Ross, Diana, 340

Ross, Haj, 4, 16, **174**

Roy, Camille, 20

Royet-Journaud, Claude (ed.), *Travail de poésie*, 170–71

Rozanov, Vasily, *Fallen Leaves*, 126, 128–39; *Solitaria*, 132–39

Rubinshtein, Lev, 320

Ruskin, John, 103

Russian Formalism, 3–4, 14–15, 26, 87, 126, 141, 143, 155,163

Russian futurism, 111, 166, 203, 257

RUSSIAN POETICS, 4, 26, 294, 320–25; and conceptualism, 422; and folklore, 9, 29, 421–22; and novelistic form, 126–39

Ruysdael, Salomon van, 403, 405, 408

Samuels, Lisa, 30

Sandmann, Manfred, 145

Sartre, Jean-Paul, 20, 47–48, 51, 233

Saussure, Ferdinand de, 66, 160, 252, 303

Scalapino, Leslie, 6, 18, 25, 27, 30, 257, **270–81**; on authoritarianism, 379, 381; on Busby Berkeley, 270, 273–74; on comic strips, 384, 385, 387, 388; and dialogue with Silliman, **378–92**; on form, 270, 271, 276–79, 378, 380, 381, 384; on genre, 272, 274, 275, 276; on McClure's work, 272–73; on simulacra, 270, 272–75; on subjectivity, 378, 379, 380, 383

Scarry, Elaine, 16

schema, linguistic: and Ceravolo's poetry, 141, 144–53; and Jakobson's "six functions" theory, 160–62

schizophrenia, 24, 202; and postmodernism, 229–30, 232, 234–38

Schjeldahl, Peter, 141–42, 152, 277, 360

Schulman, Sarah, 391

Schwenger, Peter, 345–46

SCIENCE: and experience, 297; and expository style, 49; and indeterminacy, 67; and narrative, 296; and postmodernism, 270, 274

Seagram Building (New York), 326, 328–30

Searle, John, 144, 146

Seaton, Peter, "An Example from the Literature," **282–88**

self: Buddhism and, 122, 123; critique of, 198, 217; and Dragomoshchenko's work, 321–24; and Hinduism, 321, 324n4; and lettrism, 217; and mainstream poetry, 198; in poetry, 28, 420. *See also* identity; personhood; subjectivity

semantics: and Alferi's theory of rhythm, 306; and Ceravolo's work, 143–52; and dreams, 359, 362–63; and Hejinian's work, 89; and Lemaître's work, 218, 222; and metonymy, 238; and semantic shifts, 146–55; and structuralist poetics, 174

semiotics: and narrative, 225; and Saussure's work, 252

sentence: Alferi's theory of, 303–11; and Ceravolo's work, 144, 146, 149, 150; and Hejinian's work, 89–90. *See also* New Sentence

SEXUALITY: and Acker's work, 169, 177, 314–16; and Bataille's work, 79, 83–85; and Bellamy's work, 30, 313–19; and Creeley's work, 349; and New Narrative, 5, 79, 313–19; and O'Hara's work, 374; and Pound's work, 250; and Rozanov's work, 137–39; and Tolstoy's work, 129; and Wojnarowicz's work, 313, 316–18

Shakespeare, William, 65, 96, 98, 101

Shaw, Francie, 18

Shaw, Lytle, 31

Sher, Gail, 171

Sherman, Cindy, 270, 274–75, 277, 279

Sherman, Stuart, 416

Sherry, James, 391–92n2

Shklovsky, Viktor, 3–4, 14–15, 111, **126–40**, 146; on narrative form, 126–28, 131–33

Shurin, Aaron, 9, 31, **424–25**

signifying chain, Lacan's concept of, 234

Silliman, Ron, 5, 17, 25, 26, 27, 30–31, 62, **141–57**, 158–59, 237, 238, 270, 303; on authoritarianism, 379, 381; on Ceravolo's work, 143–52; and dialogue with Scalapino, **378–92**; on frames, 141, 144, 147, 149–50; on linguistic schema, 141, 144–53; on objectivity, 381, 382; *Paradise*, 273; on poetic coherence, 141, 142–45, 147–48, 152, 155; on subjectivity, 382, 389; on titles, 143–44, 152; *Tjanting*, 5, 143, 173

Silvers, Sally, 18

simulacra, 25, 233–36, 270, 272–75, 329, 330, 335

situationism, 356

sixties culture, 12, 13, 367, 370

slavery, 335–37, 343

sleep, and time management, 355

Smith, Dave, 197, 201

Smith, Jack, 416

Smith, John, "Philadelphia Newspapers Read Crossways," **420**

Smith, Rod, 30

Smithson, Robert, 326

social codes, 191

social formation, Marxist theory of, 230–32, 238

society: and art history, 408; and expository style, 50–52; and lyric, 209–12; and meaning, 185–90, 192–94, 196; and modernism, 12; and narrative, 23; and Notley's work, 278–79; and philosophy vs. poetry, 46; and postmodernism, 278; and writing as praxis, 185–96; and Zorn's work, 417–18

Solovyov, Vladimir, 136

Sonbert, Warren, 6, 22, **289–93**, 298; *A Woman's Touch*, 291–93

Sophocles, 120

Sorrentino, Gilbert, 345

"soul," black, represented in white culture, 335–43

Soviet Union, 8, 9, 26, 29, 50, 289, 294, 320, 421–22

SPACE: and architecture, 326, 328–29; and modernism, 421; and postmodernism, 31

speech: and Jakobson's "six functions" theory, 158, 160–61; nonidentity of writing and, 72; writing as absence of, 215, 221

Spicer, Jack, 202, 212, 257

Stalin, Josef, 29

standardization of discourse, 50–51

Stanislavsky, Constantin, 263

state power, 248

Steele, Timothy, 390

Stein, Gertrude, 390; and architecture, 328; and authorship, 28; and composition, 277; and continuous present, 270; and feminism, 99; and identity, 361; and Language writing, 13, 17; Loy influenced by, 170; and metonymy, 238; and poetics, 11, 12; and postmodernism, 232; reception of, 98, 121; and reflexivity, 282; on repetition, 91

Steiner, George, 65

Stendhal, 290

Sterne, Laurence, 130, 134

Stevens, Wallace, 100, 353

Stowe, Harriet Beecher, 102, 336, 337

structuralism, 14, 37, 111, 174, 188, 202

style: critique of expository, 49–51; as cultural abstraction, 271; and Jakobson's

theory of poetics, 160; and mind-language relation, 74; and philosophy vs. poetry, 47–49, 52–54

subcultures, 203–5, 211

SUBJECTIVITY: and Creeley's work, 29, 345, 347–51; critique of poetic, 8–9; and Dickinson's work, 43, 212; and Dragomoshchenko's work, 320–25; and gender, 63; Guattari's theory of, 421; and hypersubjectivity, 28, 31; and identity, 379–80, 382–83; as ineradicable in poetry, 420; and Language writing, 27; and lyric poetry, 8, 28, 202, 208–9, 212; masculine, 34, 345–52; and narrative, 20; and Notley's work, 278; and postmodernism, 326–34; whites' representation of black identity, 335–43; and Whitman's work, 43. *See also* identity; personhood; self

sublime, the, 81, 82, 294

surface, Pop art and, 368–69

surfers, language and, 202, 203–5

surrealism, 20, 26, 177, 203, 215, 216

Suzuki, D. T., 123

Swinburne, Algernon Charles, 276, 277

symbolic order, Lacan's theory of, 60–61, 63, 95, 234–35

"Symposium on Narrative," **298**

"Symposium: Postmodern?," **298–99**

synchronicity, 119, 123

syntax: and Alferi's theory of rhythm, 306–7, 310; and Bernstein's work, 154; and dreams, 359, 362–63; and Hejinian's work, 89, 154; and Lemaître's work, 218, 222; and Palmer's work, 115–16; and Perelman's work, 154; reversed, 154

Taoism, 122, 123

Tarkovsky, Andrei, 323

Tarn, Nathaniel, 27

Templeton, Fiona, 22, 298

terrorism, 179, 180

theater, 257, 415–16; and Coates's work, 111, 112–15; and Kit Robinson's *Collateral*, 6, 22, 257–69

This (ed. Grenier and Watten), 2, 19

This Press (ed. Watten), 2

Thomas, Lorenzo, 30; and media, 393–95; and politics, 393, 395–96; "The Marks Are Waiting," **393–96**

Thoreau, Henry David, 46, 48–49, 53

TIME, 62–63, 90, 154–55, 270, 271, 277, 348, 353–57, 422; management of, 353–57

Tinker, Allan, 57

titles, as components of poetry, 143–44, 152, 403, 405, 406

Tiutchev, Fyodor, 320

Todd, Mabel Loomis, 211

Tolstoy, Leo, 127, 128, 129, 130, 146

Torres, Edwin, 257

Toscano, Rodrigo, 257, 378; "Early Morning Prompts for Evening Takes; or, Roll 'Em!," **425**

totality: poetic, 152, 155; social, 185, 186–92, 195–96, 231

Tottel's (ed. Silliman), 19

Tourneur, Jacques, 289–90

tragedy, 119, 120

Tremblay-McGaw, Robin, 5

Tu, Hung Q., 30

Tubb, Ernest, 28

Tudor, David, 124

Turgenev, Ivan, 127, 132

Turner, Lana, 374

Turner, Tina, 342

turn to language, 5, 13–15, 17, 22, 23, 29–30, 72, 79, 170, 225, 320

Tuumba Press (ed. Hejinian), 2, 361

Twain, Mark, 136

twins, private language of, 202, 206–7

Tynjanov, Jurij, 4, 91

typos, in Ceravolo's poem, 152

Tysh, Chris, 30, 177

Tzara, Tristan, 420

U.K. POETICS, 171

Umbra Workshop, 393

uncanny, the, 59

unconscious, 59, 60, 62, 67, 68, 95, 229, 234

unity, poetic, 142, 144, 145, 147, 148, 152, 155

utilitarianism, 249

utopia, 330–31, 389–90

Van Gogh, Vincent, 232–33, 415

Verlaine, Paul, 371

Vertov, Dziga, 289, 294

Vidal, Gore, 395–96

Vietnam war, 370, 382

VISUAL ART: and Ashbery's work, 397–413; Dada, 215, 216–24; in Friedman's *Space Stations*, 294; and Lemaître's work, 215–24; and Longo's work, 331–33; Pop art, 397–413; and postmodernism, 326–34; and Sherman's work, 274–75

VISUALITY: and cinema, 289–93; and experience, 297; and knowledge, 172; and material text, 38

Voigt, Andrew, 6, 22, 298

Von Hallberg, Robert, 371

voyeurism, 223

Waldman, Anne, 198

Waldrop, Rosmarie, 6

Ward, Diane, 22

Warhol, Andy, 24, 30, 232–33, 368, 397, 398–400, 402–3, 405–9, 410n11, 411n23; and Ashbery, 397–409, 411; *Popeye*, 399, 403, 405; untitled film still, 402

Watson, Craig, 48

Watten, Barrett, 2, 3, 5, 7, 10, 52, 143, **158–68**, 423; on Berkeley Poetry Conference, 15, 158, 163; as co-editor of *This*, 2; on Eagleton's work, 15, 158, 164–67; on Jakobson's work, 158, 160–61, 166; on literary autonomy, 159–62, 165–66; on Olson's work, 158, 162–67

Weiner, Hannah, 5, 198

Weininger, Otto, 170

Weiss, Jason, 7

Wesselmann, Tom, 406

Whitehead, Alfred North, 5, 119, 124, 125

Whitman, Walt: and authorship, 40, 43; and individualism, 99, 211; *Leaves of Grass*, 4, 38–40; and reading, 16

Whittier, John Greenleaf, 336

Whorf, Benjamin Lee, 94

Wilden, Anthony, 350

Williams, Raymond, 144–45, 231

Williams, William Carlos, 12, 27, 166, 348, 353

Wimsatt, W.K., Jr., 208

Winant, Howard, 389

Winet, Jon, 9

Wittgenstein, Ludwig, 5, 14, 17, 46, 48, 53, 65, 67, 148, 202, 203, 258, 363

Wolf, Reva, 30, **397–413**; and Ashbery, 397–413; and limits of knowledge, 397, 406–7, 409; and Pop Art, 406–8; and Warhol, 397, 398–400, 402–3, 405–9, 410n11, 411n23

Wolff, Christian, 124

Wojnarowicz, David: *Close to the Knives*, 316–19

women: in Creeley's work, 348–50; experimental writing of, 98–99; and Language writing, 18; and novel writing, 384; and race, 335; and representation, 55, 63–65; and symbolic order, 95; and *Women and Language* issue, 5–6, 15, 17–19

Woodall, John, 8, 9

Woolf, Virginia, 6, 16, 345, 384

Wordsworth, William, 12, 54, 358

workplace: and language, 357–59, 364; and time management, 353–57

WRITING: and critique of narrative, 228; and dreams, 359–60, 362–65; and family relations, 386; history of, 215, 218, 220; and Lemaître's work, 215–16, 218–23; and method, 46, 48–50, 52–53; and mind, 72–78; and new media, 424; nonidentity of speech and, 72, 215, 221; as praxis, 185–96; and time management, 353–54

wu-wei, 122, 123

Yeats, William Butler, 121

zaum, 166, 203

Zen Buddhism, 119, 122, 123

Žižek, Slavoj, 30

Zorn, John, 9, **414–19**; on improvisation, 414–18

Zukofsky, Louis, 13, 17, 30, 162, 282; *Bottom: On Shakespeare*, 172

Zweig, Ellen, 18